Pierre de la Rue
and Musical Life at the
Habsburg-Burgundian Court

Pierre de la Rue and Musical Life at the Habsburg-Burgundian Court

HONEY MECONI

OXFORD
UNIVERSITY PRESS

OXFORD
UNIVERSITY PRESS

Great Clarendon Street, Oxford, OX2 6DP
Oxford University Press is a department of the University of Oxford.
It furthers the University's objective of excellence in research, scholarship,
and education by publishing worldwide in

Oxford New York

Auckland Bangkok Buenos Aires Cape Town Chennai
Dar es Salaam Delhi Hong Kong Istanbul Karachi Kolkata
Kuala Lumpur Madrid Melbourne Mexico City Mumbai Nairobi
São Paulo Shanghai Taipei Tokyo Toronto

Oxford is a registered trade mark of Oxford University Press
in the UK and certain other countries

Published in the United States
by Oxford University Press Inc., New York

British Library Cataloguing in Publication Data
Data available

Library of Congress Cataloging-in-Publication Data

Meconi, Honey.
Pierre de la Rue and musical life at the Habsburg-Burgundian court / Honey Meconi.
p. cm.
Includes bibliographical references (p.) and indexes
1. La Rue, Pierre de, d. 1518–Criticism and interpretation. 2. Chapels (Music)
3. Habsburg, House of. I. Title
ML410.L135 M43 2002   781.71´2´0092–dc21   [B]   2002038106
ISBN 0-19-816554-4

1 3 5 7 9 10 8 6 4 2

Typeset by Figaro, Launton, OX26 5DG
Printed in Great Britain
on acid-free paper by
Biddles Ltd.,
Guildford & King's Lynn

For Michel and Yannick, with love

Preface

I have loved the music of Pierre de la Rue since I first heard a recording of his *Requiem* as an undergraduate, although I could hardly have foreseen at that point that I would one day write a book about him. Yet his music continued to appeal to me after that initial experience; every piece of his that I performed, heard, or studied held my interest, and it was apparent from a perusal of the bibliography that much of the material available about him was confused, inaccurate, or incomplete. It was also apparent that he was a major figure from a major period in the history of music in serious need of more comprehensive treatment than he had yet received.

Bruce Phillips, my commissioning editor at Oxford University Press, was instrumental in urging me to undertake such a project, and the request that I write the La Rue article for the revised edition of *New Grove* provided further impetus. The result, however, is somewhat different from a standard 'life and works'.

The opening chapter, treating his life, gives new information and interpretation of material and reopens the question of his identification with the tenor Peter vander Straten. The second chapter places La Rue in the context of his only identifiable place of employment, the Habsburg-Burgundian court, simultaneously revealing new information about his colleagues. The third and fourth chapters provide overviews of aspects of his sacred and secular music respectively, while the fifth chapter discusses some of the connections between La Rue and two important models for him, Ockeghem and Josquin, as well as some components of what I have elsewhere called 'Reputation History'. A series of extended appendices, intended to serve as reference material, provides comprehensive information on the events of his life, documentation of the transmission of his music throughout Europe, a collection of all known writings that mention or discuss La Rue from the late fifteenth into the seventeenth century, and an annotated catalogue of his works.

The result is a detailed yet far from comprehensive picture of La Rue; for a composer of his output and breadth, such a picture is simply not possible in a single-volume work. But it should serve as a starting place for those who wish to learn more about La Rue, demonstrating just how unusual he was in the tradition of the Habsburg-Burgundian court, showing how his early compositions seem intended for effect in their choice of subject matter and style, outlining how he has never disappeared from musical consciousness, though our knowledge of him was severely limited for many years. Throughout the writing of this book I have been very much aware of what had to be left out, especially when it came to a discussion of the music. What is here, however, will serve as the foundation for the later exploration of all aspects of the composer, which will unquestionably come.

H.M.

Acknowledgements

Many people have helped my work on La Rue and music at the Habsburg-Burgundian court over the years—so many that a complete list is scarcely possible, and I apologize if I have inadvertently omitted anyone deserving of mention. My first thanks go to those who have provided financial support for my ongoing research on La Rue, underscoring their belief in the significance of this composer; I have been fortunate to receive a Weyman Fund Travel Grant, a Fulbright Fellowship to Belgium, a National Endowment for the Humanities Summer Stipend, and an Andrew W. Mellon Postdoctoral Fellowship in the Humanities at the University of Pennsylvania. I should like to thank Bruce Phillips, who first contacted me about this book and who has done so much for the world of books on music, and I am also grateful to his successors at Oxford University Press, most recently Sophie Goldsworthy, for their patience as this project has evolved. Both Janet Moth and Jacqueline Smith at the Press deserve my thanks, too, for helping speed production of this volume. It was a special privilege to have a leading scholar of fifteenth- and sixteenth-century music, Bonnie Blackburn, as copy-editor, and I am deeply indebted to her for numerous very helpful suggestions and comments along the way. As for other individuals, when I first lived in Belgium I had the great good luck to meet two women soon to take their place as major scholars in the field, Barbara Haggh and M. Jennifer Bloxam, whose friendship and support over the years, to say nothing of their brilliant insights into this material, has been invaluable. Martin Picker and the editors of the La Rue edition, Nigel St. John Davison, J. Evan Kreider, and T. Herman Keahey, have all supplied much-appreciated assistance for many years, and I am greatly indebted to their pioneering work. Lewis Lockwood, Lawrence F. Bernstein, David Fallows, and Jaap van Benthem regularly offered stimulating discussion and argument, to say nothing of other kinds of help, and Rob C. Wegman is owed a special thank you for assistance with archival matters. Michel Godts, Leofranc Holford-Strevens, Jan Ziolkowski, Massimo Ossi, Kristine Wallace, and Marilyn de Oliveira all gave much-needed guidance on translations, though any remaining infelicities are my responsibility. Both Tess Knighton and Mary Kay Duggan were generous with material on the chapel's residence in Spain. Bonnie Blackburn, James Haar, Donna Cardamone Jackson, Noel O'Regan, Jessie Ann Owens, and Cristle Collins Judd all helped with information on theoretical treatises. For additional assistance in various matters, great and small, I wish to thank Mimi Armstrong Ferrard, Allan Atlas, Willa Collins, Jean Ferrard, Kristine Forney, Eva Haverkamp, Paula Higgins, Susan Jackson, Eric Jas, Stacey Jocoy, Marie Jorritsma, Herbert Kellman, Jacobijn Kiel, Linda Neagley, Virginia Newes, Matthew Peattie, Keith Polk, William Prizer, Eugeen Schreurs, Reinhard Strohm, L. C. J. M. Rouppe van der Voort of the Confraternity of Our Lady in 's-Hertogenbosch, Daniel Vervenne (archivist of Sint Jacobskerk, Ghent), Andrew H. Weaver, Mary Beth Winn, and especially Angela Wren Wall, whose superb computer skills lifted much of the burden of preparing the final manuscript. I also wish to acknowledge the support of my dear friends Patricia Rubin, Pam Jorgensen, Adam Jaffe, and Mark Laporta, and of course both the Meconi and Godts families.

Finally, having gone to Belgium in search of La Rue, I found there as well my beloved husband. This book is dedicated to him and to our wonderful son.

Contents

Appendices

List of Figures

List of Tables

List of Musical Examples

List of Abbreviations

LIBRARIES AND ARCHIVES

AGS   Archivo general de Simancas
   CySR   Casa y sitios reales
ASV   Archivio Segreto Vaticano
BAGR   Brussels, Archives générales du royaume/Algemeen Rijksarchief
   ASG   Archief Sint Goedele
   E&A   Papiers d'État et Audience
BNF   Paris, Bibliothèque nationale de France
NAE   Namur, Archives de l'État
RB   Bruges, Rijksarchief
RK   Rijksarchief te Kortrijk
's-HAI   's-Hertogenbosch, Archief Illustre Lieve Vrouwe Broederschap
SJG   Ghent, Archief Sint Jacob
VOS   Vienna, Österreichisches Staatsarchiv
   HHuS   Haus-, Hof- und Staatsarchiv
   OMeA   Obersthofmeisteramt
   SR   Sonderreihe

MANUSCRIPT SIGLA

AntP B 948 IV   Antwerp, Museum Plantin-Moretus, Bibliotheek, MS B 948 IV (covers)
AntP M 18.13/1   Antwerp, Museum Plantin-Moretus, Bibliotheek, MS M18.13 (fragment 1)
AntP M 18.13/2   Antwerp, Museum Plantin-Moretus, Bibliotheek, MS M18.13 (fragment 2)
AntP M 18.13/3   Antwerp, Museum Plantin-Moretus, Bibliotheek, MS M18.13 (fragment 3)
AntP R43.13   Antwerp, Museum Plantin-Moretus, Bibliotheek, R43.13
BarcBC 681   Barcelona, Biblioteca Central, MS 681
BasU F.IX.22   Basel, Öffentliche Bibliothek der Universität, MS F.IX.22
BasU F.IX.25   Basel, Öffentliche Bibliothek der Universität, MS F.IX.25
BasU F.X.1–4   Basel, Öffentliche Bibliothek der Universität, MSS F.X.1–4
BerlGS 7/   Berlin, Geheimes Staatsarchiv Preußischer Kulturbesitz, MS XX.
   KönSU 1740   HA StUB Königsberg Nr. 7
BerlPS 40013   Berlin, former Preußische Staatsbibliothek, MS Mus. 40013 (*olim* Z 13)
BerlPS 40634   Berlin, former Preußische Staatsbibliothek, MS Mus. 40634
BerlS 40021   Berlin, Staatsbibliothek zu Berlin — Preußischer Kulturbesitz, MS Mus. 40021 (*olim* Z 21)
BerlS 40026   Berlin, Staatliches Institut für Musikforschung Preußischer Kulturbesitz, Mus. MS 40026 (*olim* Z 26)

BolC B57	Bologna, Civico Museo Bibliografico Musicale, MS B57
BolC Q17	Bologna, Civico Museo Bibliografico Musicale, MS Q17 (*olim* 148)
BolSP 38	Bologna, Archivio Musicale della Fabbriceria di San Petronio, MS A.XXXVIII (*olim* CC)
BrugRA Aanw. 756	Bruges, Rijksarchief, Aanwinsten 756
BrusBR IV.90	Brussels, Bibliothèque Royale, MS IV.90
BrusBR IV.922	Brussels, Bibliothèque Royale, MS IV.922
BrusBR IV.1274	Brussels, Bibliothèque Royale, MS IV.1274
BrusBR 215–16	Brussels, Bibliothèque Royale, MS 215–216
BrusBR 228	Brussels, Bibliothèque Royale, MS 228
BrusBR 6428	Brussels, Bibliothèque Royale, MS 6428
BrusBR 7386–7394	Brussels, Bibliothèque Royale, MS 7386–7394
BrusBR 9085	Brussels, Bibliothèque Royale, MS 9085
BrusBR 9126	Brussels, Bibliothèque Royale, MS 9126
BrusBR 10572	Brussels, Bibliothèque Royale, MS 10572
BrusBR 11239	Brussels, Bibliothèque Royale, MS 11239
BrusBR 15075	Brussels, Bibliothèque Royale, MS 15075
BrusSG 9423	Brussels, Algemeen Rijksarchief, Archief van St. Goedele, No. 9423 (*olim* 29)
BrusSG 9424	Brussels, Algemeen Rijksarchief, Archief van St. Goedele, No. 9424 (*olim* 30)
CambraiBM 4	Cambrai, Médiathèque Municipale, MS 4
CambraiBM 18	Cambrai, Médiathèque Municipale, MS 18 (20)
CambraiBM 125–8	Cambrai, Médiathèque Municipale, MS 125–128 (*olim* 124)
CasAC M(D)	Casale Monferrato, Archivio e Biblioteca Capitolare, Duomo, MS M(D)
CivMA 59	Cividale del Friuli, Museo Archeologico Nazionale, MS LIX
CoimU 2	Coimbra, Biblioteca Geral da Universidade, MS M.2
DresSL 1/D/505	Dresden, Sächsische Landesbibliothek, MS Mus. 1/D/505 (*olim* Annaberg, Bibliothek der St. Annenkirche, MS 1248)
DresSL Pirna IV	Dresden, Sächsische Landesbibliothek, MS Pirna IV
EisS s.s.	Eisenach, Stadtarchiv, MS s.s. (*olim* Carl Alexander-Bibliothek)
ErlU 473/4	Erlangen, Universitätsbibliothek, MS 473/4 (*olim* 793)
FlorBN II.I.232	Florence, Biblioteca Nazionale Centrale, MS II.I.232 (*olim* Magliabechi XIX. 58)
FlorBN BR 229	Florence, Biblioteca Nazionale Centrale, MS Banco Rari 229 (*olim* Magliabechi XIX. 59)
FlorBN Magl. 178	Florence, Biblioteca Nazionale Centrale, MS Magliabechi XIX.178
FlorC 2439	Florence, Biblioteca del Conservatorio di Musica Luigi Cherubini, MS Basevi 2439
FlorC 2442	Florence, Biblioteca del Conservatorio di Musica Luigi Cherubini, MS Basevi 2442
FlorL 666	Florence, Biblioteca Medicea-Laurenziana, MS Acquisti e doni 666
FrankSU 2	Frankfurt am Main, Stadt- und Universitätsbibliothek, MS Mus. fol.-2
GhentR D 3360b	Ghent, Rijksarchief, fonds Varia D 3360b
GothaF A98	Gotha, Forschungsbibliothek Gotha, Schloss Friedenstein (formerly Landesbibliothek), MS Chart. A. 98

GreifU 640–641	Greifswald, Universitätsbibliothek, MSS BW 640–641 (*olim* Eb 133)
HeidU 318	Heidelberg, Universitätsbibliothek, MS Pal. Germ. 318
HeilbS X/2	Heilbronn, Stadtarchiv, Musiksammlung, MS X/2
's-HerAB 72A	's-Hertogenbosch, Archief van de Illustre Lieve Vrouwe Broederschap, MS 72A
's-HerAB 72B	's-Hertogenbosch, Archief van de Illustre Lieve Vrouwe Broederschap, MS 72B
's-HerAB 72C	's-Hertogenbosch, Archief van de Illustre Lieve Vrouwe Broederschap, MS 72C
HerdF 9820	Herdringen, Schloss Fürstenberg, Bibliothek, MS 9820 (*olim* Paderborn, Erzbischöflische Akademische Bibliothek)
HerdF 9821	Herdringen, Schloss Fürstenberg, Bibliothek, MS 9821 (*olim* Paderborn, Erzbischöflische Akademische Bibliothek)
HradKM 7	Hradec Králové, Krajske Muzeum, Knihovna (Regional Museum, Library), MS II A 7
JenaU 2	Jena, Universitätsbibliothek, MS 2
JenaU 3	Jena, Universitätsbibliothek, MS 3
JenaU 4	Jena, Universitätsbibliothek, MS 4
JenaU 5	Jena, Universitätsbibliothek, MS 5
JenaU 7	Jena, Universitätsbibliothek, MS 7
JenaU 8	Jena, Universitätsbibliothek, MS 8
JenaU 9	Jena, Universitätsbibliothek, MS 9
JenaU 12	Jena, Universitätsbibliothek, MS 12
JenaU 20	Jena, Universitätsbibliothek, MS 20
JenaU 21	Jena, Universitätsbibliothek, MS 21
JenaU 22	Jena, Universitätsbibliothek, MS 22
KasL 24	Kassel, Murhard'sche Bibliothek der Stadt Kassel und Landesbibliothek, MSS 4° Mus. 24/1–4
KasL 38	Kassel, Murhard'sche Bibliothek der Stadt Kassel und Landesbibliothek, MSS 4° Mus. 38/1–6
KasL 53/2	Kassel, Murhard'sche Bibliothek der Stadt Kassel und Landesbibliothek, MSS 8° Mus. 53/2
KönSU 1740 *see* BerlGS 7	
LeidGA 1443	Leiden (Leyden), Gemeentearchief, Archieven van de Kerken, MS 1443 (*olim* F; 127; 765; 866; 1008)
LeipU 49	Leipzig, Universitätsbibliothek, MS Thomaskirche 49 (1–4) (*olim* III, A. α 17–20) and MS Thomaskirche 50 (*olim* III, A. α 21)
LeipU 51	Leipzig, Universitätsbibliothek, MS Thomaskirche 51 (1–2) (*olim* III, A. α 22–23)
LeipU 1494	Leipzig, Universitätsbibliothek, MS 1494
LonBL 4911	London, British Library, Add. MS 4911
LonBL 19583	London, British Library, Add. MS 19583
LonBL 35087	London, British Library, Add. MS 35087
LonBLH 5242	London, British Library, MS Harley 5242
LonBLR 8 G.vii	London, British Library, MS Royal 8 G. vii
MechAS s.s.	Mechelen, Archief en Stadsbibliotheek, MS s.s.
MilA 46	Milan, Biblioteca Ambrosiana, MS E. 46. Inf.

MilD 1	Milan, Archivio della Veneranda Fabbrica del Duomo, Sezione Musicale, Librone 1 (*olim* 2269)
MilD 2	Milan, Archivio della Veneranda Fabbrica del Duomo, Sezione Musicale, Librone 2 (*olim* 2268)
MilD 3	Milan, Archivio della Veneranda Fabbrica del Duomo, Sezione Musicale, Librone 3 (*olim* 2267)
ModD 3	Modena, Duomo, Biblioteca e Archivio Capitolare, MS Mus. III
ModD 4	Modena, Duomo, Biblioteca e Archivio Capitolare, MS Mus. IV
ModE M.1.13	Modena, Biblioteca Estense e Universitaria, MS α .M.1.13
MontsM 766	Montserrat, Biblioteca del Monestir, MS 766
MontsM 769	Montserrat, Biblioteca del Monestir, MS 769
MontsM 773	Montserrat, Biblioteca del Monestir, MS 773
MunBS 5	Munich, Bayerische Staatsbibliothek, Musiksammlung, Musica MS 5 (*olim* H.C. 50)
MunBS 6	Munich, Bayerische Staatsbibliothek, Musiksammlung, Musica MS 6
MunBS 7	Munich, Bayerische Staatsbibliothek, Musiksammlung, Musica MS 7
MunBS 34	Munich, Bayerische Staatsbibliothek, Musiksammlung, Musica MS 34
MunBS 47	Munich, Bayerische Staatsbibliothek, Musiksammlung, Musica MS 47 (*olim* H.C. 70)
MunBS 53	Munich, Bayerische Staatsbibliothek, Musiksammlung, Musica MS 53 (*olim* H.C. 49)
MunBS 65	Munich, Bayerische Staatsbibliothek, Musiksammlung, Musica MS 65 (*olim* H.C. 48)
MunBS 260	Munich, Bayerische Staatsbibliothek, Musiksammlung, Musica MS 260
MunBS 1508	Munich, Bayerische Staatsbibliothek, Musiksammlung, Musica MS 1508
MunBS 1516	Munich, Bayerische Staatsbibliothek, Musiksammlung, Musica MS 1516
MunBS 3154	Munich, Bayerische Staatsbibliothek, Musiksammlung, Musica MS 3154
MunBS A II	Munich, Bayerische Staatsbibliothek, Handschriften-Inkunabel-abteilung, Musica MS A II
MunBS C	Munich, Bayerische Staatsbibliothek, Handschriften-Inkunabel-abteilung, Musica MS C (*olim* Cim. 210)
MunBS F	Munich, Bayerische Staatsbibliothek, Handschriften-Inkunabel-abteilung, Musica MS F
MunU 239	Munich, Universitätsbibliothek der Ludwig-Maximilians-Universität, MS 2° Art. 239
MunU 327	Munich, Universitätsbibliothek der Ludwig-Maximilians-Universität, MS 8° 327 (*olim* Cim. 44b)
MunU 328–331	Munich, Universitätsbibliothek der Ludwig-Maximilians-Universität, MS 8° 328–331 (*olim* Cim. 44c)
NapBN 40	Naples, Biblioteca Nazionale, MS VI E 40

NurGN 83795	Nuremberg, Bibliothek des Germanischen Nationalmuseums, MS 83795 (*olim* M 369m)
OxfBA 831	Oxford, Bodleian Library, MS Ashmole 831
OxfBC 213	Oxford, Bodleian Library, MS Canon. Misc. 213
OxfBLL a.8	Oxford, Bodleian Library, MS Lat. liturg. a. 8
ParisBNC 1591	Paris, Bibliothèque Nationale de France, Département de la Musique, Fonds du Conservatoire, MS Rés. 1591
RegB B220–222	Regensburg, Bischöfliche Zentralbibliothek, MS B. 220–222
RegB C 98	Regensburg, Bischöfliche Zentralbibliothek, MS C 98
RegB C120	Regensburg, Bischöfliche Zentralbibliothek, MS C 120 (*olim* D SII)
RegT 3/I	Regensburg, Fürst Thurn und Taxis Hofbibliothek, MS Freie Künste Musik 3/I
RomeC 2856	Rome, Biblioteca Casanatense, MS 2856 (*olim* O. V. 208)
SamaP 30–1	Samaden, Fundaziun Planta, MSS M 30–31
SegC s.s.	Segovia, Archivo Capitular de la Catedral, MS s.s.
SevC 5-1-43	Seville, Catedral Metropolitana, Biblioteca Capitular y Colombina, MS 5-1-43 (*olim* Z Tab. 135, N.° 33)
SGallS 461	Sankt Gallen, Stiftsbibliothek, MS 461
SGallS 463	Sankt Gallen, Stiftsbibliothek, MS 463
SGallS 530	Sankt Gallen, Stiftsbibliothek, MS 530
SienBC K.I.2	Siena, Biblioteca Comunale degli Intronati, MS K.I.2
StuttL HB 26	Stuttgart, Württembergische Landesbibliothek, MS HB VII/26
StuttL 38	Stuttgart, Württembergische Landesbibliothek, MS Musica folio I 38
StuttL 45	Stuttgart, Württembergische Landesbibliothek, MS Musica folio I 45
SubA 248	Subiaco, Monumento Nazionale dell'Abbazia di Santa Scolastica, Biblioteca Statale, MS 248
TarazC 3	Tarazona, Archivo Capitular de la Catedral, MS 3
TongerenSA 183	Tongeren, Stadsarchief, Oud regime MS 183
TourBV 94	Tournai, Bibliothèque de la Ville, MS 94
TrentBC 1947/4	Trent, Biblioteca Comunale, MS 1947/4
TrentC 89	Trent, Museo Provinciale d'Arte, Castello del Buon Consiglio, MS 1376 (*olim* 89)
TrentC 91	Trent, Museo Provinciale d'Arte, Castello del Buon Consiglio, MS 1378 (olim 91)
UlmS 237	Ulm, Münster Bibliothek, Von Schermar'sche Familienstiftung, MS 237 (a–d)
UppsU 76a	Uppsala, Universitetsbiblioteket, MS Vokalmusik i Handskrift 76a
UppsU 76b	Uppsala, Universitetsbiblioteket, MS Vokalmusik i Handskrift 76b
UtreC 47/1	Utrecht, Rijksmuseum, Het Catherijneconvent, MS 47, fragment 1
UtreC 47/2	Utrecht, Rijksmuseum, Het Catherijneconvent, MS 47, fragment 2
UtreH s.s.	Utrecht, Private Library of Peter Hecht, MS s.s.
VatC 234	Vatican City, Biblioteca Apostolica Vaticana, MS Chigi C.VIII.234
VatG XII.2	Vatican City, Biblioteca Apostolica Vaticana, MS Cappella Giulia XII.2
VatG XIII.27	Vatican City, Biblioteca Apostolica Vaticana, MS Cappella Giulia XIII.27

VatP 1976–79	Vatican City, Biblioteca Apostolica Vaticana, MSS Palatini Latini 1976–1979
VatP 1980–1	Vatican City, Biblioteca Apostolica Vaticana, MSS Palatini Latini 1980–1981
VatP 1982	Vatican City, Biblioteca Apostolica Vaticana, MSS Palatini Latini 1982
VatS 14	Vatican City, Biblioteca Apostolica Vaticana, MS Cappella Sistina 14
VatS 15	Vatican City, Biblioteca Apostolica Vaticana, MS Cappella Sistina 15
VatS 23	Vatican City, Biblioteca Apostolica Vaticana, MS Cappella Sistina 23
VatS 34	Vatican City, Biblioteca Apostolica Vaticana, MS Cappella Sistina 34
VatS 35	Vatican City, Biblioteca Apostolica Vaticana, MS Cappella Sistina 35
VatS 36	Vatican City, Biblioteca Apostolica Vaticana, MS Cappella Sistina 36
VatS 41	Vatican City, Biblioteca Apostolica Vaticana, MS Cappella Sistina 41
VatS 42	Vatican City, Biblioteca Apostolica Vaticana, MS Cappella Sistina 42
VatS 45	Vatican City, Biblioteca Apostolica Vaticana, MS Cappella Sistina 45
VatS 51	Vatican City, Biblioteca Apostolica Vaticana, MS Cappella Sistina 51
VatS 154	Vatican City, Biblioteca Apostolica Vaticana, MS Cappella Sistina 154
VatS 160	Vatican City, Biblioteca Apostolica Vaticana, MS Cappella Sistina 160
VatV 5318	Vatican City, Biblioteca Apostolica Vaticana, MS Vaticani Latini 5318
VatV 11953	Vatican City, Biblioteca Apostolica Vaticana, MS Vaticani Latini 11953
VerBC 755	Verona, Biblioteca Capitolare, MS DCCLV
VerBC 756	Verona, Biblioteca Capitolare, MS DCCLVI
VerBC 758	Verona, Biblioteca Capitolare, MS DCCLVIII
VienNB 1783	Vienna, Österreichische Nationalbibliothek, Handschriften- und Inkunabelsammlung, MS 1783 (*olim* Theol. 34; VII. A. 16)
VienNB 4809	Vienna, Österreichische Nationalbibliothek, Handschriften- und Inkunabelsammlung, MS 4809 (*olim* Theol. 35; VIII. A. 1)
VienNB 4810	Vienna, Österreichische Nationalbibliothek, Handschriften- und Inkunabelsammlung, MS 4810 (*olim* Theol. 36; VIII. A. 2)
VienNB 9814	Vienna, Österreichische Nationalbibliothek, Handschriften- und Inkunabelsammlung, MS 9814 (*olim* Rec. 1535) (fos. 132–52 only)
VienNB 11778	Vienna, Österreichische Nationalbibliothek, Handschriften- und Inkunabelsammlung, MS 11778 (*olim* Theol. 37; VIII. A. 3)
VienNB 11883	Vienna, Österreichische Nationalbibliothek, Handschriften- und Inkunabelsammlung, MS 11883 (*olim* Theol. 281; VIII. D. 20)
VienNB Mus. 15495	Vienna, Österreichische Nationalbibliothek, Musiksammlung, MS Mus. 15495 (*olim* Kunsthistorisches Staatsmuseum, Sammlung für Plastik und Kunstgewerbe, MS 5248; *olim* Series nova 2660)
VienNB Mus. 15496	Vienna, Österreichische Nationalbibliothek, Musiksammlung, MS Mus. 15496 (*olim* Kunsthistorisches Staatsmuseum, Sammlung für Plastik und Kunstgewerbe, MS 5261; *olim* Series nova 2661)
VienNB Mus 15497	Vienna, Österreichische Nationalbibliothek, Musiksammlung, MS Mus. 15497 (*olim* Kunsthistorisches Staatsmuseum, Sammlung für Plastik und Kunstgewerbe, MS 5132; *olim* Series nova 2662)

VienNB Mus. 15499	Vienna, Österreichische Nationalbibliothek, Musiksammlung, MS Mus. 15499
VienNB Mus. 15941	Vienna, Österreichische Nationalbibliothek, Musiksammlung, MS Mus. 15941 (*olim* A.N.35.H.18)
VienNB Mus. 16746	Vienna, Österreichische Nationalbibliothek, Musiksammlung, MS Mus. 16746 (*olim* A.N.33.D.76)
VienNB Mus. 18688	Vienna, Österreichische Nationalbibliothek, Musiksammlung, MS Mus. 18688
VienNB Mus. 18746	Vienna, Österreichische Nationalbibliothek, Musiksammlung, MS Mus. 18746 (*olim* A.N.35.H.14)
VienNB Mus. 18810	Vienna, Österreichische Nationalbibliothek, Musiksammlung, MS Mus. 18810 (*olim* A.N.35.E.126)
VienNB Mus. 18825	Vienna, Österreichische Nationalbibliothek, Musiksammlung, MS Mus. 18825 (*olim* A.N.35.E.133)
VienNB Mus. 18832	Vienna, Österreichische Nationalbibliothek, Musiksammlung, MS Mus. 18832 (*olim* A.N.35.H.27)
WarN 564	Warsaw, Biblioteka Narodowa, MS 564 (*olim* Poliński 564)
WarU RM 5892	Warsaw, Biblioteka Uniwersytecka, Oddział Zbiorów Muzycznych, RM 5892 (*olim* Mus. 58, MF. 2016)
WashLC M6	Washington, DC, Library of Congress, Music Division, MS M2.1.M6 Case
WeimB B	Weimar, Bibliothek der Evangelisch-Lutherischen Kirchenge-meinde, MS B
WolfA A	Wolfenbüttel, Herzog August Bibliothek, MS Guelferbytanus A Augusteus 2°
WrocU 428	Wrocław (Breslau), Biblioteka Uniwersytecka, Oddział Rękopisów, MS I-F-428
ZwiR 78/3	Zwickau, Ratsschulbibliothek, MS LXXVIII, 3

BIBLIOGRAPHICAL ABBREVIATIONS

CaulletM	Gustave Caullet, *Musiciens de la collégiale Notre-Dame à Courtrai d'après leurs testaments* (Kortrijk: Flandria, 1911)
CC	*Census-Catalogue of Manuscript Sources of Polyphonic Music, 1400–1550*, 5 vols., vol. 1 ed. Charles Hamm and Herbert Kellman; vols. 2–5 ed. Herbert Kellman (Renaissance Manuscript Studies, 1; Neuhausen–Stuttgart: American Institute of Musicology/Hänssler-Verlag, 1979–88)
ChmelH	'Bericht über die Reise des Erzherzogs Philipp von den Nieder-landen nach Spanien 1501', in Joseph Chmel (ed.), *Die Handschriften der k.k. Hofbibliothek in Wien, im Interesse der Geschichte, besonders der österreichischen*, 2 vols. (Vienna: Carl Gerold, 1840–1), ii. 554–656
DoorslaerC	Georges Van Doorslaer, 'La Chapelle musicale de Philippe le Beau', *Revue belge d'archéologie et d'histoire de l'art*, 4 (1934), 21–57, 139–65
DouillezM	Appendix II in Jeannine Douillez, 'De Muziek aan het Bour-gondische-Habsburgse Hof in de Tweede Helft der XVde Eeuw' (diss., University of Ghent, [1967])

EMH	*Early Music History*
GachardCV, i	Louis Prosper Gachard, *Collection des Voyages des Souverains des Pays-Bas*, i: *Itinéraires de Philippe le Hardi, Jean sans Peur, Philippe le Bon, Maximilien et Philippe le Beau; Relation du premier voyage de Philippe le Beau en Espagne, en 1501, par Antoine de Lalaing, Sr de Montigny; Relation du deuxième voyage de Philippe le Beau, en 1506, par un anonyme* (Mémoires de l'Academie royale de Belgique, 1; Brussels: F. Hayez, 1876)
GachardCV, ii	Louis Prosper Gachard, *Collection des Voyages des Souverains des Pays-Bas*, ii: *Itinéraire de Charles-Quint de 1506 à 1531; Journal des voyages de Charles-Quint, de 1514 à 1551, par Jean de Vandenesse* (Mémoires de l'Academie royale de Belgique, 1; Brussels: F. Hayez, 1874)
JAMS	*Journal of the American Musicological Society*
JosCon	Edward E. Lowinsky and Bonnie J. Blackburn (eds.), *Josquin des Prez: Proceedings of the International Josquin Festival-Conference held at The Juilliard School at Lincoln Center in New York City, 21–25 June 1971* (London, New York, and Toronto: Oxford University Press, 1976)
LIS	*Inventaire sommaire des archives départementales du Nord, Archives civiles, Série B*, ed. Abbé Dehaisnes, Jules Finot, and A. Desplanque, 8 vols. (Lille: L. Danel, 1872–1906)
LRE	Pierre de la Rue, *Collected Works*, 9 vols. to date, ed. Nigel St. John Davison, J. Evan Kreider, and T. Herman Keahey (Corpus mensurabilis musicae, 97; Neuhausen–Stuttgart: American Institute of Musicology/Hänssler-Verlag, 1989–)
New Grove	*The New Grove Dictionary of Music and Musicians*, ed. Stanley Sadie, 20 vols. (London: Macmillan, 1980)
New Grove II	*The New Grove Dictionary of Music and Musicians*, 2nd edn., ed. Stanley Sadie, 29 vols. (London: Macmillan, 2001)
PickerCA	Martin Picker, *The Chanson Albums of Marguerite of Austria: MSS 228 and 11239 of the Bibliothèque Royale de Belgique, Brussels* (Berkeley and Los Angeles: University of California Press, 1965)
RISM	*Recueils imprimés, XVIe–XVIIe siècles*, i: *List chronologique* (Répertoire internationale des sources musicales; Munich and Duisberg: G. Henle, 1960)
RobijnsP	Jozef Robijns, *Pierre De la Rue, circa 1560–1518: een bio-bibliographische studie* (Universiteit te Leuven, Publicaties op het gebied der geschiedenis en der philologie, Series 4/6; Gembloux: J. Duculot, 1954)
RubsamenMGG	Walter Rubsamen, 'La Rue, Pierre de', *Die Musik in Geschichte und Gegenwart*, viii, ed. Friedrich Blume (Kassel: Bärenreiter, 1960)
SG	Joseph Schmidt-Görg, 'Die Acta Capitularia der Notre-Dame-Kirche zu Kortrijk als musikgeschichtliche Quelle', *Vlaamsch jaarboek voor muziekgeschiedenis*, 1 (1939), 21–80
StaehelinNG	Martin Staehelin, 'La Rue, Pierre de', *New Grove*
TA	Herbert Kellman (ed.), *The Treasury of Petrus Alamire: Music and Art in Flemish Court Manuscripts 1500–1535* (Ghent and Amsterdam: Ludion, 1999)

TVNM	*Tijdschrift van de Vereniging voor Nederlandse Muziekgeschiedenis*
VDS	Edmond Vander Straeten, *La Musique aux Pays-Bas avant le XIXe siècle*, 8 vols. (C. Muquardt, G.-A. van Trigt, Schott, 1867–88; repr. New York: Da Capo, 1969)

CURRENCY ABBREVIATIONS

d.	denier
den. par.	denier parisis
g.	gulden
£	livre/pound/pond
£ gr.	ponds groat
£ par.	ponds parisis
mrs.	maravedís
Rg.	Rijnsgulden
s.	sols/sous
sc.	scelling
sc. par.	scelling parisis
st.	stuiver

A Note on Names

La Rue himself signed his name 'de ♯ rue' or 'P de ♯ rue', but through most of this book the rebus form of his name will be indicated as 'de *la* rue'. His masses are sometimes indicated by title rather than by the name of the pre-existent material (e.g. *Missa de sancta cruce* rather than *Missa Nos autem gloriari*) but all alternative names are included in Appendix D, the catalogue of his works. The *Missa pro fidelibus defunctis* is often referred to simply as his Requiem mass; similarly, his chanson *Incessament mon pauvre cueur lamente* is usually just cited as *Incessament*, and the mass he based on the work is called *Missa Incessament*. For multiple works on the same subjects where the second work does not seem to be by La Rue, I have used a roman numeral only for the inauthentic work: thus (inauthentic) *Missa de septem doloribus II* versus (authentic) *Missa de septem doloribus*; (inauthentic) *Magnificat quarti toni II* versus (authentic) *Magnificat quarti toni*; and (inauthentic) four-voice *Fors seulement II* versus (authentic) *Fors seulement* (one each for four and five voices). Certain procedures have been followed in tables and appendices but not the body of the text: brackets are placed around the names of works for which we have no sixteenth-century attribution to La Rue, works that remain problematic (e.g. *Missa sine nomine II*) are prefaced with a question mark, and unica are preceded by an asterisk.

1 Biography

WHO WAS PIERRE DE LA RUE?

Until recently, the question 'who was Pierre de la Rue?' seemed an easy one to answer. Any thorough synopsis of his life would have gone as follows: he was almost certainly born in Tournai, probably around 1452, and started employment as a part-time singer (a tenor) in Brussels (1469). Additional employment was found in Ghent (1471–2) and then Nieuwpoort (1472 to before 2 February 1477), and at one unspecified time he held a canonicate at St Ode. After that, he worked in Cologne (?–1489) until he was lured away by the famous Confraternity of Illustre Lieve Vrouwe in 's-Hertogenbosch (1489–92). On 17 November 1492 he was hired by Maximilian, King of the Romans and regent for his son, the archduke Philip, who would assume governance of the former Burgundian territories in the Low Countries (referred to in this book as Habsburg-Burgundy) on coming of age (see Fig. 1.1 for the Habsburg-Burgundian family tree). After Philip's unexpected death in 1506 in Spain, where he had gone to assume his new position as King of Castile, La Rue remained in that country as *premier chapelain* for the group formed from erstwhile members of Philip's chapel who remained to serve Juana, his widow. After Juana, supposed ruler of Castile, was relieved of all power in 1508, La Rue returned north to join the chapel that now served Philip's son and heir, the 8-year-old archduke Charles (future Holy Roman Emperor Charles V), which was initially overseen by Marguerite of Austria, Philip's sister and governor of the Low Countries. La Rue left the court in 1516, a little more than a year after Charles attained his majority, retired to Kortrijk, where he held a prebend, and died on 20 November 1518.[1]

Much of that synopsis remains true, including almost everything about La Rue's service at the court (references to 'the court' will refer to that of Habsburg-Burgundy unless otherwise specified). But I have rethought the material behind this compelling narrative and come up with additional evidence about La Rue that suggests that, once more, we are almost back at the start when it comes to La Rue's life before he joined the court.

Our lack of certainty about La Rue's early biography stems from the fact that, except for St Ode, all the employers from Brussels through 's-Hertogenbosch hired not Pierre de la Rue but rather Peter vander Straten (or some variant of that

---

[1] See Honey Meconi, 'Free from the Crime of Venus: The Biography of Pierre de la Rue', *Revista de musicología*, 16 (1993), 2673–2683 (*Actas del XV congreso de la Sociedad Internacional de Musicología: Culturas musicales del Mediterráneo y sus ramificaciones, Madrid, 3–10 abril 1992*, v. 121–31)

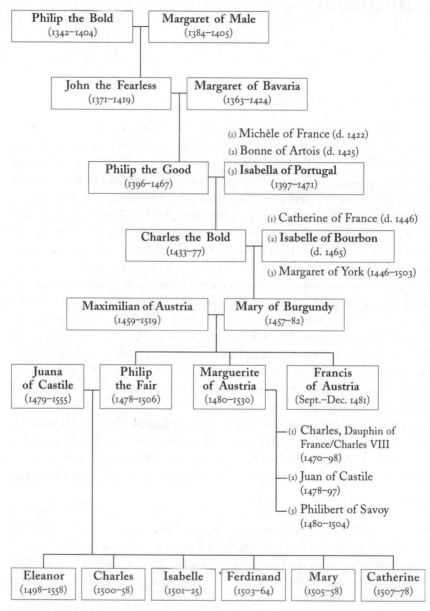

FIG. 1.1. Family Tree of Habsburg-Burgundy

name). Obviously, Peter vander Straten is the literal Flemish and Dutch translation of Pierre de la Rue. Further, all the documents using the 'vander Straten' name are themselves in Flemish or Dutch, the language of all these early places of employment (except for Cologne, but we know of Cologne only through a 's-Hertogenbosch document). In addition, this alternative appellation appears at a time when musicians are commonly found under a variety of names. Among La Rue's colleagues in the Habsburg-Burgundian chapel, for example, are Gaspar Weerbeke/Jaspart Doudemere, Jean Braconnier/Lourdault, Alexander Agricola/Alexander Ackerman, Jheronimus de Clibano/Jherome Du Four, Gilles Reingot/Gillequin de Bailleul, Nicolas Champion/Clais le Liégeois, Marbrianus de Orto/Marbrianus Dujardin, Antonius Divitis/Anthoine Le Riche, Petrus van den Hove/Pierre Alamire/Petcr Imhove. Peter vander Straten looks positively tame in this company.

We know that Pierre de la Rue appears under different forms of his name in later documents, and it is worth some perusal of these as well as discussion of the most historically accurate form of his name. Appendix A (Chronology of Events), Appendix B (Chronology of Sources), and Appendix C (Literary and Theoretical Citations) include the names by which La Rue was known in fifteenth- and sixteenth-century documents, literary works, theoretical treatises, manuscripts, and prints, and it is an incredibly varied collection. In court *escroes*,[2] with only two exceptions, he is always given with both a first and a last name. The exceptions are the *escroe* of 12 June 1497, where he is 'Pierchon'[3] (a letter of 7 April 1509 by Marguerite also uses this name), and the *escroe* for the month of October 1514, where he is 'Rue'. Last names for La Rue in contemporary court documents are limited: de la Rue, dela rue, dela Rue, de rue, and de Rue.[4]

When joined with a surname, the forms of the first name are more varied: Perchon (in one instance using the abbreviation for 'per'), Pierchon (once with an abbreviation for the 'n'), Pier chon, Piercon, Pierechon, Pierrechon, Pierre, and Pirchon. In other words, he was usually known at court by the diminutive form of his name. After returning from Spain (and occasionally before) his first name appears as Pierre, except for Marguerite's letter mentioned above and a special payment in 1514, where he is also Pierchon. This use of his full name might be a gesture of respect to a more senior member of the chapel, though the post-Spain *escroe* scribes in general seem slightly more formal than earlier ones with all the chapel members' names.

The manuscripts compiled by the court scriptorium treat La Rue's name rather differently than scribes of the *escroes* and documents. When a first name is given, it is Petrus or, much less often, Pierson, but sometimes only 'P' or 'Pe' appear.[5] Last name forms can be Rue, de la Rue, de la rue, delarue, DE LARUE, De la Rue (rare), de La Rue (once), Petrus la vie (once), or a form that uses a rebus for the

---

[2] *Escroes* were the daily pay lists for the ruler's household.

[3] Actually with a lower-case 'p'. First letters of all first-name forms in this discussion are capitalized; last-name forms are given as they actually appear. Appendices A–C give first names as they appear, with the understanding that upper- and lower-case Ps are not always easily distinguishable.

[4] The *état* of 25 Oct. 1515, which uses 'de La Rue', provides names only in a later 16th-c. copy and is not a contemporary document.

[5] FlorC2439 uses 'perison' or 'Perison' in its index, but that was compiled after the collection left the court.

'la'.[6] Manuscripts and prints from outside the court use a very wide variety of names for him.

For Latin documents in places where La Rue was known, his first name was inevitably changed to Petrus and then declined as necessary. His last name either remained de la Rue (most common) or some slight variant thereof (e.g. dela Rue) but was occasionally Latinized as well, to 'de vico' or 'de Vico'.[7] Those cases provide a parallel to the literal translation of his name into Flemish as 'Peter vander Straten'. Spanish language documents take certain liberties with La Rue's name (see App. A, October 1506 through August 1508, and App. B, inventories for 1559 and 1597).

Literary and theoretical writers, almost none of whom would have known La Rue (Molinet excepted), most often use Petrus for the first name or, in Italy, add several more variants, including Pierazzon, Piero, Pier, and Pietro. New forms of the last name include Platensis (from Glarean and his followers), à Platea (also Glarean), della Rue (Lanfranco and Zarlino), de robore (Folengo), Vicanus (Meyerus), and the garbled forms of Loroe (Martin Luther) and de Darne (the mid-seventeenth-century *Instrumentälischer Bettlermantl*).

La Rue himself signed his name 'de 卅 rue' or 'P de 卅 rue' (hereafter 'de *la* rue'),[8] but the form that most likely reflects his given name is 'Pierre de la Rue', given his probable birth in French-speaking Tournai and the overwhelming preference, in places that knew him, to use both a lower-case 'd' and 'l' and upper case 'R' when writing out the full name. When court documents or manuscripts refer to him by last name only, it is usually some form of 'de la Rue' but occasionally simply 'Rue'. The modern tendency to refer to him as 'La Rue', which dates back to the nineteenth century,[9] has no historical foundation among those who knew him personally and very little elsewhere in the sixteenth century. It is nonetheless probably the most common way of referring to him nowadays, despite its poor historical pedigree, and is the shortened form followed in this book. In any event, I trust that readers will know to whom 'La Rue' refers.[10]

To return to the problem of Peter vander Straten, we lack any document where he is unequivocally identified with Pierre de la Rue. As a result, rather than take on faith that the two are the same, as logical as that may appear, the following discussion of La Rue's life falls into three sections: first, a survey of all that we know about the unquestioned La Rue's early years; second, a treatment of Peter vander

---

[6] One particularly strange form is 'Rue de *la*', without any first name. The rebus uses a pitch in musical notation that would be solmized 'la' in a soft hexachord.

[7] Erroneously copied as 'de vito' in the 's-Hertogenbosch record of 1492–3.

[8] In the documents of 11 Oct. and 19 Dec. 1506, 19 Apr. 1507, and 19 Aug. 1508 in App. A.

[9] For example, he is alphabetized under L in both Alexandre Étienne Choron and François Fayolle, *Dictionnaire historique des musiciens artistes et amateurs, morts et vivans ... précédé d'un sommaire de l'histoire de la musique*, 2 vols. (Paris: Valade, Lenormant, 1810–11) and François-Joseph Fétis, *Biographie universelle des musiciens et bibliographie générale de la musique*, 8 vols. (1st edn., Brussels: Leroux, 1835–44).

[10] La Rue is currently listed under L in *New Grove* (both editions) and has been since the fifth edition, but was placed under R in his first appearance in the dictionary (1889), then switched to L for the second edition, and then back to R for the third and fourth editions.

Straten; third, a return to Pierre de la Rue for the years at court and thereafter. Along the way I shall point out both the problems and advantages of equating Peter vander Straten with the composer La Rue.

EARLY YEARS

Birthdate, birthplace, and family

La Rue's date of birth is, at best, an approximation. The primary constraint on establishing a date is that his mother was alive at the time of his death (20 November 1518), though his father, who was still living in August 1507, had passed away before La Rue drew up his will (16 June 1516; both parents are discussed further in this chapter). The outside limit with this constraint seems to be 1452. This would posit both pregnancy at quite a young age for his mother—about 15[11]—and longevity to at least age 81, or a somewhat later pregnancy with a correspondingly more advanced age at death. Even given the generally later menarche and younger death dates of earlier centuries, we cannot rule out that these ages are at least possible. To put them in a contemporary context, we should note that Obrecht's mother is currently thought to have borne him between the ages of 15 and 20,[12] Anne of Brittany gave birth to a stillborn son at age 16, and Marguerite was 17 at the time of her pregnancy. At the other end, current reckonings for Dufay put him at 77 at the time of his death, and Philippe Bouton, first recipient of VatC 234, lived to age 97. A birthdate of *c.*1452 fits an identification of La Rue with Peter vander Straten, whose earliest employment, as a tenor and therefore an adult singer, occurs between 1469–70 (and hence theoretically at age 17 or 18 with the suggested birthdate). If, as seems likely, La Rue is not equivalent to vander Straten, a later birthdate becomes possible.

La Rue's birthplace was almost certainly the important cathedral town of Tournai[13] (see Fig. 1.2 for a map of the Low Countries and environs), which was ruled by France at the time of his birth and upbringing, and had been for centuries.[14] Despite this technicality, the city and surrounding area (the

---

[11] One of La Rue's brothers was named Jehan, as was his father. Although we might expect Jehan to be the eldest son (therefore stretching his mother's age still more), namesakes in the 15th c. were not always the eldest sons; see the example of Étienne Petit junior given in David Fallows, "'Trained and Immersed in All Musical Delights': Towards a New Picture of Busnoys', in Paula Higgins (ed.), *Antoine Busnoys: Method, Meaning, and Context in Late Medieval Music* (Oxford: Clarendon Press, 1999), 21–50 at 42.

[12] See Rob C. Wegman, *Born for the Muses: The Life and Masses of Jacob Obrecht* (Oxford: Clarendon Press, 1994), 37.

[13] Curiously, Tournai itself was split into two dioceses, of Tournai and of Cambrai.

[14] England controlled the town from Sept. 1513 to Feb. 1519, at which time it was returned to the French. In 1521 it was taken over by Charles V for the Habsburg-Burgundian empire. For a discussion of this period see C. G. Cruickshank, *The English Occupation of Tournai 1513–1519* (Oxford: Clarendon Press, 1971). Glarean, in *Dodecachordon*, refers to La Rue as 'gallus', or French (see App. C under 1547). La Rue is described as Flemish in two other posthumous 16th-c. sources. Flemish historian Jacobus Meyerus, writing in 1531, cited Agricola, La Rue, Willaert, and Thomas Martinus as being examples of excellent Flemish singers (see App. C under 1531); all but La Rue were indeed born in Flanders. A second source, the

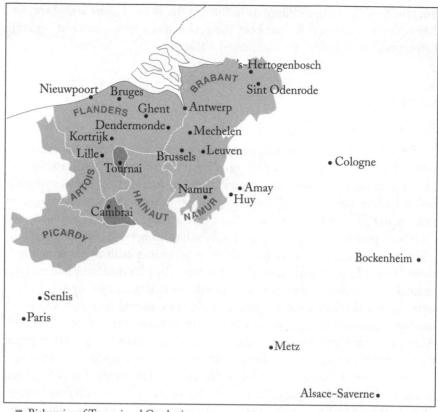

■ Bishoprics of Tournai and Cambrai
▨ Principalities

Fɪɢ. ɪ.2. The Low Countries and environs

Tournaisis) were relatively independent from the French crown[15] and it would be somewhat misleading to refer to La Rue as French; so far nothing other than his presumed place of birth connects him to France. Given that the Tournaisis was between Flanders on one side and Hainaut on the other, La Rue is probably most

Montanus and Neuber print that contains the *Lamentations* ascribed to La Rue (1549[1]), cites him as 'Petri de la Rue, flandro' on the title page and elsewhere as 'Petri de la Rue Flandri'. Early musicologists proposed varying birthplaces for La Rue. François-Joseph Fétis, *Biographie universelle des musiciens et bibliographie générale de la musique*, 8 vols. (2nd edn., Brussels: Firmin-Didot, 1860–5), v. 200, stated that La Rue was from Picardy, claiming that the diminutive 'Pierchon', by which he was frequently known, was only used there; his opinion was echoed by many later historians. Vander Straeten disagreed, citing evidence for the use of Pierchon elsewhere. He proposed instead an identification with a certain 'Petrus De Ruella' from Kortrijk who became a regent of the Sorbonne in 1510; see VDS iii. 211–12. The discovery thereafter that La Rue had held a benefice in Kortrijk and that he had died there strengthened, for Vander Straeten, the plausibility of Kortrijk as the birthplace for La Rue (VDS vii. 112–13). The question of composers' origins and the national identities of schools of composition have occupied musicologists since the origin of the discipline.

[15] See Cruickshank, *The English Occupation*, 32–5.

aptly described as Franco-Flemish, a term now usually avoided for members of his generation.

Although no incontrovertible evidence exists for Tournai as the place of birth, Gustave Caullet's publication of extensive sections of the execution of La Rue's testament showed that one of his brothers lived in Tournai and that his sister and her children presumably lived there as well.[16] To strengthen the association of La Rue with Tournai, Caullet mentioned that 'de la Rue' and his mother's birth name, 'de la Haye', were regional names and were even the names of gateways in Tournai.[17] Perhaps the most convincing evidence for the Tournai connection was provided by the Tournai archivist Adolphe Hocquet, who supplied a long list of de la Rues and de la Hayes from fifteenth-century Tournai,[18] but more importantly discovered in the 1507 *Registre de la loi* of Tournai, under the chapter *Bourgeoisies*, that Jehan de le Rue, *filetier* (maker of thread or yarn), who became a member of the bourgeoisie on 23 June 1507,[19] was a native of Tournai and the son of Jehan.[20] Since we know from the execution of La Rue's testament that he had a brother Jehan who was a *filetier*,[21] and we know from elsewhere that their father was also named Jehan,[22] this 1507 document must refer to La Rue's brother, leaving little doubt that La Rue was also a native of Tournai.[23]

In addition to the names of La Rue's father and brother Jehan, we also know the names of many other family members, furnished by the composer's testament and the execution thereof: his mother Gertrude de la Haye, his brother Jehan's daughter Jennette, another brother, Jacob,[24] and his sister Jeanne, who married Pierre de

[16] CaulletM, 52. The will was also notarized by a priest of the diocese of Tournai, but Kortrijk, where it was drawn up, is in the diocese of Tournai (as are also Ghent, Bruges, and Lille), thus removing any special significance from the priest's affiliation. The information about the priest is sometimes interpreted to mean that the will was notarized in Tournai (e.g. PickerCA, 37), but it reads 'Et ego Johannes Caen presbyter Tornacensis diocesis', i.e. 'And I, Johannes Caen, priest of the diocese of Tournai' (see CaulletM, 49).

[17] CaulletM, 41.

[18] Adolphe Hocquet, 'Archives de Tournai: Tables alphabétiques des testaments et des comptes de tutelle et d'exécution testamentaire (xve siècle)', *Annales de la Société historique de Tournai*, 10 (1906), 42–3, 46–7.

[19] Specifically an archer of the oath of Saint Meurisse; see the following citation.

[20] 'Jehan de le Rue, filetier, natif de Tournay, fil de Jehan, a accaté sa bourgeoisie et y a esté receu comme arbalestrier du serment de saint Meurisse, pour XX sols tournois et en a fait le serment en tel cas introduit. Fait le XXIIIe jour de juing l'an mil Vc et sept'; see Adolphe Hocquet, 'Un musicien tournaisien dit courtraisien', *Revue tournaisienne* (Sept. 1911), 167 8 at 168.

[21] CaulletM, 52.

[22] See App. A under 3 Nov. 1505.

[23] We are unlikely to receive positive confirmation of this. Writing in 1911, Hocquet bemoaned the condition of the Tournai archives, citing the disappearance of many documents at the beginning of the 19th c.; he was unable to find testaments for either of La Rue's parents (Hocquet, 'Un musicien tournaisien', 168). Belgium was the scene of the close of the Napoleonic Wars, and between 1815 and 1830 Tournai passed from the French to the Dutch to the newly created Belgian government, with ensuing destruction of records and organizational confusion. Bad though the situation was in 1911, it is worse now. The Archives de l'État and most of the archives of the Évêché were destroyed in 1940, while those of the cathedral had for the most part been destroyed by 'les Iconoclastes' on 24 Aug. 1566, during the time of religious and political struggles in the Low Countries; see G. Wymans, 'Un dépôt ressuscité: Les Archives de l'État à Tournai', *Archives et bibliothèques de Belgique*, 37 (1966), 186–96.

[24] On Jacob (presumably Jacques; the few references we have to him are all in Latin) see the information on La Rue's Ghent prebend given below.

le Marliere and had two children, Katherine and Anthoine.[25] La Rue's bequest to his niece Katherine raises more questions about his age, birthdate, and identification with vander Straten. At the time of La Rue's death, Katherine was still a minor; her co-guardian Jehan de la Rue received power of attorney to pick up her bequest.[26] She was thus probably born around 1500 at the very earliest, and quite possibly later. If her mother was ten years younger than La Rue (working on the assumption of a 1452 birthdate for the composer), she would have been 38 at the youngest when her daughter was born—surely old for childbearing at the time.[27] A greater gap in age between La Rue and Jeanne reduces her age when her daughter is born, but simultaneously increases the age at which her own mother gave birth. Again, separating La Rue from vander Straten eases the age limits all around.

Exactly which Jehan de la Rue was Pierre's father remains uncertain. Of the candidates put forward, the Jehan who was a bookbinder to the Count of Flanders in 1430 and 1431 can be eliminated;[28] he would have been far too old to be the same person mentioned in the documents from 1505 to 1507 concerning La Rue's father. Also unlikely is the Jean de Platea who was a singer in the chapel of Ferdinand, King of Naples, in 1480.[29] The Jehan de la Rue who was a trumpeter to Philip the Fair was a promising candidate until Jozef Robijns disproved this possibility by discovering a citation of 19 December 1505 mentioning him as deceased.[30]

This leaves two men named Jean de la Rue,[31] both *enlumineurs* in Tournai, an important centre for the production of paintings and miniatures.[32] The younger of these began his apprenticeship in Tournai on 14 September 1463, making him too young for La Rue's father. The other Jean became a master *enlumineur* on 19 May 1463, took several apprentices, and worked on the *entremets* of Bruges in 1468. Of the various people mentioned to date, he is the most likely to have been La Rue's father, although nothing confirms this supposition. Hocquet, without evidence, further identified this Jean with the Haquinet de le Rue (son of Henry de le Rue), who joined the bourgeoisie of Tournai on 14 October 1451.[33]

---

[25] CaulletM, 51–2. Knowledge of La Rue's father comes from several documents, to be discussed later, dating from the time of his second voyage to Spain with Philip the Fair.

[26] CaulletM, 52.

[27] Catherine of Aragon was just shy of 33 when she gave birth to her last child. In general we have almost no records of women's ages at childbirth except for the most famous of individuals.

[28] First mentioned in VDS iii. 211. CaulletM, 42, first considered him a possible father for La Rue.

[29] Again, first brought up in VDS iv. 29–30, and taken seriously by CaulletM, 42.

[30] Marginal note to BAGR, E&A 22, fo. 122ᵛ, cited in RobijnsP, 15. Apparently unaware of Robijns's discovery, PickerCA, 36, cited the trumpeter Jehan as La Rue's father.

[31] See Alexandre Pinchart, *Archives des arts, sciences et lettres*, 3 vols. (Ghent: L. Hebbelynck, 1860–81), iii. 73.

[32] Wim Blockmans and Walter Prevenier, *The Promised Lands: The Low Countries under Burgundian Rule, 1369–1530*, trans. Elizabeth Fackelman, rev. Edward Peters (Philadelphia: University of Pennsylvania Press, 1999), 219.

[33] Hocquet, 'Un musicien tournaisien', 168.

The Tournai 'maîtrise' and St Ode

Given La Rue's almost certain Tournaisian birth and his future as a professional singer, his musical education would doubtless have taken place at the *maîtrise* of the venerable and architecturally important Tournai cathedral. Polyphonic music was performed there since at least the fourteenth century, as we know from the famous Mass of Tournai. The *maîtrise*, which tended to go in and out of existence, was refounded in the year 1451, when three official acts were promulgated for the support of six choirboys and their master of music. These acts included a bull of Pope Nicholas V, a charter of Tournai bishop Jean Chevrot, and a charter of the French king Charles VII.[34] La Rue must have been one of the earlier choirboys to benefit from this freshly endowed *maîtrise*. Entering choirboys received the tonsure, thus becoming clerics and making them eligible for benefices.[35]

At some point, though we have no idea when, La Rue advanced up the ladder of holy orders until he became a deacon; we know this from two references in the Kortrijk records, the account of the execution of his testament, and the garments in which he was buried, which were those of a deacon.[36] That he stopped at the rank of deacon, the stage immediately below that of priest,[37] is confirmed by the almost 300 court documents that name La Rue but never accord him the title *messire*. Although this word had a variety of meanings at the time, the court chapel reserved it exclusively for priests, and the distinction was meticulously followed. La Rue is frequently referred to in prebend documents as 'Dominus', confirming his status as a canon, and occasionally as 'Magister' as well.[38] Although the latter term is most often used at the time to refer to one holding a university degree, we have no evidence of such training for La Rue. Further, he is never referred to as 'maistre' (the French equivalent) in court documents, despite their penchant for observing the proper honorifics for their singers.

La Rue's first canonicate appears to have been at the collegiate church of St Ode, though we do not know whether he was already a deacon at that point. We learn of St Ode through the account of the execution of his testament, where it is clear that it was a prebend he continued to hold at the time of his death, one of only two that he maintained into his retirement (the other being Kortrijk, where

[34] Nicolas Joachim, *Aperçu historique sur la maîtrise de la cathédrale de Tournai (Xme–XXme siècle)* (Tournai and Paris: Casterman, 1942), 19. Joachim was canon at the cathedral and the director of the Tournai *maîtrise* from 1906 to 1936. Though he drew on the cathedral archives for his material, unfortunately he rarely provided precise documentation for his statements. Cathedral archivist Chanoine Jean Dumoulin kindly informed me that the cathedral no longer had any documents from this period (pers. comm. 4 July 1984). Other information on the *maîtrise* is found in F. F. J. Lecouvet, 'Les Enfants de chœur et les maîtres de musique de la cathédrale de Tournay—Fête des Innocents', *Messager des sciences historiques des arts et de la bibliographie de Belgique* (1856), 147–76.

[35] Joachim, *Aperçu historique*, 16.

[36] See the citations in App. A for 1506 and 1508 (both otherwise undated) and 20 Nov. 1518; see also Meconi, 'Free from the Crime of Venus', which cites the pertinent bibliography and also points out the ways in which his epitaph—and for that matter, his general conduct—befitted his ecclesiastical rank.

[37] Some of the modern literature erroneously refers to him as priest, e.g. RobijnsP, 20.

[38] For citations as Magister, see App. A, 4 May 1508, 27 June 1509, 26 Apr. 1513, 22 May 1514, after 20 Nov. 1518, 1519 (undated), 3 Jan. 1522, 15 Oct. 1524, and 28–9 July 1540.

he lived). The reference states that the income for the year in which he died was sent by 'the lords, deacon, and chapter of *Roode* where the said maker of the will lived as a canon'.[39] In addition to the references to St Ode and Roode, there is also a reference to Rode in the testament.

It is not yet clear where this collegiate church was, nor how La Rue came to hold this well-paying prebend.[40] The most likely candidate is the church of Sint Odenrode in the town of the same name about twenty kilometres south-east of 's-Hertogenbosch.[41] Another possibility is the collegiate church of Sainte-Ode in Amay, a small town close to Huy in south-east Belgium.[42] Although the name of this latter church is not as promising as that of the Dutch church, Amay itself is closer to Brussels than Sint Odenrode is, a fact that becomes important in the context of a payment in the execution of La Rue's testament to 'master Nicolaus Nyspen, secretary of the venerable lord cardinal of Cambrai in Brussels for the salary of the income of Rode to be collected on behalf of the said late testator'.[43] Amay is also somewhat closer to Cologne, but that fact is only important in the context of the career of Peter vander Straten, to whom we now turn.

PETER VANDER STRATEN

Brussels/Ghent/Nieuwpoort

The account books of the collegiate church of Sint Goedele in Brussels record a miscellaneous payment to the tenor 'peteren vander straten' during the fiscal year 1469–70.[44] Sint Goedele was undergoing a period of expansion in the amount of polyphony performed there, with the result that musicians such as vander Straten were hired temporarily when need arose. Both the temporary nature of the employment, the relative proximity of Brussels to Tournai, and the early date suggest that, if La Rue were vander Straten, this may have been his earliest professional employment.

[39] CaulletM, 49.

[40] It was worth over £124 annually, which was probably the major reason La Rue maintained it for so long.

[41] According to CaulletM, 46, the *collégiale* and most of its archives were destroyed in 1583. RobijnsP, 28, citing Caullet, gives the date in a slip of the pen as 1858, saying that Protestants were responsible for the destruction. The *collégiale* is discussed in W. Heesters and C. S. M. Rademaker, *Geschiedenis van Sint-Oedenrode* (Bijdragen tot de Geschiedenis van het Zuiden van Nederland, 24; Tilburg: Stichting Zuidelijk Historisch Contact, 1972), 75–80 and *passim*.

[42] I should like to thank Barbara Haggh for bringing this church to my attention. Relatively little remains concerning the *collégiale* in the crucial two decades of the 15th c. when La Rue might have been there, the 1470s and the 1480s. The *mémoire* written by Claire Moreau, 'L'Obituaire de la Collégiale Sainte-Ode d'Amay: Édition et commentaires' (thesis, Université de Liège, 1983), contains a list of canons prior to 1500 based on the surviving material; La Rue is not included.

[43] CaulletM, 51. Brussels was an important administrative centre for the diocese of Cambrai; see Barbara Helen Haggh, 'Music, Liturgy, and Ceremony in Brussels, 1350–1500', 2 vols. (Ph.D. diss., University of Illinois at Urbana-Champaign, 1988), i. 9.

[44] See App. A, 1469–70; this document was kindly brought to my attention by Barbara Haggh. For a detailed study of musical life in Brussels (including Sint Goedele) at this time, see Haggh, 'Music, Liturgy,

Two years later 'pieter vander Straten' sings, again on an apparently temporary basis, at Sint Jacobskerk, a parish church of Ghent. The employment began sometime after 24 June 1471 (the Feast of St John the Baptist was one of the quarterly payment dates at the church, and vander Straten is absent then) and concluded sometime before 15 March 1472, another quarterly payment date on which he is not present. The temporary nature of the employment is suggested by the smaller sums he is paid than others at the time, as well as the fact that his last payment is from the miscellaneous rather than the regular singers' accounts.[45] Reinhard Strohm hypothesized that the special payment might suggest polyphonic singing,[46] and indeed a weekly polyphonic mass for the Holy Spirit had been endowed at the church in 1470.[47]

In May of 1472 'pieter van straten' showed up in the Belgian coastal town of Nieuwpoort in the records of the parish church of Onze-Lieve-Vrouw.[48] The isolated payment, which is under the monthly account, again argues for temporary employment, but in this case it led (at least initially) to something more permanent, for at the end of the church's fiscal year (which began annually on the Feast of the Purification), 'den Teneur pieter van straten' was paid for six months' service from an annual contract to total 5 pounds groot.[49] Unfortunately, the account books vanish immediately thereafter, and when they resurface again for the fiscal year 1477–8, vander Straten is no longer there. After several years of presumed itinerancy, then, vander Straten had attained some kind of resident position, however long it lasted.

Cologne/'s-Hertogenbosch

vander Straten next appears quite a few years later, in the accounts for 1489–90 of the famous Confraternity of the Illustre Lieve Vrouwe in 's-Hertogenbosch. 'Heer peteren straten tenorist' from Cologne[50] is reimbursed for his travel expenses to and from 's-Hertogenbosch because 'we really wanted him as a tenor'.[51] On 5 October 'heer peteren van straten' is now referred to as 'our tenorist' ('ons tenorist') when Ghÿsbert van roy, the confraternity's provisor in Cologne

---

and Ceremony'. The 1485 date mentioned in ii. 670 is an error.

[45] SJG, MS 1203, unfoliated; the discovery of vander Straten in Ghent was made by Reinhard Strohm. His payments can be contrasted with the much larger ones made to Pieter Bordon at the same time; see Rob C. Wegman, 'Agricola, Bordon and Obrecht at Ghent: Discoveries and Revisions', *Revue belge de musicologie*, 51 (1997), 23–62 at 57.

[46] Reinhard Strohm, private comm. 26 Mar. 1987.

[47] Rob C. Wegman, 'Ghent', *New Grove II*, ix. 806.

[48] See App. A, 5 May 1472. Again, Reinhard Strohm was responsible for discovering vander Straten in Nieuwpoort.

[49] See App. A, 1473. August to January payments, such as this presumably was, were common in West Flanders.

[50] Apart from the information in the 's-Hertogenbosch accounts, we know nothing of vander Straten's employment in Cologne, not even his institution of employment.

[51] 'Want wy hemgherne voer een tenorist hedde gehad'.

and apparently the one responsible for bringing vander Straten to the confraternity's attention, is given a sum of money to forward to him.[52]

The Confraternity at 's-Hertogenbosch was a major musical institution and certainly the most important one in town, with six to ten adult singers who performed polyphony in their chapel in the Sint Janskerk on the most important feast days of the year.[53] Vander Straten joined by what must have been late October 1489, and apparently remained until late February 1492.[54] At that point vander Straten disappears from the Confraternity's books, but very curiously, Pierre de la Rue then shows up, in two different entries, which warrant some discussion.

During the fiscal year St John's Day 1492–3, the one following the last for vander Straten (St John's Day 1491–2), La Rue and seven of his colleagues from the Habsburg-Burgundian court became members of the Confraternity, as did hundreds of people every year.[55] In the account book, the eight singers are listed individually, one below another, and then the eight names are bracketed and marked to the side as 'Cantores Regis Romanorum'—singers of the King of the Romans (i.e. Maximilian).[56] The singers are listed in the order 'heer peter du wez, presbyter/Johannes lauwier Canonicus aule valencen/dominus valennus ouger presbyter/Johannes picquavet Canonicus aule valencen/petrus de vito[57] Cantor Romanorum Regis/Gerardyn barbet/matheus de campania/michael barruyer de hanonia'.

As with all the records surviving from the Confraternity at this time, the account is a formal recopying of material that originally existed in another form,

---

[52] Although this entry precedes the reimbursement in the written records, the payment via Ghÿsbert did not necessarily precede it as well; indeed, it seems likely that the 'audition' engendering the travel reimbursement came before the confraternity's claiming of Vander Straten as 'our tenorist'. Further, the payments come from two separate sections of the accounts.

[53] For bibliography on 's-Hertogenbosch see Albert Smijers, 'De Illustre Lieve Vrouwe Broederschap te 's-Hertogenbosch', *TVNM* 11 (1923–5), 187–210; 12 (1926–8), 40–62, 115–67; 13 (1929–32), 46–100, 181–237; 14 (1932–5), 48–105; 16 (1940–6), 63–106, 216; 17 (1948–55), 195–230; Christiaan Maria van Dijck, *De Bossche optimaten: Geschiedenis van de Illustre Lieve Vrouwebroederschap te 's-Hertogenbosch, 1318–1973* (Bijdragen tot de geschiedenis van het Zuiden van Nederland, 27; Tilburg: Stichting Zuidelijk Historisch Contact, 1973); and Eric Jas, '*Sicut lilium inter spinas*: Het muziekleven te 's-Hertogenbosch rond de Illustre Lieve Vrouwe Broederschap', in *Kloosters, kronieken en koormuziek: Cultuur in bourgondisch 's-Hertogenbosch 1450–1629* (Brabantse lezingen, 6; 's-Hertogenbosch: Het Noordbrabants Genootschap, 1991), 41–60. The confraternity still exists today, and I should like to thank L. C. J. M. Rouppe van de Voort of the confraternity for his gracious assistance.

[54] The confraternity's fiscal year started on the Feast of St John the Baptist (24 June); Vander Straten's final payment record is for thirty-five weeks only, which would run to 23 Feb. of the following calendar year; see App. A, 1491–2. The records are organized by fiscal year, but precise dates are rarely noted. Vander Straten's rate of pay varies considerably during his time at the confraternity, doubtless owing to the great financial instability in the Low Countries at precisely this time. For an overview of contemporary fiscal problems, see Peter Spufford, *Monetary Problems and Policies in the Burgundian Netherlands 1433–1496* (Leiden: E. J. Brill, 1970).

[55] There were two tiers of membership, of which La Rue and his colleagues belonged to the less exclusive one. DoorslaerC, 156 and *passim*, misunderstood the entry and stated that the individuals were there with Maximilian, singing the divine offices in the chapel of the confraternity.

[56] Maximilian had held this position, which made him next in line for the title of Holy Roman Emperor, since 1486.

[57] The proper Latin form is 'vico'. Although 't' and 'c' are rather similar in the scribe's hand, the entry looks more like the former than the latter in the records.

which surely accounts for the miscopying of the Latin form of La Rue's name as 'vito' instead of 'vico'. But other curiosities about the list are much harder to explain. Most of the names and terms are given in their Latin forms, but Dutch, the usual language for the Confraternity's records, is used at the beginning of the list, with 'heer peter' rather than 'Dominus Petrus', as might be expected (the meaning of various honorifics is discussed below). Because of the extensive use of Latin, we are not surprised to see the Latin form of La Rue's name, but the scribe did not identify La Rue as a canon, which we know he was by this time (at St Ode), or as either Heer or Dominus, while vander Straten is always 'Heer' in the Confraternity records. Does that imply unfamiliarity with La Rue (i.e. evidence that he was not vander Straten) or is it simply an oversight? Or was there not enough room to include 'dominus' or 'canonicus'? After all, La Rue already had extra information added: he is the only one singled out a second time as 'Cantor Romanorum Regis'. Apparently this was considered more important than any ecclesiastical titles. Was this to indicate that he was now in a new position, no longer at the Confraternity as a singer? This is certainly possible given that this title was written first after his name and only secondarily added to encompass the other members of the group (this could also explain the incorrect spelling of his name by a scribe who initially knew him by a different name). But La Rue, if he was vander Straten, was not the only one of Maximilian's singers to be a former employee of the Confraternity. Barbet had also sung there, and for much longer, from 1471 to 1482, with a brief return in 1489.[58] Was it necessary to distinguish La Rue because he had been there so recently, in contrast to Barbet? For that matter, was the membership prompted initially by La Rue and Barbet, as former singers of the Confraternity?

The order of the list, or more precisely La Rue's position in it, is also extremely curious. The first surviving list of the Habsburg-Burgundian chapel members after La Rue joined[59] places him below all of the other seven singers included on the Confraternity list. The court chapel, although not rigid, was fairly consistent in its listing of singers according to rank, and we can observe La Rue slowly but very surely climbing up the payroll during his many years at court.[60] Does the Confraternity listing reflect an order that changed, with La Rue slipping down (the chapel list referred to earlier comes from September 1495), or was La Rue given an unnaturally high slot on the Confraternity inscription precisely because he had so recently been their favoured tenorist?

The second reference to La Rue in the Confraternity accounts comes from much later, during the fiscal year St John's Day 1511–12, when 'petrus de vico, de larue, cantor principis' is listed along with other Confraternity members as having paid his *dootschult*, literally 'death-debt'. This time the identification is triple: he is de vico, de larue, and singer of the *princeps* (the 'first in line', the 'one in charge', i.e.

---

[58] DoorslaerC, 140.   [59] See App. A, 30 Sept. 1495.
[60] See the citations in App. A beginning with 30 Sept. 1495.

the archduke Charles). Nowhere does vander Straten come in. Does the lack of identification as vander Straten here confirm that the two are different? Or has the twenty-year absence of La Rue from the Confraternity erased the need to equate 'de Vico' with the Dutch name by which he went? Or would the scribe of the later account book even have been around in 1492? Or did La Rue send in his payment by proxy? What prompted his identification as Charles's singer? All these questions remain unanswered.

Peter vander Straten makes one more appearance, but not in connection with 's-Hertogenbosch. On 15 July 1514 he became a member of the Confraternity of Our Lady in Antwerp.[61] Nothing else is known about him in this context.

Was Peter vander Straten Pierre de la Rue?

Appropriately enough, Edmond Vander Straeten was the first to suggest an identification of La Rue with Peter vander Straten, hypothesizing that the Flemish form was the original that La Rue then translated into French.[62] Given La Rue's probable birthplace, this is highly unlikely, and as we shall see, it becomes increasingly difficult to accept the identification at all. The summary that follows brings up points pro and con for the identification and rebuttals for each point.

1. (*a*) Peter vander Straten is the literal translation of Pierre de la Rue (as Petrus de Vico is the literal Latin translation), and Rue is an especially difficult French word for non-native speakers to pronounce. The name change occurs in Flemish or Dutch language documents in an age where multiple names, at least among professional musicians, almost seem to have been the norm.

(*b*) Both La Rue's first and last names were common ones, and there are numerous vander Stratens, de Vicos, and even de la Rues who could not have been the composer.[63] Neither Italians nor Spaniards (despite La Rue's multi-year residence in Spain) normally translated his name.

2. (*a*) vander Straten departs from 's-Hertogenbosch with excellent timing, avoiding any overlap with La Rue's next position at the Habsburg-Burgundian court (as we shall see in the next section, this timing could be even better than previously thought), nor does any information about any of vander Straten's appearances conflict with anything known for certain about La Rue.

(*b*) Although this does not contradict identification, neither does it provide confirmation.

---

[61] Eugeen Schreurs, 'Petrus Alamire: Music Calligrapher, Musician, Composer, Spy,' in *TA* 15–27 at 26 n. 38.

[62] VDS iii. 211, vi. 469, and vii. 123. In vi. 39, he cited the discovery by Gevaert in Toledo of a motet or motets by Pietro Ver Straete or Van der Straeten, but no such motets are known today.

[63] Possibly the most famous is the 'de la Rue' to whom numerous chansons in 16th-c. French prints were attributed; see Honey Meconi, 'French Print Chansons and Pierre de la Rue: A Case Study in Authenticity', in Jessie Ann Owens and Anthony Cummings (eds.), *Music in Renaissance Cities and Courts: Studies in Honor of Lewis Lockwood* (Warren, Mich.: Harmonie Park Press, 1997), 187–214. My own research as well as that of such generous and indefatigable archival wizards as Barbara Haggh and Rob Wegman has kept

3. (*a*) The identification of the two musicians generates a consistent and compelling biographical story. A young singer begins his career by picking up whatever temporary positions are available and gradually moves on to bigger and better things, usually farther and farther away from home, until ending up at the most important musical establishment in the Low Countries, the Habsburg-Burgundian court chapel. Rather than being just any musician, he is a tenorist, a term presumably reserved for the most highly skilled singers,[64] and thus a fitting role for someone destined to become one of the most famous musicians of his time. In his position at the court he is consistently loyal and productive, and as a result (though thanks at least in part to his financial shrewdness and frugality) he becomes rich and respected while benefiting from a forum for his enormous compositional talent. This biographical picture fits extremely well with the move from itinerancy to residency taking place in general across the Low Countries and northern France at precisely the same time, coincident with the rise of polyphonic performance in this area.[65]

(*b*) History, alas, does not always package biographies as neatly as we might wish, and any number of discoveries would derail this attractive narrative, as we shall see below.

4. (*a*) La Rue's music appears in no sources that can be firmly dated in the fifteenth century, suggesting that he is a younger musician than vander Straten.

(*b*) None of the places vander Straten worked has left any sources from the last quarter of the fifteenth century, and both Flemish and French sources are rare in any case for this period. A similarly restricted source distribution exists for the very prolific Mouton, who was at most five or six years younger than vander Straten and possibly the same age.

5. (*a*) Identifying La Rue with vander Straten requires unlikely ages for childbirth for his mother and possibly his sister, as well as an advanced age for his mother at the time of La Rue's death.

(*b*) The minuscule amount of information about the lives of medieval and early modern women, to say nothing of the extreme variability of both menarche and menopause, makes generalizations problematic.[66]

6. (*a*) The later references to La Rue in 's-Hertogenbosch documents make no mention of vander Straten.

me plentifully supplied with possible biographical leads for the composer, most of which unfortunately had to be discarded for various reasons (e.g. priesthood, marriage).

[64] David Fallows and Owen Jander, 'Tenor (2)', *New Grove II*, xxv. 285. The precise role of the tenorist has yet to be satisfactorily defined, nor was a tenorist always a tenor; see the information on Braconnier in Ch. 2. Was it significant that vander Straten went from being merely a tenor in early references to a highly desirable tenorist at 's-Hertogenbosch?

[65] See Barbara Haggh, 'Itinerancy to Residency: Professional Careers and Performance Practices in 15th-Century Sacred Music', *Early Music*, 17 (1989), 359–66.

[66] Even with a woman as famous as Catherine of Aragon it is virtually impossible to obtain accurate information about her many pregnancies—a matter of considerable historical importance.

(*b*) This might be in recognition of his new (or later, his long-held) role, because of the prominence of Latin in the specific reference, because La Rue chose to represent himself that way, or because the payments were made by proxy.

7. (*a*) The term *Heer*, always used with vander Straten in 's-Hertogenbosch, designates a priest. La Rue was only a deacon.

(*b*) *Heer* is the Dutch equivalent of the Latin *dominus*, which can mean either priest or canon.[67] We know La Rue was the latter, and we also know that he was at times referred to with the title *dominus* in documents from Kortrijk and Ghent. That said, the use of *Heer*, *Dominus*, and *canonicus* in the list of Maximilian's singers who joined the 's-Hertogenbosch brotherhood remains curious. The two called *Heer* or *Dominus* are further identified as priests. Why is this double identification necessary, if *Heer* (at least) indicated priesthood? If *Heer* is used for canon as well as priest, why aren't the canons given that honorific? Why isn't La Rue, who was a canon by then (this occurs after his time at St Ode) identified as a canon? Perhaps it is wrong to expect these short entries to provide full titular information for the singers; space surely precluded the addition of much, if anything, to these already rather complex citations. But it is also possible that at 's-Hertogenbosch the use of *Heer* was restricted to priests (just like *messire* in the court chapel) and that the use of this term for Peter vander Straten would unequivocally mark him as someone other than La Rue.

8. (*a*) Once La Rue arrives at the court, he is never referred to as a tenor or tenorist, unlike vander Straten.

(*b*) This statement, confirmed by Appendix A, may surprise those familiar with Van Doorslaer's assertion to the contrary,[68] given that author's extensive work with archival material from the court as well as his apparent unawareness of the 's-Hertogenbosch references to vander Straten. That Van Doorslaer did not get the tenor designation from court documents, however, seems clear, given that La Rue is not listed when he catalogues the vocal designations he found among court records.[69] Van Doorslaer does, however, cite Edmond Vander Straeten among his bibliographic references for information on La Rue, and this is surely where the tenor identification comes from.

As it turns out, Edmond Vander Straeten's citation of La Rue as a tenor has no foundation in fact;[70] the publication that he is quoting nowhere lists La Rue as a tenor.[71] To add another layer of absurdity, elsewhere Vander Straeten claims that La Rue is a bass because the court *escroes*, in Vander Straeten's opinion, are organ-

---

[67] For meanings of *dominus*, see 'dominus' in J. F. Niermeyer, *Mediae Latinitatis lexicon minus: A Medieval Latin-French/English Dictionary* (Leiden: E. J. Brill, 1976).

[68] DoorslaerC, 156. [69] Ibid. 161. [70] VDS iii. 213.

[71] Louis-Prosper Gachard, *Rapport à Monsieur le ministre de l'intérieur sur différentes series de documents concernant l'histoire de la Belgique qui sont conservées dans les archives de l'ancienne chambre des comptes de Flandre à Lille* (Brussels: M. Hayez, 1841), 280.

ized by order of voice part and La Rue is near the bottom.[72] *Escroes* were not organized by voice part, however, but rather by pay level corresponding to the various functions within the chapel; within each function, rank is determined by seniority as well as other now unascertainable factors. This is discussed in Chapter 2, which also demonstrates the salient point here: references to voice parts are rare in chapel records during La Rue's tenure.

That said, we have one presumed reference to a voice part for La Rue. This is in the ordinance Charles drew up for the governance of his household on 25 October 1515. La Rue appears third on the list of *Grand chapelle* members, after the two *premier chapelains* (de Orto and Antoine de Berghes alternated periods of service in this position, with de Orto, the 'first' *premier chapelain*, beginning in January and de Berghes, the 'second', starting in June).[73] After the introduction of these two, the heading 'Autres chappellains et chantres de ladict chappelle tousiours comptez' appears, followed by 'Pierre de La Rue dessus henry bredermers organiste chacung à xi sols par jour'. La Rue's citation is noteworthy for its use of the term *dessus*. Yet the first thing to mention is that the document that contains this ordinance is a posthumous sixteenth-century copy,[74] not the original, and it is faulty in some respects.

That this copy is deficient is seen by comparing it with a seventeenth-century copy of the same material.[75] This latter version lacks the names of chapel members but does include the statutes for the chapel, and we can see that it is both more complete and more accurate than the earlier copy. For example, the sixteenth-century copy twice substitutes the erroneous 'chambellain' for the correct 'chapelain', lists two feasts to be observed as 'La nativité et La nativité' instead of 'la nativite et la conception', uses an ellipsis twice where the seventeenth-century copy gives full information ('... midi et none' versus 'prime tierce mydy et none'; 'au ...' versus 'au pulpitre'), and so on. Clearly, both the sixteenth- and seventeenth-century scribes were copying from something now lost, but the earlier scribe does not seem to be especially attuned to the realities of chapel life. It is just possible that he erred when he copied *dessus*.

But let us assume that he got it right. Perhaps *dessus* merely refers to La Rue's position above Bredemers and the 'autres chappellains'; indeed, the next highest singers receive a lower salary, ten sols per day. But it is more likely that *dessus* refers to the highest voice part. Recent discussion of this sense of the term places its use in the seventeenth to early nineteenth centuries,[76] and in the famous Burgundian court document from 1469 listing the preferred combination of

[72] VDS vii. 122.

[73] The surviving *escroes* do not reinforce this division of time, however; see the discussion under de Orto in Ch. 2.

[74] In addition to being in a scribal hand found in no other contemporary court document, it also provides acute and grave accents for words and uses the more modern 'de La Rue' capitalization of the composer's name.

[75] For bibliographic information see App. A, 25 Oct. 1515.

[76] See 'Dessus', *New Grove II*.

singers, for example, the high voices are called just that, *haultes voix*.[77] Despite this, compelling evidence comes in a list of Charles V's chapel members from 1522 that lists four separate singers under the rubric *dessus* for their voice designation; further, the Burgundian court poet Jean Molinet, a musically astute writer active during La Rue's earlier court employment, uses the term to indicate a vocal part in his poem 'J'ay veu, comme il me semble'.[78]

> J'ay veu, comme il me semble,
> Ung fort homme d'honneur
> Luy seul chanter ensemble
> Et dessus et teneur;
> Olbeken, Alexandre,
> Jossequin ne Bugnois
> Qui sçavent chant espandre
> Ne font tels esbanois.
>
> I saw, it seemed to me,
> A strong man of honoor
> sing alone by himself,
> treble and tenor together.
> Ockeghem, Alexander,
> Josquin, or Busnoys,
> Who know how to deliver a song,
> Cannot entertain in such a way.

Tinctoris claimed that 'some *tenoristae* and *contratenoristae* are called *bassi* when they are recognised as suitable for singing low tenors and contratenors'.[79] This statement shows an unexpected flexibility in vocal terminology; could this flexibility have occurred in the opposite direction (for higher voices) as well? How certain are we that 'tenorist' referred exclusively to vocal range rather than some kind of performance function? Could someone who originally sang tenor have switched by the end of his performing career to the kind of falsetto singing required for superius parts? Or is it simply more reasonable to assume that La Rue was never a tenor?

It is time to turn back to the larger question. Are the negative points presented above cumulatively too great to put faith in vander Straten as La Rue? They are not only sufficient to alert us to other possibilities, they are numerous enough to

---

[77] David Fallows, 'Specific Information on the Ensembles for Composed Polyphony, 1400–1474', in Stanley Boorman (ed.), *Studies in the Performance of Late Mediaeval Music* (Cambridge: Cambridge University Press, 1983), 109–59 at 110. A chapel list from later in Charles V's reign refers to the 'vox acuta: discantus'; see Antonius Sanderus, *Chorographia sacra Brabantiae* . . . (Brussels: Philippum Vleugartium, 1659), 17, at the close of the volume.

[78] As published for the first time in Frédéric-Auguste, le baron de Reiffenberg, 'Lettre à M. Fétis, directeur du conservatoire de Bruxelles, sur quelques particularités de l'histoire musicale de la Belgique', in *Le Dimanche, récits de Marsilius Brunck,* 2 vols. (Brussels: Louis Hauman, 1834), ii. 259–329 at 284. For Charles's chapel list see Georges Van Doorslaer, 'La Chapelle musicale de Charles-Quint en 1522', *Musica sacra*, 40 (1933), 215–30 at 220.

[79] As quoted in Fallows, 'Specific Information', 115.

make us shy away from all the explaining it takes to equate the two names. Though the identification is not impossible, it is considerably less likely than the alternative, that we are dealing with two separate musicians.

THE HABSBURG-BURGUNDIAN CHAPEL UNDER MAXIMILIAN, PHILIP, AND JUANA: 1492?–1508

Maximilian, Philip, and La Rue's early years in the chapel

If La Rue had arrived at the Habsburg-Burgundian court from 's-Hertogen-bosch, as the vander Straten version of his life would have it, he would be coming as a tenorist of good reputation, a mature musician of about 40 years old with twenty-odd years of performing experience, and would certainly warrant employment immediately as a *chantre* rather than at a lower rank (see the discussion of chapel structure in Ch. 2). But professional experience equivalent to that of Peter vander Straten could be acquired elsewhere, and certainly La Rue's being hired at 10s. per day instead of 12 (he achieves the higher pay scale in January 1497, in his fifth year of service) seems an additional argument that he was instead a bit younger and slightly less illustrious than vander Straten. Yet no matter where La Rue came from, he arrived at a place well worth being. Courtly employment at this time, especially at one of the most important centres in Europe, almost always was more remunerative than that offered by sacred institutions. Moreover, singers in the chapel were eligible for miscellaneous wages and gifts, to say nothing of the lucrative prebends the rulers distributed as rewards for good service (La Rue, as his testament shows, did very well financially). If, as a professional singer, La Rue was interested in performing interesting and challenging music frequently, he could hardly have obtained a better position, and as a composer, even if not hired as such, he had found a magnificent venue for his works.

Until now, the date that La Rue joined the chapel seemed straightforward: 17 November 1492, when he and others were taken on by Maximilian, though without being paid until the chapel was switched to the *escroes* of Philip on 30 September 1495. As it turns out, there is much more to say about La Rue's entry into the chapel and his early service therein, though no new dates are forthcoming. But to explore the meaning of 17 November 1492, we need to go back much further and follow Maximilian in the period leading up to this date.[80]

---

[80] Selected material on music during Maximilian's early years is found in Otto zu Nedden, 'Zur Geschichte der Musik am Hofe Kaiser Maximilians I', *Zeitschrift für Musikwissenschaft*, 15 (1932–3), 24–32; Louise Cuyler, *The Emperor Maximilian I and Music* (London, New York, and Toronto: Oxford University Press, 1973); and Paula Higgins, '*In hydraulis* Revisited: New Light on the Career on Antoine Busnois', *JAMS* 39 (1986), 36–86. The standard work on Maximilian is Hermann Wiesflecker, *Kaiser Maximilian I.: Das Reich, Österreich und Europa an der Wende zur Neuzeit*, 5 vols. (Munich: R. Oldenbourg, 1971–86). There is also a one-volume survey; see id., *Maximilian I.: Die Fundamente des habsburgischen Weltreiches* (Vienna: Verlag für Geschichte und Politik; Munich: R. Oldenbourg, 1991), where a detailed chronology of his life appears on pp. 389–406.

When Maximilian married Mary of Burgundy, only child and heiress of the last duke of Burgundy proper,[81] Charles the Bold, he acquired an impressive array of problems. Charles was a hot-headed warrior who had managed to undo a good deal of the work of the previous and much more effective duke, Philip the Good.[82] Although Maximilian staved off immediate catastrophe with successful military campaigns, he soon proved a poor leader in other respects.[83] The death of Mary of Burgundy in a hunting accident in 1482 only added to his difficulties, and he was a thoroughly unpopular regent for his son, Philip the Fair.

Maximilian's regency was noted particularly for his almost uniformly disastrous fiscal policies.[84] Not surprisingly, the chapel fell rather by the wayside, as had happened more than once in the history of the Burgundian court. *Escroes* from September and October 1485, for example, cite as few as five members.[85] Just as in the past, however, the chapel was expanded when it was time to impress outsiders. For Maximilian, the impetus was the planned journey to Germany in December 1485 to greet his father, Holy Roman Emperor Frederick III, whom he had not seen since his marriage. Not by accident, this visit coincided with his election and then coronation as King of the Romans. Court historiographer Jean Molinet provides a fairly detailed account of the restocking of the chapel, naming specific singers and talking about their individual strengths.[86]

Although Maximilian was elected King of the Romans (the office whose holder would become the next Holy Roman Emperor) on 16 February 1486, and crowned in Aachen the following 9 April, his standing within the Low Countries did not improve. On 1 February 1488 his regency hit its lowest point, when he was imprisoned by the citizens of Bruges and kept captive until the following 16 May; this did nothing for his prestige or his authority. It comes as no surprise that in January 1489 he left the Low Countries and returned to Germany, leaving a regency council to govern in his stead. The meeting of the Golden Fleece in Mechelen on 23 May 1491 was presided over by the not quite 13-year-old Philip,[87] for by this time Maximilian had acquired a new power base in the Tyrol and his attention had turned towards the East.

What of the chapel during this time? That Maximilian did not take it with him in January 1489 is seen from a large payment (the equivalent of two months' wages)

[81] The marriage took place in Ghent on 19 Aug. 1477. Although the duchy of Burgundy reverted to the French crown on Charles's death, successive rulers of Habsburg-Burgundy often continued to identify themselves as duke of Burgundy.

[82] See Blockmans and Prevenier, *The Promised Lands*, 174–95, for an excellent summary of this period as well as numerous bibliographical references. As the full title of the book shows (and as is rarely the case), the authors correctly perceive the continuation of Burgundy as a concept as well as a political entity after the loss of the duchy proper.

[83] See Wiesflecker, *Kaiser Maximilian I.*, 113 ff., on Maximilian's basic lack of understanding of the Low Countries.

[84] Summarized in Spufford, *Monetary Problems*, 8–11, 141–6.

[85] BNF n.a.f., 5904 N° 141/53–146/58.

[86] Jean Molinet, *Chroniques de Jean Molinet (1474–1506)*, ed. Georges Doutrepont and Omer Jodogne, 3 vols. (Brussels: Palais des académies, 1935–7), i. 469–70.

[87] Ibid. ii. 222–30.

made on 17 February 1489 modern style to various members of the *grande* and *petite chapelles*.[88] This was part of a grand but yet again fiscally irresponsible gesture Maximilian had made to those many members of his household left behind.[89] But after this, no full listing of chapel members is known until the one that demarcates the period 17 November 1492–30 September 1495.[90]

The 1492–5 dates are given in the account book of 1495 as well as in two separate *mandements* (2 October 1495 and 10 December 1496). In 1841 Louis-Prosper Gachard published excerpts from the 1495 account book that were then quoted by Edmond Vander Straeten, and from there cited by almost everyone who wrote about the chapel. The relevant information in Gachard was 'dû de leurs gages, attendu qu'ils n'ont rien reçu par les écrous de la dépense ordinaire de l'hôtel, depuis le 17 novembre 1492, que le roi des Romains les retint en son service, jusqu'au 30 septembre 1495, que ledit seigneur les a fait porter sur les écrous de la dépense ordinaire de son hôtel' ('due from their wages, since they have received nothing from the *escroes* of the *dépense ordinaire de l'hôtel* since 17 November 1492, when the King of the Romans [Maximilian] retained them in his service, until 30 September 1495, when the said lord [Philip] had them carried on the *escroes* of the *dépense ordinaire* of his *hôtel*').

As it turns out, the account entry is rather more complex than Gachard's excerpt would suggest. It opens with a list of twenty-five chapel members, then provides the total amount paid out,[91] and then mentions their lack of payment for this extended period. In the original, however, it reads 'deu de leurs gaiges A cause du service que par ordonnance dicellui seigneur Ilz lui ont fait en faisant le service divin par devant lui en sadit chappelle sans avoir este comptez. Ne prins aucuns gaiges par ledict escroes de la despence ordinaire de son hostel depuis le xvii[e] jour de novembre lan iiii[xx] xii que lors Ilz vindrent devers le Roy des Romains et notre seigneur et que icellui seigneur les Retinst en son service Jusques au derrniere jour de septembre derrnierement passe ondit an iiii[xx] xv que desla en avant Il les a fait compter par les escroes de la despense ordinaire de sondit hostel ...'; it then lists the individual payments.

This fuller description goes as follows: 'due from their wages because of the service that by the ordinance of that lord they did for him in performing the divine service before him in his said chapel without having been counted, not taking any

[88] LADN B2138, according to DouillezM, no. 40, who gives the names, amounts, and specific folio numbers on which the various payments are recorded.

[89] See Spufford, *Monetary Problems*, 143. He cites BAGR, Chambre des comptes 18242, according to which some 250 household members were promised two months' wages as a parting gift.

[90] LADN B2142, the account book for 1491–2, contains a payment for overdue chapel wages for the period 1 June 1483–28 Feb. 1488, published in DouillezM, no. 34; the musicians are those for the period immediately before the one that concerns us.

[91] Described, curiously, as a loan (*en prest sur sesdit gaiges*), though surely functioning as an advance. It is clear that the payments cover only part of what was owed the singers, not least because La Rue and others, who are paid daily wages in sols, receive here amounts that end in deniers, the currency that is smaller than sols (e.g. La Rue should receive a sum divisible by 10s. with no deniers). In La Rue's case the wages come to somewhat less than two years' salary; other musicians also receive less than they were owed.

wages through the said *escroes* of the *despence ordinaire* of his *hostel* since the 17th day of November the year 1492, when they went to [literally: came towards] the King of the Romans and our lord and when that lord retained them in his service, until the last day of September recently passed of the said year 1495 when from there forward he had them counted on the *escroes* of the *despense ordinaire* of his said *hostel*'.

This is far less straightforward than we would like. As stated, the entry begins with a list of chapel members. These are identified as 'la chappelle domestique de lostel de mondit seigneur'; in the *mandement* of 2 October this person is clarified as 'larchiduc dautriche, duc de borgogne', a title that could only apply to Philip at this time (Maximilian immediately adopted the title King of the Romans upon his election). Thus the 'ordinance of that lord' would also seem to apply to Philip, although his ordinance of 10 March 1497 basically states that it is the first one he has had a chance to draw up (see the discussion in Ch. 2). Then the chapel goes to 'the King of the Romans and our lord'. Does this refer to Maximilian and Philip, or just Maximilian alone? When 'that lord retained them in his service', was it Maximilian or Philip? Certainly the one counting the singers on his *escroes* in 1495 is Philip.[92]

If the references are to Philip, why would he be with Maximilian at this time? We have no record of such a visit, and it is extremely unlikely that Molinet would not have noted one. Why would the chapel have to go to him? Wouldn't they already be with him? If the references are to Maximilian, as they would seem to be (certainly Gachard viewed it that way, and La Rue and his colleagues are described as singers of the King of the Romans when they join the Confraternity at 's-Hertogenbosch),[93] it opens up a new realm of possibilities, where 'retaining them in his service' would mean not hiring them per se, as has typically been the interpretation, but rather keeping them with him. In other words, the already extant chapel left the Low Countries where they had been more or less languishing (though not necessarily at full strength) since Maximilian's departure in 1489, and went off to join Maximilian.[94]

---

[92] The statement that Philip had them inscribed on his household rolls after 30 Sept. is literally true; various *escroes* for Philip survive before that time, none with chapel members. The Oct. 1495 *escroes* follow the same format as earlier ones for Philip's household (e.g. those in LADN B3453); recipients are listed in descending order of salary and the chapel members are simply inserted at the appropriate wage. By Nov. 1495 a new system was instituted that listed all chapel members together under their own rubric (though individual names were still given).

[93] Though even if they were resident with Philip they could be described as Maximilian's singers, since he was still regent.

[94] According to the Innsbruck account books, chapel master Nicolas Mayoul received payments during 1492, but his precise location is not specified; see Walter Senn, *Musik und Theater am Hof zu Innsbruck: Geschichte der Hofkapelle vom 15. Jahrhundert bis zu deren Auflösung im Jahre 1748* (Innsbruck: Österreichische Verlagsanstalt, 1954), 34. Joseph Schmidt-Görg, *Nicolas Gombert: Kapellmeister Kaiser Karls V.: Leben und Werk* (Bonn: L. Rohrscheid, 1938; repr. Tutzing: Hans Schneider, 1971), 31, cites a payment to Mayoul in German account books in the summer of 1492, before the significant November date. In addition, Keith Polk has found several references to the Burgundian choir in southern Germany in the early 1490s (private comm., 2 Nov. 1999).

Reading through the individual payments that follow the opening of the account shows that not all twenty-five individuals listed could have gone to Maximilian in 1492 anyway: Jehan Plouvier was hired on 1 August 1494, Anthoine François on 1 December 1494, Pierre Duret on 1 November 1494, and Martin Evrard on 1 September 1494.[95] Further, several of the twenty-five were already known as members of the court chapel, including Nicole Mayoul, Pierre Duwez, and Jacques Mouschet. Unless they were being hired again after having been let go, they would simply have been shifting residence temporarily, further reinforcing the interpretation of 'retained' as 'kept' rather than 'hired'. Finally—and here we come back to La Rue—it would certainly seem that any new singers had been recruited before 17 November. That occasion now seems to represent the day this group reached Maximilian, leaving open—wide open, as a matter of fact—the actual time that La Rue as well as many others became affiliated with the court chapel. If La Rue was Peter vander Straten, this time could have been right after he left the Confraternity (if the thirty-five weeks he was paid for in 1491–2 started on 24 June 1491 they would have ended on 23 February 1492). If La Rue is not vander Straten, the more likely possibility, he could have joined any time from late February 1489 on.

We know almost nothing about the chapel between February 1489 and November 1492, so all of this is speculation. But 17 November 1492 should now be looked on as the *terminus ante quem* for La Rue's joining the chapel rather than the precise date itself.

The phrase saying that the chapel went to Maximilian tells us nothing about how long they stayed with him or why they went to him. For that matter, we do not know exactly where Maximilian was on 17 November 1492, but we do have some clues. No publication gives much information about that month, but a handwritten list in the Vienna State Archives provides some valuable information. This list is a massive chronology drawn up in an anonymous but modern hand (i.e. nineteenth or twentieth century) that gives Maximilian's location each day (when known) for the years 1492–5 and 1498.[96] Although it is not accompanied by any critical apparatus, it was presumably drawn up in consultation with archival material, and the venues I have been able to check against the work of Wiesflecker suggest that it is largely accurate as far as it goes. Table 1.1 gives the chronology for the period November 1492–March 1495 (original spellings are retained).

As Table 1.1 and Fig. 1.2 show, in November 1492 Maximilian was, relatively speaking, closer to the Low Countries than he usually was. There was a reason for this. On 7 November a large meteorite had fallen in Ensisheim. Maximilian had interpreted it as a sign from God of coming military victory, and had begun a

---

[95] In addition, large payments clearly representing back wages are made in 1495 to members of the *chapelle domestique* who are not on the 1492–5 list; DouillezM, no. 46, names Pierre le fevre and Jehan de hont.

[96] VOS, HHuS Maximiliana 46 (alt 40b), ohne Dat., xv. 202–6.

TABLE 1.1. Maximilian's itinerary, November 1492–March 1495

Year	Month	Dates	City
1492	November	9	Metz
		19	Bockenheim
		21	Elsass . . . Zabern
	December	11	Luders
		20	Rougement
1493	January	2, 7, 14, 16, 19	Prunntrutt
		23	Altkirch
		31	Prunntrutt
	February	6, 8, 9	Prunntrutt
		24, 27	Colmar
	March	11, 21, 22, 25	Colmar
		30	Freiburg im Breisgau
	April	24	Freiburg im Breisgau
	May	7, 9, 10	Augsburg
		20, 22	Lintz
	June	3, 9	Lintz
	July	2, 4, 10, 13	Lintz
		21	Ehelsberg
		24	Lintz
	August	7	Lambach
	September	3, 11, 26	Insbruck
		27	Hall. Schwatz
		28	Schwatz
		29	Kufstein
	October	11	Wien
		27–9	Radkersburg
	November	4, 6, 9	Gratz
	December	8, 18, 25, 27, 30, 31	Wien
1494	January	6	Wien
		15	Mecheln [crossed out]
		17, 28, 29	Wien
	February	23	Ibs
	March	6	Salzburg
		10	Hall (im Innkul) [?]
		13, 17	Insbruck
		27	Memingen
		29, 30	Fuessen

TABLE 1.1. (*cont.*)

Year	Month	Dates	City
	April	8, 9, 13, 16	Fuessen
	May	1, 6–8	Kempten
		11	Pfaffenhausen
	June	13, 15	Worms
		18	Speier? [question mark by compiler]
		19	Mainz? [question mark by compiler]
		26	Cölln
	July	7	Achen
		8, 10, 17	Sittart
		22, 26, 27, 29, 31	Mastricht
	August	1	Mastricht
		5, 9, 12, 15	Gravesand
		17	Mecheln
		19	Antwerpen
		23, 25, 26	Mecheln
		27	Löwen? [question mark by compiler]
		28	Mecheln/Löwen
	September	5, 8, 9	Löwen
		13, 15, 18, 22–8, 30	Mecheln
	October	4	Mecheln
		6–8, 9, 11–15, 17–19, 21, 23–5, 27–9, 31	Antwerpen
	November	3–7, 11, 12, 16–21, 24–7	Antwerpen
	December	1, 6–15, 17–20, 22	Antwerpen
		24, 26, 27	Bergen am Sand
		31	Antwerpen
1495	January	5	Mecheln
		7, 8, 12	Antwerpen
		13–15	Bergen am Sand
		17, 18, 21	Antwerpen
		23	Mecheln
		24	Antwerpen/Mecheln
		25, 29, 30	Mecheln
	February	6	Altenbusch
		7, 9, 10	Predaro
		12–14, 22	Herzogenbusch
		27	Mastricht
		28	Mecheln/Mastricht

TABLE 1.1. (*cont.*)

Year	Month	Dates	City
	March	1	Achen
		4	Worms
		8	Cölln
		9	(Bonn) Cölln
		25	Worms

Source: VOS, HHuS Maximiliana 46 (alt 40b), ohne Dat., xv. 202–6.

campaign against France in the Franche-Comté.[97] This territory was adjacent to, and formerly owned by, Burgundy, and had been ceded to France as one of the conditions of Marguerite's dowry when she was betrothed to the future Charles VIII in 1482. Charles had since married Anne of Brittany in 1491, which was a double insult to Habsburg-Burgundy since the new Queen of France had previously married Maximilian by proxy. Having the chapel with him during this campaign may have appealed to Maximilian for symbolic reasons, and perhaps he was aware that Charles the Bold had travelled with his musicians. It certainly accorded with the standard royal desire to put on a good front for the outside world, and the chapel's twenty-odd members, possibly augmented with some of Maximilian's German musicians,[98] would have provided a show of worldly wealth that would help belie the actual financial straits in which Maximilian, as usual, found himself.

How long the chapel remained with Maximilian is exceedingly problematic. Did they leave after the conclusion of hostilities on 17 January 1493? Did they wait to return to the Low Countries until Maximilian himself turned back towards the east (Freiburg im Breisgau by the end of March; Augsburg by early May)? Did they remain until the lengthy peace negotiations concluded with the Peace of Senlis on 23 May? Were they back in Brussels in time to attend Philip when he ratified the peace on 16 August?[99] Certain factors suggest a shorter, temporary, stay: Maximilian is nowhere near 's-Hertogenbosch during this period, and his eight singers joined the Confraternity no later than 23 June 1493 (though perhaps they joined by proxy). Court account books for 1493 record several substantial sums of money (£100 and £200 at a time) to be allocated to the chapel during this period, suggesting—though not absolutely requiring—their presence nearby; these are dated 29 April, 12 May (two separate sums), and 27 July (also two separate sums).[100] And Philip would surely have needed singers to augment the ceremonial surrounding the ratification of the peace.

[97] See Wiesflecker, *Kaiser Maximilian I.*, i. 336–44, on the campaign and its aftermath.

[98] See Senn, *Musik und Theater*, 19–47, for a discussion of Maximilian's German musicians.

[99] Haggh, 'Music, Liturgy, and Ceremony', i. 35.

[100] LADN B2146, fos. 7ᵛ, 15ᵛ, 18ʳ, 18ᵛ, 59ᵛ; partial readings are published in DouillezM, no. 44, though with some errors. The entries are recorded in the section for income received, with the sum earmarked as follows:

Although most entries in the court account books during this time are made in the plural and thus refer to both Maximilian and Philip, a few special ones acknowledge Maximilian alone. Douillez published two excerpts from 1494, one for the 'archiers de corps du Roy . . . aider a vivre attendant que le prouchain estat du partement danvers seroit fait', and one for 'messire Nicole mayoul le jeusne, pierre de fontaines sebastien de bonne frenande boutins pbres chappellains et Jehannin le blanc clerc de loratoire du Roy' (none of these is on the 17 November 1492 list) for 'bons et aggreables services . . . devers la personne du Roy en ses derreniers voyaiges dallemaigne'.[101] These suggest some distinction or awareness concerning those individuals who were actually with Maximilian.

But it is possible that Maximilian kept the singers with him until he returned to the Low Countries in the summer of 1494, when Philip turned 16. Maximilian staged a series of *entrées* to remind his reluctant subjects who was still in charge and to show off his new wife, Bianca Maria Sforza of Milan.[102] On 24 August everyone attended Mass in Mechelen, where it was noted that an exquisite mass was sung by Maximilian's 'oberländischen und französischen' singers.[103] This description is enticing but reveals little. The two groups of singers are obviously those of the Habsburg-Burgundian court (*französisch*) and those from elsewhere (*oberländisch*), but whether both groups had arrived with Maximilian or whether he was augmenting his (German) travelling musicians with those resident at the court (the ones of 17 November 1492 who had since returned) is unknown.

The addition of extra members in the coming months (the four musicians given earlier) could possibly reflect renewal of the forces upon returning home. The 1494 account books also record a payment to an individual chapel member, the first in some years.[104] But nothing definitive survives, and we are left with another ambiguity in La Rue's biography. His earliest period of employment at the court—after being hired, whenever that was—presumably featured a brief tour of duty in a war arena, followed either by an extended peregrination in German lands for the next eighteen months or the relative quiet of the court of Margaret of York in Mechelen, where Philip (and after the Peace of Senlis, his sister, Marguerite)[105] were being brought up, or perhaps some combination of both.

'devers paies aux chappellains chantres et autres de la chapelle domesticque diceulx monseigneurs'; note how the chapel belongs to two lords, Maximilian and Philip (citation from LADN B2146, fo. 7ᵛ; the others are similar).

[101] DouillezM, no. 45.   [102] Molinet, *Chroniques*, ii. 390–5.

[103] 'Am Sonntag Bartholomei ritten mein g. Herre und alle ander Fürsten mit dem Römischen König zur Kirchen. Da ward von des Königs oberländischen und französischen Singern ein köstlich Meß gesungen'; see Georg Spalatin, *Friedrichs des Weisen Leben und Zeitgeschichte*, ed. Chr. Gotth. Neudecker and Ludw. Preller (Jena: Friedrich Mauke, 1851), 228. Although Maximilian was theoretically Holy Roman Emperor by this time, he was never formally crowned and continued to use the title 'King of the Romans' for many years after his father's death in Aug. 1493.

[104] LADN B2148, fos. 161ᵛ–162ʳ, under December: Fransquin de Retys receives a gift 'oultre et pardessus les gaiges quil prend deulx a cause de sondit estat de chantre de leurdit chappelle'; note the plural *leurdit*. The entry is published in part in DouillezM, no. 45.

[105] In Dec. 1482, less than a year after the death of her mother and when she was not quite 3 years old, she had been betrothed to the Dauphin Charles of France, ten years her senior. She moved to the French court

On 9 September 1494 Philip made his own *entrée* into Leuven, where he took an oath of loyalty and was received as Duke of Brabant, followed by the equivalent ceremony in Antwerp on 5 October (and others elsewhere thereafter).[106] These, if nothing earlier had already done so, mark his assumption of governance,[107] even though Maximilian did not finally leave the area until March 1495.[108] One archival entry finally acknowledges Philip's role as sole male head of the chapel: in December 1494 he pays for new clothing for its members, now thirty-three in number.[109]

Maximilian's removal from state affairs in the Low Countries had beneficial effects almost immediately. The years from 1492 to 1520 were largely peaceful and much more prosperous than any period since Philip the Good, and the chapel remained strong throughout this time.[110] But although Maximilian was finished with the regency of the Low Countries, he was far from finished with his children, who were pawns in the matrimonial diplomacy so widespread at this time. His greatest coup along these lines was the double marriage arranged between his two children and two of the offspring of Ferdinand of Aragon and Isabella of Castile, which was to have ramifications for the rest of European history. In October 1496 Philip married Princess Juana; the following January Marguerite sailed to Spain with those who had brought Juana north, and in April she married Juan, heir to the Spanish crown. But the sickly Juan passed away in October of the same year, and when the child Marguerite was carrying died shortly after birth,[111] Juan's sis-

the following year and remained there as a sort of political hostage after her supposed husband (the 'marriage' took place on 23 June 1483) espoused Anne of Brittany in Dec. 1491; see Max Bruchet and E[ugénie] Lancien, *L'Itinéraire de Marguerite d'Autriche, gouvernante des Pays-Bas* (Lille: L. Danel, 1934), 2–3. She finally returned in June 1493.

[106] See Wiesflecker, *Kaiser Maximilian I.*, i. 382–5, on the conclusion of the regency, and Molinet, *Chroniques*, ii. 395–9, on the *entrées*; he gives the date for Leuven as 10 Sept. On the significance of the *joyeuse entrée*, see Blockmans and Prevenier, *The Promised Lands*, 7 and *passim*.

[107] On the problems with defining the precise date of the transfer of power, see Jean-Marie Cauchies, 'La Signification politique des entrées princières dans les Pays-Bas: Maximilian d'Autriche et Philippe le Beau', *Publication du centre européen d'études bourguignonnes (XIVe–XVIe s.)*, 34 (1994), 19–35, esp. 20–1. Musicologists have usually placed the transfer too early; VDS vii. 177 claimed (without evidence) that it took place in Apr. 1493; DoorslaerC, 43, said 27 Mar. 1494 (for his proclamation as *Seigneur des Pays-Bas*), also without evidence.

[108] He returned only rarely thereafter. His lengthy stay in 1494–5 may have been prompted by plans to retain direct control over the Low Countries even after Philip came of age; see Wiesflecker, *Kaiser Maximilian I.*, i. 382–5. He continued to attempt to run things; VOS, HHuS, OMeA, SR, 181 contains a short ordinance drawn up by Maximilian for Philip 'sur la conduite de l'ostel' dated 28 June 1495; the chapel is not mentioned.

[109] LADN B2148, fo. 186^v: 'habiller les premier chappellain chantre fouriers et serviteurs domestiques de la Chappelle de mondit seigneur de ma dame sa seur on nombre de trente trois personnes'; a partial reading is found in DouillezM, no. 45. The official titles for the account books, which have given the names of both Maximilian and Philip since 1485 (LADN B2132), switch exclusively to Philip only in 1496 (LADN B2155).

[110] There were also far fewer breaks in the chapel's payment than before. A large one occurs between 1 May 1496 (when Philip was leaving to visit his father in Germany) and 9 Mar. 1497, immediately after which Philip reordered his household and returned to regular payments. Other gaps during La Rue's tenure were the month of May 1509 and the two-month period May–June 1515. At other times the chapel was practically the only group at court paid; during the ten months preceding Philip's death in 1506 only the chapels and archers were paid. The chapel was paid even while at sea (12 Jan. 1506).

[111] The child is often mentioned in the literature as having been stillborn, but Molinet, *Chroniques*, ii.

ter Isabella (married to the King of Portugal) became next in line for the Spanish throne. On her death in childbirth in 1498, her newborn son, Miguel, was in line to succeed Ferdinand and Isabella.

Marguerite left Spain to return to the Low Countries in 1499; by that time Philip and Juana had had a daughter, Eleanor. A second child, the future Holy Roman Emperor Charles V, arrived in February 1500. In July of the same year his cousin Miguel of Portugal died, which meant that Juana was now heiress to the crown. In reality, of course, that meant Philip, who decided to visit his would-be dominions the following year.

The first trip to Spain

The changes in political fortunes that brought Philip to an unanticipated position of importance were to have enormous ramifications for the history of Western Europe and beyond, and they also changed La Rue's life. The chapel, which had already ventured with Philip as far as Cologne in 1496[112] (and further afield under Maximilian in earlier years) was soon to become the most widely travelled musical institution of the time, exposed first-hand to leading musicians elsewhere and, in turn, providing them with a taste of the best the court had to offer.

In the light of Philip's new status, it is perhaps not surprising that in January 1501 he held the first official meeting of the Order of the Golden Fleece since attaining his majority.[113] The multi-day celebrations included a Requiem Mass and a Marian Mass; possibly La Rue's music was heard in this context.[114] In any event, in the following month La Rue, identified as a cleric in the diocese of Tournai and a chaplain in Philip's domestic chapel,[115] finally received his first formal mark of favour from the court[116] when he was awarded a prebend at the collegiate church of Saint-Aubain in Namur.[117] Philip drew up a fresh collation

441, says it 'scarcely lived' (*guaires ne vesqui*), implying a live birth. Historical records of the time are notoriously poor in dealing with such significant aspects of women's lives as pregnancy and childbirth.

[112] See ibid. 426–7.

[113] The previous official meeting took place at Sint Rombaut in Mechelen in 1491. Philip had another official meeting in 1505, but without the accompanying ceremonies. Meetings of the *petit chapitre* of the order were held much more frequently; see William F. Prizer, 'Music and Ceremonial in the Low Countries: Philip the Fair and the Order of the Golden Fleece', *EMH* 5 (1985), 113–53 for detailed information on the 1501 meeting and general background to the Order.

[114] Chaplains were required to attend the meetings; see ibid. 120.

[115] The diocese included the cities of Tournai, Lille, Kortrijk, Bruges, and Ghent.

[116] La Rue had previously been included in one of Molinet's *déplorations* for Ockeghem, the famous *Nymphes des bois*; the special conditions surrounding the creation of that poem are discussed in Ch. 5.

[117] See App. A, 8 Feb. 1501. The information was entered in the *Acta* in 1503, at the time La Rue took possession of the prebend. The citation is slightly puzzling; it copies the decree of Philip but gives the date of the decree as 8 Feb. 1501 [*sic*]. Normally the court changed years at Easter, which should make the date of the decree really 1502 modern style, but that is not possible, since it was drawn up in Mechelen, and Philip was in France in Feb. 1502. One can only assume that the Namur scribe changed the date. La Rue is often erroneously said to have received his prebend in Kortrijk in 1501 (the most recent instance being StaehelinNG), but this did not occur until 1505. The index to the extensive *Fonds Preces Primarien* concerning prebend recipients conserved in VOS, HHuS does not reveal any prebends that La Rue received under Maximilian.

list later that year, where La Rue was listed as desiring prebends at Kortrijk, Ghent, and 'la prébende du chastel', evidently also in Ghent; two of these requests were eventually honoured.[118]

Philip began preparations for the trip to Spain in mid-September; at this point relations between the court and France were excellent, since Philip's one-year-old son Charles was to marry Claude, daughter of Louis XII.[119] Philip accordingly planned to cross France to reach Spain. By early November the court was ready to embark on a journey that would last almost exactly two years. Chapel member Jean Braconnier had been sent to 'secret places' to recruit singers for the trip, and a large silver drum had been purchased.[120] Marguerite departed as well just eight days before they left, again heading towards the south to a new husband—this time Philibert of Savoy.

Philip's first excursion to Spain was chronicled by four different writers. Court historiographer Jean Molinet, who did not go to Spain, included a short, derivative account in his *Chroniques*.[121] A second account of the journey breaks off at Blois in December 1501; the author is unknown.[122] The most thorough account of the journey, with frequent references to music, was written by another anonymous author and has been almost entirely overlooked by musicologists.[123] Unfortunately, it records the trip only to 9 May 1502. The only full coverage of the journey comes from the young courtier Antoine de Lalaing, who was later to play an important role in Marguerite's court.[124] His description of the voyage is an elaborate and, for the most part, carefully dated travelogue, with much description of sights seen, important personages encountered, fancy ceremonies enacted, and gorgeous clothing worn. Music, alas, plays only a small role in the account. Although references to hearing Mass are moderately frequent, information is rarely given as to who was singing, whether Philip's chapel or the local singers.

A few non-court musical items are singled out by Lalaing. On 18 February 1502 he describes the music at Notre Dame de Burgos, 'Et se y fondèrent une grandt messe journèlement, et X ou XII basses, et les heures canoniales chantées par

[118] Although DoorslaerC made frequent references to this list, the original has not been located. A copy survives in the notes of Alexandre Pinchart in BrusBR MS II 1200, Carton 9. The information in Pinchart's copy is included in Barbara Helen Haggh, 'The Status of the Musician at the Burgundian Habsburg Courts, 1467–1506' (Master's thesis, University of Illinois, 1980), 280–92; the references are identified as 'CL2' in Table 27, which intermingles information from this collation list with an earlier one.

[119] GachardCV, i. 125; Molinet, *Chroniques*, ii. 487.

[120] See DoorslaerC, 141, and VDS vii. 147.

[121] Molinet, *Chroniques*, ii. 498–519.

[122] Published, without information as to its source, in *Louis XII et Philippe le Beau*, ed. Berthold Zeller (L'Histoire de France racontée par les contemporains, 37; Paris: Librairie Hachette, 1889), 54–96.

[123] Published in ChmelH, 554–655; the account is said to be drawn from Codex Ms. Nro. 3410 (Hist. prof. 523) in the K. K. Hofbibliothek, Vienna. The author almost invariably mentions that Philip and Juana heard Mass; the catalogue of many days is often scarcely more than that. His descriptions of the rich clothing that people wore to Mass, especially on major feasts, leaves the impression that (among other things) services were clearly the place to see and be seen, a social function that opera has sometimes served in the more recent past.

[124] The chronicle is published complete in GachardCV, i, whose introduction provides information on Lalaing's life.

XVIII, presbtres que clercs . . .'.[125] Given that the equally large court chapel sang a polyphonic mass daily, one can only assume that they were impressed to find music making on a similar scale elsewhere. Lalaing also goes into great detail about the structure of Mass at the church of Notre Dame in Toledo and how it differed from accustomed procedure.[126]

Lalaing points out two organs that made a special impression, one belonging to the parish church in Innsbruck[127] and the other situated in the chapel of the Count of Nassau in Heidelberg.[128] Since the court travelled with organ and organist at all times, this interest is understandable. Lalaing also noted a service at the cathedral in Cologne where two 'grandes messes' were sung simultaneously at two altars, one facing east and one facing west.[129]

In the four accounts, Philip's own chapel is first mentioned when they sang at the church of Notre-Dame in Noyon on 19 November;[130] three days later they performed at the church of Saint-Corneille in Compiègne[131] and then at Saint-Denis on 24 November.[132] Philip entered Paris the following day, where the chapel sang at the Sainte-Chapelle.[133]

The Parisian visit had a curious scholarly aftermath. In the last volume of *La Musique aux Pays-Bas* Edmond Vander Straeten made a passing comment about La Rue and Agricola '"qui esbahirent tout Paris"',[134] just as in the preceding volume he claimed that Agricola, like La Rue, '"ébahi tout Paris"'.[135] Earlier he had linked La Rue to the French court (on the basis of his epitaph) and claimed that there was a vogue for La Rue in Paris (on the basis of *Nymphes des bois*).[136] The phrase 'esbahirent tout Paris' is certainly familiar to modern musicologists, but not in connection with Agricola and La Rue in 1501; rather, it is from Martin le Franc's *Le Champion des dames*, written around 1438–42, and the phrase concerns three much earlier musicians: 'Tapissier, Carmen, Cesaris, / N'a pas long temps sy bien chanterent / Qu'ilz esbahirent tout Paris / Et tous ceulx qui les frequenterent.'[137]

---

[125] GachardCV, i. 154.   [126] Ibid. 186–7.

[127] Ibid. 310: 'L'église parochiale de la ville a unes orghes, les plus belles et les plus exquises que jamais je véy. Il n'est instrument du monde quy n'y joue: car ils sont tous là-dedens compris, et coustèrent plus de dix milles francs au faire.'

[128] Ibid. 328: 'Les orghes qui y sont sont les plus douces et les plus exquises que je scay, bien comparables à celles de Yzebrouch.'

[129] Ibid. 329: 'Le joedi, XXVI^c, alla Monsigneur . . . oyr la messe au Dom . . . où je vis une chose nouvelle: c'est a deux boutz d'icelle, deux autels où on chante deux grandes messes ensemble, l'une vers soleil couchant, l'aultre vers soleil levant.'

[130] *Louis XII et Philippe le Beau*, ed. Zeller, 66.   [131] Ibid. 67.

[132] GachardCV, i. 131. The anonymous writer, who is decidedly chary with punctuation, tells us more than Lalaing: 'Il fist chanter la messe par ses [Philip's] chantres qui fut bel a oyr mais le prieur et deux moines dirent la messe et furent bien esbahis les francoys doyr si bonne chapelle et de sy bonne gorge'; see ChmelH, 560.

[133] ChmelH, 562: 'De la monseigneur sen ala a la sainte capelle ou lon fist une tresbelle messe chantee par les chantres de monseigneur et orghes que cestoit une grande melodie a les oyr en la dite chapelle . . .'.

[134] VDS viii. 8.   [135] Ibid. vii. 134.   [136] Ibid. 120.

[137] The musical stanzas for the poem are given in David Fallows, *Songs and Musicians in the Fifteenth Century* (Aldershot: Ashgate, 1996), 205–8.

One might be inclined to dismiss this as another of Vander Straeten's many inaccuracies, especially since he provided no source for his quotation. But the disconnection is so dramatic—about sixty years, three singers instead of two, no similarity of names, in a context that otherwise has nothing to do with Paris—that one wonders whether there is actually some now-lost original source for Vander Straeten's quotation—and each time the phrase is placed in quotation marks. French poets—like poets everywhere at the time—continually borrowed phrases and made references to the work of others; 'Nymphes des bois', to be discussed later, provides a clear example. Possibly La Rue and Agricola did astound Paris, and perhaps their visit was memorialized in a now-lost poem that harked back to an earlier praise of singers. Although Vander Straeten knew that La Rue had travelled to Spain in Philip's entourage, his knowledge seems to be from surviving pay lists and ordinances rather than any chronicle, making it even more likely that the 'esbahirent tout Paris' quotation was from something that no longer survives.

The chapel sang for the eve and the feast of St Andrew on 30 November[138] as well as at the cathedral in Orléans on 5 December.[139] In Blois they encountered the French royal court, and on 8 December heard the royal singers: 'et chanterent et firent le service les chantres du Roy qui est fort somptueuse chappelle de belle voix tant comme dessus et y est ung chantre nomme verjus qui est le second maistre alixandre et est fort ayme du Roy et dun chacun'.[140] The implied accolade to 'maistre alixandre', Agricola, is one of the very rare instances that a chapel member is mentioned by name.

Both Philip's chapel and the French royal chapel joined forces in a mass and Te Deum.[141] The most detailed description is as follows:

La messe fut chantee par ung evesque a diacre et soubzdiacre des chantres du Roy et des chantres de monseigneur assavoir a deux estapieux Les chantres du Roy chanterent lintroite Jusques a gloria en contrepoint et les chantres de monseigneur le gloria et apres lintroite les chantres du Roy les Kyrieleison et ceulx de monseigneur et in terra Ceulx du Roy le patrem ceulx de monseigneur le sanctus et langnus ceulx du Roy quy fut fort Joyeulx et fort bien chante et regardoit le Roy dessus les chantres et monseigneur avecques et en eurent grant plaisir a les oyr et cestes cestoit triumphe.[142]

On this occasion, as on others where the Habsburg-Burgundian court was together with another major institution, it is extremely likely that the musicians of

---

[138] ChmelH, 563: 'et estoit nuyt de saint Andrieu et fut monseigneur du soir oyr le psalme lequel fut chante par les chantres de monseigneur qui fut fort beau'; 563–4 [30 Nov.], 'et firent les chantres de monseigneur le service et les orghes de mondit seigneur qui est melodie a les oyr sans Rompement de teste'. See also *Louis XII et Philippe le Beau*, ed. Zeller, 77.

[139] ChmelH, 564: 'cuida aler monseigneur oyr la messe a la grant eglise . . . et fut fait le service par les chantres et orghes de monseigneur'. See also *Louis XII et Philippe le Beau*, ed. Zeller, 81.

[140] ChmelH, 568.

[141] The date is variously given as 12 Dec. (Molinet, *Chroniques*, ii. 503–4, as the Sunday after the Feast of the Immaculate Conception), 13 Dec. (GachardCV, i. 140), or 14 Dec. (ChmelH, 570). *Louis XII et Philippe le Beau*, ed. Zeller, 96, gives 12 Dec., but only mentions Philip's singers.

[142] ChmelH, 570. The celebration was for the affirmation of the Treaty of Blois, marking the engagement of Charles and Claude.

both groups got together informally. Indeed, it may even have been expected. In later years, a court account book of 1505 records a payment to four of Philip's singers 'pour de tant mieulx les aydier a festoier [to feast or regale]' the singers of Maximilian;[143] apparently some kind of hospitality between musical groups was the norm.

La Rue may or may not have met Josquin in Blois; 'a singer named Josquin' was at that time in the city, having been sent to Flanders by Ercole I, Duke of Ferrara, to recruit new singers. Philip asked this Josquin to join him on the trip to Spain and wrote to Ercole asking to borrow him.[144] Lewis Lockwood pointed out that there is no other evidence that Josquin was in Ercole's service at this point and that it is odd that Bartolomeo de' Cavalieri, the Ferrarese ambassador to France who wrote the letter from 13 December 1501 that is our source of information, should not seem to know who this Josquin was when three months earlier he had mentioned the composer Josquin in a letter.[145]

While Richard Sherr accepted this singer as the famous Josquin,[146] Patrick Macey offered a different possibility, that the singer was in reality Josse van Steeland, also known as Josquin, stated by Macey to have joined Philip's chapel at the beginning of November 1501.[147] Macey drew on the chapel list from 1–2 November published by Edmond Vander Straeten, where van Steeland is included among the *Clers servans au grant et au petit autel*, paid 3s. a day.[148] What Vander Straeten did not indicate, however, was that van Steeland's name was an addition to the list, as perusal of the document in question shows. At periodic intervals the court drew up household *états* stating who was to receive what; these *états* then served as master lists to which additions were made in the months or years that followed.[149] The list from early November 1501 served this function; additions to it were made at least as late as 25 September 1504.

As it turns out, we know exactly when Josse van Steeland joined the chapel: it was on 22 May 1504, when he was hired not as a *cler servan* at 3s. a day, but rather as a *chantre* at 10s. a day; the document provides a precise annotation.[150] Vander Straeten's confusion stems from an inaccuracy in Gachard's publication of this document, on which Vander Straeten apparently drew. Gachard, though correctly copying the annotation that provides van Steeland's admission date, erroneously

---

[143] LADN B2191, fo. 303ʳ, cited in DouillezM, no. 63.

[144] The original document is quoted in Helmuth Osthoff, *Josquin Desprez*, 2 vols. (Tutzing: H. Schneider, 1962–5), i. 51.

[145] Lewis Lockwood, 'Josquin at Ferrara: New Documents and Letters', in *JosCon*, 103–37 at 109–10.

[146] Richard Sherr, 'Chronology of Josquin's Life and Career', in id. (ed.), *The Josquin Companion* (Oxford: Oxford University Press, 2000), 11–20 at 16.

[147] Patrick Macey et al., 'Josquin (Lebloitte dit) des Prez', *New Grove II*, 224.

[148] VDS vii. 152.

[149] The ordinance of 1 Feb. 1500 is a good example of this, with Agricola's name added in the margin when he joined on 6 Aug. of the same year.

[150] Published in GachardCV, i. 347: 'Monseigneur a retenu Josse van Seelant et Pierre Brule chantres de sa chappelle, chacun aux gaiges de X sols par jour. Fait le xxiiᵉ jour de may 1504.'

placed van Steeland (and Pierre Brule, another singer who joined at the same time) under the heading *Clers servans*.

The reason for this error becomes clear upon examination of the document. The heading for *Clers servans* is at the top of folio 1ᵛ, with two names under it (Jennet Friart and Gillet Moreau, both of whom accompanied Philip on his first voyage to Spain). The names of Josse van Steeland and Pierre Brule are placed *above* the heading *Clers servans* with the annotation on their entry in the upper left-hand corner of the folio. Although the scribe should properly have put both names and annotation on folio 1ʳ, where the other singers are listed, there was practically no room left there by May 1504, since numerous annotations and names had already been added to the recto side of the folio. If any confirmation of this interpretation is needed, it is the total absence of Josse van Steeland from any *escroe* before this date and his presence on almost every one that follows through the remainder of La Rue's service.[151] Josse van Steeland thus may or may not be the Josquin in Blois in December 1501, but if he was, he did not choose to accompany Philip.

After Blois, Philip's court continued south towards Spain. In Cognac on New Year's Day, 'pour ce que cestoit le premier Jour de lan lon y fist une tresbelle messe chantee par les chantres de monseigneur et as orgues de monseigneur, et les vespres pareillement'.[152] In Saint Milion (Saint-Émilion) on 7 January the singers again astonished those who heard them: 'Et chanterent les chantres de monseigneur la messe devant monseigneur de cambray et les contes, dont ceulx de la ville presenterent le vin de present aux seigneurs et aux chantres et furent bien esbahis de oyr si bonne chapelle.'[153] In Bayonne on 23 January the singers sang Mass and 'Le Roy [of Navarre] print plaisir a oyr chanter et jouer des orgues de monseigneur'.[154] The accolades continued after their arrival in Spain on 26 January: 'et fut fait le service . . . par les chantres de monseigneur que fut bon a oyr et avec estoient les orgues de monseigneur, dont les grans seigneurs despaignes furent bien esbahis doyr si bien chanter et jouer des orgues';[155] 'les seigneurs despaigne se esmerveillerent de veoir si belle et bonne chappelle pareillement de si bons chantres et de si bonnes orgues'.[156]

Philip's court spent the remainder of 1502 in Spain, including almost four months at the court of Ferdinand and Isabella in Toledo. Certain references to singing (or not singing) stand out. On 1 May the singers had been sent ahead to Toledo, so a low Mass was heard instead,[157] while on 4 May it was such a lovely day that the singers sang Vespers very beautifully.[158] On 8 May Lalaing makes the famous reference to Mass sung by sixty to eighty of Ferdinand's singers,[159] but the

---

[151] Like La Rue, he remains in Spain with Juana during 1506–8. He is missing from the *escroe* of 22 July 1506 as well as the declaration of money owed to the chapel drawn up in Aug. 1515.

[152] ChmelH, 581.   [153] Ibid. 584.   [154] Ibid. 594.

[155] Ibid. 601, on 2 Feb. 1502 in Sanneterre.   [156] Ibid. 613, on 14 Feb. 1502 in Burgos.

[157] Ibid. 645.   [158] Ibid. 646: 'Et pour lamour du bon Jour les chantres vindrent chanter les vespres tresbelle.'   [159] GachardCV, i. 176.

anonymous account for this day records instead, probably more accurately, that the church in Toledo where Mass was sung had sixty to eighty canons.[160] On this same day all the king's *chapelains* as well as those of Toledo's churches were presented to Philip and Juana.[161] That evening dinner lasted so long and so much meat was served that they did not bother with Vespers,[162] while the following day the news of the death of Arthur, Prince of Wales, similarly silenced singing.[163] At this point the anonymous writer breaks off, forcing us to rely exclusively on the less comprehensive Lalaing, who notes few musically significant occasions: on 15 May (Pentecost), Philip's singers sang part of the Mass, with cornettist Maistre Augustin joining in,[164] and on 6 September they sang mass at a local monastery.[165]

In the early part of 1503 Philip and his court left Spain and headed through France, where the chapel sang Mass at Avignon[166] and then proceeded to Lyons, where they stayed from 22 March to 10 April.[167] Here they are mentioned as performing at a dinner given by Philip on 26 March, and again with the French court chapel (who arrived on 29 March) at Mass on 2 April.[168] Josquin—the real one—is firmly documented at Lyons on 12 and 13 April, though his date of arrival is unknown; possibly his visit overlapped with that of La Rue and the two composers met.[169]

The court then went to Bourg en Bresse, where Philip met his sister and her husband, Philibert of Savoy. The choirs of Savoy and Habsburg-Burgundy both sang at Easter Mass (16 April) one after the other, and Maistre Augustin again played his cornett with the singers.[170] The court then took to the road once more and the chapel is recorded as singing at Dole on 30 July, Gray on 15 August (the feast of the Assumption), and Halle (Hall in Tirol) one month later.[171] Philip's

---

[160] ChmelH, 647.

[161] Ibid. 678: 'Et vindrent audevant de monseigneur et madame tous les chappellains du Roy et de la Royne aveuc ceulx des esglises de toullette.' This is another event that might have generated the numbers 60 to 80.

[162] Ibid. 655: 'le service du disner dura longhement, et furent seruy fort de grosses viandes de lapresdisner lon ne chanta point vespres'.

[163] Ibid. 655: 'Lon ne chanta point de messe ne on ne fist riens qui fut de Joye.'

[164] GachardCV, i. 178: 'Les chantres du roy chantèrent une partie de la messe, les chantres de Monsigneur l'aultre partie; avoecq lesquelz chantres de Monsigneur jouoit du cornet maistre Augustin: ce qu'il faisoit estoit bon à oyr, avoec les chantres.'

[165] Ibid. 217: 'Le mardi, VIe, Monsigneur ouyt messe chantée de ses chantres a ung très-beau et solitaire monastère des Observans.'

[166] Ibid. 277: 'Ce jour chantèrent la messe les chantres de Monsigneur ...'.

[167] See ibid. 281 on the date of arrival.

[168] Ibid. 282: 'Le dimence, XXVIe de mars, Monsigneur fist ung très-beau disné au cardinal, à monsour de Ravestain et à monsour d'Albi, frère dudit cardinal. Le service y fu beau. Monsigneur y fist venir de ses chantres de joueurs d'instrumens, pour leur doner plus plaisant passe-tampz'; and 283: 'Le dimence, deuzime jour d'apvril, le roy, la royne et Monsigneur ouyrent messe, laquèle chantèrent les chantres du roy et de Monsigneur à Sainct-Jehan ...'.

[169] Philip returned to Blois in mid-May, but Josquin was presumably in Ferrara by the end of April; see Sherr, 'Chronology of Josquin's Life and Career', 16.

[170] GachardCV, i. 287: 'Le jour de Pasques ... Monsigneur et sa soer ouyrent la messe très-solennèlement célébrée par ledict évesque en la chappelle de mondict signeur, où ses chantres et les chantres du duc chantèrent très-bien les ungs après les aultres, et avoecq les chantres jouoit de son cornet maistre Augustin, lequel faisoit bon à ouyr.'

[171] Ibid. 298, 301, and 311.

choir combined with that of Maximilian (whom Philip had joined on 12 September)[172] to sing Mass at Innsbruck on 17 September; the organ played as well.[173] After singing at Halle once more on 21 September,[174] Philip's chapel sang again in Innsbruck on 26 September.[175]

The singing on 26 September was for the funeral ceremonies for Hermes of Milan, Maximilian's brother-in-law, who had died in Innsbruck on 18 September.[176] This is a rare instance where some information about the music performed was actually provided by Lalaing. Philip's chapel sang a Requiem Mass, while Maximilian's sang a Mass for the Assumption of the Blessed Virgin Mary; Staehelin has suggested that the latter was Isaac's *Missa Virgo prudentissima*.[177] In addition, Philip's chapel sang the Offertory; one suspects that Lalaing singled this out because it was something other than the usual plainchant. He also mentioned Maximilian's sackbuts as starting the Gradual as well as playing the *Deo gratias* and *Ite missa est*—again, presumably because this was unusual and worthy of comment.

While the choice of a funeral Mass for this occasion needs no explanation, the mass for the Assumption remains puzzling. The Feast of the Assumption, on 15 August, was celebrated in Germany for thirty days thereafter (a period known as Our Lady's Thirty Days, *Frauendreissiger*), but 26 September falls outside this period. Nor was 26 September a Saturday, the traditional day for a Lady Mass. Cuyler has suggested that either the celebrations extended past thirty days or that Lalaing, the author of the court chronicle, did not remember properly.[178] Given that he made the effort to name the pieces of music—an almost unheard-of event in his chronicles—one would rather assume that they made a great impression on him and that he identified them correctly.[179]

After leaving Innsbruck—where La Rue possibly met Isaac—the chapel may have sung Mass at Heidelberg,[180] and they definitely sang Mass and vigils in

---

[172] GachardCV, i. 308.

[173] Ibid. 313: 'Les chantres du roy et de Monsigneur chantèrent la messe et jouèrent les orghes plaines de tous instrumens, come dessus a esté dit. C'est la plus mélodieuse chose que l'on pourroit oyr.'

[174] Ibid. 315.

[175] Ibid. 316–17: 'Le mardi se trouvèrent tous à l'église come devant: mais ledict sarcu estoit lors en la nef de l'église auprès du coer, et la royne et ses dames sóient audict coer; et là furent chantées solemnèlement deux messes. La première, de *Requiem*, chantèrent ledict évesque et les chantres de Monsigneur . . . La seconde messe fu de l'Assumption Nostre-Dame, chantée par les chantres du roy, et offrirent le roy et la royne et Monsigneur come devant. Et comenchèrent le Grade les sacqueboutes du roy, et jouèrent le *Deo gratias* et *Ite missa est*, et les chantres de Monsigneur chantèrent l'Offertoire.' 1 Oct. is sometimes cited as another date where the chapel is recorded as singing Mass, but it is rather Maximilian's chapel that sings: 'Le dimence, premier jour d'octobre, le roy [Maximilian] et Monsigneur [Philip], avoec grande noblesse, oyrent la messe à la grande église, chantée des chantres du roy [Maximilian]'; see ibid. 319. Maximilian's chapel similarly sings on the following day (ibid. 320).

[176] Ibid. 314.

[177] This turns up in court manuscript BrusBR 6428 later on, where it is indeed titled *Missa de assumptione beate Marie virginis*; see Herbert Kellman, 'Brussels, Bibliothèque royale de Belgique MS 6428', in *TA* 71.

[178] Cuyler, *The Emperor Maximilian I*, 66–7.

[179] He mentions an occasional performance of the Te Deum but nothing else.

[180] GachardCV, i. 328: 'Le dimence, XXe d'octobre, Monsigneur et lesdicts princeps oyrent la messe en la

Cologne on the feast of All Saints, 1 November.[181] Philip was back in Mechelen on 9 November, after more than two years away.[182] In the following month La Rue finally took possession of his prebend at Namur.[183] One wonders at what time—if at all—he learned of something that happened while he was in Germany, the publication by Petrucci on 31 October of five of his masses in the *Misse Petri de la Rue*, the fifth volume in Petrucci's series of mass prints.[184]

The second trip to Spain

The most far-reaching event of 1504 was the death on 26 November of Isabella of Castile. The crown passed to Juana by order of inheritance as well as the Queen's instructions, and in December, upon learning of Isabella's death, Philip and Juana took the titles and arms of King and Queen of Castile, León, Granada, etc.[185] This is the point at which an anonymous contemporary account of Philip's second voyage begins.[186] In complete contrast to the accounts of the first voyage, this one is almost all concerned with politics, with none of the travelogue qualities of Lalaing or his cohorts. Rather than going to Spain almost as a tourist, Philip now goes to take power. This means that references to the chapel, rare enough in Lalaing, are almost completely absent here, and at no point is there a specific reference to their singing in liturgical services.[187]

Philip was eager to return to Spain to assert his new authority, but both Ferdinand and Juana presented various roadblocks.[188] Ferdinand remarried within a year (Germaine de Foix, niece of Louis XII) and tried to produce another male heir.[189] He had Juana declared unsuitable to reign, and Juana herself was said to prefer that her father, rather than her husband, take over the royal duties. Ferdinand also forged a new alliance with France, traditional enemy of Burgundy. Interspersed with these events was Philip's war against Gueldre, carried on in the

chapelle du comte, laquèle chantèrent ses chantres, qui très-bien chantent. Les orghes qui y sont sont les plus douces et les plus exquises que je scay, bien comparables à celles de Yzebrouch.' It is not clear whether 'ses chantres' refers to those of Philip or those of the count.

[181] GachardCV, i. 332–3.   [182] Ibid. 337.

[183] See App. A, 4 Dec. 1503.

[184] La Rue's music was included in the very first volume of printed polyphonic music, Petrucci's *Odhecaton* (1501), and in various other publications during his lifetime; see Ch. 5 for a discussion of the distribution of his music.

[185] GachardCV, i. 389.

[186] Published ibid. 387–480.

[187] Molinet, *Chroniques*, ii. 566, tells us that the singers sang (obviously with relief) when they saw Philip and Juana again after everyone was separated and forced to land in England in Jan. 1506; see below on this portion of the journey.

[188] See the description of the various problems Philip faced given in GachardCV, i. 390, 399–402, as well as the letters written by Vincenzo Quirino, the Venetian ambassador, in Constantin R. von Höfler, 'Depeschen des Venetianischen Botschafters bei Erzherzog Philipp, Herzog von Burgund, König von Leon, Castilien, Granada, Dr. Vincenzo Quirino 1505–1506', *Archiv für Österreichische Geschichte*, 66 (1885), 45–256; Quirino covers the period 30 Mar. 1505–24 Aug. 1506. See also Konrad Häbler, *Der Streit Ferdinand's des Katholischen und Philipp's I. um die Regierung von Castilien 1504–1506* (Dresden: Albanns'sche Buchdruckerei [Christian Teich], 1882).

[189] He was not successful; a son born in Mar. 1509 died almost immediately.

summer of 1505. The chapel accompanied him on this campaign; although there is no mention of them in the anonymous chronicle at this point, the surviving *escroes* all match up with the places of Philip's activities during the war.

In 1505, while these political machinations were going on, La Rue received a benefice he had requested some years earlier, that for the collegiate church of Onze-Lieve-Vrouw in Kortrijk. This was to prove his preferred benefice, and he ultimately retired to Kortrijk. In November Philip helped La Rue again when he agreed to provide a pension of 4s. a day to La Rue's father during the time that the composer was in Spain.[190] This pension suggests that La Rue's parents were financially dependent upon their composer son; it also implies that if Jehan de la Rue had been a master illuminator, his guild was providing insufficient support in his old age. Certainly the picture here is of a son whose success has surpassed that of his father, and possibly that of his siblings as well.[191] It is also one of impressive filial piety, for it suggests that La Rue had previously been supplying his parents with 4s. a day—a full third of his daily allotment.

After many delays—Philip had ordered ships readied in July[192]—the court was finally ready at the end of 1505 to depart for Spain, this time by sea rather than across now-hostile France. Bad weather forced continual delays, but on 4 January 1506 most of the entourage embarked; the chapel had their own ship.[193] Philip and Juana were the last, going on board only after they had heard Mass at 2.00 a.m. on 8 January.[194] Further bad weather forced the fleet to ride at anchor for two days, but finally all set sail on 10 January.[195] In the early stage of the voyage 'it was a pleasure to hear trumpets, drums, and other instruments sounding everywhere on the ships, making good cheer',[196] but on 13 January a terrible storm blew up that lasted almost two full days. The fleet was forced to land in England, where they spent more than three months as the guests of Henry VII while making necessary repairs. Here Juana was reunited with her sister, Catherine of Aragon, who occupied a dubious position at the English court as the widow of Prince Arthur and the temporarily rejected fiancée of Prince Henry. For his part, Philip lost no time in putting the unanticipated visit to good use by concluding a treaty of alliance between his court and England and a marriage contract between his recently widowed sister Marguerite and Henry VII.[197] One assumes that musical exchanges between the two chapels took place as well.

---

[190] Two of the instalments are recorded as having been paid (Feb. and June 1506; see App. A). La Rue's father was still alive in Aug. 1507, so presumably other payments were made as well.

[191] La Rue was not the only one who received special treatment before this second voyage; various singers were provided with extra money for preparations for the trip. See the payments cited in DouillezM, no. 63.

[192] GachardCV, i. 399.   [193] Ibid. 407, 409.

[194] Ibid. 408; presumably Mass was sung by local musicians rather than the chapel, who would already have been on their ship.   [195] Ibid. 410.

[196] Ibid. 501: 'C'estoit ung plaisir d'oyr trompestes, tambours et aultres instrumens sonner partout sur les navires, où l'on faisoit bonne chière . . .'.

[197] Philibert of Savoy had died the previous September. Ratification of the two treaties took place on 1 June 1506 (VOS, HHusS, Habsburg-Lotharingische Familienurkunden, 905). Despite the contract, Marguerite refused to marry Henry.

On 22 April Philip and his retinue set sail once again and landed in Spain four days later.[198] After two tense months he was finally able to conclude a treaty with Ferdinand acknowledging his right to rule Juana's inherited lands,[199] but before three more months had passed he died of a fever, on 25 September, throwing the court into a state of confusion.[200]

Some of the chapel members, such as Braconnier, left Spain immediately,[201] but others chose to remain and serve Juana, the ostensible ruler after Philip's death, until she was deprived of power in August 1508.[202] Her new chapel was primarily staffed by northerners, though it also included Juan de Anchieta, who had served her while in the Low Countries. La Rue was among those who remained. His decision may have been the purely practical one of staying with a sure thing as opposed to venturing off to uncertain employment. While the rest of Philip's court was forced to fend for itself[203]—the chapel members were the only ones she added to her retinue—the singers were treated even better than they had been under Philip, who had already favoured them. It was claimed that for the ten months preceding his death, only the chapel and the archers had been paid by Philip.[204] Juana was even more solicitous: not only were the chapel members the only ones who were paid, but paying them was apparently the only administrative action she could bring herself to do in her grief.[205] Further, they were paid extremely well. The annual salary for one of her singers was more than half again what the highest-paid singer in Ferdinand's chapel received.[206] As if that were not enough, they were paid three months in advance, a highly unusual procedure.

La Rue was treated even better than the others, for he was rapidly promoted to *premier chapelain*. Marbriano de Orto, who had served this role under Philip, apparently initially decided to stay—he is on one of the two pay records for 11

---

[198] GachardCV, i. 431–2.

[199] Philip and Ferdinand concluded the treaty acknowledging Philip's right to the crown on 27 June 1506; a second treaty made shortly thereafter excluded Juana from the administration of the kingdom. See ibid. 438–44.

[200] Ibid. 451. The death was so convenient for Ferdinand that rumours of poisoning began circulating immediately; see ibid. 463–4.

[201] The organist Henry Bredemers arranged for the transportation of the chapel's books, presumably including music books, back to the port of Antwerp; see Georges Van Doorslaer, 'Herry Bredemers organiste et maître de musique 1472–1522', *Annales de l'Académie royale d'archéologie de Belgique*, 66 (1914), 209–56 at 220. Some of the singers who left Spain (e.g. Fransquin de Retis and Antonin François) are found back north in Charles's chapel in 1509 in the first detailed record we have of his archducal chapel (as opposed to the small chapel he had as prince). It is unclear precisely when and how the transformation of his chapel took place; Marguerite, who was to serve as his governor, left Savoy for the Low Countries at the end of October and received her official appointment the following March. The northern chapel performed at the funeral obsequies for Philip held in Mechelen in July 1507, but records of the event do not include the names of the singers, contrary to what is sometimes stated; see App. A, 18–19 July 1507.

[202] The presence of a portion of Philip's singers in Juana's chapel was first signalled by Mary Kay Duggan, 'Queen Joanna and her Musicians', *Musica disciplina*, 30 (1976), 73–95. Juana's chapel is studied in detail in Tessa Wendy Knighton, 'Music and Musicians at the Court of Fernando of Aragon, 1474–1516' (Ph.D. diss., University of Cambridge, 1983). I am grateful to Professor Knighton for kindly supplying me with copies of the relevant documents for the chapel concerning La Rue.

[203] See GachardCV, i. 452–3 and 468 on the problems faced by the courtiers.

[204] GachardCV, i. 451.   [205] Ibid. 463.   [206] Knighton, 'Music and Musicians', 106.

October 1506,[207] the first that survive—but had left by December, at which point La Rue was elevated to the top spot.[208] In La Rue's new position he received 90,000 maravedís, twice the annual salary of the other singers. This did not mean that he stopped being concerned with money; in August 1507 his father, Magister Johannes de la Rue, appeared before the assembled chapter of Onze-Lieve-Vrouw in Kortrijk with a letter written by Marguerite of Austria, excusing La Rue's absence and long distance;[209] the chapter then confirmed that La Rue would receive his income for the year 24 June 1507–8.[210] The previous year La Rue had not received it, but it was normal procedure for the second year's income (in this case for 24 June 1506–7) to go the the church itself. This is the last information we have about La Rue's father; the use of 'Magister' supports the proposed identification with the master illuminator of the same name.[211]

In August 1508 La Rue's employment in Juana's chapel came to an end, as the government finally passed from her hands to those of her father. Until mid-1508 the chapel had sung the Office of the Dead daily in memory of Philip. During much of this time they took part in a bizarre journey across Spain as Juana had Philip's coffin disinterred and moved from Burgos in the north towards Granada in the south until Ferdinand, returning in August 1507 (from Naples where he had been since shortly after Philip's death), stopped this, and had Philip reburied.[212] Little else is known of the chapel's activities except that they interacted formally with Ferdinand's choir for several months after August 1507.[213] When it was time to leave, La Rue and his fellow chapel members were given travelling expenses for their return north; as *premier chapelain* La Rue received twice what his fellow singers did. He then returned to a court dramatically changed in many respects from what he had known under Philip.

---

[207] Curiously, DoorslaerC, 155, asked whether Pierre Ronner on the 11 Oct. list was really La Rue, but La Rue already appears under a normal form of his name.

[208] Jean Moneta, who outranked La Rue on the *escroes*, was passed over. Moneta presents a very curious case of a chapel member (supposedly hired by Maximilian) omitted erroneously from most *escroes*; see DoorslaerC, 151, as well as the Maximilian–Marguerite correspondence for 29 June and 30 Aug. 1512 given in *Correspondance de l'empereur Maximilien Ier et de Marguerite d'Autriche, sa fille, gouvernante des Pays-Bas, de 1507 à 1519*, ed. M. Le Glay, 2 vols. (Paris: Jules Renouard, 1839; repr. New York: Johnson Reprint, 1966), ii. 15–16, 27–8.

[209] The letter itself does not survive; we know of it only through the chapter acts. In it La Rue is identified as *Serenissime regine castelle prothocapellani*, showing that Marguerite knew of his position. Since La Rue surely requested the letter, it indicates his knowledge that she was now in charge of the Low Countries. See Ch. 2 on his relationship with Marguerite and the song text he may have changed in connection with this letter.

[210] Additional confirmation is found in the record of 4 May 1508; see App. A under this date.

[211] Similarly, La Rue's father is identified as 'maistre' in the pay document of 18 Feb. 1506 modern style cited in App. A.

[212] M. J. Rodríguez-Salgado, 'Charles V and the Dynasty', in Hugo Soly (ed.), *Charles V 1500–1558 and his Time* (Antwerp: Mercatorfonds, 1999), 26–111 at 31.

[213] On the chapel with Juana, see Knighton, 'Music and Musicians', esp. 106–23.

THE CHAPEL UNDER MARGUERITE AND CHARLES: 1508–1516

As stated earlier, we know nothing of the northern chapel during the time that La Rue sang for Juana except that they took part in the funeral obsequies for Philip in July 1507. Pay records exist only for the years after La Rue returned, but are still far from plentiful: one for 1509, one for 1510, three for 1511, seven for 1513, one for 1514, two for 1515, and none for the first half of 1516. Only 1512, with twenty-one surviving *escroes*, is moderately well represented. In contrast to pre-Spain days, La Rue is now preceded on pay records only by the *premier chapelain*. More subtly, he is no longer referred to by his nickname, Pierchon, but rather given the dignity of his full name.[214]

The court was now ostensibly headed by an 8-year-old boy, but one who at least liked music; in 1507 he was described as wanting 'to play all instruments'.[215] The person actually in charge, at least initially, was his aunt Marguerite, who had been at the court at the same time as La Rue during the earlier periods of June 1493 to January 1497 and November 1499 to October 1501. La Rue had also visited her court at Savoy in April and May 1503 during Philip's first trip to Spain, and she herself had visited the Low Countries in 1505.[216] We know also that she was aware of La Rue's position in Juana's chapel. Further, La Rue had written more than one piece intended for her; see the discussion in Chapter 2. In 1509, however, Charles was placed under the governorship of Guillaume de Croÿ, so Marguerite was not the only one influencing the tenor of courtly life.[217]

Perhaps the most noticeable aspect of life at court from late 1508 to 1514 was its astonishing stability. Because of Charles's youth, the court spent its time mostly in Mechelen and Brussels, with travel elsewhere being unusual. The greatest exception to this was the seven-week period between 8 October and 26 November 1513 when Charles left Brussels to join Henry VIII, first in Tournai (which the English king had just conquered; would La Rue have been able to see his relatives?)[218] and then in Lille, after which Charles briefly visited Kortrijk, Peteghem lez-Deynze, Ghent, Loo, Eecloo, and Dendermonde before returning to Mechelen. The otherwise peaceful routine of the court was quite possibly very welcome to La Rue after the extended periods of travel between late 1501 and late 1508.

---

[214] The exceptions to this in court records are the two instances where he is receiving some kind of personal attention from those in charge, the letters concerning the Ghent and Dendermonde prebends (App. A, 7 Apr. 1507 and 1514, unknown date). In general, the post-Spain scribes are slightly more formal than the earlier ones.

[215] GachardCV, i. 461, 'il veult . . . à jouer de tous instrumens . . .'.

[216] See Bruchet and Lancien, *L'Itinéraire*, 5–17, as well as Höfler, 'Depeschen des Venetianischen Botschafters', 112.

[217] Marguerite was still responsible for his sisters Eleanor, Mary, and Isabelle; siblings Catherine and Ferdinand were being reared in Spain.

[218] As a French territory until 1513, Tournai was not on the usual round of court visits, and La Rue would have had few if any opportunities for returning home once he joined the court chapel. For Charles's itinerary, see GachardCV, ii. 11–12.

Most of the information we have about La Rue's life in the next few years comes from material concerning his prebends. In Kortrijk he was ineligible to receive his income for the year 24 June 1508–9,[219] but he received a special payment from them of 60 livres—close to half of his usual income there—for 'services discharged to the church'. Thereafter, for successive years until his retirement, he received his regular income from them. He soon had a new source of income as well. Within a year after his return from Spain La Rue had received a new prebend, through Marguerite,[220] at the collegiate church of Sainte-Pharaïlde in Ghent.[221] In the letter of April 1509 in which she requests the prebend from her father, she uses the conventional language of reward for good services, but also notes that La Rue performed such services for Philip and her 'these past fifteen or sixteen years', a time period that corresponds perfectly to Marguerite's return to the court in June 1493 after her upbringing in France. She also notes that he has been on the waiting list for the past twelve years and that a vacancy had only just occurred. We cannot confirm the former statement—no collation list survives from 1497—but the latter is not true, as examination of the Ghent records shows.[222] We thus have a curious combination of La Rue as someone whom Marguerite clearly knows and wishes to reward, and someone who has nonetheless not actually been at the top of the list when it came time to distribute those rewards; for more on this see the discussion in Chapter 2.

In the following year La Rue resigned his prebend in Namur, but not before creating a financial arrangement whereby his successor paid him a sum of money twice annually.[223] This evident concern with money makes one wonder why La Rue resigned the prebend in the first place; possibly the resignation is connected

---

[219] Perhaps his father had died by this time, preventing an arrangement like that of the previous year.

[220] Charles technically granted the prebend, but Marguerite wrote first to Maximilian for permission.

[221] Sainte Pharaïlde (also known as Sainte Verle and other variants) was an 8th-c. virgin from Brabant, the patron saint of Ghent whose relics were (and perhaps still are) in Sint Bavo's cathedral in Ghent. The chapter founded in her honour was one of the oldest religious organizations in Ghent; the church itself was built in 912 (Le baron Jules de Saint-Genois, *Notice sur le dépôt des archives de la Flandre orientale* (Ghent: L. Hebbelynck, 1841), 47). The church was pillaged in 1566 by the Calvinists during the 'Time of Troubles' in Belgium and was eventually destroyed in 1579 (Édouard de Moreau, *Histoire de l'église en Belgique*, 5 vols. and supplement (Brussels: L'Édition universelle, 1945–52), Suppl., 205). By 1614 it was recognized that the chapter no longer had the means to reconstruct its church since its lands (and hence its chief source of income) had been sold by the Calvinists or flooded by the sea; the chapter was thus transferred to the parish church of Sint Nicolas (Saint-Genois, *Notice sur le dépôt*, 47, and Philippe Kervyn de Volkaersbeke, *Les Églises de Gand*, 2 vols. (Ghent: Hebbelynck, 1858), ii. 196). In 1782 the Emperor Joseph II decreed the separation of the church of Sint Nicolas and the chapter of Sainte-Pharaïlde, transferring the latter to the Jesuit church of Ghent. (ibid. 196–7). Finally in 1794 the chapter was abolished (Ghent, Rijksarchief, folder 21, Inventaris van het kapittel van Sint-Veerle te Gent), doubtless as a result of the general attempt in France and French-controlled territories (which Belgium was at this time) to eradicate religious institutions in the wake of the French Revolution.

[222] Ghent, Rijksuniversiteit, MS 567, pp. 41–58, lists prebends given, some by the court, between 1497 and 1509. Of the nineteen prebends preceding La Rue's in this period, the court was responsible for eight, given in June 1499 (Johannes Braem), 7 Mar. 1502 modern style (Johannes Nilis the younger), 15 Nov. 1505 (Victor de Moro), 22 May 1506 (Petrus Van den Heyden), Aug. 1506 (Johannes De Hond), 8 May 1508 (Daniel De Heetvelde), 2 June 1508 (Petrus Clite), Sept. 1508 (Judocus Pipe), 24 Nov. 1508 (Georgius Tayspaet). Some but by no means all of these had been awarded while La Rue was in Spain.

[223] See the citations in App. A for June 1510; the arrangement required papal approval.

with another prebend that he received, at the church of Onze-Lieve-Vrouw in Dendermonde. Charles (and thus presumably La Rue) had visited Dendermonde on 22 February and 5–6 March 1509; perhaps the visit inspired La Rue to be put on the benefice rolls for the church.[224] We know neither the starting nor ending dates of the latter prebend, which was granted to him by Charles (in name) and then taken away again and given to someone else, after La Rue had already paid the fee necessary to take possession—evidence that he was still at the mercy of his employer's whims. On 30 July 1513 Charles issued letters patent authorizing reimbursement for La Rue's expense, but without providing any other information.[225] Possibly La Rue received the Dendermonde prebend in 1510 and decided to resign the Namur one; it is also possible that the Dendermonde events took place closer to 1513, the time that La Rue asked for reimbursement.[226]

The peaceful existence that La Rue had enjoyed for six years came to an abrupt end on 5 January 1515, when Maximilian, after having been paid 100,000 guilders to relinquish his rights as guardian, had the not-quite-15-year-old Charles declared of age.[227] The young ruler almost immediately embarked on a grand tour of his northern territories, making *entrées* into the major cities of his realm. After he left Brussels on 3 February, he did not return until 23 July, and then set off for more travel within a week. During his first extended period of repose during the year—a stay in Brussels from 22 September to 6 November—he drew up a new ordinance to govern his household, including his chapel. La Rue, though the highest-ranked singer after the *premier chapelain*, was not to remain in Charles's employ for much longer.

RETIREMENT: 1516–1518

Retirement and testament

During the night of 22–3 January 1516 Ferdinand of Aragon died, naming Charles his sole heir. After his formal assumption of the title King of Castile on 14 March,

---

[224] La Rue is not listed for Dendermonde on the one collation list that we know of from his period with the court, that from 1501.

[225] Knowledge of the letters patent comes only from the actual reimbursement, which took place in 1514. DoorslaerC, 156, misinterprets the Dendermonde reimbursement, saying that La Rue was granted his prebend in 1514 and left shortly thereafter, whereas we actually have no knowledge of either the starting or ending dates involved.

[226] In entries concerning property that he owned, a Pieter van der Straten appears in a Dendermonde rent book begun in 1499 and used for some years thereafter (*Rentboek van het begijnhof van Dendermonde (1499)*, ed. Jan Broeckaert (Dendermonde: Snelpersdruk Aug. de Schepper Philips, 1901)). The rent book was for the beguinage of Dendermonde, which was under the jurisdiction of the church of Onze-Lieve-Vrouw. Because the original rent book no longer survives it is not possible to tell if the van der Straten entries are from the 16th c. If this individual were La Rue, it would be a use of van der Straten unrelated to the musician cited in 's-Hertogenbosch and elsewhere).

[227] This date is given in the contemporary 'Journal des voyages de Charles-Quint'; see GachardCV, ii. 55. Written by Jacques de Herbais, the journal was expanded and claimed as original by Jean de Vandenesse. See ibid. pp. xviii–xxiii, on the authorship of the narrative.

it was only a question of time before Charles would go to Spain himself,[228] and it seems likely, as Walter Rubsamen suggested,[229] that La Rue's retirement this year was prompted at least in part by his desire to avoid a third trip to the Iberian peninsula.

The specific date of La Rue's retirement is unknown. On 21 January, when he received his back pay from the previous year, he was still described as a singer of the domestic chapel, but the record of this payment appears in the only chapel-related document that survives from the first six months of the year, leaving us no other clues in the court documents. On 17 April his request to take up residence in Kortrijk the following 23 June was presented to the chapter there, but not by La Rue. Charles was in Brussels from 9 to 20 April; one assumes that La Rue was thus still with him. However, just over two weeks later (2 May), La Rue appeared before the chapter in person to present the privilege making him eligible for his income of the preceding year. In none of the earlier years for which we have specific records of this presentation (1508, 1510, 1512–14) does La Rue deliver it personally, and since Charles was again in Brussels at this time (22 April–6 May), La Rue's personal appearance before the chapter might imply that he had indeed now made the move to Kortrijk. The request in April to begin residence on 23 June did not preclude an earlier move, since it was to satisfy a formal requirement of the chapter, which stipulated a period of forty days' residence beginning specifically on the eve of the feast of St John.[230]

If La Rue had not already gone to Kortrijk for good by 2 May, most likely he made his move on 27 May, the day Charles and his entourage were themselves in Kortrijk. Given La Rue's concern with money, he may have wished to extend his time with Charles—and thus increase his nest egg—as long as possible before his formal residence began. Another possible date for the beginning of the retirement is 9 June, when Charles and the court left Brussels for Heverlé and did not return until after La Rue is found for certain in Kortrijk. This was on 16 June, when he drew up his will in Kortrijk 'in the home of my usual residence', as he stated in the testament.[231] He was to remain there until his death.

La Rue had been thinking about the future before this; as noted under the vander Straten discussion, during the year 24 June 1511–12 he paid his 'death duty' to the confraternity at 's-Hertogenbosch for a Mass to be said after his death.[232] As his will demonstrates, La Rue was to have two other places with whom he had

---

[228] He eventually set sail on 8 Sept. 1517; see ibid. 21.

[229] RubsamenMGG, 229. RobijnsP, 20, suggested that at age 55 a singer would no longer have been much use to the chapel. However, it was precisely from age 55 to 60 that Agricola worked for the chapel, and La Rue may have been even older.

[230] Chapter records note that he completed the residence on 2 Aug.; by some means of accounting that qualified him for 'residence' for the year 1515. According to SG 23–4, every three years canons of Kortijk had to keep a 'strict residence', forty days and forty nights in Kortrijk beginning with the vigil of St John the Baptist. La Rue could not have done this every three years; 1509, 1510, 1511, 1513, and 1514 are the only possible years when he might have complied.   [231] CaulletM, 48.

[232] Since the court was not travelling at this time, La Rue either went on his own or had someone else deliver his payment.

long-term associations, St Ode and Kortrijk itself, perform Masses for his soul after his death.

La Rue's will and the account of its execution reveal several things, not least the fact that at the time he died he was quite well-to-do, if not rich. The 'separate sacks and containers with money' found in his room after he died along with the money owed to him added up to the staggering sum of £1,899. 17s.[233] When one considers that his yearly income at the court, where he was one of the better-paid employees, was about £200, one realizes with astonishment that La Rue had saved almost ten years' salary. All of his evident concern with money in the preceding years—the special services he provided in 1508–9 to the chapter at Kortrijk that enabled him to acquire almost half the income he would otherwise have lost, the special arrangement he made on giving up his Namur prebend, writing to Marguerite to intervene on his behalf (via his father) for his Kortrijk income the first year he was with Juana, asking Charles to reimburse him for his Dendermonde initiation fee, maintaining his benefice at St Ode long after he had left, keeping careful track of money owed him, even from his years in Spain—paid off handsomely.

He bequeathed the money as follows.[234] First, a great deal of it went to the church of Onze-Lieve-Vrouw in Kortrijk and his fellow chapter members. He paid for his burial place, choosing in the church the area by the left side of the altar. Arrangements were made for paying off his debts, including anything purchased on credit but not completely paid off. He paid the vice-curate for the administration of the sacraments, the chaplains for reciting the psalter after his death, the chaplains carrying his body to be interred, the chorus in the procession and in the funeral Mass, the celebrant of the funeral Mass, the altar attendants and those directing the chorus, the choirboys assigned to the candles and incense, the novices carrying the cross and holy water, the choirboys and schoolboys present at the procession, the funeral vigils, and the Mass for reading the psalms, the *Miserere*, and the *De profundis*, the master of the boys for bringing them to and from the church, and so on; in other words, 'the . . . required things just as it is customary to be done for a canon'. He arranged for bread (made from the best grain) and money to be distributed among the poor on the day of his funeral and for money to be paid to those priests at Onze-Lieve-Vrouw who prayed for the souls of his relatives and benefactors on the day of his death and to those reading the *De profundis* at his tomb. As soon as possible, for twenty-nine consecutive days after his death, a daily Requiem Mass was to be said for the souls of his relatives and benefactors, and on the thirtieth day a Requiem was to be celebrated, with the whole choir, for

---

[233] As a total, this is less money than Dufay left and more than Binchois (figures and discussion are found in David Fallows, *Dufay* (London and Melbourne: J. M. Dent, 1982), 79–82, 274) though it is difficult to say if the actual value was more or less. Musicians' testaments and executions thereof have received relatively little study and are certainly worth pursuing further, especially for comparative purposes. But as shown below, testaments do not always give the complete story of worldly possessions.

[234] The testament is given in CaulletM, 46–9; excerpts from its execution appear on 49–52.

his soul.[235] He then bequeathed money to the curate, the vice-curate, the deacon, each resident canon, each cleric, the two ushers, their staff-bearing assistant, the bellringer, and the person who lighted the candles.

La Rue then arranged for another 300 Masses to be celebrated immediately after his death, 100 in the church of Onze-Lieve-Vrouw in Kortrijk, 100 in the monastery of the Friars Minor of Kortrijk, 50 in the parish church of Sint Martin, and 50 in the convent of the Grey Sisters. Gifts of money were then given to the four orders of mendicant friars and the Grey Sisters. The revenues from his Kortrijk prebend for the year after his death, to which he was entitled, were to be divided in two. Half the money was to go to the Onze-Lieve-Vrouw church fabric and the other half to the executors of his will, to be distributed among the poor according to their discretion, but especially 'to wretched expectant women [unwed mothers?] and to other diverse poor languishing in grave illness'.

The next bequest dealt with the income from his prebend at the mysterious church of St Ode. He bequeathed half that money to the fabric of the church and the other half to the chorus (for polyphony?) so that funeral rites could be celebrated for the benefit of his soul and those of his relatives and benefactors. Two additional references in the execution of the will refer to the prebend at 'Rode'. The first is the payment of a small debt he had there, handled by Georgius Rasoris, who was going to 'Rode'. Is this evidence of continuing interaction with the place? The other is a payment of £12 'to master Nicolaus Nyspen, secretary of the venerable lord cardinal of Cambrai in Brussels for the salary of the income of Rode to be collected on behalf of the said late testator'.[236]

La Rue had bequests for his relatives. His mother was to receive his various household goods, linen, silver, clothing, etc., but no money. His brother Johannes (Jean) would get £200, and his sister's daughter, Katherine de Marliers, the same if she was unmarried and nothing if she was married. Any leftover money was to be distributed to the poor as alms.

For the executors of his will he chose two of his colleagues at Kortrijk, Jacobus van Thielt and Vincentius de Fossatis. The will was notarized by Johannes Caen, 'priest of the diocese of Tournai', but at La Rue's house in Kortrijk, as La Rue stated at the very end of his testament, in the presence of the two witnesses (a priest, Guilhelmus van den Berghe, and a cleric, Judocus vanden Broele).

The will itself dealt with the dispersal of his wealth after his death, but he had provided certain things for others earlier. On 18 June 1516 his former prebend at Sainte-Pharaïlde in Ghent, which he had resigned, was taken over by Jacob de la Rue, who must be his brother. Jacob was appointed by Charles, and the appointment was surely made at La Rue's request. Since Jacob was not assigned anything

---

[235] As we shall see, the chapter had books of polyphony that La Rue gave them, one of which may have contained his own Requiem mass.

[236] CaulletM, 51.

in La Rue's testament, this prebend must have been intended as La Rue's bequest to him.[237]

A second unnoted 'bequest' went to Vincentius de Fossatis, one of the executors of La Rue's testament, a colleague and one-time *magister cantus* at Kortrijk. La Rue gave him a parchment book of discant ('complete and not torn') that de Fossatis gave in turn (in 1524) to the chapter.[238] Other music books of La Rue's were given to the Kortrijk chapter as well. In 1540, when Johannes Pedis was deprived of the office of *magister cantus*,[239] he had to 'bring back each and every songbook belonging to the church from the gift of "magistri petri de la rue" and others'. When Pedis's successor was hired the same year, he was told that when he gave up the office he would need to return, among other things, 'the seven songbooks bound in boards, out of which one is printed, ... the gift of ... Carolus van Halewyn, and the other six are the gift of "quondam magistri petri de la Rue huius ecclesie dum viuerent canonicorum"; of these six books, one is written on parchment in *maxima forma*'.[240] The music books were not noted in the testament because they had probably been gifts during La Rue's lifetime, ensuring that during his retirement he would continue to hear the music he preferred. This was presumably his own music; a collection of six manuscripts could easily have included all his sacred works. The parchment manuscript in *maxima forma* sounds tantalizingly like something prepared by the Habsburg-Burgundian scriptorium, but all six volumes are striking evidence of manuscript ownership by a professional singer.

La Rue's retirement in Kortrijk apparently passed uneventfully, and he died there on 20 November 1518, a date given in the account of the execution of his will and on the epitaph on his tombstone (no longer surviving). The reckoning of the distribution of his Kortrijk income for the fiscal year seems to be slightly less accurate, mentioning four months and twenty-five days without specific dates (thus 24 June to 23 or 24 October—four months—followed by twenty-five days, 24 or 25 October to 17 or 18 November).[241]

The account of the execution of La Rue's testament details what happened after La Rue's death. The account deals first with the record of exactly how much money there was to be dispersed, followed by the actual dispersing of it. The people responsible for determining the amount of money were executor Vincentius de Fossatis, four other canons of the church at Kortrijk (Judocus de Scornaco, Johannes de Vico [no known relation to La Rue], Karolus van Halewyn, and

---

[237] Others resigned benefices so that relatives might profit; in Oct. 1504 Nicole Mayoul the younger resigned a benefice for Sampson Mayoul, presumably a relative; see DouillezM, no. 62.

[238] See App. A, 15 Oct. 1524.

[239] 'Because he was negligent in teaching and training the young men and because of his other demerits'; see App. A, 28 July 1540.

[240] See App. A, 29 July 1540.

[241] 'Dominus Johannes Haneton absens sed fructus hujus anni sunt magistri Petri de la Rue pro primo anno suo post mortem. Quia dominus canonicus Petrus de la Rue non vixit nisi quatuor mensibus et XXV diebus, veniunt defalcande septem menses ...'; see App. A, 20 Nov. 1518.

Martinus de Veel) plus La Rue's brother Jacob. A small chest contained two white leather purses filled with money, and in the *directorium* (armoire?) of his room were found separate sacks and containers of money. Certain money was owed to La Rue as well. 'A certain person in Spain' owed La Rue two ducats, according to a note that La Rue had kept, another example of his concern with money; it was decided that this money was not recoverable. Sampson le Roy, organist of the parish church of Sint Martin, owed La Rue £15, and from a bequest made by another Kortrijk colleague, Nicolay de Rutere, La Rue was to receive 7s. 6d. Finally, from his well-paying benefice at 'Roode' La Rue was due £124. 14s. 4d. As mentioned before, this added up to the very impressive sum of £1,899. 17s.

The payments included the following.[242] Johannes Caen, the notary who drew up the will, received £2. Johannes de Cuenick, a carpenter, was paid 'for certain rooms that he worked on in the house of the dead man'. Another payment went to 'two strangers who collected firewood for Dominus Petrus in Gavre'. This last was apparently the wooded area by the lake De Gavers, close to Kortrijk.

The Grey Sisters were paid for their help in La Rue's house at the time of his sickness, the Friars Minor were paid for their 'works, vigils, and visits', and Petrus Denis was paid for reading the canonical hours to La Rue during his illness. The apothecary Mathius de Ronneken was reimbursed for the medicines that La Rue used, and the vice-curate Piatus van Dale was paid both for his visits and for his administration of the last rites.

Another payment went to the messengers who set off after La Rue's death, one to Bruges to get Jacobus Thielt, one of the executors of the testament (explaining his absence for the tally of the money found in La Rue's house) and the other 'in the direction of Tournai' to get La Rue's brother Johannes (Jean). The presence of his other brother, Jacob, at this money-counting means that he was very near at hand, but whether he lived nearby or whether he was there because of La Rue's illness is impossible to tell. He was not a canon at Kortrijk.

Out of La Rue's savings came the money 'for the expenses made in the house of the dead man by his mother and family, from the day of his death to the day of his funeral rites'; it is from this payment that we know that his mother survived him. Other relatives, some not included in the original testament, received money. His nephew Anthonius des Marliers got £36, apparently picked up in person, while La Rue's brother Jean collected the legacies for La Rue's two nieces, one being Jean's daughter Jennette and the other their sister's daughter Katherine de le Marliere. Jean was given power of attorney to collect Katherine's inheritance on 23 November, and the money was received the following day.

The funeral was arranged by Dominus Gislenus Noppe, who was paid for his work. Payments were made for the coffin, the alb and dalmatic (the appropriate garments for a deacon, in which the body was clothed),[243] and the 'coverlet placed

[242] This is not a complete list but is drawn from the excerpts given in CaulletM, 49–52.

[243] It is assuredly to this funeral clothing that the church storeroom records for 1518 refer; see App. A,

over the body of the dead'. Various people were paid for meals given at the time of the funeral rites, including the municipal magistrate, the members of the municipal council, the canons, the chapter, the chaplains, and the vicars.

Exactly where La Rue was buried in the church is open to some question, and no trace of his grave remains in the church today. At the beginning of his testament he states that he wishes to be buried by the left side of the altar on the opposite side of the *fenestre incluse*, which can either be a stopped-up window or a window in an enclosure. Caullet has interpreted this to mean opposite the window of the dwelling of the cloister. This is not necessarily the case, however. Precisely on the left side of the altar there is a small 'chapel' that does indeed have a stopped-up window in it; it stands to reason that this is the one that La Rue meant.

According to the account of the execution of the testament, there was a cover with a white cross over the tomb; the cover was made by Jodocus Maelfait. Henricus the sculptor, staying in Menyn, was paid for engraving a *tabulatum* out of white stone, which a painter and his assistants painted gold. There was also a payment for the *clausurae* of such *tabulati* with the depiction of the epitaph in French. Further, someone was paid for painting the epitaph on a wooden *tabula*.

By Caullet's interpretation, La Rue's tomb was thus composed of an altarpiece of white polychrome stone with shutters painted probably on a panel or board, as well as an epitaph in French, plus a second funeral inscription.[244] Vander Straeten, citing no source, said that the Latin inscription marking La Rue's tomb was formerly to be found in the Chapel of St Catherine in the church.[245] Today the statue of St Catherine is to be found in the chapel to the *right*-hand side of the altar, which, furthermore, is called the Chapel of the Counts, but the statue, though large, could have been moved from elsewhere. The account of the execution of the testament states that Don Gislenus Noppe, the canon who organized the funeral and was responsible for the shroud, etc., was given a payment 'for the confraternity guild of St Katherine', so perhaps La Rue was buried in St Catherine's chapel.

The final calculation of the will was not made until 4 February 1519. Curiously enough, it does not quite tally. The amount of money paid out is recorded as £1,499. 17s., which should leave a residue of £400. The leftover money is, however, recorded as £461. 13s. 6d.

La Rue's epitaph

The form of the epitaph given below is a collated version from an earlier article in which I discussed aspects of it at length.[246] Prior to its appearance in that essay, it was available in six modern publications, none of which presented exactly the

[after 20 Nov.].

[244] CaulletM, 45.   [245] VDS vii. 115.
[246] Meconi, 'Free from the Crime of Venus'; I did not go into detail about the variant versions.

same readings.[247] The oldest printed source came from F. Van de Putte in an 1871 article in which he published material from a manuscript he described as 'Epitaphes copiées, en 1629, par Christophe van Huerne, seigneur de Schiervelde', though he did not give the current location of that manuscript.[248] According to this source, La Rue's epitaph was found on a wall in the Chapel of the Cross in the church ('in de kruiskapelle in muro').

In 1882 Vander Straeten published a version of the epitaph, citing no source and saying merely that one had previously been able to read the epitaph in the Chapel of St Catherine, and that this was stated at the beginning of the inscription.[249] The Vander Straeten version had three changes from the Van de Putte version. Caullet in 1911 included the epitaph, taking his version from an eighteenth-century copy after the van Huerne manuscript, which he identified as *Collectio epitaphiorum Belgicorum*.[250] The copy was made by the bibliophile Goethals and was evidently to be found on folio 79 of book 311 of the Goethals-Vercruysse library. Caullet cited Vander Straeten as well, but the version he printed incorporated only two of Vander Straeten's changes and added seven more. Tirabassi presented three unique readings but otherwise his version is the same as Vander Straeten's.[251] In Robijns's book the situation is even more confused.[252] His copy of the epitaph accepted most but not all of the Caullet version and included two new variants as well. Further, he claimed that Vander Straeten drew his text from van Huerne (which may be true, but is not stated by Vander Straeten himself) and that the van Huerne volume was in the Bibliothèque Goethals-Vercruysse (in the municipal archive of Kortrijk), which, if true at one point, is no longer the case. Finally, the version printed in *MGG*[253] was drawn from (and cited) Van de Putte (though the name of the journal rather than the author) but still made one change in orthography.

The situation thus seems to be as follows. Only one person made a copy from the original, and that was van Heurne, but his copy cannot currently be located.[254] Both Goethals and Van de Putte made copies from van Heurne, and possibly

[247] A seventh publication, John Evan Kreider, 'The Masses for Five and Six Voices by Pierre de la Rue', 2 vols. (Ph.D. diss., Indiana University, 1974), i. 10, copies Robijns exactly and is thus not treated separately here.

[248] F. Van de Putte, 'Epitaphes copiées, en 1629, par Christophe van Huerne, seigneur de Schiervelde', *Annales de la Société d'Émulation pour l'Étude de l'Histoire et des Antiquités de la Flandre*, ser. 3, 16/4 (1871), 280.

[249] VDS vii. 115.   [250] CaulletM, 45.

[251] Antonio Tirabassi, 'L'Interprétation traditionelle des œuvres de Pierre de la Rue', *Musica sacra*, 42 (1935), 250–7; 43 (1936), 37–41, 116–30; here (1935), 252.

[252] RobijnsP, 30.   [253] RubsamenMGG, 229.

[254] It is possible that van Huerne's manuscript is today part of the library of Count Frederic de Limburg Stirum of the Chateau of Huldenberg in Huldenberg. The Count is the great-grandson of the famous Belgian bibliophile Thierry-Marie-Joseph, comte de Limburg Stirum (1827–1911), about whom see Vicomte Terlinden, 'Limburg Stirum (Thierry-Marie-Joseph, comte de), *Biographie nationale* [Belgium], xxxiii. 443–6. The possibility that he owned the van Huerne manscript comes from Le Baron Bethune, *Épitaphes et monuments des églises de la Flandre au XVIme siecle d'après les manuscrits de Corneille Gailliard et d'autres auteurs* (Bruges: L. De Plancke, for the Société d'émulation pour l'étude de l'histoire et des antiquités de la Flandre, 1900), 36 n. 1. Referring to a discussion of epitaphs in Kortrijk, Baron Bethune mentions that these are 'D'après une copie du ms. de C. van Huerne, qui possède M. le comte de Limburg-

Vander Straeten as well, but the correctness of these readings can only be confirmed by comparison with the currently untraceable van Heurne. The collated version given below is thus based on what is now available, mostly taken from Van de Putte.[255]

> In tumulo Petrus de Vico conditur isto,
> nobile cui nomen musica sacra dedit.
> Pannonios[256] reges[257] coluit, gallos et hiberos;[258]
> omnibus ob cantum[259] gratus et ipse fuit.
> sed virtute magis clarus pietate parentes[260]
> fovit, et in[261] miseros munera[262] larga tulit.[263]
> assiduus superi[264] cultor Christique minister,
> castus et a[265] Veneris crimine[266] mundus erat.
> hujus[267] canonicus templi sua tempora clausit;
> posce[268] Deum, lector, spiritus astra colat.
> Obiit[269] anno Domini 1518, xx die[270] novembris.

> In this tomb is buried Petrus de Vico
> to whom sacred music gave a noble name.
> He worked for the rulers of Pannonia, Gallia, and Hiberia;
> to all of them he was pleasing because of his singing/song.
> But renowned rather for his virtue, he cherished his relatives with piety,
> and conferred generous gifts on the needy.
> Tireless worshipper of God and minister of Christ,
> he was pure and free from the crime of Venus.
> He concluded his days as a canon of this temple;

Stirum . . .'. Bethune himself does not include La Rue's epitaph. Unfortunately I received no reply to my inquiry to Count Frederic about this manuscript.

255 My thanks to Leofranc Holford-Strevens for suggestions as to editorial corrections.

256 Van de Putte: *Pannonus*; Caullet: *pannonios*; Robijns: *panonios*. Leofranc Holford-Strevens notes that *Pannonus* must be mistaken, being an incorrect form, a false quantity, and the wrong case (private comm., 22 July 1991).

257 Tirabassi: *reget*.

258 The reading *Hibernos* (Ireland) is found in vander Straeten, Caullet, and Tirabassi.

259 Caullet and Robijns: *cantu*, but *ob* requires the accusative case, making *cantum* correct.

260 Both Robijns and Caullet, who give the reading *parente*, say that this must be an error and that *parentes* must be meant. Vander Straeten sticks with *parente* (as does Tirabassi), mentioning 'the virtue that breeds piety', but does not offer a translation for the full passage.

261 Caullet and Robijns eliminate *in*.

262 Tirabassi: *numera*.

263 Caullet and Robijns: *dedit* instead of *tulit*, but the meaning is the same.

264 *Superni* in the sources, but *superi* is required by the metre; my thanks to Leofranc Holford-Strevens for this correction. Caullet and Robijns substitute *ipse* for this word, changing the meaning to 'tireless worshipper himself and minister of God'.

265 Robijns eliminates the necessary *a*.

266 Caullet and Robijns have the incorrect reading *crimina* instead of *crimine*, *criminis* being a third-declension noun.

267 Rubsamen has *huius*.

268 The reading by Vander Straeten, Van de Putte, Tirabassi, and Rubsamen of *post* instead of *posce* makes no sense. Caullet and Robijns have *posce*.

269 Tirabassi: *obijt*.

270 Vander Straeten and Tirabassi omit the *die*.

pray God, reader, that his spirit will inhabit the stars.

He died in the year of the Lord 1518, the 20th day of November.

The epitaph presents no surprises and fits well with what we know of his life. La Rue was famed for sacred music and song, worked for the Habsburg-Burgundian court (represented by its three major components at this time, the equivalents of Austria, Belgium, and Spain),[271] was generous to his relatives and others, and morally upright. His fiscal prudence enabled his generosity, and his testament shows his concern for others both in his gifts of money and in having Masses said for souls in addition to his own. Indeed, at Onze-Lieve-Vrouw his is the last of the initial thirty Masses said (though he clearly wanted all possible forces involved in its celebration). Nuns as well as male clerics sing for his soul.

We have some partial ideas about what certain famous composers of the fifteenth and earlier sixteenth centuries were like: Dufay, at least in his old age, seems to have been 'a difficult and mean man';[272] Busnoys was feisty and pugnacious;[273] Josquin was a bit of a prima donna who only composed when he wanted to, while Isaac was much more amenable in this matter;[274] Obrecht kept running into difficulties with his employers;[275] Gombert molested a choirboy;[276] and Ockeghem was 'alone of all the singers . . . free from vice and abounding in all virtues'.[277] La Rue seems to come closer to the Isaac/Ockeghem style of behaviour, with a corresponding intense loyalty to his employer—he is on every surviving *escroe* and pay document from the court during his years of service. Perhaps he was simply a sanctimonious prig, but it is equally likely that he was a genuinely devout and honourable person—no bloody brawls, no illegitimate children, no inappropriate relations with choirboys—whose religious faith governed his life and generated the lion's share of his work.

[271] See Meconi, 'Free from the Crime of Venus', for an explanation of these geographical designations and other ways the epitaph represents the major parts of his life.

[272] Fallows, *Dufay*, 81.

[273] Paula Higgins, 'Busnoys, Antoine', *New Grove II*, iv. 666.

[274] Lockwood, 'Josquin at Ferrara', 114.

[275] Rob C. Wegman, 'Obrecht, Jacob', *New Grove II*, xviii. 291.

[276] George Nugent and Eric Jas, 'Gombert, Nicolas', *New Grove II*, x. 119.

[277] Leeman L. Perkins, 'Ockeghem, Jean de', *New Grove II*, xviii. 315, quoting Francesco Florio.

2 The *Grande chapelle* and Musical Life at the Habsburg-Burgundian Court

Now that it seems unlikely that La Rue was the same musician as Peter vander Straten, the Habsburg-Burgundian court assumes even greater significance in his career. Placing La Rue in context within the court chapel requires an understanding of the chapel's functions and duties, an overview of his colleagues who were also composers of polyphonic music, some thought as to what music the chapel had at its disposal, and a re-evaluation of the received understanding of La Rue's significance to the chapel and its rulers. Each of these components is treated in turn in this chapter.

STRUCTURE AND DUTIES OF THE CHAPEL

Statutes governing the chapel

The Habsburg-Burgundian court employed many musicians, both singers and instrumentalists.[1] La Rue was a member of the largest and most prestigious group of singers, the *grande chapelle*, also known as the *chapelle domestique*, which accompanied the ruler everywhere, even on hunting trips or during war. Throughout this book the term 'chapel' refers to this specific one unless otherwise indicated.[2]

The duties of the court chapel are known through large-scale *états de l'hôtel* drawn up periodically by court rulers to regulate their household. Three survive from La Rue's tenure at court, two from Philip (10 March 1497 and 1 February 1500) and one from Charles (25 October 1515).[3] In each case a list of current members of the chapel is provided along with instructions as to their duties, which, as we shall see, varied greatly in degree of specificity.

Although Philip had assumed governance of the Low Countries in 1494, he did not attempt a significant reorganization of his household until more than two

---

[1] For overviews of musical life at the court, see DoorslaerC; Jeannine Douillez, 'De Muziek aan het Bourgondische-Habsburgse hof in de tweede helft der XVde eeuw' (diss., University of Ghent, [1967]); Martin Picker, 'The Habsburg Courts in the Netherlands and Austria, 1477–1530', in Iain Fenlon (ed.), *The Renaissance from the 1470s to the End of the 16th Century* (Englewood Cliffs, NJ: Prentice Hall, 1989), 216–42; and Haggh, 'The Status of the Musician'.

[2] Other chapels included a *petite chapelle* in service of the ruler, which said low Mass (as opposed to the high Mass sung by the *grande chapelle*) as well as small groups associated with other important personages such as Juana, Charles before the death of his father, and later Marguerite. Chapelains also served other units within the court (e.g. Pierre Barbry was chapelain for the archers; see DoorslaerC, 140). These smaller musical groups have received very little attention.

[3] See App. A under these dates for bibliographic citations.

years later. In the introduction to his *état* of 10 March 1497, he states that since coming of age and being received in his country, he has always had a conspicuous desire to attend to the great disorder that has previously been in his household and elsewhere during his minority and past wars.[4] The organization begins with his chapel: 'First, that our *grande chapelle* be henceforth served, governed, and led by the persons thus and in the manner that follows'.[5]

The members of the *grande chapelle* are then listed by name, divided into five categories, to be discussed below. The layout of *grande chapelle* members is followed by an extremely long list of all the other members of the household, interspersed with information about the duties of these other groups. Finally, approaching the end of the *état*, the chapel reappears: 'Item, we wish and command that those of our said *grande chapelle* conduct and regulate themselves, as for their occupation and affairs concerning the said chapel, according to the ordinance to this effect made by our very dear late lord and grandfather the duke Charles, may God absolve him, which ordinance will be made known to them to this end by our said *grand maître d'hôtel*, and we wish that this ordinance be maintained and followed by them in all its points, under the penalties announced there, as if it were inserted here verbatim.'[6] Still further on, even closer to the end, one more brief statement addresses the chapel: 'The *premier chapelain* will be held to do the same concerning those of the chapel',[7] that is, to report absences daily to the *maître d'hôtel*, on pain of losing his office otherwise.[8] The 1497 *état*, then, relies almost completely on the previous set of regulations, adding only the stipulation about reporting absences.[9] This reliance on a document of almost thirty years earlier is perhaps surprising, but no other known *état* comes even close to approaching the detail of these earlier regulations.[10] As Fallows has pointed out, in 1469 the

[4] '[D]epuis que sommes venus en âge et être receu en nos pays, nous avons toujours eu singulier désir, vouloir et affection de pourvoir au grand désordre, qui, à l'occasion de notre minorité et des guerres et divisions passées, a été par ci-devant, tant en notre maison qu'ailleurs ...'; see Frédéric Auguste le Baron de Reiffenberg, 'État de l'hôtel de Philippe-le-Bel, duc de Bourgogne, en l'an 1496, à Bruxelles', *Compte-rendu des séances de la Commission royale d'histoire ou Recueil des ses bulletins*, 11 (1846), 677–718 at 678.

[5] 'Premiers, que notre grande chapelle sera doresnavant déservie, gouvernée et conduite par les personnes, ainsi et par la manière qui s'ensuit'; ibid. It is noteworthy that Philip begins with the chapel, perhaps because of its primary association with the sacred service; at this time it was not yet listed at the top of the daily *escroes*.

[6] 'Item, voulons et ordonnons que ceux de notredite grande chapelle se conduiront et règleront, quant a leurs états et affaires concernant ladite chapelle, selon l'ordonnance sur ce faite par feu notre très-cher seigneur et grand-père le duc Charles, que Dieu absoude, laquelle ordonnance leur sera à cette fin déclarée par notredit grand maître d'hôtel, et voulons qu'icelle ordonnance soit par eux entretenue et ensuivie en tous ses points, sous les peines y déclarées, comme si elle étoit icy insérée de mot à autre'; ibid. 716. For the 1469 ordinance of Charles the Bold, stated to be a codification of previous practices, see Fallows, 'Specific Information'.

[7] 'Le premier chapelain sera tenu de faire le semblable touchant ceux de la chapelle'; see Reiffenberg, 'État de l'hôtel', 717.

[8] These were the instructions given to other household officials immediately before the citation of the chapel.

[9] This was clearly an important one financially, for the pay of absent members was docked. The threatened dismissal from office must have been necessary to counter loyalty to the chapel that might otherwise prompt the *premier chapelain* to falsify reports in favour of the absent chapel members.

[10] As shown below, the chapel did not attend strictly to the 1469 rules, as for example in the distribution

rules for the chapel (those to which Philip refers in 1497) comprise a full 25 per cent of the *état* of which they are a part.[11] Contemporaries recognized the definitive nature of this document; in the next *état*, written five years later for England's Edward IV by Olivier de la Marche, the chapel was summed up neatly in a single paragraph.[12] La Rue, then, joined a chapel with a long-standing commitment to a specific set of regulations, though as we shall see, not all of the original 1469 statutes could have been followed during his time at the court.

On 1 February 1500, close to three years after his first household reorganization, Philip drew up a second *état*. The chapel once again heads the *état*, and from this point on all the daily *escroes* will also lead off with the *grande chapelle*. This time the instructions for the chapel follow immediately after the list of chapel names, and they are considerably more detailed, though they still fall back on Charles the Bold's 1469 chapel regulations. The 1500 *état* gives nine 'statutes and ordinances' as follows.

[1][13] First, that the said *chapelains* and members of the said chapel will be held to perform, in all honour and reverence, the divine service, to sing [*chanter*] Mass, Vespers, and Compline, each day, at the appropriate time and at the place where my lord will be, or elsewhere where it pleases him, having and wearing clerical dress, round caps, and surplices, on all eves of feasts and feasts themselves and on triple and grand double feasts, with shaved faces, losing their wages each day that they will be found at fault in this.[14]

[2] Item, that the said *chapelains* and other members, when they enter and behold the said chapel, will genuflect and bow to the Saviour, the Virgin Mary, and the patron of the said chapel.[15]

[3] Item, that in performing the office they will be standing, and in singing [*chantant*] the Introit of the Mass, the Kyries, Gloria, the Gospel, the Credo, Sanctus, Pater Noster, the Agnus Dei and similarly the Introit [beginning] of Vespers and Compline in the Chapters, Magnificat and Nunc dimittis, in prayers and orations, the said *chapelains* will have their

of roles within the chapel. Aspects of the 1469 ordinances apparently persisted into the time of Philip II: see Bernadette Nelson, 'Ritual and Ceremony in the Spanish Royal Chapel *c.*1559–*c.*1561', *EMH* 19 (2000), 105–200.

[11] Fallows, 'Specific Information', 110.

[12] 'En sa chapelle a quarante hommes, à comprendre ung evesque, son confesseur, et trois autres Jacopins prestres et confessours, autres chappellains et autres officiers, organistes et sommeilliers, lesquels chappellains, chantres et officiers sont gouvernez par le premier chappellain. Et tous les jours, où qu'ilz soient, chantent les heures du jour et la grant messe solennel. Ouquel service et à toutes heures est le prince quant ils sont devers lui, et principalement à la messe et aux vespres. Et n'est pas à oublier que l'evesque dessusdit et les freres Jacopins sont grans clercs, doctes et prescheurs, et preschent très souvent'; see Olivier de la Marche, *Mémoires d'Olivier de la Marche, Maître d'hotel et capitaine des gardes de Charles le téméraire*, 4 vols., ed. Henri Beaune and J. d'Arbaumont (Paris: Renouard, 1883–8), iv. 2. De la Marche's *état* takes up ninety-four pages in its modern edition.

[13] No numbers are given in the *état* itself.

[14] DoorslaerC, 45: 'Premiers que lesd. chappellains et suppoz de lad. chappelle seront tenuz de en tout honneur et reverance faire le service divin, chanter messe vespres et complies, chacun jour, à heure deue et au lieu ou Mond. Sgr. sera, ou ailleurs ou il lui plaira, ayans et portans habis clericaux bonnetz rondes suppliz en toutes veilles et festes et en triples et grans doubles, la barbe rase à peine destre royez pour chacun jour quilz seront trouvez en faulte.'

[15] Ibid.: 'Item que leds. chappellains et suppoz quant ilz entreront et vuyderont lad. chappelle se mectront a genoulx et salueront le Saulveur, la Vierge Marye, et le patron de lad. chappelle.'

heads bared, and in Advent and Lent and daily offices they will kneel at prayers as well as at all accustomed times.[16]

[4] Item, that during the office they will be silent and keep from laughing, talking, and other disorderly deportment on pain of being corrected by suspension of their wages or otherwise as the case requires.[17]

[5] Item, that the said *chapelains* and other members and each of them in his place will employ and acquit himself diligently and carefully do in the office that which he should and is held to do. And the *premier chapelain* will remain continuously in the pulpit to oversee everything and likewise see if everything is going as it should.[18]

[6] Item, the said *chapelains* and other members should assemble and hold chapter at least once each week in order to surrender and correct those who have erred and to levy and carry out the penalties assigned to him for the good of the community of the said chapel, of which same penalties and punishments the said *premier chapelain* will have charge and knowledge, and the said *chapelains* and other members will be held to obey him in all things concerning the doings and service of the said chapel.[19]

[7] Item, that if the said *premier chapelain* is negligent in carrying out the punishments and corrections of the said *chapelains* and other misbehaving members according to their faults and demerits, in this case Monseigneur de Salubrye, confessor to my lord, will carry out the punishments against the said *chapelains* and other members as well as against the said *premier chapelain* as the case requires.[20]

[8] Item, that the said *premier chapelain* will be held to indicate each day at the office of the *maistres d'ostel* those said *chapelains* and other members who will serve, in order to count those present and dock the pay of those absent each hour that they will be in default. And if the said *premier chapelain* is negligent or at fault in doing this he will similarly be deprived of his wages whenever that is the case.[21]

[9] Item, that the said *chapelains* and other members conduct and regulate themselves in addition in all things concerning the doings of the said chapel and their service in it, accord-

[16] DoorslaerC, 45: 'Item que en faisant loffice ilz seront drois et en chantant lintroyte de la messe, les kyries, gloria, leuvengille, le credo, sanctus, pater noster, l'agnus dei et semblablement lintroyte des vespres et complyes aux capitaulx, magnificat et une dimistis [Nunc dimittis], aux preces et oroisons lesd. chappellains auront les testes descouvertes, et es avens et karesme es offices feriaulx ils seront tenuz eulx agenouillier aux preces ainsi quil est accoustume de tout temps.'

[17] Ibid.: 'Item que durant loffice ilz feront scilence et se abstiendront de riz, devises et autres manières desordonnees à peine destre corrigez par suspension de leurs gaiges ou autrement selon le cas le requerra.'

[18] Ibid. 46: 'Item, que lesd. chappellains et suppoz et chacun deulx en son endroit se emploieront et acquiteront diligemment et soigneusement a faire en loffice ce quilz doivent et sont tenuz de faire. Et se tiendra continuelement le premier chapellain au pulpitre pour avoir le regard sur tout, et mesmement si toutes choses se feront et conduiront deuement et ainsi quil appartient.'

[19] Ibid.: 'Item, se assembleront lesd. chappellains et suppostz et tiendront chappitre toutes les sepmaines une fois pour le moins afin de capituler et corrigier ceulx qui auront mesprins et mesce et se lèveront et executront les peines par lui commises a lutilité dela communaulte de lad. chappelle desquelz mesmes peines et delictz led. premier chapellain aura la charge et congnoissance et seront lesd. chappellains et suppostz tenuz lui obeir en toutes choses concernans le fait et service de ladite chappelle.'

[20] Ibid.: 'Item que si led. premier chappellain estoit negligent de faire les pugnicions et corrections desd. chappellains et suppostz mesb sans [meschans] selon leurs faultes et demerites, en ce cas monsgr de Salubrye, confesseur de Mond. Sgr, fera lesd. pugnicions aussi bien contre lesd. chappellains et suppostz comme contre led. premier chappellain selon que le cas le requerra.'

[21] Ibid.: 'Item, que led. premier chappellain sera tenu de signifier chacun jour au bureau des maistres d'ostel ceulx desd. chappellains et suppostz qui serviront afin de faire compter les presens et faire royer les absens a chacune heure quilz seront deffaillans. Et se led. premier chappellain estoit negligent ou en faulte de ce faire il sera mesmes roye de ses gaiges toutes et quanteffois que le cas y escherra.'

ing to the statutes and ordinances to this effect made by the late lord duke Charles of Burgundy, may God absolve him, [that were] not included or declared above.[22]

Of the nine items contained here, the last two essentially duplicate the only information given about the chapel in the 1497 list. Items 4 and 6 are very similar to two given in the 1469 *état* (nos. 19 and 24 respectively);[23] misbehaviour and its consequences obviously needed addressing specifically.[24] The remaining items (1–3, 5, and 7) are all basically new, but are mostly just the obvious laying out of duties: sing (appropriately attired) when and where instructed to, and stand, kneel, and genuflect at the appropriate places. The *premier chapelain*, who has the most important post, has some major duties listed and again is threatened with the consequences if they are not carried out. Nothing about the performance of the actual music is spelled out.

On 25 October 1515, within a year of attaining his majority, Charles also had an *état* for the governance of his household drawn up. After the introduction the *état* proceeds to enumerate the members of the household; the chapel is listed first. Once all household members have been cited, the *état* goes immediately to 'Statutz et Ordonnances sur le faict de nostre grande Chapelle'. Again the list is completely derivative, but this time there is no mention of the 1469 *état*. Instead, items 1–5 of the thirteen on the list are taken from the first four of the 1469 ordinance.[25] The remaining eight items, 6–13, are almost literal repeats of items 1–8 of 1500.

The five 'new' items are as follows:

[1][26] First, we command and decree that the *chapelains*, *chantres*, and other members of this chapel be obedient to our said *premiers chapelains*, treating their superiors with honour and reverence, complying with their commands and orders concerning the doings and condition of the said chapel. And if some are rebellious and disobedient, they will be suspended from their wages for as many days as seems reasonable and fair that the rebellion and disobedience requires, for which days the said rebels and disobedient ones will lose their wages.[27]

---

[22] Ibid.: 'Item que leds. chappellains et suppostz se regleront et conduiront au surplus en toutes choses concernans le fait de lad. chappelle et leur service en icelle selon les statuz et ordonnances sur ce faictes par feu monsgr. le duc Charles de Bourgoingne que Dieu absoille, cydessus non comprinses ne declairees.'

[23] The numbering is that of Fallows, 'Specific Information', 151–3.

[24] Injunctions against misbehaviour must have been necessary, as singers in general seemed to be an unruly lot. André Pirro provides an amazing list of improper goings-on among the singers at Cambrai Cathedral, from such simple matters as inappropriate attire (long hair and white hose) and falling asleep during the service, to bringing a dog to church or throwing bones and pieces of meat from one side of the choir to the other. Illicit relations with women also seem to have been rampant, which may have prompted the assertion in La Rue's epitaph that he never succumbed in this manner. See André Pirro, 'Jean Cornuel vicaire à Cambrai', *Revue de musicologie*, 10 (1926), 190–203. Closer to home, SG 23 notes similar problems with quarrels during services, drunkenness, and unwed paternity among the members of the *collégiale* at Kortrijk.

[25] The wording is often, though not always, exact on the two lists. Item 4 of 1469 is divided into items 4 and 5 for 1515.

[26] No numbers are given in the original.

[27] GachardCV, ii. 495: 'Premièrement, ordonnons et statuons que les chapellains, chantres et aultres suppostz d'icelle chapelle soyent obéyssans à nosdicts premiers chapellains, leur portent honneur et révérence comme à leurs chefz, obtempèrent à leurs commandemens et ordonnances, mesmement touchant

[2] Item, that each day of the year, at the appropriate time, will be said and celebrated [*dicte et célébrée*] in our chapel, by those *chapelains, chantres, clercs*, and other servants of this chapel, a customary high Mass [*une haulte messe ordinaire*], in chant and polyphony [*à chant et deschant*], for whichever saint has his or her feast that day, and if no feast is known, the said Mass will be ferial according to the Sunday office of the week.[28] [The 1469 *état*—but not that of 1515—further stipulates that the use of Paris will be followed.]

[3] Item, similarly at the appropriate time for Vespers, Vespers and Compline will be said and sung [*dictes et chantées*] with such office as will have been that of the Mass [of that day] unless the next day is a double or solemn feast, in which case Vespers will be of the solemnity following that observed at such times, and the second Vespers of all feasts shall be as solemn in ceremony, ornament, and other things as the first.[29]

[4] Item, on the feasts and days designated hereafter will be said and celebrated [*dicte et célébrée*] Matins together with all the hours of the day up to but excluding Vespers, which hours, namely Prime, Tierce, Midi, and None, will be said immediately after Matins, without making any break after the said Matins until None inclusively, except on Christmas day after Matins, on which day, because the office is long, there will be an appropriate interval until Prime, at the discretion of our *premier chapelain* serving then. And in regard to Vespers on these days, they will be said [*dictes*] at the time ordered above in the preceding article.[30]

[5] Here follow the feasts and days mentioned above: first, the Nativity, the Circumcision of Our Lord, Epiphany, the Purification of Our Lady, her Annunciation, Visitation, Assumption, Nativity, and Conception, the feasts of Easter, the Ascension of Our Lord, the eve and the day of Pentecost, the feast of the Trinity, that of the Holy Sacrament [Corpus Christi], the Nativity of St John the Baptist, the feast of St Peter in June, the feast of All Saints, the Commemoration of the Dead [All Souls], the feasts of St Catherine, St Andrew, and St Barbara, and each day of Lent and Advent.[31] [The 1469 *état* differs by decreeing that Matins is to be reinstated on the days during Advent when the 'O' antiphons are sung. This seems like a superfluous injunction since Matins was supposed to be sung on each day of Advent anyway].

le faict et estat de ladicte chapelle. Et s'aulcuns estoyent rebelles et désobéyssans, ilz seront suspenduz de leurs gaiges pour aultant de jours qu'il semblera en bonne raison et équité que la rébellion et désobéyssance exigera, pour lesquelz jours desdicts rebelles et désobéyssans perderont leursdicts gaiges.'

[28] Ibid.: 'Item, que chascun jour de l'an à heure compétente, sera dicte et célébrée en nostre chapelle, par iceulx chapellains, chantres, clercqz et aultres servans en icelle chapelle, une haulte messe ordinaire, à chant et deschant, de tel sainct ou saincte dont la feste écherra à icelluy jour; et si feste n'y eschiet, ladicte messe sera du férial selon l'office dominical de la sepmaine.'

[29] Ibid.: 'Item, semblablement à heure compétente de vespres, seront dictes et chantées vespres et complies de tel office que aura esté celuy de la messe, si avant que le lendemain ne soit jour de feste double ou solennelle: auquel cas les vespres seront de la solemnité séquente selon l'ordinaire en ce observé de tout temps, et que les secondes vespres de toutes festes soyent aussi solemnelles en cérémonie, paremens et aultres choses, que les premières.'

[30] Ibid.: 'Item, aux festes et jours cy-après désignez seront dictes et célébrées matines, ensemble toutes les heures du jour jusques aux vespres exclusivement, lesquelles heures, à sçavoir prime, tierce, mydy et none, se diront incontinent après matines, sans faire aucune intermission depuis lesdictes matines jusques à none inclusivement, excepté au jour de Noël après les matines: duquel jour, pour ce que l'office est long, aura intervalle compétent jusques à prime, à la discrétion de nostre premier chapellain lors servant. Et au regard des vespres d'iceulx jours, elles seront dictes à l'heure ordonnée cy-dessus en l'article précédent.'

[31] Ibid.: 'S'ensuyvent les festes et jours dessus mentionnez: Premièrement, la Nativité, Circomcision de Nostre-seigneur, l'Apparition, la Purification de Nostre-Dame, l'Annonciation, la Visitation, l'Assumption, la Nativité et la Conception d'icelle, les festes de Pasques, l'Assension de Nostre-Seigneur, la veille et le jour de Pentecouste, la feste de la Trinité, celle du Sainct-Sacrement, la Nativité sainct Jehan-Baptiste, la feste de Sainct-Pierre en juing, la feste de Toussaincts, la Commémoration des trespassez, les

Charles has thus elided what Philip thought needed reiterating with the first—and presumably the most important—sections of the long-followed 1469 ordinance of his great-grandfather Charles the Bold. The emphasis is first and foremost on duty and obedience—these are servants, after all—followed by the musical heart of the matter: a daily polyphonic Mass and daily Vespers and Compline,[32] with the remaining offices on twenty-one important feasts as well as daily during Advent and Lent. La Rue's primary duty within the Habsburg-Burgundian court was to sing.

Makeup of the chapel

The *grande chapelle* functioned as a self-sufficient ecclesiastical unit with duties divided among its members. The ruler needed to be able to hear Mass and receive the sacrament without recourse to any local church (although he would attend services in local churches when appropriate), and the chapel's primary function was to provide these services.

The chapel served a second, more subliminal, function, and that was as a projection of the ruler's wealth and power. In the fifteenth and sixteenth centuries, power was most readily perceived when it was visible, which was one reason why the leaders of Habsburg-Burgundy were almost constantly on the move. A large musical force, well-attired and performing the newest and most complex polyphony, was an important element in the theatre-state that constituted the Habsburg-Burgundian court.[33] As seen above, the rules governing the chapel dealt with appearance and demeanour as well as music, for the chapel was often visually as well as aurally on display.

As a result, the chapel typically increased its numbers when it was about to accompany the sovereign on his travels, and often—though not always—scaled down upon return. This long-standing tradition dated back at least as far as John the Fearless.[34] Fluctuations in membership of the *grande chapelle* during the time La Rue was at court are shown in Appendix A, where the number of chapel members (and La Rue's position therein) is included along with each court pay record.[35] We know from the December 1494 purchase of cloth for the chapel

festes de Saincte-Catherine, Sainct-Andrieu et de Saincte-Barbe, et chascun jour de quaresme et de l'advent.'

[32] That these were sung in polyphony as well is suggested by a special payment made in 1509 for 'singing, daily in discant hours and Masses of the day before monseigneur'; see App. A, June? 1509. La Rue's numerous polyphonic Magnificats and Salves suggest this as well.

[33] On the court as a theatre state, see Walter Prevenier and Wim Blockmans, *The Burgundian Netherlands* (Cambridge: Cambridge University Press, 1986), 223–5; and Blockmans and Prevenier, *The Promised Lands, passim*. The comments on the chapel's performances during their travels noted in Ch. 1 show that they were indeed noticed and admired.

[34] On music under John the Fearless see Craig Wright, *Music at the Court of Burgundy 1364–1419: A Documentary History* (Musicological Studies, 28; Henryville, Ottawa and Binningen: Institute of Mediaeval Music, 1979), 85–110.

[35] I have included all individuals listed under the rubric *grande chapelle* on each list; these lists usually start with the name of a high-ranked ecclesiastic and then proceed to the *premier chapelain*. Some of the lists

members that there were thirty-three at that time;[36] this large number was surely to add splendour to the various *joyeuses entrées* of Philip in connection with his assuming power. By the time the chapel switched to his daily *escroes* (30 September 1495), they were down to twenty-five or so, and continue to fall in number immediately thereafter. Membership remained relatively low until shortly before the birth of the future Charles V in February 1500, when it picked up again. After that, chapel numbers remained high until right before Philip embarked for Spain the first time, when certain members decided not to go along on what was sure to be a long and arduous journey.[37] Despite this unpromising start—the initial chapel list for the voyage had only twenty-two people, and two of this small group dropped out as well—Philip simply recruited as he went along and bolstered the numbers again. The numbers remained high after the first trip and during the second one. Although Juana inherited a reduced northern chapel on Philip's death, since many did not wish to remain in Spain, the reconstituted institution of Archduke Charles rarely had fewer than twenty-five members, and swelled to thirty-four by the time of his 1515 household ordinance. The court chapel was a decidedly robust group for most of La Rue's employment.

Not all of these large numbers were singers. Individual *escroes* list chapel members under the rubric *grande chapelle* from the highest-paid to the lowest, and thus implicitly by function, but the specific names of each rank within the chapel during La Rue's tenure come from three other kinds of sources: (1) the three *états* themselves, which, in listing the members of the *grande chapelle*, group them under their specific functions; (2) the personnel list for the first trip to Spain, which similarly orders the members; and (3) three special payments for back wages, organized in like fashion.[38]

Charles the Bold's 1469 *état*, the most detailed of those that survive, explicitly states how many of each kind of member the chapel should have: twenty-five members consisting of thirteen *chapelains*, six *clercs*, five *sommeliers*, and one *fourrier*.[39] None of the *états* made during La Rue's years at court gives such a *desideratum*, and none of the combinations recorded in these later sources matches Charles the Bold's ideal; moreover, as shown below, both the names of the various ranks within the chapel and the numbers constituting those ranks were of considerable fluidity during La Rue's time. The seven sources providing this information are given here.

have names crossed off to indicate the individual's absence; I have counted these crossed-off names, since they were supposed to be present and were thus officially members of the chapel.

[36] LADN B2148, fo. 186ᵛ, cited in DouillezM, no. 45.

[37] In addition, two singers initially signed up for the voyage dropped out at the start and then rejoined in Apr. 1502; see the list given in GachardCV, i. 345–6.

[38] Of the payments for back wages during La Rue's time, only that for May–June 1515 (declaration drawn up on 4 Aug. 1515) does not give a breakdown of names by function.

[39] 'Premierement mondit seigneur veult et ordonne que . . . sa chapelle domestique soit entretenue et gouvernee en son hostel par le nombre de 25 personnes cy dessoubz desclarés: c'est ascavoir 13 chapelains, 6 clers, 5 sommeliers et 1 fourrier'; see Fallows, 'Specific Information', 146.

Special payment of back wages for the period 17 November 1492–30 September 1495 (25 total)

    Chantres: 18[40]

      premier chapelain at 24s. per day

      seven at 12s. per day (including organist Godefroid Nepotis)

      ten at 10s. per day (including La Rue, next to last in this section)[41]

    Sommelier: one at 8s. per day

    Fourriers: three at 6s. per day

    Porteurs d'orgues: three at 4s. per day

10 March 1497: État (23 total)

    Chapelains: fourteen

      premier chapelain at 24s. per day

      thirteen at 12s. per day (including La Rue and the organist Fleuriquin)

    Clercs: two at 10s. per day

    Sommeliers: two at 10s. per day

    Fourriers: two (each serves six months at 6s. per day)

    Porteurs d'orgues: two (each serves six months at 4s. per day)

    Porteur de livres et chappes: one at 3s. per day

1 April 1497: special payment of back wages (1 May 1496–9 March 1497) (22 total)

    Chantres: 13

      premier chapelain at 24s. per day

      six at 12s. per day

      six at 10s. per day from May to December; 12s. per day thereafter (including La Rue)

    Organistes: three at 12s. per day

    Sommeliers: two at 8s. per day May–December; 10s. per day thereafter

    Fourriers: two at 6s. per day; only one serves at a time

    Porteurs d'orgues: two at 4s. per day; only one serves at a time

1 February 1500: État (25 total)

    Chappellains: 17

      premier chappellain at 24s. per day

      fourteen at 12s. per day (including La Rue and the organist Henry Bredemers)

      two *clercs* at 10s. per day; only one serves at a time[42]

    Sommeliers: three at 10s. per day

    Fourriers: two at 6s. per day (each serves six months)

---

[40] After the first eighteen names are listed, the indication 'tous chantres' appears.

[41] In this group Jacques Mouchet is also listed as 'disant les haultes messes' (in the initial listing of names) and 'chappelain des haultes messes' (in the listing of individual payments).

[42] The *clercs* are specifically listed under the heading 'Chappellains'. Only the first is actually identified as a *clerc*.

Porteurs d'orgues: two at 4s. per day (each serves six months)

Porteurs [sic] *des livres et chappes*: one at 3s. per day

1 November 1501: personnel list for the first trip to Spain (22 total)[43]

at head of list: 'grant et souverain de la chapelle' and one 'soubs luy', both at
24s. per day,

Chappelains: twelve at 12s. per day (including La Rue and the organist Henry
Bredemers)

Chappelains des haultes messes et sommeliers: four at 10s. per day

Fourier: one at 6s. per day

Porteur d'orghes: one at 4s. per day

Clers servans au grant et petit autel: two at 3s. per day

?June 1509: back pay for May 1509[44] (25 total)

Chantres: sixteen (including La Rue)

Organiste: one

Priests and *Chappellains*: two

Fourrier: one

Clercs: two

Porteur et souffleur des orghes: two

Escripvain: one

25 October 1515: État (34 total)

Premiers chappelains: two at 18s. per day

Autres chappellains et chantres:

two at 11s. per day (La Rue and the organist Henry Bredemers)

three at 10s. per day

sixteen at 9s. per day

two at 8s. per day

Autres deux chappellains:

two at 5s. per day (each serves half a year)

Forier: one at 6s. per day

Clercqz: two at 6s. per day (each serves half a year)

Souffleurs d'orgues: two at 4s. per day (each serves half a year)

Garde des livres: one at 3s. per day

Porteur dorgues: one at 3s. per day

The relatively simple five-part division of Charles the Bold's chapel is long
gone by the time of Archduke Charles in 1515, but even by 1495 different arrangements were in order. With Charles the Bold,[45] both *chapelains* and lesser-paid

---

[43] Based on the original list; numerous additions and changes were made and notated as the journey
proceeded. None of the published versions of this list is completely accurate.

[44] This somewhat confusing payment was to be divided equally among the chapel members.

[45] See Fallows, 'Specific Information', esp. 155–9, for a description of the various ranks and duties.

clercs could sing. Some of the five *sommeliers* could sing, too, when they were not busy with their many duties, which included serving at the altar at high Mass. The lowest rank of all was the *fourrier*, who took care of the chapel's accommodations and other mundane matters.[46]

During La Rue's time at court the *sommelier* eventually ceased to exist, with his duties presumably divided among other chapel members (*clers servans au grant et petit autel* in 1501? *Autres deux chappellains* or *clercqz* in 1515?) One or more organists always appear in the chapel membership, ranked equally with the *chapelains* and always supported by at least an organ carrier and eventually a special *souffleur d'orgues* as well.[47] There is also usually, though not always, one person specially assigned to the books in some form or another: *porteur de livres et chappes* in 1497 and 1500; *escripvain* in 1509 and *garde des livres* in 1515, the latter two roles filled by the famous music scribe Petrus Alamire. Although La Rue did not enter at the very highest rank—he is first listed as a *chantre* at 10s. per day instead of 12s.—he is promoted to the higher-paying slot in January 1497. Since the 1497 *état* denotes those at 10s. per day as *clercs*, perhaps La Rue ranked with this less elite group upon joining the chapel.

Voice designations and the balance of singers

Voice designations for singers are never given in *escroes*, but instead are found only in account books and other special lists. They are not especially common anywhere, at least during La Rue's time at the court. Of the dozens of singers among La Rue's colleagues, only fourteen are known by their voice parts. Gérard Barbet was a 'contratenorist' while Jacques Buckel and Weerbeke both sang hault-contre; Weerbeke's vocal assignment has been almost completely overlooked in the scholarly literature.[48] Pierre Barby, Valentin Hongher, and Roger van Gheldrop were all tenorists; Gilles de Formanoir sang haulteneur.[49] Guillaume Chevalier, Jean Moneta, Guiot Prézet, Alard Theoderici, and Joes Willebroot sang basse-contre.[50] Braconnier appears in court records as a tenorist three times[51] and is also

---

[46] On the *sommelier* and *fourrier* see ibid. 112, 114.

[47] Although organists were not on the 1469 *état*, they were not unknown at the court; see e.g. Wright, *Music at the Court of Burgundy*, 111–21. Their position under Philip the Fair and his successors seems more formal than previously.

[48] Barbet is listed as a contratenor in the records of the confraternity at 's-Hertogenbosch; see e.g. Smijers, 'De Illustre Lieve Vrouwe Broederschap', 13 (1931–2), 181–237 at 187. Buckel's part is listed on the special payment for the period 17 Nov. 1492–30 Sept. 1495 (see App. A for bibliography); Weerbeke's is given in an account book from 1497, LADN B2159, fo. 190ᵛ, published in DouillezM, no. 49.

[49] Barbry and Hongher were listed as such on the special payment for the period 17 Nov. 1492–30 Sept. 1495 (see App. A for bibliography), among other places, while Gheldrop is identified as a tenorist in the 's-Hertogenbosch confraternity records (see e.g. Smijers, 'De Illustre Lieve Vrouwe Broederschap', vol. 13, p. 187). Gilles de Formanoir is marked as a haulteneur in the chapel list drawn up in 1522 for Charles's second trip to Spain; see Van Doorslaer, 'La Chapelle musicale de Charles-Quint en 1522', 220.

[50] DoorslaerC, 143, cites the voice part for Chevalier. For Moneta, see *Correspondance de l'empereur Maximilien Iᵉʳ*, ed. Le Glay, ii. 15. Prézet was identified by his voice part when he was hired; see GachardCV, i. 346. Theoderici and Willebroot as listed under their voice designation in Charles's 1522 chapel list; see Van Doorslaer, 'La Chapelle musicale de Charles-Quint en 1522', 220.

[51] LADN B2159, fos. 196ᵛ and 200; LADN B2162, fo. 200ᵛ, as cited in DouillezM, nos. 49–50.

cited as a basse-contre by Crétin,[52] confirming Tinctoris's statement that 'Some *tenoristae* and *contratenoristae* are called *bassi* when they are recognised as suitable for singing low tenors and contratenors.'[53] Jheronimus de Clibano is known from Bruges as a tenorist, and Pasquier Pastoris was a *dessus*.[54] La Rue himself now seems to have been a *dessus*, singing the highest line.

Without knowing all the singers' voice assignments we cannot specify what kind of balance was used for the performance of sacred music. Charles the Bold's *état*—supposedly in effect for most of La Rue's tenure—is famous for stipulating the ideal balance of singers as being 'at least 6 high voices, 3 tenors, 3 basses, and 2 mid-range voices'.[55] Some of the time there were simply not enough voices of any kind to meet this ideal; the special payment on 1 April 1497 detailed above shows a dozen regular singers instead of the necessary fourteen, though perhaps the *sommeliers* joined in.[56] But even when the chapel waxed larger, such as during the trips to Spain and when Charles came of age, it is not clear that this ideal would still have held, in part because of the compositional preferences of La Rue. The most prolific creator of sacred music associated with the court, he was a major force for its expansion, both in terms of the numbers of parts (with an increasing preference for five- and six-voice works) and in terms of range, which he dramatically extended downwards. The 'ideal' 6/2/3/3 distribution probably fell by the wayside as much for musical as for practical reasons.[57]

LA RUE'S COLLEAGUES

The court had a very long tradition of employing noted composers, though no evidence suggests that any were hired specifically for their compositions. Johannes Tapissier, Nicolas Grenon, Jacobus Vide, Pierre Fontaine, Binchois, Cardot, Simon le Breton, Gilles Joye, Robert Morton, Adrien Basin, Hayne van Ghizeghem, Constans Breuwe, and Busnoys all worked for the dukes of Burgundy at some point in their careers. But at the time La Rue joined the chapel, no one there

[52] Guillaume Crétin, *Œuvres poétiques*, ed. Kathleen Chesney (Paris: Firmin-Didot, 1932), 210–17, ll. 47 and 109; see also l. 39, 'Car voix avoit tresbelle, bas et hault'.

[53] As quoted in Fallows, 'Specific Information', 115.

[54] Reinhard Strohm, *Music in Late Medieval Bruges* (Oxford: Clarendon Press, 1985), 50, mentions Clibano, while Pastoris is identified in Charles's 1522 chapel list; see Van Doorslaer, 'La Chapelle musicale de Charles-Quint en 1522', 220.

[55] 'Item pour le chant du livre y aura du moyns six haultes voix, troys teneurs, troys basses contres et deux moiens'; see Fallows, 'Specific Information', 149. This distribution was for sacred music; secular works were presumably performed as chamber music, with one musician to a part.

[56] The 1469 *état* allows the *sommeliers* to sing if not otherwise occupied (ibid. 114); on the other hand, Philip had far fewer *sommeliers* than Charles the Bold.

[57] The chapel list drawn up in 1522 (six years after La Rue's retirement) for Charles's upcoming journey to Spain lists (by name) four bascontres, four hautecontres, five haulteneurs, and four dessus, as well as four 'chappellains de haultes messes', eight unidentified 'enffans de chappelle', and at least one other musician known to have been a singer. All are listed as members of the *grande chapelle*; see Van Doorslaer, 'La Chapelle musicale de Charles-Quint en 1522', 219–20. How such an ensemble would have realigned itself for five- or six-voice music is unclear.

was known as a composer of polyphony, nor did another join him until several years into his employment.[58]

Weerbeke (c.1445–after 1516)

Gaspar van Weerbeke was the first to join La Rue; he shows up almost immediately after Philip assumed responsibility for the payment of the chapel musicians on 30 September 1495. Weerbeke is on the first surviving *escroe* after that date, on 8 October 1495, and appears on all those that follow until 3 July 1498, giving him a chapel tenure much longer than previously thought.[59] Often listed as 'Jaspart doudemere' in court records,[60] he is not, however, the 'Messire Jaspart' found on various chapel *escroes* in 1502 and 1503, as Van Doorslaer thought possible;[61] he is found in the papal choir at this time and was not, in any event, known to have been a priest.

By the time that he came to Habsburg-Burgundy, Weerbeke was somewhat older than La Rue and already a very well-known musician.[62] Prior to his arrival at court, he had served at the famous Sforza court in Milan as *vice-abbate*, as well as at the papal chapel. Hired immediately by Philip at the highest pay level for a singer (other than that of the *premier chapelain*), and thus above La Rue, he rises at one point to the number 2 position on the daily *escroes* (first reached on 5 June 1497) before falling slightly in the ranks shortly thereafter. He is always listed above La Rue.

Weerbeke's compositional credentials were impressive. Too often overshadowed in the scholarly literature by his contemporaries, he was an extremely important composer in the history of the late fifteenth-century mass. Before Josquin's belated appearance in the sources, only Obrecht's masses were more widely circulated,[63] and Weerbeke was eventually to warrant a complete collection in Petrucci's mass series (though four years later than La Rue's volume); see Table 2.1 for the early circulation of his music. He was also a significant figure in the *motetti missales* tradition cultivated in Milan, possibly influencing La Rue in this respect (La Rue's motet *O salutaris hostia* assumes the place of the first Osanna in his *Missa de Sancta Anna*). Author of eight masses, two mass movements, three

---

[58] Pierre Duwez was the winner of the contest to provide chant for a new office of the Feast of the Seven Sorrows, but no polyphonic music by him is known. See 'La Vierge aux sept glaives', *Analecta Bollandiana*, 12 (1893), 333–52 at 341.

[59] The last surviving *escroe* on which he is found is that of 10 June 1498. DoorslaerC, 158, documented him at the court in 1496–7 only. There is no evidence for the statement that 'Up to 1495 Weerbeke's life was dominated by a longstanding connection with the court choir of Philip the Fair' given in Gerhard Croll and Andrea Lindmayr-Brandl, 'Weerbeke, Gaspar van', *New Grove II*, xxvii. 207. Unless otherwise indicated, all information about appearances in court *escroes* is from my overview of the documents.

[60] Weerbeke was born in Oudenaarde.

[61] DoorslaerC, 158.

[62] For a general overview of his life see Croll and Lindmayr-Brandl, 'Weerbeke, Gaspar van'.

[63] For the early distribution of Obrecht's music, see Honey Meconi, 'Josquin and Musical Reputation', in Barbara Haggh (ed.), *Essays on Music and Culture in Honor of Herbert Kellman* (Paris and Tours: Minerve, 2001), 280–97 at 296–7.

TABLE 2.1. Pre-print distribution of music by or attributed to Weerbeke

prob. 1474	VatS 14 (Naples)[a] Missa Ave regina coelorum (Gaspar)
*c.*1475–80	VerBC 755 (Naples) Missa O venus banth (anon.)
1480–1	ModE M.1.13 (Ferrara) Missa O venus banth (Guaspar uuarbec)
early 1480s	SevC 5-1-43 (probably Naples) ?O venus banth? (Gaspar)
1484?[b]	MunBS 3154 (probably Innsbruck; perhaps also Augsburg) ?O venus banth? (anon.)
*c.*1484–90	MilD 1 (Milan) Ave mundi domina (Gaspar) Ave stella matutina (Gaspar) Christi mater ave sanctissima (Gaspar) Mater digna dei (Gaspar) Quam pulchra es (Gaspar)
*c.*1484–91	VatS 51 (Rome) Credo (anon.) Missa O venus banth (Gaspar)
1485–8[c]	BerlinS 40021 (Leipzig?) Missa O venus banth (anon.)
*c.*1487–90	VatS 35 (Rome) Missa Princesse d'amourettes (Gaspar) Missa Se mieulx ne vient (Gaspar)
early 1490s	FlorBN Magl. 178 (Florence) Anima mea liquefacta est (Gaspar) Vray dieu quel payne (anon.) by Compère?
*c.*1490–1500	MilD 2 (Milan) Ave domina angelorum (Ave regina caelorum) (anon.) Ave regina caelorum mater (anon.) Missa Ave regina coelorum (Gaspar) O Maria clausus ortus (anon.) Quam pulchra es (Gaspar) Quem terra pontus aethera (anon.)
*c.*1490–1504	LeipU 1494 (Leipzig?) Missa O venus banth (V.b) Missa Se mieulx ne vient (anon.)
1492–3	FlorBN BR 229 (Florence) Anima mea liquefacta est (anon.) Missa O venus banth (anon.) Et incarnatus, Pleni, Benedictus only

TABLE 2.1. (*cont.*)

1492–4	VatG XIII.27 (Florence) Vray dieu quel payne (Qia doi) (anon.) by Compère?
*c.*1495[d]	VatS 15 (Rome) Magnificat octavi toni (Gaspar)
after 1495[e]	SegC s.s. (Spain) La stangetta (Ortus de celo) (Ysaac) by Weerbeke SienBC K.I.2 (Siena) O virginum praeclara (anon.) Virgo Maria (anon.)
*c.*1495–7	VatS 15 (Rome) Ave regina caelorum mater (Gaspar) Dulcis amica dei (Gaspar)
*c.*1497–1503	VatS 41 (Rome) Missa Et trop penser (Gaspar)
*c.*1498–1503	VatC 234 (HB scriptorium) Stabat mater dolorosa/Vidi speciosam (Gaspar)
1498 or later	BolC Q17 (probably in or near Florence) Vray dieu quel payne (anon.) by Compère?
late 15th/early 16th c.	HradKM 7 (Bohemia) Missa O venus banth (anon.) Et incarnatus, Pleni, Benedictus only
*c.*1500	MilD 3 (Milan) ?Sancti spiritus adsit nobis gratia (anon.) VerBC 758 (Verona) Mater digna dei (anon.) WarU RM 5892 (Silesia or Bohemia) Anima mea liquefacta est (anon.) Missa O venus banth (anon.) Quem terra pontus aethera (anon.) WashLC M6 (Florence? N. Italy?) Anima mea liquefacta est (anon.)

[a] The ascription in the manuscript is given in parentheses. Dates are from *CC* unless otherwise indicated.

[b] Cason, 'The Dating of Munich 3154 Revisited'.

[c] Date from Just, *Der Mensuralkodex Mus. ms. 40021*.

[d] Refinements for datings of Vatican manuscripts are taken from Sherr, *Papal Music Manuscripts*.

[e] For SegC s.s. see Meconi, 'Art-Song Reworkings', 16; for SienBC K.I 2 see Wegman, *Born for the Muses*, 100.

motet cycles, twenty-two or twenty-three other motets, a Magnificat, a set of Lamentations, and perhaps seven secular works, Weerbeke had some music circulate in court manuscripts: two of his masses (*Missa brevis* and *Missa Princesse d'amourettes*), one chanson attributed to 'Jaspar' (*Sans regrets/Allez regretz*), and three motets (*Anima mea liquefacta est, Stabat mater dolorosa/Vidi speciosam,* and *O salutaris hostia*). Since Weerbeke occasionally appears in court records with his first name spelled 'Jaspar',[64] the chanson with this ascription may be his.

Braconnier (? to before 22 January 1512)

The next composer to join the court—very minor as a composer, though very popular as a performer—was the tenorist Jean Braconnier, known as Lourdault, who had previously served at the court of Lorraine and the ducal chapel in Nancy.[65] The scholarly literature almost unanimously provides an incorrect date—1496—for his joining the chapel; the confusion appears to stem from Vander Straeten's quotation of Philip's '1496' *état*,[66] which is really from 10 March 1497.[67] Braconnier is on no list prior to this *état*, nor is he included in the payment for back wages for the extended period 1 May 1496 to 9 March 1497. All references to him in court records date from the 1497 *état* or thereafter. Curiously, even though he is on the *état* from 10 March 1497 (where he is last of the *chapelains*), he is missing from the pay lists that survive from immediately thereafter: 16 March, 8, 12–14, 16, and 26 April. He first appears on the daily *escroes* on 1 June 1497. Given that Philip's *état* survives only in an eighteenth-century copy, it is highly likely that Braconnier's name was an addition to the original *état*—it is the last name in the section for *chapelains*—and that he actually joined the chapel between 27 April and the end of May. He remained with the chapel (excepting the absences noted below) until Philip's death in Spain in September 1506; he is found several months thereafter at the French court.

During the first trip to Spain he was involved in a fight that has been completely overlooked in the musicological literature.[68] It is extraordinarily rare to have a singer mentioned specifically in such an account, and it is telling that it has nothing to do with music. The account goes as follows:

This day Monseigneur de Boussut, the bastard of Trazegnies, and Lourdault, singer of Monseigneur, dined at their lodgings, where a woman dropped in with her husband. The above-named bade them good cheer. Then other Castilians dropped by, full of pranks and quarrels; the Seigneur de Boussut, to avoid a quarrel, made them leave. And after supper, the aforementioned, without staffs, walking on the Marchié at 10.00 at night, were assaulted by

---

[64] e.g. *escroes* for 26 Feb., 23 and 26 Mar., 1, 3, 5, 6, and 11 Apr. 1498.

[65] The *déploration* written on his death by Crétin is an unusual mark of esteem for a contemporary musician. For general information on Braconnier, see Lewis Lockwood and John T. Brobeck, 'Braconnier, Jean', *New Grove II*.

[66] VDS vii. 498.

[67] The introduction to this *état*, quoted above, shows clearly that this was the first *état* Philip was to draw up.

[68] Published in GachardCV, i. 196.

twenty or more Castilians, armed with rapiers, shields, and spears. But the attacked fought back so well that they deprived them of some of their sticks, and turned them in flight and wounded them so much that one of them died the next day. Because of that, it was advisable for the aforementioned to take sanctuary in a monastery called Monastery of St Bernard, half a league from Toledo, and the next day they transported themselves for no reason to the Abbey of St Jerome, where they were until the departure from Toledo of Monseigneur, who pardoned them, hearing that they had acted in self-defence. And the Queen was satisfied, saying that she would have punished these people severely, had they been wrong, but agreed with their rights, and so the Queen pardoned them and they were free. But Francequin, *potagier* of Madame, who had been wounded in the said altercation, died in the said monastery on the twenty-seventh of August.[69]

Also new is the fact that Braconnier assumed the priesthood while in court service. He is known to Crétin as *maistre*, a title normally associated with a university degree; on the court *escroes* he assumes the priestly designation *messire* on the paylist of 4 January 1506, the date that the court entourage began going on board for the voyage to Spain; all remaining court records use this title for him. As the honorific is missing on the immediately preceding *escroe* of 31 December 1505, we can safely assume that he was elevated to the priesthood at the very beginning of January 1506.

Braconnier was initially ranked lower than La Rue on the chapel lists (albeit at the same salary), but by 8 July 1500 he had leapfrogged over La Rue. In the surviving lists from 1501 and the first half of 1502 La Rue is again more highly ranked, but Braconnier eventually assumes and remains in a higher position. He is not consistently on the *escroes*; in addition to an absence between 13 January and 9 March 1498 for which he was reimbursed[70] he is missing for an extended period of more than a year; after 17 September 1498 he does not reappear until 30 January 1500.[71]

---

[69] Ibid.: 'Ce jour mons^r de Boussut, le bastardt de Trazegnies et Lourdault, chantre de Monsigneur, soupoient à leur logis, où une femme avoec son mari sourvinrent. Les prénommés leur firent bone chière. Puis sourvinrent aultres Castillans plains de bragues et de querelles, lesquels le signeur de Boussut, pour éviter noise, fist yssir hors de l'hostel. Et, après souper, les prédits, desgarnis de bastons, spacians sur le Marchié et pourmenans à X heures de nuict, furent assaillis de vingt ou plus Castillans, munis de raspières, bouclets et javelines. Mais les assaillis besongnèrent sy bien qu'ilz leurs ostèrent parties de leurs bastons, et les tournèrent en fuyte, et les bléchèrent tèlement que l'ung d'euls morut lendemain. Par quoy il convint les prédits prendre franchise au couvent nommé monastère de Sainct-Bernardt, demie lieue de Toulette; et lendemain se transportèrent, pour aulcune cause, à l'abaye de Sainct-Jhérôme, où ils furent jusques au partement de Monsigneur de Toulette, qui leur pardona, entendu que c'estoit sur leurs corps deffendans. Et se contenta la royne, disant qu'elle eusist prins de ses gens griève punition, s'ilz eusissent eut le tort, mais en leur droict les voloit bien porter: pour quoy la royne leur pardona, et eulrent leur grâce. Mais Francequin, potagier de Madame, qui avoit estet bléchié audit débat, morut audit monastère le XXVIIe d'aoust.'

[70] The document is given in VDS vii. 138; DouillezM, no. 50, cites this as LADN B2162, fo. 200^v, and incorrectly gives the ending date as 3 Mar. (the payment was for fifty-six days' absence). Braconnier is indeed missing from the *escroes* during this period.

[71] He is not documented as being at Nancy, where he had an ongoing association, during this time; see Richard Freedman, 'Music, Musicians, and the House of Lorraine during the First Half of the Sixteenth Century' (Ph.D. diss., University of Pennsylvania, 1987), 42, 522–3. Professor Freedman kindly informs me that the Nancy records for this period are skimpy, and that Braconnier may have been there in some capacity (private comm. 12 July 2001).

Braconnier is known for a single composition, the chanson *Amours me trocte par la pancé* in the style of a 'four-part arrangement' that appears in *Canti B* (RISM 1502[2]) and features a text whose continual and barely veiled references to sexual intercourse in several positions can scarcely be missed. Given the date of its first appearance, it is possible that Braconnier wrote it while in court service; given the song's subject matter, La Rue's reputation as 'free from the crime of Venus', and his own preference for more refined topics, one wonders what La Rue would have thought of it.

Agricola (c.1446–1506)

On 6 August 1500 La Rue and Braconnier were joined by Alexander Agricola, a composer who already had a significant list of works to his credit as well as an impressive professional career that included as places of employment Cambrai Cathedral, the French royal court, and the cathedral in Florence.[72] He was much sought after as a singer and was able to command a high salary for his services; at one point he was offered an annual salary of 300 ducats to serve at the court of Naples. It is somewhat surprising, then, to see his position on the court *escroes*, where, though receiving the same salary as La Rue, he is consistently ranked below him for the entire period that he was there (in contrast to Braconnier, who surpasses La Rue after several years despite having joined the chapel five years later than La Rue). He was surely valued, at least for his singing—one of the anonymous chronicles of the first trip to Spain praises French court singer Verjus as *le second maistre alixandre*[73]—but this did not translate itself into a higher rank on the *escroes*.

Agricola disappears from the court *escroes* for an extended period when the court was first in Spain. He is on the *escroe* of 23 February 1502; he may or may not be on the almost illegible *escroe* of 19 March 1502, the next that survives. He is gone from the one that follows, from 9 May, and is missing through the *escroe* of 12 August. He is back on the following *escroe*, from 31 August. Wherever he happened to be, his absence was evidently excused by the court, which gave him a gift of £96 in September 1502.[74]

Court *escroes* also now reveal that the recently heralded date for his death, 15 August 1506, is in fact incorrect. The date of 15 August is based on a strict interpretation of the phrase *my-aoust* given in his epitaph as his date of death.[75] Such an

[72] Agricola is added to the *état* of 1 Feb. 1500 in a marginal note indicating that he joined on 6 Aug. 1500 (misread by DoorslaerC, 139, as 5 Aug.). For an overview of his life and works see Rob C. Wegman, Fabrice Fitch, and Edward R. Lerner, 'Agricola, Alexander', *New Grove II*.

[73] ChmelH, 568.

[74] BAGR E&A 22, fo. 179[v], published in DouillezM, no. 57.

[75] 'Et fut par la mort desolé / En my-aoust, mil cincq cens et six.' The epitaph and accompanying poem were discovered by Bonnie Blackburn and are discussed in Wegman, 'Agricola, Bordon and Obrecht at Ghent', 48–50 and 61–2. Agricola's death engendered considerably more reaction than La Rue's seems to have done; in addition to the poem and epitaph discovered by Blackburn, he is the subject of the elegiac motet *Musica quid defles?* and mourned by Jean Lemaire de Belges in his plainte *Désiré* (see DoorslaerC, 139,

interpretation is not by itself unjustified; court chronicles sometimes use this precise term when giving the date for the Marian Feast of the Assumption, which occurs on 15 August.[76] The author of the epitaph could not have meant 15 August, however, for Agricola received his usual salary on the *escroe* of 16 August 1506, the day after his supposed death.[77] He may already have been ill—court singers were paid during illness—but he could not have died on 15 August.[78] The court under Philip was painstaking in its daily accounts; the chapel ordinances given above demonstrate that the proper representation of who was to be paid was considered one of the most important duties of the *premier chapelain*, and *escroes* exist where the names of singers were entered and then crossed out,[79] which is not the case for Agricola's here. Clearly, Agricola did not die on 15 August. He might, however, have died late in the day on the 16th, after daily payments had been noted; with thirty-one days in the month, August has a technical mid-point of the sixteenth, with fifteen days on either side of that date. Or perhaps the citation for 'my-aoust' was poetic licence for a somewhat later date.

In contrast to Braconnier, Agricola was a prolific composer—twelve masses or mass movements, twenty-five other sacred works, more than seventy-five secular pieces—whose music had already received wide distribution throughout Europe by the time he joined the chapel; Petrucci was later to publish a book of his masses (though again, later than La Rue's mass print).[80] He is best known today—and probably then as well—for his secular music, and in the earliest court chansonnier to survive intact, FlorC 2439, he is the featured composer.[81] His sacred music was also known at court: four masses, a Credo, a Magnificat, and five motets all appear in court manuscripts; in addition, the hymn *Nobis sancti spiritus* was possibly written for the Order of the Golden Fleece connected to the court.[82] Agricola must surely have proved a stimulating colleague for La Rue, and vice versa. La Rue's *Si dormiero* is part of a tradition of 'Si' pieces started by Agricola's best-known work, *Si dedero*.[83] Both composers used *Je ne vis oncques* and *D'ung aultre aymer* as the basis for new works, both linked the Benedictus and second Osanna in a mass (in La Rue's *Missa Assumpta est Maria* and Agricola's *Missa In myne zin*), a formal procedure so unusual at the time it can hardly be coincidental, both wrote

and Martin Picker, 'Musical Laments for King Philip of Castile and his Musician Alexander Agricola', *Revista de musicología*, 16 (1993), 2684–95 (*Actas del XV congreso de la Sociedad Internacional de Musicología: Culturas musicales del Mediterráneo y sus ramificaciones, Madrid, 3–10 abril 1992*, v. 132–43).

[76] e.g. GachardCV, i. 195, 397.

[77] VOS, HHuS, OMeA, SR 181, N°. 2.

[78] See Fallows, 'Specific Information', 154, on singers being paid although ill.

[79] e.g. 3 June 1505.

[80] See the list of the pre-1501 distribution of Agricola's works given in Meconi, 'Josquin and Musical Reputation', 289–91.

[81] See Honey Meconi, Introduction to *Basevi Codex: Florence, Biblioteca del Conservatorio, MS 2439* (Peer: Alamire, 1990).

[82] See Prizer, 'Music and Ceremonial', 129.

[83] See Honey Meconi, 'Sacred Tricinia and Basevi 2439', *I Tatti Studies: Essays in the Renaissance*, 4 (1991), 151–99. Other composers who wrote 'si' pieces include Ninot le Petit, Craen, Obrecht, and Divitis.

art-song reworkings, one of the court's favourite genres, and so on. Very likely La Rue knew Agricola's work even before the latter joined Philip's chapel, for Agricola was active at the French court for part of the time that Marguerite lived there. The various diplomatic activities surrounding Marguerite's residency there (and its termination) were surely the occasion for musical exchange, and some of Agricola's compositions doubtless came to Habsburg-Burgundy when Marguerite returned in 1493 if not before.

Clibano (c.1459–1503)

Joining the chapel at precisely the same time as Agricola (6 August 1500) was another, considerably less well-known composer, Jheronimus de Clibano, also known as du Four.[84] He is on most of the surviving *escroes* until 6 May 1503,[85] beginning below Agricola on these lists but ultimately overtaking him, though always remaining below La Rue. He is the composer of the four-voice motet *Festivitatem dedicationis* that was published in *Motetti libro quarto* (RISM 1505²), and possibly the author as well of the *Credo de villagiis* (in Petrucci's *Fragmenta missarum*, 1505¹) and the four-voice cantus-firmus work *Missa Et super nivem dealbabor*, based on *Asperges me*, that appears in VatS 51, although both of these may be by his father Nycasius.[86] As the motet is for the dedication of a church, Clibano presumably wrote it while not in Philip's service, since the court would have no need of such a work. Curiously, the motet is preceded in its source by an Agricola motet and followed by a Weerbeke work.

Reingot (fl. early 16th c.)

Gilles Reingot, another composer with a small surviving output, first appears in the *grande chapelle* on the list of singers accompanying Philip to Spain that was drawn up at the beginning of November 1501; earlier in the same year he was a *sommelier* for the chapel of the infant Charles.[87] With few exceptions,[88] Reingot (who was also known as Gillequin de Bailleul) appears on all following pay records throughout La Rue's time at court, always ranked below La Rue. He remained in Spain as part of Juana's chapel for the full time that it was maintained. Only two works by him survive, a florid four-voice *Fors seulement* setting in *Canti C* (RISM 1504³), and a *Salve regina* contained in court manuscript MunBS 34. La Rue, of course, wrote multiple settings of both *Fors seulement* and *Salve regina*.

---

[84] DoorslaerC, 143 incorrectly gives the date of entrance as 5 Aug. 1500. For a general overview of Clibano, see Stanley Boorman and Eric Jas, 'Clibano, Jheronimus de', *New Grove II*.

[85] Not 16 May, the *terminus ante quem* given for his death in Boorman and Jas, 'Clibano, Jheronimus de'. He is missing from the *escroes* of 17 and 20 July 1502.

[86] Ibid.

[87] The best sources for information about Reingot remain DoorslaerC, 154–5, and id., 'Gilles Reyngoot: chantre-compositeur—xvᵉ–xviᵉ siècles', *Mechlinia*, 7 (1928–9), 167–71.

[88] e.g. 12 and 15 May 1512.

Champion (c.1475–1533)

Not long into Philip's first Spanish journey—on 13 November 1501, to be precise—the composer Nicolas Champion joined the *grande chapelle*.[89] More frequently recorded as Clais le Liégeois or some variant thereof, he appears thereafter on almost all court pay lists until after La Rue retired.[90] Prior to the death of Philip the Fair, his position on the *escroes* varied wildly, with him often lower but sometimes higher than La Rue; by the time of Charles's chapel, he is consistently one of the highest singers on the *escroes*, though always below La Rue. He was one of the singers to remain with Juana in Spain throughout the period that she maintained the northern chapel.

Only half a dozen works attributed to Champion survive, but they are of impressively high quality.[91] Nors Josephson praised Champion's works as 'outstanding examples of Franco-Flemish polyphony in the high Renaissance';[92] certainly the best-known to modern listeners is the stunning four-voice motet *De profundis clamavi*, also attributed to Josquin and because of that both studied and recorded. Using stylistic and other evidence, Patrick Macey has recently argued that the attribution to Champion, found in court partbooks VienNB Mus. 15941, trumps the ascriptions to Josquin elsewhere.[93] Three others survive in court manuscripts: a four-voice psalm motet *Deus in adiutorium* (also in VienNB Mus. 15941) and two five-voice masses, *Missa Ducis saxsonie: Sing ich niet wol* and *Missa Maria Magdalena*, both in more than one court source. The remaining pieces known by Champion are another psalm motet, *Beati omnes* (for six voices), and a four-voice Flemish song, *Noch weet ick*. With Champion, La Rue had another superb composer as colleague for more than fourteen years at the court.

De Orto (c.1460–1529)

In late 1504 or the earlier part of 1505 another significant composer entered the chapel. Marbriano de Orto is typically cited as joining the court on 24 May 1505,[94] but this is merely the first surviving *escroe* on which he is listed. Since the preceding *escroe* (where he is absent) dates from 31 October 1504, there is a period of almost seven months during which he could have begun his new employment.

---

[89] A short overview of Champion is found in David Fuller, David Ledbetter, and Nors S. Josephson, 'Champion', *New Grove II*. Two articles should be added to the bibliography cited there: DoorslaerC, and id., 'La Chapelle musicale de Charles-Quint en 1522'. Champion is added to the 1 Nov. 1501 chapel membership list with an annotation giving the 13 Nov. date of hire; see GachardCV, i. 346.

[90] Exceptions include the *escroe* of 31 Oct. 1504.

[91] It is possible that some of these, attributed only to 'Champion', are by his brother Jacques, who worked for the court after La Rue's death.

[92] Fuller, Ledbetter, and Josephson, 'Champion', 461.

[93] Patrick Macey, 'Conflicting Attributions for *De profundis*: Josquin and Champion', in conference packet for *Josquin: International Conference, New Directions in Josquin Scholarship, Princeton University, 29–31 October 1999*, pp. 99–121.

[94] Most recently in Martin Picker, 'Orto, Marbrianus de', *New Grove II*, which provides an overview of his life.

Like La Rue, de Orto was apparently from Tournai; after early employment with the Cardinal-Bishop of Tournai, he sang in the papal chapel and was eventually appointed dean of the collegiate church of Sainte-Gertrude in Nivelles. Upon joining the chapel he immediately assumed a position very close to the top of the *escroes*, though at only 12s. per day, the same as La Rue, Braconnier, and Agricola; he appears on court *escroes* as both *messser* and *maistre*. His entrance into the chapel at a very high level is striking, for even though a newcomer and perhaps younger than La Rue, he always ranks above him. At the beginning he is preceded on the lists only by Jean de Nivelles (Philip's confessor and ostensible head of the chapel)[95] and former *premier chapelain* Nicole Mayoul the elder. De Orto's name is written and then crossed out on *escroes* of 8, 10, 17, and 18 November 1505; on the next surviving list, 30 November, Mayoul has disappeared and de Orto has assumed the salary, and surely thus the duties, of the *premier chapelain*.

After Philip's death de Orto was apparently prepared to assume that position for Juana as well, since he is listed at the top of one of the two pay lists drawn up for her newly expanded chapel on 11 October 1506; he also signed for his wages (again at the top of the list) on the same day. In each case the salary is that of the *premier chapelain*. He did not remain with Juana, however, despite statements to this effect in the scholarly literature.[96] He is already gone from the next pay list for Juana's singers (19 December 1506) and La Rue is now in the position of *premier chapelain*, where he will remain until the disbanding of the chapel in August 1508.

De Orto probably headed back north after leaving Juana, but there is no evidence that he 'helped to reorganize the chapel for Philip's son Charles',[97] logical as that assumption might be. Indeed, apart from the chapel's singing at the funeral services for Philip in the summer of 1507, we have almost no evidence at all about their activities—certainly no *escroes*—until after La Rue himself returns. De Orto is listed as *premier chapelain* on the first northern chapel record to survive after Philip's death, the belated payment (in June?) for the wages of May 1509; he alternates the post with Anthoine de Berghes and is thus often missing from the few surviving later pay lists.[98] He is still functioning in this capacity at the time of La Rue's retirement.

Though not as active a composer as Agricola, de Orto still has a respectable body of music, including nine masses or mass movements, nine motets or other sacred works, and ten secular pieces; Petrucci published a volume of his masses (again, later than the La Rue volume). Some of de Orto's works were included in court sources: two masses, one Credo, two motets, a secular work, and a setting of *Dulces exuvie* that is striking in its notated accidentals, just like some of La Rue's

[95] On Jean de Nivelles, see DoorslaerC, 48.
[96] See Picker, 'Orto, Marbrianus de', 765.
[97] Ibid.
[98] He is present on the *escroes* of 4, 12, and 15 May 1512, 24 July 1512, 2 and 18 Aug. 1512, 31 Jan. 1513, and 4, 10, 18, 23, 24, and 25 Feb. 1513; he is also on the documents of 4 Aug. and 25 Oct. 1515.

compositions. His borrowed material, like La Rue's, includes *L'homme armé*, *D'ung aultre aymer*, and *Fors seulement*.

Divitis (c.1470–c.1530)

By the time of Philip's second trip to Spain, the various composers in his chapel had been joined by yet another, Anthonius Divitis, also known as Le Riche. Employment prior to the court included stints at Sint Donaas (Donatian) in Bruges and Sint Rombaut in Mechelen, acting as master of the boys in both churches.[99] The date 24 October 1505 was erroneously cited by Van Doorslaer (and thus much quoted in later literature) as Divitis's entry date into the chapel, but he first appears not on that *escroe* but rather on the next surviving one, that of 2 November 1505.[100] Positioned just below Agricola, at 12s. per day, he remains beneath Agricola (and thus La Rue, Braconnier, and de Orto) for the duration of his service. He is missing from the list of 17 November 1505, but is back on the next day. Other than that he is on the surviving lists until Philip's death. He then continued in Juana's service, though not for the entire time her northern chapel remained together; he is missing from the last quarterly payment, for the period 25 June–25 September 1508, and is next found working for Anne of Brittany. His output includes five masses or mass sections, eight motets, three Magnificats, and one secular composition, a five-voice setting of *Fors seulement*.[101] Five of his works, all sacred, survive in court manuscripts: one mass, two Magnificats, a Credo, and a motet.

Rogier Herben (fl. early 16th c.)

Rogier Herben appears as a last-minute addition to the *grande chapelle* for Philip's second trip to Spain; he is normally named in court records as 'Messire Rogier' and has thus been identified with the composer 'Rogier', whose only known works appear in FlorC 2442.[102] Rogier is found on all court *escroes* of 1506, always below La Rue but above Agricola, and he remained in Spain with Juana's northern chapel. After the breakup of the chapel in August 1508 he disappears from court records, surfacing instead in Antwerp in 1514. Curiously, Rogier's two chansons in FlorC 2442, *Noble fleur excellente de mon cuer* and *Sans mot sans nulz mot*, are preceded by Braconnier's only surviving work and followed by two chansons attributed to de Orto.

---

[99] See Martin Picker, 'Divitis, Antonius', *New Grove II*, for an overview of his life and works.

[100] DoorslaerC, 155.

[101] Though settings of *Fors seulement* were extremely popular at court, Divitis's may date from after his service there; the work is not included where we might expect it, in court manuscript VienNB Mus. 18746, which concludes with a highly unusual unit, a series of five-voice *Fors seulement* settings.

[102] For biographical information on Herben, see DoorslaerC, 146, and Eugeen Schreurs, 'Petrus Alamire: Music Calligrapher, Musician, Composer, Spy', in *TA* 15–27 at 16. Herben, selling his house to Alamire on 29 Dec. 1505, is cited in the deed as a singer in Philip's chapel but he is on no pay lists of 1505, not even the one of 31 Dec.

Molinet (fl. early 16th c.)

The composer Johannes Molinet, sometimes confused with the court poet Jean Molinet (who died in 1507), first shows up in court records on the 1509 late payment for wages due. He appears on every surviving list thereafter during La Rue's tenure at court, always well below him on the *escroes* as one of the lowest paid singers (8s. per day). His only known work is a five-voice *Salve regina* in MunBS 34; La Rue set this text six separate times.

Alamire (c.1470–1536)

The colourful and versatile music scribe Petrus van den Hove, better known as Alamire, began his formal association with the Habsburg-Burgundian court in 1509 and remained with the court until pensioned off in 1534.[103] With the exception of 4, 12, and 15 May 1512, he is on all the surviving *escroes* and pay records (at the bottom of the chapel list) from La Rue's last years at court. He is not the composer of La Rue's *Missa Sancta dei genitrix* (to be discussed in Ch. 3), but he is the author of a four-voice *Tandernack* setting in VienNB Mus. 18810.[104] La Rue himself used *Tandernaken* as the basis of one of his masses.

During much of his time at the court an impressive number of La Rue's colleagues were composers of polyphonic music.[105] Quite possibly other musicians in the chapel composed as well; the organist Henry Bredemers seems a likely candidate for one. Not far removed from the *grande chapelle* was another composer, the Spaniard Juan de Anchieta, who served in Juana's private chapel from 1504 on and who became La Rue's immediate colleague after Philip's death.[106] As noted in Chapter 1, La Rue surely encountered other major composers such as Isaac on his travels with the court, and musicians visiting the court perhaps interacted with La Rue. In short, with few but notable exceptions La Rue found himself in the company of others who were creators as well as performers while in Habsburg-Burgundian service. Table 2.2 provides a chronology of known composers of polyphony among La Rue's colleagues in the *grande chapelle* between 1492 and 1515.

---

[103] See *TA* for the most detailed information on his life and work; in some cases it is supplemented or superseded by material in the present book.

[104] On this see David Fallows, 'Alamire as a Composer', *Yearbook of the Alamire Foundation*, 5 (forthcoming). My thanks to Professor Fallows for kindly providing me with a copy of his article before its publication.

[105] DoorslaerC, 161 also mentions Jean Baudouin as a composer, but without providing any evidence for this asssertion. Was it a confusion with Noel Bauldeweyn? The composer Gilles Mureau is sometimes cited as being associated with the chapel, but this is a confusion with the court singer Gilles Moreau (see Richard Freedman, 'Mureau, Gilles', *New Grove II*).

[106] On Anchieta, see Robert Stevenson, 'Anchieta, Juan de', *New Grove II*.

TABLE 2.2. La Rue's composer colleagues, 1492–1515

Only composers of polyphonic music are included, and only those in the *Grande chapelle* or in Juana's chapel.

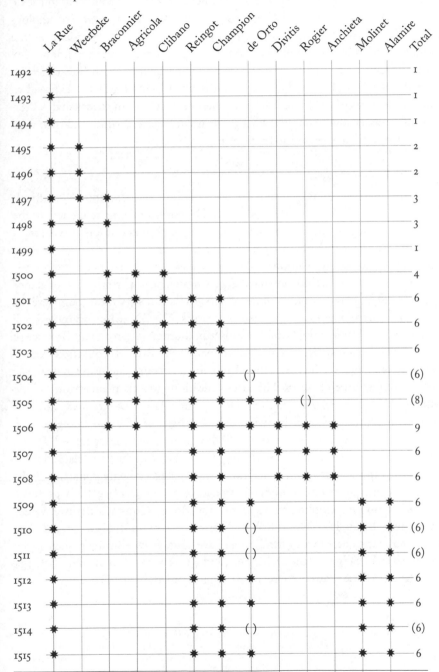

MUSIC AVAILABLE AT THE COURT

Even if we were confident about the details of La Rue's biography prior to his joining the court, we would probably still know next to nothing about what music he
knew and performed while growing up and during his pre-court years of employment. Very few sources survive from either France or the Low Countries from the
last quarter of the century, and much of the polyphony may have been improvised
anyway. Unless La Rue had a secular patron before Maximilian, the music he performed was assuredly sacred, though that is not to say he was not exposed to
popular melodies of the time. It is only when he arrives at the court that we can
make some assertions about just what made up his musical world, and then with
confidence only some years into his tenure.

Court music before 1492

The court's musical holdings—or more precisely, its active repertoire—is difficult
to determine at the time of La Rue's arrival. Despite tantalizing references to the
copying or giving of books of music,[107] very few such manuscripts survive from
fifteenth-century Burgundy; a recent survey lists a mere half dozen.[108] Leaving
aside the ostentatiously luxurious collection of basse-danse tenors BrusBr 9085—
as a singer, La Rue would not have taken part in the performance of dance
music—the two manuscripts compiled closest to La Rue's arrival at court were the
collection of six anonymous *L'homme armé* masses (NapBN 40) and the choirbook
BrusBR 5557. Although the Naples manuscript journeyed to recipient Beatrice of
Aragon long before La Rue joined the chapel,[109] the Brussels collection, copied
from the mid-1470s to the late 1470s,[110] remained at court, and some of its music
was possibly still being sung. The latest additions to this manuscript include
Dufay's *Missa Ave regina caelorum*, Ockeghem's *Missa Quinti toni*, and five
Busnoys motets on such well-known texts as *Regina caeli*, *Victimae paschali laudes*,
and *Anima mea liquefacta est*. It seems highly likely that at least some Busnoys
compositions remained in the repertoire, for less than a decade had elapsed since
he vanished from court records, his music was still exceedingly popular in Italy,
and no one of equal talent or productivity had yet taken his place. Perhaps music
of other composers employed by Charles the Bold—Constans Breuwe, Gilles
Joye, Adrien Basin, Hayne, and Robert Morton—was also still being heard. Any
newer music the chapel was getting must have come from elsewhere, such as the
French court or Soignies (the Ockeghem and Regis works contained in VatC 234
from the end of the 1490s or thereabouts suggest precisely these venues).

---

[107] e.g. DoorslaerC, 21, 24.
[108] Craig Wright and David Fallows, 'Burgundy', *New Grove II*, iv. 622.
[109] See *CC* ii. 247. It is possible, of course, that the music remained in the repertoire of the court.
[110] See Rob C. Wegman, Introduction to *Choirbook of the Burgundian Court Chapel: Brussel, Koninklijke
Bibliotheek Ms. 5557* (Peer: Alamire, 1989), 8.

Court music 1492–1516

We know or can guess which art music was available at court during La Rue's working years through a variety of sources. The most obvious place to find repertoire is the collection of manuscripts compiled by the court scriptorium.[111] Our understanding of the relationship between the Habsburg-Burgundian court and the more than fifty surviving manuscripts or fragments that emanated from its circle is imprecise at best, but the common-sense notion that their contents represented music available to the court is followed here. Some of these manuscripts will be discussed in greater detail later, but the earliest surviving one, the just-mentioned VatC 234, provides no real surprises in its repertoire: an extensive series of masses by Ockeghem, who was already present in BrusBR 5557, motets by Regis (also represented in the earlier collection), works by the court composers Weerbeke, La Rue, and Agricola, a series of *L'homme armé* masses (by Josquin, Brumel, Compère, and the former court composer Busnoys), and so on. Although certain works, especially those by La Rue, appeared in multiple court manuscripts, by and large the repertoire was continually refreshed with new and up-to-date pieces. La Rue would have kept perpetually abreast of the latest compositional innovations through performance of these works.

A second source of music would be the compositions of La Rue's colleagues. The overview presented above lists some of their music that circulated in court manuscripts, but notes numerous other works that did not. Were these neglected works known at court but simply not included in the surviving court manuscripts? We still have very little idea about who 'owned' a piece of music in the fifteenth and early sixteenth centuries; was it the composer or the patron/place of employment for whom the work was written? When a composer left one job for another, did he take copies of his music with him? Weerbeke provides a very small test case in this matter. Of the few pieces of his that were copied into court manuscripts, his *Missa Princesse d'amourettes* was written and circulated in Italy[112] before he joined the court in 1495 (see Table 2.1). It seems very likely that he brought the mass with him when he came north. While one would hardly wish to generalize from this single case, it offers the possibility that others retained copies of their own music as well, and that La Rue's colleagues brought with them pieces to add to the court repertoire that they had written elsewhere.[113]

---

[111] See *TA* for the latest information on court manuscripts as well as indexes of their repertoire. The term 'court scriptorium', though useful, is somewhat misleading, implying as it does either a physical place (usually not possible, since the court was itinerant for a good part of La Rue's tenure) or a fixed group of people on salary from the court working steadily on the production of manuscripts, for which there is no firm evidence.

[112] In VatS 35 from *c*.1478–90. *Anima mea liquefacta est*, from a motet cycle, also dates from his Italian days, but it is a late addition to BrusBR 228, suggesting that it might not have been readily to hand.

[113] Agricola might seem to be an even more promising test case, since he was a prolific composer whose work was very well known before he joined the court, where many of his pieces found their way into manuscripts. The court, however, very likely received some of his music via the French court before Agricola signed on in 1500 rather than getting it specifically from him.

Considerably more controversial is the repertoire of manuscripts compiled not at court but possibly within its orbit. LonBL 35087, compiled before 1509, is a potential candidate in this regard; its owner, Hieronymus Laurinus, or Jérôme Lauweryn, was counsellor and treasurer general under Philip the Fair from 1497 on (having previously served Maximilian and Philip as receiver general for Bruges and vicinity) who maintained a home in Mechelen until 1508, one year before his death.[114] The thirty-six chansons in his collection share four concordances with Marguerite's slightly later chansonnier BrusBR 228,[115] and it would seem quite likely that Lauweryn's court contacts generated most if not all of the other thirty-two chansons in the collection, which include Josquin's *Quant je vous voye*, *En l'ombre d'ung buisonnet*, and *Mon mary m'a diffamée*, Hayne van Ghizeghem's *Mon souvenir*, Agricola's *C'est mal cherché*, Ghiselin's *J'ayme bien mon amy*, the future court composer Benedictus Appenzeller's *Tout plain d'ennuy* and *Buvons, ma comere*, Févin's *Adieu solas, tout plaisir, Petite camusette, Fuyés regretz*, and *On a mal dit de mon amy*, Mouton's *James n'aymeray mason, Je le laray puisqu'il m'y bat*, and *Dieu gard de mal de deshonneur*, Ninot's *C'est donc par moy*, Brumel's *Vray dieu d'amour*, and others. The Habsburg-Burgundian court is also the most likely conduit for other kinds of works found in Lauweryn's collection, such as Prioris's *Consumo la mia vita* and *Dulcis amica dei*, Agricola's *Da pacem domine*, and Mouton's *Salve mater salvatoris*. Quite possibly even some of the Flemish works were known at court; see the discussion in Chapter 4 of La Rue's *Mijn hert*.

A more problematic case is that of the northern repertoire in the Spanish-compiled SegC s.s. (hereafter Segovia). Scholars have long noted that the presence of an extensive group of accurately texted Flemish pieces can only mean that a portion of the repertoire came from the north. Norma Baker thought that these works were transmitted during Philip's first stay in Spain, in 1502, but other scholars, including myself, have suggested dates somewhat earlier, in part because of the complete absence of any music by La Rue.[116] If the court was a possible conduit for the entry of northern repertoire into Spain, a more likely time than 1502 for the introduction of such repertoire is the arrival of Marguerite and her entourage in March 1497 for her marriage to Juan of Castile the following month. If this hypothesis is correct, some of the contents of Segovia, with their rich repertoire of art-song reworkings, could reflect still more of the court repertoire in the 1490s.[117] This would also account for the extensive amount of French court connected

[114] William McMurtry, Introduction to *Chansonnier of Hieronymus Lauweryn van Watervliet: London, British Library Ms. Add. 35087* (Peer: Alamire, 1989), 5.

[115] Three works by Compère and one by Josquin; four of the three are motet-chansons.

[116] Discussed in Honey Meconi, 'Art-Song Reworkings: An Overview', *Journal of the Royal Musical Association*, 119 (1994), 1–42 at 16, and *Fortuna desperata: Thirty Six Settings on an Italian Song*, ed. Meconi (Recent Researches in the Music of the Middle Ages and Early Renaissance, 37; Middleton, Wisc.: A-R Editions, 2001), *passim*. See also Amanda Zuckerman Wesner, 'The Chansons of Loyset Compère: Authenticity and Stylistic Development' (Ph.D. diss., Harvard University, 1992), 36–40.

[117] That the court was fond of art-song reworkings is already known through the repertoires of the later chansonniers FlorC 2439 and VienNB Mus. 18746.

music in Segovia, such as the compositions by Compère and Agricola, which Marguerite would have learnt in her childhood and brought back to the Habsburg-Burgundian court (still largely reliant on other institutions for any influx of new material) when she returned in 1493,[118] and took with her from there to Spain.

Recent arguments against any possible Habsburg-Burgundy/Segovia connection are readily answered.[119] The first of these, that the Habsburg-Burgundian court would have propagated La Rue's music (absent from Segovia) energetically in 1497, is dealt with below and in Chapter 5. The second, Agricola's presence in court-related material prior to his joining in 1500, has already been explained via the French court connection. The third, that few of Segovia's composers have direct connections with the court, is moot; a direct connection with a composer is not required for an institution to acquire or perform his music, and we have already noted that the court was forced to rely on other venues for new music for almost a decade prior to La Rue's arrival. The fourth, that few of Segovia's pieces find concordances in the court manuscript complex, reflects a misunderstanding of those manuscripts. With certain exceptions, the court sought newer music for its collections, putting Segovia's contents out of consideration for inclusion in most later manuscripts, about 80 per cent of which date from almost two decades or more after Marguerite's arrival in Spain. Further, manuscripts prepared at the court scriptorium—especially those containing secular music, which accounts for far more than half of Segovia's contents—were normally tailored very specifically for their recipients (sometimes apparently at the recipients' request), virtually guaranteeing that the repertoire that survives in the court-generated manuscripts does not represent everything the court had at its disposal.[120] In addition, there is no particular reason to expect Segovia's northern repertoire to be recopied, since many pieces within collections generated at court appear within a single manuscript only. Finally, that the large repertoire of Flemish works in Segovia distances it from Marguerite, who did not speak Flemish well and who had but a single Flemish work in her personal chansonnier BrusBR 228, merely confirms that she was not personally responsible for choosing the music to accompany the court retinue—as we would hardly expect her to be.[121]

As I have stated before, many problems remain with Segovia's contents, and we cannot rule out, for example, Italian connections (which could explain the

[118] Mary Beth W[inn] Marvin, '"Regrets" in French Chanson Texts of the Late XVth Century', *Fifteenth-Century Studies*, 1 (1989), 193–217 at 208–9, suggests that the taste for regret chansons came to Habsburg-Burgundy with Marguerite when she returned from France.

[119] See Joshua Rifkin, 'Busnoys and Italy: The Evidence of Two Songs', in Paula Higgins (ed.), *Antoine Busnoys: Method, Meaning, and Context in Late Medieval Music* (Oxford: Clarendon Press, 1999), 505–71 at 524–8.

[120] See Honey Meconi, 'The Function of the Habsburg-Burgundian Court Manuscripts', *Yearbook of the Alamire Foundation*, 5 (forthcoming). I pursue the question of the manuscripts' repertoire in forthcoming work on the court complex.

[121] Nor, obviously, was Segovia intended as her personal collection.

presence of Tinctoris and Isaac, for example); indeed, I am unaware that anyone has argued that the non-Spanish repertoire came from a single venue.[122] But the hypothesis that the court was one of the contributors to Segovia's contents is still viable, and the manuscript may well reflect aspects of the court repertoire in the 1490s.

Once the court began travelling, La Rue was exposed to even more music than the court already owned. Leaving aside the possibility of travel with Maximilian in German lands from November 1492 on, by mid-1494 he was in the Low Countries for the various tours that Maximilian undertook with Philip in tow. Once Maximilian returned to Habsburg lands, Philip spent certain extended periods of time in Brussels[123] but increasingly toured his various territories, with the result that La Rue and the rest of the chapel probably visited every musically important town in the Low Countries at some point in their travels. I bring this up because unless the chapel was cordoned off and forbidden contact with any but their fellow travellers, an unlikely restriction, they would surely have encountered a great deal of music, if not individual composers, at many places along the way. Further, unless we believe that only a composer had access to his own music (which is not the corollary to saying that a composer could retain copies of his music), La Rue and the chapel would have come across music by composers in places where they had once been but were no longer employed. In other words, contact with, say, Obrecht's music was not restricted to 25 July 1497, when both the court and Obrecht were in Bergen op Zoom. I would suggest that the court ran across much of the musically worthwhile material that was circulating in the Low Countries during their periods of active travel, with the more stationary period from 1508 through 1514 (autumn 1513 excepted) providing rather fewer musical contacts. At this time and earlier, however, new music could still reach the court via the travels that individual chapel members made on their own to their various prebends. Perhaps Braconnier, for instance, brought music by Josquin back from Condé (see Ch. 5 for more on this). Alternatively, composers may have come to the vicinity of the court on their own, creating still other channels for the distribution of music.

In its travels outside the Low Countries, the chapel was especially fortunate in encountering many of the most important courtly musical establishments (and a number of ecclesiastical ones) outside Italy: those of the French court, the Spanish court, the Savoyard court, and the English court, to say nothing of Maximilian's German chapel. The almost continual flow of ambassadors to and from the

---

[122] Meconi, 'Art-Song Reworkings', 16. Strohm, *Music in Late Medieval Bruges*, notes several interesting possibilities in his discussion of the manuscript; see esp. 142–4.

[123] Surviving *escroes* between 2 Oct. 1495 and 6 Apr. 1496 are, with one exception, from Brussels, as are those between 7 Sept. 1497 and 26 Mar. 1498, between 4 June and 10 Dec. 1498 (except for one day spent hunting), and between 10 Mar. and 1 June 1499 (again with one exception); see App. A. Since the *escroes* are not complete, we cannot guarantee that every day for which a record is missing was also in Brussels, but they do suggest extended periods of residence there.

court's home base in the Low Countries also provided opportunities for fresh supplies of music. Finally, the chapel may have purchased printed music; the canonic resolutions of Josquin masses found in VienNB 11778 may have been copied from his Petrucci mass prints.[124] In short, the chapel provided La Rue with an unending stream of music to examine and perform, almost certainly a dramatic contrast to his pre-court days.

LA RUE'S SIGNIFICANCE AT THE COURT

The preceding discussion of the chapel structure and duties, court-affiliated composers, and available sources of art music provides the background for assessing La Rue's position. For many years now scholars have recognized his role as leading court composer during his years of employment with the various Habsburg-Burgundian rulers. The following will attempt to elucidate the complexities that underlie this broad generalization while acknowledging that La Rue and his colleagues were hired to sing, not compose.

La Rue is on every *escroe* and special group payment or *état* that survives for the period of his employment of approximately twenty-four years. This grand total of 270 documents (fourteen of which come from Juana's period of leadership) is unmatched by any other court composer during this time. His employment was of greater duration than that of his composer colleagues and of greater regularity than for most of them; almost all the others are missing for short or long periods within the surviving records.[125] Hired at 10s. per day, possibly as a *clerc*, he started receiving 12s. per day during his fifth year of employment and only descended in salary with the reductions made under Charles (even then he still was paid more than all but the *premier chapelain*).

La Rue also rose slowly but surely up through the ranks, yet the rationale behind a given position on court *escroes* is a tricky matter to ascertain. As demonstrated above, Weerbeke, arriving at court several years after La Rue, was hired above him, but whether for his singing, compositional talent, or more impressive pre-court résumé is impossible to tell. Agricola, on the other hand, with glowing testimonials as to his desirability and an even lengthier list of compositions, remains below La Rue and many other presumably less-talented individuals; he is even overtaken by as minor a figure as Clibano, hired on exactly the same day. Braconnier, despite being that supposedly much valued commodity, a *tenoriste*, enters at the bottom of his pay rank, yet after five years he has surpassed La Rue.

---

[124] Eric Jas, 'Vienna, Österreichische Nationalbibliothek, Handschriftensammlung, MS 11778', in *TA* 147. Bonnie Blackburn suspects that Josquin's *Missa Une mousse de Biscaye* in court manuscript VienNB Mus. 15495 was copied from Petrucci as well; see ead., 'Masses Based on Popular Songs and Solmization Syllables', in Richard Sherr (ed.), *The Josquin Companion* (Oxford: Oxford University Press, 2000), 51–87 at 76.

[125] Though sometimes La Rue must have been missing, too, for he left court occasionally in connection with his prebends; we just happen to be lacking the *escroes* that would correspond with his absences.

Champion fluctuates wildly on the lists at two different pay ranks; de Orto is immediately placed above La Rue on the *escroes*, even though he was possibly younger. While La Rue's steady advancement on the lists indicates some kind of positive evaluation, we would have to conclude that Weerbeke, Braconnier, de Orto, and Clibano, as well as others not known as composers, were sometimes valued more highly for reasons we can no longer discern. Loyalty and service to the court were surely important for advancement, but one can scarcely fault La Rue in these areas.

La Rue also never achieved the position of *premier chapelain* in the north, despite having held this position for almost two years under Juana in Spain. Did he want to serve in this capacity under Juana or was he forced into it? He could hardly have objected to the splendid pay; did he wish to continue in this capacity upon his return north but missed his chance because de Orto (the previous *premier chapelain*) and Anthoine de Berghes (the other *premier chapelain*) presumably got to Marguerite before him? Was he sick of the administrative nature of the job or did he attempt to have himself placed in the position but was rebuffed by Marguerite? These questions are impossible to answer.

The scholarly literature since the nineteenth century has cast La Rue as a favourite of Marguerite. Once enshrined, such claims are difficult to shake off, even when they are not founded in fact. In reality, the precise relationship between these two is something that we will never be able to uncover. Moreover, placing La Rue in the broader context of the court and its chapel makes some of the supposed favours and signs of esteem (by both Marguerite and others) lose significance. The court's specific attentions to La Rue consist of seven items:

1. Granting of the prebend in Namur in February 1501. La Rue had worked for the court for possibly almost nine years; they were obviously in no special hurry to reward him.
2. Granting of a prebend in Kortrijk in April 1505.
3. Providing a small pension for his father beginning in November 1505 to last for the expected two years of the second trip to Spain. While not insignificant, this occurs at the same time that Philip is bestowing gifts on numerous members of the chapel in connection with the upcoming journey; in other words, La Rue is not the only one benefiting from Philip's generosity at this time.[126]
4. Providing a letter for La Rue's father to take to Kortrijk in August 1507 to explain La Rue's absence. This cost Marguerite nothing and was surely done at La Rue's initiative; Marguerite would scarcely have kept abreast of her *chapelains'* responsibilities for their prebends.
5. Granting a prebend in Ghent in April 1509. With one exception (to be discussed below), the letter requesting the prebend uses standard formulae; virtu-

---

[126] As noted in Ch. 1; relevant citations for granting the pension are found under 3 Nov. 1505 in App. A. Although La Rue is described by Philip as 'nostre bien amé ... chantre de nostre chapelle domestique', this is the language of convention.

ally everyone receiving a prebend or gift was noted for having performed 'good services'. Marguerite's request to Maximilian for this prebend was merely standard operating procedure: the prebend fell open, La Rue was next on the list, Marguerite (on site, and thus responsible for getting the process going) needed permission from Maximilian (permanently out of town though *de facto* head of the court) and thus wrote the letter requesting permission to give it to La Rue. More important, La Rue had been waiting twelve years for this prebend. During this period there were twenty openings, nine of which were at the disposition of the court rulers, who consistently passed him over (see the information given in Ch. 1). Rather than falling into the special treatment category, this comes under the heading of 'it's about time'.

6. Arranging for a reimbursement in July 1513 for fees that La Rue had paid to take possession of a prebend (granted by Charles) that was then taken away from him. This document, by demonstrating that the court deprived La Rue of what should have been his, shows negative rather than favourable treatment of La Rue. The restoration of his money was the least Charles could do, and it was surely Marguerite rather than the 13-year-old Charles who reneged on the promised prebend.

7. Providing La Rue's brother Jacob with the prebend in Ghent after the composer's resignation in June 1516.

La Rue was therefore granted four prebends by the court, of which one was taken away, and received three special favours, two of which cost the court nothing. Reading through the brief biographies of other chapel members given by Van Doorslaer, one sees immediately that the dispersal of prebends and miscellaneous gifts was extremely common among the members of the chapel, and that it is not as easy as we might expect to make a case for preferential treatment of La Rue, especially during Marguerite's stewardship.[127] Other assumptions must also fall upon closer scrutiny. Court manuscripts BrusBR 15075 and MechAS s.s., replete with La Rue and previously thought to have been prepared especially for Marguerite, are now considered more ambiguous in their origins and thus may have nothing to do with her preferences.[128] These manuscripts were the primary impetus for the long-held assumption that La Rue was especially esteemed by Marguerite, but they actually offer no direct evidence for that claim. In a different matter, sometime court poet and musically au fait Jean Lemaire de Belges never mentions La Rue in any of his writings, in contrast to citations of Josquin, Agricola, and Compère, among others,[129] and the even more musically astute court historiographer and poet Jean Molinet names him just once, and then by default (see the discussion of *Plorer, gemir, crier/Requiem* in Ch. 5).

[127] DoorslaerC, 139–59.
[128] See the relevant entries in *TA*.
[129] In *La Concord des deux langages* of 1511; see PickerCA, 17.

And yet it is very difficult and surely wrong to reject the idea that the court, including Marguerite, liked La Rue, or more specifically, his music. The facts assembled above appear to fall in the same category as the information about the *escroes*: while they do not necessarily place La Rue above his colleagues, most of them indicate approval of some sort. Further, all those whom La Rue served at court were true lovers of music. Certainly in 1508, when La Rue returned north and was quite probably at the height of his compositional powers, he arrived at a court led by one of the most artistically sophisticated patrons of the time. It is extremely difficult to believe that, in some form, Marguerite would not have appreciated La Rue's gifts.[130]

In the first place, this was not her first contact with La Rue. She had previously been at court between June 1493 and January 1497[131] and then again from November 1499 to October 1501; Philip and his chapel sojourned in Savoy while she was living there in 1503, and she visited the north again in 1505. Moreover, Marguerite's and La Rue's musical tastes appear to have been similar.[132] But neither residence at the same court nor comparable tastes are as important as the impressive series of pieces that La Rue seems to have written specifically for her or others close to her. This begins with the chansons *Tous les regretz* and *Tous nobles cueurs*, both set to texts by Octavien de Saint-Gelais and drawn from a longer poem that the poet wrote on her leaving the French court. Surely La Rue composed these works as a gesture of welcome for the young princess shortly after her return from France.[133] A third early piece intended for her was *De l'oeil de la fille du roy*. The daughter of the king can only be Marguerite, daughter of the king of the Romans, Maximilian. The song must date from before January 1497, when she went to Spain to marry Prince Juan. When she returned north in 1499 she was a widow and the mother of a child who had died; a chanson treating her as the stereotypical unattainable woman in the context of courtly love seems highly unlikely under these circumstances.[134] This is especially true given the song's lines 'Car elle fiert du dart d'amer / Souvent pour ung homme tuer' (For with love's arrow she often strikes to kill a man). One of the rumours surrounding her husband's death was that it was caused by excessive love-making; writing such a song after the death of Juan would have been in the poorest possible taste.[135]

---

[130] The literature on Marguerite is extensive; an excellent introduction to her artistic milieu is found ibid. 9–31. One change to material usually cited in connection with Marguerite is that the composer Pierrequin Thérache was not employed at her court in Savoy, as previously thought; this was instead Perroctus Terrache. See Freedman, 'Music, Musicians, and the House of Lorraine', 43.

[131] Although La Rue may have been with Maximilian until some point in 1494.

[132] See Honey Meconi, 'Pierre de la Rue and Secular Music at the Court of Marguerite of Austria', *Jaarboek van het Vlaamse Centrum voor Oude Muziek*, 3 (1987), 49–58.

[133] Or alternatively upon first coming back to the Low Countries, if he had been with Maximilian in June 1493 when Marguerite returned.

[134] Molinet, *Chroniques*, ii. 488, now gives her titles as 'princesse de Castile, vefve de feu Jehan, filz du roy Fernande de Castille'; note the emphasis on her widowhood.

[135] This is not to say that Marguerite forswore the literary delights of courtly love—her chansonnier BrusBr 228 is clear evidence that she did not—but rather to suggest that the sentiments of the poem bespeak a time before her first real marriage.

That these early pieces were special to Marguerite is clear from their position in her personal chansonnier, BrusBr 228. After the opening motet, La Rue's *Ave sanctissima Maria* (the basis for one of his masses), the first secular work is *Tous les regretz* (also the foundation for a La Rue mass), followed immediately by *De l'oeil de la fille du roy*, while the three-voice section of the manuscript opens with a setting of one of her poems (*Pour ung jamais*) and is immediately followed by *Tous nobles cueurs* and then *A vous non autre*, another work with a special meaning for Marguerite (see below). The placement of these works hardly seems coincidental.

La Rue's attentions were very much in evidence as well after the unexpected death of Philip. His mourning motets *Absalon fili mi* (written for Maximilian)[136] and *Considera Israel* (for Marguerite) were possibly joined by *Delicta iuventutis* and perhaps even the Requiem mass.[137]

Other works of La Rue's could hardly fail to draw Marguerite's attention. His chanson *Incessament* was based on a poem included in one of Marguerite's poetry albums.[138] His *Missa O gloriosa domina*, a middle- or late-period mass on the hymn of the same name, was ostentatiously titled *Missa O gloriosa Margareta* (or Margaretha) in two court manuscripts, VatS 36 (sent to Pope Leo X) and MontsM 773 (which may have been intended for her). The motet *Salve mater salvatoris* refers to Marguerite in her capacity as governor of the Netherlands. He altered the text of his chanson *A vous non autre* to read 'A vous non autre servir m'abandone / Bien quatorze ans me suis en toute place' (to you and no other I have given myself to serve everywhere well-nigh fourteen years),[139] surely referring to his service for her within the broader context of the court. The most likely time for such an alteration was La Rue's contact with Marguerite in 1507 requesting the letter of excuse for Kortrijk. With this in mind, Marguerite's letter requesting approval of the Ghent prebend for La Rue two years later suddenly becomes more personal, for embedded within the formulaic request is the remark that he has served her late brother and her for fifteen or sixteen years. Either Marguerite had been prodded by La Rue—possibly she enquired if he were still interested before composing the letter—or she remembered on her own the approximate time he had been with the court (she, of course, returned from France in 1493, exactly sixteen years before 1509). Either case is more evidence for something approaching a real personal relationship between ruler and composer. Indeed, when she writes her letter requesting his Ghent prebend, she uses the familiar diminutive of his name rather than the more formal full name that is now being used in other court documents. In addition, she could hardly have failed to notice La Rue's works for various courtiers, specifically *Dedans bouton* (surely referring to the same Bouton

---

136 Although this work is a less-than-perfect stylistic fit, La Rue is at the moment the best prospect for the composer. Alternative suggestions (other than Josquin) have not yet been explored.

137 On the motets see Honey Meconi, 'Another Look at *Absalon*', *TVNM* 48 (1998), 3–29, esp. 21–2.

138 BrusBR 10572.

139 This textual change was first noted by André Pirro, *Histoire de la musique de la fin du XIV⁰ siècle à la fin du XVI⁰* (Paris: Librairie Renouard, 1940), 229; see also Meconi, 'Sacred Tricinia', 155–8.

family associated with VatC 234) and the motet-chanson *Cueurs desolez/Dies illa* on the death of Jean de Luxembourg.

Even more telling is the evidence of collaboration between the gifted ruler and the prolific composer. La Rue provided a polyphonic setting of Marguerite's words in *Pour ung jamais*, and he is the most likely author for the anonymous work *Me fauldra il*, again to her text. This last song generated the *réponse Il me fait mal*, for which La Rue is probably creator of the music and perhaps the text as well. Marguerite may also have written the texts for La Rue's *Secretz regretz* and *Il est bien heureux*.[140] She can scarcely have been unaware of who was setting her poems. The possibility also exists that La Rue worked with her on composition. Much of the text for the motet-chanson on Philip's death *Se je souspire/Ecce iterum* was written by Marguerite, and Martin Picker has suggested that the music was as well.[141] La Rue is, of course, only one of several possible tutors; five other known composers were in Charles's chapel after Philip's death.[142] But none wrote pieces for Marguerite that we know of and none set her texts. She may well have turned to La Rue instead of anyone else because of this more personal relationship.

It looks extremely likely, then, that La Rue's achievements were—ultimately— not ignored at court, even if they did not translate into better treatment with prebends or cash gifts (possibly his undisputed spot on the *escroes* from 1509 on, immediately below the *premier chapelain*, was a subtle acknowledgement of his contributions as well as a testament to his seniority). The material assembled above shows that the court was by no means hasty in bestowing its favours; noth- ing suggests that it singled La Rue out in the 1490s as their coming compositional star. Any bonuses he received in the way of prebends and high ranks were earned only gradually over a period of many years. His reputation, both within courtly circles and in the outside musical world, was built very slowly but very surely. With this in mind, I should like to explore additional ways in which La Rue stood out at court, ways that may or may not have been apparent to anyone but his fellow musicians.

La Rue was the most productive composer associated with the court during the years between 1492 and 1516. At times he was the only known composer of polyphony on the staff (1492 to September 1495, and again in 1499).[143] As much as the presence of fellow composers may have spurred him to friendly competition and mutual influence, his complete creative isolation may have been an even greater incentive to production. Even when he had as many as seven composer colleagues (in 1506) it is extremely doubtful that anyone was producing at the same rate (his mass output, for example, averages more than one per year); only

---

[140] Martin Picker, 'Three Unidentified Chansons by Pierre de la Rue in the *Album de Marguerite d'Autriche*', *Musical Quarterly*, 46 (1960), 329–43 at 334–5.

[141] Picker, 'Musical Laments'.

[142] She may also have turned to the court organist Henry Bredemers, who also functioned as a music tutor; see DoorslaerC, 142.

[143] Although other singers not now known as composers may have written some works, it is unlikely that the court harboured an anonymous producer generating as much music as La Rue.

Agricola can begin to rival him in works produced, and then not at all in the realm of sacred music.

Furthermore, it is quite likely that all the work by La Rue that survives was written at court. This is not to say that he started composing there; he probably began as a choirboy. But there is currently no compelling reason to place any of it elsewhere. The same cannot be said of all his colleagues, though this is a question still little explored. Divitis and Rogier Herben, because of their relatively short tenures with the court, could well have produced their music elsewhere, and Clibano's motet gives no reason for an association with court. Braconnier's chanson possibly originated at court, and Reingot's extended employment there may have generated his secular pieces. Molinet's sole work and those by Champion quite probably came from court, but neither musician even begins to approach La Rue in terms of quantity. Many of the works of the more prolific composers—Weerbeke, Agricola, de Orto—can definitely be linked with earlier places of employment.[144] Again, La Rue stands out for the quantity of work generated specifically at court; none of his fellow composers approaches him in this regard.

To continue with this thread, possibly as many as fifteen of La Rue's pieces can be linked to specific events or people at court; works by other composers fail altogether in this category. Champion's *Missa Ducis saxsonie: Sing ich niet wol*, whose title honours Frederick the Wise, Duke of Saxony, comes nearest in that Frederick maintained close relations with the court, but that is not precisely the same as being a member (or more significantly, ruler) of the court. Further, many of La Rue's sacred compositions enhanced the court's liturgical celebrations (to be discussed in Ch. 3). The same holds true for certain works by his colleagues, but again, never to the same degree.

At this point I hasten to add that the pre-eminence of the achievements of La Rue outlined above—sustained productivity while at court with firm or very promising ties to specific events or personnages—could all be overturned if anonymous works in court manuscripts were to receive attributions to La Rue's colleagues (whether because of stylistic similarities or newly uncovered concordances) or if their various apparently neutral compositions prove to have hidden and important links to courtly events or individuals. It is worth pointing out, however, that so far La Rue is overwhelmingly the composer who has been named in connection with anonymous court-transmitted works, and that his compositions have equal if not greater potential to reveal hitherto unsuspected meanings.

Perhaps the most important factor in crediting La Rue with greater significance than his colleagues is his unquestioned dominance of the court manuscript repertoire.[145] No one else even comes close in either the number of individual

144 For Weerbeke see Table 2.1; for Agricola see Meconi, 'Josquin and Musical Reputation', 289–91; for de Orto see Picker, 'Orto, Marbrianus de'.

145 First pointed out in Herbert Kellman, 'Josquin and the Courts of the Netherlands and France: The Evidence of the Sources', in *JosCon*, 181–216.

pieces included or the amount of times pieces were recopied. Surprisingly, the composer who places second in this regard never worked for the court at all: Josquin.

Many factors account for this greater attention, including the ones just presented. La Rue simply wrote more than his colleagues (and, for that matter, most of his contemporaries), and he did it while at court, not elsewhere, over a period of many years. As stated before, those requesting or organizing the collections show a preference for new music, and La Rue's sustained productivity generated fresh material regularly. In his last seven or eight years at the court, he is really the only one composing with any frequency. With many of the court manuscripts produced at the very end of his employment or shortly thereafter, it is no surprise that they drew heavily on his output. He was also the most versatile composer at the court, at least in the genre that was most often featured in the manuscripts, the mass.[146]

Another possibility, unfortunately not verifiable, is that La Rue had some hand in determining the contents of the very manuscripts that emphasized his creations.[147] We know far too little about what exactly went on in the preliminary stages of a manuscript's production, and Alamire was, after all, a composer himself and fully competent to make musical decisions. But certainly in the stage of manuscript production between La Rue's return north in 1508 and his retirement in 1516 he would have been the most logical person to turn to for advice, were any needed.

La Rue's dominant position in the court manuscript complex leads the question of his significance at court in another direction. As stated earlier, many of the best fifteenth-century composers had worked for the court, though the court provided no formal recognition of their compositional ability. Almost immediately after Busnoys leaves the court, we find—elsewhere—the beginnings of recognition by employers for composers as creators and not merely performers. Isaac is paid as a composer on 15 September 1484, Obrecht is actively sought for his compositional skill at the court of Ferrara in the late 1480s, Isaac is hired as a composer by Maximilian in 1496, and the compositional skills of Josquin and Isaac are contrasted by an agent of the Duke of Ferrara in 1502.[148] In 1501 Petrucci's first publication hails the commodification of music and hastens the cult of the composer.

Not only did the Habsburg-Burgundian court play no part in this, its reputation for musical eminence for much of the fifteenth century now seems to have been based far more on performance and display than on creativity. David Fallows

---

[146] On the reasons for this, see Meconi, 'The Function of the Habsburg-Burgundian Court Manuscripts'.

[147] Though this is not true, obviously, for manuscripts compiled posthumously, such as SubA 248. Whether or not he was a scribe is uncertain, but in any event he is not the Peter Pierson in Antwerp in 1516, as suggested in Schreurs, 'Petrus Alamire', 17; see Honey Meconi, 'Style and Authenticity in the Secular Music of Pierre de la Rue' (Ph.D. diss., Harvard University, 1986), 18–20.

[148] For Isaac see Reinhard Strohm and Emma Kempson, 'Isaac, Henricus', *New Grove II*, xii. 576–7; for Obrecht see Wegman, *Born for the Muses*, 138–47; for Josquin see Lockwood, 'Josquin at Ferrara', 114.

first pointed out the problems with compositional activity during Philip the Good's reign by noting that few besides Binchois did much composing: the totals he provided were Joye, five songs, Simon le Breton, two songs, and Constans Breuwe, two textless songs.[149] He further sketched a picture of Philip as a less than involved patron of music, in dramatic contrast to Charles the Bold.[150] A recent article elaborates on this theme:

The court chapel seems to have appointed no new composers of any stature between the 1430s and 1457. . . . Effectively, the picture that begins to emerge is of a court establishment heavily aware of its history, more inclined to revere that history . . . it is . . . no surprise that the Burgundian court, the only one with an uninterrupted tradition going back many years, should retain an interest in its earlier musical achievements.[151]

Although the court had a richer musical life under Charles the Bold, even Busnoys, Charles's most famous composer, produced a good deal of his work before joining the Burgundian team. As Fallows noted, one 'could almost make a case that fewer than a dozen of his [Busnoys's] known songs are likely to date from his years at the court'.[152] While his sacred music presents greater problems of chronology and thus fewer assurances as to what is Burgundian and what is not, motets such as *In hydraulis* and *Anima mea/Stirps Jesse* hail from pre-court days, and much evidence points to dating his *Missa L'homme armé* from then as well.[153] But no matter how much Busnoys may have composed for Burgundy's rulers, he was gone by mid-1483. The court then reverted to its previous position of consumer rather than creator of music.

By the time La Rue had retired from court, that passive role was long gone. Whether the court made a conscious decision to hire more composers or whether there were simply more composers of polyphonic music available is impossible to determine, but in any event La Rue was the first of the dozen known composers of polyphony, four of whom garnered individual mass prints from Petrucci, to work with the court over a period of twenty-four years. No musical establishment received as great exposure as the Habsburg-Burgundian court during the period La Rue was there, initially through their unrivalled 'tours' of Europe and later by means of the extensive series of presentation and commissioned manuscripts. La Rue, more than anyone else, led and sustained the transformation of court musical culture.

LaRue's single greatest contribution to court musical life, then, may have been to propel a seemingly moribund court back into the thick of innovative

[149] David Nicholas Fallows, 'Robert Morton's Songs: A Study of Styles in the Mid-Fifteenth Century' (Ph.D. diss., University of California, Berkeley, 1978), 290 n. 17.

[150] Ibid. 299–324.

[151] David Fallows, 'Jean Molinet and the Lost Burgundian Court Chansonniers of the 1470s', in Martin Staehelin (ed.), *Gestalt und Entstehung musikalischer Quellen im 15. und 16. Jahrhundert* (Quellenstudien zur Musik der Renaissance, 3; Wiesbaden: Harrassowitz, 1998), 35–42 at 40.

[152] Fallows, '"Trained and Immersed in All Musical Delights"', 24.

[153] Paula Higgins, 'Busnoys, Antoine'.

compositional activity.[154] He knew some of Binchois's music and doubtless more of Busnoys's, but even were he unaware of their contributions he surely noticed that anything new being performed at court came from somewhere else, the French court (where Marguerite lived at the time he was hired) being the most likely provider. By the time La Rue arrived, the court was also far less peripatetic than before, further reducing its opportunities for acquiring new music. After Maximilian left for German lands in early 1489, the primary courtly seat was the stationary household in Mechelen of Margaret of York, who was Charles the Bold's widow and Philip's step-grandmother. Except for the time of undetemined duration that the chapel travelled with Maximilian from late 1492 on, there would have been an uninterrupted period of several years in one locale. Even after Philip assumed control of the choir in 1494 there were extended periods of stasis, as noted above.

Paradoxically, it may have been the court's former habit of constant motion that cut down on its earlier composers' productivity and forced it to rely on the music of outsiders. The heavy performance schedule of the chapel has been noted many times; this combined with the burdens of travel surely provided less time than ideal for creative pursuits. The extended periods of single-place residence in the 1490s and again from 1509 through 1514 may also have proved a boon for La Rue's own work, a possibility I shall discuss briefly in the chapters on his music.

La Rue, then, started his position at court in an environment that had a long tradition of superior music making and, in its performance resources, the equivalent of a ready library of important works from which to learn. He may also have been aware that two of the greatest and most productive of all fifteenth-century composers, Binchois and Busnoys, preceded him at the court, and perhaps he recognized the possibility of following their example. But more importantly, he was faced with both a *tabula rasa* and an unequalled opportunity: a place with both an unquenchable appetite for music and no competition to meet that appetite, as well as extended periods where the predictability of daily life facilitated creative endeavour. It is from that environment that his music grew.

---

[154] Innovative in several senses: producing new music, following the latest compositional trends, and, in some cases, leading them; see the discussion of music in the next two chapters.

3 Aspects of the Sacred Music

Sacred music occupies the largest portion of La Rue's output, and was even noted in his epitaph as being responsible for his 'noble name'. We see here some of his most significant contributions to the changing face of late fifteenth- and early six-teenth-century music: the move to a texture for more than four voices, pioneering especially in works for six voices; the frequent exploration of ranges outside the gamut, with a unique emphasis on low ranges and an evident pleasure in the sound of many low voices together; a preference not merely for imitation but for strict canon; an apparently systematic exploration of the possibilities of parody tech-nique, including the use of all motifs of a polyphonic model; a (for us, frustrating) fondness for obscure models, most often drawn from chant, that are then further disguised by a penchant for paraphrase and ongoing motivic transformation; and an evident desire to fill perceived gaps in the polyphonic liturgy of the court.

In not all of these traits was La Rue alone. Févin, for example, plays a similarly significant role in the history of the early parody mass, and Isaac enacts a curious kind of *Doppelgänger* function at Maximilian's court, the Germanic twin to Habsburg-Burgundy, where he too ventures often into multi-voiced and espe-cially six-voice textures, and displays a preoccupation with liturgically correct masses, though in a very different way than La Rue. But only La Rue demon-strates the fascination with low ranges and canonic foundations, at least in the masses; no other composer adopts these ranges and this structural device as often as he.

Full treatment of La Rue's sacred music would require a book in itself. The fol-lowing presents some material necessary for such discussion: an overview of vari-ous constructive aspects, the implications of some of these traits for a chronology of the masses, examples of particularly striking borrowings, and a survey of the liturgical function of much of this music. Ideally, these beginnings will serve as jumping-off points for later investigation.

OBSERVATIONS ON THE STRUCTURE AND CHRONOLOGY OF LA RUE'S MASSES

Structure

La Rue's masses are of especial importance, both within his body of work and for the early sixteenth century in general. Of his contemporaries, only Isaac and Obrecht wrote more mass ordinary cycles and individual movements. The current count for La Rue stands at thirty-two surviving masses, two Kyries, and five Credos. Of these, the five-voice *Kyrie pascale* (not to be confused with the four-voice *Kyrie in festo pasche*), the *Missa L'homme armé II*, and the *Missa sine nomine II* all survive without attribution and have been suggested as La Rue's on the basis of style; only the last-named still remains suspect as providing a less-than-ideal stylistic match, but I have included it here for purposes of comparison. A fourth work, the eight-voice *Credo Angeli archangeli*, was previously considered problematic because it survived only in a late German source,[1] but its authenticity receives confirmation in the 1597 inventory of manuscripts owned by Philip II, direct heir to Habsburg-Burgundian musical holdings in Spain.[2] The garbled inscription for the *Missa Sancta dei genitrix* in its primary source has led some to question its authorship and assign it instead to Alamire (whose name, it was claimed, was written first and then altered to La Rue's), but Flynn Warmington has recently stated that the inscription never read Alamire in the first place,[3] and stylistically there is no reason to question the attribution to La Rue. All other works have secure attributions in sources prepared by the Habsburg-Burgundian scriptorium, an enviable source situation that none of La Rue's major contemporaries can match.

Although La Rue's masses and mass movements are enormously varied in many aspects of their style, for the most part they follow fairly standard layouts. With three exceptions, all Kyries have tripartite Kyrie/Christe/Kyrie divisions. Two of the exceptions are the individual Kyrie movements, each of which consists of the division Kyrie/Christe/Kyrie/Kyrie, implying *alternatim* performance with repetition of the first Kyrie. Non-polyphonic sections could have been sung as chant or performed on the organ; the chapel always travelled with both organ and organist. The third exception is the *Missa Almana*, whose Kyrie is divided Kyrie/Christe/Christe/Kyrie; perhaps this was also performed alternatim with chant/organ taking the odd-numbered elements of the movement. This is one of several ways in which the *Missa Almana* departs from the norm; another is the reduction to three-voice texture for the second Christe section. The *Missa Sancta dei genitrix* similarly goes down to three voices in its Christe section, but that is the only other mass to do so. In contrast, the *Requiem* expands to five voices for the second Kyrie, but this is a unique mass in almost every feature, as will become obvious.

The normal structure for the Gloria is a bipartite division with the second section at Qui tollis. The *Missa de beata virgine* has the second of its two sections at Qui sedes instead. Three masses use a tripartite division: Et in terra/Domine deus/Qui tollis for the *Missa L'homme armé I*; Et in terra/Qui tollis/Qui sedes for the *Missa Ave sanctissima Maria*, and Et in terra/Qui tollis/Cum sancto for the *Missa Sancta dei genitrix*. A single mass, *Missa Tandernaken*, has the entire Gloria in one section, but it is the shortest of all La Rue masses.

[1] See LRE vii, p. lxiii.   [2] VDS viii. 373.
[3] Flynn Warmington, private comm., 28 Nov. 1999.

In the Credo, a bipartite Patrem/Crucifixus division is the most frequent sectionalization, but Patrem/Et resurrexit is also common (*Missa Assumpta est Maria, Missa de Sancta Anna, Missa de Sancto Job, Missa Conceptio tua, Missa de sancta cruce, Missa pascale, Missa Alleluia, Missa sine nomine I*, and *Missa Tandernaken*). The division Patrem/Et incarnatus is used in the *Missa Inviolata* and *Credo L'amour du moy*. Of the tripartite divisions, the six-voice Credo, *Missa L'homme armé I, Missa Cum iocunditate, Missa Sub tuum presidium, Missa Ave Maria, Missa de feria*, and *Missa sine nomine II* all use Patrem/Et incarnatus/Crucifixus. Of the other tripartite possibilities, the *Missa Sancta dei genitrix* and *Credo Angeli archangeli* use Patrem/Et incarnatus/Et in spiritum; the *Missa O salutaris hostia* uses Patrem/Visibilium/Et resurrexit; and the *Missa Incessament* divides at Patrem/Et incarnatus/Et resurrexit. A fourfold division occurs in the *Missa L'homme armé II*: Patrem/Et incarnatus/Crucifixus/Et resurrexit; the interior two sections shrink to two voices, a rarity in La Rue's Credos. The most complex structure of all is found in the *Missa Ave sanctissima Maria*, with five sections: Patrem/Visibilium/Cruxifixus/Et resurrexit/Et iterum. Both the Cruxifixus and Et resurrexit sections reduce to two voices. The only other works that reduce voices within sections are the *Missa Sancta dei genitrix* (down to three for Et incarnatus) and *Credo Angeli archangeli*, whose eight voices subside to six for the same section. Both the *Missa Cum iocunditate* and the *Missa Ave Maria* expand the entire Credo to five voices, another uncommon procedure.

Similar variety exists for the Sanctus. The standard formula in La Rue's masses is for separate Sanctus, Pleni, Osanna, and Benedictus sections, followed by a repeat of the Osanna. Eight masses vary this by having a separate In nomine section as well: *Missa Almana, Missa de Sancto Antonio, Missa O gloriosa domina, Missa Conceptio tua, Missa pascale, Missa Incessament, Missa sine nomine I*, and *Missa de virginibus*. Six other masses have individual layouts. The *Missa Sub tuum presidium* has the standard Sanctus/Pleni/Osanna/Benedictus layout followed by a new second Osanna. The *Missa de beata virgine* also has a separate final Osanna, but combines the Pleni and the first Osanna into a single section. The *Missa Assumpta est Maria* divides the Pleni into two sections (Pleni and Gloria tua), and joins the Benedictus with the final Osanna. The *Missa de septem doloribus* divides the Benedictus into two sections (Benedictus and In nomine) and has a new second Osanna. An unusual treatment of this movement is found in the *Missa de Sancta Anna*, which substitutes the motet *O salutaris hostia* for the first Osanna, divides the Benedictus into Benedictus and In nomine sections, and includes a separate Osanna for the close. The *Missa Tous les regretz* presents a particularly complex situation. The Sanctus, Pleni, and Osanna are followed in the earliest court source, VienNB Mus 15497, by duos for the Benedictus and In nomine; the second Osanna is a repetition of the first. In the two other court sources for the full mass, JenaU 12 and SubA 248, the Benedictus is a single three-voice section, and in JenaU 12, it is followed by the indication 'Osanna supra Kyrie ultimum'. Since both JenaU 12 and SubA 248 appear to post-date La Rue's death, it is not clear whether the three-voice Benedictus is his.[4]

Reduced texture is the norm for the Pleni, Gloria tua, Benedictus, and In nomine. Only five masses depart from this procedure. Neither the *Missa de Sancto Antonio* nor the *Missa sine nomine II* reduces voices for the Benedictus (though the former cuts back for the In nomine). The *Missa beata virgine* joins the Pleni and Osanna and does not reduce voices. Similarly, the *Missa Assumpta est Maria* unites the Benedictus and Osanna, with no reduction in texture. Finally, though the *Requiem* technically 'reduces' the Pleni and Benedictus, their four-voice texture is the norm in other movements; it might be more fitting to say that the Sanctus and Osanna expand to five voices.

La Rue normally wrote two sections for the Agnus. Eight masses have a third section as well: *Missa Almana*, *Missa L'homme armé I*, *Missa O gloriosa domina*, *Missa Tous les regretz*, *Missa O salutaris hostia*, *Missa de feria*, *Missa Tandernaken*, and the *Requiem*. The *Missa Sancta dei genitrix* has an implied third section (a canonic instruction plus indications that two voices are tacet) but no music.[5] One mass, the *Missa Nuncqua fue pena maior*, has but a single Agnus section, possibly for modal reasons. La Rue's model, the famous *canción* by Urrede, has two sections, the A section ending on E, the B section ending on G; the song itself closes with the A section, which means its final sonority is E. In each of the first four movements of La Rue's mass the song appears once, with the sections in the order AB, which means that those movements all close on G. In the Agnus, La Rue presents just the A section, which makes the mass end on E, matching the song. Whether the section would have been repeated is not clear, though at a mere twenty-two breves it would provide a very concise ending without repetition. It is similarly unclear whether Agnus movements with two sections would repeat one (and if so, which).

La Rue sometimes highlights the Agnus by use of a special procedure or technique, a common practice for masses at this time. Examples of this in his masses include the expansion to five-voice texture (*Missa L'homme armé II* and the *Requiem*), the use of canon (*Missa L'homme armé I*, with its 4 ex 1 mensuration canon, as well as the *Missa de septem doloribus*, *Missa de Sancto Job*, *Missa Conceptio tua*, and *Missa Sancta dei genitrix*, whose Agnus II canon is now lost), the use of new borrowed material in addition to the mass's primary model (*Missa Ave sanctissima Maria*, *Missa L'homme armé I*), the culmination of a primary structural element (*Missa de feria*, with the expansion of the canonic interval to four breves; *Missa Incessament* and *Missa Nuncqua fue pena maior*, with the greatest amount of polyphonic borrowing), and the unique treatment of borrowed material (*Missa Alleluia* and *Missa Conceptio tua*, with the placement of the model tune in the very audible top voice).

---

[4] Several non-court sources for the mass present a considerably revised and modernized version; there is no evidence that these revisions are La Rue's, despite the view presented in LRE vi, p. lii.

[5] See ibid., p. xvii.

Other elements of mass construction and implications for chronology

Table 3.1 is a listing of the masses and mass movements ordered by very approximate chronological first appearance in sources. The table is divided into three sections, the first consisting of works that appear in sources before Philip's second voyage to Spain. For court sources, these are the ones commonly identified with 'Scribe B', a term now used more for convenience than to identify a single individual. The second section includes works appearing in sources prepared until just before La Rue's retirement in 1516. The third section contains works that appeared either after his retirement or immediately before.[6] This list is far from a strict chronology of La Rue's masses and mass movements, nor will I attempt to construct one here. The material presented, however, can contribute to questions of compositional timing, and there are chronological implications not to be ignored in the three divisions of material. Table 3.2, though ordered alphabetically, provides similar material for the motets and Magnificats.

The first two pieces in Table 3.1 both come from VatC 234, the 'Chigi Codex' compiled at the turn of the century. These are followed by the four additional masses from the Petrucci mass volume of 1503 (Petrucci also published the *Missa Almana*). Within the next two years, three collections produced at the court (JenaU 22, VienNB 1783, and BrusBR 9126) contained most of these works as well as some new ones: *Missa Assumpta est Maria*, *Missa Cum iocunditate*, and *Missa de Sancto Antonio*. In what was probably the last of this group, BrusBR 9126, another mass appears, the *Missa Sub tuum presidium*. It is tempting to view this work, which has considerable rhythmic excitement, as a 'hot off the press' addition to this last manuscript; its prominent position as the first La Rue piece in the manuscript (immediately after the opening mass by Josquin) is also suggestive in this respect.

Regardless of whether other compositions should be added to this group or not, these are surely early works. Taken as a whole, they suggest a composer trying to make his mark at the beginning of his courtly career with a set of compositions designed to draw attention by a series of canny choices in borrowed material, performing forces, structural design, and other elements of composition.

Most of the pieces share two characteristics that later composers (and seemingly La Rue as well) moved away from: the use of an open fifth for the final sonority of a movement, and extensive employment of *tempus perfectum*.[7] Of the masses that provide a third in a final sonority, only the *Missa Puer natus est*

---

[6] I have in mind here compositions in JenaU 4 (*Kyrie pascale*, *Missa Ave sanctissima Maria*, *Missa Incessament*). Flynn Warmington has recently suggested that this collection was compiled not long after Charles was proclaimed King of Spain in mid-March 1516; see Flynn Warmington, 'Jena 4, Charles V, and the Conquest of the Infidels', in *Abstracts of Papers Read at the Meeting of the American Musicological Society: Sixty-Seventh Annual Meeting, November 15–18, 2001*, ed. Mark Evan Bonds (n.p.: American Musicological Society, 2001), 48–9.

[7] Interestingly, movement from *tempus perfectum* to *imperfectum* is observed in other early works of La Rue's, his motets *Gaude virgo* and *Salve regina VI*.

TABLE 3.1. Overview of the mass music

Pieces are listed in approximate chronological order by surviving source, subdivided into three groups. These contain works from sources (1) before 1506, (2) between 1506 and March 1516, (3) after March 1516. Pieces in the second group, except for the first three compositions and the final one, are arranged alphabetically.

Compositions in bold survive only in Habsburg-Burgundian (HB) sources.
[ ] No sixteenth-century ascription to La Rue.
 ? Work is of problematic authenticity.
 * Piece survives in a single source.
F All movements built on canonic foundation.
T Mass is canonic throughout.

	Triple to duple mvts.	3rd in final –	number of mvts.	Number of canons	Number of breves[a]	HB manuscripts	Other sources of full pieces	Sources w/single mvt. or excerpts[b]	Total sources
Missa Almana, 4v	—	—	—		873	5	2	—	7
Credo, 6v	—	yes	—			3	2	—	5
Missa de beata virgine, 4v	2	1	—		612	4	3	5	12
Missa L'homme armé I, 4v	all	1		4	737	3	3	12	18
Missa Nuncqua fue pena maior, 4v	all	—	—		703	1	6	1	8
Missa Puer natus est, 4v	all	2	—		670	4	6	1	11
Missa Assumpta est Maria, 4v	all	—	—		613	4	—	—	4
Missa Cum iocunditate, 4–5v	all	—	—		597	4	8	7	19
Missa de Sancto Antonio, 4v	all	—	—		622	4	5	2	11
Missa Sub tuum presidium, 4v	4	1	—		656	3	4	1	8
*Credo, 4v	—	—	—			—	1	—	1
Missa Ave Maria, 4–5v	—	1	—		733	6	8	1	15
Credo de villagiis, 4v	—	yes	—			2	1	—	3
***Kyrie in festo pasche, 4v**	yes	—	—			1	—	—	1
Missa Alleluia, 5v	4	2	—		711	5	—	—	5
Missa Conceptio tua, 5v	all	4		1	676	7	—	—	7
Missa de feria, 5v	—	4		F	787	7	—	2	9
Missa de Sancta Anna, 4v	all	—	—		659	4	1	—	5
Missa de sancta cruce, 5v	all	2	—		730	7	—	—	7
Missa de Sancto Job, 4v	all	—		2	655	4	—	1	5
Missa de septem doloribus, 5v	—	5		1	668	6	—	—	6
Missa Inviolata, 4v	—	3	—		718	3	—	1	4
Missa Ista est speciosa, 5v	3	1	—		826	7	—	1	8
[Missa L'homme armé II], 4v	4	2		F	677	2	—	—	2
Missa O gloriosa domina, 4v	2	1	—		737	4	2	—	6
Missa O salutaris hostia, 4v	2	1		T	773	1	1	6	8
Missa pascale, 5v	3	3	—		887	6	—	—	6
Missa Tous les regretz, 4v	—	—	—		683	4	6	—	10
Missa pro fidelibus defunctis, 4–5v	some	some	—		616	2	4	—	6

TABLE 3.1. *(cont.)*

Missa Ave sanctissima Maria, 6v	I	4	T	791	7	—	I	8
Missa Incessament, 5v	—	2	F	994	3	7	2	12
[Kyrie pascale], 5v	—	yes	F		2	—	—	2
*Missa sine nomine I, 4v	—	2	—	596	I	—	—	I
?[Missa sine nomine II], 4v	2	I	—	735	I	I	—	2
*Missa de virginibus, 4v	I	—	—	737	I	—	—	I
Credo l'amour du moy, 4v	—	—	—		2	—	—	2
Missa Sancta dei genitrix, 4v	all	3	2	450	I	—	I	2
Missa Tandernaken, 4v	I	—	—	427	2	—	I	3
*Credo Angeli archangeli, 8v	yes	yes	—		I	—	—	I

[a] Osanna but not Agnus repetitions have been counted.
[b] Excluding Habsburg-Burgundian(HB) sources.

includes one in the Agnus; the others all restrict the third to an interior move-ment. As for use of *tempus perfectum*, the table shows that most of these early works open each movement in *tempus perfectum*; later sections within movements typically switch to *tempus imperfectum* and then sometimes back again. It is ironic, however, that the two pieces copied first (as far as surviving sources go) are more forward looking in their use of duple metre and, for the Credo, a full triad at the close.

The works are also mostly for four voices, the exceptions being the *Missa Cum iocunditate* (five voices in a single movement, the Credo) and the more impressive use of six voices in the free-standing Credo. This picture suggests that La Rue was first mastering four-voice mass texture before moving on to fuller forces, with his experiments beyond four voices confined to individual movements. Also worth pointing out is his avoidance of canon in the six-voice Credo; all the other surviv-ing six-voice works of unquestioned authenticity use a canonic foundation. For that matter, in this early group canon is found only in the *Missa L'homme armé I*, though already displayed with virtuosity: each section of the Kyrie is founded on a two-voice mensuration canon, while the second Agnus is the famous 4 ex 1 men-suration canon that proved a favourite throughout the sixteenth century and again in modern times. Again, it seems as if canon was something La Rue moved into gradually (see Table 3.3 for a list of canons in La Rue's output).

As noted above, this early group seems to represent a desire on La Rue's part to prove what he can do, and not merely with mensuration canons. His choice and treatment of borrowed material provide considerable variety within this group, though there are some frequently used procedures. His preferred models are chant (this remains true throughout his career), and it is most common for him to place the borrowed melody in the tenor voice, often entering last and in longer note values, but typically speeding up, growing ever freer in its relationship to the origi-nal, and usually being thoroughly integrated into the texture. The model often

TABLE 3.2. Overview of the motets and Magnificats

Compositions in bold survive only in Habsburg-Burgundian (HB) sources.
[ ] No sixteenth-century ascription to La Rue.
 ? Work is of problematic authenticity.
 * Piece survives in a single source.
 T Totally canonic.

	Number of sections	Sections in triple metre	Use of canon	Number of breves	HB sources	Other sources	Total sources
Magnificats							
*Magnificat primi toni, 3–6v	6	—	×ᵃ	218	1	—	1
Magnificat secundi toni, 2–4v	6	—	—	233	1	2	3
Magnificat quarti toni, 3–4v	6	—	—	309	—	3	3
Magnificat quinti toni, 2–4v	6	1	—	226	2	—	2
Magnificat sexti toni, 3–5v	6	1	—	289	2	2	4
Magnificat septimi toni, 3–4v	6	—	—	200	1	1	2
*Magnificat octavi toni, 2–4v	6	1	—	310	1	—	1
Motets							
?[Absalon fili mi], 4v	1	—	—	85	1	3	4
Ave regina celorum, 4v	1	—	—	87	3	2	5
[Ave sanctissima Maria], 6v	1	—	T	79	2	1	3
Considera Israel, 4v	4	—	—	273	3	1	4
Da pacem Domine, 4v	1	—	T	25	—	2	2
Delicta iuventutis, 4v	2	—	—	233	1	1	2
*Gaude virgo, 4v	2	1	—	164	1	—	1
Lauda anima mea dominum, 4v	2	—	×	180	—	2	2
*Laudate dominum, 4v	1	—	—	107	—	1	1
[Maria mater gratie/Fors seulement], 5v	2	—	—	76	2	—	2
*O domine Jhesu Christe, 4v	1	—	—	92	1	—	1
[O salutaris hostia], 4v	1	—	—	34	4	1	5
Pater de coelis deus, 6v	2	—	×	283	—	2	2
*Quis dabit pacem, 4v	2	—	—	139	—	1	1
*Regina celi, 4v	2	—	—	139	—	1	1
Salve mater salvatoris, 4v	2	—	—	300	2	—	2
Salve regina I, 4v	2	—	T	137	1	1	2
Salve regina II, 4v	3	—	—	244	1	2	3
*Salve regina III, 4v	2	—	—	136	1	—	1
*Salve regina IV, 4v	4	2	—	118	1	—	1
*Salve regina V, 4v	4	1	—	161	1	—	1
Salve regina VI, 4v	2	1	—	98	1	1	2
Sancta Maria virgo, 3v	2	—	—	144	1	1	2
Si dormiero, 3v	1	—	—	115	1	13	14
Vexilla regis/Passio domini, 4v	1	—	—	54	2	1	3

ᵃ Two of the six sections are totally canonic.

TABLE 3.3. La Rue's use of canon

[ ] No sixteenth-century ascription to La Rue.

Missa Ave sanctissima Maria, 6v
Entirely canonic throughout; all canons $\uparrow 4^{\text{th}}$

6 ex 3 canon

Kyrie I	S2/S1, T2/T1, B2/B1	@ 2 breves
Christe		@ 4 breves
Kyrie II		@ 3 breves
Gloria Et in terra		@ 3 breves
Qui sedes		@ 2 breves
Credo Patrem		@ 1 breve
Visibilium omnium		@ 4 breves
Et iterum		@ 2 breves
Sanctus		@ 11 breves
Osanna		@ 2 breves
Agnus I		@ 9 breves
Agnus II		@ 3 breves

4v section: double canon

Benedictus	@ 1½ breves

2v section (2v canon)

Qui tollis	B2/B1	@ 2 breves
Crucifixus	S2/S1	@ 1½ breves
Et resurrexit	B2/B1	@ 1½ breves
Pleni	B2/B1	@ 1 breve

Missa Conceptio tua, 5v

1 foundation canon in Agnus I	T1/T2	$\downarrow 4^{\text{th}}$@ 1 breve

Missa de feria, 5v
Built on canonic foundation except for duos and trios

Kyrie I	T2/T1	$\uparrow 5^{\text{th}}$ @ the semibreve
Christe	T1/T2	$\downarrow 5^{\text{th}}$ @ the semibreve
Kyrie II	T2/T1	$\uparrow 5^{\text{th}}$ @ the semibreve
Gloria Et in terra	T2/T1	$\uparrow 5^{\text{th}}$ @ 1 breve
Qui tollis	T2/T1	$\uparrow 5^{\text{th}}$ @ 1 breve
Credo Patrem	T2/T1	$\uparrow 5^{\text{th}}$ @ 2 breves
Et incarnatus	T2/T1	$\uparrow 5^{\text{th}}$ @ 2 breves
Crucifixus	T1/T2	$\downarrow 5^{\text{th}}$ @ 2 breves
Sanctus	T2/T1	$\uparrow 4^{\text{th}}$ @ 3 breves
Osanna	T1/T2	$\downarrow 4^{\text{th}}$ @ 3 breves
Agnus I	T1/T2	$\downarrow 5^{\text{th}}$ @ 4 breves
Agnus III	T2/T1	$\uparrow 5^{\text{th}}$ @ 4 breves

TABLE 3.3. (*cont.*)

___

Missa de Sancto Job, 4v
2 foundation canons

Agnus I	B/T	↑5th @ 1 breve
Agnus II	T/B	↓5th @ 2 breves

Missa de septem doloribus, 5v
1 foundation canon

Agnus I	A/T2	↓4th @ 4 breves

Missa Incessament, 5v
Built on canonic foundation, except for Pleni/Benedictus

All canons	B/T2	↑4th @ 2 breves

Missa L'homme armé I, 4v
4 canons, 3 of which are foundation canons

Kyrie I	T/B	mensuration canon @ octave
Christe	A/T	mensuration canon @ 5th
Kyrie II	T/B	mensuration canon @ octave
Agnus II	4 ex 1	mensuration canon @ 5th, 4th, 5th

[Missa L'homme armé II], 4v
Built on canonic foundation, except for duos

Kyrie I & II	S/B	↓12th @ 1 breve
Christe	S/B	↓12th @ 4 breves
Gloria Et in terra	S/B	↓12th @ 2 breves
Qui tollis	S/B	↓12th @ 4 breves
Credo Patrem	S/B	↓12th @ 2 breves
Et resurrexit	B/S	↑12th @ 5 breves
Sanctus	A/B	↓5th @ 7 breves
Osanna	T/B	↓5th @ 2 breves
Agnus I	A/S	↑4th @ 2 breves
Agnus II	S/A	↓5th @ 3 breves

Missa O salutaris hostia, 4v
Entirely canonic throughout

4 ex 1 canon

___

Kyrie I	SATB	↓5th ↓4th ↓5th @ 2, 8, 2 breves
Christe	TBSA	↓5th ↑12th ↓5th @ 2, 6, 2 breves
Kyrie II	SATB	↓5th ↓4th ↓5th @ 1, 3, 1 breves
Gloria Et in terra	SATB	↓5th ↓4th ↓5th @ 2, 11, 2 breves
Qui tollis	TBSA	↓5th ↑12th ↓5th @ 2, 6, 2 breves
Credo Patrem	SATB	↓5th ↓4th ↓5th @ 2, 4, 2 breves
Visibilium	SATB	↓5th ↓4th ↓5th @ 2, 11, 2 breves
Et resurrexit	TBSA	↓5th ↑12th ↓5th @ 2, 11, 2 breves

TABLE 3.3. *(cont.)*

Sanctus	SATB	↓5th ↓4th ↓5th @ 1, 5, 1 breves
Osanna	SATB	↓5th ↓4th ↓5th @ 2, 4, 2 breves
Agnus I	TBSA	↓5th ↑12th ↓5th @ 1, 4, 1 breves
Agnus II	SATB	↓5th ↓4th ↓5th @ 2, 6, 2 breves
Agnus III	TBSA	↓5th ↑12th ↓5th @ 2, 4, 2 breves

2v sections

Pleni	T/B	↓5th @ 1½ breves
Benedictus	S/A	↓5th @ 1 breve

Missa Sancta dei genitrix, 4v
'2' canons

Pleni, 3v

3 ex 1 canon	BAS	↑4th ↑4th @ 1 breve

Agnus II, 2v

'duo Discantus In corpore uno' supposedly a canon, but no music exists

[Kyrie pascale], 5v
Built on canonic foundation

Kyrie I	T1/S	↑octave @ 2 breves
Christe	T1/T2	↑5th @ 6 breves
Kyrie II	T1/T2	↑5th @ 4 breves
Kyrie III	T2/S	↑octave @ 2 breves

Magnificat primi toni, 6v

Sicut locutus	6 ex 3	mensuration canon @ unison
Sicut erat	6 ex 3	canon ↓5th @ 4 breves

[Ave sanctissima Maria], 6v

6 ex 3 canon	S2/S1, T2/T1, B2/B1	↑4th @ 1 breve

Da pacem domine, 4v

Double canon	A/S, B/T	↑4th @ the semibreve

Laudate dominum, 4v

3 ex 1 canon plus free voice	SAT	↓4th ↓5th @ 2 then 4 breves

Pater de coelis deus, 6v
3 ex 1 canon plus 3 free voices

Prima pars	T2, A2, S	↑5th ↑5th @ 3 breves each
Secunda pars	T2, A2, S	↑5th ↑5th @ 2 breves each

Salve regina I, 4v
4 ex 1 canon

Salve	SATB	↓4th ↓5th ↓4th @ 2, 6, 2 breves
Et Jesum	ASBT	↑5th ↓12th ↑5th @ 2, 7, 2 breves

TABLE 3.3. (*cont.*)

[Adieu comment] 5v Foundation canon	T2/B	↓4th @ 7 breves
Cent mille regretz, 5v Foundation canon	B/T2	↑4th @ 3 breves
[Dueil et ennuy] 5v Foundation canon	B/T2	↑4th @ 4 breves
En espoir vis, 4v Double canon	A/S, B/T	↑5th @ 3 breves
For seulement, 5v Foundation canon	B/T2	↑5th @ 1 breve
Incessament, 5v Foundation canon	B/T2	↑4th @ 2 breves
[Je n'ay regretz] 5v Foundation canon	B/T1	↑4th @ 2 breves
[Je ne dis mot] 6v 6 ex 3 canon	S2/S1, T2/T1, B2/B1	↑4th @ 2 breves

generates material in the other voices as well. It is also extremely common (though not universal) for movements to begin in a similar manner, creating a polyphonic motto with references to the model. Significantly, La Rue almost invariably makes alterations rather than literally repeating a previous opening, and in several masses, the motto weakens and eventually disappears by the final movement or movements. Both La Rue's typical treatment of the chant model and the use of a varied motto opening continue throughout his compositional life.

But in addition to this common operating procedure, La Rue explored other possibilities as well. Throughout his life he was to write several masses with multiple chant models. *Missa de beata virgine* appears to be the earliest of these, and it is appropriate that it has the simplest structure; again, the implication is that La Rue got his feet wet first before attempting trickier stuff. The mass employs a different and liturgically appropriate chant model for each movement, a straightfoward procedure adopted by others who wrote *de beata virgine* masses.[8] Studies of the *de beata virgine* mass complex, however, suggest that La Rue's mass is quite possibly the first of its kind. It was certainly the first to appear in print, and it appears to pre-date the versions of both Josquin and Brumel.[9] Its presumably widespread

[8] For a concise overview of *de beata virgine* masses, see Gustave Reese, 'The Polyphonic "Missa de Beata Virgine" as a Genre: The Background of Josquin's Lady Mass', in *JosCon*, 589–98. La Rue's mass would seem to be one of the first to use Credo IV for its Credo movement.

[9] Both the Josquin and Brumel works are generally considered late masses. Nors Sigurd Josephson, 'The Missa De Beata Virgine of the Sixteenth Century' (Ph.D. diss., University of California, Berkeley, 1970), 65, identifies La Rue's mass merely as the first to appear in print, but none of the other full-fledged masses he presents can be shown to pre-date La Rue's. Earlier works are either composite masses or just pairs of movements, while Isaac's *Beata virgine* masses are all *alternatim* settings. It is possible that La Rue's *Missa de beata virgine* was written by 1496, since in that year Alamire copied, for the 's-Hertogenbosch confraternity, a new

dissemination via Petrucci may have made it a kind of model for later masses of this sort. In other words, La Rue not only started his own series of multiple cantus-firmus masses with this work; he apparently also played a major role in generating the *de beata virgine* complex as a whole.

In another change from the usual chant mass La Rue builds his *Missa Cum iocunditate* on a chant-derived ostinato that normally begins on one of two possible pitches and undergoes ceaseless rhythmic changes, in keeping with the composer's decided preference for constantly varied material. As we shall see later, the mass may have been influenced by Josquin. The expansion to five voices in the Credo also sets it apart from the usual mass procedures.

Three of these ten early works are based on secular (or presumed secular) models. *L'homme armé* comes as no surprise for a model; not only was there a particularly rich tradition of masses built on this, there was clearly interest at the court in these masses. Habsburg-Burgundian manuscript VatC 234, containing material known at court during the 1490s, includes *L'homme armé* masses by Josquin (*sexti toni*), Brumel, Busnoys (possibly the earliest of all *L'homme armé* works), and Compère. It only makes sense for La Rue to have joined in the fray at an early stage of his mass production, given his employers' obvious enjoyment of this subgenre. La Rue's entry into the game would surely have impressed his listeners, and not merely because it was one more treatment of a favourite tune: this is one of his very best works, with fragments of the tune permeating the entire texture and generating a spectacular example of a paraphrase mass. This mass also provides an early instance of something La Rue liked to do from time to time, to include a short quotation from an unrelated model. In this case he puts the melody *Tant que nostre argent durra* in the Bassus of Agnus III.

A more unusual choice for a model was *Nuncqua fue pena maior*, but this was surely also done to draw the attention of a listener, in this case Juana. *Nuncqua fue pena maior* was probably the most popular Spanish song outside of Spain, and the court unquestionably had a copy; it appears in the fragmentary manuscript OxfBA 831 and was likely to have come north either with Juana's entourage or with one of the many ambassadors during the multi-year negotiations preceding Philip's wedding. It is less likely to have been written for the betrothal or wedding than for sometime thereafter, mainly because of the text of the song, which deals with unfaithful love. It certainly would have resonated strongly some years later, with Juana's growing jealousy. She could scarcely have failed to notice the model, for La Rue opens each movement of the mass borrowing polyphonically from Urrede's song.

La Rue's third choice for a secular model remains speculative, for we simply do not know to what the *Missa Almana* refers.[10] There seems to be some borrowed

mass on *Salve sancta parens* (the title by which La Rue's work is known in the early manuscript VienNB 1783). On Alamire and this mass, see Schreurs, 'Petrus Alamire', 26 n. 9.

[10] The name apparently provided some puzzlement in the 16th c. as well, for it was changed in two non-court sources.

melody here,[11] presumably a German secular tune (encountered while La Rue was with Maximilian?), but since he normally treats his models extremely freely, the original has so far proved impossible to trace. In any event, this earliest group of mass compositions shows La Rue dealing with single- and multiple-chant models, canon and ostinato, secular monophonic and polyphonic models, normal and expanded textures, well-known and obscure models (at least to us, but possibly to them as well), and techniques of cantus-firmus, paraphrase, polyphonic borrowing, and motto construction. This is not a bad start for someone wishing to establish himself as a composer of some versatility.

This early group of mass music is also striking in that almost all of it circulated outside of court manuscripts, and often for quite some time, in contrast to much of the later music (see Table 3.1).[12] The six-voice Credo, for instance, was still in use in Germany in the mid- to late 1530s (KasL 38), and the *Missa de Sancto Antonio* was printed in 1539². The *Missa de beata virgine* was being revised in Pirna in 1554 (DresSL Pirna IV). As a complete mass, the *Missa L'homme armé I* was still being copied in Leipzig c.1555 (LeipU 51), with its famous canon in circulation even longer. The *Missa Nuncqua fue pena maior* appeared in full in half a dozen non-court sources, the last from c.1543 in Augsburg (MunU 327). The *Missa Puer natus est* surfaces at mid-century in Amsterdam (LeidGA 1443). The *Missa Cum iocunditate* was extraordinarily popular; apart from numerous excerpts, four court and eight non-court manuscripts kept it in circulation to mid-century in both Germany (StuttL 38) and presumably Italy (MilA 46, where it is mistakenly ascribed to Josquin). The same manuscript also contains the *Missa Sub tuum presidium*. Only the *Missa Assumpta est Maria* was restricted to court manuscripts—or at least that is what survives.

The second group of masses in Table 3.1 starts with three works that first survive in non-court sources. The four-voice Credo appears in MunBS 53, a manuscript compiled around 1510 for Maximilian's court chapel. The *Credo de villagiis* and *Missa Ave Maria* first appear in papal chapel collection VatS 45. Following are fifteen works from court sources compiled prior to March 1516; these works are listed alphabetically, followed in Table 3.1 by the *Requiem*, which first appears in a manuscript from Munich from about the same time. One manuscript not contributing to this second group is BrusBR 6428. The date 'perhaps ca. 1512' is still given in conjunction with this collection in the latest work on the court manuscripts,[13] but this hypothetical date needs revision. All the scribes currently identified in the manuscript have work dating clearly from 1521 or later, essentially generating a later date for this manuscript as well.

As is quite clear, then, there is little room for certainty about the chronological ordering of this second group—not that there was all that much in the first group.

[11] See LRE i, p. xxxi.

[12] This is not merely owing to the widespread distribution of the masses via Petrucci; stemmata for the relevant masses given in LRE usually show little reliance on printed versions.

[13] Herbert Kellman, 'Brussels, Bibliothèque royale de Belgique MS 6428', in *TA* 71.

Nor is it a given that all of these works post-date Philip's second trip to Spain. In addition, almost all of these works are bunched up in sources from the last few years of La Rue's service. Some sources from these very late years resulted from Charles's attainment of his majority and the increased need for the court to use manuscript diplomacy as one of several tools in the establishment of his presence on the political stage.[14] But not all of these collections served the purpose of 'illuminated bribery', and it is a striking coincidence that there is an outpouring of La Rue's work in court-related sources in the period just before he is scheduled to depart. Was there, somehow, a sense of ownership involved here, that these were 'his' works that he was only ready to release on the brink of retirement for use elsewhere? Although too little is known about who 'owned' music at the time, La Rue is writing in the period when compositions are gradually beginning to be defined as commodities, when both the mechanism for distributing them (print) and the economic basis behind their creation changed. Composition went from being ancillary to a musician's life to being an important component of it as the independent identity of 'composer' solidified, separating him from a mere performer and leading to the beginnings of a 'publish or perish' mentality. Whether La Rue sensed any of this is completely unknown, but so much of his music stands out from its surroundings that he could hardly have been unaware of how special it was; its differences must have been part of an intentional plan to distinguish himself.

The years between late 1508 and the beginning of 1515 would have been an ideal period for La Rue to compose, since the court was virtually stationary during this time.[15] This is not to imply that it is impossible to compose while 'on the move', but it is surely easier to write when one does not have to pack up and travel to a different town every day or so. As mentioned earlier, the court's traditional penchant for continuous movement may have been a factor contributing to its reliance for so many years on music created elsewhere.[16] It is therefore quite possible that this roughly six-year period could have spawned more masses than La Rue's earlier, and considerably busier, sixteen years in court employment. Further, because the court was no longer visiting new places on a regular basis, there was greater need to generate new music from within. Although ambassadors and other visitors were a probable conduit for music from outside, as noted in Chapter 2, there were simply fewer opportunities for the musicians to encounter new pieces than there had been previously. As with some of the earlier part of La Rue's

---

[14] For an overview of this process, see Honey Meconi, 'Foundation for an Empire: The Musical Inheritance of Charles V', in Francis Maes (ed.), *The Empire Resounds: Music in the Days of Charles V* (Leuven: Leuven University Press), 18–34.

[15] Richard Schaal, 'Zur Methodik quellenmäßiger Datierung der Werke Pierre de la Rues', in *Kongress-Bericht Gesellschaft für Musikforschung Lüneburg 1950*, ed. Hans Albrecht, Helmuth Osthoff, and Walter Wiora (Kassel and Basel: Bärenreiter, [1950]), 80–2, arrived at precisely the opposite conclusion, claiming that most of La Rue's works were composed before Philip's death; he felt the uncertainty of government afterwards would have made it more difficult to compose.

[16] Most other major musical institutions were more stable in terms of location.

career at the court, this lack of regular outside contact may have been an impetus for additional composition.

The second group of masses suggests an ever more confident composer. The *Missa Ave Maria* shows another effort at five-voice composition in its Credo, but there are now many full-fledged five-voice masses standing by themselves. Canon is more prominent as well: in the *Missa O salutaris hostia* all movements are derived from a single canonic voice, an impressive contrapuntal achievement rarely attempted by others.[17] On a smaller scale, the *Missa de septem doloribus*, *Missa Conceptio tua*, and *Missa de Sancto Job* each have one or two sections built on a canonic foundation (for each of them the first Agnus; for the *Missa de Sancto Job* the second Agnus as well), while both the *Missa de feria* and the *Missa L'homme armé II* have canonic foundations for each movement. While this might be expected for the second *L'homme armé* mass, fitting within the tradition of contrived structures for those masses,[18] it comes as a surprise in the supposedly lowly ferial mass, as does the use of a rich five-voice texture. In another element of complexity, the *Missa de feria* increases the rhythmic distance of the canon from movement to movement (Kyrie, at the semibreve; Gloria at the breve, Credo at two breves, Sanctus at three, and Agnus at four). It is as if La Rue wanted his work for even the simplest of liturgical events to radiate a sense of importance. This is particularly significant, because once again La Rue plays a major role in the definition of a compositional genre, in this case the ferial mass.[19] Apart from being the first composer to treat the mass as a full-fledged liturgical work rather than a kind of *Missa brevis*, La Rue's work was surely the model for Févin's own version.

The *Missa de feria* is also a mass using multiple models. Although the ones identified to date are liturgically appropriate (as are those of La Rue's earlier multiple-model mass, the *Missa de beata virgine*), the aspects noted above clearly separate it from the earlier work. The other multiple-model masses transmitted in this second group also distinguish themselves in some manner from the earlier work. The *Missa de septem doloribus* uses a series of unidentified chants[20] (would they

---

[17] An earlier example of a 4 ex 1 canonic mass appears in TrentC 91 from *c.*1460–80 (no. 1353 in 'Thematischer Katalog der sechs Trienter Codices', in Guido Adler and Oswald Koller (eds.), *Trienter Codices I: Geistliche und weltliche Kompositionen des XV. Jahrhunderts* (Denkmäler der Tonkunst in Österreich, 14–15; Vienna: Artaria, 1900)).

[18] I wonder, however, whether this mass might have preceded what we call *Missa L'homme armé I*, an idea that would change our profile of the composer's canonic use in his earlier works. The mensuration canons of the 'first' mass are harder to write, and the mass in general is a melodic and rhythmic tour de force. Was the 'second' mass in reality a warm-up for the better work?

[19] On the ferial mass and La Rue's position in the tradition, see Andrew H. Weaver, 'Aspects of Musical Borrowing in the Polyphonic *Missa de feria* of the Fifteenth and Sixteenth Centuries', in Honey Meconi (ed.), *Early Musical Borrowing* (New York: Garland, forthcoming). It is possible that Pipelare's incomplete ferial mass, which employs some canonic writing, may have provided the inspiration for La Rue's own mass. If this were so, it would be another connection between La Rue and Pipelare, from whom La Rue borrowed the material for his *Missa de Sancto Job*. Pipelare's ferial mass was known at court, though it appears only in a manuscript that post-dates La Rue's death. In another interesting parallel, Isaac's ferial mass also makes use of canon, though it is an incomplete mass for four voices only. On the connections with Ockeghem, see Ch. 5.

[20] Jennifer Bloxam has speculated that the auxiliary texts provided for these chants in the mass may be

have been known to court musicians, or were they unfamiliar to them as well?) in addition to a surprising quotation from Josquin's famous motet *Ave Maria*. While the *Requiem* employs the expected chants as models, the composition shifts throughout between four- and five-voice texture in unpredictable ways, with duos for the opening of the Tract rather than as interior sections. Mixing Proper and Ordinary sections, as is standard for the Mass for the Dead, it also includes numerous chant intonations and a marked shift—unknown in other La Rue masses—between movements for high tessitura and those using a much lower range, descending to the cavernous pitch of B♭ below the staff (again, not found in any other of his masses).

All the chant models for the *Missa pascale* are associated with Easter, but they are drawn from very disparate parts of the liturgy, including Matins, Lauds, Compline, and the Introit for the day, thus generating a mass that is indeed unified liturgically (as was the *Missa de beata virgine*) but in an unexpected and much less readily discernible way.[21] This dazzling variety of model sources is in striking contrast to more usual kinds of Easter masses. For example, instead of La Rue's intricate borrowings, Agricola merely used Kyrie I, Gloria I, Sanctus XVII, and Agnus XXII in his *Missa paschalis*, written for only four voices. An even more complex situation is found in the *Missa de Sancto Job*, where La Rue uses chant models that are drawn from Pipelare's use of the same models in his Livinus mass rather than from the original chants themselves.[22]

Perhaps La Rue's most unusual treatment of a model (for him) occurs in his *Missa Alleluia*, where the unidentified borrowed voice is treated strictly throughout, using diminutation, augmentation, and retrograde. While these techniques are standard fare in the masses of other composers, they are virtually unknown in La Rue's mass music. This has prompted suggestions that the model is borrowed from a polyphonic work, but it still forms a marked contrast with the treatment of polyphonic models in La Rue's other masses, such as the early *Missa Nuncqua fue pena maior* and the *Missa Tous les regretz* from this middle group of sources, both of which treat the borrowed voices with considerable freedom.

Another important and different aspect of model treatment in this second group is the addition of extra text derived from the cantus firmus. I do not refer here to text given merely to reflect the desire of a manuscript's patron, such as the altered text for *Missa de Sancto Antonio* found only in VerBC 756. Rather, in works such as *Missa de Sancto Job* and *Missa de sancta cruce*, the extra text is clearly meant to replace that of the mass ordinary and provide an additional level of meaning to

contrafacts of models actually drawn from some other feast (pers. comm., 13 Feb. 1996).

[21] For an excellent discussion of this work, including the musical unification of the chosen models, see Mary Jennifer Bloxam, 'A Survey of Late Medieval Service Books from the Low Countries: Implications for Sacred Polyphony 1460–1520' (Ph.D. diss., Yale University, 1987), 399–408.

[22] See M. Jennifer Bloxam, 'In Praise of Spurious Saints: The *Missae Floruit egregiis* by Pipelare and La Rue', *JAMS* 44 (1991), 163–220. Pipelare's mass appears to date from the 1480s or perhaps even earlier (see the communications by Rob C. Wegman and M. Jennifer Bloxam in *JAMS* 45 (1992), 161–7), making La Rue's mass one of several instances where he felt no hesitation in drawing on an older model.

the work, creating a more complex entity than found in the masses from the earliest sources.

Masses from this second group of sources are likely to be more expansive than those from the earliest sources; see the numbers provided in Table 3.1. Because of the uncertainty of Agnus repetition, I have tabulated only the number of breves in that movement for written-out music; that is, works with only two written Agnus sections do not include a possible repeated Agnus section in their tally of breves.[23] Thus, the 'total' number of breves given for each mass is doubtless not exact, but these figures still suggest a more leisurely treatment of the material in this second group of masses. Perhaps this is another demonstration of confidence, or perhaps it is just the result of more time to compose. One curious point is that the longest masses in the earliest group are those that use (or seem to use) secular models, yet the two based on secular models in this second group are both among the shorter works.

Masses from this middle group feature *tempus perfectum* much less often than those from the earliest sources, and there is, as well, much greater use of the full triad for final sonorities. Rather surprising, however, is the considerably more restricted circulation of these mass compositions outside of court sources, with a total of eleven confined to manuscripts originating from the court scriptorium (not including the transmission of isolated movements or individual sections from movements, which represent a different phenomenon). Even the ones generated in full elsewhere are often found only once or twice in non-court sources: the *Credo de villagiis* in VatS 45, the *Missa de Sancta Anna* in UppsU 76b, the *Missa O salutaris hostia* in 1516[1], the *Missa O gloriosa domina* in FrankSU 2 and 1539[2]. The only ones with significant non-court circulation were the *Requiem* (though all of its extra manuscripts originated in Munich), *Missa Tous les regretz* (on La Rue's own very popular chanson), and *Missa Ave Maria*. This is hardly to say that this batch of La Rue's masses was unknown outside the court; most of them had a healthy distribution to other musical centres and chapels throughout Europe via the dispersal of court manuscripts as gifts or commissions. But it is nonetheless a distinct contrast with the earlier subset of masses.

The third group of masses—those that may have first appeared in sources after La Rue's retirement—includes an incredibly diverse group of pieces. Most are for four voices, with two for five, one for six, and one for eight (a texture virtually unknown at this time; the work exists today only in a late German source). Two are quite short, the *Missa Sancta dei genitrix* and the *Missa Tandernaken*,[24] while the *Missa Incessament* is the longest of any of La Rue's masses. *Tempus perfectum* is not common but not unknown, and three works still close on an open fifth. In the choice of models, a mere three works use or appear to use chant: the *Missa Sancta*

---

[23] The tallies do include, however, Osanna repetitions, since there is no question about what was to be repeated.

[24] Rubsamen puts these in the very earliest layer of his chronology of La Rue's masses; see RubsamenMGG, 236.

dei genitrix (another ostinato mass), the *Missa de virginibus* (unknown model, presumably chant), and the *Kyrie pascale*. The two *Sine nomine* masses use no known model, while secular monophony, something La Rue has largely ignored except for the *L'homme armé* masses, shows up rather unexpectedly in the *Credo L'amour du moy* and *Missa Tandernaken*. Polyphonic models make a strong showing in the *Missa Incessament* (on La Rue's own song) and the *Missa Ave sanctissima Maria* (on his own motet) as well as in the *Credo Angeli archangeli*, on Isaac's six-voice motet of the same name. Canon is quite popular: the *Missa Sancta dei genitrix* has a 3 ex 1 canon in the Pleni, while the second Agnus, as noted above, was intended to be a two-voice canon, though no music was notated. The *Kyrie pascale* and *Missa Incessament* each use a canonic foundation throughout (as does the model for the mass), and the *Missa Ave sanctissima Maria*, again like its model, is entirely canonic.

An especially striking feature of this third group of pieces is the limited distribution of most of these works, even within court sources: one or two is the usual number of manuscripts. The two exceptions are the *Missa Ave sanctissima Maria*—though here the distribution is essentially via the court—and the popular *Missa Incessament*, which again mirrors its very widely distributed model. Thus the total picture for the three groups of masses shows, oddly enough, an ever-shrinking general circulation, going from masses disseminated widely in both court and non-court sources, to masses known broadly but predominantly through court manuscripts, to those hardly known anywhere.

This last group of masses and mass movements is the most problematic in terms of chronology. Do these pieces represent genuinely late works or are they works that for one reason or another simply didn't make it into earlier sources? Or are earlier sources in which they appeared simply lost? As noted above, for example, Rubsamen considered the pithy *Missa Tandernaken*, with its atypically straightforward handling of the cantus firmus, to be one of the earliest of La Rue's masses. Both the *Missa Incessament* and *Missa Ave sanctissima Maria*, on the other hand, certainly seem like later works, with their impressive handling of the compositional challenges they presented.

Aspects of the mass music that provide few clues to chronology are the finals, ranges, and cleffing combinations of the works. Table 3.4 provides an overview of these; it is organized by final rather than chronological grouping by source, but chronological reordering by earliest source does not demonstrate any particular patterns (for comparison, Table 3.5 presents material for the motets and Magnificats).[25] Moreover, the finals are sometimes deceptive, as La Rue occasionally veers from one presumed pitch centre to another in the course of a movement (a trait also observable in non-mass music). As it stands, Table 3.4 shows

---

[25] Interestingly, *Missa pascale* and *Kyrie in festo pasche* share the same range and almost identical cleffings, and sometimes the same final. *Kyrie pascale* has a wider range than either, but shares a G final and similar cleffings with the mass.

TABLE 3.4. Cleffing, range, and final in La Rue's mass music

{ } High and low pitches exceeding the gamut.
[ ] No sixteenth-century ascription to La Rue.
  ? Work is of problematic authenticity.
  * Piece survives in a single source.

	Signature accidentals	Cleffing	Low pitch	High pitch
C final				
*Credo, 4v	—	g2-c2-c3-c4	B♭	{g''}
Missa Inviolata, 4v	—	g2-c2-c3-c4/f3	c	{g''}
Missa Assumpta est Maria, 4v	♭	c3-c4/c5-f4-f5	{C}	a'
D final				
Missa O gloriosa domina, 4v	—	g2-c2-c3-c4	c	{g''}
Missa de septem doloribus, 5v	—	c1-c4-c4-c4-f4	{D}	d''
Missa Tous les regretz, 4v	—	c2-c4-c4-f4	{D}	d''
Missa L'homme armé I, 4v	—	c2/c3-c4-c5-f5	{C}	a'
?[Missa sine nomine II], 4v	—	c2/c3-f3-f4-f5	{D}	b'
Missa Conceptio tua, 5v	—	c3-c4/f3-f3-f4-f5	{C}	a'
E final				
Missa de feria, 5v	—	c1-c4-c3/c4-f4	{E}	d''
Missa Ista est speciosa, 5v	—	c1/c2-c4-c3/c4-f3/f4-f5	{D}	d''
Credo, 6v	—	c2-c2-c4-c5-f4-f5	{D}	c''
F final				
*Missa de virginibus, 4v	—	g2/c1-c2/c3-c3-c4/f3	{F}	{f''}
*Credo Angeli archangeli, 8v	♭	g2/g2-c1/c3-c4/c4-f3/f4	{F}	{g''}
Credo l'amour du moy, 4v	♭	c1-c2-c3-f3	B♭	{f''}
Missa de Sancta Anna, 4v	♭	c2-c2-c3-f3	{F}	{f''}
Missa Alleluia, 5v	♭	c2-c3/c4-c4-c4/f3/f4-f4	{C}	c''
Missa Almana, 4v	♭	c2-c4-c4-f4	{F}	c''
G final				
Missa Cum iocunditate, 4–5v	—	c1-c1-c3/c4-c4-f4	G	d''
*Kyrie in festo pasche, 4v	—	c1-c3-c4-f4	{F}	d''
Missa Incessament, 5v	—	c1-c3-c4-f4	G	e''
[Kyrie pascale], 5v	—	c1-c3-c4-c4-f4	G	e''
M. Ave sanctissima Maria, 6v	—	c2-c4-f4	{F}	e''
[Missa L'homme armé II], 4v	—	c3-c4-c4-f4	{F}	e''
Missa Puer natus est, 4v	♭	c1-c3-c3-c4/f3	G	{f''}
*Missa sine nomine I, 4v	♭	c1-c3-c4-f4	G	e''
Missa de Sancto Job, 4v	♭	c1-c3-c4-f4	{F}	{g''}
Missa O salutaris hostia, 4v	♭		{F}	d''

TABLE 3.4. (*cont.*)

A final

Missa Ave Maria, 4–5v		—	g2-c3-c3-c3-f3	A	{g´´}
Missa de Sancto Antonio, 4v		—	c1-c3-c3-c4	A	{f´}
Missa de sancta cruce, 5v		♭	g2-c2-c3-c3-f3	A	{f´}
Credo de villagiis, 4v		♭♭	g2-c2-c3-f3	A	{f´}

Mixed final

Missa de beata virgine, 4v					
4 different finals, w&w/o flat			g2/c1-c3-c3/c4-c4/f3/f4	{F}	{g´´}
Missa pro fidelibus, 4–5v					
4 different finals, various accidentals, each mvt. w/new cleffing				{B♭}	d´´
M. Tandernaken, 4v					
various accidentals	A/D		c2-c4-c4-f4	{F}	d´´
Missa Sub tuum, 4v	E/A	—	c1-c3-c4-f4	{E}	d´´
Missa Sancta dei, 4v	E/A	—	c1-c3/c4-c4-f4	G	d´´
Missa Nuncqua fue, 4v	G/E	—	c1-c3-c3-f3	G	{f´}
Missa pascale, 5v	G/E	—	c1/c2-c3-c4-c4-f4	{F}	d´´

La Rue's expected penchant for continual variety, with finals on six different scale degrees, with and without signature accidentals, and with an extraordinary list of cleffing combinations. Although various cleffing combinations recur, none predicts a specific final or range. Further, Table 3.4 also shows that La Rue freely changes clefs between movements, and in the concluding group of pieces shifts finals between movements at will. While this is to be expected in the *Missa de beata virgine* and the *Requiem*, based on the liturgically appropriate chants, it is quite surprising in most of the other masses.

Table 3.4 also clearly demonstrates how often La Rue transgressed the traditional gamut.[26] Although two of his immediate predecessors, Ockeghem and Tinctoris, made noteworthy contributions to the extension downwards of the written range,[27] no one in La Rue's generation or at any time earlier tapped the lower depths with the frequency that La Rue did. Table 3.4 highlights infractions of the gamut with curly brackets; while most of these are merely to low *F* (and none is higher than *f´´* or *g´´*), La Rue also stooped to *E*, *D*, *C*, and *B♭* in a full dozen of these works. I do not plan to argue that fixed pitch is intended here[28] (though we should remember that Mahler's Second Symphony consigns the

---

[26] Similar transgressions in the motets and Magnificats are demonstrated in Table 3.5.

[27] See Kenneth Kreitner, 'Very Low Ranges in the Sacred Music of Ockeghem and Tinctoris', *Early Music*, 14 (1986), 467–79 at 467. Kreitner also provides a list of earlier experiments in extreme ranges; see p. 470.

[28] Although the court always travelled with an organ and thus had the potential for a fixed-pitch reference, and the accounts of the first trip to Spain mention organ playing during the services, it is not clear exactly what the organ's role was. Further, positive organs of the time (which is what the court would have used while travelling, and perhaps even when not) usually began at *B*, too high for the lowest notes of many of these works.

TABLE 3.5. Motet and Magnificat cleffing, range, and final

{ } High and low pitches exceeding the gamut.
[ ] No sixteenth-century ascription to La Rue.
 ? Work is of problematic authenticity.
 * Piece survives in a single source.

	Third in final	Low pitch	High pitch	Final	Signature	Cleffing
Magnificats						
*Magnificat primi toni, 3–6v	—	{D}	c''	D	—	c2-c3-c4-c4-f4-f5
Magnificat secundi toni, 2–4v	—	d	{g''}	D	—	g2-c1/c2-c2/c3-c3/c4
Magnificat quarti toni, 3–4v	—	G	e''	E	—	g3-c3-c4-f4
Magnificat quinti toni, 2–4v	—	A	{f''}	A	—	c1-c3-c3-f3
Magnificat sexti toni, 3–5v	—	{F}	d''	F	—	c1/c2-c2-c3/c4-c4/f4-f4
Magnificat septimi toni, 3–4v	—	d	{g''}	G	♭	g2-c2-c3-c4/f4
*Magnificat octavi toni, 2–4v	—	{F}	d''	G	—	c1-c3-c4-f4
Motets						
?[Absalon fili mi], 4v	—	{B♭}a♭'		B♭	♭♭	c3-c4-f4-f5
Ave regina celorum, 4v	×	{F}	d''	F	♭	c1-c3-c4-f4
[Ave sanctissima Maria], 6v	×	{F}	d''	G	—	c2-c4-f4
Considera Israel, 4v	—	{F}	d''	E	—	c1-c3-c4-f4
Da pacem Domine, 4v	—	c	e''	G	—	c2-f4
Delicta iuventutis, 4v	—	G	d''	E	—	c2-c3-c4-f4
*Gaude virgo, 4v	—	A	{g''}	D	—	g2-c2-c3-c4
Lauda anima mea dominum, 4v	—	{F}	{f''}	D	♭	g2-c3-c4-f5
*Laudate dominum, 4v	—	{D}	d''	D	—	c1-c2-c4-f4
[Maria mater gratie/Fors seulement], 5v	—	A	{f''}	A	♭	g2-c2-c4-[ ]-f4
*O domine Jhesu Christe, 4v	—	A	{f''}	D	—	g2-c2-c3-f3
[O salutaris hostia], 4v	—	A	c''	F	♭	g2-c2-c3-f3
Pater de coelis deus, 6v	×	{D}	d''	D	—	c1-c3-c3-c4-c4-f4
*Quis dabit pacem, 4v	—	{E}	d''	E	—	c1-c4-c4-f4
*Regina celi, 4v	—	{F}	d''	E	—	c1-c3-c4-f4
Salve mater salvatoris, 4v	—	{D}	a'	D	—	c3-c4-f4-f5
Salve regina I, 4v	—	{D}	d''	D	—	c1-c3-c4-f4
Salve regina II, 4v	—	{F}	d''	D	—	c1-c3-c4-f4
*Salve regina III, 4v	—	A	{g''}	A	—	g2-c2-c3-c4
*Salve regina IV, 4v	×	A	{g''}	D	—	g2-c2-c3-c4
*Salve regina V, 4v	—	A	{f''}	A	—	g2-c2-c3-f3
Salve regina VI, 4v	—	G	d''	G	♭	c1-c3-c4-f4
Sancta Maria virgo, 3v	—	A	e''	A	—	c1-c4-f4
Si dormiero, 3v	—	G	e''	A	—	c1-c4-f4
Vexilla regis/Passio domini, 4v	—	{F}	b♭'	D	♭	c1-c4-c4-f4

basses to low *B*♭ at one point), but the extension of the range in three-quarters of this mass music strongly suggests that the court chapel had excellent low basses, and that La Rue regularly took advantage of this special sonority.[29]

EXAMPLES OF BORROWING
IN LA RUE'S SACRED MUSIC

No models were more favoured by La Rue than those drawn from the vast reper-toire of plainchant that still constituted the bulk of sacred music throughout his lifetime. All too often, however, we cannot pinpoint the precise versions used in his masses. One would think this task might be fairly simple; the court, where he spent his last two dozen years of employment and which presumably formed the original venue for all of his surviving sacred music, followed the liturgical use of Paris, as stated in the various *états* governing the function of the chapel. But not only is it exceedingly difficult to reconstruct liturgies of this time, there was more than one use of Paris.[30] As a result, little progress has been made in determining just what his chant models were.[31]

The process is further complicated by the knowledge that La Rue was surely exposed to other chant traditions and may have been drawing on them rather than the use of Paris. His presumed Tournai upbringing, and probable training in the Tournai *maîtrise*, would make the use of Tournai his first chant repertoire. The years prior to joining the court, wherever they were spent, doubtless exposed him to other traditions as well. In addition, an inventory of Marguerite's possessions lists two missals of the use of Rome, one a manuscript and the other a printed version.[32] Was the use of Rome another possible source for La Rue? To add to the difficulties, his propensity for paraphrasing his models adds another layer of chal-lenge to sorting out what they really looked like originally.

In contrast to the uncertainty surrounding many of his chant models, his poly-phonic models—with the exception of that for the *Missa Alleluia*—are readily known and thus much easier to trace within his derived works. The following two sections examine several of the more unusual examples of La Rue's use of poly-phonic models.

---

[29] Low ranges are also found in motets and secular works, heightening this probability. Three masses and two motets have works whose highest clef is c3, giving an overall dark sound to the timbre; these are *Missa Assumpta est Maria, Missa Conceptio tua, Missa L'homme armé II, Absalon fili mi,* and *Salve mater salvatoris.* On the other hand, six sacred works eschew the bass clef altogether: the four-voice Credo, *Missa O gloriosa domina, Missa de Sancto Antonio, Gaude virgo,* and *Salve Regina III* and *IV.*

[30] See Barbara Haggh, 'Binchois and Sacred Music at the Burgundian Court', in Andrew Kirkman and Dennis Slavin (eds.), *Binchois Studies* (Oxford: Oxford University Press, 2000), 1–25.

[31] The best work so far is found in Bloxam, 'A Survey of Late Medieval Service Books', and ead., 'In Praise of Spurious Saints'.

[32] VOS, HHuS, Habsburg-Lotharingisches Familienarchiv, Familien-Urkunden, 827.

Salve regina IV *and the web of tradition*

Two of La Rue's motets use secular polyphonic models. The first, *Maria mater gratie/Fors seulement*, draws on Ockeghem's famous song, using the tenor voice.[33] The model voice is notated at its original pitch, thus emphasizing the connection to Ockeghem's song. The indication *in dyapason* instructs the performer to transpose it down an octave. The borrowed melody is presented with minor variants only and essentially retains the original rhythms and pitches. The A and B sections of the chanson tenor are fitted into the first and second parts of the motet, but the switch in genre obviously precludes rondeau performance. As we shall see in Chapter 4, the procedures used here match those of four secular works also based on Ockeghem chansons. These works and La Rue's motet belong to the large families of art-song reworkings so popular at the time, and all are straightforward in their references.

The other motet based on secular polyphony is considerably more complex, not in its treatment of the borrowed material but rather in its intricate web of connections to other pieces and traditions. La Rue's *Salve regina IV*,[34] an *alternatim* setting, borrows from the Marian antiphon of the same name as well as Dufay's rondeau *Par le regard* in its first polyphonic section (*Vita dulcedo*) and Binchois's *Je ne vis oncques la pareille* in the third and fourth parts (*Et Jesum* and *O pia*). Both of these highly popular courtly models, with their love-inspired texts, fitted well symbolically in their new Marian context. The first and third sections of the motet use the superius of their respective polyphonic models, placed in the highest (and thus most audible) voice. La Rue follows *Par le regard* closely, both in terms of melody and rhythm, for most of the first section. Only when he gets to the final verse of the original rondeau does he begin to alter the material rhythmically, with some stretching out of note values. But the melodic borrowing remains almost exact, allowing for easy recognition of the tune. He transposed the line up a fifth, making it even more prominent; it ascends to G above the treble staff. There is no mistaking this song. In the third section, *Je ne vis oncques la pareille*, likewise placed up a fifth, is treated even more literally, with only the merest of alterations present.

The fourth section proceeds somewhat differently. Here the first nine breves of the tenor from *Je ne vis oncques la pareille* (again transposed up a fifth) appear in the altus at twice *integer valor*. Apart from the augmentation, both melody and rhythm of the borrowed voice are exactly like the original. Motifs derived from the superius of Binchois's work direct the other voices in imitative play, but the contrast between the rapid, freely treated motifs and the slow-moving altus makes this not the usual polyphonic borrowing.

---

[33] Although anonymous in its two sources, VienNB Mus. 18746 and BrusBR 228 (both from the Habsburg-Burgundian court), the work's style and provenance argue strongly for La Rue's authorship.

[34] I follow the numbering used in LRE ix, which in this case, though not the others, accords with the earlier system used in StaehelinNG.

TABLE 3.6 Relationships among La Rue's *Salve regina IV* and other pieces

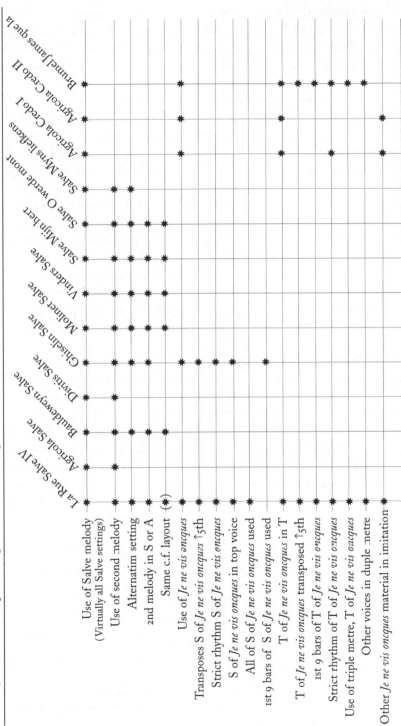

What traditions is La Rue involved with here? As it turns out, several simultaneously (see Table 3.6). Polyphonic *Salve reginas* between 1425 and 1550 typically paraphrased the chant melody, sometimes beyond recognition.[35] La Rue follows that practice here as well as in his other *Salve* settings,[36] but it is his favourite way of treating a borrowed melody anyway, as we have already noted for the masses. The strictness of his polyphonic model treatment in *Maria mater gratie/Fors seulement* as well as in secular works (to be discussed in Ch. 4) is in strong contrast to his preferred practice. Further, the songs trump the chant in that all other material in the motet must accede to the structure imposed by the *cantus firmus*.

A second tradition involved here is that of using another melody in addition to the chant. This is not all that common; of the 129 polyphonic *Salves* from 1425 to 1550 only fifteen pieces besides La Rue's do this.[37] Yet it is possible, if not likely, that La Rue knew nine of the fifteen.[38] Eight pieces appear in the same manuscript as La Rue's *Salve regina IV*: MunBS 34, prepared at the Habsburg-Burgundian court (albeit after La Rue's death) and devoted exclusively to polyphonic *Salves*. An additional work La Rue could have known is one of Agricola's settings, which uses the tenor of Walter Frye's *Ave regina caelorum* strictly; it was apparently written before Agricola became La Rue's colleague at the Habsburg-Burgundian court[39] and may have accompanied him when he joined the court chapel.

The eight pieces on secular models that accompany La Rue's in MunBS 34 are works by Bauldeweyn (on *Je n'ay deuil*), Divitis (on *Adieu mes amours*), Ghiselin (on *Je ne vis oncques*), Molinet (on *O werde mont*), and Vinders (on *Ghy syt*) as well as anonymous works based on *Mijn hert* (drawing on La Rue's song of the same name), *O werde mont*, and *Myns liefkens*. Divitis and Molinet were both La Rue's colleagues in the court chapel, and Bauldeweyn worked in the same city for several years (as *Magister cantorum* at Sint Rombaut's in Mechelen from 1509 to 1512). Ghiselin's compositions were well known at court, and Vinders's piece may have entered the court repertoire before La Rue's retirement in 1516. We thus have a group of ten pieces (including La Rue's) that possibly reflect compositional connections.

Eight of the ten works are *alternatim* settings of the text,[40] with chant used for the even verses and polyphony for the odd (*Vita dulcedo, Ad te suspiramus, Et Jesum,*

---

[35] On polyphonic *Salve regina* settings see Sonja Stafford Ingram, 'The Polyphonic Salve Regina, 1425–1550' (Ph.D. diss., University of North Carolina, 1973).

[36] La Rue wrote six *Salve regina* settings, more than any other composer of the time. One can easily surmise that borrowing the songs was one way he could create variety in the context of his many settings.

[37] See the discussion of borrowed tunes in Ingram, 'The Polyphonic Salve Regina', 106–19.

[38] La Rue is less likely to have known the works by Senfl and Gombert or the settings in OxfBC 213, TrentC 89, and MunBS 3154.

[39] Martin Just, *Der Mensuralkodex Mus. ms. 40021 der Staatsbibliothek Preußischer Kulturbesitz Berlin: Untersuchungen zum Repertoire einer deutschen Quelle des 15. Jahrhunderts*, 2 vols. (Würzburger musikhistorische Beiträge, 1; Tutzing: Hans Schneider, 1975), ii. 32, places it in a section of BerlS 40021 completed by 1498.

[40] Agricola's and Divitis's settings are of the full text.

and *O pia*). The two that are not *alternatim* settings, those by Agricola and Divitis, differ in another way from most of the other settings in that they place their model melody in the tenor voice. One of the *alternatim* settings, that using *Myns liefkens*, also puts its tune in the tenor. All the remaining, including La Rue's work, display the borrowed secular melody prominently and in a straightforward manner in either the highest or second highest voice.[41]

Sonja Ingram noted that five pieces (the works by Molinet, Vinders, and Bauldeweyn, and the anonymous ones on *Mijn hert* and *O werde mont*) follow a similar layout of the cantus firmus: the tune spread once over the first two sections while appearing complete in the third section and in part in the fourth—remember how the *Myns liefkens* setting, which does not match this, had its secular tune in the tenor. Ghiselin's setting also differs (though the tune is in the top voice); we shall return to this setting shortly.

While not matching the layout shared by these works precisely, La Rue's setting presents a variant of it. He uses two secular melodies and puts the first in the initial section only, but the third presents *Je ne vis oncques* complete and the fourth gives it in part. Thus La Rue's work fits within not only the general polyphonic *Salve* tradition but also a much smaller group of works using borrowed secular melodies in the top voices of *alternatim* settings.

But there is more. La Rue's choice of *Je ne vis oncques* was not just made as a generational match to *Par le regard* but as another gesture to another group of related pieces. These are works built on *Je ne vis oncques*, a small but rather interesting collection. The song was extremely popular in its own right, and had a surprising appeal for composers of La Rue's generation, with derivative works including two Credos by Agricola, Josquin's *L'amye a tous*, Brumel's *James que la*, Obrecht's *Missa Plurimorum carminum I* (all using the tenor), Ghiselin's *Salve regina* on the superius, and La Rue's setting, which uses both superius and tenor.[42] Whether La Rue would have known Josquin's chanson or Obrecht's mass is unclear, but he certainly knew the works just mentioned by Ghiselin, Brumel, and his colleague Agricola (for at least one of the settings) since they all appear in court manuscripts; it is extremely likely that he knew Agricola's other setting as well.[43]

Ghiselin's *Salve* setting, like La Rue's, places the superius of the model in the top voice. Each transposes the melody up a fifth; each follows the original rhythm strictly. They differ in that Ghiselin places the tune in the opening section while La Rue puts it in the third, and Ghiselin stops after the first nine breves (first phrase) of the original whereas La Rue uses the whole tune.

Brumel's setting, like La Rue's, places the tenor of the model in an interior

---

[41] Molinet's work sets the tune in the secundus discantus, but this voice often crosses its supposedly higher neighbour and is, in the *Ad suspiramus*, the highest voice, since the superius drops out.

[42] For additional settings see the list in David Fallows, *A Catalogue of Polyphonic Songs 1415–1480* (Oxford: Oxford University Press, 1999), 216.

[43] The works appear respectively in MunBS 34, FlorC 2439, VienNB 1783 (for Agricola's second Credo), and *Fragmenta missarum* (1505[1]) (for Agricola's first Credo).

voice; in La Rue it is the altus, in Brumel the tenor, though the tenor usually sounds above the altus in his setting. Each transposes the melody up a fifth, and each uses only the first nine breves. Each follows the original rhythm strictly and each maintains the triple mensuration of the original for that voice. More striking, each surrounds the borrowed voice with more rapidly moving lines in duple metre, so both employ metric tension within a similar texture. They differ in that Brumel also presents the borrowed phrase in retrograde motion, and his is a secular work.

Agricola's two Credo settings each employ the tenor; the first setting uses it strictly while the second uses it freely. Both settings commence with imitative entries in superius and altus that draw on the melodic material of the model's superius; La Rue does this too, including the bassus in the imitation as well and bringing back related motifs later in the *O pia* section. The settings differ in that Agricola's tenors are silent during the use of the superius material in other voices, while La Rue cannot afford in such a short section to leave out his borrowed cantus firmus.

In this complex web of influence, then, La Rue draws on the general tradition of *Salve* settings as well as a much more limited one employing borrowed secular melodies, and he makes reference to the four other pieces built on *Je ne vis oncques* that he is likely to have known from court.

Both *Maria mater gratie/Fors seulement* and *Salve regina IV* shun polyphonic borrowing, with one brief exception. It is evident that La Rue was closely adhering to the generic norms for these motets based on secular models. Within the large *Fors seulement* family, an unambiguous cantus-firmus setting is standard procedure, and La Rue composed accordingly.[44] Similarly, *Salve* settings normally incorporate the chant melody, making polyphonic borrowing from a model much less likely, and we find almost none in this *Salve* setting. La Rue's adherence to almost fanatically literal borrowing in these works is even more striking given his overwhelming preference for paraphrasing his models. Indeed, as noted before, normally one of the major problems in analysing La Rue's music is the difficulty of unearthing the original in his heavily paraphrased versions.

These motets, with their strict cantus-firmus treatment, provide an interesting contrast to La Rue's masses based on polyphonic models. Four of these masses demonstrate an extremely logical continuum in terms of the treatment of the model. The *Missa Nuncqua fue pena maior*, in the earliest group of sources, is a four-voice mass based on Urrede's three-voice song, but normally it only uses two of the model's three voices. The *Missa Tous les regretz*, also for four voices, is based on La Rue's own four-voice model and uses all four voices of the original material. The *Missa Incessament* and *Missa Ave sanctissima Maria*, five and six voices respectively, draw on La Rue's own five- and six-voiced models (all voices) and emulate the canonic structures of their models: a foundation canon in *Incessament* and total

---

[44] On *Fors seulement* and other art-song reworkings see Meconi, 'Art-Song Reworkings'.

canonic texture in *Ave sanctissima Maria*. It is as if La Rue kept raising the compositional bar with the number of voices borrowed continually rising and canonic restrictions going from non-existent to totally controlling. No work uses any voice of its model in strict cantus-firmus fashion, as the motets did; rather each paraphrases its material, borrows polyphonically, and is increasingly dependent on the model for its polyphonic construction.

Lacking knowledge of the *Missa Alleluia*'s borrowed material, it is difficult to know just where to place that work within La Rue's borrowing practice. The *Credo Angeli archangeli*, on the other hand, seems to occupy a middle ground between the two motets with polyphonic models and the masses. The model is Isaac's six-voice motet of the same name (copied in VatC 234), which uses texts for the Feast of All Saints. La Rue expands the six voices to eight, giving himself at least something of a creative challenge, and again borrows polyphonically in prominent places. In contrast to the masses, two of the three sections of the work are built on fairly strict cantus-firmus treatment of one of the voices of the model, but the selection of borrowed voice was not an accident; it is the tenor, itself drawn from Binchois's famous and much copied song *Comme femme* (which, interestingly enough, generated more motets than usual for the average big art-song reworking family).[45] La Rue, then, makes a kind of compromise between genres by using a strict cantus firmus, the way he does when he takes part in a compositional tradition such as that of *Comme femme* settings, but larding it with polyphonic borrowing the way he usually does when taking over a polyphonic model. We have a kind of parallel here with the *Missa de Sancto Job*; although the chants are the borrowed material in that mass, it is really Pipelare's use of them that is borrowed. The same goes for the Binchois model: Isaac's setting of the melody and resultant polyphony are the source for La Rue's Credo rather than the Binchois song itself.

La Rue, Josquin, and hidden borrowing

The masses just cited have a trait in common: their borrowing occurs in prominent places, leaving no doubt aurally as to the identity of their models. In marked contrast to this, several of La Rue's masses employ a kind of hidden borrowing, where pre-existent material from something other than the main model occupies a secondary and fleeting existence within the mass.[46] In several instances these subsidiary models seem to be unidentified plainchant (see the annotations in App. D), but others are from well-known pieces: *Tant que nostre argent durra* shows up in the final Agnus of the *Missa L'homme armé I*, and a bit of the *L'homme armé* melody in the *Missa Sancta dei genitrix* (both, interestingly enough, appear in the lowest voice, which might be the most likely place to search for other examples).[47]

---

[45] See the lists ibid. 26–36.

[46] This kind of hidden borrowing is different from that of the *Missa de Sancto Job* or *Credo Angeli archangeli*, where La Rue borrows original material via an intermediary, though all of these examples indicate a kind of cleverness that is quite different from that employed in traditional cantus-firmus manipulation.

[47] La Rue practises subsidiary borrowing in secular music, too: his setting of Ockeghem's *Ma bouche rit* also uses material from that composer's *Je n'ay deuil* (first noted in Pirro, *Histoire de la musique*, 229).

Ex. 3.1. Comparison of (*a*) Josquin, *Ave Maria ... virgo serena*, conclusion (from SegC s.s., fos. 84ᵛ–85ʳ), with (*b*) La Rue, *Missa de septem doloribus*, Osanna II (from VatS 36, fos. 29ᵛ–30ʳ)

(*a*)

(*b*)

Ex. 3.1. (*cont.*)

Both of those melodies, however, are anonymous and monophonic in origin. In decided contrast are two mass sections where a polyphonic work by Josquin was the inspiration.

In the first example, the model is Josquin's famous motet *Ave Maria . . . virgo serena*; the new piece is La Rue's *Missa de septem doloribus* (see Ex. 3.1). La Rue borrows only a short portion of a single voice, the closing of the superius line with the words 'O mater dei, memento mei, amen'.[48] This melody is used just once, in the tenor primus of the second Osanna. La Rue's use of it presents a curious mixture of hesitation and boldness, if one may use such terms in describing a kind of borrowing. The tune is transposed down a twelfth; the borrowing is otherwise exact both rhythmically and melodically. Both La Rue and Josquin supply it with a largely homorhythmic texture, though La Rue has both more motion (in altus and tenor secundus) as well as greater stasis (fermatas at the end of *dei* and *mei*). But the registral shift demotes Josquin's line from being the easily audible top of four voices to the less readily perceived interior of a thicker five-voice texture. Even more striking is the change in harmonization; with Josquin the phrase provides the root of both initial and final harmonies (as well as several in between); with La Rue it forms the third in the opening and closing sonorities. Josquin's work is centred on C, with the resulting major-sounding harmonies; La Rue's on D, generating a 'minor' or 'Dorian' feel. Nor is there any use of polyphonic borrowing. In these respects La Rue did an excellent job of masking his new material.

---

[48] This phrase appears in the illumination of Marguerite that occurs at the opening of her personal chansonnier, BrusBR 228. The *Missa de septem doloribus* is first found in the group of manuscripts compiled during Marguerite's governorship of the Low Countries; was La Rue's quotation of this text another subtle gesture towards Marguerite?

At the same time he called attention to it in other ways. Most sources for this part of La Rue's mass[49] include the 'O mater mei, memento mei' text underlaid to the tenor primus at this point. This text is obviously not part of the Osanna; more to the point, it is not part of the extensive auxiliary texting (mostly drawn from the sequence for the feast) that accompanies this mass in its sources. It is a completely extraneous addition.

Second, the very presence of a second Osanna is unusual for La Rue. As noted earlier, in most of his masses the first Osanna is simply repeated after the Benedictus. Exceptions are rare. For the *Missa Tous les regretz,* one court source indicates that the music for the second Kyrie is used for the second Osanna. With the *Missa Assumpta est Maria* the second Osanna is contained within the Benedictus. A separate and newly composed Osanna II section appears only in the *Missa de beata virgine, Missa de Sancta Anna, Missa Sub tuum presidium,* and the mass under discussion. Even in this small group the *O mater dei* Osanna stands out by virtue of its brevity. In the *Missa de Sancta Anna* the first Osanna is the subsitution motet *O salutaris hostia,* obviously an inappropriate choice for repetition. The second Osanna there lasts twenty-seven perfect breves; for the *Missa de beata virgine* and *Missa Sub tuum presidium,* the lengths are eighteen and twenty-one perfect breves respectively. The *O mater dei* Osanna, on the other hand, lasts a mere dozen imperfect breves, making it one of the shortest subsections in any La Rue mass.

A third means of calling attention to this Osanna was not compositional. Simply because the piece is so short it takes up very little room on its manuscript opening, meaning that in some sources it is surrounded by empty parchment. This is especially true in BrusBR 6428. The presentation is visually arresting, and the rubricated text makes it stand out even more. Although it is highly unlikely that La Rue was thinking along these lines as he composed, the singers who performed the work would have noticed it immediately. Even though the resulting performance would hardly draw attention to the borrowed tune (in contrast to the *Salve regina* setting), the musicians would know it was there.

The Pleni of La Rue's *Missa de sancta cruce* provides another example of a 'hidden' model. The rest of the mass is based on the chant *Nos autem gloriari,* the Introit for two feasts for the Holy Cross and thus an obvious choice as model. The Pleni, however, takes as its source the *Missa L'ami baudichon* attributed to Josquin, most specifically the second Agnus, a section that does not use the popular tune at all (see Ex. 3.2).[50]

[49] BrusBR 15075 omits the 'O mater dei' text; VienNB Mus. 18832 has the Pleni only.

[50] This connection was first noticed in Edgar H. Sparks, *Cantus Firmus in Mass and Motet 1420–1520* (Berkeley and Los Angeles: University of California Press, 1963; repr. New York: Da Capo, 1975), 355. For a complete edition of the Josquin mass see Josquin des Prez, *Werken,* ed. Albert Smijers, Myroslaw Antonowycz, and Willem Elders (Amsterdam and Leipzig: Vereniging voor Nederlandse Muziekgeschiedenis, 1921–69), *Missen,* ii. 67–91.

Ex. 3.2. Comparison of (*a*) Josquin, *Missa L'ami baudichon*, Agnus II, bars 1–11 (from *Missarum Josquin liber secundus*), with (*b*) La Rue, *Missa de sancta cruce*, Pleni, bars 1–8 (from MechAS s.s., fos. 75ᵛ–76ʳ)

Both sections are for superius, altus, and bassus, dropping the tenor voice (Josquin) or voices (La Rue). Josquin's Agnus is built on a dotted-rhythm stepwise motif occurring in all voices. La Rue's Pleni can be described the same way, but he constructs his movement somewhat differently. Josquin's initial motif rises three steps and then falls; La Rue extends and repeats the ascending line before introducing downward motion. Both composers play against the inherent triple pulse of the motif, and each brings in the new voices at the rhythmic distance of three semibreves. But while Josquin stretches the motif out over a breve and a half of *tempus imperfectum*, La Rue compresses it into half a perfect breve. La Rue's piece is corresponding brisker in its tumult of motifs, and he gives us two appearances of the motivic kernel before bringing in his second voice.

Once all voices enter (both composers introduce them imitatively) both Josquin and La Rue employ full-voice texture for approximately the first half of the piece. After a sustained C/E sonority in bars 22–4, however, Josquin moves to duet texture for the work's latter half. The superius/bassus duet that first results starts in strict imitation; it then switches to a quasi-pedal point bassus that ultimately leads to a cadence on G at bar 42. Following this, tenor and superius then join in strict imitation until the re-entry of the bassus just before the close of the work. This second half of the work is marked by somewhat less use of the initial motif.

In contrast, La Rue uses all three voices throughout almost the entire piece, and makes much more constant use of the defining motif. He also works with a related, stepwise motif built of semiminims, first seen in the middle voice in bar 3. He makes increasing use of this semiminim motif in the second half of the work, where few measures go by without its presence. The result is, much more than with Josquin, a kind of perpetual motion with a sense of drive and urgency.

Neither work has frequent cadences, yet both Josquin and La Rue display harmonic planning typical for their compositional styles. Josquin generates a C tonal centre right from the start, with two voices beginning on G and rising to C, followed by a third entering on C itself. The linear motion at bar 11 emphasizes C (with the bassus dropping a fifth to C), and the long sustained sonority in bars 22–4 is built on C. The classic suspension cadence at the close leads to C; the bassus again drops a fifth, and the piece concludes on octave Cs. In contrast, La Rue shows his usual harmonic freedom. As frequently happens in his work, the initial imitative entries are on three different pitches, in this case F, B♭, and C. None of these is the final sonority, which is instead A (three octaves in the same registral spacing that Josquin uses).

That La Rue's piece came after Josquin's is highly likely. Unvaried reiteration of a motif, especially for the duration of an entire movement, is rare for La Rue.[51]

---

[51] Though masses (not just those by La Rue) tend to use this kind of motivic interplay in sections that have abandoned the model. One wonders about stylistic connections with sacred tricinia: were the composers of these pieces trying to imitate free mass sections, or the other way around?

His use of such a procedure here makes most sense if he is attempting to outdo Josquin, who eases up on the texture and motif in the second half of his Agnus.

With both the *Missa de septem doloribus* and the *Missa de sancta cruce* we have unexpected treatments of the model. In each case the polyphonic model (one from a motet, one from another mass) is used for a mass whose primary borrowed material is plainchant; in each case this secondary borrowed material inspires a section late in the mass that does not use chant. We receive no clues about the connection to *Missa L'ami baudichon* and not many more for the motet model, since it is the last rather than the first phrase of *Ave Maria* that is borrowed. In the *Missa de septem doloribus* La Rue quotes directly from the *Ave Maria* in a strict cantus-firmus setting of the final phrase; in contrast, the Pleni of the *Missa de sancta cruce* takes the material from the *Missa L'ami baudichon* as a jumping-off point for something that is stylistically similar to the original but is neither cantus firmus nor paraphrase, or even parody. Compared with his treatment of other polyphonic models, these two do not shout out their source but rather operate as extremely clever references for those in the know.

LITURGICAL FUNCTIONS OF LA RUE'S SACRED MUSIC

As outlined in the preceding chapter, the Habsburg-Burgundian court chapel during La Rue's time had a steady performance schedule of a daily polyphonic mass as well as daily services for the final two offices of the day, Vespers and Compline, and these two offices were apparently polyphonic as well, at least in part. On major feast days, as well as during Advent and Lent, the performance requirements were increased to include the other offices as well, sung consecutively at the beginning of the day.

Perhaps the most impressive thing about La Rue's sacred music is the extent to which it fulfils these ongoing musical needs. Table 3.7 aligns La Rue's sacred compositions with the fixed liturgical requirements of the court (presented in bold)[52] and lists his other sacred works as well. Although not every feast has a work by La Rue to suit the occasion, a considerable number do, with multiple works presented in some instances. La Rue wrote a complete cycle of polyphonic Magnificats (surely one of the first) as well as six separate *Salve regina* settings, perhaps used in general Salve services as well as at the end of Compline. The only one of the four major Marian antiphons for which we do not have a setting by La Rue is *Alma redemptoris mater*.

Apart from marking major liturgical dates, other functions for La Rue's masses are readily comprehensible. The Feast of the Seven Sorrows was widely celebrated in votive commemorations, especially by confraternities, and both Philip and

---

[52] Movable feasts are clustered together after 25 Mar.

TABLE 3.7. Liturgy and La Rue's sacred music at the Habsburg-Burgundian court

The *grande chapelle* was required to perform a daily polyphonic mass as well as Vespers and Compline. All offices were to be sung on major feast days (given in bold below) and on each day of Lent and Advent.

[ ] No sixteenth-century ascription to La Rue.
? Work is of problematic authenticity.

	Feast	Work by La Rue
	Daily Vespers	Magnificats I–VIII
	Daily Compline	Ave regina celorum, Regina celi, Salve regina I–VI
	Daily polyphonic mass	Missa de feria
25 Dec.	**Nativity**	Missa Puer natus est
1 Jan.	**Circumcision**	
6 Jan.	**Epiphany**	
17 Jan.	St Anthony Abbot	Missa de Sancto Antonio
2 Feb.	**Purification of the BVM**	Missa Inviolata?
25 Mar.	**Annunciation**	Missa Ave Maria
	Passion Sunday	Vexilla regis/Passio domini
	Saturday before Palm Sunday[a]	Missa de septem doloribus
	Easter	Missa pascale, Kyrie in festo pasche, [Kyrie pascale]
	Eastertide	Missa Alleluia
	Ascension	
	Eve and day of Pentecost	
	Trinity	Pater de coelis deus
	Corpus Christi	O salutaris hostia, Missa O salutaris hostia
3 May	Finding of Holy Cross	Missa de sancta cruce
10 May	St Job	Missa de Sancto Job
24 June	**St John the Baptist**	
29 June	**St Peter**	Petre amas me
2 July	**Visitation**	
20 July	St Margaret	Missa O gloriosa domina
26 July	St Anne	Missa de Sancta Anna
15 Aug.	**Assumption of the BVM**	Missa Assumpta est Maria, Salve mater salvatoris
8 Sept.	**Nativity of the BVM**	Missa Cum iocunditate
14 Sept.	Exaltation of Holy Cross	Missa de sancta cruce
1 Nov.	**All Saints**	Credo Angeli archangeli
2 Nov.	**All Souls**	Requiem
25 Nov.	**St Catherine**	
30 Nov.	**St Andrew**	
4 Dec.	**St Barbara**	
8 Dec.	**Conception of the BVM**	Missa Ave sanctissima Maria, Missa Conceptio tua

TABLE 3.7. (*cont.*)

General Marian masses	Missa Ave sanctissima Maria
	Missa de beata virgine
	Missa Ista est speciosa
	Missa Mediatrix nostra[b]
	Missa Sancta dei genitrix?
	Missa Sub tuum presidium
Other general mass music	Credo, 6v
	Credo, 4v
	Credo de villagiis, 4v
	Requiem
	Missa sine nomine I and ?[II][c]
	Missa de virginibus
Masses on secular models	Credo l'amour du moy
	Missa Almana
	Missa Incessament
	Missa L'homme armé I & [II]
	(Order of the Golden Fleece?)
	Missa Nuncqua (presumably for Juana)
	Missa Tandernaken
	Missa Tous les regretz (presumably for Marguerite)
Political/court-specific motets	
Death of Philip the Fair	?[Absalon fili mi]
	Considera Israel
	Delicta iuventutis?
For peace	Da pacem domine
	Quis dabit pacem?
For Marguerite	Salve mater salvatoris
General Marian motets	[Ave sanctissima Maria]
	Gaude virgo
	[Maria mater gratie/Fors seulement]
Motets for Christ	O domine Jhesu Christe
	Salve Jesu
Psalm motets	Lauda anima mea dominum
	Laudate dominum
Sacred tricina	Sancta Maria virgo
	Si dormiero

[a] See LRE iii, p. xlvii.

[b] Known only from the inventory HeidU 318.

[c] The mass without name listed in HeidU 318 might have been one of these *Sine nomine* masses.

Marguerite had a special veneration for the Virgin of the Seven Sorrows.[53] The long-suffering Saint Job had great significance throughout the Low Countries as well as specifically for Marguerite.[54] The Holy Cross was another familiar votive subject, as was the Holy Sacrament.[55] The court may have followed the common practice of assigning individual days of the week to specific votive subjects (e.g. Monday, the departed; Tuesday, the Holy Spirit; Wednesday, the Trinity; Thursday, the Holy Sacrament; Friday, the Holy Cross; Saturday, Our Lady).[56] If so, certain of La Rue's works might have received performances on a weekly basis.

Other works could speak for more than one occasion. The Marian *Missa O domina gloriosa*, based on a hymn of the same name, was sometimes retitled *Missa O gloriosa Margaretha*, suggesting performance on the feast day of Marguerite's patron saint (20 July) or at any time that the chapel wished to pay special homage to their acting ruler. The *Missa de virginibus*, though technically a mass for the Feast of Virgins, possibly had resonance for the widowed Marguerite as well, for the text of the cantus-firmus, from Wisdom 4: 1, certainly described her: 'O how beautiful is the chaste generation with glory: for the memory thereof is immortal.' One wonders, too, whether the *Missa Puer natus est* would have been performed after the birth of Charles, or whether that would have seemed too sacrilegious.

The mass for St Anne most probably reflects the standard veneration for the mother of the mother of God.[57] More problematic is the third saint's mass that La Rue wrote (three saints' masses are a relatively high number for the time). St Anthony Abbot was the patron saint of the first Duke of Burgundy, Philip the Bold; how long this feast had special meaning at the court is difficult to say. Interestingly, the virtuosic motet *Anthoni usque limina* by Busnoys (whose patron saint was also Anthony Abbot) was copied into BrusBR 5557 and thus known at court (and possibly by La Rue, though no musical connections between Busnoys's motet and La Rue's mass have been traced).

In addition to works meeting specific occasional needs, of course, a number of others were by design multi-purpose, including the *Sine nomine* masses, the general Marian works, and especially the *Missa de feria*, one of the earlier examples of

---

[53] For the latest on this feast and music specifically for it see Barbara Haggh, 'Recovering Meaning in a Manuscript: Brussels, Bibliothèque Royale, MS 215–216, and its Repertory for the Seven Sorrows of the Virgin', *Yearbook of the Alamire Foundation*, 5 (forthcoming).

[54] See Bloxam, 'In Praise of Spurious Saints', 198–9.

[55] See Haggh, 'Music, Liturgy, and Ceremony', i. 383.

[56] See Strohm, *Music in Late Medieval Bruges*, 3. It is possible, however, that the court held to the stipulation in the chapel ordinances to celebrate the appropriate saint's feast day during the week, or failing that, to take its cue from the preceding Sunday; see Item 2 under the discussion of Charles's ordinance in Ch. 2.

[57] Although the court did interact with two contemporary Annes, it is unlikely that either of them would have inspired the work. In July 1515 Anne of Hungary married Charles's younger brother, Ferdinand, by proxy in Vienna, an occasion at which neither La Rue nor the chapel was present. Although the mass is copied only in sources compiled after that date, its consistent use of open fifths as final sonorities and its beginning of each movement in *tempus perfectum* suggest that it is not from the very end of La Rue's compositional career. The other significant Anne the court knew was Anne of Brittany, Queen of France at the time the Habsburg-Burgundian and French courts met in 1501 and 1503. As the former 'wife' of Maximilian (by proxy only), it is unlikely that the court would wish her honoured in such an overt manner.

this genre. Because of their flexibility, these works were arguably even more valuable than the others mentioned above. In addition, the court would also occasionally 'mix and match' movements from different masses, thus increasing the versatility of certain compositions. A striking example is La Rue's *Credo de villagiis*, which usurps the original Credo of Obrecht's *Missa Sicut spina rosam* in that mass's appearance in VatS 160, thereby sabotaging the original compositional layout of the cycle.

La Rue's chant masses obviously suited the needs of the court extremely well, but we must also ask ourselves if a desire for personal salvation generated such an intensive concentration on sacred models. What little we know of him as a person indicates a devout man and one who took major religious orders; no evidence exists of violating choirboys or beating up priests. His testament shows careful plans for the care of his soul after his death, and it hardly seems surprising that the line he took from Josquin's *Ave Maria* was 'O mater dei, memento mei'. Moreover, at least in the case of his motet *Ave sanctissima Maria* and the mass based on it, indulgences might have accrued from its performance.[58] It is almost as if La Rue's relatively limited use of secular models represented a kind of private Counter-Reformation before the actual Reformation itself.

He did, of course, use secular models on occasion. While he probably had some purely musical desires for reworking secular material, extra-musical motivations are possible and in some cases likely. As noted, in the *Missa Nuncqua fue pena maior* the model was surely chosen for Juana's attention. Similarly, the *Missa Tous les regretz* must have been yet another work destined for Marguerite's ear, since it is based on the chanson La Rue undoubtedly wrote for her when she returned from France. The *L'homme armé* masses enabled La Rue to take his place in the already venerable tradition, and they might also have been performed at gatherings of the Order of the Golden Fleece. Although only two major meetings were held during La Rue's time at court, and one of them without the traditional ceremonies, lesser ones still occurred regularly. The liturgical services typically included both a Requiem mass and a Marian mass, presenting more possibilities for La Rue's music to be performed.[59]

The impetus behind the other secular-derived works is more difficult to make out, though the *Missa Incessament*, as noted above, forms part of a continuum of compositional challenge and was based on an extremely popular work. Both *Tandernaken* and *L'amour du moy* were well-known monophonic tunes; that may have been sufficient justification for new works, though perhaps the resultant masses had a now-lost significance related somehow to the court's travels (and similarly for the *Missa Almana*).

---

[58] On this possibility, at least for the motet, see Bonnie J. Blackburn, 'For Whom Do the Singers Sing?', *Early Music*, 25 (1997), 593–609 at 595.

[59] On the meetings of the Order of the Golden Fleece, at which the chapel was required to be present, see Prizer, 'Music and Ceremonial'. The Requiem mass performed was apparently that of Dufay (ibid. 133),

With none of La Rue's contemporaries do we find an apparent preoccupation with full-fledged mass settings for specific liturgical functions; certainly the cycles of neither Obrecht nor Josquin demonstrate this. Even Isaac, who has a vast quantity of liturgically appropriate music (even more than La Rue), appears to be working from a different aesthetic: masses that fit obviously into the service are typically either cyclic settings of the Proper (the *Choralis Constantinus* collections) or multiple settings of series of mass Ordinary chants (e.g. four for Easter, five *de beata virgine* masses, and so on), normally in *alternatim* settings. By and large, too, Isaac's works in this area seem to come from the later part of his life and were in part generated by a commission,[60] whereas a liturgical focus seems both to have been a near-constant with La Rue and to have come from his own impulses.

This statement, with the implication that his compositions were not generated at the request of his employers, is of course not provable. But if the successive leaders of the chapel were the spur to La Rue's compositional efforts, he was being rather dramatically singled out, for his colleagues at the court contributed little towards specific liturgical occasions. Not only were they conspicuously less prolific than he when it came to sacred music, they also normally preferred secular models for their masses, though there are various multi-purpose masses such as de Orto's *Missa domenicalis*. None of Weerbeke's or de Orto's masses suits a specific liturgical occasion, and for Agricola only the *Missa paschalis* has a precise liturgical fit. One of Champion's two masses, his *Missa supra Maria Magdalena*, would be appropriate for her feast day. In one other case, Divitis's *Missa Gaude Barbara* would be a match for the Feast of St Barbara, a major day at the court.

As for La Rue's numerous predecessors at the court, most are known today primarily or exclusively for secular music. One piece that matched a specific liturgical connection is Busnoys's *Missa O crux lignum triumphale*, which, like La Rue's *Missa de sancta cruce*, is suitable for both the Finding of the Holy Cross and the Exaltation of the Holy Cross, or a possible weekly votive service. This work may post-date Busnoys's Burgundian service, however.[61] Only with Binchois do we find a significant amount of sacred music, some of it recalling the important feasts listed in the court ordinances, e.g. the two psalm antiphons *Inter natos mulierum* for the feast of St John the Baptist. But certainly the scale of the mass music is much smaller than that of La Rue, with no complete cycles but rather a collection of paired and single movements.

We have already seen, of course, that the chapel often needed to rely on composers outside the chapel for their repertoire, and the collection BrusBR 5557, the only sacred manuscript that survives from the chapel before the time of Philip the

meaning that La Rue would have known and performed it; the requirement for a Marian mass could easily have been met by one of La Rue's, though chant as well as music by other composers could have been used.

[60] See discussion of his mass music in Strohm and Kempson, 'Isaac, Henricus', 577–80.

[61] See Antoine Busnoys, *Collected Works, Part 3: The Latin Texted Works*, ed. Richard Taruskin (Masters and Monuments of the Renaissance, 5; New York: Broude Trust, 1990), Commentary vol., 46.

Fair, offers a sample of what they had.[62] Several works here suit exact times in the liturgical calendar: Frye's *Missa Summe trinitati* (Trinity Sunday) and his *Missa Nobilis et pulchra* (St Catherine of Alexandria), the already mentioned *Anthoni usque limina*, Dufay's *Missa Ecce ancilla domini* (for both the Annunciation and the Visitation), Regis's *Missa Ecce ancilla/Ne timeas* (also suited for the Annunciation), and a series of Easter and Christmas motets by court-employed Busnoys (*Noel noel, Ad cenam agni, Victimae paschali laudes, Alleluia verbum caro*) as well as other pieces fitting more generally into the liturgy, such as a Kyrie by Dufay.

We cannot know what would have been in other, now lost, collections of polyphony, and it is highly likely, too, that much of the sacred polyphony performed by the chapel in the fifteenth century, or at least before 1469, was improvised, in which case a suitable repertoire did not have to be on hand. In addition, we have already noted the example of the *Missa de assumptione beate Marie virginis* (cited in Ch. 1) that was performed after the appropriate time. Clearly, perfect liturgical matches and overt functionality were by no means required for religious music in the fifteenth or sixteenth centuries.

We know far too little about music making under the earlier Burgundian dukes, despite stellar work by numerous scholars. Is it possible that there was a steady progression over the decades from a chant mass to one of improvised polyphony to one based on written polyphony? Was La Rue's expansion of the repertoire the culminating step in a process leading to a full, rich collection of masses? Certainly much of La Rue's sacred output seems to be an attempt to fill a perceived vacuum and to create full-fledged, appropriate works for most of the days of the court's greatest ceremony. In this he is unique for his time.[63]

---

[62] NapBN 40 is also from Burgundy, though it was not compiled for use by the chapel. Still, its six *L'homme armé* masses may have been known to the singers. On BrusBR 5557, see the discussion in Howard Mayer Brown, 'Music and Ritual at Charles the Bold's Court: The Function of Liturgical Music by Busnoys and His Contemporaries', in Paula Higgins (ed.), *Antoine Busnoys: Method, Meaning, and Context in Late Medieval Music* (Oxford: Clarendon Press, 1999), 53–70.

[63] As noted above, Isaac differs in writing many *alternatim* masses (typically multiple ones for the same purpose) and much work on commission.

4 Aspects of the Secular Music

OVERVIEW

La Rue's secular music presents a very different picture from his sacred music, and not merely because the latter was used for devotional purposes. In contrast to the masses and mass movements, the secular music seems to have circulated much less widely, even though there are slightly more total pieces (probably between forty-one and forty-three secular works, in contrast to a probable thirty-eight or thirty-nine masses and mass movements, though the sacred pieces are obviously far more commanding in length). The reason for this is simple: the manuscripts from the Habsburg-Burgundian scriptorium were the major outlet for La Rue's music, and the scriptorium generated far fewer chansonniers than mass collections.[1] Despite this somewhat lesser dissemination, certain of the songs made a considerable impact, especially *Mijn hert*, *Pourquoy non*, and *Incessament*. Furthermore, La Rue was one of the most productive and significant secular composers in the first two decades of the sixteenth century, noteworthy in part for making little use of secular monophony, a major source of borrowed material for most of his contemporaries. The author of his epitaph may have considered his secular music important, too, for it contains the ambiguous line 'he was pleasing because of his "cantum"', which can mean either his 'singing' or simply his 'song', with the implication of secular music. Finally, secular music is another realm where La Rue was apparently intent on making his compositional mark at the court from the very beginning.

Three major chansonniers survive from the court, along with three other collections containing secular music.[2] These latter three are VienNB 9814 (predominantly a collection of motets, with one anonymous chanson), VienNB Mus. 18832 (a collection of bicinia, some still unidentified, including one secular work attributed elsewhere to La Rue), and OxfBA 831, a fragmentary source that now only contains three secular works, none by La Rue. The major court chansonniers are the ones that contain the bulk of La Rue's secular music: FlorC 2439, compiled for an unknown member of the Agostini-Ciardi family of Siena around 1505–8; BrusBR 228, written for Marguerite sometime between 1508 and 1516; and VienNB Mus. 18746, a set of partbooks of five-voice works owned by (and pre-

---

[1] There are various reasons for this, including the fact that mass music was more impersonal and thus more versatile, as it were. Manuscript chansonniers of the time tended to be highly personal and very individualized collections. For more on this, see Meconi, 'The Function of the Habsburg-Burgundian Court Manuscripts'.

[2] For an overview of secular music at the court, see Meconi, 'Pierre de la Rue and Secular Music'.

sumably prepared for) the avid music collector Raimund Fugger the Elder; the collection is dated 1523.

Table 4.1 lists La Rue's secular music in the approximate chronological order in which it appears in surviving sources. As with the source chronology for the mass music, the ordering of pieces here should not automatically be interpreted as representing early, middle, and late works (not least because there are four subsections). Again, however, certain patterns are suggestive, with early pieces often standing out through unusual or special texts or elements of composition.

Five of the first six pieces are works that definitely preceded the compilation of FlorC 2439. Most appeared in Petrucci's alphabet series of chansonniers: *Pourquoy non* in the *Odhecaton* (1501), *Ce n'est pas jeu* and *Tous les regretz* in *Canti B* (1502²), and both *Mijn hert* and *Pourquoy tant* in *Canti C* (1504³). Except for *Mijn hert*, these works and another chanson, *Il viendra le jour désiré*, are all in the problematic collection BrusBR 11239. Although it was ultimately owned by Marguerite (it is in the 1523 inventory of her books but cannot be confirmed in the 1516 inventory), it is unclear at what point it came into her possession. The coat of arms is that of Savoy, but it also matches that of more than two dozen other contemporary families, and the lack of any armorial device for Marguerite makes it extremely unlikely that it was intended as a bridal gift. The second-rate, generic decoration seems more likely to stem from northern France,[3] though it is too early to rule out Savoyard origin (the manuscript is not listed in the latest surviving inventory of the Savoy ducal library, that of 1498).[4] The date of ca. 1500 usually suggested for the collection comes from the lack of armorial representation of Marguerite, who married the Duke of Savoy in 1501, but it is more likely just slightly later (and as we have just seen, four of the works in it were already in circulation far from Habsburg-Burgundy by the early years of the sixteenth century).

Two different hypotheses would account for the presence of Savoyard arms (if that is really what they are), the absence of any armorial reference to Marguerite, and the presence of a large number of works by La Rue (his motet *Vexilla regis/ Passio domini* is also included). The book may have been first owned by Marguerite's future husband Philibert himself,[5] put together before his marriage from pieces at hand as well as music obtained via ambassadors during the negotiations for Philibert's marriage (thus the date suggested in App. B, 1501). Marguerite would then have acquired the book following Philibert's death in 1504. Or could the book have been owned first by Philibert's successor, Charles III? If this were the case, perhaps the collection—though not originally intended for her and thus

---

[3] This statement is difficult to document because of the concentration of art historical scholarship on the exceptional rather than the mundane. My assertions are based on my own observations as well as conversations with art historians; I am especially grateful to Rowan Watson and Jeffrey Hamburger for their help.

[4] The library of the dukes of Savoy was one of the great ones of the era; see Sheila Edmunds, 'The Medieval Library of Savoy', *Scriptorium*, 24 (1970), 318–27; 25 (1971), 253–84; 26 (1972), 269–93.

[5] That Philibert was the original owner was assumed without discussion in W[inn] Marvin, '"Regrets" in French Chanson Texts', 208.

TABLE 4.1. Overview of secular music

Compositions are ordered in four groups arranged chronologically by source. The four groups contain pieces that appear first in (1) very early sixteenth-century sources, (2) FlorC 2439, arranged by number of voices, (3) BrusBR 228, arranged by number of voices, plus VatV 11953 (*Saulliés avant*), (4) sources from after *c*. 1516.
Compositions in bold survive only in Habsburg-Burgundian (HB) sources.

{ }	Full text survives only in a poetic source.
[ ]	No sixteenth-century ascription to La Rue.
?	Work is of problematic authenticity.
*	Piece survives in a single source.
R4	*rondeau quatrain*.
R5	*rondeau cinquain*.
TC	Triple canon.
DC	Double canon.

	Third in final	Use of canon	Number of breves[a]	Structure	HB sources	Other sources	Total sources
Ce n'est pas jeu, 4v	—	—	52	R4	1	5	6
Il viendra le jour désiré, 4v	—	—	50	—	1	1	2
Mijn hert, 4v	—	—	54	—	2	11 ?	13?
Pourquoy non, 4v	—	—	67	—	1	8	9
Pourquoy tant, 4v	—	—	53	R4?	1	2	3
Tous les regretz, 4v	—	—	54	{R5}	1	8	9
A vous non autre, 3v	—	—	42	R5	2	1	3
Tous nobles cueurs, 3v	—	—	46	R5 text	2	1	3
Autant en emporte le vent, 4v	—	—	41	—	2	—	2
*****Dedans bouton**, 4v	—	—	38	—	1	—	1
De l'oeil de la fille du roy, 4v	—	—	64	R5	2	—	2
Fors seulement, 4v	—	—	67	c.f.	1	2	3
*****Ma bouche rit**, 4v	—	—	149	c.f.	1	—	1
*****Plorer, gemir, crier/Requiem**, 4v[b]	—	—	51	c.f.	1	—	1
Pour ce que je suis, 4v	—	—	58	R5?	2	—	2
Trop plus secret, 4v	—	—	55	—	2	8	10
Pour ung jamais, 3v	—	—	56	strophic	1	3	4
*****[Il me fait mal]**, 3v	—	—	45	—	1	—	1
*****[J'ay mis mon cueur]**, 3v	—	—	52	c.f.	1	—	1
*****[Je ne scay plus]**, 3v	—	—	47	—	1	—	1
*****Il est bien heureux**, 4v	×	—	56	—	1	—	1
Secretz regretz, 4v	—	—	54	—	1	2	3
*****[Aprez regretz]**, 4v	×	—	64	R5	1	—	1
*****[Ce m'est tout ung]**, 4v	—	—	48	{R5}	1	—	1
*****[C'est ma fortune]**, 4v	—	—	57	R5	1	—	1
*****[Changier ne veulx]**, 4v	—	—	45	R4	1	—	1
?**[Dulces exuvie]**, 4v	—	—	80	—	2	—	2
*****[Helas, fault il]**, 4v	—	—	52	—	1	—	1
*****[Las, helas, las]**, 4v	—	—	53	R5	1	—	1
*****[Me fauldra il]**, 4v	—	—	54	strophic	1	—	1
*****[Plusieurs regretz]**, 4v	—	—	54	{R5}	1	—	1
*****[Quant il survient]**, 4v	—	—	44	R4	1	—	1

TABLE 4.1. *(cont.)*

*[Cueurs desolez/Dies illa], 5v	×	—	88	R5/c.f.	I	—	I
[Dueil et ennuy], 5v	×	×	50	—	2	—	2
*[Je ne dis mot], 6v	×	[TC]	42	—	I	—	I
?[Sailliés avant], 5v	×	×	135	—	I	I	2
*?Il fault morir, 6v	×	—	75	—	—	I	I
*En espoir vis, 4v	—	[DC]	31	—	—	I	I
Cent mille regretz, 5v	×	×	61	—	I	2	3
Incessament mon pauvre cueur, 5v	×	×	53	R5 text	I	14	15
*D'ung aultre aymer, 5v	×	—	54	c.f.	I	—	I
*Fors seulement, 5v	×	×	76	c.f.	I	—	I
*[Adieu comment], 5v	—	×	63	—	I	—	I
*[Je n'ay regretz], 5v	—	×	44	—	I	—	I

ᵃ Includes the repetitions in *Il me fait mal* and *Je ne scay plus* but not in forme-fixe works.
ᵇ In triple metre.

lacking her arms—might have been given to Marguerite after Charles had owned it for a while. Opening as it does with a series of 'regret' chansons, it would have been especially meaningful at any point after Philibert's death. Or perhaps it was a parting gift when she left Savoy for good in the autumn of 1506—also under sad circumstances.

The second group of secular works comprises those appearing for the first time in FlorC 2439, arranged here by number of voices and then alphabetically. This is followed by the third group, works from BrusBR 228 (compiled no earlier than 1508, and completed for the most part before March 1516), again ordered alphabetically by number of voices, to which is added at the end *Sailliés avant*, found in VatV 11953 (connected to Maximilian's court) from *c.*1515–16. The pieces given in brackets here are those that lack ascription to La Rue in any source (most are unique to BrusBR 228) and have been suggested as La Rue's by modern scholars.[6] These anonymous works are in general consistent with his secular style; the brackets serve as a reminder that we cannot prove they are his, with question marks given for pieces that are more troublesome as far as authenticity goes. Not surprisingly, Marguerite's chansonnier (BrusBR 228) has a number of pieces appearing for the first time that are probably the result of collaboration between La Rue and his employer (e.g. *Pour ung jamais, Il me fait mal, Me fauldra il*). The most likely time for this shared creativity, of course, is precisely during the period when Marguerite was in charge of the court, rather than during her earlier residences.

The final subdivision holds those pieces surfacing only after La Rue's retirement. It opens with *Il fault morir*, known only from a posthumous source now connected with Maximilian's court, the first part of RegB C120. The next work, *En espoir vis*, appears only in a printed collection of double canons (1520³); the last

6 See App. D for information on these modern attributions.

four are only in VienNB Mus. 18746. The other two, while both in the Vienna source, are also in other, possibly earlier, manuscripts.

Several aspects of Table 4.1 immediately stand out. One is that there are no five- or six-voice works in the two earlier groups. FlorC 2439 and the early prints all include five-voice works by other composers, suggesting that La Rue's secular ventures into fuller forces happened rather further along in his compositional career. The chronology of mass sources also suggested such a tendency as a general trend, even though the six-voice Credo was an earlier work (*Il fault morir*, if it is really by La Rue, would be another exceptional early work for six voices).

Also appearing in the latter half of the table (and thus the later sources) are works that include canons: a double and a triple canon (the latter an anonymous work) and seven works built on a canonic foundation. Again, the table of masses suggested a similar later involvement with canons, but differed in that the early *Missa L'homme armé I* made important use of canon. Perhaps more significant is that except for the double canon, all La Rue's secular works that use canon are for five or six voices. Canons in the masses lacked that specific association (again, the four-voice *Missa L'homme armé I* is a good example of La Rue's freedom in using canon in four-voice works).

Another curious observation is that the use of a third in the final cadence is largely, though not entirely, restricted to works for more than four voices. The exceptions here are *Il est bien heureux* and the anonymous *Aprez regretz*, both in BrusBr 228.[7] While we saw that, with masses, final triads happen more frequently in works from later rather than earlier sources, the distinction does not seem to be as clear-cut as it is here. Similarly, while five- and six-voice masses are more likely to have final triads than works for four voices only, the difference is rather less noticeable than in the secular works. In general, it looks as if La Rue was more inclined to use canon and final triads when he had more than four voices at his disposal, with the secular works proving rather stricter in this regard than the masses. At the same time, it is very striking that he almost completely eschews *tempus perfectum* in his secular music, calling it into play only in the second part of *Plorer, gemir, crier/Requiem* (to be discussed in Ch. 5). Two possible reasons for this come to mind. The first is that secular music would seem to be a likelier realm than sacred music to present the newest style (duple metre was far more fashionable than triple by the end of the fifteenth century); tradition would arguably count more in the sacred realm (though we have just seen that at least as far as final triads are concerned, La Rue seems to have been more forward-looking in his masses). A second possible reason is that some of the secular music might have been per- formed by courtly amateurs, and *tempus imperfectum* is much easier to read than *tempus perfectum*.

---

[7] In FlorC 2439, *Pourquoy tant* has a third in the final cadence, but its two concordances have an open fifth, suggesting that the Florence reading is an error.

While most of the secular compositions are standard French-texted chansons, La Rue's output also extended into the realm of art-song reworkings,[8] Flemish song, and the motet-chanson; this last category will be discussed separately in Chapter 5. He may also have sampled Latin secular composition in the currently anonymous *Dulces exuvie*. Although Picker saw no reason to associate the work with La Rue, Milsom gave this an unqualified affirmative for the composer.[9] Even though the texture is fairly continuous and the imitation rather more sparing than usual for La Rue, the individual lines themselves seem very much in keeping with the composer's style, generating the rhythmic counterpoint so prominent in his writing. The work has duly been noted with a question mark on the various lists and tables where it appears.

Art-song reworkings were apparently quite popular at court. FlorC 2439 is one of the major sources for this type of piece, and Agricola is undoubtedly the most prolific composer within this genre. As observed in Chapter 2, other colleagues of La Rue's also wrote this kind of composition. La Rue's four unproblematic secular art-song reworkings, all of which circulated with textual incipits only,[10] are remarkably unified in their treatment of the pre-existent material (a fifth piece, *Il fault morir*, will be discussed later). All are based on Ockeghem chansons and all are strict cantus-firmus compositions. La Rue's settings of *D'ung aultre aymer* (five voices) and *Ma bouche rit* (four voices) as well as his four- and five-voice versions of *Fors seulement* (the latter built on a canon between the two lowest voices) all present their borrowed voices with their original rhythmic values.[11] The four-voice *Fors seulement* transposes Ockeghem's superius[12] down a fifth, while *D'ung aultre aymer* requires the same for Ockeghem's tenor.[13] The other two maintain their original pitches (Ockeghem's superius in the superius of the five-voice *Fors*

[8] On these see Meconi, 'Art-Song Reworkings'.

[9] PickerCA, 96, and John Milsom, Review of Pierre de la Rue, *Opera omnia*, vols. 2–3, in *Early Music*, 21 (1993), 479–82 at 482.

[10] La Rue's *Sancta Maria virgo* and *Si dormiero*, technically motets because of their Latin 'texts', also exist with incipits only. It is very likely that they were sometimes, perhaps usually, performed in secular settings, since they fall into an unusual category of works I have labelled sacred tricinia. For more on both these individual works as well as sacred tricinia themselves, see Meconi, 'Sacred Tricinia and Basevi 2439'. Although lack of text does not necessarily imply instrumental performance, the court had a full array of instruments and instrumentalists at their disposal; see for example DoorslaerC 25, 39; SG 30–1; VDS vii. 196, 268–9.

[11] Modern editions in Meconi , 'Style and Authenticity', 301–5, 359–67, 325–8, and 329–35 respectively. The *Fors seulement* works are also in *Fors seulement: Thirty Compositions for Three to Five Voices or Instruments from the Fifteenth and Sixteenth Centuries*, ed. Martin Picker (Recent Researches in the Music of the Middle Ages and Early Renaissance, 14; Madison: A-R Editions, 1981), 12–14 (4v.) and 37–41 (5v.).

[12] In the original version, the superius voice sometimes circulated as the tenor and vice versa. I follow the practice of Picker (ibid.) in calling the tenor the voice that approaches the final cadence stepwise from above.

[13] The indication for the transposition has caused some confusion in the past. In the sole source for the work, VienNB 18746, the second tenor is marked 'Canon In dyatessaron descendendo', leading earlier scholars to assume that a sixth voice would be generated canonically (e.g. StaehelinNG lists the work as being for six voices). The instructions, however, concern the transposition to be applied to the second tenor voice, which presents Ockeghem's untransposed tenor. Not only does nothing work in canon, but the untransposed second tenor creates horrible dissonances with the other voices; only transposed down a fifth does it work. It was surely copied at Ockeghem's original pitch to emphasize the connection to its model.

seulement and Ockeghem's tenor in the tenor of *Ma bouche rit*). This last work doubles the rhythmic values of Ockeghem's line, resulting in an immensely long work (149 breves, one of the longest through-composed secular creations before Janequin), while *D'ung aultre aymer* inserts rests that were not present in Ockeghem's line (the insertions are between the A and B sections of the rondeau and in the middle of the final phrase; the former pause permits a cadence on a non-cantus-firmus pitch; the latter is more difficult to account for). La Rue does not borrow polyphonically in these works (though the model voice sometimes inspires other material), and the borrowed voice is usually harmonically subservient to other considerations. Interestingly, La Rue uses a motif from the bassus of Ockeghem's *Je n'ay deuil* extensively in *Ma bouche rit*—another example of 'hidden borrowing'.

La Rue typically sabotages Ockeghem's formal structures; *Ma bouche rit* must end with the B section of the original bergerette rather than the normally required A,[14] and *D'ung aultre aymer* and the four-voice *Fors seulement* are impossible to perform as rondeaux. Nonetheless, in all instances the identity of the borrowed line could not be clearer. As we have already seen with the mass music, this kind of clarity in his treatment of borrowed material is unusual for La Rue, though in this case it is the norm for art-song reworkings, especially those based on such favoured models as these three Ockeghem works. Once again, as with his *Salve Regina IV*, La Rue is sensitive to generic expectations.

La Rue's sole Flemish work, *Mijn hert*, needs some explanation. It exists with a conflicting attribution to Obrecht, who might initially seem the more promising author given that he is the most prolific composer of Flemish songs at this time and that La Rue has nothing else of this sort to his credit. Further, La Rue was surely originally francophone, may not have worked at any Flemish-language musical centres, and spent much of his court employment under Marguerite, whose Flemish was not strong.[15] But the attribution of the work to La Rue in FlorC 2439 insures that the work is his, since the manuscript is from the court complex. La Rue is also given as the author of the work in *Canti C* (1504³), while the Obrecht ascription comes from *c*.1540, a full thirty-five years after that composer's death.

Flemish was unquestionably the original language of the work; if 'Mijn hert' were a contrafact for a French text, the latter would surely have appeared with the song when it was copied into BrusBR 228, Marguerite's chansonnier. Further, the choice of Flemish is not as unusual as it might seem. Not only did the court travel frequently to places where Flemish was the preferred language, Flemish was far

---

[14] The A section of La Rue's setting closes insubstantially (there is no cadence proper; the music just stops on a C-E-G triad) while the ending of B is strong, clear, and all that we need from a true conclusion (superius/tenor suspension cadence on A with the bassus dropping a fifth to A for additional emphasis). Obviously La Rue intended an A/B performance rather than AbbaA, the usual structure for a bergerette rendition.

[15] PickerCA, 13.

from unknown at court. While Marguerite herself was not fluent in it, she did use the language in dealing with some individuals,[16] and in any event she was not in charge when the work was written; Philip was. Both Philip the Good and Charles the Bold spoke Flemish,[17] and it would not be surprising if Philip had known it as well, for he was brought up where Flemish was the language spoken everywhere but court (unlike Marguerite), and he knew from childhood that he would be dealing with the leading citizens of such cities as Ghent and Bruges, where the first language was Flemish (again, unlike Marguerite, who was raised to be queen of France). Certainly Flemish tunes formed the foundation for a surprising number of works known at court: Agricola's *Missa In myne zyn*, Bauldeweyn's *Missa Myn liefkens bruyn oghen*, Isaac's *Missa Een vrolic wesen*, the Credo from his *Missa Tmeisken was jonck*, La Rue's own *Missa Tandernaken* (which Rubsamen thought was an early work, that is from Philip's time),[18] Molinet's *Salve regina* on *O werde mont*, Strus's *Sancta Maria* on the same tune, Vinder's *Salve regina* on *Ghy syt de liefste boven al*, an anonymous *Missa O werde mont*, anonymous *Salve regina* settings on *Mijn hert* (on La Rue's piece), *O werde mont*, and *Myns liefkens bruyn ooghen*, Gascongne's *Missa Mijn hert* (also on La Rue's work), to say nothing of eight other secular pieces in addition to La Rue's work. As noted in Chapter 2, the manuscript LonBL 35087 had an original owner closely connected to the court, and it has a large repertoire of Flemish-language works. So La Rue's choice of Flemish for a single work is not as unexpected as it might initially seem; it is certainly more likely that he would have written a Flemish work than, say, Josquin.

Mijn hert is one of the highest-lying of La Rue's works; in two sources (VatV 11953 and UlmS 237) it is transposed down a fifth to put it in a more normal range. Several other La Rue pieces also reach this high (up to g''): *Tous nobles cueurs* (which has a very slightly lower range and which is actually one of La Rue's earlier works, despite not appearing till FlorC 2439), the double canon *En espoir vis*, and the anonymous works *Helas, fault il*, *Las, helas, las*, *Me fauldra il*, and *Il me fait mal* (the last going even higher, to a''). The formal structure is unusual for La Rue in bringing back the initial material in varied form at the close, but a similar (though not exact) plan is followed in *Trop plus secret*. Another interesting feature is that the musical repetition begins at a textually awkward spot (a subordinate clause); that and the fact that the supposed popular song is rhythmically complex have led Leon Kessels to argue convincingly that La Rue is not working with a pre-existent song here.[19]

The song is extremely attractive and was deservedly popular, then as well as now; no other secular work by La Rue has been recorded as often. During the sixteenth century, only *Incessament* was more widely circulated among the secular

[16] Ibid.

[17] Blockmans and Prevenier, *The Promised Lands*, 121–2.

[18] RubsamenMGG, 236.

[19] Leon Kessels, 'The Brussels/Tournai Partbooks: Structure, Illumination, and Flemish Repertory', *TVNM*, 37 (1987), 82–110 at 99.

works. In addition to the two sacred pieces noted above, two secular works were based on this song, a three-voice reworking by Cornelius Rigo de Bergis and an anonymous work also written for three voices. While obviously not rivalling the offspring of Ockeghem's *Fors seulement*, *Mijn hert*'s four derived pieces are a significant number, especially considering that most contemporary works inspired no later pieces at all.

La Rue's French-texted pieces were written at a time of significant stylistic transition and reflect his individual response to the demands of courtly writing of the time. One of their most noteworthy features is his evident reluctance to base pieces on popular songs of the day, in contrast to other major composers of secular works such as Josquin and Févin; only his *Credo L'amour du moy* and the anonymous three-voice *J'ay mis mon cueur* are built this way. Furthermore, his choice of these two models is telling: neither one has a bawdy or suggestive text (not that the secular text would have been heard in the Credo, but its associations would surely have been present). This fits well with the picture obtained from La Rue's biography of a religious man 'free from the crime of Venus'. That the reluctance seems prompted by textual rather than musical considerations is suggested by his incorporation in other works of various elements associated with the style of contemporary settings of popular melodies. These include extensive use of repeated notes, syllabic text setting, and short phrases, found in works such as *Autant en emporte le vent* and *Dedans bouton*.

As is often the case in this period, the authors of most of La Rue's secular texts are unknown, although in a few cases we can identify the individual responsible. The texts for both *Tous les regretz* and *Tous nobles cueurs* were part of a larger poem written by Octavien de Saint-Gelais to mark Marguerite's departure from the French court.[20] *Pour ung jamais*, a typically melancholy text, is a strophic poem written by Marguerite herself ('One sorrow forever stays with me which, ceaselessly, night and day, at every hour torments me so much that I should dearly wish to die . . .').[21] The text for this work (in a somewhat varied form) appears in the court poetry manuscript BrusBR 10572 described as 'chanson faite par semadams', obviously Marguerite,[22] and the work appears in RegB C120 as 'fraw margretsen lied'.

Marguerite again seems to be the poet for the anonymous song *Me fauldra il?*[23] ('Must I always languish thus? Must I finally thus die?')[24] whose textual beginning is reminiscent of the very famous *Pourquoy non*, to be discussed below. In BrusBr 228, *Me fauldra il* is immediately followed by the anonymous three-voice *Il me fait*

[20] See Mary Beth Winn, 'Octavien de Saint-Gelais: Complainte sur le départ de Marguerite', *Le Moyen Français*, 5 (1979), 65–80; and ead., '"Regret" Chansons for Marguerite d'Autriche by Octavien de Saint-Gelais', *Bibliothèque d'humanisme et Renaissance: Travaux et documents*, 39 (1977), 23–32.

[21] 'Pour ung jamais ung regret me demeure / Qui sans cesser nuyt et jour a toute heure / Tant me tourmente que bien vouldroy morir'.

[22] PickerCA, 54.

[23] Ibid. 55.

[24] 'Me fauldra il tousjours ainsi languir? Me fauldra il enfin ainsi morir?'

mal, which seems out of place in this otherwise four-voice section of the manuscript. Picker has noted the correspondence of the two poems in formal outline, metre, and rhyme scheme, and has suggested that the latter is intended as a response to the former, justifying its placement in the manuscript.[25] La Rue is the likely creator of the music in both works, and he might be the author of the latter poem as well, a passionate response to the pain expressed in the first poem ('It makes me ill to see you languish . . .').[26] If he is the poet, that is yet another thread between Marguerite and him.

An earlier pairing of poems seems to occur in the attributed works *Pourquoy tant* and *Il viendra le jour désiré*. Again, we have a despairing cry answered in the affirmative, but this time the viewpoint is that of a single author: 'Why must I wait so long? Whence can such resistance come? Why must I endure so much? Such pains I cannot understand',[27] answered by 'It will come, the desired day. It will come, what I wish. God protect me from need. It is a great affliction to be deceived.'[28] Another textual association surely occurs with the anonymous songs *Quant il advient* and *Quant il survient*, but the latter setting suits La Rue's style better than the former; perhaps in this pairing he collaborated with another of the many composers at court.

Two songs are in a woman's voice and were thus most likely to have been written by female poets, presumably women at court. *Ce n'est pas jeu* includes the lines 'Et sy suis sceure que pas de luy ne vient . . . De tout cecy je le porteray bien / Mais que de luy je ne soye oublyee' (And thus I am certain it isn't his fault . . . I will bear all of this well / But may he not forget me), while the anonymous *Changier ne veulx* states 'A tousjours je luy veulx complaire' (Always I wish to please him). Although these songs are from a woman's point of view, the sentiment is the standard courtly one, found as well in songs from a masculine or neutral position, such as *Incessament mon pauvre cueur lamente* (Incessantly my poor heart laments; ceaselessly memory torments me . . .)[29] or *Je ne scay plus* (I no longer know what I should say if not to curse fortune . . .).[30]

But scattered among the clichés are several poems that make one stop and ponder their meaning (and not merely because of the problems that late fifteenth- and early sixteenth-century poetry presents). *Pour ce que je suis* is one: 'Since I am no longer one of the lovers of whom they speak as having no hope or assurance, I wonder when I am angry whether this is my great honour or shame?'[31] Another is

[25] PickerCA, 56. The correspondence extends to extreme similarities between lines: 'Mestier en ay, je le prens sur ma foy' (*Me fauldra il*); 'J'a mestier n'est, je le prens sur ma foy' (*Il me fait mal*).

[26] 'Il me fait mal de vous veoir languir . . .'.

[27] 'Pourquoy tant me fault il attendre / Dont peut telle riguer venir / Pourquoy tant fault il soustenir / De maulx je ne le puis entendre'.

[28] 'Il viendra le jour desire / Il viendra ce que je demande / De la faulte Dieu me defende / C'est grand paine d'estre abuze'.

[29] 'Incessament mon pauvre cueur lamente / Sans nul repos souvenir me tormente'.

[30] 'Je ne scay plus que je doy dire / Si non de fortune mauldire'.

[31] 'Pour ce que je suis hors du compte / Des amoureux dont on raconte / Sans espoir ou entretenue / Je demande quant je m'argue / Se ce m'est grant honneur ou honte'.

Trop plus secret: 'Much more secretive than my beloved am I now, I note. For two or three years, out of madness, I haven't believed it.'[32] And the anonymous *Ce m'est tout ung* is astonishing in its tone: 'It's all one to me, by our Lady / Whether you are a poor woman or a great lady / I wish you neither well nor ill / Whether you have much or nothing / I neither hate you nor love you.'[33] These atypical sentiments suggest a cool objectivity towards the game of love, a perfect stance for a composer 'free from the crime of Venus'.[34]

Poetic rhyme schemes invariably follow the standard patterns *abba* for *quatrains* and *aabba* for *cinquains*, but larger formal structures show that La Rue was increasingly willing to abandon the fixed forms of the fifteenth century. The songs that are demonstrably *rondeaux* (the only fixed form La Rue used) are, for three voices, *A vous non autre*; for four voices, *Ce n'est pas jeu*, *De l'oeil de la fille du roy*, the anonymous *Aprez regretz*, *C'est ma fortune*, *Changier ne veulx*, *Las, helas, las*, and *Quant il survient*; and, for five voices, the anonymous *Cueurs desolez/Dies illa*. Two of the attributed ones come from the earliest layer of sources, and *A vous non autre*, with its three-voice texture, is quite probably an early song as well. Regardless of their dating, these pieces mark La Rue as one of the very last composers to write *rondeaux*.

Several other works look as if they were intended as *rondeaux*. *Tous les regretz*, another work that is surely early, sets the refrain of a *rondeau cinquain*; the full text appears only in poetic sources.[35] The piece has the requisite division into A and B sections and was presumably intended as a complete *rondeau*, but it is odd that none of the many musical manuscripts containing the work gives more than the refrain text (especially considering that one of these manuscripts is BrusBR 228, Marguerite's own collection, which normally supplies all additional texts for its works). *Ce m'est tout ung* is similar in having a full *rondeau* text known only in a poetic source,[36] but no medial break is indicated in its sole musical source, BrusBR 228 (though it is easy enough to create one).[37] *Plusieurs regretz* is like the preceding except that the *rondeau* text found for it has a slightly different textual incipit.[38]

Certain works raise the possibility that they might have been intended as *rondeaux*. The text of *Pourquoy tant* (another early work) could be the refrain of a *rondeau quatrain*, and it divides into clear A and B sections, but no additional text

---

[32] 'Trop plus secret que ma partie / Suis maintenant je m'en perchois / Des ans y a bien deux ou trois / Que ne l'ay creu par ma folye'.

[33] 'Ce m'est tout ung par nostre Dame / Soyes povre femme ou grant dame / Je ne vous veuil mal ne bien / Ayez des biens ou nayez riens / Je ne vous hais ne ne vous ayme'.

[34] Another superb example of uncourtly—yet not uncouth—sentiment is found in *Autant en emporte le vent* (discussed at length in Meconi, 'French Print Chansons'), which basically states that physical affection is meaningless without love.

[35] Lille, Bibliothèque municipale, MS 402, and Moritzburg (Dresden), MS Jean de Saxe, no. 253.

[36] BNF, MS nouv. acq. fr. 7559.

[37] See PickerCA, 217.

[38] 'Tous les regretz qui sur la terre sont' (found in BNF, MS nouv. acq. fr. 7559) instead of 'Plusieurs regretz qui sur la terre sont'; see PickerCA, 136.

is known. *Pour ce que je suis* is analogous in structure except that it has a five-line text.

Full *rondeau* texts exist for both *Tous nobles cueurs* and *Incessament*, but neither work breaks successfully into the two sections necessary for the repetition scheme of a *rondeau*; La Rue has ignored the poetic structure. The remaining compositions similarly fail to divide into precise A and B sections, and they lack any kind of additional text as well. With these works La Rue turns his back unequivocally on the past.

The move away from *rondeaux* had a dramatic effect on the overall length of the secular works. Although a work such as *A vous non autre* was a mere forty-two total breves, taking all the necessary repetitions would lengthen it to the equivalent of 167 breves; a longer work such as *De l'oeil de la fille du roy* (sixty-two breves for the refrain) would turn into 267 breves. In contrast, pieces that not only were through-composed but also tended towards syllabic text setting, such as *Autant en emporte le vent*, *Dedans bouton*, or *En espoir vis*, would zip by in a mere forty-one, thirty-eight, and thirty-one breves respectively—a fraction of earlier compositions in their duration. Whereas in music for the mass La Rue seemed in general to move towards longer settings, his secular works evince the opposite trend.

As with the masses, La Rue does not hesitate to explore the lower depths (see Table 4.2). When he goes below the gamut, it is normally merely to *F*, but he also reaches *E* (the anonymous *C'est ma fortune*), *D* (*Ce n'est pas jeu*, *A vous non autre*, *Trop plus secret*, and the anonymous *Plusieurs regretz*, *Je n'ay regretz*, and *Sailliés avant* if it is his), *C* (*Tous les regretz* and *Il fault morir* if it is his, and the anonymous *Aprez regretz* and *Adieu comment*) and even *Bb´* in the spectacular *Pourquoy non*. Low ranges appear slightly more often in works from the earlier sources. Cleffing combinations are also as varied as they were with the masses; only two of the three-voice works, for example, share a cleffing combination, and the anonymous *J'ay mis mon cueur* is striking in using c4 in all voices, a very rare combination for this time. High-lying works transmitted without use of the F clef include *Mijn hert*, *Tous nobles cueurs*, *Il me fait mal*, and *En espoir vis*; low-lying works whose highest clef is only c3 or even c4 are *Pourquoy non* and *Adieu comment*.

In contrast to the masses, La Rue concentrates his tonal centres much more narrowly, with D as the overwhelming favourite (usually without a signature flat, but occasionally with one), followed by G, almost invariably with a single flat, making it the transposed equivalent of D-mode works. The only exceptions for G are *Incessament*, without flat, *Me fauldra il* (anonymous), with two signature flats, and *Je ne dis mot* (also anonymous), with a partial signature. Works on A are the other major category for La Rue's secular pieces; here only the five-voice *Fors seulement* uses a signature flat, and then only in the bassus. The five works not finishing on D, G, or A explore the other possible finals: the anonymous *C'est ma fortune* and *Dulces exuvie* on E, *Adieu comment* (also anonymous) on C, *Plorer*,

TABLE 4.2. Cleffing, range, and final in La Rue's secular music

{ } High and low pitches exceeding the gamut.
[ ] No sixteenth-century ascription to La Rue.
 ? Work is of problematic authenticity.

	Signature accidentals	Cleffing	Low pitch	High pitch
A final				
Il viendra le jour désiré, 4v	—	c1-c3-c4-f4	G	e″
Pourquoy tant, 4v	—	c1-c4-c4-f4	A	d″
Ma bouche rit, 4v	—	c1-c4-c4-f4	{F}	d″
Pour ung jamais, 3v	—	c1-c3-f4	G	e″
Secretz regretz, 4v	—	c1-c3-c4-f4	A	d″
[Aprez regretz], 4v	—	c1-c3-f4-f5	{C}	d″
[Ce m'est tout ung], 4v	—	c1-c3-c4-f4	A	{f″}
Fors seulement, 5v	♭a	g2-c1-c4-c4-f4	G	{f″}
?Il fault morir, 6v	—	c1-c2-c4-c4-f4-f5	{C}	d″
B-flat final				
Pourquoy non, 4v	♭♭	c4-c5-f4-f5	{B♭}	g′
C final				
[Adieu comment], 5v	♭b	c3-c4-f4-f4-f5	{C}	g′
D final				
Mijn hert, 4v	♭c	g2-c2-c3-c4	d	{g″}
Tous les regretz, 4v	—	c2-c4-c4-f5	{C}	c″
A vous non autre, 3v	—	c2-c5-f5	{D}	g′
Tous nobles cueurs, 3v	—	g2-c2-c4	c	{g″}
De l'oeil de la fille du roy, 4v	—	c1-c4-c4-f4	{F}	d″
Trop plus secret, 4v	—	c2-c4-c4-f5	{D}	c″
[Il me fait mal], 3v	♭	g2-c2-c4	c	{a″}
[Je ne scay plus], 3v	—	c1-c3-f3	A	d″
Il est bien heureux, 4v	—	g2-c1-c2-f3	c	{f″}
[Helas, fault il], 4v	—	g2-c2-c4-f3	G	{g″}
[Las, helas, las], 4v	—	g2-c2-c3-f3	c	{g″}
[Cueurs desolez/Dies illa], 5v	—	g2-c3-c4-f4-f4	{F}	{f″}
[Dueil et ennuy], 5v	—	c1-c3-c3-X-f4	G	d″
En espoir vis, 4v	♭	c2-c4	d	{g″}
Cent mille regretz, 5v	—	c1-c3-c4-c4-f4	G	d″
[Je n'ay regretz], 5v	—	c2-c4-c4-f4-f4	{D}	b′
?[Sailliés avant], 5v	♭	g2-c3-c4-c4-f4	{D}	{f″}
E final				
[C'est ma fortune], 4v	—	c1-c4-c4-f4	{E}	d″
?[Dulces exuvie], 4v	—	c1-c4-c4-f4	{F}	d″

TABLE 4.2. (*cont.*)

F final

Plorer, gemir, crier/Requiem, 4v	♭	c2-c4-c4-f4	{F}	c″

G final

Ce n'est pas jeu, 4v	♭	c2-c4-f3-f5	{D}	c″
Autant en emport le vent, 4v	♭	c1-c3-c4-f4	G	d″
Dedans bouton, 4v	♭	c1-c3-c4-f4	G	d″
Fors seulement, 4v	♭	c1-c2-c4-f4	G	d″
Pour ce que je suis, 4v	♭	c1-c3-c4-f4	{F}	d″
[J'ay mis mon cueur], 3v	♭	c4-c4-c4	A	g′
[Changier ne veulx], 4v	♭	c1-c3-c4-f4	G	d″
[Me fauldra il], 4v	♭♭	g2-c2-c3-c4	B♭	{g″}
[Plusieurs regretz], 4v	♭	c2-f4-f4-Γ	{D}	b♭′
[Quant il survient], 4v	♭	c2-c4-c4-f4	G	c″
[Je ne dis mot], 6v	♭d	c2-c4-f4	G	d″
Incessament mon pauvre cueur, 5v	—	c1-c3-c4-c4-f4	G	d″
D'ung aultre aymer, 5v	♭	c1-c3-c4-c4-f4	G	d″

[a] Flat in B only.
[b] Flat in SAT2 only.
[c] Flat in A only.
[d] Flat in TB only.

gemir, crier/Requiem on F, and *Pourquoy non* on B♭. The last two are unusual pieces in many respects, as we shall see later.

TWO EXAMPLES

Maximilian may have been La Rue's first secular employer, but all of La Rue's secure surviving secular works display a polish that suggests either that his very earliest efforts were discarded or that he transferred skills already honed in the sacred realm to this more intimate genre. To give more explicit examples of his style than was possible in the overview, the following discussion looks at two very different works, both from earlier in his courtly career and both demonstrating a concern with the comprehension of the text to a degree that scholars have not usually associated with La Rue.

Tous nobles cueurs

One of the conditions of the Peace of Senlis, signed on 23 May 1493, was the return of Marguerite from France to Habsburg-Burgundy. As a parting gift for the princess, French court poet Octavien de Saint-Gelais penned a farewell poem that contained within it three separate rondeaux (*Tous nobles cueurs, Le cueur la suyt*, and

Tous les regretz), the first and last of which were set by La Rue.[39] Although the texts can easily double as expressing the typical sentiments of courtly love, La Rue's settings were surely intended as a musical gesture of homage or welcome to the young princess. They were most probably written either shortly after her return in June 1493 (if La Rue was then resident at court) or shortly after his own return, if he was travelling with Maximilian.

Tous nobles cueurs is one of La Rue's few three-voice works, and he set it rather higher than usual for this texture (see Ex. 4.1); when it appeared in the print 1538[9] it was transposed down a fifth to a more normal range.[40] The work begins with a call to 'all nobles hearts'; La Rue has laid out the opening for maximum effect. The voices enter one at a time, each with the same imitative motif. No voice enters until the preceding has given its initial cry, set syllabically for clear understanding. The lines build up from the bottom, successively on *d*, *a'*, and *d''*, each one entering in the high—and thus readily audible—part of its range. Though neither of the two texted sources (BrusBR 228 and FlorC 2439) writes out textual repetition at this point, such repetition is more than likely, which would place the final call to 'all noble hearts' on *f''*, on the second-highest pitch of the work. The high pitch is further emphasized by its breve rhythm (preceded by a pickup to the tactus); the line then glides down from this powerful and attention-getting opening. This beginning has already moved outside the gamut, but La Rue goes even higher later on, to *g''*, when he sets the word *passeroute*, the matchless one, a reference to Marguerite that is hard to miss because of this highlighting.

Features of La Rue's writing are present from the start. The highly unusual off-tactus beginning becomes a unifying motif throughout; no phrase in the entire piece begins on a strong beat, and syncopation is frequent. The melodic lines continually change direction, repeated notes are less frequent than they will be in later works, and predominantly stepwise motion is continually enlivened by leaps (most often of a third, but with other intervals as well), typically signalling a momentary change in direction. The phrases are constantly varied in length; contrast the short segments of the top voice with the longer opening line of the lowest voice. Note, too, the clever construction of the section beginning with the pickup to bar 7; at the pickup to bar 10 the top two voices transpose and switch their previous material, joined by a varied, transposed version of the lowest voice.

Rhythmic counterpoint is the norm; homorhythm is shunned (in general, La Rue keeps homorhythm in reserve for special points). The work clearly begins in D, and will end there as well, which is not always the case for La Rue. All three voices are equally important, and all contibute to forming cadences (e.g. bars 8–9 between the two lowest voices; bars 11–12 between the two highest). These cadences are on different pitches, A and E, and later cadences will explore other

[39] See Winn, 'Octavien de Saint-Gelais'; ead., '"Regret" Chansons'; and Martin Picker, 'More *Regret* Chansons for Marguerite d'Autriche', *Le Moyen Français*, 5 (1979), 81–101.
[40] The print also includes significant alterations in the closing of the piece.

Ex. 4.1. La Rue, *Tous nobles cueurs*, bars 1–12 (from BrusBR 228, fos. 51ᵛ–52ʳ)

areas as well: F, G, and D; this variety in cadential pitches is the norm for La Rue. And despite the fact that the original poem was a *rondeau cinquain*, La Rue has chosen to set only the refrain; it would be awkward to carve out separate A and B sections to generate the repetition necessary for a fixed form.

Pourquoy non

As impressive a work as *Tous nobles cueurs* is, it still functions within expectations for a late fifteenth-century chanson. The same cannot be said for *Pourquoy non*, one of the most amazing secular works of the entire period. Almost everything about it seems intended to demolish preconceived norms.[41]

Before the singers even opened their mouths they would have known something unusual was happening (see Ex. 4.2). The clef for the highest voice, the superius line, is c4, sometimes used for the altus but more normally for the tenor line—and almost never for the superius. The altus is written in the c5 clef, the tenor in f4, and the bassus in f5. The work promises to be deep and dark.[42]

But the pre-performance surprises are not over. All voices have two signature flats, for B and E. Two signature flats are not unknown in the fifteenth century, but

---

[41] For similarities with *Absalon fili mi*, another unusual work, see Jaap van Benthem, 'Lazarus versus Absalon: About Fiction and Fact in the Netherlands Motet', *TVNM* 39 (1989), 54–82 at 67–9.

[42] Five sources transpose the work up a fifth to a more normal range.

Ex. 4.2. La Rue, *Pourquoy non*, bars 1–15 (from BrusBR 228, fos. 11ᵛ–12ʳ)

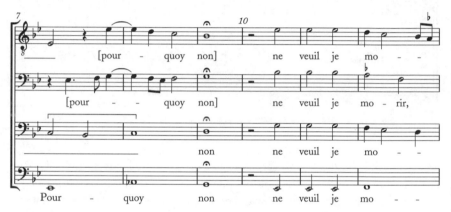

they normally occur in the lowest voice of a work with partial signatures. *Pourquoy non* is one of the earliest examples of a work with two flats in all voices.

When the singers finally began to sing, something else extremely unusual took place: the altus, after entering alone on an E♭, then moved directly to a signed A♭, an accidental used only very rarely at this time. By just the second note of the piece it is undeniably clear that this is not a normal chanson. In retrospect, this second pitch will be recognized as a forerunner of an even more unusual aural move that sets this piece far apart from the average chanson.

The rest of the opening proceeds in a reasonable manner. The altus is followed by the superius, then the tenor, then the bassus, each at the interval of two breves, on the pitches B♭, B♭, and E♭. Each enters imitatively (the bassus also gets a signed A♭), but as is often the case with La Rue, variation creeps in almost immediately after the imitative relationship has been established; note how the third bar of each line is different. The altus and superius lines, the only ones that continue for any length of time, move from longer to shorter note values (a characteristic by no means confined to La Rue), and the altus line shows the combination of stepwise motion and small leaps that is a hallmark of his style.

But by bar 9—only two breves after the last voice has entered—all this has ground to a halt, with a solid close on a G minor triad[43] marked in all voices by both a breve and a fermata. Once again alarm bells would go off for anyone used to the conventions of the French chanson. Why this sudden stop? We are instantly alerted to the fact that this piece is not going to follow a fixed form, and the opening text, 'why not', is emphasized by its segregation in this manner—these are the only two words heard so far.

This is followed by a pause in all voices, by no means a common practice for La Rue, but one that gives even greater emphasis to this sectionalization—as if any more were needed. All four voices then enter simultaneously in homorhythm and with repeated notes, all techniques La Rue reserves for special emphasis. Not only has the first mini-section ended in a highly atypical manner, this second area commences unexpectedly as well. And no sooner has it begun than it has ended: superius and bassus move to pitches marked by fermatas while altus and tenor meander a bit before also settling under fermatas. The first complete line of text, 'Pourquoy non ne veuil je morir' (literally 'Why don't I want to die', but obviously in the sense of 'Why shouldn't I want to die?'), has thus been chopped into two short segments, sharply contrasted in terms of texture but each firmly delineated and commanding the listener's attention.[44]

The second line of text mirrors the first, 'Why shouldn't I seek . . .',[45] and La Rue responds with a corresponding musical treatment. The second 'Pourquoy non' is an almost literal repeat of the first, again coming to a complete halt, marked by fermatas in all voices, after nine breves. La Rue moves to the second half of the second phrase in a manner very similar to the way he completed the first phrase, with a pause before the entry of the voices, together again in homophony and

---

[43] I do not intend to imply the presence of functional harmony by the use of this convenient terminology.

[44] See PickerCA, 71, for additional details on the opening of the work.

[45] 'Pourquoy non ne doy je querir'.

repeated notes, but a few slight changes lead into a longer phrase that leads to the first real cadence of the work, on E♭.

As remarkable as this opening segment is, the beginning of third line is the most incredible part of the piece. La Rue has lavished much musical time on his first two lines; they take up approximately half of the work, leaving the remaining three lines of text to be fitted into the latter half of the work (it is typical for La Rue to allot different amounts of time for different lines of text rather than treating them evenly). The third line of text continues the thought begun in the second line, '. . . the end of my sorrowful life' ('La fin de ma doulente vie'). La Rue marks the words 'La fin' by a striking harmonic shift from what we have just heard (see Ex. 4.3). The preceding phrase concluded on E♭, first accompanied by B♭ and then G. Suddenly we hear a D♭ major triad (built over low D♭) moving to a first inversion C minor triad, with the third doubled. Only someone who was asleep would fail to be struck by this astonishing colour change, seemingly coming from nowhere. It would have been even more striking for a listener than for a performer, since the former would have had no awareness of either the two signature flats or the move to A♭ at the start of the piece, whereas an astute performer would have expected that something was afoot right from the start.

As if to atone for the first half of the work, with one surprise after another, La Rue continues the composition in a much more straightforward manner until the very end, when the final cadence plunges to low *B♭′* (for performers who could not reach it, the octave above was given as an alternate pitch), one of the rarest of all possible pitches for this period.

This unique work was fully appreciated at the time. It is the only work of La Rue's that was included in *Odhecaton*, a collection that in many respects gathers the most significant secular works of the late fifteenth century. In addition to this print (which was reissued on several occasions) it is included in an organ tablature and six other manuscripts and was intended to be copied into a seventh,[46] for a total of nine sources (a large number for the time) over a period of about forty years, far beyond the lifespan of the average late fifteenth-century song. It served as the model for Gascongne's parody mass (he also wrote a mass on the equally famous *Mijn hert*).

People knew who wrote it, too. Six of the nine sources contain attributions (one of the three that does not is Marguerite's BrusBR 228; as noted below, only one piece is ascribed in the manuscript, and she surely knew who the author of *Pourquoy non* was in any case). The work is mentioned in both the Del Lago correspondence (in 1520) and Pietro Aaron's treatise *Toscanello* from 1529. Its fame is probably best confirmed by the appearance of La Rue's *Missa Almana* in the Sistine Chapel manuscript VatS 45, compiled between 1511 and 1514, a decade or more after the song was written. As already noted, the model for the mass and the reason for its name are unknown. But the scribe of the Vatican manuscript

<hr />

[46] It is cited in the index of SGallS 463, but was never copied into the partbooks.

Ex. 4.3. La Rue, *Pourquoy non*, bars 32–5 (from BrusBR 228, fos. 11ᵛ–12ʳ)

thought he knew what the model was, for he named it *Missa Pourquoy non. Missa Almana* begins in a manner very similar to *Pourquoy non*; the four voices enter in imitation in the same order (A, S, T, B), always at the distance of two breves, and with the same opening motif as the chanson: a rising fourth followed by a falling second. The pitch durations are even the same, though not the exact rhythm. Although the mass is a whole tone higher than the chanson, the imitative intervals are very similar: up a fifth for the superius, then down an octave for the tenor entry. In the chanson, the bassus enters a fifth below the tenor; in the mass, the bassus is the same pitch as the tenor. To the scribe (or to whoever wrote his exemplar), a mass that began this way must surely be based on the famous song *Pourquoy non*.

PROBLEMS OF AUTHENTICITY

One of the major differences between La Rue's mass music and his secular music are the problems of authenticity in the latter. As noted in Chapter 3, all but a handful of masses or mass sections circulated with an attribution to La Rue in manuscripts from the court scriptorium, establishing a degree of certainty for these works almost unknown for his contemporaries or earlier composers. Because far fewer chansonniers came from the scriptorium, the situation is quite different for secular music; a significant number of works attributed to La Rue appeared only in sources unrelated to the court.[47] Further, with the exception of FlorC 2439, the secular music was usually copied into court sources without attribution. In BrusBR 228, for example, only one piece has a name attached to it: *Plus nulz regretz*, marked as Josquin's. VienNB Mus. 18746 has a few more attributions,

---

[47] Table 4.1 does not reflect this, since it omits works no longer deemed authentic; these are included in App. D.

including two to La Rue (*D'ung aultre aymer* and the five-voice *Fors seulement*), but these seem intended merely to distinguish these from other works on the same borrowed material. Some of the issues of authenticity that this situation presents have been treated in detail elsewhere,[48] but new interpretations, new material, and pieces not discussed previously warrant a re-examination of certain elements of the various problems.

Conflicting attributions

Several of the conflicting attributions appear to come from a confusion of names. *Adieu florens* appears in FlorBN BR 229 and FlorBN Magl. 178, attributed to Pietrequin and Pietraquin, respectively. This composer is Pietrequin Bonnel, who has six other songs to his name. Because *Adieu florens* is also attributed to 'petri de la rue' in VienNB Mus. 18810,[49] La Rue was considered at one time to be the author of all seven works, but this identification was questioned by Rubsamen and has been dismissed by Martin Staehelin.[50] As it turns out, *Adieu Florens* is unusual for Bonnel (his other works are all *rondeaux*, while this is free in form), but it is even odder for La Rue, with an essentially homophonic texture (normally used sparingly by La Rue), almost constant use of all four voices (La Rue prefers greater textural variety), and cadences formed almost exclusively by superius/tenor pairs; while La Rue always uses these voices for his final cadence in secular works, internal cadences typically involve pairs of voices in many combinations. It seems obvious that the German scribe ran across this piece with a 'Pietrequin' attribution and interpreted it to signify La Rue. Bonnel, a minor figure active towards the end of the fifteenth century, must have been completely unknown in Germany in the early 1530s, whereas La Rue's music was extremely popular there at that time (see App. B). If additional proof were needed, the documented employment of Bonnel in Florence stands in sharp contrast to the lack of any evidence for La Rue's presence in Italy.

A second four-voice *Fors seulement*[51] (not included in Tables 4.1 or 4.2) might also suffer from a contemporary confusion over names. This popular work appears thirteen times, with one of its earliest attributions being to 'Pe.de.la rue' in 1502[2]. But in five other sources it is given to Pipelare. The names are certainly similar, and each sometimes was written with a rebus for 'la' (although Pipelare's usually had a rebus for 're' as well). Even apart from the much more promising source situation for Pipelare, the work displays many traits not normally associated with La Rue's secular music, such as a far lengthier opening duet than his norm, the extensive presence of homorhythm, and the frequent use of long note values (La

---

[48] Meconi, 'Style and Authenticity', and ead., 'French Print Chansons'.
[49] It appears anonymously in MunU 328–331.
[50] RubsamenMGG, 230; StaehelinNG.
[51] The piece is related only second-hand to Ockeghem's progenitor. It is built on the original tenor of an anonymous work in LonBL 35087 that is itself built on Ockeghem's song.

Rue prefers snappier rhythms). Petrucci (or his music editor) unquestionably got this one wrong.

A much odder situation exists with another work that is surely by Pipelare, a four-voice setting of *Een vrolic wesen* that is attributed to him in FlorC 2439.[52] This alone is enough to reject it out of hand for La Rue; although the court scriptorium often left La Rue's works anonymous, they never mistakenly assigned one of his works to someone else. Even without the attributions to Pipelare (RegB C120 also assigns it to him), traits such as the lack of imitation and almost unvaried four-voice texture would speak against La Rue.

The attribution to him in VienNB Mus. 18810 might stem from name confusion, possibly combined with the typical German enthusiasm for La Rue's music. But another, more circuitous and interesting route might be responsible for this attribution. That route begins with the collection TrentBC 1947/4, probably the earliest surviving source for the composition. Here only the lower three voices are written out. The top, unwritten, voice is the borrowed voice, the superius of the original setting by Barbireau. That the scribe did not write it out confirms that it was so well known that it did not need to be written down.[53] It would have helped the performers if he had written it, however, because the melody must be transposed up a fifth to fit the setting. The transposed melody goes up to a'', a fourth above the gamut and an unusual pitch for the time (and for a very long time thereafter). In FlorC 2439, the only source where the melody is noted at this pitch (at least three other sources transpose the whole piece down a fifth)[54] the scribe resorted to an extremely rare clef, the symbol 'dd' placed on the second lowest line of the staff to indicate d'', a ninth above middle C.[55] Perhaps the scribe of the Trent collection was also faced with something that seemed odd to him, prompting him to omit this voice and assume that it was well enough known for him to get away with it.

And here La Rue comes in again. The scribe left a comment about this missing part; at the end of the bassus voice he wrote 'Der alt Discant gehört da Rue' (the old discantus is by La Rue). For whatever reason, the scribe believed the cantus-firmus for this song—and thus presumably the original version—to be La Rue's rather than Barbireau's. This unusual claim is not supported by any other source, and yet this manuscript is one of the oldest to contain any version of *Een vrolic*

[52] Of the works attributed to La Rue in FlorC 2439, only *Mijn hert* has a conflicting attribution, noted and dismissed above.

[53] The most popular models of the time, of which *Een vrolic wesen* is one, were probably known by heart by numerous musicians. Some of the implications of this for *Fortuna desperata* are explored in *Fortuna desperata*, ed. Meconi, pp. xxii–iii and *passim*.

[54] SGallS 530, RegsB C120, and VienNB Mus. 18810 all place it down a fifth; I have not seen the last source, SamaP 30–1. Richard Taruskin, in *Een vrolic wesen* (Miami: Ogni Sorte, 1979), 12, implies that the lower version is the original. The Trent manuscript and FlorC 2439 contain the higher version, however, and these two manuscripts are the earliest sources for this piece, lending greater credence to their readings. Furthermore, transposing a piece up to a stratospheric range makes no sense, while transposing a piece from an unusual range to a normal one is standard procedure.

[55] At the time, 'dd' was the standard letter notation for d''.

wesen, either original or derived. Also interesting is the possibility of a connection between this manuscript and Maximilian's court,[56] especially considering that Barbireau, presumably the author of the famous setting, was employed by Maximilian as an envoy at one point.

It is the Maximilian connection that might explain the later attribution for the entire piece to La Rue, though it is based on a series of 'ifs' and 'mights' (including the initial premiss that the Trent collection might be connected with Maximilian at all). An exemplar that gave one voice part to La Rue might easily be copied as one giving the whole piece to La Rue. Both Munich and Augsburg are possible places for the compilation of VienNB Mus. 18810, and the latter city at least had numerous imperial connections. It is not unthinkable that the initial, curious assignment of *Een vrolic wesen*'s superius to La Rue led to the attribution of Pipelare's version to La Rue some thirty years later.

The attribution of the combinative work *Amours fait moult/Il est de bonne heure ne/Tant que nostre argent durra* seems again to stem from Germanic enthusiasm for La Rue's compositions. This widely disseminated song appears with two attributions to Japart as well as one to Busnoys; the former composer is the likely author of the work, given both his propensity for this kind of composition as well as the fact that he is named as composer in the earliest source for the piece, RomeC 2856, compiled in Ferrara at exactly the same time he was employed there. The chanson does not match La Rue's preferences in any event, with its simultaneous use of two borrowed popular tunes. *Il est de bonne heure ne* has a particularly direct text that could hardly have been to La Rue's taste: 'He was born at a favourable time / Who has his lady in a meadow / On the fine grass',[57] nor is *Amours fait moult* any better: 'Love does much as long as money lasts / When money is lacking, love is hard / And says quite frankly to her friend: "Since your money is gone / Go find another adventure"'.[58]

This work appears among a cluster of authentic La Rue works in VatV 11953, with *Pourquoy non, Trop plus secret*, and *Tous les regretz* preceding this one, the first three all attributed to La Rue. In BasU F.X.1–4 the same four works appear, this time with *Pourquoy non* at the end of the three authentic works but with all four works, including *Tant que nostre argent durra*, ascribed to the composer. The readings for this cluster of works are extremely similar in each source, even down to coloration and ligatures. This suggests a common exemplar, perhaps a fascicle containing these four works, and makes it rather likely that the Basel scribe, the only one to give this work to La Rue, assumed that it, too, was by the composer of the three preceding pieces.

---

[56] Reinhard Strohm, *The Rise of European Music 1380–1500* (Cambridge: Cambridge University Press, 1993), 523.

[57] 'Il est de bonne heure ne / Qui tient sa dame en ung pre / Sur l'erbe jolye'.

[58] 'Amours fait moult tant qu'argent dure / Quant argent fault amour est dure / Et dit tout franc à son amy / Puis que vostre argent est failly / Alles querir aultre aventure'.

BasU F.X.1–4 is also the only source to attribute *Ach hülff mich leid* to La Rue. This *Tenorlied* follows standard *Stollen/Stollen/Abgesang* form and confines the use of the fourth voice to the *Abgesang* section. Once the fourth voice is in, the texture is almost unremittingly for the full four voices, with imitation quite rare. Traits such as these, combined with attributions to other composers elsewhere,[59] argue convincingly against La Rue's authorship. The real author is surely Hans Buchner, to whom the work is given in SGallS 530, a manuscript compiled by Fridolin Sicher, a pupil of Buchner's at precisely the time the source was being copied.

One large group of works with 'conflicting' attributions are the eight pieces assigned to La Rue in French prints from the 1530s on. These have been discussed in detail elsewhere, and none matches La Rue's style.[60] All, in fact, look exactly like 'Parisian' chansons of the time period matching these sources. While some of these works have genuine conflicting attributions (e.g. the selfish, indeed misanthropic *Je suys a moy* attributed to both La Rue and Mittantier in 1536[5]), most are given only to 'La Rue' or 'de la Rue'. With the almost complete stylistic discord between these works and unquestionably authentic ones, it is virtually certain that the 'de la Rue' intended here is Robert de la Rue, master of the boys at Meaux in June 1533, rather than Pierre de la Rue.

All other conflicting attributions are to Josquin. For three of these works—*Tous les regretz*, *Incessament mon pauvre cueur lamente*, and *Cent mille regretz*—both the source situation and style favour La Rue, and no one today accepts the attribution to Josquin. For the last two works, confusion with Josquin's own *Incessament livre* and *Mille regretz* may have generated the misattributions.

Two other works present a different picture. *Dicte moy bergère* and *Leal schray tante* were both known only as La Rue's until very recently, when David Fallows discovered attributions to Josquin for each piece (in HerdF 9820 and ZürZ Z.XI.301 respectively).[61] Even prior to these discoveries, however, the style of the works had already banished them from La Rue's corpus. *Dicte moy bergère* is a double canon; although La Rue was fond of canonic procedures, only four works under his name are double canons, and only one has a decent source pedigree, the Benedictus from the *Missa Ave sanctissima Maria*. The motet *Da pacem domine* appears in two late German prints, 1540[7] and 1567[1], both from a generation or more after La Rue's death. The chanson *En espoir vis* is in 1520[3], a collection of double canons, and *Dicte moy bergère* is first found in FlorC 2442, a set of partbooks probably from France that transmits the canon next to two of La Rue's most popular works, *Pourquoy non* and *Tous les regretz*.

The form and tone of *Dicte moy bergère*'s text are unknown among La Rue's authentic chansons. 'Tell me, shepherdess / Where will I have to pass / And where

---

[59] Hans Buchner, Noel Bauldeweyn, and Josquin.

[60] Meconi, 'Style and Authenticity', 100–13, and ead., 'French Print Chansons'.

[61] My thanks to Professor Fallows for alerting me to these discoveries.

will I leave? / Tell me shepherdess / I have come from the river'[62] is sung and then partially repeated. The bucolic text and lack of regular rhyme scheme suggest a popular model, but no appropriate text or tune is known. With the repetition of text comes a varied repetition of music, generating an ABA´ musical structure such as we saw with *Mijn hert*, which, however, brought back the music in a more subtle manner. The text determines the layout of the music; each line of text generates a phrase of music. Every phrase has a clear contour, starts on the tactus, and closes with a double cadence (altus/bassus, then superius/tenor a fourth away) followed by rests; the layout could not be clearer. The text is largely syllabic, with frequent use of semibreves. The underlying canonic structure is quite simple. Superius and altus are in canon at the fourth and at the breve; tenor and bassus are identically built. As noted, the canons interlock at cadences and they also share some imitation, while the large repeated section at the end makes the layout even simpler. This extremely clear-cut structure, the modal clarity present from the start, the preference for semibreves, and the bucolic subject matter all speak against La Rue's authorship.

These differences become even more pronounced in comparison with *En espoir vis*. Working under the same constraints, La Rue produced a work more in keeping with his usual style. The short text, whose poetic scheme is a standard *abba*, expresses La Rue's normal courtly sentiments: 'In hope I live and therefore languish / Having a marvellous sorrow / I would not know how to be joyous / As long as I see her, I think.'[63] Each line of text generates a phrase of music, with some repetition at the end (though just a few words rather than a full line or more). The text setting is primarily syllabic, with some short melismas intermingled. La Rue has given himself more leeway in the canonic structure by having both canons at the fifth and at a distance of three breves. As is often the case for him, the work does not open decisively in what will be its eventual mode; the tonal direction only becomes clear as the piece progresses, with the bassus helping to establish it. Although the work is extremely short, La Rue manages to squeeze in cadences on four different pitches, in keeping with his preferred cadential variety. In contrast, *Dicte moy bergère*, though almost twice as long, cadences on only three different pitches.

The phrases of *En espoir vis* are varied in length and in rhythmic profile, with much greater use of minims than in *Dicte moy bergère* and a greater emphasis on rhythmic counterpoint (a favourite practice of La Rue's) than homorhythm. Phrases begin both on and against the tactus. We find textural differentiation here,

[62] 'Dictez moy bergère / Par ou passerai-ge / Et par ou m'en irai-ge / Dictez le moy bergère / Je suis venu de la riviere'.

[63] 'En espoir vis et si languis / Ayant ung merveilleux regret / Estre je ne scauroye dehet / Tant que la voye se m'est advis'. Lawrence F. Bernstein, 'Josquin's Chansons as Generic Paradigms', in Jessie Ann Owens and Anthony Cummings (eds.), *Music in Renaissance Cities and Courts: Studies in Honor of Lewis Lockwood* (Warren, Mich.: Harmonie Park Press, 1997), 35–55 at 39, demonstrates that the usual French secular double canon was built on a popular tune; how typical of La Rue to have avoided this expectation!

more so than in *Dicte moy bergère*; despite the expected emphasis on pairs, three- and four-voice sections appear as well. There are even motivic connections between phrases. *En espoir vis* is readily believable as a work of La Rue's, and it shares similarities with both the Benedictus from the *Missa Ave sanctissima Maria* and *Da pacem domine*, such as the textural variety in the Benedictus, the cramming of three cadential centres into a mere twenty-five breves in the case of *Da pacem domine*, and the willingness to begin phrases on the off-beat.

The last work, *Leal schray tante*, appears in two separate sources with an attribution to La Rue; both are posthumous and German (RegB C120 and VienNB Mus. 18810). Lacking any text other than incipits, the work is impossible to judge in terms of text–music relationship, though it looks more like La Rue's works that circulate with text that those without (e.g. *Fors seulement* or *Sancta Maria virgo*). Although many features of the work fit comfortably with La Rue's secular style, the cadences are very problematic. The final cadence is atypical; it finishes with all voices, as is standard for La Rue, but the work only moves to full four-voice texture a mere six minims before the final breve; in his unquestioned works La Rue gives himself more lead time going into the final cadence. The cadential layout is significantly off, too. All cadences are on A or D, while La Rue normally prefers more variety. All but the last produce unison or octave harmonies only (La Rue is much more likely to include fifths and/or thirds), all but one are superius/tenor constructions (La Rue frequently depends on altus and bassus), all but one are conclusive (La Rue often undercuts the sense of closure by a variety of means), and all but one are delineated by rests after the cadence, not a favourite La Rue device. There is really no difficulty in discarding this work from La Rue's output.

Works attributed only to La Rue

Of the works attributed only to La Rue but which receive their attributions outside of court sources, *Pourquoy non*, *Ce n'est pas je*, *Il est bien heureux*, *Secretz regretz*, and *Pour ung jamais* all fit readily into La Rue's output. The others do not. *Le renvoye*, a bicinium that receives its attribution to La Rue only in 1549[16] (where it appears as a sacred contrafactum), is also transmitted in the court partbooks VienNB Mus. 18832, without text. The true title comes from MunBS 260, which provides the clue as to its construction. The top voice of the work is the superius of Compère's *rondeau* of the same name, transposed down an octave but otherwise unaltered. The work is thus a cantus-firmus bicinium of the sort often used in the sixteenth century for pedagogical purposes, since it involves a small number of voices and uses material possibly already familiar to the performer.[64] La Rue is not known to have written any of this kind of work. Though he has fifty-six bicinia, all are from his masses, and only seven are for equal voices (as this work is). Of these

---

[64] See Lawrence F. Bernstein, 'French Duos in the First Half of the Sixteenth Century', in John Walter Hill (ed.), *Studies in Musicology in Honor of Otto E. Albrecht* (Kassel: Bärenreiter, 1980), 43–87, for an excellent overview of this genre.

seven, five are canonic, and neither of the other two uses pre-existent material. Although it is possible that this is his unique venture into the genre, the newly written voice argues strongly against that idea, as it has extremely long lines, few cadences, and little imitation. The attribution to La Rue again seems to stem from posthumous German appreciation for his music—obviously coupled with an inexact understanding of his style.

Il fault morir is another work that draws on Compère, presenting the tenor of his motet-chanson *Tant ay d'ennuy/O vos omnes* (which also survives with the text 'O devotz cueurs') in the tenor, with the same rhythmic values and at the same pitch as the original. Compère's motet-chanson was his most widely disseminated venture in this genre, but it is unclear whether it was written by the early 1490s, the time that *Il fault morir* must date from if it is La Rue's, as we shall see. None of the sources that contain Compère's work appeared before the late 1490s at the earliest, though this does not preclude composition at an earlier date.[65] Compère's piece is included in both BrusBR 228 and the somewhat earlier LonBL 35087, as well as many other sources.

Il fault morir exists in a single source, RegB C120, where only the gloomy-sounding incipit remains (literally: 'it is necessary to die'). The first part of this source, where the song appears, has recently been connected to the court of Maximilian,[66] thereby strengthening the attribution and prompting a re-evaluation of the work. As we shall see, it still presents problems.

The 'Maximilian' portion of the manuscript also includes La Rue's *Pour ung jamais*, here indicated as 'fraw margetsen lied' but otherwise transmitted anonymously. This work's lack of attribution to La Rue does not really lessen the possible value of the *Il fault morir* attribution; Marguerite, as Maximilian's daughter, was obviously far more important as the author of *Pour ung jamais*'s text than La Rue was as the piece's composer. Furthermore, both the low range of *Il fault morir* (down to *C*) and the six-voice texture are completely in keeping with a possible authorship by La Rue,[67] since he explored lower depths and fuller textures more than almost anyone of his generation (Isaac also is noted for full-textured works, but not for the lower depths).

It becomes rather problematic to judge the work after that, however, since there are no precise parallels in his output. La Rue normally uses a canonic foundation for his six-voice works; this has none. Neither does the early Credo, but that is a sacred work, and it is furthermore a work without pre-existent material. La Rue

---

[65] Wesner, 'The Chansons of Loyset Compère', unfortunately does not cover the motet-chansons, but does list the sources. The portion of UppsU 76a including *Tant ay d'ennuy/O vos omnes* is from *c.*1515–20; see Howard Mayer Brown, Introduction to *Uppsala Universitetsbiblioteket Vokalmusik i handskrift 76a* (Renaissance Music in Facsimile, 19; New York and London: Garland, 1987), p. vi.

[66] Rainer Birkendorf, *Der Codex Pernner: Quellenkundliche Studien zu einer Musikhandschrift des frühen 16. Jahrhunderts (Regensburg, Bischöfliche Zentralbibliothek, Sammlung Proske, Ms. C120)*, 3 vols. (Collectanea musicologica, 6/1; Augsburg: Bernd Wißner, 1994), i. 27.

[67] Six-voice works by La Rue include one Credo, one mass (*Missa Ave sanctissima Maria*), the motets *Ave sanctissima Maria*, *Pater de coelis deus*, and *Salve Jesu* (now lost), and the chanson *Je ne dis mot*; sections for six voices are found in *Credo Angeli archangeli* and *Magnificat primi toni*.

Ex. 4.4. La Rue?, *Il fault morir*, bars 1–16 (from RegB C120, pp. 10–11)

has numerous pieces built on polyphonic secular models, but none of these is for six voices. Perhaps closest to *Il fault morir* are *D'ung aultre aymer* and the anonymous *Maria mater gratie/Fors seulement*, since both are built on a strict cantus firmus drawn from a polyphonic model and have five voices (the five-voice *Fors seulement*, built on a canonic foundation, is too dissimilar in its basic premiss for adequate comparison).

Unfortunately, *Il fault morir* does not look much like either *D'ung aultre aymer* or *Maria mater gratie/Fors seulement* (see Ex. 4. 4). There is much emphasis on homorhythm at long note values, very few cadences, little imitation, and a fairly thick texture. All voices come to a complete halt at bar 10—shades of *Pourquoy non*—and then again at bar 48 (the work is seventy-five bars in modern transcription). These pauses are presumably text-generated, though it is impossible to give more information than that. The entrance of the lowest voice before the first fermata is also quite similar to the entrance of the bassus in *Pourquoy non*. The initial fermata pause is then followed by the entry of all voices in repeated-note homorhythm (again like *Pourquoy non*, though rather more ponderous). By comparison, the anonymous *Maria mater gratie/Fors seulement* looks much more like La Rue, with its more interesting rhythmic counterpoint, shifting textures, and continual titbits of imitation. *D'ung aultre aymer*, though having less imitation than is usual for La Rue, nevertheless opens with three voices imitatively introducing the same motif as the borrowed melody; further, the extensive use of free counterpoint is surely intended as a stylistic reference to Ockeghem, whose work La Rue is borrowing and who similarly makes very little use of imitation in the original work. In contrast, imitation is a major structural feature of Compère's motet-chanson, in which superius and tenor are prominently linked in imitation at the start and return to that device again and again throughout the work, and there are several catchy motifs that the composer of *Il fault morir* failed to pursue in other voices.

Although (not surprisingly) La Rue's six-voice pieces tend to have a generally thicker texture than works with smaller forces, his other non-canonic writing for these resources allows for more frequent textural contrast. In the six-voice Credo, for example, the work begins with two voices only, rapidly joined by a third. In the first five bars of the piece the texture changes from two to three to four to five voices, then continues with five voices (one of the intial voices drops out, but the sixth voice, previously unheard, enters at just that point) and then drops to two voices. Full six-voice texture is not reached until bar 8, and then it only lasts for a semibreve. Similarly, the six-voice section (the middle part) of the eight-voice *Credo Angeli archangeli* opens with a single voice, then moves to three-voice texture, then adds a fourth and fifth voice, with all six voices not sounding together until the eleventh bar, and then only for a semibreve. In contrast, *Il fault morir* opens with four voices, keeps all sounding for the first five bars (no rest in any of these voices), and adds the remaining two voices in bar 6 to lead up to the first fermata.

Il fault morir could only be La Rue's if it were the earliest work of his to survive,[68] an experiment that did not completely come off. It certainly makes a strong contrast with his other early works, such as *Tous nobles cueurs*, with its polished

[68] In which case it would presumably have remained with Maximilian after La Rue returned to the Low Countries, showing up only years later in RegB C120.

sophistication. If *Il fault morir* is his, it would represent an attempt to make a splash through its outsized texture and sepulchral range, as well as the unusual grand pause shortly after the work had started—a pause whose effect was probably undercut by the more normal division occuring about two-thirds of the way through the composition. In its treatment of the borrowed material the work seems to present a series of missed opportunities, with the composer ignoring promising melodic material in the model in favour of non-imitative and rhythmically uninspired counterpoint, two traits not normally associated with La Rue but perhaps generated by his unease with so many voices.

If we see this as an experiment, it is one that La Rue learned something from. His six-voice Credo is far more assured in its handling of the multiple lines, incorporating imitation to a greater degree and generating continual textural contrast.[69] Despite the greater success of the Credo, however, La Rue still seems to have set aside the exploration of big textures after this work until somewhat later, and then he normally turned to canon as a foundation for anything with six voices. The idea of the short opening phrase set off by a fermata and then followed by homorhythm is similarly handled with infinitely greater care in *Pourquoy non*.[70]

It is also possible that one of his colleagues wrote *Il fault morir*, imitating certain more obvious aspects of La Rue's style without really succeeding in capturing its spirit. This view would eliminate any worries about the date of Compère's work, and would substitute a different interpretation for the work. Rather than being La Rue's early, not especially successful attempt to achieve compositional distinction, it would represent instead someone else's effort to borrow two of the most distinctive elements of La Rue's music—many-voiced texture and deep ranges—as well as aspects of one of his most striking and unusual secular works, *Pourquoy non*. That the work ended up with La Rue's name attached in a posthumous source, even one connected to Maximilian's court, is by no means impossible. It is quite easy to imagine the scribe receiving an anonymous exemplar coming from the Habsburg-Burgundian court and assuming that a work with this many voices and this span could only be by La Rue. In short, there is no easy answer to the problem this work poses, and it has been identified with a question mark on the various lists of works.

The last work presents rather different problems. *En l'amour d'une dame* survives today in an incomplete collection (LonBL 19583) compiled in Ferrara almost two decades after La Rue's death; most of its works are by composers of a later generation. Only one of the work's original five voices, the altus, survives

---

[69] Perhaps the thick texture of *Il fault morir* represented insecurity on the part of the composer—a fear that lightening the texture would lessen the impact of the six voices. At the time the work must have been written if La Rue were the composer, the early 1490s, six-voice texture was almost unknown on the Continent; Isaac's *Missa Wolauff Gesell von hinnen* is a rare example.

[70] In two of his masses, La Rue also brings everything to a halt very early in the Credo movement, much earlier than normally done. These two are *Missa Ave sanctissima Maria* (pausing after a mere nine breves) and *Missa O salutaris hostia* (after fifteen breves). Neither mass seems particularly early, and both, interestingly, are completely canonic.

today.[71] Both the rhyme scheme of the text (*aabb*) and the overall formal structure of the work (AAB) are unknown in La Rue's authentic secular works. The initial gesture has a prominent melodic augmented fourth; while La Rue is no stranger to dissonance, he does not normally display it in this manner. The very wide-ranging melody spans a thirteenth; this is true also of the altus of *Plorer gemir crier/Requiem*, but unlike that work, *En l'amour d'une dame* includes two phrases that sweep through all or most of the entire range in descending line. While it is obviously difficult to make an assessment on the basis of a single voice, what remains hardly speaks for La Rue's authorship.

Anonymous works

The court scriptorium often transmitted La Rue's works (both secular and sacred) without attribution, raising the possibility that some of the many anonymous works in these collections are by La Rue even though no contemporary attribution has come down to us. Scholars have been suggesting some of these works as La Rue's since the nineteenth century, but the most thorough treatments have been undertaken by Picker and Bernstein, whose ideas about which anonymous chansons are by La Rue are convincing (see the citations in App. D), and whose views on *Soubz ce tumbel* (not La Rue), *Se je souspire/Ecce iterum* (also not; perhaps by Marguerite instead), and *Sailliés avant* (perhaps) I have also followed. More recently, John Milsom mentioned several other chansons in BrusBr 228 as possibilities or probabilities for La Rue's authorship. *Dulces exuvie* was already noted earlier as promising; *Quant il advient*, which Milsom thought was a maybe, is much less likely. Apart from the various criticisms that Picker raises about this work, two other points make it unlikely to be La Rue's. The final cadence is formed by the top two voices, something I do not recall ever seeing in La Rue's output (final cadences are invariably classic superius/tenor pairs). Furthermore, at two separate points in the piece a breve begins on a weak beat. Perhaps one instance might be excused as a highly unusual aberration (though again, nothing else like this comes to mind with La Rue), but twice in the same piece is too much to dismiss.

In a rather different vein, Rainer Birkendorf proposed an anonymous *Plus aultre* in RegB C120 (the second part, which lacks a definite connection to the imperial court) as probably being by La Rue.[72] Only the incipit of the text remains, but it is a variant of the motto of Charles, *Plus oultre*. He adopted this motto only in 1516, and possibly not until the summer of that year.[73] This timing decreases the likelihood that La Rue wrote the work, unless Charles was using the motto before La

---

[71] Based on her work on this manuscript, Jessie Ann Owens kindly informed me that the music appears in the five-voice section of the original collection. For more on this collection and its scattered components, see the entry in *CC*.

[72] Birkendorf, *Der Codex Pernner*, i. 233.

[73] Ibid.

Rue retired. Nor, as it turns out, does the style of the piece argue convincingly for La Rue's authorship.

Although only a textual incipit is given with the work, it is quite possible that the work was never intended to be paired with a complete text; its frequent use of motivic repetition and sequential motion matches other untexted works of this time (though these attributes are by no means restricted to 'instrumental' works of the period). But it does not look much like La Rue's untexted works, such as *Si dormiero*, *Sancta Maria virgo*, or the various secular art-song reworkings (and not simply because this is work in a slightly different genre). Cadences are sometimes missing where we would expect them, awkward in construction, or surprisingly old-fashioned for what would presumably be La Rue's very last work (see Ex. 4.5). The melodic writing at times is uncharacteristic; see Ex. 4.6, where both the descending line in the tenor and the downward octave leap with dotted rhythm in the altus are odd in the context of the composer's usual style. Similarly, the bassus line in Ex. 4.7 is very unexpected, with the continuation of the rising line after the flatted B. Even the opening of the piece sends a warning. After a straightforward point of imitation put forth by bassus, tenor, altus, and superius (perfectly normal for La Rue), the altus then returns with an exact repetition of the opening motif; this is very unlike La Rue, who would be far more likely this early in the piece to present an altered version of this material were he to bring it back right away. Overall, the writing speaks against La Rue's authorship.

OBSERVATIONS ON TIMING AND DISTRIBUTION

Perhaps the first thing to note is that in the secular music, La Rue had already covered a wide stylistic range by the time he returned from Spain in the latter part of 1508; FlorC 2439 was probably compiled around this time at the latest. Between the secular works transmitted somewhat earlier and those contained in this manuscript we can find both *rondeaux* and through-composed works, largely melismatic compositions and those stressing syllabic underlay, traditional-sounding works versus those imitating popular arrangements. The suggestion here is that La Rue explored different styles more readily in secular than in mass music, at least based on the appearance of these works in sources. Lacking a firm chronology, such a suggestion is obviously tentative, and yet it is not an unreasonable one. Secular works, much shorter and surely more susceptible to rapid changes of fashion, seem a more accessible venue for experimentation than the weightier and more conservative genre of the mass.

At the same time, the secular works that circulated earliest have something significant in common with the sacred works appearing at the same time: taken as a whole, they seem intended to make a significant impression right from the start. Three songs were unquestionably directed towards Marguerite: *Tous nobles cueurs*,

Ex. 4.5. Anonymous, *Plus aultre*: (*a*) bars 55–8; (*b*) bars 67–9; (*c*) bars 85–6 (from RegB C120, pp. 198–9)

(*a*)

(*b*)   (*c*)

Ex. 4.6. Anonymous, *Plus aultre*, bars 90–4 (from RegB C120, pp. 198–9)

Tous les regetz, and *De l'oeil de la fille du roy*. One, *Mijn hert*, was surely a gesture to those whose first language was Flemish. *Dedans bouton* could hardly fail to attract the attention of anyone who knew the Bouton family, closely connected to the court. *Fors seulement* and *Ma bouche rit* fed the court's apparent love of art-song

Ex. 4.7. Anonymous, *Plus aultre*, bars 16–18 (from RegB C120, pp. 198–9)

reworkings. *Ce n'est pas jeu*, in a woman's voice, quite probably set a poem by one of the various noblewomen present at the court. The paired songs *Pourquoy tant* and *Il viendra le jour désiré* were an unusual novelty at the time. *Plorer, gemir, crier/Requiem* was probably an answer to the court poet Molinet's demand to mourn Ockeghem, as we shall see in the next chapter. *Autant en emporte le vent* captured the latest style without degenerating into coarse lyrics. *Pourquoy non* was probably the most egregious attention-getter, but even a more traditional song such as *Tous nobles cueurs* demonstrates careful consideration of the text and some thought about how best to bring it out. Surely all these songs were pleasing to his audience.

Some of them were pleasing to those outside the court as well. It is striking to note that we find the same overall pattern for distribution of the secular music that we did for distribution of the sacred music: by and large, it is the earliest pieces that fare the best, with the later sources including pieces distributed far less often. The most popular ones appeared mainly before FlorC 2439: *Ce n'est pas jeu* (six sources), *Pourquoy non* and *Tous les regretz* (nine sources each), *Mijn hert* (thirteen sources?).[74] Some early pieces remained in circulation for quite some time: *Ce n'est pas jeu* appears in two sources from the 1530s, *Pourquoy non* is still of interest around 1540 (it is listed in the index of SGallS 463, though never copied into the collection), *Mijn hert* was copied in 1551 (UlmS 237), and even *Tous nobles cueurs* was considered worth including in 1538[9] (admittedly a collection with many 'oldies but goodies').[75] To this early group of popular works we can add *Trop plus secret* (from FlorC 2439) with ten sources, and the favourite of all, *Incessament mon pauvre cueur*, in fifteen sources. It is not necessarily a given that works appearing earlier would circulate longer; *Incessament*, which surely seems like a later work with its greater number of voices, canonic foundation, and final triad, wins the

---

[74] The Saint-Gelais poems were popular in their own right; see Winn, 'Octavien de Saint-Gelais', 66, and ead., '"Regret" Chansons', 26. *Tous les regretz* was also in a now-lost manuscript owned by Palatine Count Ottheinrich at Neuberg, as we know from the inventory of his library contained in HeidU 318.

[75] Other works circulated for an equally long time, e.g. *Trop plus secret*, which is in the mid-century RegT 3/I. *Incessament* was included in retrospective collections as late as 1572[2] .

prize for most sources for a La Rue chanson. In any event, we cannot really say what is normal for this time since we lack this kind of distribution survey for any of La Rue's contemporaries.

In short, the picture that emerges is that of a composer making shrewd choices in his decisions of what to set and how to set it, making important compositional moves early on, and covering all his bases.

5 Patterns of Influence

This final chapter explores certain patterns of influence during La Rue's lifetime and after his death, taking as subjects two composers whose example affected the way his music sounded, the paths by which his music became known in the sixteenth century, the writers who cited him and his music from the late fifteenth into the seventeenth century, and the renewal of awareness first prompted by the stirrings of musicology at the end of the seventeenth century and continuing up to our time. All have influenced our current understanding of the composer, an understanding that nonetheless remains incomplete five centuries after La Rue's time.

OCKEGHEM AND JOSQUIN

Ockeghem and Josquin were far from the only composers whose music La Rue knew and emulated; Pipelare and Isaac, for example, immediately spring to mind as others who influenced La Rue. For now at least, however, Ockeghem and Josquin appear as the ones figuring most prominently in an understanding of La Rue's borrowings. This may well change, for the tapesty of interconnection among composers of this time grows continually in richness and complexity.

This talk of influence presupposes that La Rue knew who wrote the pieces that inspired him.[1] Perhaps this was not always the case, but Ockeghem and Josquin are attributed with some regularity in court manuscripts: the early sources VatC 234, FlorC 2439, VienNB 1783, and BrusBR 9126, for example, are all thorough in their ascriptions.[2] I suspect that La Rue's extensive and well-documented travels also increased his chances of knowing who wrote individual pieces.

Ockeghem

La Rue is sometimes cited as a pupil of Ockeghem because Molinet calls on him (among others) to mourn the passing of Ockeghem in his famous poem 'Nymphes des bois'. Although no particular reason exists to put La Rue anywhere

---

[1] Nor do we always know who wrote these works; a number of the Josquin pieces cited below have been questioned by various writers as to their authenticity. The matter of influence for La Rue works in several ways, however. If La Rue thought a work was by Josquin, then his concept of 'Josquin' included that work. By the same token a work could influence him regardless of his knowledge of the composer. *Planxit autem David* (a work that shows up with some regularity on 'suspicious' lists for Josquin) influenced *Considera Israel* whether or not La Rue thought it was by Josquin.

[2] Josquin's *Missa Ave maris stella* was left anonymous in BrusBR 9126 but appears with his name in VienNB 1783.

other than Tournai in his youth, he possibly had contact with Ockeghem at some other point. While various superficial biographical resemblances exist between the two composers (each remarkably loyal to a major musical institution for decades at a time when most composers changed venue frequently, each assuming the guise of leading composer at that institution, each having visited Spain, neither known to have been in Italy), it is naturally the more significant musical ones that interest us.

Whether or not La Rue knew any of Ockeghem's music in his youth, he was certainly exposed to it at the Habsburg-Burgundian court. The early court manuscript VatC 234 is the major source of Ockeghem's mass music, containing as it does every mass except the early one for three voices; it also includes his motet *Intemerata Dei mater*.[3] With the court performing a polyphonic mass daily, La Rue would probably have become intimately acquainted with these major works. He also knew at least some of the secular music. FlorC 2439 has several secular works: *Baisiés moy dont fort*, the second *Fors seulement* setting (*Fors seulement contre ce qu'ay promys*), *Je n'ay deuil*, and *Petite camusette*. More directly, La Rue certainly knew three of Ockeghem's most famous works—*Ma bouche rit*, *D'ung aultre aymer*, and *Fors seulement*—since he wrote strict cantus-firmus settings based on these models, using the last on three separate occasions. In *Ma bouche rit* he drew as well on material from *Je n'ay deuil*. One wonders, too, whether La Rue's interest in chansons that responded to an earlier one (e.g. *Il viendra le jour désiré* as a response to *Pourquoy tant*) was prompted by knowledge of Ockeghem's two *Fors seulement* settings, the second of which is sometimes seen as a reply to the first.

La Rue is one of the leaders in writing masses for five or more voices and is also extremely well known for his exploration of written low pitch. In each of these realms Ockeghem is his most important predecessor. Ockeghem has two five-voice masses (one without model and one on *Fors seulement*); he also has a five-voice motet, *Intemerata Dei mater*. These works are the same that explore low ranges, down to low C' in all three, and each of these works is contained in VatC 234. This manuscript also includes five-voice works by Barbireau (*Missa Virgo parens*), Josquin (*Stabat mater*), Weerbeke (also a *Stabat mater*), and especially Regis (five separate motets) as well as six-voice works by Isaac (*Angeli archangeli*) and anonymous (the second part of a textless work plus the motet *Ave rosa speciosa*). Of these full-textured works, four stand out for their low ranges: Weerbeke's *Stabat mater* descends to E below the staff, and three of the Regis motets sink to the D below that (*Lux solempnis adest*, *Lauda Syon salvatorem*, and *Clangat plebs flores*). La Rue was clearly familiar with both works exceeding the standard four-voice texture and with those exploring low ranges.

It is hard to escape the conclusion that La Rue was influenced by these pieces, especially those of Ockeghem, which were the most striking in their use of the low range. Certainly La Rue's ferial mass would seem connected in certain respects to

---

[3] A later addition to the collection was his motet *Ave Maria*.

Ockeghem's unnamed five-voice mass: the use of five voices, the low range, and the treatment of the chant model in the Gloria all suggest as much.[4] But La Rue seems determined to surpass Ockeghem by writing a full work (Ockeghem's is only three short movements) and underpinning everything with a canonic foundation at increasing rhythmic distance between dux and comes. One can also imagine a desire to outdo Ockeghem in other works by using six-voice texture and extending the range even lower, to Bb'. Works by La Rue that go one better than Ockeghem in these components are found within the earliest sources to contain his music—the six-voice Credo in VatC 234 itself and *Pourquoy non* in several early collections, enhancing the idea put forth earlier that La Rue was intent from the start on making his mark and creating pieces that would cause a sensation.

Ockeghem used his own songs as models for the *Missa Fors seulement*, *Missa Ma maistresse*, and possibly *Missa Au travail suis*; La Rue used his own works as models in the *Missa Tous les regretz*, *Missa Incessament*, and *Missa Ave sanctissima Maria*. Because composers since Dufay had been doing this as well, La Rue was not necessarily inspired by Ockeghem in this practice, but it is worth noting. Similarly, La Rue's occasional use of non-imitative counterpoint could be an influence from Ockeghem or just a basic generational influence from older music (although in a work such as La Rue's setting of *D'ung aultre aymer* that texture would seem to be an intentional reference). As for treatment of a pre-existent melody, La Rue's overwhelming tendency to handle his model freely connects him much more to Ockeghem's manner of composing than to that of Busnoys. The mensuration canons in La Rue's *Missa L'homme armé I*, though derived more immediately from Josquin, would also seem a nod in the direction of Ockeghem's *Missa prolationum*, the tour-de-force mass that consists entirely of this most difficult kind of canonic writing.

Ockeghem's *Requiem*—the earliest to survive—clearly influenced La Rue's own mass for the dead, itself one of the very earliest cycles (his contemporaries Brumel, Prioris, and Févin wrote polyphonic settings as well). At a time when the Requiem was not standardized, La Rue's and Ockeghem's masses are similar though not identical in what they set to polyphony. Both set the Introit, Kyrie, Offertory, and Tract with the text *Sicut cervus* (this last a rarity at the time); neither set the sequence (Brumel's is the only early setting of this). La Rue did not set the Gradual, though Ockeghem did, while La Rue's mass includes the Sanctus, Agnus, and Communion; if Ockeghem ever set these parts, they have not survived.

La Rue uses the liturgically appropriate chants, freely embellished, as does Ockeghem; he proceeds with stricter treatment of the chant in the Osanna and

⁴ Ronald Cross, 'Matthaeus Pipelare: A Historical and Stylistic Study of his Works' (Ph.D. diss., New York University, 1961), 150–60, was the first to include Ockeghem's work with La Rue's in the ferial tradition; Kreider, 'The Masses for Five and Six Voices', i. 45, first noticed the similar models and treatment in the Gloria movements of the two composers.

Agnus I, two parts that do not survive for Ockeghem. He makes far more textural shifts in this mass than he does anywhere else, and at highly unusual places, expanding from the basic four voices into five-voice texture for Kyrie II, *Quam olim Abrahae* from the Offertory, the Sanctus and Osanna, and all sections of the Agnus, while cutting back to duos for the first two sections of the Tract (*Sicut cervus* and *Sitivit anima*), starting first with a duo for high voices and following with one for low voices. Although Ockeghem is working primarily with three voices, he too expands the texture for his last Kyrie, going to four voices.[5] Ockeghem also makes the unusual gesture of starting the Tract with duos for both *Sicut cervus* and *Sitivit anima* (similarly opening with one for high voices and then one for low), and uses fuller texture for his *Quam olim Abrahae* (though he employs four voices for the beginning of the Offertory, unlike La Rue). La Rue also switches between movements using higher cleffing combinations and those using lower, as does Ockeghem (though this is another work where La Rue frequently plunges below the gamut, to low *B♭ʹ* at one point, unlike Ockeghem). These highly unusual correlations between the two works—each of which is atypical in many ways for its composer—cannot be coincidental, and the similarities must have been evident to contemporaries who knew both settings, such as La Rue's colleagues.

Josquin

The precise relationship of Josquin to the court of Habsburg-Burgundy has been a matter of dispute for quite some time. No evidence exists for any kind of formal link between the composer and the institution, and probably none ever existed. Yet the informal connections are hard to ignore, starting with the significant position of Josquin's music in the court manuscript complex. Although La Rue is far and away the composer most frequently featured in this collection, Josquin is second in quantity despite lacking any obvious reason for holding this position. Of the masses most often considered Josquin's, for instance, all but *Missa ad fugam*, *Missa di dadi*, and *Missa D'ung aultre amer* are included,[6] along with numerous motets and secular works. Although many of these works appear only in later court collections, it is impossible to tell at what point the music entered the court repertoire, and his compositions are present right from the earliest surviving source. With his *Missa L'homme armé sexti toni* and his five-voice *Stabat mater* he is an equal presence with La Rue in VatC 234 (Josquin's mass follows immediately after La Rue's two works in the manuscript).

Other early court collections include him as well. VienNB 1783 has the *Missa Ave maris stella*, BrusBr 9126 opens with that mass and also contains the *Missa Hercules dux ferrarie* (altered to read *Missa Philippus rex castillie*), *Missa Malheur me*

---

[5] Ockeghem's Kyrie has seven sections in all.

[6] Also missing is the *Missa Mater patris*, which is unlikely to be by Josquin; see M. Jennifer Bloxam, 'Masses Based on Polyphonic Songs and Canonic Masses', in Richard Sherr (ed.), *The Josquin Companion* (Oxford: Oxford University Press, 2000), 151–209 at 186–95.

bat, the *Stabat mater* again, *Huc me sydereo descendere*, *Missus est Gabriel angelus*, and *Gaude virgo mater Christi*. FlorC 2439 includes *Entrée je suis* and the motet-chansons *A la mort/Monstra te esse matrem* and *Fortune d'estrange plummaige/Pauper sum ego*. The slightly later BrusBR 228 transmits the latter motet-chanson as *Ce povre mendiant/Pauper sum*, along with *Plaine de dueil*, *Entrée je suis* again, *Plus nulz regretz*, and an anonymous song and motet that Martin Picker thought might also be Josquin's: *Soubz ce tumbel* and *Proch dolor/Pie Jhesu*.[7] *Plus nulz regretz* is the only song in the otherwise entirely anonymous collection to receive an ascription, and thus it stands out unexpectedly from its surroundings. And, as noted, the later manuscripts contain much more of Josquin's output. Whether any personal relationship with the composer existed or not, the court was not averse to the sound of his music.

Josquin's connections with court poets are part of the puzzle surrounding his relationship with the court. He is the one to set Molinet's *Nymphes des bois*, not La Rue, who would seem the more logical choice since he was resident at the court when the poem was written and was also named within.[8] *Plus nulz regretz* sets a political poem written specifically for the court after 1 January 1508 by Jean Lemaire de Belges, and *Soubz ce tumbel*, written in 1505 on the death of Marguerite's pet parrot, is another poem by that poet. Although *Soubz ce tumbel* was written in 1505, while Marguerite still lived in Savoy, it would (if it is really by Josquin) provide a connection with Lemaire de Belges (and thus, tangentially at least, Marguerite). Lemaire de Belges is certainly a far more likely contact with Josquin for the unquestioned *Plus nulz regretz* than Marguerite herself, since she was apparently unaware in May 1508 that Josquin was provost at Condé.[9] In another possible literary connection, Lemaire de Belges may be the author of *Cueurs desolez*, given a motet-chanson setting by Josquin.

As noted in Chapter 1, Josquin may have come in personal contact with the court once, twice, or never. Regardless of a meeting with the composer or not, Philip the Fair may have had a hand in providing Josquin with the provostship of Condé in 1504.[10] The Condé connection is an extremely interesting one, for Paula Higgins has discovered that Braconnier became a canon there at the same time as Josquin in May 1504.[11] For a short period of time thereafter Braconnier might have been a conduit for the music of Josquin to the court. A further potential court connection was brought up by William Prizer, who speculated that Josquin's *Ut*

---

[7] PickerCA, 76, 89–90.

[8] Although the interpolation of an additional line of text suggests that Josquin is not setting the work specifically at Molinet's instigation. On this interpolation, see Edward E. Lowinsky, *The Medici Codex of 1518: A Choirbook of Motets Dedicated to Lorenzo de' Medici, Duke of Urbino*, 3 vols. (Monuments of Renaissance Music, 3–5; Chicago and London: University of Chicago Press, 1968), text vol., 214. For another Molinet/Josquin connection see Blackburn, 'For Whom Do the Singers Sing?', 604 and 609 n. 26.

[9] See Kellman, 'Josquin and the Courts of the Netherlands and France', 207–8.

[10] See Kellman's comments ibid. 207. His cautious assessment of the chapter's politics changed to a more direct claim in id., 'Brussels, Bibliothèque royale de Belgique MS 9126', in *TA* 73: 'it was he [Philip] who nominated the composer to the provostship . . . in Condé . . .'.

[11] Private comm., 18 Oct. 1988. The document is BNF lat. 9917.

Phoebi radiis was 'associated in some way with the meetings of the order [of the Golden Fleece] and with its Marian Office'.[12]

The output of La Rue demonstrates various similarities with that of Josquin.[13] We have already noted the strict borrowing from Josquin's *Ave Maria* in La Rue's *Missa de septem doloribus* as well as the more general modelling of the Pleni from the *Missa de sancta cruce* on the Agnus II of the *Missa L'ami baudichon*. Both drew more heavily on Ockeghem than any other composer for direct cantus-firmus borrowing (in Josquin's case four works based on *D'ung aultre amer*). Both set the text *Gaude virgo*, both set most of the same text in Josquin's *Planxit autem David* and La Rue's *Considera Israel*, both wrote a *Credo de villagiis* (Josquin possibly more than one), both wrote a *Missa de beata virgine*, both used the chant *Inviolata* as the basis for a work (Josquin for a motet, La Rue for a mass), both borrow from *Je ne vis oncques* (Josquin in his five-voice song *L'amye a tous*), both use *Comme femme* as a cantus firmus (Josquin in his five-voice *Stabat mater*; La Rue in his *Credo Angeli archangeli*, where he derives it from Isaac's motet of the same name), both wrote at least one *Ave Maria* work (again, a mass for La Rue and a motet for Josquin), both wrote not one but two *L'homme armé* masses (this doubling up was not previously seen in the tradition), both wrote ostinato masses (*Missa Cum iocunditate* and *Missa Sancta dei genitrix* for La Rue; *Missa Faisant regretz*, *Missa La sol fa re mi*, and *Missa Hercules dux ferrariae* for Josquin), both explored the relatively restricted genre of motet-chanson and both wrote such a motet-chanson using the text *Cueurs desolez*, both included a motet within a Sanctus (La Rue in his *Missa de Sancta Anna*, Josquin in the *Missa D'ung aultre amer*, *Sanctus de passione*, and *Sanctus D'ung aultre amer*), Josquin wrote a chanson *Mille regretz* and La Rue one called *Cent mille regretz*, both may have set the text *Dulces exuvie*, both were extremely important in expanding textures beyond four voices, each frequently changed the internal texture of a piece or mass movement, with duo texture favoured by both, each wrote tightly unified melodic lines, and both were masters of canon. The most obvious differences occur in such things as their choice of models and treatment thereof (La Rue's preference for chant and heavy use of paraphrase setting him apart), La Rue's exploration of low ranges and signed accidentals, his somewhat lesser use of syllabic text setting, balanced phrases, homorhythmic texture, and exact repetition, and Josquin's greater reliance on hierarchical harmonic layouts.[14]

---

[12] Prizer, 'Music and Ceremonial', 133.

[13] Similarities were noticed as far back as Ambros in the 19th c. (August Wilhelm Ambros, *Geschichte der Musik*, 5 vols. (Breslau: F. E. C. Leuckart, 1862–82), iii. 234–40); see the discussion below.

[14] Writing in the *Oxford History of Music* in 1905, Wooldridge observed that 'Pierre de la Rue, for instance, the master who perhaps among the contemporaries of Josquin stands next to him in talent, prefers to compete with him in general in the field of canonic and proportional contrivance, while in respect of clear and intelligible harmonic progressions, such as are constant and well sustained in the work of Josquin, his compositions do not even apparently invite comparison'; see H. E. Wooldridge, *The Oxford History of Music* ii: *The Polyphonic Period, Part II, Method of Musical Art, 1300–1600* (Oxford: Clarendon Press, 1905), 240. Although the differences and similarities between La Rue and Josquin have never been treated in full, some discussion can be found in various places, including PickerCA, 72–3 and especially Walter H. Rubsamen,

Some of the similarities cited above are more apparent than real, and none has been explored in detail. Numerous composers wrote a *Credo de villagiis*, and it is more likely that La Rue got the idea of using a motet in *Missa de Sancta Anna* from his colleague Weerbeke than from Josquin (though the shared use in a Sanctus is interesting). La Rue's use of *Comme femme* was inspired by Isaac more than (if at all) by Josquin. La Rue's *Missa de beata virgine* seems to be one of the earliest polyphonic settings written as an entity, and it probably precedes Josquin's. The latter's mass is widely considered a hybrid, and in any event uses a somewhat different combination of chant models than does La Rue's. As for *Ave Maria*, La Rue's mass is built on the chant *Ave Maria . . . benedicta tu* while Josquin's more famous motet (which La Rue knew, since he quotes it in the *Missa de septem doloribus*), uses *Ave Maria . . . Virgo serena*; Josquin's *Ave Maria . . . benedicta tu* setting was much less well known. Curiously, however, even though La Rue's mass is not based on the same chant as Josquin's famous motet, its opening presents a much clearer imitative point than is usually found in his mass beginnings, and even reverses the opening pitches of Josquin's work (breve C down to semibreve G in the mass versus semibreve G up to breve C in the motet); could La Rue's choice of texture and initial motif be some kind of reference to the opening of Josquin's motet?[15]

A stronger connection is found between two of the ostinato masses; the structural similarities between La Rue's *Missa Cum iocunditate* and Josquin's *Missa La sol fa re mi* (the latter of which circulated in early court manuscript BrusBR 9216) are rather more than we might expect. Each uses a five-note ostinato figure,[16] each brings it back constantly, and each places it in all voices. Each continually varies the rhythmic value of the figure, and each normally places it on either the natural or the hard hexachord (both works, interestingly, were very popular masses).

The connection between *Planxit autem David* and *Considera Israel* is undeniable; both are in four sections and make a textual break at precisely the same awkward spot, in the middle of a sentence.[17] La Rue omitted the opening of the text to make it more appropriate as a mourning motet for Marguerite[18] and adopted a considerably more syllabic style than was his wont, in keeping with the similar style of *Planxit autem David*.

Although Josquin's *Missa L'homme armé super voces musicales* does not appear in a court manuscript until the late collection VienNB 11778, La Rue seems to have known it (just as he knew various other works not in court manuscripts, which

'Unifying Techniques in Selected Masses of Josquin and La Rue: A Stylistic Comparison', in *JosCon*, 369–400.

[15] While the pitches of each are chant-derived, the rhythm is not.

[16] La Rue's is chant-derived while Josquin's is freely composed.

[17] 'A sanguine interfectorum, ab adipe fortium / Sagitta Jonathae nunquam rediit retrorsum' (From the blood of the slain, from the fat of the mighty / The bow of Jonathan turned not back). For Josquin this break is between the second and third sections; for La Rue between the first and second. Both composers start the final section at 'Doleo super te'.

[18] See Meconi, 'Another Look at *Absalon*', 22.

obviously do not contain the complete repertoire available to the chapel). La Rue's first *L'homme armé* mass is surely related to it, and again La Rue's seems to be the later work. Among other features, Josquin's mass is noted for its extensive use of mensuration canons. Each section of the Kyrie has a two-voice mensuration canon plus two free voices; the Benedictus is a series of three duos, each of which is a mensuration canon, and the second Agnus, for three voices, is a 3 ex 1 mensuration canon. La Rue's mass, though doing nothing fancy in the Benedictus, is otherwise similarly structured as far as its canons go. Each section of the Kyrie is based on a two-voice mensuration canon; in the Christe and Kyrie II the voices involved are exactly the same as those chosen by Josquin, altus/tenor for the former and tenor/bassus for the latter. In the Kyrie I, La Rue also uses tenor/bassus, while Josquin instead involves superius/tenor. In the Agnus II, La Rue again exceeds Josquin in complexity by adding another voice and writing a 4 ex 1 mensuration canon (both composers begin this canon simultaneously in all voices).[19] As these are almost the only mensuration canons in La Rue's output[20] and are placed in precisely the same spots that Josquin chose, the obvious conclusion is that La Rue modelled the canonic features of his mass on Josquin's, with the implied intention of outdoing him. Glarean certainly saw the Agnus II as being 'undoubtedly in emulation of Josquin', though he pronounces La Rue's canon 'far more astonishing'.[21] Jeremy Noble has also suggested that another unusual feature of La Rue's mass, the presentation of the melody on, successively and imitatively, D, E, and F at the opening of the first Agnus, may reflect the changing modes of the cantus firmus in Josquin's mass.[22]

Josquin's mass possibly influenced La Rue's *Missa Alleluia* as well. One of the most striking features aurally of the *Missa L'homme armé super voces musicales* is the placement of the cantus firmus, in augmentation, in the superius for the final Agnus section.[23] La Rue follows precisely this feature for the concluding Agnus of his *Missa Alleluia*. This is already a highly unusual mass for La Rue, involving as it does strict cantus-firmus procedure, a process he normally reserves for smaller-scale works based on very well-known secular models (the model here is unknown and presumably sacred polyphony). Placing the augmented cantus firmus in the top voice for the final section of the mass (as opposed to the middle of the five-voice texture, where it has previously resided) instantly changes the focus of the movement. The lower voices are heavily motivic and imitative in nature, as are those of Josquin's movement, and passages such as the descending sequence under

---

[19] Ockeghem's *Missa prolationum* again comes to mind here; although he did not include any 4 ex 1 mensuration canons in the mass, his double mensuration canons (which constitute the bulk of the mass) use four prolations simultaneously, as La Rue's movement does.

[20] The only other one appears in the Sicut locutus section of the *Magnificat primi toni*.

[21] See App. C, 1547 Glarean, Citation 10.

[22] LRE iv, p. lv.

[23] Josquin is by no means the only composer to treat a cantus firmus in this manner, but given La Rue's knowledge of *Super voces musicales* and his other borrowing from it, that mass is the most obvious of the possible models.

the descending cantus firmus (see Ex. 5.1(*a*)), where La Rue uses only three of the lower voices (thus equalling the four-voice texture of Josquin's mass), call Josquin's Agnus to mind as well (see Ex. 5.1(*b*)). Although there appears to be no melodic borrowing, a listener who knew Josquin's very popular mass would hardly fail to observe the overall resemblance between the two movements.[24] La Rue also places a cantus firmus in long note values in the superius of the final Agnus in his *Missa Conceptio tua*, where the opening motif of the other voices bears a striking resemblance to the Pleni of his *Missa de sancta cruce*, which itself draws on the second Agnus of Josquin's *Missa L'ami baudichon*.

Whether La Rue's second *L'homme armé* mass was intended as a response to Josquin's other *L'homme armé* mass is more problematic. Writing a second *L'homme armé* mass is significant by itself (no one besides Josquin had done so up to then), but resemblances between La Rue's second mass and the *Missa L'homme armé sexti toni* are less obvious than in the earlier pair. Josquin's mass has several notable features: the melody is placed on F instead of G, canonic foundations are used for the Osanna and the initial Sanctus, and the final Agnus has an incredibly intricate construction with its expansion to six voices, four of which make up a double canon at the minim, with simultaneous retrograde and forward-motion presentation of the cantus firmus (its sections slightly rearranged) in the remaining two voices. La Rue's work is much tamer. It follows the mensural layout of Josquin's mass almost exactly (the major, though not the only, difference being the use of La Rue's preferred c2 instead of ₵)[25] and also increases the number of voices in the Agnus, a very rare practice for La Rue.[26] Here, however, the entire Agnus, not just the final one, goes to more voices, and only a fifth voice is added, not a sixth as well. The major difference with La Rue's mass is that each movement is built on a canonic foundation (except the sections that drop to two voices).

If La Rue is trying to outdo Josquin in his second *L'homme armé* mass, the choice of a canonic foundation might seem a rather unspectacular means of achieving this goal, and one that pales in comparison with Josquin's final Agnus. But it is possible that La Rue thought his structure was something Josquin had never tried. Of the two Josquin masses built on canons, one (*Missa ad fugam*) does not appear in court manuscripts at all, and the other (*Missa sine nomine*) appears in court manuscripts compiled after La Rue's death. La Rue may not have known either mass, which would mean that this canonic foundation for a *L'homme armé*

[24] LRE ix, p. lxvii, suggests still another possible *Super voces musicales* influence, this time in the conclusion of both *partes* of La Rue's motet *Regina celi*, where the tenor is silent while the other three voices cadence, a highly unusual (though not unknown) procedure at this time. Seven sections of Josquin's mass end in this manner. Rubsamen, 'Unifying Techniques', 371, notes that La Rue presents the ostinato in the Sanctus of the *Missa Cum iocunditate* on descending steps while Josquin places the cantus firmus in the *Missa L'homme armé super voces musicales* on ascending steps, but does not draw any inferences from this.

[25] Though this is not necessarily an indication of borrowing, since the pattern (perfect *tempus* changing to imperfect *tempus* in the course of a movement) is found frequently in La Rue, and the main deviation from this, the use of Ɵ for the last Kyrie, is a common pattern for him (see the final Kyries in the *Missa Puer natus est*, *Missa Cum iocunditate*, *Missa Sub tuum presidium*, and others).

[26] The only other place where this happens is his *Requiem*.

Ex. 5.1. Comparison of (*a*) La Rue, *Missa Alleluia*, Agnus II, bars 87–95 (from VatS 36, fos. 48^v–50^r), with (*b*) Josquin, *Missa L'homme armé super voces musicales*, Agnus III, bars 100–10 (from *Liber primus missarum Josquin*)

Ex. 5.1. (*cont.*)

mass could appear to be going beyond Josquin. Further, Josquin's *Sexti toni* mass appears in VatC 234 minus both its Sanctus and Agnus (it appears complete in the late collection VienNB 11778); La Rue may have been unaware of any of Josquin's use of canon in that work. If La Rue's mass were written in a spirit of competition, what seems to us like a less challenging mass in its construction may have appeared to him as one that outdid Josquin's in multiple ways.

Although both La Rue and Josquin frequently expanded textures and explored the possibilities of canonic construction, their efforts in these directions differed somewhat, in part because their overall production did as well. La Rue has almost twice as many secure masses as Josquin does (a proportion that would be even greater if we limited Josquin's masses to those that everyone agrees are his), while Josquin exceeds La Rue in the number of both motets and secular works. We have already noted La Rue's seeming intent to fill in perceived gaps within the liturgy, a goal of no interest to Josquin. While Josquin was endlessly innovative in his masses, he very rarely wrote for more than four voices in this genre, and then only for individual movements; his multi-voice works are confined to other realms. La Rue, by contrast, is a leader in both the five- and six-voice mass, applying these textures less frequently in his other works. His *Credo Angeli archangeli* uses the extremely unusual combination of eight voices, almost unknown at the time. (Mouton's *Nesciens mater*, which first appears in FlorL 666, is another example.)

Canon likewise plays slightly different roles for each. Although the two are probably the most frequent users of strict canon among their contemporaries, La Rue again concentrates on it more in his masses, while it is more frequent in Josquin's motets and chansons. La Rue has two masses that are entirely canonic; Josquin has none. La Rue has three masses built on canonic foundations throughout; Josquin has two. Josquin never writes either a 4 ex 1 canon or a 6 ex 3 canon; La Rue writes a mass movement, a motet, and an entire mass using 4 ex 1 canons, and a chanson, a motet, two Magnificat sections, and an entire mass on 6 ex 3 canons.

As noted before, in La Rue's case the use of canon is often apparently inspired by the presence of an additional voice or voices, whereas Josquin is more willing to incorporate canon within a four-voice texture (and indeed seems to be the progenitor of the secular four-voice double canon).[27]

Motet-chansons

One work that offers a connection to both Josquin and Ockeghem is La Rue's motet-chanson *Plorer, gemir, crier/Requiem*, which was probably written to mark Ockeghem's death. This event spawned no fewer than four poetic laments, of which the most famous is *Nymphes des bois*, written by none other than the Habsburg-Burgundian court poet Jean Molinet. In it Molinet calls on four composers—Josquin, Perchon, Brumel, Compère—to mourn their 'bon père', Ockeghem. Josquin's response was to set Molinet's text to music, in one of the most beautiful of all fifteenth-century compositions. Given what we have already seen of La Rue's attempts to meet the musical needs of those at court, he must surely have responded to Molinet's imperative. Although his *Requiem* might initially seem the most obvious answer to this call, it is rather more likely that his smaller-scale motet-chanson fitted the bill, although this idea cannot be proven.

Ockeghem himself was the author of a work that marked the death of Binchois, *Mort tu as navré de ton dart/Miserere*. Though not the first fifteenth-century motet-chanson, it seems to have set generic norms and instituted an ongoing musical exchange between the courts of France and Habsburg-Burgundy in this kind of work, with assorted shared textual and musical material.[28] It is, of course, extremely difficult to know which composer saw what piece in this genre, but it is impossible to explain the numerous interconnections among these works without assuming some knowledge of this generic tradition on the part of composers .

Although motet-chansons were almost always serious in nature (and when they were not, they seemed to be poking fun at the tradition), Josquin was the first since Ockeghem to use the genre to mourn the death of a composer, and his idea to turn Molinet's poem into a motet-chanson via the addition of material from the Latin Introit for the Requiem mass was surely to create a connection with Ockeghem's earlier work of mourning. After Josquin, numerous composers marked the death of a colleague by using this chant as a cantus firmus; examples include Jheronimus Vinders's *O mors inevitabilis/Requiem* for Josquin, the anonymous *Absolve, quaesumus, Domine/Requiem*, also for Josquin, *Eheu dolor/Requiem* for Johannes Lupi (by Josquin Baston?), Jacobus Vaet's *Continuo lacrimas/Requiem* for Clemens non Papa, Regnart's *Defunctorum charitates Vaetem/Requiem* for

---

[27] Though it seems unlikely that La Rue would have known that. On Josquin's role, See Bernstein, 'Josquin's Chansons as Generic Paradigms', 47.

[28] On the motet-chanson as well as Ockeghem's and Josquin's position in the tradition, see Honey Meconi, 'Ockeghem and the Motet-Chanson in Fifteenth-Century France', in Philippe Vendrix (ed.), *Johannes Ockeghem: Actes du XL*ᵉ *Colloque international d'études humanistes, Tours, 3–8 février 1997* (Paris: Klincksieck, 1998), 381–402.

Vaet, and possibly Josquin's *Absolve, quaesumus, Domine/Requiem* for Obrecht.[29] Even though all of these works post-date *Nymphes des bois*, the connection is clear: one used the Requiem chant for a work of mourning.

La Rue's work is a motet-chanson of mourning, then, of which only two others are known to exist, the ones already cited by Ockeghem and Josquin. It seems likely that La Rue knew Josquin's work, and the latter's stunning composition essentially precluded any attempt to provide another setting of the same text. The text La Rue did end up setting, however, seems like a direct answer to Molinet, who proclaims 'Chantres expers de toutes nations / Changer voz voix . . . / En cris trenchantz et lamentations. . . . / Et pleurez grosses larmes doeil' (Expert singers of all nations / Change your voices / Into trenchant cries and lamentations . . . / And cry great tears of grief). La Rue's text is 'Plorer, gemir, crier, et braire / Me commant grant desplaisir / Quant la mort . . .' (To cry, to moan, to scream, and to blubber / A great anguish commands me / When death).

The text breaks off precisely at this point, leaving us in the dark as to what was intended. Curiously, however, this lack of text is not evidence against a possible dedication to Ockeghem. The sole source to contain the piece is FlorC 2439, where texting of individual pieces was altered to suit the tastes of its Italian patron.[30] A text offering a specific reference to Ockeghem would have been inappropriate in these surroundings. Indeed, Obrecht's *Mille quingentis*, a mourning work for his father, was similarly stripped of any such identifiying text in this same collection.[31]

Although motet-chansons always have at least one Latin-texted voice, usually drawing on plainchant set in longer note values, La Rue's is the only motet-chanson beside Josquin's to use the Introit of the Requiem mass (though their readings diverge by the time they get to 'dona eis'. Ockeghem's work also draws text and music from the Requiem mass, but from the Sequence rather than the Introit. La Rue uses Latin text for the lower two of four voices; Ockeghem uses Latin for the bottom three of his four voices. These two are the only composers to use Latin texting in more than one voice in the motet-chanson—except again for Josquin, who switches to exclusively Latin texting to conclude his work.

In La Rue's composition the chant is placed in the lower two voices, in long note values, and in such close imitation that it is almost in canon; is this canonic treatment an attempt to outdo Josquin? Even the top voice joins in briefly, as its opening motif is the same as that of the chant, also presented in somewhat longer note values than much of the rest of its line. Ockeghem also uses imitation to highlight his use of chant, and in his work the lower two voices are often paired

---

[29] For details see ibid. 399–402. Prior to Josquin, Obrecht used the chant in the mourning work *Mille quingentis* (for his father, also a musician); both Josquin and Obrecht transposed the chant to Phrygian.

[30] See Honey Meconi, 'The Manuscript Basevi 2439 and Chanson Transmission in Italy', in *Atti del XIV congresso della Società Internazionale di Musicologia (Bologna 1987)*, ed. Angelo Pompilio et al. (Turin: EDT, 1990), 163–74.

[31] Although the work was a later addition to the manuscript, the same texting principles applied.

rhythmically or melodically. All three composers limit their use of borrowed material. With La Rue, it appears only in the first part of the work (except that superius and bassus use the first three pitches of the chant to open the second part); with Ockeghem, it only appears towards the end of his work (though his strophic setting would bring it back several times). With Josquin, like La Rue, it figures in the first part of the work, and his second part opens—and for the most part remains—completely free, just like La Rue's second part. Josquin also cuts back to four voices at this point, the same texture La Rue uses throughout. Josquin, however, closes his work not just with a complete Latin texting for 'Requiescat in pace', but also brings back the chant—the fifth voice—for that phrase.

Another similarity between La Rue's work and that of Ockeghem is that each changes metre between their first and second sections (all three works have two sections of music), though La Rue reverses Ockeghem's procedure. La Rue moves from *tempus imperfectum* to *tempus perfectum*; Ockeghem does the opposite. This mensural shift is unique for a La Rue secular work. Josquin remains in duple time throughout. Like Josquin, however, La Rue's second part is much more homorhythmic than its first, and again like Josquin, La Rue moves to exclusively French text for the second part, where it breaks off a mere three words after it begins, 'Quant la mort'. It is unlikely that La Rue returns to Latin texting at the close of the second part, as Josquin does; nothing in the music suggests the return of chant, and in any event La Rue's work is considerably shorter than Josquin's, which is one of the longest of all motet-chansons.

These various interrelationships among these three mourning motet-chansons notwithstanding, La Rue's short composition, pitched slightly lower than its counterparts and clearly on F with one signature flat (creating the same effect as the chant, which is in mode 6 but flats all its Bs), may seem like a poor relation to its much longer and arguably more overtly effective cousins. But it is an extremely attractive work, poignant in its own way, and closing with a well-wrought drive to the cadence in stretto based on a motif that is—interestingly—very similar to one of the few lively gestures found in *Nymphes des bois*. The motif is highlighted in Josquin's work by the dropping out of three voices when it starts. This two-voice texture quickly moves to a three-voice texture, still one of the thinner sections of *Nymphes des bois*; it is further emphasized by the lack of movement in the other two voice parts while it sounds its last three notes. The motif outlines a fifth in descending stepwise motion and the rhythm is the same in both works, though the melodies are not strictly identical; Josquin outlines the fifth from A down to D, La Rue from C down to F. Perhaps the similarity is merely accidental, but perhaps not, for in *Nymphes des bois* the text at that point is 'Ochghem'.[32]

---

[32] La Rue's other motet-chanson, *Cueurs desolez/Dies illa*, shares the same French text (with the addition of a separate final stanza) with Josquin's *Cueurs desolez/Plorans ploravit*. Both settings are for five voices, but their overall styles are rather different; see the discussion in PickerCA, 88.

Why Ockeghem and Josquin?

There is no simple answer to the question of why La Rue's music makes reference to or resembles Ockeghem's and Josquin's, though we can hardly fault his taste. Ockeghem was one of the two most important composers of his generation and was a major figure in mass composition, and La Rue's inclinations seemed to lean more towards Ockeghem's style than that of Busnoys. While it is possible that La Rue's many strict borrowings from Ockeghem were simply a means of joining in the lively traditions of art-song reworkings, which found a ready home at the Habsburg-Burgundian court, they may also indicate a genuine personal attraction to his music, exhibited in other ways by the exploration of low ranges and full textures.

Josquin's appeal for La Rue is not hard to understand; La Rue's style is probably closer to that of Josquin than to any of his other contemporaries. Both enjoyed a posthumous vogue in German lands, and scribes and printers of the time mixed up their works with some regularity. But even though they were possibly chronologically the same age, Josquin's career got off to a much faster start than did La Rue's, with his music circulating some two decades earlier. By the early sixteenth century Josquin had already begun his ascent to a kind of adulation that no one else reached,[33] even though La Rue was often hailed in the same breath as Josquin when music of the day was discussed.

The interesting mixture of borrowings that La Rue takes from Josquin suggests a kind of one-sided competition, with La Rue in his own way trying to match or outdo Josquin. This is not merely an idea of our time; Glarean, who was well acquainted with the music of each composer, thought so in at least one instance, as already noted.[34] Again, however, the psychological reason behind this is impossible to determine. Is this homage or jealousy or both or neither? For all the ambiguities surrounding Josquin's relationship to the court, La Rue could hardly have failed to notice that both Molinet and Lemaire de Belges mentioned Josquin in their poetry—indeed, seemed to appeal to him to set it—and ignored La Rue, with the exception of *Nymphes des bois*, an aberration to be discussed below. But perhaps that meant nothing to him. Perhaps borrowing from or outdoing Josquin was simply part of one aspect of La Rue's creative personality, which seemed intent on writing works that stood out from their surroundings in some way. During La Rue's time, Josquin was often the composer embodying the latest trends, and his endless invention would certainly make him worthy of the respect of La Rue, himself no slouch when it came to continual innovation.

---

[33] See Meconi, 'Josquin and Musical Reputation'.
[34] App. C, 1547 Glarean, Citation 10.

DISSEMINATION OF MUSIC
AND THE JOSQUIN GENERATIONS

Court manuscripts

Appendix B lists all manuscripts and printed collections that contain either La Rue's music or music attributed to the composer, indicating as well which pieces survive in a single source and which pieces have a single attribution (a fair number in each of these categories). The list is arranged in a very approximate chronological order that is obviously partly subjective. Dependent as it is upon current interpretations of dates of compilations, it would shift correspondingly with any new insights or discoveries, including reattributions of individual works. Despite the lack of precision in this respect, it tells us a great deal about the popularity of La Rue's music, extending as it does through the entire sixteenth century and beyond in almost 200 sources across Europe.

The most important sources for La Rue's music are the manuscripts associated with the Habsburg-Burgundian court scriptorium, since they were compiled at or near his place of employment, many of them during his lifetime. La Rue is extremely well represented in these collections; of forty-nine complete manuscripts, thirty-six include one or more of his works, while eight of the dozen fragmentary collections contain something of his as well. No composer figures more prominently therein. Through these collections, which were commissioned or sent as gifts to recipients across Europe, La Rue's works spread to a large audience of wealthy or even princely owners. A certain amount of his music must already have been disseminated through the frequent travels of the court, both within the Low Countries and abroad on its two trips to Spain, especially the first. Although we lack any evidence of what that music might have been, it is possible that some of those who received his music in manuscript form had already heard it sung live by the chapel itself on one of its travels.

La Rue's continued and major presence in court collections, even after his death, is significant given that the court—at least in what it collected into manuscripts—reflected an interest in the latest musical trends and frequently pruned more old-fashioned works.[35] Thus for example we find little Ockeghem and no Regis after VatC 234, which appears to have been a largely retrospective collection in any event, and relatively little Agricola after his death.[36] A steady influx of new material, especially from the French court, mingled with La Rue's creations and selected other works. La Rue's preferred compositional habits, which normally meant avoiding the older style of strict cantus-firmus procedure, kept his work sounding fresh and up-to-date with his constant use of paraphrase and gradually increasing interest in polyphonic borrowing.

---

[35] A statement open to numerous qualifications, but still generally true.

[36] Agricola, for example, is the major figure in FlorC 2439, compiled during his lifetime or shortly after his death, but is much less prominent in the later BrusBR 228. The relationship between VatC 234 and the

Four manuscripts, all containing masses, are devoted exclusively to La Rue;[37] they are VienNB Mus. 15496 (for Charles),[38] MontsM 773 (for Marguerite?),[39] SubA 248 (for an unknown recipient), and BrusBR 15075 (for John III and Catherine of Portugal); a fifth mass manuscript, JenaU 12 (for Frederick the Wise of Saxony),[40] contains the problematic *Missa sine nomine II* in addition to a series of unquestioned works. Although Petrucci had pioneered the concept of a collection of masses devoted to a single composer, similar manuscript collections were still far from common at this point, making manuscripts of La Rue's masses especially noteworthy. Five other mass manuscripts add a single work by another composer to a group of La Rue's works. These collections are JenaU 5 (for Frederick the Wise), VatS 34 and 36 (for Pope Leo X),[41] MechAS s.s. (for Charles),[42] and BrusBR 6428 (for Marguerite?). His music also took pride of place in various collections, including BrusBR 215–16, 's-HerAB 72B, JenaU 2, JenaU 7, JenaU 8, JenaU 22, MontsM 766, VerBC 756, BrusBR 228, JenaU 20, and VienNB Mus. 18746. His position in BrusBR 228, made for Marguerite, is of considerable importance, given that the manuscript opens with thirteen works that are definitely or probably his, with batches of his compositions appearing later as well. The prominence of works of his that had special meaning for Marguerite has already been observed.

Other recipients of La Rue's music via court manuscripts include the Agostini-Ciardi family of Siena (FlorC 2439), Raimund Fugger the Elder of Augsburg (?VienNB 9814, VienNB Mus. 18832, VienNB Mus. 15941, and VienNB Mus. 18746),[43] Pompeius Occo of Amsterdam (BrusBR IV 922), the Confraternity at 's-Hertogenbosch ('s-HerAB 72B), courtiers Philippe Bouton (VatC 234) and Charles le Clerc (BrusBR 215–16), Ulrich Pfinzing, treasurer at Maximilian's court (?VienNB Mus. 15947), and rulers Philip and Juana (BrusBR 9126), Manuel I of Portugal and Marie of Spain (VienNB 1783), Henry VIII and Catherine of Aragon (LonBLR 8 G. vii), Wilhelm IV of Bavaria (MunBS 34), Anne and Ferdinand of Bohemia and Hungary (VatP 1976–79); his music also went to the unknown (Italian?) recipient of VerBC 756. Fragmentary court manuscripts suggest that La Rue's music was used as well in Tongeren, Antwerp, Wingene, the

court collections that come shortly thereafter remind one a bit of that between the *Odhecaton* (1501) and *Canti B* (1502²), with the latter, though coming on the heels of the former, presenting the more up-to-date repertoire.

[37] It is interesting to think that, if La Rue's father were indeed an illuminator, the composer would have been surrounded by beautifully illuminated manuscript leaves since his childhood, as his music was later surrounded in these manuscripts.

[38] He was possibly also the recipient of MontsM 766.

[39] Marguerite was the recipient of BrusBR 228.

[40] Frederick was the recipient of a great deal of La Rue's music in other manuscripts as well.

[41] He also received VatS 160.

[42] Interestingly, the contents are almost identical to those of VienNB Mus. 15496, also for Charles and copied about the same time. Was one for home, the other for the road? Strong repertorial overlap exists in other manuscripts as well.

[43] La Rue's mass print of 1503 is listed in the 1566 inventory of Raimund Fugger the Younger (see Kellman, 'Josquin and the Courts', 202); one wonders whether it was already in the possession of his father.

church of Sint Goedele in Brussels, and no doubt other places as well.[44] That La Rue's music was still being performed at court long after his departure is shown by the inclusion of his *Magnificat septimi toni* in MontsM 769, compiled post-Alamire (around 1540) for Marguerite's successor, Mary of Hungary.[45]

The readings of La Rue's music in court manuscripts often differ from collection to collection. Though the reasons for this are not clear, I wonder whether this diversity was in part generated by the nature of La Rue's music itself. Although his compositions are often motivically unified, he tends to eschew exact repetition in favour of constant variation. In a broad sense, the court sources reflect this precisely. Did La Rue's penchant for *varietas* extend to a tendency for minor reworkings of pieces he had already finished? In works that already stressed change, did the singers feel free to introduce further departures from the original?

Outside the court

La Rue's music had a very wide dissemination outside of court circles from the very beginning of the sixteenth century. Even after the court dissemination of his music ceased around 1530, about ninety manuscripts, prints, and theoretical treatises containing his music (almost half of the total number of sources) were still to be produced.[46] Most of these were made by the century's mid-point, but a surprising fifteen sources come from the 1550s. After that, almost everything is a theoretical treatise or related kind of compilation (e.g. 1590[30] and 1594[3], two collections of canons). The exceptions to this are few: *Incessament* was published in two related retrospective collections and reissued in tablature (1560 *Livre de mélanges*, 1572[2], and 1562[24] respectively), and *Da pacem domine*, itself a double canon and thus of some intellectual interest, was printed in 1567[1]. A copy of Plantin's *Biblia polyglotta*, published in 1569–72, used old manuscript leaves from La Rue's *Missa de beata virgine* as part of its cover, showing that the music was considered outdated by that time, as this chronology suggests.[47] Curiously, however, text alterations were made to the copy of *Missa Cum iocunditate* in VatS 45 around 1576–7, indicating that it was still being performed in the Sistine Chapel at that late date.[48]

---

[44] See Eric Jas, 'Choirbook Fragments', in *TA* 166–7; many of the fragments were taken from manuscripts apparently dismantled in the 17th c. Places of destination for fragments UtreC 47/1 & 2 are not known. GhentR D 336ob was recovered from a rent book of the Ghent abbey Ter Haeghen; since these were Cistercian nuns, it is unclear whether this order would have been singing La Rue's *Missa Ave sanctissima Maria* that the fragment contains.

[45] Jacobijn Kiel has recently associated the scribe of CoimU 2 (which contains the *Missa Ave Maria* and *Missa Cum iocunditate*) with the post-Alamire court (see App. B, after 1530).

[46] Although datings are so approximate it is difficult to be precise, the second decade of the 16th c. seems to be the busiest in terms of the dissemination of La Rue's music, with about 25 per cent of his sources from that time. That was the decade, of course, that saw tremendous activity on the part of the court scriptorium.

[47] Other court fragments were used as binding material in the 17th c.

[48] Musicians elsewhere were losing their ability to read the notation of the early 16th c.; see the discussion in Jessie Ann Owens, 'Music Historiography and the Definition of "Renaissance"', *Notes*, 47 (1990–1), 305–30 at 319–23.

Although La Rue's music had widespread distribution, little of it is found on the geographical fringes of Europe. Nothing, for example, remains of whatever might have been left in England when the court entourage was forced to stay there in early 1506.[49] The English knew La Rue's music—several motets are in LonBLR 8 G.vii—but after that only the very late theoretical treatises have anything (Morley's *Plaine and Easie Introduction* from 1597 and the presumably Scottish treatise LonBL 4911 from *c*.1580).

In Spain, a depressing number of manuscripts that once contained La Rue's music have been lost, as the inventory of Philip II's choirbooks compiled late in the sixteenth century makes clear.[50] La Rue is listed in connection with ten manuscripts, of which seven appear to be devoted entirely (or almost so) to his music. These include three illuminated parchment manuscripts (of seven, nine, and ten masses),[51] two paper manuscripts (one of seven masses[52] and one of Magnificats on all eight tones plus several hymns),[53] and two of unspecified material, one of which opens with La Rue's *Missa Cum iocunditate* and the other of which opens with his eight-voice Credo (doubtless the one on *Angeli archangeli*).[54] In three other collections (one paper, two without specification of material) La Rue is but one of several authors, though he is listed as being first in the collections. One opens with his *Missa Tous les regretz*, one (a book of motets) with a now-lost six-voice *Salve Jesu*, and the last, a collection of 'Regina Salve y motetes', simply says the first (*el primero*) is by La Rue.[55] Philip's library may have contained a complete run of La Rue's masses (this was almost the case for Frederick the Wise), possibly

---

[49] One reference so far untraced is that given by Robert Eitner, *Biographisch-bibliographisches Quellen-Lexikon der Musiker und Musikgelehrten der christlichen Zeitrechnung bis zur Mitte des neunzehnten Jahrhunderts*, 10 vols. (Leipzig: Breitkopf & Härtel, 1900–4), vi. 55, for a song found in British Museum MS 630, two 16th-c. partbooks. Location in the British Museum, of course, says nothing about the origin of a collection.

[50] The contents of the inventory are published in Alfonso Andrés, 'Libros de canto de la Capilla de Felipe II', *Musica Sacro-Hispana*, 10 (1917), June, 92–5; July, 109–11; Aug.–Sept., 123–6; Oct.–Nov., 154–6; Dec., 189–90; where La Rue appears in numbers 3, 4, 27, 31, 65, 71, 76, 87, 122, 170. The contents also appear, somewhat less accurately, in VDS viii. 365–83. Various dates for the inventory are given in the literature; the date of 1597, used here, appears at the end of the inventory as published by Andrés, 'Libros de canto', 189, 'a diez y seys dias del mes de Agosto de mill y quinientos y noventa y siete'. VDS viii. 383 publishes the date of 1602, found in a letter drawn up prior to selling what was then seen as useless but would now be a priceless collection. Robert Stevenson, 'Josquin in the Music of Spain and Portugal', in *JosCon*, 217–46 at 229 n. 68, gives the inventory's date as 13 Sept. 1598 without further explanation. The manuscripts in the inventory that contain La Rue are not necessarily all from the Habsburg-Burgundian court. My thanks to Bonnie Blackburn for kindly providing a copy of the Andrés article.

[51] Andrés, 'Libros de canto', 94 no. 3, 126 no. 122 (which appears to be the same as MontsM 773), and 95 no. 27. The relevant entries in VDS viii. are 365 no. 8, 375 no. 16, and 367 no. 32.

[52] Andrés, 'Libros de canto', 94 no. 4; VDS viii. 365 no. 9.

[53] The hymns may or may not be by La Rue, as the entry separates the two items: 'de ocho tonos de Magníficat de música de Pedro de la Rua, con algunos ynnos'; see Andrés, 'Libros de canto', 109 no. 31; VDS viii. 367 no. 36.

[54] Andrés, 'Libros de canto', 156 no. 170, 123 no. 71; VDS viii. 379 no. 28, 373 no. 35.

[55] Andrés, 'Libros de canto', 123 no. 76, 124 no. 87, 111 no. 65; VDS viii. 369 no. 48, 370 no. 61, 372 no. 13. In his discussion of the inventory, Vander Straeten mistakenly lists two manuscripts under La Rue's name that are not indicated as such in the inventory; the first is ibid. 354–5, which corresponds to p. 373 (after no. 35 but no number given); the second is ibid. 359, the second collection listed under La Rue's name by Vander Straeten but not given so in the inventory, 375–6, where it is given to Manchicourt instead.

with duplicate copies or with still other completely unknown masses by the composer; whether his chapel performed them or whether they were simply left over from earlier court repertories is impossible to say.[56]

As for Spanish collections not connected with the court, only La Rue's six-voice Credo is found in such a manuscript; it appears in BarBC 681, compiled sometime during the first half of the century in Vich, north of Barcelona. This work is also contained in VatC 234, which is thought to have been in Spain early in the sixteenth century. Curiously, the reading of the work in BarBC 681 is apparently closer to that in another court manuscript never known to have been in Spain, VatS 36.[57] Obviously all readings ultimately derive from the court, since that is where La Rue worked, and it seems here as if the version that inspired BarBC 681 probably entered Spain on one of Philip's two trips there rather than via VatC 234.

La Rue has some presence in French sources, but is still not especially well represented (though relatively few sources from this time survive).[58] Several chansons appear in collections from about the second decade of the century (LonBLH 5242, for the future mistress of Francis I, and FlorC 2442, which erroneously attributed the double canon *Dicte moy bergère* to La Rue, perhaps because the scribe was aware of his penchant for canonic writing). Sacred works appear at Cambrai Cathedral (CambraiBM 4 and 18) and elsewhere (UppsU 76b). Misattributions occur in later French prints; I refer here not to those works now assigned to Robert de la Rue[59] but rather to *Ave sanctissima Maria* in 1534[5] (where both Verdelot and Claudin, each equally unlikely, are named instead of La Rue) and to *Incessament* and *Cent mille regretz*, given to Josquin in Attaingnant's 1550 collection dedicated to that composer. Attaingnant's misattribution is especially interesting given that Le Roy and Ballard managed to get the composer right in their later collections of 1560 and 1572, both of which contain *Incessament*.

As would be expected, La Rue's music was known in various centres throughout the Low Countries, including Bruges, Kampen, Leiden (where his *Missa Puer natus est* was used in the church of St Peter in mid-century),[60] and Leuven (where *Incessament* was published as a lute song and a lute intabulation in the 1550s) as well as those places noted above in connection with court manuscripts, 's-Herto-

---

[56] At least part of Mary of Hungary's library was absorbed into Philip's. The section of Philip's inventory that lists books from her library includes the parchment collection of nine masses. VDS vii lists several other La Rue manuscripts that Mary had (ibid. 473 in his discussion; 481, 482, 488, 489, 491 in the inventory, which gives seven La Rue manuscripts instead of the five that Vander Straeten gives in the discussion, though the last two items appear to duplicate the first two); these look as if they might also have counterparts in Philip's inventory: a paper book of seven masses, a paper book of all eight Magnificats, and a parchment book of seven masses. The inventory lists a book of eight masses as well; perhaps this is the collection that started with *Missa Cum iocunditate*.

[57] LRE vii, p. lvi.

[58] If BrusBr 11239 turns out to be from France rather than Savoy, this would increase La Rue's representation in French sources.

[59] See Meconi, 'French Print Chansons'.

[60] LeidGA 1443; the manuscript was probably copied in Amsterdam.

genbosch and presumably Antwerp, Brussels, Ghent, Tongeren, Utrecht, and Wingene, where fragments of court manuscripts have turned up.[61]

La Rue's music is surprisingly well represented in Italian sources,[62] starting right away with Petrucci's earliest prints.[63] He appears in the *Odhecaton* (1501), *Canti B* (1502²; in addition to two authentic works by La Rue, Pipelare's *Fors seulement* was erroneously attributed to him in the print rather than to its proper author), and *Canti C* (1504³), and in 1503 he was one of the first composers favoured with a volume in the publisher's series of mass prints, preceded by Josquin, Obrecht, Brumel, and Ghiselin. Unless there was some patron behind La Rue's mass print—an idea for which there is no evidence—Petrucci would not have undertaken such a publication without a belief that this print would sell, which is some indication of his contemporary reputation.[64]

Many of his pieces in these early prints were ultimately to prove extremely popular, and Petrucci (or his editor) chose some of La Rue's most distinctive music: *Pourquoy non, Mijn hert, Tous les regretz, Ce n'est pas jeu, Missa Puer natus est*, and *Missa Nuncqua fue pena maior*. Other publications followed: *Salve regina II* in 1505², the *Missa de Sancto Antonio* in 1509¹ (actually published in 1508), and the *Missa Sub tuum presidium* in the Févin mass collection of 1515. Three other Venetian publishers printed La Rue: Antico, who published his double canon *En espoir vis* in 1520, and, much later, Girolamo Polo and Gardano, who printed theoretical treatises by Zacconi (1592) and Rossi (1618) respectively, and thus small samples of La Rue's music. It is unclear where or how Petrucci got hold of La Rue's music,[65] and equally unclear whether La Rue ever knew that any of his music was being published. One wonders what any early sixteenth-century composer would have thought about seeing a work of his in print.

Rome was another important place for La Rue's music. In addition to the three court manuscripts sent to Pope Leo X, several other Sistine collections contained his work, possibly starting in the first decade of the century: VatS 23 (*Missa Puer natus est*), VatS 41 (*Missa de beata virgine*), VatS 42 (*Regina caeli*), VatS 45 (a significant collection, including *Credo de villagiis, Missa Almana, Missa Ave Maria, Missa Cum iocunditate*, and *Missa Nuncqua fue pena maior*), and the much later

---

[61] In addition, Henri Vanhulst has kindly informed me that music by 'Petri de la Rue' was included in the auction catalogue of the library of Philippe de Croÿ, sold in Brussels in 1614 (private comm., 18 Mar. 1997).

[62] Could Weerbeke have taken some of La Rue's music with him when he returned to Italy in 1498?

[63] For citations by Italian theorists, see the discussion below on literary and theoretical writings.

[64] B. Kahmann, 'Antoine de Févin: A Bio-Bibliographical Contribution', *Musica disciplina*, 4 (1950), 153–62; 5 (1951), 143–55 at (1951), 153, claimed that Petrucci's mass print of La Rue ran to six editions, but gave no evidence; only a single edition is currently known.

[65] Bonnie Blackburn has presented a plausible hypothesis that the music lover Girolamo Donato functioned as a conduit for repertoire for Petrucci. Donato served as the Venetian ambassador to numerous courts, including that of Maximilian from March to July 1501; he was at the French court in Nov.–Dec. of the same year, at precisely the time that Philip's court was passing through. See Bonnie J. Blackburn, 'Lorenzo de' Medici, a Lost Isaac Manuscript, and the Venetian Ambassador', in Irene Alm, Alyson McLamore, and Colleen Reardon (eds.), *Musica Franca: Essays in Honor of Frank A. D'Accone* (Stuyvesant, NY: Pendragon, 1996), 19–44, esp. 38–41.

VatS 154 (from the 1540s or thereafter; it contained *Missa Incessament*). This last mass also appeared in the Cappella Guilia collection VatG XII.2 (from *c*.1518–21). Prior to assuming the papacy, Giulio de Medici had two collections containing La Rue: VatP 1982 (with *Cent mille regretz*, *Missa Ave Maria*, and *Missa Tous les regretz*), and VatP 1980–1, containing the *Missa Ave Maria* again as well as both *Incessament*[66] and its mass. In Rome Antico printed both the *Ave Maria* and *O salutaris hostia* masses in his gorgeous woodcut edition of 1516;[67] the former of these masses was reprinted by Giunta in 1522.

Other Italian centres have rather more modest showings when it comes to La Rue's music, but there are a fair number of places where it was known, and for a surprising amount of time. *Pourquoy non* was copied around the turn of the century, possibly in Florence (BolC Q17); the *Odhecaton* was not the inspiration for this, as the version there is transposed up at fifth while the Bologna version is at the original low pitch; it seems that this justly famous work was circulating independently in Italy about the time of Petrucci's print. The later Florentine manuscript FlorBN II.I.232 has *Considera Israel* (interestingly, the collection also contains Josquin's *Planxit autem David*) and the mysterious *Quis dabit pacem*, for which only the incipit remains. Because the incipit is the same as that for the poem used by Isaac to mark the death of Lorenzo de' Medici (8 April 1492), various scholars have speculated that La Rue's work was written for the same purpose. No one has come up with any reason why La Rue should have been prompted to write such a piece, however (no evidence exists of a sojourn in Florence), and there seems no particular reason to assume La Rue's original text was the same as the poem for Lorenzo. Certainly cramming the text in produces a rather tight fit. Given that the surviving text is the rather general question 'Who will give peace?', it is far more likely that the work was inspired by a northern, court-related conflict (such as the war with Gueldre in the summer of 1505) than the death of Lorenzo.

Further places in Italy that knew La Rue's music include Casale Monferrato (CasAC M [D]), possibly commissioned by the Marquis of Monferrato, with the *Missa Ave Maria*), the cathedral in Modena (ModD 4, with the Credo from the *de beata virgine* mass), the church of San Petronio in Bologna (BolSP 38, with the same Credo), and the collegiate church of Santa Maria Assunta in Cividale (CivMA 59, with the *Missa de Sancto Antonio*). Probably also Italian is the mid-century collection MilA 46, with the *Missa Cum iocunditate* (but here attributed to Josquin) and the *Missa Sub tuum presidium*. Of considerable interest are Italian misattributions to La Rue. In the discussion of *En l'amour d'une dame* we noted its misattribution to La Rue in a Ferrarese collection of 1535; another error is found in ModD 3 (from the 1520s; for the cathedral of Modena), where a spurious *Magnificat quarti toni* is given to La Rue. But both of these manuscripts are from

---

[66] The song was also contained in [c. 1521]⁷, formerly thought to have been printed in Rome.

[67] Antico's print was listed in the 1559–66 inventory of the papal chapel; see Jeffrey J. Dean, 'The Repertory of the Cappella Giulia in the 1560s', *JAMS* 41 (1988), 465–90 at 473.

the time when La Rue's fame was already established, and this is far from the case for MilD 3, compiled for the cathedral choir of Milan at the beginning of the six-teenth century. Here, Brumel's *Missa sine nomine I* is ascribed in the index to 'petricon de la rue' (a unique form of his name, but it can only refer to him). The ascription was then crossed out and replaced by 'de Brumel'. This is reminiscent of the inscription in the early manuscript TrentBC 1947/4, which claimed that La Rue wrote the superius to *Een vrolic wesen*. La Rue's name—and presumably some of his music—was known at a considerable distance from the court by the turn of the century.

La Rue's music thus has a not insignificant presence in Italy over several dec-ades. As is the case with Josquin's work, however, little remains after the 1530s. From this time on, the centre of dissemination is Germany and other German-speaking areas.[68] Although La Rue's popularity in Germany never equalled Josquin's, his was a real and long-lasting presence over a widespread area.[69] His significance there was doubtless fanned by the connections Maximilian main-tained with the Low Countries as well as the presentation/commission manu-scripts generated by the court.

Collections now believed to have a possible or definite connection to Maximilian's court include TrentBC 1947/4 (site of the curious inscription about La Rue and *Een vrolic wesen*), MunBS 53 (the only source for the four-voice Credo), the important, largely secular collection VatV 11953, and the first part of RegB C120. We have already noted two major German collectors of court manu-scripts, Frederick the Wise of Saxony and Raimund Fugger the Elder, but it is worth pointing out other La Rue sources from the places associated with these collectors. Frederick lived in both Torgau and Wittenberg; from the former we find NurGN 83795, with *Incessament* (as a contrafactum motet) and its mass, as well as three Magnificats; BerlPS 40013, which duplicates the La Rue contents of the preceding except for the mass; WeimB B, with the *Incessament* contrafactum and, interestingly, Josquin's *de beata virgine* mass attributed to La Rue; and GothaF A98, again with the *Incessament* contrafactum. From Wittenberg we have (probably) DresSL 1/D/505, which incorrectly attributes a setting of the Passion to La Rue (possibly a sign of the esteem in which he was held in Wittenberg); UtreH s.s., with the motet *Lauda anima mea dominum*; the two editions of Hermann Finck's *Practica musica* (to be discussed below); and a series of publica-tions by Georg Rhau (1538[8], 1542[8], 1544[4], 1545[6], 1545[7]) that presents a group of contrafacta along with *Ave regina caelorum*, *Magnificat quarti toni*, and the spuri-ous *Salva nos domine* (in reality a mass section by Isaac).

Augsburg, which was home to the Fuggers, had strong imperial connections as well and an intense musical life. In addition to the manuscripts that Fugger

---

[68] Contrafact texts are encountered fairly frequently here.
[69] Whether German composers tried to imitate La Rue (as they did Josquin) is an interesting question that has never been explored.

commissioned, La Rue's work is also found in the following collections known or suspected to have come from Augsburg: 1520⁴, with his *Pater de coelis deus* (the collection was edited by Senfl, who had been employed by Maximilian until the ruler's death); the second part of RegB C120, which misattributes *Leal schray tante* (possibly Josquin's) to La Rue and which gives La Rue's *Tous les regretz* to Josquin; MunU 328–31, with *Secretz regretz*; VienNB 18810, all secular, which misattributes four works to La Rue and gives his genuine *Si dormiero* to Isaac (two other works are correctly identified); 1540⁷ (*Da pacem domine*); MunBS 1516 (two songs); MunU 327 (*Missa Nuncqua fue pena maior*); and the mid-century ParisPNC 1591 (*Salve regina I*).

Wilhelm IV, Duke of Bavaria, presents an interesting case when it comes to the collecting of La Rue's music. As the recipient of court-generated manuscript MunBS 34, a collection compiled in the early 1520s, he came into possession of five of La Rue's six *Salve regina* settings. But in contrast to other collectors he also had several non-court manuscripts with La Rue's music, some preceding MunBS 34. These are MunBS 65, with the *Missa Cum iocunditate* and the *Requiem*; WolfA A, again with the *Requiem*, this time coupled with the *Missa Incessament* (both of these manuscripts preceding MunBS 34); MunBS 5, with another copy of the *Missa Cum iocunditate*; and MunBS 47, again with the *Requiem*; this last collection was copied in the 1540s. MunBS C, originating in Munich at the same time as MunBS 47 and probably commissioned in memory of the Duke's sister, contains both the *Requiem* and *Missa Incessament*. La Rue's music was obviously much appreciated at Wilhelm's court.

One city that generated a good bit of La Rue's music was Nuremberg, a major printing centre. In addition to an early series of tablatures that included La Rue's secular works (Brown 1532₂, reprinted as Brown 1537₁; Brown 1533₁, where *Si dormiero* is misattributed to Isaac; and 1536¹³, where *Si dormiero* is misattributed to Finck), Nuremberg printers also published music by La Rue, or thought to be by La Rue, in 1538³ (*Delicta iuventutis*), 1538⁹ (*Tous nobles cueurs* and the two sacred tricinia), 1539¹ (*Missa Tous les regretz*), 1539² (a major collection that contained the *Missa Cum iocunditate*, *Missa de Sancto Antonio*, *Missa O gloriosa domina*, and *Missa Sub tuum presidium*), 1549¹ (where a set of Lamentations is mistakenly attributed to La Rue), 1549¹⁶ (a series of mass bicinia plus the erroneously attributed *Le renvoye*, here with contrafactum text), 1553⁶ (*Lauda anima mea Dominum*), 1555¹¹ (*Pater de coelis deus*), 1559² (*Absalon fili mi*, attributed here as elsewhere to Josquin), and 1567¹ (*Da pacem domine*).

Another city that at one time had significant La Rue holdings was Heidelberg. HeidU 318, the inventory of the disbanded court chapel of Palatine Count Ottheinrich, shows that the chapel holdings included La Rue's popular *Tous les regretz*, two motets (*Pater de coelis deus* and an otherwise unknown *Petre amas me* in two separate copies) and the large sum of fifteen different masses (plus an extra copy of the *Missa Ave Maria* and two extra copies of the *Missa Sub tuum presidium*, one of which was in the court's copy of 1515[1], Petrucci's 'Févin' mass print), making this one of the largest collections of La Rue's music outside Habsburg-Burgundy.[70] One of the masses in this now-lost collection, the *Missa Mediatrix nostra*, is not known from anywhere else; another, attributed to La Rue but given without name, cannot be securely identified; it could be either 'new' or 'old'. Curiously, the collection contains an entire volume devoted to five-voice masses of La Rue that is an exact duplicate of the contents of BrusBR 15075, in exactly the same order, with a single exception: the Brussels collection contains the six-voice *Missa Ave sanctissima Maria*, missing in the Heidelberg collection. Because all other manuscripts devoted to La Rue's music come from Habsburg-Burgundy, I wonder whether this, too, might have had its origins in the court scriptorium, especially given the very curious overlap with BrusBR 15075 (much of its repertoire is shared with other court collections as well, i.e. a five-mass overlap with BrusBR 6428, and four-mass overlaps with JenaU 4, MechAS s.s., and VatS 34).

No other cities have this kind of plentitude, but again the geographical spread within German lands is impressive (though some of this geographic diversity is due to the popularity of a single piece, the sacred tricinium *Si dormiero*). La Rue's music was known (or probably known) in Barth on the Baltic coast (GreifU 640–641), Eisenach, Frankfurt an der Oder, Frankfurt am Main, Heilbronn (ErlU 474/4, for the Cistercian monastery, containing the *Missa Tandernaken*), Kassel (where Count Philip of Hesse owned three manuscripts that included La Rue's works, including both the six- and eight-voice Credos), Königsberg (BerlGS 7/KönSU 1740, with the *Missa Cum iocunditate*, *Missa L'homme armé I*, and the motet *Domini est terra*, erroneously attributed to La Rue), Lauingen (where the late canon collections 1590[30] and 1594[3] were printed),[71] Leipzig (where the late collections LeipU 49 and 51 contain the *Missa L'homme armé I*, the Marian antiphon *Ave regina caelorum*, retexted to be more acceptable to Lutherans, and the *Missa Tous les regretz*, shorn of its last three movements to generate a proper Lutheran mass), Pforzheim, Pirna, Stuttgart (where the Duke had both the *Missa Nuncqua fue pena maior* and *Missa Cum iocunditate* in his manuscripts; the mid-century collection BerlPS 40634, possibly from Stuttgart, included the *Missa Tous les regretz* and *Missa de Sancto Antonio*), and Zwickau. In addition to these German cities,

[70] On the inventory, see Jutta Lambrecht, *Das "Heidelberger Kapellinventar" von 1544 (Codex Pal. Germ. 318): Edition und Kommentar*, 2 vols. (Heidelberger Bibliotheksschriften, 26; Heidelberg: n.p., 1987); my thanks to Bonnie Blackburn for supplying the relevant passages from this reference. For earlier bibliography, see Martin Bente, *Neue Wege der Quellenkritik und die Biographie Ludwig Senfls: Ein Beitrag zur Musikgeschichte des Reformationszeitalters* (Wiesbaden: Breitkopf & Härtel, 1968), 353; and Siegfried Hermelink, 'Ein Musikalienverzeichnis der Heidelberger Hofkapelle aus dem Jahre 1544', in Georg Poensgen (ed.), *Ottheinrich: Gedenkschrift zur vierhundertjährigen Wiederkehr seiner Kurfürstenzeit in der Pfalz (1556–1559)* (Heidelberg: n.p., 1956), 247–60. Lambrecht, *Das "Heidelberger Kapellinventar"*, 574, mistakenly includes the *Missa Jam non dicam vos servos* as a work of La Rue's; it is instead by Loyset Piéton.

[71] Alphonse Goovaerts, 'Delarue (Pierre)', *Biographie nationale*, v. 325–8 at 328, mentions 'le recueil de fugues, mis au jour en 1587 à Lauingen, contient, de lui, des morceaux pour orgues'. This must be the volume (now lost) that was the predecessor for 1590[30], a collection of canons in mensural notation, including two by La Rue. Although Jacob Paix, the compiler, was an organist, it is unlikely that the works themselves were arranged for organ.

La Rue's music was known in Austria and especially Switzerland. Several other manuscripts containing La Rue's music appear to be of Germanic origin but lack more precise indications of provenance. Two of special interest are HerdF 9820 and 9821, a collection of works or excerpts put into score format, apparently to facilitate study. Bits and pieces of three La Rue masses appear here: the *Missa O salutaris hostia*, *Missa Ave Maria*, and *Missa Sub tuum presidium*. But the most important of these general Germanic collections is unquestionably FrankSU 2, possibly from the second decade of the century, which includes an astonishing number of La Rue masses for a German manuscript of this time: the *Missa Nuncqua fue pena maior*, *Missa O gloriosa domina*, *Missa Puer natus est*, *Missa Sub tuum presidium*, *Missa Tous les regretz*, and the problematic *Missa sine nomine II*. Unless the collection really dates from somewhat later, it is testimony to the rapid dissemination of La Rue's works into German lands.[72]

As various remarks above and earlier in the book have indicated, La Rue's works were at times transmitted in altered forms and formats.[73] Even within the court, where we might expect a fair degree of consistency, numerous differences exist among the various exemplars that were generated over the years, differences that could reflect a combination of artistic revision, performance practices, scribal inattention, or other factors. Other differences tend to occur outside the court complex, such as the transposition of La Rue's extreme ranges into more normal ones, the resetting of text for greater precision, and compositional rewriting to thicken the texture, as happened with the *Missa Tous les regretz*. An extremely large number of La Rue's masses are known by alternative titles in different sources, a phenomenon that appears to occur far more often with his works than with those of his contemporaries, though it is unclear why this might be. In addition, a number of works were intabulated; see Table 5.1.

As might be expected, many of La Rue's works circulated without attribution; performers and listeners probably often had no idea whose music they were hearing. But his name continued to be attached to works throughout the entire sixteenth century, and, as we shall see shortly, both literary and theoretical citations kept his name in view during this period. At the same time, confusion about who wrote what began as soon as his music started going out, with La Rue's name connected to works that were not his (especially in later German sources), while legitimate works were at times given to other, usually equally famous, composers. Such misattributions confirm that his was one of numerous recognized names at the time, but also that scribes could copy names blindly or have a very flexible view of individual styles.

---

[72] Lothar Hoffmann-Erbrecht, 'Ein Frankfurter Messenkodex', *Archiv für Musikwissenschaft*, 16 (1959), 328–34 at 329, thought the manuscript was from the Habsburg-Burgundian court scriptorium, but the German layout of the choirbook (bassus under superius) rules this out.

[73] For details see the various volumes of LRE; Meconi, 'Style and Authenticity'; and App. B, where some of the major changes are listed.

The Josquin generations

This exhausting yet far from exhaustive[74] overview of the dissemination of La Rue's music reminds us in many respects of the dissemination of Josquin's music, although there are major differences. One, of course, is the sheer volume of works either written by or claimed to be by Josquin; few if any could surpass him in this regard—certainly not La Rue—and there is another, significant difference that we shall return to shortly. Yet it is surprising in many ways that La Rue's music survived as long as it did. It has a thinner texture than was fashionable after his death (even with the multiple voices), and in many respects—including his interest in canonic writing—it is challenging to sing. Its significant presence throughout the first half of the century bears witness to its genuine popularity.

If La Rue were really born as early as 1452, it might appear odd that few or none of his works were copied into surviving sources before the sixteenth century. But regardless of his birthdate—which is now probably as open as Josquin's—we should remember that the last quarter of the fifteenth century is very poorly represented by manuscripts from the Low Countries.[75] Nor do we have anything from the court until the turn of the century. Yet La Rue's early works seem designed to make an impression, and they eventually did. By the early sixteenth century his name was known far from the court, and even within the court the rewards were finally starting to appear.

As we have just demonstrated, once his works began to reach a wider audience they continued to be disseminated for decades thereafter. Since no one has prepared a similar sixteenth-century chronology of sources for other composers, it is difficult to make precise comparisons. But the work has been done for selected composers in the fifteenth century,[76] and that leads to some perhaps unexpected conclusions.

The usual composers with whom La Rue is ranged include Josquin, Agricola, Brumel, Compère, Isaac, and Obrecht. These are probably the first names to come to mind when we think of the 'Josquin Generation', though certainly others could be added. But what we are really dealing with are multiple 'Josquin Generations', for both in terms of style and chronology there are some very strong differences within this presumably homogeneous group.[77] This is not to claim that scholars have lumped all of these musicans together with no awareness of compositional differences, but rather to state that it is appropriate to observe some rather crucial distinctions when we attempt to make comparisons.

Two composers who unquestionably belong in an earlier tier of this group are Obrecht and Agricola. Each died early in the sixteenth century (1505 and 1506,

---

[74] For example, the famous *Si dormiero* made it as far as Poland, as shown by its inclusion in the keyboard tablature WarN 564 from 1548.

[75] See *CC* v. 287.

[76] See Meconi, 'Josquin and Musical Reputation', 287–97.

[77] Scholars, including myself, have obviously used the term 'Josquin Generation' for convenience.

TABLE 5.1. Intabulations of La Rue's music

Source	Tablature	Date	Provenance	Piece (attribution)
BasU F.IX.22	keyboard	by 1513?	Basel and/or Freiburg	Si dormiero (Isaac)
BerlS 40026	German keyboard	c.1520–4	Pforzheim	Tous les regretz (anon.) Trop plus secret (anon.)
SGallS 530	German keyboard	c.1512–21	Konstanz	Pourquoy non (anon.) ↑fifth Si dormiero (Alexander) Trop plus secret (anon.)
VienNB Mus. 18688	German lute	1523 or later	Ebenfurt	Trop plus secret (anon.)
WarN 564	keyboard	1548	Kraków?	Si dormiero (Josquin)
Brown 1523₂	German lute	1523	Vienna	Mijn hert (anon.) Trop plus secret (anon.)
Brown 1532₂	lute and gamba	1532	Nuremberg	Ce n'est pas jeu (anon.)
Brown 1533₁	German lute	1533	Nuremberg	Si dormiero (Isaac)
1536¹³	German lute	1536	Nuremberg	Si dormiero (Hainricus Finck) Mijn hert (anon.)
Brown 1537₁ (reprint of Brown 1532₂)	lute and gamba	1537	Nuremberg	Ce n'est pas jeu (anon.)
1552²⁹	French lute	1552	Leuven	Incessament (anon.)
1553³³	lute songs	1553	Leuven	Incessament (anon.)

Brown 1556₅	German lute	1556	Strasburg	Incessament (anon.)
1558[20]	lute	1558	Heidelberg	Absalon fili mi (Iosquin de Pres)
1562[24] (later edition of Brown 1556₅)	German lute	1558	Strasburg	Incessament (anon.)

Summary of intabulated works

Piece	Number of times intabulated
Absalon fili mi	1
Ce n'est pas jeu	2
Incessament	4
Mijn hert	2
Pourquoy non	1
Si dormiero	5
Attributions: Isaac twice, Josquin, Finck, anon.	
Tous les regretz	1
Trop plus secret	4

respectively), each received widespread dissemination of his music in the fifteenth century,[78] and each relied heavily on cantus-firmus construction; Obrecht in particular is famous for his brilliant variations on traditional cantus-firmus design.[79] A third composer who could readily be included with these earlier two is Compère, whose music was also distributed very widely in the fifteenth century. Although Compère lived until 1518, as long as La Rue, relatively little of his music appears to date from the sixteenth century, unlike La Rue's.

Although neither I nor anyone else has attempted to construct sixteenth-century dissemination profiles for these three composers, it seems unlikely that any one of them would generate two hundred manuscripts, prints, and theoretical citations throughout the century, that is, the equivalent of La Rue's source chronology; at the same time they each have a vital presence in the fifteenth century, when La Rue is essentially unknown. In other words, a Venn diagram for the dissemination of Agricola, Compère, Obrecht, and La Rue would show a restricted amount of overlap.

In contrast, two composers often overlooked in discussions of this generation are Antoine de Févin[80] and Mouton, who have certain crucial aspects in common with La Rue. Like La Rue, they are virtually absent from the fifteenth century in terms of their music. Mouton in particular might well match La Rue in terms of sixteenth-century dissemination; again, this kind of survey remains to be done. The relatively lesser amount of attention these composers have received may be owing to the correspondingly lesser access scholars have had to their music (especially Mouton's). Yet both are crucial in the history of polyphonic borrowing and other important early sixteenth-century compositional trends.

In still a third group we would find Isaac, Josquin, and to a rather lesser extent Brumel (this last, an excellent composer, has never received the attention his music deserves). The music of all these composers was known in the fifteenth century (especially that of Isaac, who is a major presence in the last two decades) and all continued their creative activity well into the sixteenth century. They thus straddle the two 'halves' of this generation musically, the earlier half of which, by death or disinclination, ceased their contributions early in the sixteenth century, while the latter half, because of youth or restricted opportunities, made their mark only in the sixteenth century.

[78] See Meconi, 'Josquin and Musical Reputation', 289–91 and 296–7.

[79] Obviously, this is not to claim that either composer should be identified solely by this preference.

[80] Févin was one of six composers Glarean linked to classical authors, in his case to Claudian. The others were La Rue (Horace), Josquin (Virgil), Obrecht (Ovid), Isaac (Lucan), and Brumel (Statius). Leofranc Holford-Strevens has kindly pointed out to me that Virgil (like Josquin) was slow to produce, whereas Ovid (like Obrecht) worked much more rapidly. It is likely that Glarean intended a dual hierarchy in his pairing of composers and poets, with Virgil, Ovid, and Horace (and thus Josquin, Obrecht, and La Rue) on a higher rung than Lucan, Statius, and Claudian (and thus Isaac, Brumel, and Févin). The precise quote is given in App. C under 1547 Glarean, citation 9.

As every scholar of this period knows, accidents of survival give us only a limited picture of when music was known or composed, but the pictures created by observing what remains are nonetheless suggestive and should be reflected in our assessment of this time. Thus, even though Compère may be an almost exact contemporary of La Rue's, and both are major chanson composers, comparison between the two is inappropriate in many ways. Compère's style undergoes a sharp change between his three-voice chansons (of which there are many) and his four-voice works (of which there are few),[81] and there are none for more than four voices. In contrast, there is little stylistic distinction between La Rue's (few) three-voice chansons and his (many) four-voice chansons, and he readily explored larger textures in his secular works. The main reason for this is that they are essentially in different compositional generations, despite their potentially similar ages or the fact that they both lived until 1518. We need to remember divisions such as these when dealing with the composers who constitute the several 'Josquin Generations'.

LITERARY AND THEORETICAL CITATIONS

La Rue is respectably represented among theorists and writers of the sixteenth century; Tables 5.2 and 5.3 provide lists of citations in literary and theoretical sources, and Appendix C includes the texts and translations for these citations, as well as indications of reprint editions. In general these citations place La Rue where we would expect him to be, among the most famous composers of his time, and serve as well to help justify that fame. From the approximate time of his retirement onwards they recur in a fairly steady progression throughout the sixteenth century and a bit beyond. We shall briefly examine first the literary and then the theoretical citations.

Molinet

The first time La Rue is mentioned is in Molinet's famous elegy for Ockeghem, 'Nymphes des bois', in the line 'Josquin perchon brumel compere'.[82] Interpretations of this coterie of composers has varied over the years, from their being literal pupils of Ockeghem (so far no hard evidence for that), to figurative pupils of the composer (plausible), to simply great musicians of the time.[83] In any event, no one

---

[81] See Wesner, 'The Chansons of Loyset Compère'; and ead., 'The Chansons of Loyset Compère: A Model for a Changing Aesthetic', in Jessie Ann Owens and Anthony Cummings (eds.), *Music in Renaissance Cities and Courts: Studies in Honor of Lewis Lockwood* (Warren, Mich.: Harmonie Park Press, 1997), 483–501.

[82] Other combinations of musicians could easily match the scanning here, e.g. 'Josquin Lourdault Brumel Compère' or 'Josquin Agricola Compère'.

[83] e.g. Ludwig Finscher, *Loyset Compère (c. 1450–1518): Life and Works* (Musicological Studies and Documents, 12; n.p.: American Institute of Musicology, 1964), 21: 'In the lamentation on the death of Ockeghem, Molinet includes Compère among the greatest masters of his time.' VDS vii. 120 wondered why La Rue was

TABLE 5.2. Citations of La Rue in literary works

Only first editions or appearances are cited.

Date	Person or source	Work and genre	Geographical area
*c.*1498	Jean Molinet	*Nymphes des bois* Poem	Habsburg-Burgundy
1517	Pierre Moulu	*Mater floreat florescat* Motet	France
*c.*1520	*S'ensuivent . . .*	*Sus nimphe des bois* Chanson	Switzerland
1521	Teofilo Folengo (Cocaius)	*Opus . . . Macaronicorum* Poem	Italy
*c.*1523?	Jean Daniel	*Ung gracieulx oyselet* Noel	France
1531	Jacobus Meyerus	*Flandricarum rerum tomi x* History	Flanders
1537	Martin Luther	*Tischreden* 'Table talk'	Germany
1552	François Rabelais	*Le Quart Livre des faicts et dicts* *heroïques du bon Pantagruel* Novel	France
1565–70	Hans Müelich	Medallion in MunBS A II	Germany
1607	Giulio Cesare Monteverdi	Introduction to Claudio Monteverdi, *Scherzi musicali*	Italy

TABLE 5.3. Citations of La Rue in theoretical treatises

Only first editions or appearances are cited.

Date	Person/source	Theoretical writing	Geographical area
1516	Heinrich Glarean	*Isagoge in musicen*	Switzerland
1517	Andreas Ornithoparchus	*Musice active micrologus*	Germany
1520	Giovanni del Lago	letter to Giovanni da Legge	Italy
	mentions:	*Pourquoy non*	
1525	Pietro Aaron	*Trattato della natura*	Italy
	mentions:	*Ce n'est pas jeu* *Fors seulement II* *Missa de beata virgine*	
1529	Pietro Aaron	*Toscanello in musica*	Italy
	mentions:	*Il est bien heureux* *Pourquoy non*	
1533	Giovanni Maria Lanfranco	*Scintille de musica*	Italy

TABLE 5.3. (*cont.*)

1537	Sebald Heyden	*Musica, id est Artis canendi*	Germany
	gives music for:	Agnus II from *Missa L'homme armé I* Pleni from *Missa O salutaris hostia*	
1540	Sebald Heyden	*De arte canendi*	Germany
	gives music for:	Agnus II from *Missa L'homme armé I*	
1547	Heinrich Glarean	*Dodecachordon*	Switzerland
	mentions:	*Missa Puer natus est nobis* *Missa de Sancto Antonio*	
	gives music for:	Pleni from *Missa O salutaris hostia* Christe from *Missa de Sancto Antonio* Agnus II from *Missa L'homme armé I* Kyrie I from *Missa O salutaris hostia*	
after 1547	Giovanthomaso Cimello	*Della perfettione delle quattro* *note maggiori*	Italy
	gives music for:	Agnus II from *Missa L'homme armé I* Kyrie I from *Missa O salutaris hostia*	
1552	Adrianus Petit Coclico	*Compendium musices*	Germany
1554	Johann Zanger	*Practicae musicae praecepta*	Germany
	gives music for:	*Et incarnatus* section of Credo from *Missa Cum iocunditate* (missing A) Agnus II from *Missa L'homme armé I*	
1556	Hermann Finck	*Practica musica* (original and enlarged editon)	Germany
	gives music for:	initial Sanctus of *Missa Cum iocunditate* Kyrie I from *Missa de beata virgine*	
1558	Gioseffo Zarlino	*Le istitutioni harmoniche*	Italy
	mentions:	*Pater de coelis deus* *Missa O salutaris hostia* *Missa Ave Maria*	
*c.*1560	StuttL HB 26		Germany
	gives music for:	*Et incarnatus* section of Credo from *Missa Cum iocunditate* (missing A)	
1563	Claudius Sebastiani	*Bellum musicale*	Germany
1565–74	Pietro Gaetano	*Oratio de origine et dignitate musices*	Italy
*c.*1580	LonBL 4911		Scotland
	gives music for:	initial Sanctus from *Missa Cum iocunditate* Agnus II from *Missa L'homme armé I*, T only	
1592	Lodovico Zacconi	*Prattica di musica*	Italy

TABLE 5.3. *(cont.)*

Date	Person/source	Theoretical writing	Geographical area
	gives music for:	Credo fragments from *Missa Cum iocunditate*, T only Agnus I fragment from *Missa Cum iocunditate*, T only Credo fragment from *Missa de Sancto Antonio*, A only	
1597	Thomas Morley	*A Plaine and Easie Introduction to Practicall Musicke*	England
	gives music for:	Kyrie I from *Missa O salutaris hostia*	
1618	Giovanni Battista Rossi	*Organo di cantori*	Italy
	mentions:	*Missa de beata virgine* *Missa L'homme armé I* *Missa Nuncqua fue pena maior* *Missa O salutaris hostia* *Missa Puer natus est nobis*	
	gives music for:	Kyrie I from *Missa L'homme armé I*, T and B only	
1618	Pedro Thalesio	*Arte de canto chão*	Portugal
	mentions:	*Missa Ave Maria*	
mid-17th c.		*Instrumentälischer Bettlermantl*	Germany
1662	João Álvares Frouvo	*Discursos sobre a perfeiçam do diathesaron*	Portugal
	mentions:	*Missa de beata virgine*	

has questioned La Rue's position in this quartet. If nothing else, Molinet's status as court poet for Philip at the time of Ockeghem's death, 6 February 1497, and La Rue's ongoing employment by Philip made such a citation seem entirely natural. But the evidence suggests that this citation is actually anomalous: La Rue is not quite yet a famous musician. He is cited nowhere else until the year of his retirement, and his music does not yet seem to be circulating outside court circles (although that will soon begin). He is not even particularly favoured by the court in 1497. The most plausible reason for his inclusion is that Molinet wished to represent the court in his line-up.[84]

not cited by Crétin, obviously assuming that someone of his stature should have been included in that poet's list of composers; he then proceeds to hypothesize that the 'Barizon' Crétin mentioned was 'Perizon' La Rue, claiming that 'Basiron', whom others thought this referred to, could hardly qualify as 'very noteworthy', the description Crétin applies to the musician. RobijnsP, 7, remarks that in *Nymphes des bois* La Rue is named on an equal footing with 'Josquin himself, Brumel, Compère' and then proceeds to wonder why he was not included in the list of singers in Compère's *Omnium bonorum plena*.

[84] I first explored the aspects of *Nymphes des bois* considered below, including the relationship between Molinet and Crétin, in 'What is La Rue Doing in *Nymphes des bois*?', paper presented at Conference on

Molinet's was not the first poem for Ockeghem, whose death prompted numerous elegies; the most substantial of these was the lengthy poem by the French court poet Guillaume Crétin. In a famous passage in this work, Crétin called on a series of living musicians to mourn Ockeghem; he had earlier presented a list of departed musicians (including Busnoys and Regis) who were to welcome the composer to heaven. Those to mourn Ockeghem were instructed as follows: 'Agricolla, Verbonnet, Prioris / Josquin Desprez, Gaspar, Brunel, Compere / Ne parlez plus de joyeux chantz ne ris / Mais composez ung Ne recorderis / Pour lamenter nostre maistre et bon pere / Prevost, Ver Just, tant que Piscis Prospere / Prenez Fresneau, pour voz chantz accorder / La perte est grande et digne a recorder.'[85] La Rue is noticeably absent.

Earlier in the poem Crétin had also noted poets whom he thought were remiss in not mourning Ockeghem, including Molinet. The precise passage reads: 'Sus Molinet, dormez vous, ou resvez? / Vos sens sont ilz si pressez ou grevez / Que ne pouez prendre papier et plume? / A quoy tient il que aujourd'huy n'estrivez / Contre la mort, et soubdain n'escripvez / De Okergan quelque petit volume?'[86] Crétin badgers Molinet—has he been sleeping, or dreaming? What's wrong? Why hasn't he written something to commemorate Ockeghem?

Molinet eventually responded to Crétin's chastisement by writing not one but two elegies for Ockeghem; these are exceptional works within his output for several reasons. All of Molinet's other poems of mourning were for people directly connected to the Habsburg-Burgundian court, and the only other person who received multiple elegies from Molinet was Philip the Good. In addition, the two elegies for Ockeghem are the two shortest of Molinet's commemorative poems. He seems to have been trying to satisfy the call to write 'quelque petit volume' without too great an effort.[87]

In his two poems he mirrored Crétin's disposition of composers.[88] In 'Johannis Obghem Epitaphium', in Latin (still a living language, but no longer anyone's

Medieval and Renaissance Music, London, Aug. 1986. A more recent investigation of *Nymphes des bois*, which also posits a connection between Molinet and Crétin, is found in Jaap van Benthem, 'La Magie des cris trenchantz: comment le vray trésorier de musique échappe à la trappe du très terrible satrappe', in *Théorie et analyse musicales/Music Theory and Analysis 1450–1650: Actes du colloque international Louvain-la-Neuve, 23–25 septembre 1999/Proceedings of the International Conference Louvain-la-Neuve, 23–25 September 1999*, ed. Anne-Emmanuelle Ceulemans and Bonnie J. Blackburn (Publications d'histoire de l'art et d'archéologie de l'Université catholique de Louvain, C; Musicologica Neolovaniensia, Studia 9; Louvain-la-Neuve: Département d'histoire de l'art et d'archéologie, Collège Érasme, 2001), 119–47. My thanks to Bonnie Blackburn for bringing this article to my attention, and to Jaap van Benthem for kindly supplying a copy of the article before its publication.

[85] 'Déploration . . . sur . . . Okergan', ll. 397–404, after Crétin, *Œuvres poétiques*, ed. Chesney, 72.

[86] Ibid. 69, ll. 277–82.

[87] By 1497 Molinet had the use of only one eye; see Noël Dupire, *Jean Molinet: La Vie—Les Œuvres* (Paris: E. Droz, 1932), 24–5.

[88] Molinet and Crétin were unquestionably in contact with each other; a short correspondence between the two falls sometime between 1498 and 1502. It opens with Crétin praising Molinet's skill and then complaining that he never hears from him, sentiments similar to those expressed in the *déploration*; see Jean Molinet, *Les Faictz et dictz de Jean Molinet*, ed. Noël Dupire, 3 vols. (Paris: Société des anciens textes français, 1936–9), ii. 834–41.

native tongue, and rarely used by Molinet), he named two departed composers, Busnoys and Regis (just as Crétin included a section for deceased musicians with these two composers), while in 'Nymphes des bois', in the more modern French, he called on 'Josquin perchon brumel compere'.[89] That Molinet was practically quoting from Crétin at this point should be obvious.[90] Literature at the time was typically interlarded with quotations or semi-quotations, borrowings, and references to earlier works, and there are various phrases that reappear in works of mourning from as far back as the previous century; 'nimphes des bois', for example, is found in Deschamps's elegy for Machaut.[91] Certainly in 'Nymphes des bois' the identical order of the composers, with the substitution of 'perchon' for 'Gaspar', can leave little doubt of Molinet's source. The line Molinet was mimicking included a composer he knew personally (Compère), a composer working at the Habsburg-Burgundian court (Gaspar, who must be Weerbeke), and the composer who was ultimately to set Molinet's poem to music (Josquin).

But if Molinet was borrowing from Crétin here, why didn't he simply use the name of Gaspar? Weerbeke was already noted in Chapter 2 for the widespread distribution of his music in the fifteenth century, his prominent places of employment prior to joining the court, and his higher salary and position on the pay lists than La Rue's despite La Rue's greater seniority. In terms of reputation in 1497, Weerbeke was head and shoulders above La Rue, and the other composers on the list were as well. Certainly they all had a much greater presence in contemporary manuscripts than La Rue did.[92] Gaffurius, writing in 1496 or earlier in Book III of his *Practica musicae*, includes among his list of 'very pleasing composers' 'Jusquin despret, Gaspar . . . Loyset . . . Brumel';[93] La Rue is nowhere in sight. Nor, as

---

[89] The order is switched in 1545[15], the Susato print of Josquin's setting, so that Brumel precedes La Rue. There is no particular evidence that Brumel was viewed more highly than La Rue at this time; I suspect the opposite was true.

[90] The passages are so similar that the poems have sometimes been confused. CaulletM, 39, for example, quotes Molinet but assigns the poetry to Crétin, and Friedrich Blume, *Renaissance and Baroque Music: A Comprehensive Survey*, trans. M. D. Herter Norton (New York: W. W. Norton, 1967), 46, obviously conflating the two poems, said 'To conclude from Guillaume Crétin's *déploration* for Ockeghem that Josquin, La Rue, Weerbecke, and Compère were his pupils is hardly plausible.' Hocquet, 'Un musicien tournaisien', 167, claims that Crétin wrote an elegy on La Rue, a statement lacking any foundation.

[91] Lowinsky, *The Medici Codex*, text vol., 215. Crétin echoes himself in his elegy for Braconnier, where Prioris is now called 'bon pere' and instructed to 'Prenez l'ardoyse et de vostre faczon / Composez cy un "ne recorderis"'; see Crétin, *Œuvres poétiques*, 215. Both Crétin and Molinet mention the mythological Atropos (a common figure in elegiac writing), and there are various other similarities as well. See van Benthem, 'La Magie des cris trenchantz', for an extended discussion of *Nymphes des bois* and its relations to other works, including Molinet's own.

[92] See above, Table 2.1 for Weerbeke, and Meconi, 'Josquin and Musical Reputation', 287–9, 292–4 for Josquin and Compère. Brumel had appeared twenty-seven separate times in manuscripts by the turn of the century.

[93] 'Tinctoris, Gulielmus guarnerius, Jusquin despret, Gaspar, Alexander agricola, Loyset, Obrech, Brumel, Isaac, and other very pleasing composers', in Franchinus Gaffurius, *Practica musicae*, trans. Clement A. Miller (Musicological Studies and Documents, 20; n.p.: American Institute of Musicology, 1968), 144. Clement A. Miller, 'Gaffurius's *Practica Musicae*: Origins and Contents', *Musica disciplina*, 22 (1968), 105–28, esp. 105–9, suggests that the work published in 1496 is really a collection of four separate earlier treatises revised for publication.

Appendix C indicates, is he anywhere else in poetical or theoretical sources until the time of his retirement.

Moreover, we have no other mention of La Rue anywhere within Molinet's copious literary output. Not only was Molinet himself musically astute, he frequently named musicians and works of music in his writings,[94] yet La Rue is completely absent. Around 1496, for example, Molinet mentions 'Okeguem, Alexandre, Jossequin . . . Busnois';[95] again no La Rue. While we modern scholars may find Molinet's apparent lack of insight inexplicable, we must remember that everything noted so far shows that La Rue's rise in the estimation of the court was a gradual one, and that courtly rewards do not seem to accrue to him until the sixteenth century. Molinet seems consistently to cite only those active in the earlier of the 'Josquin generations' just outlined.

Since Molinet is surely borrowing from Crétin in his poem, Weerbeke would seem a more logical choice for him to include than La Rue, being far more important than La Rue in court circles—and anywhere else, for that matter—at the time of Ockeghem's death. Molinet must have been 'forced' to include La Rue if he wanted to represent the court in this poem.[96] The most likely catalyst for this is not, I think, any intervention from Philip or Marguerite, but rather the departure of Weerbeke from the court in June or July of 1498, which would imply that the poem was written after this date. This is by no means an unreasonable delay; mourning works could easily be written some time after the fact. Molinet's commemorative poem for Charles the Bold, for example, was written almost ten years after the duke's death.[97] Crétin's poem of more than 400 lines was not dashed off in a day, and some time must have elapsed before it reached Molinet and spurred him to action. Only if we allow for a belated date for the poem's creation does La Rue's presence make sense therein, for Molinet seems otherwise to have snubbed La Rue—still in the throes of establishing himself—completely.

A final possibility exists, that Molinet did indeed write 'Gaspar' and that this was changed to 'perchon' at a later date, to reflect the rise of La Rue's reputation. While this is possible (the poetry source dates from 1512 or later,[98] as do the

---

[94] These include poems to Compère, Busnoys, and Verjus; see Molinet, *Les Faictz et dictz*, ii. 779, 781, 788–95, 798–9. He is also apparently composer of the song *Tart ara mon cueur*, which was widely distributed in the 15th c. in three different versions, and is noteworthy for using two signature flats in each voice in two separate sources. Cited in Compère's motet *Omnium bonorum plena*, his name appears along with Compère's in the anonymous quodlibet *Vous qui partes/He Molinet*.

[95] In *J'ay veu, comme il me semble*, the poem and translation are given in Ch. 1.

[96] Josquin's whereabouts at this time are unknown, with the French court one possibility. Brumel was at Notre-Dame in Paris (as of Jan. 1498), and Compère was in Cambrai (as of late Apr. 1498); Molinet (consciously or not) could be representing major musical centres in this short list of composers if the poem is from the summer of 1498 or later, as is most likely.

[97] *L'Arbre de Bourgonne sus la mort du duc Charles* comes from after 9 Apr. 1486; Charles died in 1477. See Jean Devaux, *Jean Molinet: Indiciaire Bourguignon* (Bibliothèque du XVe siècle, 55; Paris: Honoré Champion, 1996), 602.

[98] The manuscript, BNF fr. 24315, is a poetry collection that includes Crétin's *déploration* for Braconnier, entered immediately after the Molinet poem. Since the Crétin work is copied in the same hand as 'Nymphes des bois', this section of the manuscript must date from after Braconnier's death in 1512.

musical sources including this text),[99] it presupposes either that the change was made before Josquin composed his setting or that the copies of Josquin's piece were changed after he had written a setting that included 'Gaspar'. The latter scenario seems unlikely just from a logistical point of view, and the former is also problematic, given that Weerbeke remains a significant figure for quite some time after he left the court. The desire to represent the court in the poem, and the need to substitute someone (with a two-syllable name) after Weerbeke departed, remains the most plausible impetus behind La Rue's inclusion in the poem.

Later literary citations

Almost two decades after Molinet wrote 'Nymphes des bois', La Rue showed up again in a list with other musicians, but this time there is no question about his right to be included. Pierre Moulu's four-voice ceremonial motet *Mater floreat florescat* was most likely written for the triumphant entry of Queen Claude of France into Paris on 12 May 1517.[100] The text calls on two dozen musicians, divided into two groups, to praise the King and Queen. Although it is not specifically stated in the text that it is the sovereigns of France who are being praised, the second group of musicians is drawn mostly from the contemporary French royal chapel. The first group is composed of musicians from the past in a semi-chronological order. It is here that La Rue's name is found, in the company of 'the incomparable Josquin', and Compère, as before (but no Gaspar), along with Agricola ('the magnificent Alexander'), Obrecht, Hayne, Busnoys, Baziron, Regis, and Dufay. 'The eloquent Brumel' is listed in the second group of musicians, as are La Rue's former colleagues Braconnier and Divitis. La Rue and others are described as 'memorable'. The likely audience for this motet would be the French royal court, and, slightly later, members of the Medici family; for neither group would La Rue be an unfamiliar name.

Around the year 1520 La Rue's name appeared in an anonymous poem in a collection of chanson verse printed in Geneva, *S'ensuivent plusieurs belles chansons*. The poem (for which no music survives) is headed 'Sus nimphe des bois', essentially announcing its debt to Molinet. The new poet is now apparently mourning the departure of Brumel from the court of Savoy in July 1502[101] (which is thus the likely date of the poem's conception), and seems to be making (untranslatable) punning references to the names of the four composers Molinet called up. Since the new poem refers back to Molinet, it does not itself provide additional evidence for awareness of La Rue's achievements, but it does add to the argument that Molinet included La Rue's name rather than Weerbeke's right from the start.

La Rue is disguised in his next literary appearance as 'Petrus de robore'. As odd as this version of his name is, he is the most likely candidate for the context. The

---

[99] The piece is given without French text in 1508[1] and with complete texting in FlorL 666 and 1545[15].
[100] Lowinsky, *The Medici Codex*, text vol., 73–5.
[101] See van Benthem, 'La Magie des cris trenchantz', 124.

work in question is the *magnum opus* of Teofilo Folengo (1491–1544), which appeared under his pseudonym of Merlinus Cocaius. This immense poem, *Opus . . . macaronicorum*, was written in Latin, with Italian words (and the dialect of his native Mantua) latinized.[102] The poem is a satire on the chivalric epics so popular at the time, of which the best-known is Ariosto's *Orlando furioso*, first published in 1516. Folengo's work first appeared the following year; three other main versions followed in 1521, *c*.1539–40 and 1552, but only the 1521 version has the passage in question. This version had many reprints, even after the revised editions appeared.[103]

References to music and composers are sprinkled throughout the work,[104] but the most famous selection is the passage that calls on Josquin to usher in a new age of music, and, in the process, provides a partial list of his compositions. Ambros called it 'eine unverkennbare Parodie einer berühmten Ekloge Virgils';[105] the one in question must be Eclogue IV, the famous Messianic eclogue that was viewed by Christians as foretelling the coming of Christ. If Ambros is correct in his interpretation,[106] the excerpt would represent an essentially blasphemous equation of Josquin with Christ (although Folengo was possibly satirizing the current adulation for the composer). In any event, La Rue, in the guise of Petrus de Robore, plays an extremely minor role as a kind of acolyte of the Great Man, but at least he is mentioned, which is not the case for Compère or Gaspar. Brumel is cited as well, and noted as being 'Magnus'. Interestingly, it is Festa, not La Rue, who 'often will be thought to be Josquin'. The passage's excision from the 1539/1540 and 1552 versions suggests that it no longer held much resonance for readers, matching our earlier observations that Josquin's music (and La Rue's) is hardly to be found in Italian sources after the 1530s. It is similarly unlikely that 'Petrus de robore' or any of the other musicians cited meant anything to the poem's readers in the later reprints of 1572, 1581, 1618, or 1692.

La Rue's next literary appearance is in a charming noel for which music no longer survives, written about 1523 and included in Jean Daniel's *S'ensuyvent plusieurs noels nouveaulx*. La Rue and other composers (predominantly French ones) all take part in music making for the infant Jesus. La Rue is preceded in the song by Agricola, Prioris, and Josquin, and followed by Compère and others. Neither Brumel nor Weerbeke is included. This song was apparently quite

---

[102] See the introduction to Teofilo Folengo, *Histoire maccaronique de Merlin Coccaie*, ed. Gustave Brunet (Paris: Adolphe Delahays, 1859), pp. i–li, for background information.

[103] The 1521 edition was reprinted in 1522, 1572, 1581, 1613, 1692 and possibly at other times. Of the three early editions I have seen—those of 1521, 1572, and 1581—all place the quoted passage in Book 20. However, in only one of the four modern editions I consulted was the passage to be found there; this was [Teofilo Folengo] Merlin Cocai, *Le opere maccheroniche*, 2 vols., ed. Attilio Portioli (Mantua: C. Mondovi, 1882–3).

[104] See Giulio Cattin, 'Canti, canzoni a ballo e danze nelle Maccheronee di Teofilo Folengo', *Rivista italiana di musicologia*, 10 (1975), 180–215. He does not discuss the passage in question.

[105] Ambros, *Geschichte der Musik*, iii. 12.

[106] None of the three classicists to whom I showed the excerpt thought the relationship between Folengo and Virgil's fourth eclogue was especially strong.

popular, for it reappeared (sometimes with various textual changes) in six known later editions, the last from *c.*1595.[107]

Just as La Rue functioned as a performer in Daniel's noel, he was also cited, and more directly, for his singing in Flemish historian Jacobus Meyerus' history of Flanders, published in 1531.[108] La Rue, as 'Petrus Vicanus', appears in Book 9, among a discussion of famous Flemings. Here he is listed as a singer of Charles V. Meyerus is obviously going on reputation alone, since La Rue is hailed for his singing sixteen years after he stopped working for Charles V. Agricola is also noted for his singing in the same excerpt, where he is identified as a singer for Philip the Fair. The longevity of a reputation for performance is quite striking, especially given that La Rue's music was still being copied and performed in Flanders at this time. One would assume that his reputation as a composer would have overtaken any reputation as a singer (especially given that this is the only firm evidence we have that he was an 'excellent singer', as Meyerus calls him; the reference in the epitaph is ambiguous). Interesting, too, is the assumption that he was Flemish.

La Rue is one of the very few musicians mentioned by name by the musically astute Martin Luther (Josquin and Finck are the only others), appearing in one of the accounts of dinner and after-dinner conversations assiduously compiled by his followers. On New Year's Day, 1537, after singing 'exceptional songs', Luther remarked that Josquin, La Rue, Finck and others ('fine' and 'excellent' musicians) had died within the past ten years. Although Luther was off by almost a decade on La Rue's death date, the passage is telling. Again, La Rue is mentioned in the same breath as Josquin, and he is obviously someone whose music Luther knew and valued highly. Luther's general musical knowledge was sufficient for him to know that La Rue was no longer living, and it is possible that La Rue's were among the 'exceptional songs' that Luther, a skilled practitioner, and his guests were singing. As noted above, La Rue's music was well-known in Germany at this time, with Wittenberg, where Luther lived for much of his adult life, an especial outpost for the composer's music, both via Frederick the Wise (Luther's protector) and others. Lutheran churches continued to use his music, as seen in the various Torgau manuscripts.

In La Rue's remaining literary citations he is simply one of a list of famous composers. This is especially true in the prologue to the fourth book of Rabelais' *Pantagruel*, where he is one of almost sixty musicians Rabelais trots out to sing a song. In this large crowd we find Josquin (listed first), Brumel, and Compère (among many, many, others) listed with La Rue, but no Weerbeke. As we saw with

---

[107] See App. C for the list of editions.

[108] For a discussion of the book see Victor Fris, 'Tableau de la Flandre au début du xvie siècle d'après Antonio De Beatis et Jacques de Meyere', *Bulletin de la Société d'histoire et d'archéologie de Gand*, 18 (1910), 42–91; the section on Meyerus is on pp. 71–91 and includes a French translation of the passage on p. 86. La Rue was not included twenty-five years later in Ludovico Guicciardini, *Descrittione di tutti i paësi bassi* (Antwerp, 1556); see RobijnsP, 10.

Moulu, the composers are divided into two roughly chronological groups, with La Rue in the earlier group. It is this generational divide that lets us say with confidence that it is Pierre rather than Robert de la Rue whom Rabelais is including.

A slightly more select group of musicians appears in the late (around 1565–70) illuminated manuscript MunBS A II, where painter Hans Müelich arrayed the names of twenty-eight 'Distinguished and Most Excellent Authors of Music' under a picture of Lasso's Munich choir. Josquin, as usual, is included here, but Obrecht is the first on the list (which is divided into three columns). Brumel is there too, but neither Compère nor Weerbeke. La Rue is given as 'Petrus pirson de la Rue', incorporating a version of his name by which he was commonly (albeit sometimes erroneously) cited in earlier German manuscripts.

The final 'literary' citation is a quasi-theoretical one (indeed, one could quibble about its categorization), Giulio Cesare Monteverdi's introduction to his brother's 1607 collection of *Scherzi musicali*. In this instance La Rue is simply one of a group of *prima prattica* composers; it seems unlikely that either of the Monteverdi brothers knew any of his music unless it were one of the canons that kept his name alive at the end of the century. Josquin, as usual, is named with La Rue, but not Brumel, Compère, or Weerbeke.

While this is hardly a copious list of literary citations, its longevity (more than a century) is significant, as is its geographical spread—France, Italy, Flanders, Switzerland, and Germany. The earlier French citations are particularly welcome, given the relative paucity of both French sources by themselves and the appearance of La Rue's music therein; they attest nicely to his name recognition in France. Although the citations from after 1550 are merely the rote repetition of his name (especially in Rabelais, where the urge for completeness seems the major goal of the list), in both the Munich manuscript and the Monteverdi introduction La Rue is one of the very few from his generation to be included. Unlike most of his contemporaries, his reputation survived the demise of the performance of his music, even if not for long.

Theoretical citations

Theoretical citations of La Rue and/or his music are much more common than literary ones, and like the former, they exhibit a similar chronological and geographical spread.[109] They are testimony for a greater dissemination of his music than the musical sources alone can tell us. For example, in his 1529 treatise Pietro Aaron cites La Rue's chanson *Il est bien heureux*, a song that exists today only in Marguerite's private collection BrusBR 228. Without Aaron's citation it would be easy to assume that this song, though extremely attractive, had a limited circulation within the confines of Marguerite's court circle; instead, it was known as far

---

[109] On theorists' borrowing from each other and their reliance on printed sources of music, see Cristle Collins Judd, *Reading Renaissance Music Theory: Hearing with the Eyes* (Cambridge: Cambridge University Press, 2000).

away as Italy, suggesting that other songs (and works) were as well. Similarly, the six-voice motet *Pater de coelis deus*, which survives only in posthumous German printed sources, was known by Zarlino in Italy in the latter half of the century.[110]

A number of the citations are of the 'name list' type, with some being more generic than others. The first of these is Andreas Ornithoparchus' *Musice active micrologus* (Leipzig, 1517), an extremely popular treatise with numerous reprints and ultimately an English translation in 1609 by none other than Dowland. Here La Rue is in the company of (among others) Compère, Josquin, and Brumel, but not Weerbeke. Some of the musicians on the list receive an additional 'citation' in the margin of the print (just the way modern textbook publishers emphasize the most important figures); La Rue is one of the chosen (though indicated merely as 'Pe.') Although Ornithoparchus travelled extensively, all of his travels seem to have been in German-speaking lands, and it appears unlikely that either he or his collaborator, Georg Brack, the second Kapellmeister at Stuttgart, had met La Rue (the composer's German travels were probably too early). Hence, by 1517 his music and/or reputation were well enough known in German lands for him to be included in this star-studded list.

Adrianus Petit Coclico divided musicians into several groups (essentially chronological), of which his favourite was the third group, 'the most outstanding musicians and almost as kings of the others'; he continues in this vein with lavish praise. While 'the chief is easily Josquin des Prez', La Rue leads the list of the other 'most skilled musicians and artful symphonists'; he is immediately followed by Brumel and many others (but this time not by Compère or Weerbeke). Claudius Sebastiani (*Bellum musicale*, 1563) takes over Coclico's groups of musicians with few alterations; La Rue is listed after Josquin and before Brumel. Coclico mentions La Rue three other times, each time in company with others. With Josquin 'and others' he is cited as a teacher—a role not documented by anyone other than Coclico—and called a prince of music and one 'whom the world esteems and admires'. In another reference to his teaching (and performing), La Rue, along with Josquin and 'Iacobus Scampion', are all called princes of music 'who have performed the smoothest and [most] elegant passages that must be admired'. Their influence 'is still preserved and is continued by scholars of music, since their pupils faithfully imitate their teachers'. In a final reference to the art of counterpoint, La Rue is again matched with Josquin 'and their successors'; they all had 'ears . . . most delicate'.

Hermann Finck includes La Rue in a list of musicians supposedly from around 1480 who were 'far ahead of their predecessors'. Josquin is praised separately, then La Rue (and Brumel) are included in a small group of 'other skilled musicians'. Pietro Gaetano (*Oratio de origine et dignitate musices*, between 1565 and 1574) puts La Rue in a *tertiam aetas* with Josquin, Brumel, and a few others. A final list, from

---

[110] Judd, *Reading Renaissance Music Theory*, 232, suggests that Zarlino had access to 1520[4], which contains this motet.

the anonymous mid-seventeenth-century *Instrumentälischer Bettlermantl* (a compendium of treatises and descriptions of instruments apparently from southern Germany or Austria), is drawn from Gallus Dressler's *Praecepta musicae poeticae* (1564), which itself does not include La Rue.[111] The anonymous writer added several musicans, however, and La Rue is surely the 'Petro de Darne' newly incorporated here—a surprising addition at this late date. It is not difficult to see the scribal transition from 'Larue' to 'Darne', and, as so often happens, the other composer cited is Josquin. Both are noted for constructing their music from *fugae* and chastised for their thin texture.

An unusual 'list' appears in Pietro Aaron's *Toscanello in musica*, 1529, where individual pieces are cited, first those by *moderni*, then those by *antichi*; in between the two groups is a specific list of *antichi*. La Rue (Pierazzon de larue) is on this *antichi* list, which also includes Compère (but no Josquin, Brumel, or Weerbeke). The citation is amusing in one respect: La Rue (Piero de larue) has just been listed in a series of *moderni* (that series included Josquin). Aaron cites two different pieces for La Rue, *Pourquoy non* under the *antichi* examples and *Il est bien heureux* under the *moderni* examples (coincidentally, the songs are adjacent to each other in BrusBR 228, a manuscript Aaron could not have known). La Rue is also one of the *antichi* in Giovanni Maria Lanfranco's *Scintille di musica* (1533), where he is listed with Josquin and others.

Music examples drawn from La Rue's works are relatively few. The most popular is the second Agnus from his *Missa L'homme armé I*, the famous 4 ex 1 mensuration canon; it appears in six separate treatises (Heyden 1537 and 1540, *Dodecachordon* (where it is identified as Hypodorian), Giovanthomaso Cimello (apparently derived from the preceding), Johann Zanger (1556), and LondBL 4911). Giovanni Battista Rossi's *Organo di cantori* from 1618 has the tenor and bassus from the opening Kyrie of the same mass; this is also a mensuration canon, albeit for two voices.[112] Two other examples come from La Rue's canonic *Missa O salutaris hostia*. Heyden 1537 and the *Dodecachordon* both give the Pleni, a 2 ex 1 canon. For some reason this work was dropped from Heyden 1540; he also dropped the statement in his 1537 introduction that the music examples were from the 'best and most praiseworthy musicians', which included Josquin, who was cited first, Obrecht, La Rue, and Isaac.[113] The presence of their 'miraculous examples', he claimed, made the book even more valuable.

[111] All information on this collection is from Noel O'Regan, 'The *Instrumentälischer Bettlermantl* and Gallus Dressler's *Precepta Musicae Poeticae* of 1563/4', in J. P. Campbell (ed.), *Proceedings of the International Interdisciplinary Conference on Instrumentälischer Bettlermantl, August 1997* (forthcoming). My thanks to Professor O'Regan for kindly providing me with a copy of his essay before its publication.

[112] Rossi gives the date of completion of the treatise as 5 May 1585; see Gio. Battista Rossi, *Organo di cantori* . . . (facs. edn., Bibliotheca musica Bononiensis, Sez. II, 57; Bologna: Arnaldo Forni, 1984), 79. For more on Rossi, see Tim Carter, 'Rossi, Giovanni Battista', *New Grove II*.

[113] Curiously, the preface to the second part of the treatise also mentions the most esteemed musicians, but this time they are Josquin, Obrecht, Brumel, and Isaac, bringing to mind the switch in name order (between La Rue and Brumel) in Susato's 1545 print of *Nymphes des bois*. This little list in the second part remains intact in 1540 Heyden.

The other example from *Missa O salutaris hostia*, the first Kyrie (a 4 ex 1 canon), appears in the *Dodecachordon* (marked as Hypodorian) and the derivative Cimello, as well as Thomas Morley in 1597. The ostinato mass *Missa Cum iocunditate* generates six citations: the initial Sanctus, where the ostinato starts on successively lower pitches (in Finck's *Practica musica* of 1556 and in LonBL 4911), the Et incarnatus (in Zanger and in the derivative StuttL HB 26; in each source it is missing the altus), and twice in Lodovico Zacconi (1592), with brief excerpts from the Confiteor and first Agnus. Two other examples are taken from the *Missa de Sancto Antonio*. The Christe is presented in the *Dodecachordon* as an example of the Hypoaeolian mode, which Glarean suggests 'escaped the composer involuntarily', while Zacconi includes a small excerpt from the Credo. Finally, Finck uses the first Kyrie of the *Missa de beata virgine* to demonstrate major tactus.

Although the examples are often of canon or cantus-firmus procedure, they are cited for a variety of things. Heyden 1537 uses the Pleni from the *Missa O salutaris hostia* as an example of Mode 2, an interesting choice since it is transposed Dorian. Glarean uses the same example in the *Dodecachordon* but acknowledges the transposition. LonBL 4911 uses the Agnus II from the *Missa L'homme armé I* to show 'the progression of diverss conceptis of harmony'. Zanger, Zacconi, and Finck (in his excerpt from the *Missa de beata virgine*) all use La Rue's music to illustrate various components of notation.

In citations without the use of musical examples, Glarean mentions La Rue's use of mixed modes in a single melody and his unusual harmonies; he makes the interesting suggestion that La Rue employed the latter 'more perhaps in order that the highest voices should be brought into play than that they should make beautiful consonances'. These two citations are in his youthful classroom treatise *Isagoge* (1516), where La Rue and Obrecht are the only two non-theorists he mentions. This is the earliest theoretical mention of La Rue, and prefigures his appearance in the later *Dodecachordon*. In this later treatise, the *Missa Puer natus est nobis* is noted as an example of modal transposition from the seventh to the first mode (La Rue is said to set the melody 'most elegantly'), while the tenor of the *Missa de Sancto Antonio* is described as Aeolian. Interspersed between these modal citations are several paeons to La Rue's skill, always in Josquin's (and others') company. La Rue is 'a most pleasing musician', his is a 'happy genius', he is one of those who 'have expressed the nature of song with ingenuity and artistry, and . . . justly merited surpassing praise'. He has 'a high degree of talent' and 'uncommon erudition in musical matters'. In the most famous citation, Glarean asks 'to whom shall we compare Petrus Platensis, a wonderfully pleasing composer, other than to Horace?', thereby linking La Rue with one of the most famous lyric poets of ancient Rome, whose work was well known to humanists such as Glarean. Perhaps the comparison was inspired by two typical traits of Horace, his frequent changes of mood and his habit of withholding the true identity of a speaker until the end of the poem. Were La Rue's shifts of modal direction and his occasional surprise endings seen as the musical equivalent?

The theorist Giovanni del Lago (correspondence, 1520) mentions *Pourquoy non* in his list of works using *conjunctae*, transposed hexachords. Aaron (*Trattato*, 1525)[114] gives *Ce n'est pas jeu* as an example of Mode 2 on G, as well as the Sanctus and Agnus of *Missa de beata virgine* as being in Mode 5 with the B♭ added, and the Gloria of the same mass as an example of Mode 7.[115] In the second edition of his *Toscanello* (1529) he mentions both *Il est bien heureux* and *Pourquoy non* to demonstrate the use of a signed accidental to avoid a dissonance.[116] Zarlino (1558) says that it is 'admirable to write four voices on one . . . as P. della Rue did' in *Missa O salutaris hostia*, a mass also mentioned by Rossi for its unusual construction. Zarlino placed La Rue's *Missa Ave Maria* in the ninth mode,[117] and noted that the imitative beginning of La Rue's *Pater de coelis deus* was acceptable despite going against compositional norms for the opening of a piece.[118] Writing in 1585, Rossi directed his readers to the *Missa L'homme armé I* when discussing points of division, and to three separate masses to see perfect breves: *Missa de beata virgine*, *Missa Nuncque fue pena maior*, and *Missa Puer natus est nobis* (all works, of course, appearing in the Petrucci mass print from 1503). Two seventeenth-century Portuguese theorists likewise mentioned specific works of La Rue: Pedro Thalesio observed that the *Missa Ave Maria* was in the ninth mode, while João Frouvo noted a consonant fourth in the *Missa de beata virgine*. Thalesio was perhaps drawing on Zarlino, but it sounds as if Frouvo actually had access to La Rue's mass.

Between literary and theoretical citations, then, La Rue's name and music were kept before interested readers with a fair degree of continuity from about the time of his retirement until around a century later. Although Cimello, Finck, StuttL HB 26, and LonBL 4911 all present his music anonymously, everyone else included his name.[119] There are many sixteenth-century 'name lists' and theoretical treatises where he is absent, but Josquin is the only contemporary of La Rue's who is listed everywhere; everyone else was subject to the vagaries of an individual writer's taste and experience.[120]

[114] For the latest on the examples in this treatise, see Cristle Collins Judd, 'Reading Aron Reading Petrucci: The Music Examples of the *Trattato della natura et cognitione di tutti gli tuoni* (1525)', *EMH* 14 (1995), 121–52.

[115] Following Petrucci, he erroneously cites Pipelare's *Fors seulement* as La Rue's.

[116] For a discussion of the musical examples in the *Aggiunta* to *Toscanello*, see Margaret Bent, 'Accidentals, Counterpoint and Notation in Aaron's *Aggiunta* to the *Toscanello in Musica*', *Journal of Musicology*, 12 (1994), 306–44.

[117] This reference is dropped in the revised 3rd edn. of 1573.

[118] Zarlino also mentions his own *Virgo prudentissima* in this connection, which has confused some writers, who think he is ascribing it to La Rue (e.g. VDS iii. 213).

[119] Finck includes La Rue's name in his 'composer list' but does not give La Rue as the composer when he cites his music.

[120] See Owens, 'Music Historiography'. These citations can be helpful in establishing the trajectory of a composer's musical or mythical presence, but they hardly offer a complete picture, nor are the images always precise. Weerbeke, for example, is conspicuously absent from most composer lists of the 16th c., yet he is a

GROWTH OF A REPUTATION

La Rue's participation in the modern historiographical tradition begins not long after the citation of his *Missa de beata virgine* by Frouvo in 1662 (see Table 5.4). He is included in the first known biographical dictionary of music, part of the Danish writer Matthias Henriksen Schacht's manuscript *Musicus danicus eller Danske sangmester* from 1687. Here La Rue is listed simply as 'Petrus Platensis Musicus Symphetta, citatur à Glareano'.[121] Glarean, as will soon become evident, was one of the primary sources cited by writers on earlier music for a good two centuries beyond this early endeavour. Very shortly thereafter La Rue makes a brief appearance in the first major German history of music, Wolfgang Caspar Printz's *Historische Beschreibung*, where he is noted simply for his inclusion in the 1549 *Lamentations* collection (for a work now thought not to be his) and for the designation as being from Flanders.[122] Starting with Walther, later writers will misinterpret 1549 to be the date of composition of the *Lamentations*, leading to problems reconciling this late date with evidence of considerably earlier activity.

The information from these two earliest entries is combined in Johann Gottfried Walther's *Musicalisches Lexicon* (1732), the first major German music dictionary.[123] To this earlier material Walther adds information about 'Petrus de Ruimonte' (Pedro de Rimonte), a Spanish composer active in the later sixteenth and early seventeenth centuries whom Walther erroneously believed to be the same person as La Rue; this misidentification persists for some time thereafter. Walther also added that Glarean identified La Rue as French, noting the 1549 citation of La Rue as being from Flanders.

Glarean was again the impetus behind La Rue's inclusion in John Hawkins's *A General History of the Science and Practice of Music*, originally published in 1776. Here La Rue, as Petrus Platensis, is listed with other composers as being included in the *Dodecachordon*; he seems not to be found elsewhere in the history.[124] In contrast, Charles Burney's rival coverage, *A General History of Music from the Earliest Ages to the Present Period* (vol. 2, 1782), offers the most copious discussion of La Rue so far. He even includes a music example, the first for La Rue in modern historiography; this is the three-voice *Benedictus* from the *Missa de beata virgine*. Burney calls La Rue (whom he identifies both as Pierre de la Rue and Petrus

greater presence than La Rue in Heyden, 1540 (two examples to La Rue's one), and we have already noted the unexplained switching of La Rue's and Brumel's names in Susato's publication of *Nymphes des bois*.

[121] Matthias Henriksen Schacht, *Musicus danicus eller Danske sangmester*, ed. Godtfred Skjerne (Copenhagen: H. Hagerup, 1928), 66. Glarean was a major source for most writers on early music but was not published in a modern edition until 1888, by Peter Bohn.

[122] Wolfgang Caspar Printz, *Historische Beschreibung der edelen Sing- und Kling-Kunst* (Dresden: Johann Georgen, 1690), ch. 11, no. 19; repr. in id., *Ausgewählte Werke*, 3 vols., ed. Helmut K. Krausse (Berlin and New York: Walter De Gruyter, 1974–93), ii. 385.

[123] Johann Gottfried Walther, *Musikalisches Lexicon, oder Musicalische Bibliothec* (Leipzig: W. Deer, 1732), under 'Rue (Petrus de la)'.

[124] John Hawkins, *A General History of the Science and Practice of Music*, 2 vols., 2nd edn. (London: J. Alfred Novello, 1853; repr. New York: Dover, 1963), i. 320.

TABLE 5.4. Historiography of La Rue to 1900

Date[a]	Author/Editor/Piece	Publication
1687	Matthias Henriksen Schacht	*Musicus Danicus*
1690	Wolfgang Caspar Printz	*Historische Beschreibung*
1732	Johann Gottfried Walther	*Musicalisches Lexicon*
1776	Sir John Hawkins	*A General History of the Science and Practice of Music*
1782	Charles Burney	*A General History of Music* includes Benedictus from *Missa de beata virgine*
1792	Ernst Ludwig Gerber	*Historisch-biographisches Lexicon der Tonkünstler*
1801	Johann Nicolaus Forkel	*Allgemeine Geschichte der Musik* includes *prima pars* of *Lauda anima mea dominum*
1806?	Johann Nicolaus Forkel, ed. Joseph Sonnleithner	*Geschichte der Musik in Denkmälern* includes the conclusion of the Gloria and Agnus II from *Missa de Sancto Antonio*[b]
1810–11	Alexandre Choron and François Fayolle	*Dictionnaire historique des musiciens*
1813	Ernst Ludwig Gerber	*Neues historisch-biographisches Lexikon der Tonkünstler*
1828	Giuseppe Baini	*Memorie storico-critiche . . . di Giovanni Pierluigi da Palestrina*
	Pierre Jean Suremont	*Opuscule apologétique sur les mérites des célèbres musiciens belges*
1829	François-Joseph Fétis	*Mémoire sur cette question*
	Rafael Georg Kiesewetter	*Die Verdienste der Niederlaender um die Tonkunst* includes Benedictus from *Missa de beata virgine*
	Frédéric-Auguste, baron de Reiffenberg	'Lettre à M. Fétis'
1830	William Cooke Stafford	*A History of Music*
1834	Rafael Georg Kiesewetter	*Geschichte der europäisch-abendländischen . . . Musik*
1838	Auguste Bottée de Toulmon	*Agnus dei de la Messe super l'homme armé de Pierre de Larue* includes Agnus II of *Missa L'homme armé I*
	Gustav Schilling (ed.)	*Encyclopädie der gesammten musikalischen Wissenschaften*

TABLE 5.4. *(cont.)*

Date	Author/Editor/Piece	Publication
1840	François-Joseph Fétis	*Biographie universelle des musiciens*, 1st edn.
1843	Charles-Edmond-Henri Coussemaker	*Notice sur les collections musicales*
1848	Agnus II of *Missa L'homme armé I*	published in *Caecilia*[c]
1849	Edouard Fétis	*Les Musiciens belges*
1858	Heinrich Bellermann	*Die Mensuralnoten und Taktzeichen des XV. und XVI. Jahrhunderts* includes Agnus II of *Missa L'homme armé I*
1860–81	Alexandre Pinchart	*Archives des arts, sciences et lettres*
1863	François-Joseph Fétis	*Biographie universelle des musiciens*, 2nd edn.
1864	Adrien de la Fage	*Essais de diphthérographie musicale*
1867–88	Edmond Vander Straeten	*La Musique aux Pays-Bas* includes beginning of Qui tollis from *Missa de Sancto Antonio* in vol. 7 (1885)
1868	August Wilhelm Ambros	*Geschichte der Musik*
	Arrey von Dommer	*Handbuch der Musik-Geschichte*
1871	F. Van de Putte	'Epitaphes copiées en 1629 par Christophe van Huerne'
1875	Hermann Mendel and August Reissmann	*Musikalisches Conversations-Lexikon*
1876	Alphonse Goovaerts	entry for La Rue in *Biographie nationale*
1877	Robert Eitner	*Bibliographie der Musik-Sammelwerke des XVI. und XVII. Jahrhunderts*
1879	Kyrie of *Missa Conceptio tua*	published in *Cäcilienkalender*[d]
1882	Otto Kade (ed.)	Vol. 5 of August Wilhelm Ambros, *Geschichte der Musik* includes *O salutaris hostia* and Sanctus, Pleni, and Osanna from *Missa Tous les regretz*
	Hugo Riemann	*Musik-Lexikon*
1882–93	Robert-Julien Van Maldeghem (ed.)	*Trésor musical* includes numerous sacred and secular works by La Rue
1886	Jean-Baptiste Weckerlin	*La Chanson populaire*

TABLE 5.4. *(cont.)*

1888	Peter Bohn (ed.)	*Glareani Dodecachordon* includes Kyrie I and Pleni from *Missa O salutaris hostia*, Christe from *Missa de Sancto Antonio*, and Agnus II from *Missa L'homme armé I*
1889	William Sterndale Bennett	entry for La Rue in *A Dictionary of Music and Musicians*
1893	Charles Bordes (ed.)	*Anthologie des maîtres religieux primitifs* includes *O salutaris hostia*
1895	Charles Bordes	publishes *Il me fait mal* with attribution to La Rue[e]
1898	Henry Expert (ed.)	*Les Maîtres musiciens de la Renaissance française* includes *Missa Ave Maria*
1899	Robert Eitner (ed.)	*Sechzig Chansons zu vier Stimmen* includes *Au feu d'amour*

[a] In the case of multi-volume works, the date listed is that of the volume containing the reference to La Rue.
[b] According to Wagner, *Geschichte der Messe*, 167.
[c] According to Eitner, *Verzeichnis neuer Ausgaben*, 175.
[d] According to RubsamenMGG, 237.
[e] According to Eitner, *Biographisch-bibliographisches Quellen-Lexikon*, vi. 54.

Platensis, as do many later writers; the ongoing list of multiple names thus begins in the eighteenth century) 'One of the most voluminous composers of the period', and 'a very learned Contrapuntist'. He mentions the Petrucci mass print and also that La Rue was one of many who set *L'homme armé*. Acknowledging the problem of origin (French vs. Flemish vs. Spanish), he continues to identify La Rue with Rimonte. In the first modern attempt to discuss the music, he points out examples of dissonance in the Benedictus, going so far as to mark them in the score with the name of the offending interval. Nonetheless, he later says that the masses of La Rue (along with those of Josquin and Févin) are superior in melody, rhythm, and design to those of Mouton.[125]

Johann Nikolaus Forkel's *Allgemeine Geschichte der Musik*, whose second volume (the one mentioning La Rue) was published in 1801, goes even further than Burney, though still citing Printz and Walther (including the Ruimonte material, this time conflating the *Lamentations* by that composer with those ascribed to La Rue in 1549).[126] Forkel notes La Rue among the composers cited by Coclico and Finck, and he too was aware of the Petrucci print. He places La Rue in the 'French school' and calls him a contemporary of Josquin, among the first and oldest

[125] Charles Burney, *A General History of Music from the Earliest Ages to the Present Period (1789)*, 2 vols. (New York: Harcourt, Brace, 1935), i. 709, 740, 764–5, 770.
[126] Johann Nicolaus Forkel, *Allgemeine Geschichte der Musik*, 2 vols. (Leipzig: Schwickertschen, 1788–1801), ii. 516–9, 615–16.

contrapuntalists, and a very industrious composer.[127] He mentions by name the four music examples given by Glarean, but gives a completely separate work in transcription, the *prima pars* of the motet *Lauda anima mea dominum* from 1553[6].[128] Forkel's *Geschichte der Musik in Denkmälern* (edited by Joseph Sonnleithner (1806?)) is said to contain two sections from *Missa de Sancto Antonio*, the second Agnus and the end of the Gloria.[129] Forkel is also noteworthy for discussing La Rue immediately after Josquin, which will happen with a certain amount of frequency thereafter.

La Rue is very briefly mentioned in Choron and Fayolle's *Dictionnaire historique* of 1810–11: 'LARUE (Pierre de) *Petrus Platensis*, français de nation, maître de chapelle à Anvers, a composé des messes et des motets en 1549', followed by a reference to Glarean.[130] It is not clear where the Antwerp chapel master reference comes from (though that reference will continue to pop up for some time thereafter), and no evidence for that exists today. The *Dictionnaire* is important for the recognition that Ruimonte is a separate composer, who was accordingly given his own entry. This separation may have been derived in part from the earlier separation of Petrus de Ruimonte and Petrus Platensis in Gerber's *Historisch-biographisches Lexicon der Tonkünstler* (1790–2),[131] but Gerber does not identify Platensis (described as a famous contrapuntist) with La Rue, and refers only to Hawkins for information. Curiously, in Gerber's later *Neues historisch-biographisches Lexikon der Tonkünstler* (1812–14),[132] La Rue (now identified with Platensis) and Ruimonte are again conflated, and although the entry is now much longer, the only information not already found elsewhere is a list of manuscripts in Munich that contain his music.[133] Further information on the sources for La Rue's music was provided by Giuseppe Baini in his book on Palestrina (1828).[134]

La Rue shows up in all of the essays that were published following the competitions sponsored by the Koninklijk-Nederlandsche Instituut van Weteschappen,

---

[127] Forkel, *Allgemeine Geschichte der Musik*, ii. 615–16.

[128] Ibid. 616–28.

[129] According to Peter Wagner, *Geschichte der Messe* (Kleine Handbücher der Musikgeschichte nach Gattungen, ii/1; Leipzig: Breitkopf & Härtel, 1913), 167.

[130] Choron and Fayolle, *Dictionnaire historique*, i. 401. The entry was taken over almost word for word in John S. Sainsbury, *Dictionary of Musicians, from the Earliest Ages to the Present Time*, 2 vols. (London: Sainsbury, 1825; repr. New York: Da Capo, 1966), 'LARUE, (Pierre de) a Frenchman by birth, called sometimes Petrus Platensis, was chapel-master at Antwerp. He composed some masses and motets about the year 1549.'

[131] Ernst Ludwig Gerber, *Historisch-biographisches Lexicon der Tonkünstler*, 2 vols. (Leipzig: J. G. I. Breitkopf, 1790–2)

[132] Ernst Ludwig Gerber, *Neues historisch-biographisches Lexikon der Tonkünstler*, 4 vols. (Leipzig: A. Kuhnel, 1812–14).

[133] Three of these correspond to today's MunBS 5, 47, and 53. A fourth manuscript, which Gerber calls Cod. 57, is evidently the one now known as MunBS 65.

[134] Giuseppe Baini, *Memorie storico-critiche della vita e delle opere di Giovanni Pierluigi da Palestrina*, 2 vols. (Rome: Società tipografica, 1828; repr. Hildesheim: Georg Olms, 1966), i. 96–9, 139–40, 144–5, 225–7, 354–5. Except for VatS 36 and the Petrucci mass print, however, Baini merely includes La Rue among a list of many composers who are found in contemporary Vatican manuscripts. Baini also included the relevant section from Folengo; he identified de Robore as La Rue and then further equated him with Pierazzon della Ruellien, a name that will be listed as an alternate for La Rue by later writers.

Letterkunde en Schoone Kunsten in the 1820s. The first of these was by Pierre Jean Suremont, a loser in the 1824 event who decided to forego the 1828 competition (since the question was the same) and publish his earlier essay that same year. The first- and second-place winners in the 1828 competition were two who were among the most important musicologists of the nineteenth century, Rafael Georg Kiesewetter and François-Joseph Fétis, whose essays were duly published the following year.

The contestants were asked to identify the merits of the Netherlanders (principally those of the fourteenth, fifteenth, and sixteenth centuries) in music and to discuss their later influence on Italian schools of composition. Suremont's single-sentence reference to La Rue provided no new information,[135] but Kiesewetter names La Rue in several places and introduces new material. With a series of others, he is called 'unquestionably' a pupil of Ockeghem's; he is plucked from Forkel's French school and deposited in the Netherlands; he is identified as the 'Pierchon' in *Nymphes des bois* and thereby again reiterated as a pupil of Ockeghem's.[136] With Compère he shares a short *Anhang*, where he is described as a 'sehr berühmten Meister' and noted for his appearance in a Petrucci print of 1508 and in Aaron's two treatises.[137] The Benedictus from the *Missa de beata virgine* (copied from Burney) is included among the musical examples.

Fétis gave the lengthiest discussion of the composer to date.[138] Each of the twenty-seven sections of his essay was devoted to one or more composers; La Rue received his own section. Noting that Glarean and others placed him among the great musicians of his time, he rejects that theorist's identification of him as French and, tellingly (given the nature of the competition), aligns him with the Netherlanders, just as Kiesewetter did. He points out the problems of associating a musician supposedly active in the first part of the seventeenth century (Petrus de Ruimonte) with one whose masses were published by Antico in 1516 and suggests that the similarity in names caused the confusion. He continues by saying that La Rue is known mainly by the two masses published by Antico, the *Missa Ave Maria* and *Missa O salutaris hostia*, by the four fragments from the *Dodecachordon*, and by

---

[135] 'Un autre compositeur flamand des plus fertiles de cette époque, fut Pierre De la Rue, nomme *Petrus Platensis* maître de chapelle à Anvers où il composa des messes et des motets et où il publia en 1549 un recueil de diverses espèces de compositions'; see Pierre Jean Suremont, *Opuscule apologétique sur les mérites des célèbres musiciens belges, inventeurs ou régénérateurs de la musique aux 14ᵉ, 15ᵉ, et 16ᵉ siècles* (Antwerp: Veuve J. S. Schoesetters, 1828), 8. This single-sentence reference (about a paragraph in the original) contrasts markedly with almost three pages devoted to Josquin.

[136] Rafael Georg Kiesewetter, 'Die Verdienste der Niederlaender um die Tonkunst', in *Verhandelingen over de vraag: Welke verdiensten hebben zich de Nederlanders vooral in de 14ᵉ, 15ᵉ en 16ᵉ eeuw in het vak der toonkunst verworven; en in hoe verre kunnen de nederlandsche kunstenaars van dien tijd, die zich naar Italien begeven hevven, invloed gehad hebben op de muzijkscholen, die zich kort daarna in Italien hebben gevormd?* (Amsterdam: J. Muller, 1829), 21, 25.

[137] Ibid., *Anhang*.

[138] Suremont's essay was twenty pages long, preceded by a nine-page introduction complaining about the judging of the competition and justifying his essay's publication. Fétis's essay, in contrast, stretched to fifty-six pages, while Kiesewetter's winning entry ran to 120 pages of text (including seven *Anhangen* and five *Nachtragen*) plus seventy-three pages of music examples.

the motet that Forkel had published. He then proceeds to make an evaluation of La Rue's music: 'We notice in these pieces a fuller and more sustained harmony than in the compositions of Josquin, joined to a great elegance in the movement of the voices, but we do not see enough study in imitations or in canonic forms [!] The style of the celebrated Palestrina seems to be formed subsequently by the union of the particular merits of each of these two Netherlandish masters.'[139]

Fétis's essay prompted a response from the Baron de Reiffenberg, a scholar who was later to publish, among other things, the 1497 *état de l'hôtel* of Philip the Fair.[140] Reiffenberg's response was merely a list of details he had uncovered in the course of his readings, but he is the first to mention the appearance of 'Petrus Vicanus' as singer to Charles V in the 1531 *Flandricarum rerum* of Jacobus Meyerus.[141] He also includes La Rue in a list of 'célèbres musiciens belges'.[142] La Rue is described rather differently in William Stafford's *A History of Music* (1830): 'Pierre de la Rue, a learned and excellent contrapuntist, and one of the most volu-minous composers of the age, resided principally in Germany; but it is not known whether he was a native of that country'; Stafford gives no clue as to the reasoning behind this statement.[143] La Rue then makes a brief appearance in Kiesewetter's major work, *Geschichte der europäisch-abendländischen oder unsrer heutigen Musik* (1834), a book unabashedly devoted to the 'great man' approach to history. La Rue falls in the 'Epoche Josquin' (1480–1520),[144] described merely as one of the superior masters from Ockeghem's school (though Kiesewetter now separates him from Rimonte). He is listed first among the contemporaries of Josquin, a position that he already occupied with Forkel, one that became commonplace in discussions of this generation, and one that echoed so many sixteenth-century theorists.

In all of the encyclopedias, dictionaries, and histories named so far, La Rue was

---

[139] 'On remarque dans ces morceaux une harmonie plus pleine, plus nourrie que dans les compositions de Josquin, jointe à une grande élégance dans le mouvement des voix, mais on n'y remarque pas autant de recherche dans les imitations, ni dans les formes canoniques. Le style du célèbre Palestrina semble s'être formé, dans la suite, de la réunion des mérites particuliers de chacun de ces deux maîtres Neerlandais'; see François-Joseph Fétis, 'Mémoire sur cette question: "Quels ont été les mérites des Neerlandais dans la musique, principalement aux 14ᵉ, 15ᵉ et 16ᵉ siècles; et quelle influence les artistes de ce pays qui ont séjourné en Italie, ont-ils exercée sur les écoles de musique, qui se sont formées peu après cette époque en Italie?"' in *Verhandelingen over de vraag: Welke verdiensten hebben zich de Nederlanders vooral in de 14ᵉ, 15ᵉ en 16ᵉ eeuw in het vak der toonkunst verworven; en in hoe verre kunnen de nederlandsche kunstenaars van dien tijd, die zich naar Italien begeven hevven, invloed gehad hebben op de muzijkscholen, die zich kort daarna in Italien hebben gevormd?* (Amsterdam: J. Muller, 1829), 32.

[140] After the founding of Belgium as an independent nation in 1830, numerous writers, including vari-ous wealthy and titled amateurs, worked to piece together the past history of the country, especially its former period of great glory before the centre of government transferred to Spain during the time of Charles V.

[141] Reiffenberg, 'Lettre à M. Fétis', ii. 288–9.

[142] Ibid. 286, drawn from a 'mémoire de M. de Laserna sur la bibliothéque [*sic*] de Bourgogne'.

[143] William Cooke Stafford, *A History of Music* (Edinburgh: Constable, 1830), 234.

[144] R. G. Kiesewetter, *Geschichte der europäisch-abendländischen oder unsrer heutigen Musik: Darstellung ihres Ursprunges, ihres Wachsthumes und ihrer stufenweisen Entwickelung; Von dem ersten Jahrhundert des Christenthumes bis auf unsre Zeit. Für jeden Freund der Tonkunst* (Leipzig: Breitkopf & Härtel, 1834), 56. Ear-lier epochs were named after Hucbald (10th c.), Guido (11th c.), Franco (13th c.), Marchettus and de Muris (1300–80), Dufay (1380–1450), and Ockeghem (1450–80). The 12th c. was designated as 'Ohne Namen'; Hildegard was not yet on the musicological radar.

but one of several (sometimes several hundreds) being discussed. This treatment was continued in 1838, when the entry for him in Gustav Schilling's *Encyclopädie der gesammten musikalischen Wissenschaften* calls him 'einer der ältesten berühmten Contrapunktisten' and notes the confusion among various writers' treatment of him.[145] But in the same year that this derivative entry appeared, La Rue was the sole focus of attention in a curious but significant little book. This remained the only volume devoted to La Rue that was not simply the publication of a dissertation until this current book, written more than 150 years later.

The work in question, a slender volume of twelve pages and five plates that barely warrants its description as a book, is by Auguste Bottée de Toulmon, *bibliothécaire et chef honoraire* of the Paris Conservatory. It takes the form of a letter to Kiesewetter and opens with a description of the contents of VienNB 1783, which contains six of La Rue's early masses. After the briefest of introductions, Bottée de Toulmon turns to the *Missa L'homme armé I*, and most specifically, the 4 ex 1 mensuration canon that constitutes the second Agnus. The challenge of transcribing it into modern notation is the impetus behind the book; he notes that few works present difficulties as great as this one, and that it is the most remarkable specimen of its type (an evaluation with which few would disagree). The book is devoted to a discussion of the problems involved in interpreting the notation and provides the first modern transcription (which, apart from the opening of the tenor, is correct).

Bottée de Toulmon wrestles with the challenge in exhausting detail, criticizing Glarean at several points along the way. He takes issue with Glarean's description of the Agnus as 'admirabilius', complaining that that word expresses admiration and arguing that 'mirabilius', which merely admits astonishment, is a better choice. This far from positive opinion of the work at hand emerges still more strongly in the following: 'According to Glarean, de Larue thus composed his Agnus Dei, prevented from sleeping as he was by the triumphs of Josquin, who, despite an incontestable genius, was as crazy as the others in the genre of which we speak.'[146] But he gets angriest at Glarean's failure to provide a resolution of the canon, unaware that Glarean assumed that readers had access to Heyden (a theorist still unknown in 1838). After sputtering about this for a bit, he finally decides that Glarean could not really understand the musical notation of his time (if he did, Bottée de Toulmon argues, he would have provided the canon's resolution), claiming a sense of suffocation and oppression every time he looks at Glarean's resolution of Josquin's Agnus from the *Missa L'homme armé super voces musicales*.[147]

---

[145] *Encyclopädie der gesammten musikalischen Wissenschaften oder Universal-Lexikon der Tonkunst*, ed. Gustav Schilling, 6 vols. (Stuttgart: Franz Heinrich Köhler, 1835–8; repr. Hildesheim and New York: Georg Olms, 1974), under 'Rue, Pierre de la'.

[146] 'D'après Glarean, de Larue aurait donc composé son Agnus Dei, empêché de dormir qu'il était par les triumphes de Josquin, lequel, malgré un génie incontestable, était aussi fou que les autres dans le genre dont il s'agit'; see Auguste Bottée de Toulmon, *Agnus dei de la Messe super l'homme armé de Pierre de Larue: Lettre adressée à M. le Conseiller G.-R. Kiesewetter* ([Paris: Imprimerie royale, 1838]), 5.

[147] 'En un mot, ce que je vais dire va paraître *énorme: il n'entendait rien à lire la musique de cette époque, de la*

He finally obliquely accuses Glarean of being a charlatan[148] and then gets to work on the actual transcription.

When he finishes, he addresses Kiesewetter directly: 'Now have we succeeded? It's not up to me to decide ... you know also through how many disappointments I had to pass, how many nights without sleep, worried musings on my errands around town. In effect, all these little tribulations weighed so heavily on me in this instance that I hope that by the favour of your pity you will pardon me for all the boredom that my observations must have inspired in you. In order to encourage you in this generous idea, I will attest that I found my repose day and night only when I could believe I had overwhelmed the monster ... it remains to be seen if my hope is presumptuous.'[149] Few, if any, have suffered such torments over a mere transcription.[150]

La Rue appears as expected in Fétis's *Biographie universelle*; the volume containing 'L' arrived in 1840. Although little new material is presented, its format more closely resembles what we have come to expect in such kinds of dictionary entries, and it is the longest general treatment of the composer up to its time. La Rue is placed at the end of the fifteenth and beginning of the sixteenth centuries, he is acknowledged as being cited by Glarean as French, 'but the majority of other writers who have spoken of him agree in placing him among the musicians of the Low Countries'.[151] Fétis questions both the identification with Ruimonte and the idea that La Rue composed the *Lamentations* in 1549, and mentions the various sources of his music that earlier scholars have provided (a typographical error places the Petrucci mass print in 1513, not 1503) and adds 1509[1], 1505[2], BrusBR 15075 and 215–216 to this list and details their contents; he also provides the contents of the Petrucci mass print for the first time. As obvious as this material may appear to us, it is easy to forget how valuable such references were and remained for an

---

sienne [italics original]. En effet, j'ai toujours éprouvé une espèce de suffocation et d'oppression toutes les fois que j'ai examiné la traduction qu'il présente pour l'*Agnus* de Josquin'; ibid. 6.

[148] 'J'avais la simplicité de croire que le charlatanisme n'avait pas encore cours au XVIe siècle'; Auguste Bottée de Toulmon, *Agnus Dei de la Messe super l'homme armé de Pierre de Larue: Lettre adressée à M. le Conseiller G.-R. Kieswetter* ([Paris: Imprimerie royale, 1838]), 8.

[149] 'Maintenant avons-nous réussi? ce n'est pas à moi à le décider ... vous savez aussi par combien de désappointements j'ai dû passer, combien de nuits sans sommeil, de rêveries soucieuses dans mes courses de la ville. En effet, toutes ces petites tribulations se sont tellement appesanties sur moi à cette occasion que j'espère qu'à la faveur de votre pitié vous me pardonnerez l'ennui qu'ont dû vous inspirer mes observations. Pour vous encourager dans cette généreuse idée, je vous avouerai que j'ai retrouvé mon repos du jour et de la nuit seulement lorsque j'ai pu croire avoir terrassé le monstre ... Reste à savoir si mon espoir est de la présomption'; ibid. 12.

[150] Bottée de Toulman's unpublished transcriptions of numerous 16th-c. masses were drawn on by J. B. Weckerlin, *La Chanson populaire* (Paris: Firmin-Didot, 1886). For masses by La Rue on popular themes he cites the *Missa Tous les regretz*, *Missa L'homme armé*, and, interestingly, *Missa Fortuna disperata*. Weckerlin claims that the transcriptions were made from libraries in Vienna and Munich; it is not clear whose *Fortuna desperata* mass got mixed up with La Rue. Referring specifically to La Rue's 4 ex 1 mensuration canon, Weckerlin rather cheekily wonders whether composers of the time (who had to earn their living as singers) wrote their complicated canons specifically to annoy their non-composer colleagues in the chapel choirs; see ibid. 116–17.

[151] 'Mais la plupart des autres écrivains qui en ont parté s'accordent à le placer parmi les musiciens des Pays-Bas'; see Fétis, *Biographie universelle* (1st edn.), vi. 48.

extremely long time. Fétis mentions that he scored the opening Kyrie of the *Missa Ave sanctissima Maria* from BrusBR 15075 and that it is 'a masterpiece of construction' (*un chef-d'œuvre de facture*). He repeats the claim that La Rue was chapel master in Antwerp, but now (on the basis of his presence in the Vatican manuscripts and Italian prints) posits an Italian sojourn as well. He concludes, 'All that we know of this master proves that he was one of the best composers of his time.'[152]

By 1840, an astute reader would know names of more than a dozen of La Rue's masses, even though the masses themselves remained almost completely inaccessible except for the smallest of excerpts. Given this handicap, it is understandable that scholars made errors in the identification of his music. Coussemaker, for example, asserted incorrectly that the unattributed *Missa Ave Maria* in CambraiBM 18 was not the same as La Rue's mass found in Antico's 1516 print.[153] He also identified La Rue as Belgian, said that his works were greatly valued in his time, and that he died in Antwerp (again, without any evidence for this last).

With his current identification as specifically Belgian (as opposed to Netherlandish; the two countries were separated in 1830), La Rue makes an appearance in *Les Musiciens belges* (1849), written by Edouard Fétis,[154] eldest son of François-Joseph Fétis. Though virtually unknown now, the book's discussion of La Rue was significant in that it was the first to identify La Rue's connection with the Habsburg-Burgundian court, and in many ways it set the tone for much later writing about La Rue's relationship with the court. Just three years before the publication of *Les Musiciens belges*, the Baron de Reiffenberg had published the 1497 *état de l'hôtel* of Philip the Fair (1496 o.s.), with its list of Philip's chapel members.[155] Eduoard Fétis was the first to draw on this information, connecting La Rue with Philip and then Marguerite.[156] His comments about Marguerite and La Rue are significant: 'Pierre de la Rue [was] one of the musicians that Marguerite of Austria was fond of . . . Marguerite had a particular esteem for his compositions. Catherine of Austria, sister of Charles V, married to John III, King of Portugal, had requested that Marguerite have composed for her a collection of masses

---

[152] 'Tout ce qu'on connait de ce maître prouve qu'il fut un des meilleurs compositeurs de son temps'; ibid. 50.

[153] Charles-Edmond-Henri de Coussemaker, *Notice sur les collections musicales de la bibliothèque de Cambrai* (Paris, 1843; repr. Hildesheim and New York: G. Olms, 1975), 55–6.

[154] Edouard Fétis, *Les Musiciens belges* (Brussels: Jamar, [1849]).

[155] Just as 19th-c. scholars were filling in the blanks on music of the 15th and 16th cc., so too was knowledge of the Habsburg-Burgundian court coming into focus at the same time. Because of the somewhat different emphases—political vs. cultural history—musicologists did not always immediately tap into these potential sources of information. For example, Molinet's *Chroniques* were first published in 1828 (as part of Georges Chastellain, *Chronique des ducs de Bourgogne*, 6 vols. (Collection des chroniques nationales françaises, 42–7; Paris: Verdiere, 1827–8), and in 1841 Gachard published the information about the 1495 overdue payment to Philip's (previously Maximilian's) chapel; see Gachard, *Rapport*. To my knowledge neither was used by musicologists for some time thereafter. Important material published later in the century includes Gachard's *Collection des voyages* of 1876–82 (GachardCV).

[156] Fétis erroneously puts Compère, Isaac, and Agricola in her service as well; the last of these had died before Marguerite took over the governing of the court in 1507. See E. Fétis, *Les Musiciens belges*, 116.

by one of those clever Flemish musicians whose fame was indeed European. The princess cast her eyes on Pierre de la Rue as surely the most capable of sustaining, in this circumstance, the glory of the Flemish school.'[157] Fétis proceeds to a discussion of BrusBR 15075, the manuscript that prompted this completely fictitious account. When discussing VatS 36, which contains the *Missa O gloriosa domina* with its alternative title, *Missa O gloriosa Margaretha*, Fétis further states, 'The text of this last proves that at the time when P. de la Rue visited Italy, he was already honoured by the protection of Marguerite of Austria.'[158] Scholarly understanding of La Rue's relationship with the court was thus plagued by inaccuracies and romantic fiction right from the start.

Ten years after Bottée de Toulmon's wrestling match with La Rue's mensuration canon, it appeared in the last volume of the journal *Caecilia: Eine Zeitschrift für die musikalische Welt* (1848),[159] and another ten years later the same piece figured in the first modern book on mensural notation, Heinrich Bellermann's *Die Mensuralnoten und Taktzeichen des XV. und XVI. Jahrhunderts* of 1858.[160] Bellermann cites both Glarean and Heyden as containing the work; though he does not go into transports of despair over the piece, he calls it 'impracticable' (*unausführbar*).[161]

The second edition of Fétis's *Biographie universelle* was, once again, the most substantial writing on La Rue at the time of its publication (the volume containing 'L' appeared in 1863). Fétis incorporated a variety of new information, not all of it accurate. He claimed (erroneously) that the diminutive 'Pierchon' by which La Rue was sometimes known was only used in Picardie and that La Rue was thus born there, but he was still from the Low Countries since this was in Burgundian hands until 1477 when it was retaken by France, thus accounting for Glarean's identification of La Rue as French.[162] He put La Rue in the chapel of Mary of Burgundy in 1492 (he justified this by saying that even after her death the chapel

---

[157] 'Pierre de la Rue, un des musiciens qu'affectionait Marguerite d'Autriche. . . . Marguerite avait pour ses compositions une estime toute particulière. Catherine d'Autriche, sœur de Charles-Quint, mariée à Jean III, roi de Portugal, avait prié Marguerite de lui faire composer un recueil de messes par un de ces habiles musiciens flamands dont la renommée était alors européenne. La princesse jeta les yeux sur Pierre de la Rue, comme sur le plus capable de soutenir hautement, dans cette circonstance, la gloire de l'école flamande'; E. Fétis, *Les Musiciens belges*, 117.

[158] Ibid. 118: 'Le texte de cette dernière prouve qu'à l'époque où P. de la Rue visita l'Italie, il était déja honoré de la protection de Marguerite d'Autriche.'

[159] Cited in Robert Eitner, *Verzeichnis neuer Ausgaben alter Musikwerke aus der frühesten Zeit bis zum Jahre 1800* (Berlin: T. Trautwein [M. Bahn], 1871), 175; the piece was supposedly on p. 4 of the journal.

[160] Heinrich Bellermann, *Die Mensuralnoten und Taktzeichen des XV. und XVI. Jahrhunderts* (Berlin: Georg Reimer, 1858), 62–3. The work has reappeared in later works on notation, including Willi Apel, *The Notation of Polyphonic Music 900–1600*, 5th edn. (Cambridge, Mass.: Mediaeval Academy of America, 1953), 181 (Apel includes other examples from La Rue's mass as well); Antonio-Maria-Giuseppe Tirabassi, *La Mesure dans la notation proportionnelle et sa transcription moderne* (Brussels: Maison Delvigne, 1927), 49–50; and id., *Grammaire et transcription de la notation proportionnelle et sa transcription moderne: Manuel des ligatures* (Brussels: Van Damme & Duquesne, 1930), 53, 80–1.

[161] Bellermann, *Die Mensuralnoten*, 64.

[162] Fétis also took issue with Glarean's Latinization of La Rue's name, noting that Platea (large street or public place) was first declension; see Fétis, *Biographie universelle* (2nd edn.), v. 200.

was considered hers until Philip came of age) and though he correctly noticed La Rue's *Missa Sub tuum presidium* in Petrucci's Févin mass print of 1515 (named there *Missa quarti toni*), he wrongly considered a collection of four-voice madrigals by 'Perisone' published by Gardane in 1544 to be La Rue's. Fétis was the first to call him a priest, another error, and dated his Kortrijk prebend from 1501 (also incorrect), but he had begun looking in the Royal Archives in Brussels and came up with important material for the first time, including chapel records from 1499, 1500, 1502, and 1505, the prebend list of 1501 (now lost), and the date of resignation from the Namur prebend (1510, the last date Fétis found for La Rue). He garbled the date of Philip's trip to Spain, putting it in 1504, and thought that La Rue did not accompany him. He originates the idea that La Rue was the musician most in favour with Marguerite (quite possibly true) because of the care she took to have his works copied in especially luxurious manuscripts (no firm evidence for this type of attention). Fétis introduces the Mechelen manuscript, MechAS s.s.[163] (he identifies the subject of the famous miniature, now thought to be Charles, as Maximilian), MunBS 34, 1539[1], and 1539[2] for the first time in the literature and outlines the La Rue pieces in MunBS 5, 53, and 57 (mentioned earlier but not detailed; the last seems to be MunBS 65 today). Fétis notes that the total number of masses for La Rue thus stands at twenty-nine. Although this is just one short of the number of securely attributed masses, some of these twenty-nine were actually the same mass under different names. Nonetheless, it is striking that so many were known so early. Fétis is also the first to mention secular works by La Rue, starting with those in Petrucci prints.

Still more extensive than Fétis was the treatment given to La Rue by Ambros (Kiesewetter's nephew) shortly thereafter in his pioneering *Geschichte der Musik* (volume 3, which contains the discussion of La Rue, was published in 1868).[164] He draws on Fétis for his biographical information and repeats the idea that Marguerite showed her favour for La Rue by having his music copied in lavish manuscripts. As a result of his extensive research, his listing of pieces and sources goes beyond that of Fétis. The total of masses has climbed to thirty-six; this too high number stems from a variety of inaccuracies, such as describing the *Credo L'amour du moy* as a complete mass[165] and claiming a *Missa Pater noster* and *Missa Fors*

---

[163] Adrien de la Fage provided a more detailed discussion of the manuscript not long thereafter; see Adrien de la Fage, *Essais de diphthérographie musicale*, 2 vols. (Paris: O. Legouix, 1864), text vol., 352. According to La Fage, the manuscript was uncovered only when the archives began to be put in order (he does not provide a date) and he mentions that Reiffenberg attempted to acquire the manuscript for the Royal Library in Brussels but was rebuffed. He also (p. 354) brings up the 1492–5 pay list and subjects it to greater analysis than before, though erroneously concluding that the eight singers on the list without voice designations must be basses.

[164] Ambros's achievement is underscored by the treatment of La Rue in another historical work published the same year, Arrey von Dommer's *Handbuch der Musikgeschichte* (Leipzig: Fr. Wilh. Grunow, 1868), 88, 95–6, where La Rue is twice referred to as a pupil of Ockeghem; his 1503 mass print is also mentioned. The encyclopedia *Musikalisches Conversations-Lexikon* of Hermann Mendel and August Reissmann (Berlin: Robert Oppenheim, 1870–9; the volume containing La Rue was published in 1875) has a twenty-nine-line entry on La Rue that is completely derivative.

[165] This goes back to Baini, *Memorie storico-critiche*, i. 98.

seulement for La Rue (the latter apparently the one by Pipelare transmitted anonymously in MechAS s.s.).[166] His list of motets is much shorter but still surpasses that of Fétis, who knew of only three works. Similarly, he is able to add a number of previously unknown secular pieces, especially those from FlorC 2439.[167]

Ambros is the first scholar to have any real knowledge of La Rue's music and he is impressed by the quantity and quality of his output and the diversity of his style, as indeed is everyone who knows more than just a handful of the compositions. He is also the first to be genuinely enthusiastic about La Rue's music, an enthusiasm rarely missing from later commentators.[168] La Rue to him is a serious composer whose work is raised to heights not merely because of his technique but also because of his intellectual power. This was felt by his contemporaries, Ambros notes, though 'very often they also remain stuck in their admiration of canons and other contrapuntal elaborations'.[169] He mentions numerous pieces specifically; though he starts with the *L'homme armé* mensuration canon, he rapidly moves on to works no one has described before. The motet *Delicta juventutis* is 'one of the most excellent works for getting to know the master's individuality and worth',[170] but the canonic *Da pacem domine* is 'insignificant and less pleasing'.[171] In the motet *O salutaris hostia* 'the most ideal harmony in pure perfection and the so-called Palestrina style are there completely, long before Palestrina'.[172] He notes 'the intimate final Agnus of the great Missa *De S. Cruce*',[173] while in somewhat flowery terms he contrasts 'the fine-pointed texture of his Missa *De S. Anna . . .* against the powerful, massive forms of the Missa *L'omme armé*, the dryness of the mass *Cum jocunditate* against the intellectual breath that blows through the mass *De S. Cruce*, the arabesque work of the Christe of the Missa *Tous les regrets*, delicately and symmetrically carved, as if out of stone, against the more beautiful raising of the swelling storm of songs in the Christe of the mass *De S. Antonio*'.[174]

---

[166] Ambros's citation is not clear; the contents of the manuscript he is describing most closely match those of MechAS s.s., but he includes it in his discussion of Brussels manuscripts. He similarly assumes that the anonymous *Stabat mater* in BrusBR 215–216 is by La Rue, when it is in fact Josquin's; see Ambros, *Geschichte der Musik*, iii. 237.

[167] This manuscript would be discussed in detail in 1882 in Léon de Burbure, 'Étude sur un manuscrit du xvie siècle, contenant des chants à quatre et à trois voix; suivie d'un *Post-scriptum* sur le *Bellum musicale*, de Cl. Sebastiani', *Mémoires couronnés et autres mémoires publiés par l'Academie Royale des Sciences, des Lettres et des Beaux-Arts de Belgique*, 33/6 (1882), 1–44.

[168] As noted earlier, writers such as Bottée de Toulmon seem bewildered by La Rue.

[169] 'Sehr und oft sie auch in der Bewunderung von Canons und anderen contrapunktischen Aussenwerk stecken blieben'; Ambros, *Geschichte der Musik*, iii. 238.

[170] 'Eines der vorzüglichsten Werke, um den Meister in seiner Eigenthümlichkeit und seinem Werthe kennen zu lernen'; ibid. 237.

[171] 'Unbedeutend und wenig erfreulich'; ibid. 238.

[172] 'Der idealste Wohlklang in reiner Vollendung offenbart und der sogenannte Palestrinastyl lange vor Palestrina vollständig da ist'; ibid. 235.

[173] 'Das sehnsuchtsvoll innige letzte "Agnus" der grösseren Missa *De S. Cruce*'; ibid.

[174] 'Das feine Spitzengewebe seiner Missa *De S. Anna . . .* gegen die mächtigen, massiven Formen der Missa *L'omme armé*, die Trockenheit der Messe *Cum jocunditate* gegen den Geistesathem, der durch die Messe *De S. Cruce* weht, das wie aus Stein zierlich und symmetrisch ausgemeisselte Arabeskenwerk des "Christe" in der Missa *Tous les regrets* gegen den in schöner Steigerung schwellenden Strom des Gesanges im "Christe" der Messe *De S. Antonio*'; ibid.

Ambros does not hesitate to contrast La Rue with Josquin, though he considers the two to be completely different. His discussion of La Rue is the first in the section devoted to Josquin's Netherlandish contemporaries, and he opens by saying that if anyone could rival the mastery of Josquin, it would be La Rue. He contrasts their *L'homme armé* masses (the first one by La Rue, *Super voces musicales* by Josquin) and claims readily that La Rue loved to surpass the special accomplishments of other composers. Josquin writes his *Missa ad fugam* so that two voices are always in canon, so La Rue writes his *Missa O salutaris hostia* so that he derives all four voices from a canon. Josquin's *Missa La sol fa re mi* is answered by La Rue's *Missa Cum iocunditate*.[175] La Rue's four-voice mensuration canon in the *Missa L'homme armé* surpasses Josquin's 3 ex 1 canon in *Super voces musicales*, though Ambros thinks La Rue's tour de force is no longer music.[176] Ambros does not hesitate to criticize other aspects of La Rue's writing; he cannot write 'light, cheerful, charming works' like the chansons of Josquin and Compère, though he notes the spritely nature of the Osanna in the *Missa Tous les regretz*.[177] His *Missa Assumpta est Maria* fails in comparison with that of Palestrina,[178] as does his *Missa de beata virgine* when contrasted with the 'charming' (*anmuthigem*) work of the same name by Josquin.[179]

Ambros's familiarity with La Rue's music came from transcribing it (still an excellent method for learning music). His collection now resides in the Österreichische Nationalbibliothek (ÖNB) in Vienna; pieces (or portions thereof) noted by Robijns and the editors of the collected works edition[180] include the *Missa de Sancta Anna* and *Missa de sancta cruce* (ÖNB, Sammlung Ambros [SA], MS 1580, dated 1863); the Kyrie and Benedictus from the *Missa Alleluia*, the Kyrie from the *Missa Assumpta est Maria*, the Kyrie and Agnus from the *Missa Ave Maria*, *Missa Cum iocunditate*, *Missa de Sancto Antonio*,[181] *Missa L'homme armé I*, *Missa O gloriosa domina* (incomplete), the Kyrie I and Pleni from the *Missa O salutaris hostia* (via the *Dodecachordon*), the beginning of the Sanctus from the *Requiem*, the Agnus II from the *Missa Puer natus est nobis*, the Pleni from the *Missa Sancta dei genitrix* (but copied from 1545[6] and thus as the contrafactum motet *Miserere*), the Kyrie, Christe, Benedictus, and Et incarnatus from the *Missa Sub tuum presidium*, *Missa Tous les regretz* (signed and dated 9 August 1865), *Mijn hert,*

---

175 In addition to these Josquin examples, Ambros connects the *Missae Mi Mi* of Ockeghem and de Orto with the *Missa Ut fa* of La Rue; he was unaware that this title (more properly *Missa Sexti ut fa*) appeared in the Petrucci mass print as a replacement for the more accurate (even if not understandable) *Missa Almana*; ibid. 239.

176 Ibid. 238.

177 Ibid. 239.

178 VDS vii. 130 criticizes this comparison: 'Of what use, we ask, is this comparison of two compositions separated by an abyss? ('A quoi bon, nous le demandons, ce rapprochement de deux compositions qu'un abîme sépare?')

179 Ambros, *Geschichte der Musik*, iii. 239.

180 RobijnsP, 45–6; LRE, *passim*.

181 This is not listed in LRE but only in RobijnsP, 46. I suspect that the folio number given by Robijns on which the mass begins should be 78[v] instead of 68[v], since he has the *Missa Tous les regretz* transcription starting on 67[v]; according to LRE, vi, p. xlviii, that mass continues up through 77[v].

Plorer, gemir, crier/Requiem, the *Lamentations* (now no longer thought to be his), *Da pacem domine*, and incomplete copies of *Delicta iuventutis* and *Pater de coelis deus* (all from ÖNB, SA, MS 1567); three copies of all or part of *Fors seulement* (ÖNB, SA, MSS 1595, 1596, and 1597);[182] another copy of *Plorer, gemir, crier/Requiem* (ÖNB, SA, MS 1596).[183] This list is obviously not complete, since Ambros mentions other works besides these, but one wonders whether he based some of his opinions on excerpts rather than complete pieces.

Ambros was neither the only nor even the first to leave manuscript transcriptions of La Rue's music. A copy of the first Kyrie of the *Missa O salutaris hostia* was supposedly made in the eighteenth century,[184] and the copy of the Et incarnatus and Benedictus from the *Missa Cum iocunditate* have been said to date from around 1820.[185] Undated but presumably nineteenth-century transcriptions include all of the *Missa O salutaris hostia* (BrusBR, Fétis Collection, 1641, transcribed by F.-L. Perne),[186] *Missa Cum iocunditate*, *Missa Incessament*, the *Requiem*, *Salve Regina II* and *III* (MunBS Ms. Mus. 880, 881, 882, 98, and 883 respectively, made or presumably made by A. J. F. Thibaut),[187] and the first part of *Salve regina III* (MunBS Ms. Mus. Cod. Lat. 1511),[188] while the Sammlung Kiesewetter in the ÖNB contains *Lauda anima mea dominum*, the Benedictus from the *Missa de beata virgine*, and the Agnus from the *Missa L'homme armé I*.[189] Just as in the sixteenth century, we find a certain emphasis on canonic works in many of these transcriptions, in part because early musicologists were drawn to the major theoretical treatises from the sixteenth century.

La Rue's epitaph was published in 1871, thus making known the date of his death,[190] and in 1876 a small amount of new material appeared in the largely derivative article on La Rue by Alphonse Goovaerts in the Belgian *Biographie nationale*;[191] his appearance in this encyclopedia is another step in the establishment of his national reputation. Goovaerts introduced the composer as 'one of the justly celebrated artists who established the superiority of the Low Countries in the art of music'[192] and once again listed him as the favourite composer of Mar-

---

[182] RobijnsP, 45, does not indicate which versions these are.

[183] Ibid. ÖNB Ms. 19328 contains, very curiously, precisely the La Rue examples found in LonBL 4911: the Agnus II from *Missa L'homme armé I* (quite common, of course) but also the tenor line only of the opening of the Sanctus from *Missa Cum iocunditate*. Philipp Naegele, 'Ambros, August Wilhelm', *New Grove II*, lists no London visit for Ambros, so perhaps this is merely a coincidence.

[184] Berlin, Staatsbibliothek zu Berlin — Preußischer Kulturbesitz, MS 30326; see LRE v, pp. xxvii, xxx.

[185] See ibid. ii, p. xxiv.   [186] Ibid. v, p. xxvii.

[187] Ibid. ii, p. xxiv; RobijnsP, 49; LRE v, p. xlviii; ix, pp. lxxv, lxxx.   [188] LRE ix, p. lxxx.

[189] RobjnsP, 45. Other interesting items include a copy of the altus partbook (from the 1503 mass print) for the *Missa L'homme armé I* (Barcelona, Biblioteca Musical de la Disputació, MS 115 [*olim* 426]; see LRE iv, p. li) and a collection of four partbooks containing the *Missa de Sancto Antonio* (ÖNB MS 18742; see LRE iii, p. xxiv).

[190] Van de Putte, 'Epitaphes copiées', 280. Vander Straeten was the first to pick up on this; the date of birth remains uncertain.

[191] Goovaerts, 'Delarue (Pierre)'. Some of the new material is erroneous; the correct material introduces new sources.

[192] Ibid. col. 325: 'un de ces artistes justement célèbres qui établirent la supériorité des Pays-Bas dans l'art musical'.

guerite. Similarly derivative is Riemann's *Musik-Lexikon* (1882), which calls the composer 'master of the most extreme arts of imitative counterpoint'.[193] In 1877, Eitner's *Bibliographie der Musik-Sammelwerke des XVI. und XVII. Jahrhunderts* listed forty-six works by La Rue that had appeared in sixteenth-century printed collections (he did not include those in the 1503 mass print), but many of these have since proven to be either excerpts from larger works, contrafacta, or inauthentic.[194]

La Rue is barely mentioned in Pinchart's *Archives des arts, sciences et lettres*, whose three volumes appeared between the years 1860 and 1881, though his erroneous claim that La Rue was on the court payroll by 2 April 1485 was frequently repeated thereafter in the literature.[195] Pinchart gathered far more material on early music than appeared in this publication, with the intention, never realized, of writing a book on music at the court. His notes, conserved today in the Royal Library in Brussels, contain information that is no longer to be found elsewhere.[196]

The publication of La Rue's music received a huge boost from the ongoing series *Trésor musical*, edited by Robert-Julien Van Maldeghem. Although the biannual collections started in 1865, La Rue's works first appeared in 1882, when Van Maldeghem began a series of issues largely or entirely devoted to his music.[197] In the *Musique religieuse* series, both the 1882 and 1883 volumes were given over completely to La Rue's music, or in some cases to music that Van Maldeghem thought was La Rue's. The works now available were *Salve regina I, Gaude virgo, Vexilla regis/Passio domini, Doleo super te* (the *quarta pars* of *Considera Israel*), *Si dormiero* (as *Cum coelum mutatur*), and *Salve regina VI*, in addition to *Ave sanctissima Maria* and *Maria mater gratie/Fors seulement*, which lack contemporary attributions to La Rue but are surely his. Eight other works that are probably or definitely not his were also published under his name in these two collections (e.g. Obrecht's *Si sumpsero*). In 1893, Van Maldeghem republished *Salve regina VI* along with the *Magnificat Sexti toni*.

La Rue's secular music received similar attention on the *Musique profane* side of Van Maldeghem's *Trésor musical* in the years between 1884 and 1888. Authentic

---

[193] 'In dem extremsten Künsten des imitierenden Kontrapunkts Meister'; Hugo Riemann, *Musik-Lexikon* (Leipzig: Bibliographisches Institut, 1882), 505.

[194] Robert Eitner et al., *Bibliographie der Musik-Sammelwerke des XVI. und XVII. Jahrhunderts* (Berlin: L. Liepmannssohn, 1877).

[195] Pinchart, *Archives des arts, sciences et lettres*, iii. 165.

[196] BrusBR MS II 1200, Carton 9.

[197] The biographical essay that Van Maldeghem includes when he first publishes music by La Rue is entirely derivative and manages to garble some earlier material; La Rue, described as Flemish, is now said to resign his Namur prebend in 1501 (the correct date is 1510, as earlier writers noted) to take on that of Kortrijk in the same year. He perpetuates the idea that he was a priest and that Marguerite had 'admiration without bounds' (*admiration sans bornes*) for his works. Although he does not publish any of La Rue's masses, he does say that they are of 'très-grand caractère'. See *Trésor musical: Collection authentique de musique sacrée et profane des anciens maîtres belges recueillie et transcrite en notation moderne*, 29 vols. each of *Musique profane* and *Musique religieuse*, ed. Robert-Julien Van Maldeghem (Brussels: C. Muquardt, 1865–93), *Musique religieuse*, xviii. [23].

pieces published (often under different titles or with altered texts) were *Tous les regretz*, *De l'oeil de la fille du roy*, *Ce n'est pas jeu*, *Secretz regretz*, *Trop plus secret*, *Autant en emporte le vent*, *Pourquoy non*, *Il est bien heureux* (but attributed by Van Maldeghem to Agricola), *Pour ce que je suis*, *Mijn hert*, *Tous nobles cueurs*, and *A vous non autre* (these last two published anonymously). Van Maldeghem also freely added La Rue's name to anonymous pieces he transcribed from BrusBR 228 (the source of almost all of the music listed above); many, though not all, of these works are now believed to be La Rue's.

The historiographical survey given so far shows only half a dozen short bits of La Rue published before 1882: the Benedictus from the *Missa de beata virgine* that Burney and then Kiesewetter published, the motet *Lauda anima mea dominum*, and the two excerpts from the *Missa de Sancto Antonio* in Forkel and Forkel/Sonnleithner,[198] the canonic Agnus from the *Missa L'homme armé I* (published three times), and the Kyrie of the *Missa Conceptio tua*, which appeared in the *Cäcilienkalender* of 1879.[199] This last was the only new thing by La Rue to appear in the forty-four years between 1838 and 1882, the year that Van Maldeghem began to print the composer's music. In that same year, after Ambros's death, Otto Kade edited the final volume of *Geschichte der Musik*, which consisted of musical examples and included *O salutaris hostia* and the Sanctus, Pleni, and Osanna from the *Missa Tous les regretz*.[200] Other pieces published later in the nineteenth century were the beginning of the Qui tollis from the *Missa de Sancto Antonio* (in vol. 7 of Vander Straeten's *La Musique aux Pays-Bas*, 1885),[201] *O salutaris hostia* (in Bordes, *Anthologie des maîtres religieux primitifs*, 1893),[202] *Il me fait mal* (anonymous, but published as La Rue's by Bordes, 1895),[203] *Au feu d'amour* (1899, now thought to be by Robert de la Rue),[204] and the *Missa Ave Maria* (in 1898, in Expert's series *Les Maîtres musiciens de la Renaissance française*), the last-named the first complete mass by La Rue to be published in a modern edition.[205] In addition, La Rue's

---

[198] Johann Nikolaus Forkel and Joseph Sonnleithner (eds.), *Geschichte der Musik in Denkmälern von der ältesten bis auf die neueste Zeit* (Leipzig? 1806?), according to Wagner, *Geschichte der Messe*, 167.

[199] According to RubsamenMGG, 237 (RobijnsP, 156, incorrectly gives 1873 as the date).

[200] Ambros, *Geschichte der Musik*, v. 137–45.

[201] VDS vii, facing p. 130.

[202] *Anthologie des maîtres religieux primitifs des XVᵉ, XVIᵉ et XVIIᵉ siècles*, ed. Charles Bordes, 6 vols. (Paris: Bureau d'édition de la Schola Cantorum, 1893; repr. New York: Da Capo, 1981), vi. 68–9.

[203] According to Eitner, *Biographisch-bibliographisches Quellen-Lexikon*, vi. 54.

[204] *Sechzig Chansons zu vier Stimmen aus der ersten Hälfte des 16. Jahrhunderts von französischen und niederländischen Meistern*, ed. Robert Eitner (Publikationen älterer praktischer und theoretischer Musikwerke, 23; Leipzig: Breitkopf & Härtel, 1899), 68–9.

[205] *Liber quindecim missarum: Brumel Missa 'De beata virgine', P. de la Rue Missa 'Ave Maria'*, ed. Henry Expert (Les Maîtres musiciens de la Renaissance française, 8; Paris: Alphonse Leduc, 1898). Expert's edition inspired a discussion of this work in Michel Brenet, *Palestrina* (Paris: Félix Alcan, 1906), where she states 'l'on se sentira en présence d'une œuvre d'art achevée, qui contient, sous un aspect très rapproché de la perfection, presque toutes les beautés du style palestrinien' and continues to praise his writing throughout her description (ibid. 21). On the basis of the 'poetry and expression' of this mass and other contemporary works, Brenet argues against the 19th-c. predilection to view these 'old artists', i.e. pre-Palestrina, as 'absorbed in the cold calculation of combination techniques' ('absorbés dans le froid calcul des combinaisons techniques'); ibid. 25. Palestrina learns from them not just the art of arranging voices in in-

excerpts in the *Dodecachordon* were published in Bohn's 1888 edition of the treatise.[206] Although Van Maldeghem's editorial procedures have been justly criticized, he almost single-handedly put La Rue within the reach of performers and scholars.[207]

Similar credit must go to Edmond Vander Straeten. While previous writers did a surprisingly good job of producing a works list (especially for the masses) and a very creditable compilation of sources,[208] Vander Straeten paved the way for a real biography of La Rue. Although his massive, eight-volume study *La Musique aux Pays-Bas* has countless errors, many of which were repeated by later writers, it provided far more information on the composer, including many new documents, than anyone heretofore. Mentioned in passing in volumes 1 (1867) and 4 (1878), La Rue makes a more significant appearance in volumes 3 (1875), 6 (1882), 8 (1888), and especially 7 (1885). Appearing here for the first time (mostly in the extended discussion in volume 7)[209] is the possible identification of La Rue with vander Straten, discussion of the epitaph in connection with La Rue as the composer (it was published previously merely as part of a collection of epitaphs), evidence that La Rue accompanied Philip to Spain on two separate journeys, numerous lists of chapel personnel, information on his father's pension from Philip (described in the usual romanticized manner), suppositions as to his father's identity and profession (and suggestion of La Rue's birthplace as Kortrijk on the basis of his father's presumed place of activity), the first information about the Dendermonde benefice, and the inventories of the libraries of Mary of Hungary and Philip II. Vander Straeten suggests that La Rue must have had pupils attracted to him by his brilliant reputation, thereby founding or consolidating an important music school, a thread of thought not followed by later scholars (though possibly influenced by Coclico's claims). He also claims that La Rue had some influence on Spanish composers. At the same time, he is the first to suggest that Ockeghem was not literally La Rue's teacher.

La Rue appears in the appendix to volume 4 of Grove's *A Dictionary of Music and Musicians* (first published 1889).[210] Sterndale Bennett, the author of the article, was apparently unaware of Vander Straeten's work and thus presented a much

---

genious counterpoint, but also how to translate the affections of the spirit into sound ('et ce n'est pas seulement dans l'art d'associer les voix en contrepoints ingénieux, mais bien en même temps dans celui de traduire par des sons les affections de l'âme, que Palestrina a été leur disciple'); ibid.

[206] *Glareani Dodecachordon: Basileae MDXLVII*, trans. and ed. Peter Bohn (Publikationen älterer praktischer und theoretischer Musikwerke, 16; Leipzig: Breitkopf & Härtel, 1888).

[207] On Van Maldeghem's editing, see Gustave Reese, 'Maldeghem and his Buried Treasure: A Bibliographical Study', *Notes*, 6 (1948–9), 75–117. To his credit, Van Maldeghem simultaneously published performing editions to facilitate actual performance, not just study.

[208] Eitner, *Biographisch-bibliographisches Quellen-Lexikon*, vi. 54–5 (from 1902), summarizes and adds to what was known in the 19th c.

[209] VDS vii. 108–31.

[210] William Sterndale Bennett, 'Rue, Pierre de la', in *A Dictionary of Music and Musicians (A.D. 1450–1889)*, 4 vols. (London: Macmillan, 1879–89), iv. 778. By the time of the second edition (1904–10), La Rue had been shifted to the 'L' section of the dictionary.

less complete biography than was possible. He observed 'Most writers on music accord him a position as a contrapuntal composer scarcely second to that of Josquin ... Indeed, considering his great reputation, it is somewhat surprising that so little is known of the events of his life, and that so little of his music has been printed', a statement (even taking Vander Straeten into account) that remained largely true a full century after its publication.[211]

By the end of the nineteenth century, then, La Rue was in the major French, German, and English language music encyclopedias[212] and had taken his position as a composer to be mentioned in any musical work that aspired to comprehensiveness. Already entrenched were numerous biographical errors, a somewhat one-sided reputation as a master contrapuntist, and the unsupported claim of personal protection and attention on the part of Marguerite, all of which has proved stubbornly tenacious in the literature. Although little work had been directed specifically towards understanding his life or music, ongoing general research, including the publication of library catalogues, the examination of individual manuscripts, and the study of musical life at the Habsburg-Burgundian court continued to add to knowledge of his output and career, as would be the case throughout much of the twentieth century.

Major twentieth-century bibliographic breakthroughs came in the earlier part of the century with the work of Hocquet on Tournai as the probable birthplace for the composer, Caullet and Schmidt-Görg on musicians of Kortrijk, and Van Doorslaer on music under Philip the Fair.[213] Dissertations devoted to La Rue came from Rubsamen (masses), Robijns (life and works), Davison (motets), Kreider (five- and six-voice masses), and Meconi (secular music).[214] Two dissertations on broader topics made very significant contributions to our understanding of the composer, Picker's work on BrusBr 228 and 11239, and Bloxam's study of masses with multiple cantus firmi, including two of La Rue's.[215] Comprehensive

---

[211] The various entries in later editions of Grove alter very little. The second edition (1911 for the volume containing 'L') adds his date of death, places him in the service of Charles V until 1512, at which point he is said to switch to Marguerite's service, and directs the reader to Eitner's *Quellenlexikon* for a list of manuscript sources. The third edition (1928 for the 'R' volume, where La Rue is again listed) adds some bibliographical information but nothing else; the entry is repeated verbatim in the fourth edition (1940). The fifth edition (1954) switches him back to 'L', where he has remained ever since, and finally adds some different material, claiming that his father worked for Philip the Fair between 1496 and 1501, saying 'He may have been a pupil of Okeghem's but this is uncertain', connecting him with 's-Hertogenbosch in 1490–1, making him a canon in Mechelen (which should actually be Namur) on 8 Feb. 1501, giving 1502 and 1503 as the dates of the Spanish trips, and various other inaccuracies. Until the 1980 edition of *New Grove*, all of the articles were still attributed to Sterndale Bennett, with the qualification that additions had been made. Only with StaehelinNG (1980) did La Rue receive a serious scholarly treatment in this dictionary.

[212] He does not appear in the first important Italian dictionary, Carlo Schmidl, *Dizionario universale dei musicisti* (Milan: G. Ricordi, 1887).

[213] Hocquet, 'Un musicien tournaisien'; CaulletM; SG; DoorslaerC.

[214] Walter Howard Rubsamen, 'Pierre de la Rue als Messen-Komponist' (Ph.D. diss., University of Munich, 1937); RobijnsP; Nigel St. John Davison, 'The Motets of Pierre de la Rue' (D.Mus. diss., University of Edinburgh, 1961); Kreider, 'The Masses for Five and Six Voices by Pierre de la Rue'; Meconi, 'Style and Authenticity'.

[215] Martin Picker, 'The Chanson Albums of Marguerite of Austria: Manuscripts 228 and 11239 of the

surveys of knowledge to date appeared successively in *MGG* (1960, Rubsamen), *New Grove* (1980, Staehelin), and *New Grove II* (2001, Meconi),[216] and numerous specialized articles have appeared, especially in the last forty years.

Yet always the major handicap to scholarship and (especially) performance was the absence of modern editions.[217] Although Ambros had signalled the importance of the masses in La Rue's output as early as 1868, only one was available in modern edition by the end of the nineteenth century, and other editions were slow to follow. Not until 1931 did another mass appear, in the *Chorwerk* edition of the *Requiem* (as volume 11, one of the earliest in the entire series;[218] even earlier than this, four chansons of La Rue[219] appeared in volume 3, dedicated to 'Josquin des Prés und andere Meister'). A decade later Tirabassi produced his edition of the seven masses in BrusBR 15075, but the use of original clefs, among other things, limited its practicality for performance.[220] In 1950 Feininger published the *Missa Ave sanctissima Maria* in a striking edition that gave the voices derived from canon in red, and in 1960 Robijns and René Lenaerts brought out the *Missa de beata virgine*, *Missa de Sancta Anna*, and *Missa de virginibus* in *Monumenta musicae Belgicae*.[221] In 1968 the *Missa Assumpta est* appeared in the series *Musica divina*, and only in 1972 was La Rue's first *L'homme armé* mass published; the *Missa Cum iocunditate* came out in 1978.[222] Kreider's dissertation included editions of all the five- and six-voice masses; though unwieldy for performance they at least permitted study.[223] Both Rubsamen and Robijns generated transcriptions of the masses for their dissertations, but these editions were not generally available. The same is true for the editions of motets Davison prepared as part of his dissertation; those who purchased a copy of his thesis did not receive the music as well. Study and

Bibliothèque Royale de Belgique, Bruxelles' (Ph.D. diss., University of California, Berkeley, 1960); Bloxam, 'A Survey of Late Medieval Service Books'.

216 RubsamenMGG; StaehelinNG; Honey Meconi, 'La Rue, Pierre de', *New Grove II*.

217 Performances of La Rue's music were taking place by 1911 if not before; see the programme given in Paul Bergmans, *Les Musiciens de Courtrai et du Courtraisis: Notes d'une conférence faite au Cercle historique et archéologique de Courtrai le 30 mars 1911* (Ghent: C. Vyt; Courtrai: L. Beyaert-Sioen, 1912), 2. The Gloria from the *Missa Ave Maria* was performed, as well as a chanson no longer considered his, *Ma mère hellas*.

218 Pierre de la Rue, *Requiem und eine Motette zu 4–5 Stimmen*, ed. Friedrich Blume (Das Chorwerk, 11; Wolfenbüttel: Möseler, 1931).

219 *Autant en emporte le vent*, *Pourquoy non*, *Quand il survient*, and *Cueurs desolez/Dies illa* (the latter part titled *Dies irae*). The last two, published there under La Rue's name, are actually anonymous. Friedrich Blume, editor of the volume, characterizes La Rue as 'neben Isaac der genialste und vielseitigste unter Josquins zeitgenössischen Landsleuten, heute noch viel zu wenig gekannt, ein unruhiger Geist'; see *Josquin des Prés und andere Meister: Weltliche Lieder*, ed. Friedrich Blume (Das Chorwerk, 3; Berlin: Kallmeyer, 1929), 2.

220 P[ierre] de la Rue, *Liber Missarum*, ed. [Antonio] Tirabassi (Mechelen: Maison Dessain, [1941]).

221 P[ierre] de la Rue, *Missa Ave sanctissima*, ed. Laurence Feininger (Documenta polyphoniae liturgicae Sanctae Ecclesiae Romanae, ser. I. B. 1; Rome: Societas universalis S. Ceciliae, 1950); id., *Drie Missen*, ed. René Bernard Lenaerts and Jozef Robijns (Monumenta musicae Belgicae, 8; Antwerp: Vereniging voor Muziekgeschiedenis, 1960).

222 Pierre de la Rue, *Missa Assumpta est Maria*, ed. Ludwig Finscher (Musica divina, 18; Regensburg: Friedrich Pustet, 1966); id., *Missa L'Homme armé I zu 4 Stimmen*, ed. Nigel Davison (Das Chorwerk, 114; Wolfenbüttel and Zürich: Möseler, 1972); id., *Missa Cum iocunditate for 4 and 5 voices*, ed. Nigel Davison (Mapa Mundi Series B: Franco-Flemish Church Music, 3; London: Bruno Turner, 1978).

223 Kreider, 'The Masses for Five and Six Voices by Pierre de la Rue'.

performance of the motets was thus limited to various individual editions that continued to appear, of which the most significant was the *Chorwerk* collection of *Considera Israel* and three other motets that appeared in 1964.[224] Picker's edition of BrusBR 228 and 11239 (1965) made many of La Rue's secular works available (as with the motets, various ones had appeared elsewhere previously); all other secular works then ascribed to La Rue appeared in Meconi (1986).[225] It is only with the advent of the collected works edition, whose volumes began appearing in 1989, that those interested in his music have had ready access to his works.[226]

WHO IS PIERRE DE LA RUE?

In hindsight we can see La Rue's historical position, or at least part of it: a major composer, one of the most prolific of his generation, his music widely transmitted in almost two hundred sources—including one of the earliest Petrucci mass prints and numerous court manuscripts where he was the featured composer—over the course of a century or so, cited by writers and theorists over an even longer period of time, with a slow build-up of his rediscovery in modern times. We see a series of firsts, onlys, mosts, or near-firsts: author of one of earliest polyphonic Requiems, originator of possibly the earliest true *de beata virgine* mass, one of the first to produce a complete Magnificat cycle, the most prolific creator of *Salve regina* settings, perhaps the author of the earliest full-fledged ferial mass, one of the few to write two *L'homme armé* masses, the creator of the first canonic six-voice work, a leader in the aural expansion of music (in terms of both range, number of voices, and chromaticism),[227] the contriver of the only known 4 ex 1 mensuration canon, and so on. Certain of his compositions served as models for works by other composers: *Missa de feria*, *Absalon fili mi* (if it is his), *Sancta Maria virgo*, *Mijn hert*, *Pourquoy non*,[228] perhaps *Salve regina IV* and *Missa Ave sanctissima Maria*,[229] and probably others. A major writer of masses, a master of paraphrase, an innovator in polyphonic borrowing, a canonic wizard, a liturgically conscious creator, a

---

[224] Pierre de la Rue, *Vier Motetten zu 4 Stimmen*, ed. Nigel Davison (Das Chorwerk, 91; Wolfenbüttel: Möseler, 1962).

[225] PickerCA; Meconi, 'Style and Authenticity'.

[226] LRE; as of 2001, all volumes except the last (secular music) had appeared.

[227] In examining the relationship between the 15th- and 16th-c. mass, it is not too far-fetched to see an analogy with the 18th- and 19th-c. symphony, where in each case the earlier century saw the gradual establishment of formal norms, used smaller performing forces with more limited ranges, and maintained a more conservative harmonic language, while the following century saw formal expansion (in the case of the mass, complete five-movement works with multiple interior sections), increase in performing forces, new extremes of range, and greater chromaticisim in harmonic language.

[228] Both *Pourquoy non* and *Mijn hert* were among his most widely disseminated songs. Still unexplored are more general influences such as a possible influence on the northern chanson, or the next generation of Franco-Flemish composers, such as Gombert.

[229] Benedictus Appenzeller, who worked at the court of Marguerite of Austria's successor, Mary of Hungary, wrote a now-lost six-voice *Missa Ave sanctissima Maria*. One wonders whether La Rue's identically titled mass, also for six voices, was its inspiration.

compositional leader and probable inspiration at one of the most important musical institutions of the day, the Habsburg-Burgundian court: all describe La Rue.

But many questions still remain. Did La Rue's individual style develop because, like Haydn, he was largely on his own as a young musician and forced to solve compositional problems by himself? Does his preference for currently untraceable chant models reflect formative years spent in musical backwaters? What prompted him to borrow wholesale from Pipelare, to write *Si dormiero* and interact musically in a special tradition of sacred tricinia, to generate a large number of works that parallel those of Josquin? Did his exploration of low sonorities inspire others, especially at court, to do so as well?[230] Did he influence Isaac in the expansion of forces, or vice versa? Or did each develop the interest individually? Why did it take so long for the court to acknowledge him, especially in view of the extremely impressive series of early works he generated for them?

Despite the general statements we can make about La Rue, and a considerable bibliography as well, his music remains far too little known, for several reasons. One is that his masses (by implication the most prestigious of genres for his generation) present certain difficulties when it comes to analysis. The precise models are unknown for many of them, and La Rue prefers paraphrase to strict cantus-firmus treatment in any event. The latter is easier to trace, and thus to discuss; La Rue's very compositional process has slowed our understanding of it. But a larger reason is, until very recently, the lack of a critical edition. Those wishing to study the masses (and to a lesser extent, the motets and secular music) were surely deterred by the time-consuming process of compiling and transcribing the material. It is no accident that the composers who have been most studied have been those who received editions—at least of the masses—fairly early on: Obrecht, Ockeghem, and Josquin, all of whom had significant material available by the 1920s.[231] And this says nothing about the enormous psychological impact of a collected works edition, even if incomplete: it conveys an authority and prestige otherwise lacking. Acknowledged or not, the unspoken thought is that a composer without such an imprimatur is less important than those receiving this attention.

The questions that frame this book will remind readers of two essays appearing within the last fifteen years with the title 'Who was Josquin?'[232] Each author who addressed that question could count on his readers' intimate knowledge of numerous works by or attributed to that composer. The same cannot be said for the works of La Rue, or for that matter, of any of his peers. La Rue and all of his

---

[230] This was suggested earlier as possible in the case of *Il fault morir*, for example. Could this be true for the *Missa sine nomine II*, an anonymous work that is discordant with La Rue's style in certain respects but that does explore the lower depths?

[231] By the late 20th c., both Ockeghem and Josquin were in the process of acquiring a second collected works edition, while Obrecht's third was completed.

[232] Willem Elders, 'Who Was Josquin?', in id. (ed.), *Proceedings of the International Josquin Symposium, Utrecht 1986* (Utrecht: Vereniging voor Nederlandse Muziekgeschiedenis, 1991), 1–14; Rob C. Wegman, 'Who Was Josquin?', in Richard Sherr (ed.), *The Josquin Companion* (Oxford: Oxford University Press, 2000), 21–50.

contemporaries, even Josquin, have suffered from the way in which our work is sometimes conducted. As crowded as the field may seem at times, there are actually relatively few of us working on this music, and (far more significant) even fewer performers involved in bringing it back to life. But scholarship is competitive; we must build a case for grants, for publication, for presentation of papers, on the perceived significance of the subject at hand; we are all competing for the same limited resources. Too often we act as if forced into a kind of zero-sum game with a silent subtext: if my paper/grant proposal/article/book proposal is accepted, yours cannot be—and therefore, my composer can only be significant at the expense of your composer. In reality, we have an astonishing series of incredibly interesting composers active at the same time (or, as noted earlier, with overlapping periods of activity). Agricola, Brumel, Compère, Isaac, La Rue, Josquin, Obrecht—aren't these the Beethoven, Schubert, Mendelssohn, Schumann, Chopin, Berlioz, Liszt of their time? Don't they all have rich and exciting music for us to enjoy? In reading over the 'Reputation' section of the *New Grove II* article on Josquin, I was struck by how much the article described La Rue as well; the differences are more of volume (more theoretical references, more works in German prints for Josquin) than of kind. In some respects it is increasingly hard to compare these two, and almost pointless.

This brings me to what I believe is the most important element of what La Rue is for us today, and the aspect that should be the most important in creating his reputation. He is a superb composer whose music is still waiting, by and large, to be discovered, or at least by more than just a few specialists. One of the factors that propelled me (and perhaps others as well) into the study of early music was the desire to find new pieces of music to love after having explored what one might still call the standard repertoire. La Rue offers an especially exciting opportunity in this regard.

He is certainly an exciting composer to perform. The unexpected twists of his melodic lines, his lively, shifting rhythms, and his penchant for landing at a different centre for each cadence make singing his music challenging but immensely satisfying, though I sometimes wonder whether the frequent references in the literature to parallel intervals and his casual use of dissonance (a criticism we now know goes back to Burney) have not deflected some of the attention he might otherwise have received. The fame of his *L'homme armé* mensuration canon has also, I think, led to misunderstandings, for this is probably the least appealing part of his entire *Missa L'homme armé I*, an otherwise irresistible frolic on the well-known melody.

I cannot predict what pattern of influence this book will have by itself. Its almost Rabelaisian appetite for lists will, I hope, answer questions about many different aspects of La Rue's life, his musical surroundings, elements of his works, his influences, and his reception and reputation over the past five centuries. Ideally it will inspire greater curiosity about his music and especially new performances, now that the collected works are at hand. I am tempted to list works to explore that barely appeared in earlier chapters but that are still wonderfully interesting—*Missa Sub tuum presidium, Considera Israel, Delicta iuventutis*—but the list would soon prove unwieldy. Suffice it to say that it is a rare La Rue composition that does not offer both intellectual and aural delights. I hope, then, that the material presented here will lead in as many ways as possible to renewed explorations of La Rue and his music—not, in fact, to conclusions, but rather to a series of new and fruitful beginnings.

Appendix A
Chronology of Events

In the chronology that follows, all known contemporary documents that mention La Rue or Peter vander Straten are listed, with brief comments on conflicts and inaccuracies in the published literature and in the documents themselves. Selected information about the chapel in general is included, as well as dates of various political and courtly events. Dates for Easter are given for the years at the Habsburg-Burgundian court, since this is when the year changed. Abbreviations have been silently expanded, except in the case of La Rue's name. Curly brackets around a form of his name mean either that I have not seen the original myself or that the name appears in a later copy of the original document.

c.1452? later?
born, probably in Tournai

St. John's 1469–70
'peteren vander straten den tenor' paid £3 g. d. by the collegiate church of Sint Goedele, Brussels. BAGR, ASG 1390, fo. 156ʳ (Accounts of the Villicus, 1458–77, within the section for miscellaneous expenses 'De acciden' for 1469–70)

1471
1 Oct. (Feast of Sint Baaf): 'pieter vander Straten' paid 56 sc. 6 den. par.

24 Dec.: 'pieter vander Straten' paid 12 sc. par. Both payments listed in quarterly accounts for the singers of the parish church of Sint Jacobskerk, Ghent. SJG, MS 1203, unfoliated (Accounts of the Cotidiane, 1471–2)

1472
between 1 Jan. and 15 Mar.: 'pieter vander Straten' paid 30 sc. par. (shared with Pieter Claus). Payment listed in miscellaneous accounts for singers of the parish church of Sint Jacobskerk, Ghent. SJG, MS 1203, unfoliated (Accounts of the Cotidiane, 1471–2)

5 May: 'pieter van straten' paid 7 sc. 6 den. par. by the parish church of Onze-Lieve-Vrouw, Nieuwpoort. RB, Stad Nieuwpoort, Oud Archief 3147, Register 1, fo. 17ʳ (Kerkrekeningen 2 Feb. 1472 mod. style–2 Feb. 1473 mod. style)

Aug. (probably): vander Straten begins employment as tenor at the parish church of Onze-Lieve-Vrouw, Nieuwpoort

1473
'den Teneur pieter van straten' paid £30 par. (£5 par. per month for 6 months, from an annual contract of £5 gr.) by the parish church of Onze-Lieve-Vrouw, Nieuwpoort. RB, Stad Nieuwpoort, Oud Archief 3147, Register 1, fo. 26ᵛ (Kerkrekeningen 2 Feb. 1472–3 mod. style). Although the payment is undated, it is at the conclusion of the account book for the period Candlemas 1472 mod. style to Candlemas 1473 mod. style and thus presumably covers the period Aug. 1472 to Jan. 1473. Payment records are missing from Feb. 1473 to Jan. 1477.

before 2 Feb. 1477

vander Straten leaves church of Onze-Lieve-Vrouw, Nieuwpoort

before employment at Habsburg-Burgundian court; dates uncertain

Resident canon at Church of St Ode; kept prebend until death

1489

5 Oct.: payment by the Confraternity of Illustre Lieve Vrouwe, 's-Hertogenbosch to Ghysbert van Roy, provisor from Cologne, for 'heer peteren van straten ons tenorist' 'who had not yet been received at that time'.[1] 's-HAI, Rekeningen 1485–95, fo. 157^v

'heer peteren straten tenorist' from Cologne, paid 4½ Rg. as reimbursement for expenses for his journey to and from 's-Hertogenbosch, made at the invitation of the brothers of the Confraternity of Illustre Lieve Vrouwe 'because we really wanted him as a tenor.'[2] Ibid., fo. 159^v

1489–90

'heer peter van straten onsen tenorist' paid by the Confraternity of Illustre Lieve Vrouwe, 's-Hertogenbosch, for 9 weeks' service (presumably 30 Oct.–31 Dec. 1489) at the rate of 24 st. per week for a total of 10 Rg. 16 st. Ibid., fo. 161^r[3]

'heer peter van straten' paid 21 st. for cloth (part of a joint payment along with 13 others) by the Confraternity of Illustre Lieve Vrouwe, 's-Hertogenbosch. Ibid., fo. 178^v[4]

'heer peteren van straten' paid by the Confraternity of Illustre Lieve Vrouwe, 's-Hertogenbosch, for 25 weeks' service (presumably 1 Jan.–24 June 1490) at the weekly rate of 14 st. for a total of 17½ Rg. Ibid., fo. 179^v[5]

1490–1

'heer peteren vander straten' paid £3 for cloth (part of a joint payment with others) by the Confraternity of Illustre Lieve Vrouwe, 's-Hertogenbosch. Ibid., fo. 200^v[6]

'heer peteren vander straten onsz tenorijst' paid by the Confraternity of Illustre Lieve Vrouwe, 's-Hertogenbosch, for 52 weeks' service at the weekly rate of 4 st., for a total of 36 Rg. 8 st. Ibid., fo. 203^v[7]

1491–2

'heer peteren vander straten onsz tenorist' paid by the Confraternity of Illustre Lieve Vrouwe, 's-Hertogenbosch, for 35 weeks' service (from 24 June 1491 to 23 Feb. 1492?) at a weekly rate of 14 st., for a total of 23 Rg. 16 st. Ibid., fo. 228^v[8]

1492 (Easter = 22 Apr.)[9]

17 Nov.: Habsburg-Burgundian court chapel, including La Rue, comes to Maximilian; not paid before 30 Sept. 1495[10]

---

[1] 'Die noch doen nyet ontvangen en was'; published in Smijers, 'De Illustre Lieve Vrouwe Broederschap ... Sint Jan 1475 tot Sint Jan 1500', 13 (1931–2), 187. The entry is identified as the Monday after the feast of Sint Baaf (1 Oct.); in 1489 this was 5 Oct.

[2] 'Want wy hem gherne voer een tenorist hedde gehad'; published ibid. 188, with 'Straten' misread as 'Strak'.

[3] Ibid.   [4] Ibid. 189.   [5] Ibid.   [6] Ibid. 190.   [7] Ibid.   [8] Ibid. 192.

[9] At the court the year changed at Easter; e.g. all documents written between 1 Jan. and 21 Apr. in 1492 bear the date 1491. The date of Easter each year is given below for reference. Unless otherwise indicated, all following payments are from the Habsburg-Burgundian court.

[10] See the documents cited for 30 Sept. 1495, 2 Oct. 1495, and 10 Dec. 1496.

1492–3
'petrus de vito Cantor Romanorum Regis' becomes a member of the Confraternity of Illustre
Lieve Vrouwe, 's-Hertogenbosch, with 7 of his colleagues. 's-HAI, Rekeningen 1485–95,
fo. 242[v11]

1493 (Easter = 7 Apr.)
23 May: Peace of Senlis, according to which Marguerite is to leave the French court and be
returned to her family[12]
12 June: Marguerite returns to Habsburg-Burgundian territories[13]
19 Aug.: death of Holy Roman Emperor Frederick III[14]
20 Nov.: Maximilian marries Bianca Maria Sforza by proxy in Milan[15]

1494 (Easter = 30 Mar.)
July: Maximilian returns to the Low Countries and is reunited with Philip and Marguerite[16]
24 Aug.: Frederick the Wise attends church in Mechelen with Maximilian, whose
'oberländischen und französischen' singers perform 'ein köstlich Meß'[17]
9 Sept.: Philip makes his joyous entry into Leuven[18]

1495 (Easter = 19 Apr.)
30 Sept.: date cited as the end of the non-payment period for the chapel; 'pierchon de la Rue'
listed among the *chantres* (17th of 25 chapel members);[19] then 'pierchon de la Rue' paid at
the daily rate of 10s. for the period beginning 17 Nov. 1492, for a total of £315 4s. 6d. LADN
B2151, fo. 110[v], for the chapel list; fo. 111[r-v] for the individual payment (account book of the
Receiver General, Simon Longin, for 1495)[20]
2 Oct.: 'pierchon de la Rue' listed among the *chantres* (17th of 25 chapel members); then
'pierchon de la Rue' paid at the daily rate of 10s. for the period beginning 17 Nov. 1492, for a
total of £315 4s. 6d. LADN B2152, N° 70529 (*mandement* for material recorded in the preceding document)[21]

[11] Published in Smijers, 'De Illustre Lieve Vrouwe Broederschap . . . 1475–1500', 192–3. PickerCA, 36,
gives no source for his citation of Jan. 1493 as the date of this event.
[12] Bruchet and Lancien, *L'Itinéraire*, 4; see also Molinet, *Chroniques*, ii. 354–71.
[13] Bruchet and Lancien, *L'Itinéraire*, 5; Molinet, *Chroniques*, ii. 371–3.
[14] Molinet, *Chroniques*, ii. 376; Wiesflecker, *Maximilian I.*, 392.
[15] Wiesflecker, *Maximilian I.*, 392; Molinet, *Chroniques*, ii. 387–8.
[16] Molinet, *Chroniques*, ii. 390–1.
[17] 'Am Sonntag Bartholomei ritten mein g. Herre und alle ander Fürsten mit dem Römischen König zur
Kirchen. Da ward von des Königs oberländischen und französischen Singern ein köstlich Meß gesungen.'
Spalatin, *Friedrichs des Weisen Leben*, 228.
[18] Cauchies, 'La Signification', 30; see also Molinet, *Chroniques*, ii. 395–7, where the date is given as 10
Sept..
[19] Numbers given in court documents include all members of the *grand chapelle* (e.g. *sommeliers*,
fourriers), not just singers. Numbers on *escroes* include names that were written and then crossed out (not a
common occurrence), since those individuals were supposed to be there and thus should be included in the
total number.
[20] Titled 'Compte dix[me]', but the 'dix' is crossed out; in reality this is the fourth book. The chapel list has
been published several times, beginning with Gachard, *Rapport*, 280. Gachard's somewhat inaccurate copy
formed the basis for almost all succeeding publications, which include VDS iii. 213–14, who at one point
gives the starting date as 2 Nov. 1492 and who calls La Rue a *tenoriste*; RobijnsP, 240, who mistakenly cites
the document number for the material from 2 Oct. 1495; Haggh, 'The Status of the Musician', 161; and
DouillezM, no. 46, whose partial transcription is based on the original. Douillez also notes (ibid.) income
received on 26 Sept. 1495 that was to be directed to the chapel wages; the document itself (LADN B2151, fo.
39[v]) further states that the money was from Jehan vander Eycken of Brabant.
[21] DoorslaerC, 42–3 publishes the chapel list derived from this document but does not provide the information about the individual amounts. He incorrectly lists the date in 1492 as 16 Nov., and indeed the origi-

8 Oct., Thursday, Brussels: 'pierchon de la Rue' paid 10s. LADN B3453 N° 120492 (*escroe*)[22]

12 Oct., Monday, Brussels: 'pierchon de la Rue' paid 10s. Ibid. N° 120494 (*escroe*)[23]

15 Oct., Thursday, Brussels: 'pierchon de la Rue' paid 10s. Ibid. N° 120496 (*escroe*)[24]

20 Oct., Tuesday, Brussels?: 'pierchon de la Rue' paid 10s. Ibid. N° 120498 (*escroe*)[25]

1 Nov., Sunday, Mechelen: 'pierchon de la Rue' paid 10s. (12th of 19 members). Ibid. N° 120500 (*escroe*)[26]

27 Nov., Friday, Brussels: 'perchon de la Rue' paid 10s. (12th of 19). Ibid. N° 120501 (*escroe*)

1496 (Easter = 3 Apr.)

7 Mar., Monday, [1496] mod. style, [Brussels]: 'pierchon de la Rue' paid 10s. (13th of 18). LADN B3454 N° 120506 (*escroe*)[27]

11 Mar., Friday, 1496 mod. style, [Brussels]: 'pierchon de la Rue' paid 10s. (13th of 18). Ibid. N° 120507 (*escroe*)

15 Mar., Tuesday, 1496 mod. style: 'pierchon de la Rue' paid 10s. (13th of 18). Ibid. N° 120509 (*escroe*)

20 Mar., Sunday, 1496 mod. style, Brussels: 'pierchon de la Rue' paid 10s. (13th of 18). Ibid. N° 120510 (*escroe*)

21 Mar., Monday, 1496 mod. style, Brussels: 'pierchon de la Rue' paid 10s. (13th of 18). Ibid. N° 120511 (*escroe*)

23 Mar., Wednesday, 1496 mod. style, Brussels: 'pierchon de la Rue' paid 10s. (13th of 18). Ibid. N° 120512 (*escroe*)

29 Mar., Tuesday, 1496 mod. style, Brussels: 'pierchon de la Rue' paid 10s. (11th of 18). Ibid. N° 120515 (*escroe*)

1 Apr., Friday, 1496 mod. style, Brussels: 'pierchon de la Rue' paid 10s. (11th of 18). Ibid. N° 120516 (*escroe*)[28]

2 Apr., Saturday, 1496 mod. style, Brussels: 'pierchon de la Rue' paid 10s. (11th of 18). Ibid. N° 120517 (*escroe*)[29]

4 Apr., Monday, Brussels: 'pierchon de la Rue' paid 10s. (11th of 18). Ibid. N° 120519 (*escroe*)

6 Apr., Wednesday, Brussels: 'pierchon de la Rue' paid 10s. (11th of 18). Ibid. N° 120521 (*escroe*)

21 Apr.: lost paylist. Ibid. [N° 120522][30]

nal is very difficult to read at this point, though it does say the 17th. Prizer, 'Music and Ceremonial', 127 n. 39, incorrectly gives this document number for the *escroe* of 9 Apr. 1501 (modern style).

[22] This document number is listed in RubsamenMGG, 226, for *escroe*s from the years 1495–6. In fact, LADN B3453 contains *escroe*s from 1495 only. On no. 120492 there is no separate entry for chapel members; rather, all employees of the archduke's household are listed in descending order of salary. La Rue is seventh from the bottom of column 1.

[23] This *escroe* follows the same format as the preceding; La Rue is twelfth in column 2.

[24] This *escroe* follows the same format as the preceding La Rue is eighth in column 2.

[25] This *escroe* follows the same format as the preceding; La Rue is second in column 2.

[26] The chapel members are now listed together under their own heading, as they will be in all following *escroe*s. They appear towards the end of the *escroe*, as they will on all successive *escroe*s until Feb. 1500 (modern style).

[27] Published in DouillezM, no. 48, and Haggh, 'The Status of the Musician', 162. The year of the document is no longer legible, but context (the specific singers given and their order) and consultation with a perpetual calendar make 1496 the correct year.

[28] The list is published in VDS vii. 178; Haggh, 'The Status of the Musician', 162; and Georges Van Doorslaer, 'Aperçu sur la pratique du chant à Malines au xvᵉ siècle', *Annales de l'Académie royale d'Archéologie de Belgique*, ser. 7, vol. 7 (1930), 479.

[29] This is the correct date of the *escroe* previously thought to be 2 Apr. 1485.

[30] This date was cited by RobijnsP, 235, 240, as forming part of LADN B3454. There is no list currently under that number in Lille, but the document that should be N° 120522 (Robijns does not give that number) is missing, and the handwritten index accompanying LADN B3454 confirms that there was at one time an *escroe* for this date.

30 Apr., Saturday, Tongres: 'pier chon de Rue' paid 10s. (11th of 18). BAGR E&A 13 N° 330 (*escroe*)[31]

20 Oct.: marriage of Philip the Fair and Juana of Castile in Lierre[32]

10 Dec.: authorization of the payment to 'pierchon de la Rue' (17th of 25) for the period between 17 Nov. 1492 and 30 Sept. 1495; paid 10s. per day for total of £315 4s. 6d. LADN B2156 N° 70811 (*mandement*)[33]

1497 (Easter = 26 Mar.)[34]

22 Jan.: probable date of departure of Marguerite for Spain[35]

6 Feb.: death of Ockeghem

[10] Mar.[36] 1497 mod. style, Brussels: {'Pierchon dela rue'} listed among chapelains receiving 12s. per day (10th of 23). BAGR E&A N° 22bis (*olim* BrusBR 19519), fo. 1ᵛ (*État de l'Hôtel* of Philip)

16 Mar., Thursday, 1497 mod. style, Ghent: 'pierchon de la Rue' paid 12s. (9th of 18). LADN B3455[37] N° 120605 (*escroe*)

1 Apr.: 'pierchon dela Rue' listed (10th of 22) with other *chantres* as being owed wages; 'pierchon dela Rue' then paid £163 6s. for the period 1 May 1496–9 Mar. 1497, at 10s. per day through Dec. and 12s. per day thereafter.[38] LADN B2159, fo. 97ᵛ for the chapel list; fo. 98ʳ for the payment (Compte viᵉ de Symon Longin, [1497])[39]

3 Apr.: marriage of Marguerite and Juan in Burgos[40]

8 Apr., Saturday, Audenarde: 'pierchon de la Rue' paid 12s. (11th of 19). LADN B3455 N° 120607 (*escroe*)

---

[31] Published in Haggh, 'The Status of the Musician', 163, after Pinchart's notes; the latter has various errors, including the order of musicians.

[32] Molinet, *Chroniques*, ii. 431.

[33] DoorslaerC, 163, mistakenly gives the number as B2256.

[34] Philip's itinerary for 1497 is given in GachardCV, i. 115–20; it supplies the bracketed place names below.

[35] Bruchet, *L'Itinéraire*, 7.

[36] The surviving document is not the original but an 18th-c. copy, possibly made in England, as suggested by the watermarks 'Pro patria' and 'GR', George Rex. The manuscript gives only Mar. 1497 (modern style) as its date, but the precise date is found in Kortrijk, Public Library, Goethals-Vercruysse Codex 357 (Compte iiiiᵉ de Jehan naturel), fos. 11ᵛ–12ʳ: 'Vendredy xᵉ jour de mars. Lan mil iiiiᶜ iiiiˣˣ xvi Monseigneur larchiduc daustrice duc de bourgogne tout le jour a bruxelles Et cedit jour fit Renouveller les ordonnances de son hostel.' The document is frequently misdated in the literature, often as 1496, which is its o.s. date, but also as 1 Mar. (DoorslaerC, 56) and 14 Mar. (Andreas Walther, *Die burgundischen Zentralbehörden unter Maximilian I. und Karl V.* (Leipzig: Duncker & Humblot, 1909), 166). Similarly, La Rue is sometimes stated as having been engaged by Philip at this time at a salary of 12s. per day (DoorslaerC, 156); in reality he had been working for Philip for quite some time by this date, and his salary was raised to 12s. per day as of the beginning of Jan. 1497, as the document of 1 Apr. 1497 makes clear. The complete *état* was published shortly after it came into possession of the Brussels Bibliothèque royale; see Reiffenberg, 'État de l'hôtel', 677–718. A partial list of the *chapelle* was published in VDS vii. 498; a fuller list appeared in DoorslaerC, 44–5. Reiffenberg, 'État de l'hôtel', 677, mentions two earlier publications as listing members of the court of Philip the Fair (Christophe Butkens, *Supplement aux Trophées tant sacrés que profanes du Duché de Brabant* (The Hague: Chrétien Van Lom, 1726); Sanderus, *Chorographia sacra Brabantiae*), but neither includes the chapel.

[37] RobijnsP, 235 mistakenly gives the document number for all 1497 *escroes* as B3453.

[38] The amount corresponds precisely to the period between the *escroe* of 30 Apr. 1496 and the reordering of Philip's household on 10 Mar. 1497. Other singers received similar raises.

[39] Published in DouillezM, no. 49, where the information from the two sections is amalgamated; also published in Haggh, 'The Status of the Musician', 165, after DouillezM.

[40] Bruchet and Lancien, *L'Itinéraire*, 8. Molinet, *Chroniques*, ii. 437, claims that Juan and Marguerite secretly married first on Easter Monday (27 Mar.) before the official public ceremony.

12 Apr., Wednesday, Ghent: 'pierchon de la Rue' paid 12s. (11th of 19). Ibid. N° 120608 (*escroe*)

13 Apr., Thursday, Ghent: 'pierchon de la Rue' paid 12s. (11th of 19). Ibid N° 120610 (*escroe*)

14 Apr., Friday, to Bruges: 'pierchon de la Rue' paid 12s. (11th of 19). Ibid. N° 120612 (*escroe*)

16 Apr., Sunday, Bruges: 'pierchon de la Rue' paid 12s. (11th of 19). Ibid. N° 120613 (*escroe*)

26 Apr. [Bruges]: 'pierchon de la Rue' paid 12s. (11th of 19). Ibid. N° 120615 (*escroe*)

1 June, Baudeloo: 'pierchon de la Rue' paid 12s. (11th of 20). Ibid. N° 120618 (*escroe*)

2 June, Friday, Baudeloo: 'pierchon de la Rue' paid 12s. (9th of 18). Ibid. N° 120621 (*escroe*)

3 June, Saturday, Tamise: 'pierchon de la Rue' paid 12s. (9th of 19). Ibid. N° 120623 (*escroe*)

4 June, Sunday, slept at Antwerp: 'pierchon de la Rue' paid 12s. (9th of 19). Ibid. N° 120624 (*escroe*)

5 June, Antwerp: 'pierchon de la Rue' paid 12s. (10th of 19). Ibid. N° 120626 (*escroe*)

10 June, slept at Breda: 'pierchon de la Rue' paid 12s. (10th of 19). Ibid. N° 120628 (*escroe*)

11 June, Sunday, [Oosterhout, 1497][41]: 'pierchon de la Rue' paid 12s. (10th of 19). LADN B3458 N° 120972 (*escroe*)

12 June, Dordrecht: 'pierchon' paid 12s. (10th of 19). LADN B3455 N° 120629 (*escroe*)

19 June, Monday, The Hague: 'pierchon de la Rue' paid 12s. (9th of 18). Ibid. N° 120631 (*escroe*)

22 June, Thursday, hunting in Tellinghe: 'pierchon' paid 12s. (7th of 15). Ibid. N° 120633 (*escroe*)

24 June, Saturday [Harlem]: 'pierchon' paid 12s. (7th of 15). Ibid. N° 120635 (*escroe*)

6 July, Thursday, The Hague: 'pierechon de Rue' paid 12s. (9th of 18). BAGR: E&A 13 N° 331 (*escroe*)

14 July, Friday, The Hague: 'pierechon de Rue' paid 12s. (10th of 19). LADN B3455 N° 120637 (*escroe*)

25 July, Tuesday, Bergen op Zoom: 'pierechon de Rue' paid 12s. (10th of 19). Ibid. N°120638 (*escroe*)

7 Sept., Thursday, Brussels: 'pierechon de Rue' paid 12s. (11th of 21). BAGR E&A 13 N° 332 (*escroe*)

4 Oct.: Juan dies in Salamanca[42]

12 Nov., Sunday, Brussels: 'Pierchon de Rue' paid 12s. (11th of 21). BNF n.a.f. 5904, N° 138/70

1498 (Easter = 15 Apr.)

16 Jan., Tuesday, 1498 mod. style, Brussels: 'pierchon de Rue' paid 12s. (11th of 19). LADN B3456 N° 120689 (*escroe*)[43]

11 Feb., Sunday, 1498 mod. style, Brussels: 'pierchon de Rue' paid 12s. (12th on the list).[44] Ibid. N° 120695 (*escroe*)

26 Feb.,[45] Monday, 1498 mod. style, Brussels: 'pierchon de Rue' paid 12s. (11th of 20). Ibid. N° 120696 (*escroe*)

23 Mar., Friday, 1498 mod. style, Bruges: 'pierchon de Rue' paid 12s. (11th of 20). Ibid. N° 120700 (*escroe*)

26 Mar., Monday, 1498 mod. style, Bruges: 'pierchon de Rue' paid 12s. (11th of 20). Ibid. N° 120702 (*escroe*)

1 Apr., Sunday, 1498 mod. style, Bruges: 'pierchon de Rue' paid 12s. (11th of 20). Ibid. N° 120705 (*escroe*)

[41] The year on the document is indecipherable, but of the years on which 11 June was a Sunday, only 1497 would have had the particular group of singers on the list in the specific order in which they appear. The chapel is still towards the end of the list.

[42] Bruchet and Lancien, *L'Itinéraire*, 8.

[43] Published in DouillezM, no. 51, and Haggh, 'The Status of the Musician', 165, after DouillezM.

[44] Only an incomplete list survives; there are at least twenty people on it.

[45] RobijnsP, 235, 240, incorrectly gives the date as 16 Feb.

3 Apr., Tuesday, 1498 mod. style, Bruges: 'pierchon de Rue' paid 12s. (11th of 20). Ibid. N°
120706 (*escroe*)

5 Apr., Thursday, 1498 mod. style, Ardembourg: 'pierchon de Rue' paid 12s. (11th of 20). Ibid.
N° 120708 (*escroe*)

6 Apr., Friday, 1498 mod. style, Damp and Bruges: 'pierchon de Rue' paid 12s. (11th of 20).
Ibid. N° 120709 (*escroe*)

11 Apr., Wednesday, 1498 mod. style, Bruges: 'pierchon de Rue' paid 12s. (11th of 20). Ibid. N°
120711 (*escroe*)

12 May, Saturday, Bruges: 'pierchon de Rue' paid 12s. (11th of 21). Ibid. N° 120712 (*escroe*)

13 May, Sunday, Bruges: 'pierchon de Rue' paid 12s. (11th of 21). Ibid. N° 120713 (*escroe*)

4 June, Monday, Brussels: 'pierchon de Rue' paid 12s. (11th of 21). Ibid. N° 120717 (*escroe*)

10 June, Sunday, Brussels: 'pierchon de Rue' paid 12s. (11th of 21). Ibid. N° 120722 (*escroe*)

3 July, Tuesday, Brussels: 'pierchon de Rue' paid 12s. (10th of 19). Ibid. N° 120723 (*escroe*)

6 July, Friday, Brussels: 'pierechon de Rue' paid 12s. (10th of 20). Ibid. N° 120724 (*escroe*)

2 Aug., Thursday, Brussels: 'pierchon de Rue' paid 12s. (10th of 19). Ibid. N° 120725 (*escroe*)

21 Aug., Tuesday, Brussels: 'pierchon de Rue' paid 12s. (10th of 19). Ibid. N° 120728 (*escroe*)

28 Aug.,[46] Tuesday, hunting at Moerbeke: 'pierchon de Rue' paid 12s. (10th of 19). BAGR
E&A 13 N° 333 (*escroe*)

15 Sept., Saturday, Brussels: 'pierchon de Rue' paid 12s. (10th of 19). LADN B3456 N° 120732
(*escroe*)

17 Sept., Monday, Brussels: 'pierchon de Rue' paid 12s. (10th of 19). Ibid. N° 120734 (*escroe*)

between 18 Sept. 1498 and 29 Jan.1500: 'pierchon de Rue' paid 12s. (10th of 19). LADN B3458
N° 120966 (*escroe*)[47]

4 Dec., Tuesday, Brussels: 'pierchon de Rue' paid 12s. (10th of 19). LADN B3456 N° 120736
(*escroe*)

5 Dec., Wednesday, Brussels: 'pierchon de Rue' paid 12s. (10th of 19). Ibid. N° 120737 (*escroe*)

10 Dec., Monday, Brussels: 'pierchon de Rue' paid 12s. (10th of 19). Ibid. N° 120740 (*escroe*)

1499 (Easter = 31 Mar.)

12 Jan.,[48] Saturday, 1499 mod. style, Burnoult?: 'pierchon de Rue' paid 12s. (10th of 19). LADN
B3457 N° 120750 (*escroe*)

17 Jan., Thursday, 1499 mod. style, 's-Hertogenbosch: 'pierchon de Rue' paid 12s. (10th of 19).
Ibid. N° 120752 (*escroe*)

20 Jan., Sunday, 1499 mod. style, Grave: 'pierchon de Rue' paid 12s. (9th of 18). Ibid. N° 120753
(*escroe*)

21 Jan., Monday, 1499 mod. style, Grave: 'pierchon de Rue' paid 12s. (9th of 18). Ibid N° 120755
(*escroe*)

25 Jan., Friday, 1499 mod. style, Grave: 'pierchon de Rue' paid 12s. (10th of 19). Ibid. N° 120756
(*escroe*)

8 Feb., Friday, 1499 mod. style, Brussels: 'pierchon de Rue' paid 12s. (10th of 19). Ibid. N°
120758 (*escroe*)

1 Mar. 1499 mod. style, Antwerp: escroe[49]

[46] RobijnsP, 235, 239, incorrectly gives the date as 28 Apr.

[47] This *escroe* lacks all introductory material, including the date. The specific singers on the list and their
order give us the general time period during which it must have been drawn up. The *escroe* is quite possibly
before 8 Feb. 1499, when the spelling of the *premier chapelain*'s first name switches to Nicole.

[48] RobijnsP, 236, 241, mistakenly gives the date as 7 Jan.

[49] Cited by Louis-Prosper Gachard, 'Notice sur quelques collections d'états de la maison des princes, et
spécialement sur celle qui est conservée aux Archives du Royaume', *Compte rendu des séances de la Commis-*

3 Mar., Sunday, 1499 mod. style, Antwerp: 'pierchon de Rue' paid 12s. (11th of 19). LADN B3457 N° 120761 (*escroe*)

7 Mar., Thursday, 1499 mod. style, Mechelen: 'Pierchon de Rue' paid 12s. (11th of 19). Ibid. N° 120763 (*escroe*)

10 Mar., Sunday, 1499 mod. style, Brussels: 'pierechon de Rue' paid 12s. (11th of 19). Ibid. N° 120765 (*escroe*)

31 Mar., Sunday, Brussels: 'Pierchon de Rue' paid 12s. (10th of 19). Ibid. N° 120769 (*escroe*)

5 Apr., Friday, Brussels: 'pierchon de Rue' paid 12s. (10th of 19). Ibid. N° 120772 (*escroe*)

7 Apr., Sunday, Brussels: 'pierchon de Rue' paid 12s. (10th of 19). Ibid. N° 120773 (*escroe*)

16 Apr., Tuesday, Brussels: 'pierechon de Rue' paid 12s. (12th of 19). Ibid. N° 120775 (*escroe*)

17 Apr., Wednesday, Brussels: 'pierechon de Rue' paid 12s. (12th of 19). Ibid. N° 120777 (*escroe*)

18 Apr., Thursday, Brussels: 'Pierchon de Rue' paid 12s. (10th of 19). Ibid. N° 120779 (*escroe*)

4 May, Saturday, Brussels: 'pierchon de Rue' paid 12s. (13th of 19). Ibid. N° 120781 (*escroe*)

6 May, Monday, Brussels: 'pierechon de Rue' paid 12s. (13th of 19). Ibid. N° 120782 (*escroe*)

10 May, Friday, Sept-Fontaines: 'pierechon de Rue' paid 12s. (10th of 19). Ibid. N° 120786 (*escroe*)

20 May, Monday, Brussels: 'pierechon de Rue' paid 12s. (13th of 19). Ibid. N° 120789 (*escroe*)

21 May, Tuesday, Brussels: 'pierchon de Rue' paid 12s. (12th of 18). Ibid. N° 120791 (*escroe*)

28 May, Tuesday, Brussels: 'pierchon de Rue' paid 12s. (12th of 18). Ibid. N° 120794 (*escroe*)

29 May, Wednesday, Brussels: 'pierchon de Rue' paid 12s. (12th of 18). Ibid. N° 120796 (*escroe*)

30 May, Thursday, Brussels: 'pierchon de rue' paid 12 sols (12th of 18). Ibid. N° 120798 (*escroe*)

1 June, Saturday, Brussels: 'pierchon de Rue' paid 12s. (10th of 19). Ibid. N° 120800 (*escroe*)

29 June, Saturday, Arras: 'pierchon de Rue' paid 12s. (13th of 19). Ibid. N° 120801 (*escroe*)

28 Sept. (probably): Marguerite leaves the Spanish court to return north, arriving in Feb.[50]

1500 (Easter = 19 Apr.)

30 Jan., Thursday, 1500 mod. style,[51] Ghent: 'pierchon de Rue' paid 12s. (11th of 20). LADN B3457 N° 120802 (*escroe*)

1 Feb., 1500 mod. style, Ghent: 'piercon de la Rue' (9th of 25) listed as chapelain at 12s. per day in *état* regulating Philip's household. BAGR E&A 22, fo. 103ᵛ (*état*)[52]

24 Feb.: Charles born in Ghent

29 Feb., Saturday, 1500 mod. style, Ghent: 'pierrechon de Rue' paid 12s. (10th of 26). BAGR E&A 22, fo. 139ʳ[53] (contemporary copy of *escroe*)

13 Apr., Monday, 1500 mod. style, Ghent: 'pierchon de Rue' paid 12s. (10th of 26). BNF n.a.f. 5904 N° 160/72 (*escroe*)

sion Royale d'Histoire ou Recueil de ses Bulletins, 2nd ser., 6 (1854), 435–48 at 447, as being in the possession of M. du Fresne, Conseiller de préfecture in Metz. Lucie Roux, Conservateur en Chef des Archives pour la Région de Lorraine and Directeur des Archives départementales de la Moselle, kindly informs me on behalf of those archives as well as the Archives communales de Metz (letter of 17 Aug. 1990) that the document in question is not in those archives and that furthermore, 'Dufresne était un voleur d'archives célèbre'.

50 Bruchet and Lancien, *L'Itinéraire*, 8–9.

51 RobijnsP, 241 incorrectly gives the date as 30 June 1499.

52 This call number is a miscellaneous collection of documents bound together at a later date. The complete ordinance is found on fos. 102–32; chapel members are listed on fos. 103–4, with the statutes that apply to the *Grande chappelle* on fos. 104–5. Fo. 122ᵛ is where Robijns found the marginal note stating that the trumpeter Jehan de la Rue was dead; see RobijnsP, 239. The chapel is listed at the very beginning of the ordinance (fo. 102 is a modern 'title page'), and henceforth will lead all *escroes* as well. DoorslaerC, 45–7, publishes both the list of chapel members and the statutes, as does DouillezM, no. 54. RobijnsP, 239, publishes a portion of the document, and Haggh, 'The Status of the Musician', 166, publishes the chapel list.

53 Not fo. 134 as RobijnsP, 236 states, nor fo. 137 as Walther, *Die burgundischen Zentralbehörden*, 137, claims.

8 July, Wednesday, Brussels: 'pierchon de Rue' paid 12s. (12th of 28). BAGR, E&A 13 N° 334 (*escroe*)

11 July, Saturday, Quesnoy: 'pierchon de Rue' paid 12s. (12th of 28). Ibid. N° 335 (*escroe*)

13 July, Monday, Quesnoy: 'pierchon de Rue' paid 12s. (12th of 28). Ibid. N° 336 (*escroe*)[54]

20 July: death of Miguel (b. 1498), son of Juana's older sister Isabella; Juana becomes heiress to Castile

1501 (Easter = 11 Apr.)

8 Feb.: Philip the Fair gives to 'dilecto nostro petri de vico, clerico Tornacensis diocesis musico et capellano nostre capelle domestiqe' the prebend at the collegiate church of Saint-Aubain, Namur, left vacant by the death of Barthelemy Saulchoit. NAE, Archives ecclésiastiques 103, fo. 95ᵛ (Acta Capitularia St. Albani Namurcensis, 1490–1507)

9 Apr., Friday, 1501 mod. style, Bruges: 'pierchon de la Rue' paid 12s. (10th of 28). LADN B3459 N° 121039 (*escroe*)[55]

10 Apr., Saturday, 1501 mod. style, Bruges: 'pierchon de la Rue' paid 12s. (10th of 28). Ibid. N° 121040 (*escroe*)

1 June, Tuesday, Middelburg: 'pierchon de la Rue' paid 12s. (9th of 27). Ibid. N° 121041 (*escroe*)[56]

27 Oct.: Marguerite leaves for Savoy[57]

1–2 Nov.: ordinance giving the entourage and salaries for the trip to Spain; 'Piercon dela Rue' listed at 12s. per day (8th of 21). LADN B3334, fo. 1ᵣ[58]

4 Nov.: the court sets out for Spain[59]

25 Nov. 1501: the court in Paris; La Rue and Agricola 'esbahirent tout Paris'?[60]

2 Dec.: wedding of Marguerite and Philibert of Savoy[61]

1502 (Easter = 27 Mar.)

23 Jan., Sunday, 1502 mod. style, Bayonne: 'pierchon de Rue' paid 12s. (6th of 25). LADN B3460 N° 121225 (*escroe*)

4 Feb., Friday, 1502 mod. style, Vittoria: 'piercon de Rue' paid 12s. (6th of 25). BNF n.a.f. 5904, N° 162/74 (*escroe*)

6 Feb., Sunday, 1502 mod. style, Vittoria: 'pierchon de Rue' paid 12s. (6th of 25). Ibid. N° 163/75 (*escroe*)

20 Feb., Sunday, 1502 mod. style, Burgos: 'pierchon de Rue' paid 12s. (7th of 26). BNF 8255, fo. 62ᵣ (*escroe*)

21 Feb., Monday, 1502 mod. style, Burgos: 'pierchon de Rue' paid 12s. (7th of 26). Ibid., fo. 63ᵣ (*escroe*)

22 Feb., Tuesday, 1502 mod. style, Burgos: 'pierchon de rue' paid 12s. (7th of 26). Ibid., fo. 64ᵣ (*escroe*)

---

[54] Published in Prizer, 'Music and Ceremonial', 126.

[55] Ibid. 127 n. 39 incorrectly gives the document number for this as B2152 N° 70529, which is the number for 2 Oct. 1495, and also incorrectly says it is for 1 Apr. 1501.

[56] Published in VDS vii. 108; DouillezM, no. 56; Haggh, 'The Status of the Musician', 166.

[57] Bruchet and Lancien, *L'Itinéraire*, 11. Molinet, *Chroniques*, ii. 489, gives the date as 22 Oct.

[58] This was started on 1 Nov. and finished the next day (both dates appear in the literature) but changes and additions were made for years thereafter (to at least 25 Sept. 1504). The complete ordinance is published in GachardCV, i. 345–72; portions of it also appear in LIS vii. 229–31. The list of chapel members is given in VDS vii. 151–2 and Haggh, 'The Status of the Musician', 168.

[59] GachardCV, i. 126. ChmelH, 554, says they left on 3 Nov.

[60] GachardCV, i. 131; they remain until 28 Nov. For La Rue and Agricola see Ch. 1 and VDS viii. 8.

[61] Bruchet and Lancien, *L'Itinéraire*, 12.

23 Feb., Wednesday, 1502 mod. style: 'pierchon de Rue' paid 12s. (7th of 26). Ibid., fo. 65ʳ (*escroe*)

19 Mar.,⁶² Saturday, 1502 mod. style, Madrid: 'pierchon de Rue' paid 12s. (6th of 25?). BAGR, E&A 13 N° 336a (*escroe*)

9 May, Monday, Toledo: 'pierchon de Rue' paid 12s. (8th of 27). Ibid. N° 336aa (*escroe*)⁶³

10 May, Tuesday, Toledo: 'pierchon de Rue' paid 12s. (8th of 27). Ibid. N° 336ab (*escroe*)

27 May, Friday, Toledo: 'pierchon de Rue' paid 12s. (8th of 27). LADN B3460 N° 121232 (*escroe*)

28 May, Saturday, Toledo: 'pierchon de Rue' paid 12s. (8th of 27). Ibid. N° 121233 (*escroe*)

6 June, Monday, Toledo: 'pierchon de Rue' paid 12s. (8th of 27). Ibid. N° 121234 (*escroe*)

6 July,⁶⁴ Wednesday, Toledo: 'pierchon de Rue' paid 12s. (8th of 27). Ibid. N° 121238 (*escroe*)

17 July, Sunday, Toledo: 'perchon de Rue' paid 12s. (9th of 27). Ibid. N° 121239 (*escroe*)

20 July, Wednesday, Toledo: 'perchon de Rue' paid 12s. (9th of 27). Ibid. N° 121240 (*escroe*)

30 July, Saturday, Toledo: 'pierchon de Rue' paid 12s. (8th of 27). Ibid. N° 121241 (*escroe*)

4 Aug., Thursday, Toledo: 'pierchon de Rue' paid 12s. (8th of 27). Ibid. N° 121243 (*escroe*)

12 Aug., Friday, Toledo: 'pierchon de Rue' paid 12s. (12th of 27). Ibid. N° 121245⁶⁵ (*escroe*)

31 Aug., Wednesday, Aranjuez: 'pierchon de Rue' paid 12s. (12th of 28). Ibid. N° 121246 (*escroe*)

3 Sept., Saturday, Ocaña: 'pierchon de Rue' paid 12s. (12th on the list).⁶⁶ Ibid. N° 121247 (*escroe*)

4 Sept., Sunday, Ocaña: 'pierchon de Rue' paid 12s.⁶⁷ Ibid. N° 121248 (*escroe*)

5 Sept., Monday, Ocaña: 'pierchon de Rue' paid 12s. (12th of 28). Ibid. N° 121250 (*escroe*)

6 Sept., Tuesday, Ocaña: 'pierchon de Rue' paid 12s. (12th of 29). Ibid. N° 121252 (*escroe*)

7 Sept., Wednesday, Ocaña: 'pierchon de Rue' paid 12s. (12th of 29). Ibid. N° 121253 (*escroe*)

11 Sept., Sunday, Ocaña: 'pierchon de Rue' paid 12s. (12th of 29). Ibid. N° 121255 (*escroe*)

9 Oct.,⁶⁸ Sunday, Guadalajara: 'pierchon de Rue' paid 12s. (11th of 29). Ibid. N° 121258 (*escroe*)

12 Oct., Wednesday, Jadraque: 'pierchon de Rue' paid 12 sols (11th of 29). Ibid. N° 121259 (*escroe*)⁶⁹

26 Oct., Wednesday, Saragossa: 'pierchon de Rue' paid 12s. (11th of 29). Ibid. N° 121261 (*escroe*)

27 Oct., Thursday, Saragossa: 'pierchon de Rue' paid 12s. (11th of 30). BAGR E&A 13 N° 336b (*escroe*)

1 Nov., Tuesday, Saragossa: 'pierchon de Rue' paid 12s. (11th of 28). Ibid. N° 336c (*escroe*)

15 Nov., Tuesday, Madrid: 'pierchon de Rue' paid 12s. (11th of 28). BAGR E&A 33 N° 9 (*escroe*)⁷⁰

17 Nov., Thursday, Madrid: 'pierchon de Rue' paid 12s. (11th of 28). BAGR E&A 13 N° 336d (*escroe*)

20 Nov., Madrid: *escroe*?⁷¹

---

⁶² Incorrectly cited by DoorslaerC as 19 May 1502. This list is extremely difficult to read, but the date on it is 'samedy xixᵉ jour de mars l[an mil cinq cents et] ung'. The portion of the date reading 'mil cinq cents et' is missing, but a perpetual calendar and the year 'ung' that is present leave no doubt as to its correctness. 19 May was a Thursday, not a Saturday, in 1502. The confusion is compounded by Lalaing, who gets his dates off by a week in Mar. 1502 (noted by GachardCV, i. 169). Lalaing would have the court in Segovia on 19 Mar. (ibid.), arriving in Madrid on 25 Mar. (ibid. 171); in reality the court arrived in Madrid on 18 Mar. The Madrid locale for 19 Mar. is confirmed in ChmelH, 635.

⁶³ RobijnsP, 239, incorrectly gives the date as 1500 for this *escroe* as well as for those of 10 May, 27 Oct., 1, 15, and 17 Nov., and 8, 10, 11, 13, and 24 Dec. 1500.

⁶⁴ Misread by RobijnsP, 236, 241, as 7 July 1502.

⁶⁵ Misread ibid. as 7 Aug. 1502.

⁶⁶ The list is almost illegible.

⁶⁷ The list is almost illegible.

⁶⁸ Misread by RobijnsP, 236, as 2 Oct. 1502.

⁶⁹ Published in part in VDS vii. 156–7, and Haggh, 'The Status of the Musician', 168.

⁷⁰ RobijnsP, 239, incorrectly gives the date as 1500 and the document number as 13.

⁷¹ Gachard, 'Notice', 444, says that there is an *escroe* in BAGR from 20 Nov. 1502, drawn up in Madrid. I

8 Dec., Thursday, Alcala: 'pierchon de Rue' paid 12s. (11th of 28). BAGR E&A 13 N° 336e (*escroe*)

10 Dec., Saturday, Madrid: 'pierchon de Rue' paid 12s. (11th of 28). Ibid. N° 336f (*escroe*)

11 Dec., Sunday, Madrid: 'pierchon de Rue' paid 12s. (10th of 27). Ibid. N° 336g (*escroe*)

13 Dec., Tuesday, Madrid: 'pierchon de Rue' paid 12s. (11th of 28). Ibid. N° 336h (*escroe*)

24 Dec., Saturday, Siguenza: 'pierchon de Rue' paid 12s. (11th of 28). Ibid. 13 N° 336i (*escroe*)

1503 (Easter = 16 Apr.)

1 Jan., Sunday, 1503 mod. style, Calatayud: 'Pierchon de Rue' paid 12s. (10th of 27). BNF n.a.f. 5904, N° 164/76 (*escroe*)

16 Jan., Monday, 1503 mod. style, Molins de rey: 'pierchon de Rue' paid 12s. (10th of 26). BAGR E&A 13 N° 336j (*escroe*)

18 Feb., Saturday, 1503 mod. style, Perpignan: 'pierchon de Rue' paid 12s. (11th of 27). Ibid. N° 336k (*escroe*)

20 Feb., Monday, 1503 mod. style, Perpignan: 'pierchon de Rue' paid 12s. (11th of 27). BNF n.a.f. 5904, N° 169/81 (*escroe*)

1 Mar., Wednesday, 1503 mod. style, Narbonne: 'pierchon de Rue' paid 12s. (12th of 27). BAGR E&A 13 N° 336l (*escroe*)

5 Mar., Sunday, 1503 mod. style, Montpellier: 'pierchon de Rue' paid 12s. (12th of 27). BNF n.a.f. 5904, N° 170/82 (*escroe*)

6 Mar., Monday, 1503 mod. style, Montpellier: 'pierchon de Rue' paid 12s. (12th of 27). Ibid. N° 171/83 (*escroe*)

8 Mar., Wednesday, 1503 mod. style, Montpellier: 'pierchon de Rue' paid 12s. (12th of 27). BAGR E&A 13 N° 336m (*escroe*)

22 Mar., Wednesday, 1503 mod. style, Lyons: 'pierchon de Rue' paid 12s. (12th of 27). Ibid. N° 336n (*escroe*)

25 Mar., Saturday, 1503 mod. style, Lyons: 'pierchon de Rue' paid 12s. (12th of 27). Ibid. N° 336o (*escroe*)

11 Apr.: Philip meets his sister Marguerite and her husband Philibert of Savoy at Bourg en Bresse[72]

6 May, Saturday, Pont d'Ain: 'pierchon de Rue' paid 12s. (12th of 26). LADN B3461 N° 121412 (*escroe*)[73]

21 May, Sunday, Pont d'Ain: 'pierchon de Rue' paid 12s. (12th of 25). Ibid. N° 121413 (*escroe*)

3 June, Saturday, Lyons: 'pierchon de Rue' paid 12s. (13th of 27). Ibid. N° 121415 (*escroe*)

13 June, Tuesday, Lyons: 'pierchon de Rue' paid 12s. (12th of 25). Ibid. N° 121418 (*escroe*)

22 July, Saturday, Vauldry: 'pierchon de Rue' paid 12s. (13th of 27). Ibid. N° 121422 (*escroe*)

28 July, Friday, Dole: 'pierchon de Rue' paid 12s. (13th of 27). Ibid. N° 121424 (*escroe*)

19 Aug., Saturday, château de Héricourt: 'pierchon de Rue' paid 12s. (13th of 28). Ibid. N° 121425 (*escroe*)

13 Sept., Wednesday, Hall: 'pierchon de Rue' paid 12s. (13th of 28). Ibid. N° 121432 (*escroe*)

14 Sept., Thursday, Hall: 'pirchon de Rue' paid 12s. (13th of 28). Ibid. N° 121434 (*escroe*)

15 Sept., Friday, Hall to Innsbruck: 'pierchon de Rue' paid 12s. (12th of 26). Ibid. N° 121435 (*escroe*)

was unable to locate this list.

[72] GachardCV, i. 285.

[73] Published in DouillezM, no. 60, and Haggh, 'The Status of the Musician', 170. Gerhard Pietzsch, *Quellen und Forschungen zur Geschichte der Musik am kurpfälzischen Hof zu Heidelberg bis 1622* (Wiesbaden: F. Steiner, 1963), 746, mistakenly claims that this document contains information about the stay of the chapel in Schloss Heidelberg, 20–3 Oct. 1503.

19 Sept., Tuesday, Hall: 'pierchon de Rue' paid 12s. (13th of 28). Ibid. N° 121437 (*escroe*)

28 Sept., Thursday, Innsbruck: 'pierchon de Rue' paid 12s. (13th of 28). Ibid. N° 121439 (*escroe*)

29 Sept., Friday, Innsbruck: 'pierchon de Rue' paid 12s. (13th of 28). Ibid. N° 121440 (*escroe*)

6 Oct., Friday, Nazaret: 'pierchon de Rue' paid 12s. (13th of 28). Ibid. N° 121442 (*escroe*)

21 Oct., Saturday, Heidelberg: 'pierchon de Rue' paid 12s. (13th of 28). Ibid. N° 121444 (*escroe*)[74]

31 Oct.: *Misse Petri de la Rue* published by Petrucci in Venice

4 Dec.: 'petri de vico' takes possession of his prebend at the collegiate church of Saint-Aubain, Namur. NAE, Archives ecclésiastiques 103, fo. 95ᵛ (Acta Capitularia St. Albani Namurcensis, 1490–1507)

1504 (Easter = 7 Apr.)

10 Sept.: Philibert of Savoy dies[75]

31 Oct., Thursday, Ghent: 'pierchon de Rue' paid 12s. (9th of 35). LADN B3461 N° 121449 (*escroe*)

26 Nov.:[76] Isabella of Castile dies; the crown of Castile goes to Juana by order of inheritence and by the Queen's instructions

1505 (Easter = 23 Mar.)

8 Apr.: 'petri de la Rue cantoris principis' invested as canon at the collegiate church of Onze-Lieve-Vrouw, Kortrijk. RK, O.L.V. 5, 1505, p. 4 (Computus Fabricae 1500–1530)[77]

24 May, Saturday, 's-Hertogenbosch: 'pierchon de Rue' paid 12s. (9th of 34). BAGR E&A 13 N° 336q (*escroe*)

3 June, Tuesday: 'pierchon de Rue' paid 12s. (9th of 32). BNF n.a.f. 5904, N° 172/84 (*escroe*)

5 June, Thursday, Cleves?: 'pierchon de Rue' paid 12s. (9th of 32). Ibid. N° 173/85 (*escroe*)

24 June, Nijmegen: 'pierchon de Rue' paid 12s. (9th of 35). BAGR E&A 13 N° 336r (*escroe*)

26 June, Nijmegen: 'pierchon de Rue' paid 12s. (9th of 35). Ibid. N° 336s (*escroe*)

6 July, Sunday, Arnhem: 'pierchon de Rue' paid 12s. (9th of 32). Ibid. N° 336t (*escroe*)

8 July, Tuesday, camp before Arnhem: 'pierchon de Rue' paid 12s. (9th of 32). Ibid. N° 336u (*escroe*)

11 July, Friday, camp by the village of Ree: 'pierchon de Rue' paid 12s. (9th of 30). Ibid. N° 336v (*escroe*)

19 July, Saturday, Brummen: 'pierchon de Rue' paid 12s. (9th of 32). Ibid. N° 336w (*escroe*)

23 July,[78] Wednesday, Brummen: 'pierchon de Rue' paid 12s. (9th of 32). Ibid. N° 336x (*escroe*)

---

[74] Published in Pietzsch, *Quellen und Forschungen*, 746, where he erroneously gives the document number as B121412.

[75] Bruchet and Lancien, *L'Itinéraire*, 16.

[76] Bruchet and Lancien, ibid., give the date as 24 Nov., but the funeral account that appears in BrusBR 7386–7394, fos. 17–25, gives the date of 26 Nov.

[77] Published in CaulletM, 155, no. 165, and RobijnsP, 243 (less complete). CaulletM, 43, cites additional material noted by the earlier canon-archivist de Meulenaere in 'Documenta capituli, II, 38', a presumably handwritten collection of information: 'D. {Petrus de Vico}, capellanus domini ducis, canonicus. D. {Petrus de la Rue}, cantor capelle regis et canonicus fundavit anniversarium pro quo dedit VII lb. p. cum dimidiâ in pane et pecunia distribuenda; item 30. prebendas 30 pauperibus erogandas in toto 15 lb. p. annue; vide Calendarium fo. iii articulo i; vide capsam Y, n. . . et antiquum repertorium ad litt. x nu. iii. Item dedit reditum de 6 lb. p. annue irredimibilem pro salve cothidiserotino, per obitum domini Nicolai Majoul canonici et prepositi; canonicus die 8 aprilis 1505; vide 12 janv. 1518; vide testamentum ejus in n. 13; vide acta 1521, fo. 156', which, among other things, notes La Rue's contributions to two charitable distributions and the daily Salve service. CaulletM, 145 no. 8 (and RobijnsP, 242 but less completely), quotes de Meulenaere's (again, presumably handwritten) 'Notanda ex computibus prebendarum et mense capitularis, 1500–1580' on the luncheon for the new canons: 'Domini prandentes cum novis canonicis domino {Petro de la Rue} et domino Jacobo van Thielt et Carolo de Hallewyn'.

[78] Mistakenly read by DoorslaerC, 57, as 22 July.

24 July, Thursday, Brummen: 'pierchon de Rue' paid 12s. (9th of 32). Ibid. N° 336y (*escroe*)

1 Aug., Friday, Emmerich: 'pierchon de Rue' paid 12s. (9th of 35). Ibid. N° 336z (*escroe*)

18 Sept., Thursday, Brussels: 'pierchon de Rue' paid 12s. (9th of 35). Ibid. N° 336za (*escroe*)

24 Oct., Friday, Brussels: 'pierchon de Rue' paid 12s. (9th of 36). LADN B3462 N° 121495 (*escroe*)[79]

2 Nov., Sunday, Brussels: 'pierchon de Rue' paid 12s. (9th of 37). Ibid. N° 121497 (*escroe*)

3 Nov.: Philip grants Jehan de la Rue, father of 'pierre de la Rue', a daily payment of 4s. for the two years projected for Philip's second trip to Spain; the payments were to be every three months with the first trimester beginning immediately. LADN B2192 N° 74030 (*mandement*)[80]

5 Nov., Wednesday, Brussels: 'pierchon de Rue' paid 12s. (8th of 36). LADN B3462 N° 121499 (*escroe*)

8 Nov., Saturday, Mechelen: 'pierchon de Rue' paid 12s. (9th of 37). Ibid. N° 121502 (*escroe*)

10 Nov., Monday, Mechelen: 'pierchon de Rue' paid 12s. (9th of 37). Ibid. N° 121503 (*escroe*)

17 Nov., Monday, Middelburg: 'pierchon de Rue' paid 12s. (9th of 36). Ibid. N° 121504 (*escroe*)

18 Nov., Tuesday, Vlissingen: 'pierchon de Rue' paid 12s. (9th of 37). Ibid. N° 121505 (*escroe*)

30 Nov., Sunday, Ghent: 'pierchon de Rue' paid 12s. (9th of 38). Ibid. N° 121509 (*escroe*)[81]

27 Dec., Saturday, Middelburg: 'pierchon de la Rue' paid 12s. (4th of 31). Ibid. N° 121512 (*escroe*)

28 Dec., Sunday, Vlissingen: 'pierchon de la Rue' paid 12s. (4th of 31). Ibid. N° 121513 (*escroe*)

31 Dec., Wednesday, Middelburg: 'pierchon de la Rue' paid 12s. (4th of 31). Ibid. N° 121514 (*escroe*)

1506 (Easter = 12 Apr.)

4 Jan., Sunday, 1506 mod. style, Zoobourg: 'pierchon de la Rue' paid 12s. (8th of 36). LADN B3463 N° 121661 (*escroe*)[82]

10 Jan.: the fleet sets sail for Spain; embarkation began on 4 Jan.[83]

12 Jan., Monday, 1506 mod. style, at sea: 'pierchon de la Rue' paid 12s. (8th of 36). LADN B3463 N° 121662 (*escroe*)

15 Jan.: Philip's ship lands at Dover; the court remains as guests of Henry VII during the repair of the vessels[84]

21 Jan., Wednesday, 1506 mod. style, Blancfort in England: 'pierchon de la Rue' paid 12s. (8th of 36). LADN B3463 N° 121664 (*escroe*)

23 [Jan.], Friday, [1506 mod. style],[85] Salisbury in England: 'pierchon de Rue' paid 12s. (8th of 36). LADN B3458 N° 120984 (*escroe*)

1 Feb., Sunday, 1506 mod. style, castle of Windsor: 'pierchon de Rue' paid 12s. (8th of 36). LADN B3463 N° 121669 (*escroe*)

2 Feb., Monday, 1506 mod. style, Windsor: 'pierechon de la Rue' paid 12s. (8th of 36). Ibid. N° 121670 (*escroe*)

---

[79] Published in DouillezM, no. 64; Haggh, 'The Status of the Musician', 170; and LIS viii. 93–4 (CaulletM, 138, mistakenly gives this volume number as III).

[80] This is a copy of the original document, which was itself drawn up on 6 Nov. The document is given, with minor omissions, in VDS vii. 109–11. The citation in LIS iv. 312 merely lists the document as being 'à Pierre De la Rue, chantre de la chapelle domestique, qui doit accompagner le Roi en Espagne'. The copy is made on paper with a watermark similar to that of court partbooks VienNB Mus. 18832.

[81] Published in VDS vii. 161–2, and Haggh, 'The Status of the Musician', 172.

[82] Printed in DouillezM, no. 67, and Haggh, 'The Status of the Musician', 172.

[83] GachardCV, i. 407–10.

[84] Ibid. 502; date incorrectly given as 13 Jan.

[85] Only 'Vendredi xxiiie' is left of the date on this *escroe*, but the format, the locale, the musicians listed, and the order in which they are listed make 23 Jan. 1506 the only feasible date.

15 Feb., Sunday, 1506 mod. style, Richmond: 'pierchon de Rue' paid 12s. (8th of 36). Ibid. N°
121673 (*escroe*)

18 Feb. 1506 mod. style: Jehan de la Rue, father of 'pierre de la Rue', received £18, 8s. from the
court for the period 3 Nov. 1505–2 Feb. 1506 mod. style. LADN B2192 N° 74031
(*mandement*);[86] LADN B2197, fo. 97ʳ (Compte Quinziesme de Simon Longin [1506])[87]

1 Mar., Sunday, 1506 mod. style, Windsor: 'pierchon de Rue' paid 12s. (8th of 36). LADN
B3463 N° 121677 (*escroe*)

5 Mar.,[88] Thursday, 1506 mod. style, Reading: 'pierchon de Rue' paid 12s. (8th of 35). Ibid. N°
121679 (*escroe*)

16 Mar., Monday, 1506 mod. style, with a gentlemen named Romez Palet: 'pierchon de Rue'
paid 12s. (8th of 34). Ibid. N° 121682 (*escroe*)

19 Mar., Thursday, 1506 mod. style, Exeter: 'pierchon de Rue' paid 12s. (8th of 35). Ibid. N°
121684 (*escroe*)

20 Mar., Friday, 1506 mod. style, Kierton: 'pierchon de Rue' paid 12s. (8th of 35). Ibid. N°
121685 (*escroe*)

22 Mar.,[89] Sunday, 1506 mod. style, Lauston: 'pierchon de la Rue' paid 12s. (8th of 35). Ibid. N°
121688 (*escroe*)

27 Mar., Friday, 1506 mod. style, Perinne: 'pierchon de Rue' paid 12s. (8th of 35). Ibid. N°
121690[90] (*escroe*)

1 Apr., Wednesday, 1506 mod. style, Perinne: 'pierchon de Rue' paid 12s. (8th of 35). Ibid. N°
121692 (*escroe*)

7 Apr., Tuesday, 1506 mod. style, Perinne in Cornwall: 'pierchon de Rue' paid 12s. (8th of 35).
Ibid. N° 121694 (*escroe*)

15 Apr., Wednesday, Perinne: 'pierchon de Rue' paid 12s. (8th of 35). Ibid. N° 121696 (*escroe*)

17 Apr., Friday, [Perinne][91]: 'pierchon de Rue' paid 12s. (8th of 35). Ibid. N° 121697 (*escroe*)

18 Apr., Saturday, [Perinne]: 'pierchon de Rue' paid 12s. (8th of 35). Ibid. N° 121698 (*escroe*)

21 Apr., Tuesday, [Perinne]: 'pierchon de Rue' paid 12s.[92] Ibid. N° 121699 (*escroe*)

26 Apr.: the fleet arrives in Spain after leaving England on 22 Apr.[93]

8 June, Monday, Orense, in Galicia: 'pierchon de Rue' paid 12s. (7th of 34). LADN B3463 N°
121701 (*escroe*)[94]

10 June, Wednesday, Allaríz in Galicia: 'pierchon de Rue' paid 12s. (8th of 34). Ibid. N° 121702
(*escroe*)

13 June: Jehan de la Rue, father of 'pierre de la Rue', received £17 16s. from the court, the sec-
ond instalment of his 'pension', for the period 3 Feb. 1506 mod. style to 2 May 1506. LADN
B2200 N° 74732 (*quittance*); LADN B2197, fo. 108ʳ⁻ᵛ (Compte Quinziesme de Simon
Longin [1506])[95]

---

86 Given in VDS vii. iii. CaulletM, 42, mistakenly cites the date as 13 Feb.
87 An excerpt appears in DouillezM, no. 65.
88 RobijnsP, 237 incorrectly gives the date as 3 Mar.
89 RobijnsP, 241 incorrectly gives the date as 21 Mar.
90 Printed in Haggh, 'The Status of the Musician', 174, and LIS viii. 100 (not VDS viii. 100, as stated by
DoorslaerC, 57).
91 Not all of the year is legible, only 'lan mil cinq cens', but 1506 was the only year that had this combination of chapel personnel. The locations on this and the next two *escroe*s are all very difficult, if not impossible,
to read, but the court was at Perinne 26 Mar.–22 Apr.; see GachardCV, i. 431.
92 The list is almost illegible and it is impossible to tell how many people are on it.
93 GachardCV, i. 431–2.
94 Printed in VDS vii. 163–4; GachardCV, i. 524–33; and Haggh, 'The Status of the Musician', 174.
95 Printed in part in DouillezM, no. 65.

22 July, Wednesday, Valladolid: 'pierchon de Rue' paid 12s. (8th of 34). LADN B3463 N° 121703 (*escroe*)[96]

16 Aug., [Sunday], Tudéla de Duéro: 'pierchon de Rue'[97] paid 12s. (7th of 34). VOS, HHuS, OMeA, SR 181, No 2 (*escroe*)

25 Sept.: Philip the Fair dies[98]

11 Oct., Burgos: {Pierchon de la Rue, cantor}[99] paid 11,125 mrs. (3rd of 18). AGS, Casa real, leg° 1°, fos. 420 and 421 (pay list)

11 Oct.: 'pierchon de la rrue cantor' paid in advance 11,125 mrs. for 25 Sept.–25 Dec. (3rd of 20).[100] AGS, CySR, leg° 14, fo. 1/24 (pay list)

11 Oct., Burgos: 'pierchon' included on receipt list for wages (3rd of 20); signs name 'Ita est de *la* rue' (2nd of 20). AGS, CySR, leg° 14, fo. 1/25 (receipt)

29 Oct.: Marguerite leaves Savoy to return to the Low Countries[101]

19 Dec., Burgos: 'pierchon dela Rue primo Capellan' paid in advance 22,625 mrs. for 25 Dec. 1506–25 Mar. 1507 mod. style (1st of 19). 'pierchon dela Rua primer Capellan' to sign for the money; signs name 'Ita est P de *la* rue'. AGS, CySR, leg° 14, fo. 1/21 (pay list); fo. 21ᵛ (receipt and signature)

undated: {Dominus Petrus de la Rue} declared absent from the chapter of Onze-Lieve-Vrouw, Kortrijk, for the year 1506;[102] income of {diaconalis domini Petri de la Rue} goes to the chapter treasury[103]

1507 (Easter = 4 Apr.)

18 Mar. 1507 mod. style: Marguerite designated as regent for Charles, as well as governor for Charles and his sisters[104]

24 Mar.: 'piarchon delarrue' paid in advance 22,500 mrs. for 25 Mar.–25 June (1st of 20); also mentioned as 'maestre pier . . . primer capellan'. AGS, CySR, leg° 14, fo. 1/66 (pay list); fo. 66ᵛ (citation as *primer capellan*)

19 Apr., Madrid: 'P de *la* rue' signs receipt for wages (1st of 17). AGS, CySR, leg°14, fo. 1/[67]? (receipt)

[96] Printed in VDS vii. 164–5; DoorslaerC, 53–4; and Haggh, 'The Status of the Musician', 176.

[97] The list also includes 'alexandre agricola', thus showing he did not die on 15 Aug., as claimed in Wegman, 'Agricola, Bordon and Obrecht', 50.

[98] The date of 15 Sept. given in DoorslaerC, 54 is a typographical error but has unfortunately been copied widely in the musicological literature. For 25 Sept. see, among other places, LADN B3463 N° 121704 (the *état journalier* for the day) as well as GachardCV, i. 451.

[99] I have not seen this list, which is printed in VDS vii. 167–8; Haggh, 'The Status of the Musician', 176; and RobijnsP, 242, where he incorrectly cites the date as 1507. The list is not, however, included in Knighton, 'Music and Musicians'. It has many similarities but some striking differences with the next list, drawn up on the same day. Presumably at least some of the court chapel members no longer found on this list returned north and entered the service of Charles directly, but no pay record from the north survives until 1509, after La Rue's return. All following Spanish documents are for Juana's chapel.

[100] This list is very similar to, but nonetheless different from, the preceding document. It has more names in a somewhat different order, and includes de Orto (first on the list) as well as Messire Rogier and Messire Guillaume l'anglois, none of whom is on the preceding list.

[101] Bruchet and Lancien, *L'Itinéraire*, 20.

[102] 'Dominus Petrus de la Rue, absens ad bursam 1506', from CaulletM, 158, no. 221, who cites de Meulenaere, 'Notanda ex computibus', 'Tableau de résidence et d'absence. Reverendi admodum domini decanus et canonici residentes et absentes ab anno Domini 1500 . . . [ad 1609].' It is also given in RobijnsP, 243.

[103] 'Item fructus prebende diaconalis domini Petri de la Rue deducto servitio Iᶜ XXVIII lib. VII sc. . . .', from CaulletM, 146, no. 11, who cites de Meulenaere, 'Notanda ex computibus prebendarum et mense capitularis, 1500–1580'; also given in RobijnsP, 242. The citation is likely to date from spring 1507, close to the end of the fiscal year, which began on 24 June each year.

[104] Prevenier and Blockmans, *The Burgundian Netherlands*, 384.

23 June: 'petrus dela Rue primero Capellan' paid in advance 22,500 mrs. for 25 June–25 Sept. (1st of 18). AGS, CySR, leg° 14, fo. 2/88 (pay list)

23 June: La Rue's brother Jehan becomes a *bourgeois* of the city of Tournai[105]

18–19 July: funeral services for Philip the Fair held in Mechelen[106]

24 Aug.: Magister Johannes de la Rue, venerable father 'viri domini petri de la Rue canonicj huius ecclesie Serenissime regine castelle prothocapellani', appeared before the assembled chapter of Onze-Lieve-Vrouw in Kortrijk with a letter written by Marguerite of Austria, excusing La Rue's absence and long distance; the chapter states that La Rue will receive his income for the year 24 June 1507–8. RK, Onze-Lieve-Vrouwekerk 169, fo. 57ʳ (Acta Capituli 1489–1532)[107]

23 Sept.: 'petrus dela rrue primero capellan' paid in advance 22,500 mrs. for 25 Sept.–25 Dec. (1st of 16). AGS, CySR, leg° 14, fo. 2/97 (pay list)

23 Dec.: 'petrus dela Rue primo capellan' paid 10,000 mrs. to help with expenses (1st of 18). AGS, CySR, leg° 14, fo. 2/162 (record of payment)

23 Dec.: 'petrus dela Rue primo capllan' paid 22,500 mrs. in advance for 25 Dec. 1507–25 Mar. 1508 mod. style (1st of 18). AGS, CySR, leg° 14, fo. 2/113 (pay list)

undated: {Dominus Petrus de la Rue}, absent from the chapter of Onze-Lieve-Vrouw, Kortrijk, is entitled to his income for the year 1507[108]

1508 (Easter = 23 Apr.)[109]

23 Mar.: 'petrus dela Rue primero Capellan' paid 22,500 mrs. in advance for 25 Mar.–25 June (1st of 18). AGS, CySR, leg° 14, fo. 4/315 (pay list)

15 Apr.: 'pierchon dela Rue primero Capellan' provided with silk (1st of 14). AGS, CySR, leg° 14, fo. 4/209 (record of allotment)

4 May: *significamus* of 'magistri Petrj de vico dominis' for 1507 is presented to and accepted by the chapter of Onze-Lieve-Vrouw, Kortrijk, by 'magistrum Fernandum boutins'. RK, Onze-Lieve-Vrouwekerk 169, fo. 60ʳ (Acta Capituli 1489–1532)[110]

5 July: 'petrus dela Rue primero capellan' paid 22,500 mrs. in advance for 25 June–25 Sept. (1st of 14). AGS, CySR, leg° 14, fo. 4/216 (pay list)

19 Aug.: 'Monseigneur pierson' is given 20 ducados for expenses for the return trip to Flanders (1st of 13); 'perizon dela Ria primer capellan' to sign for the money; signs as 'Ita est P de *la* rue'. AGS, CySR, leg° 14, fo. 3/172 (record of payments and receipts)

without precise date: {Dominus Petrus de la Rue}, absent from the chapter of Onze-Lieve-Vrouw, Kortrijk, is not entitled to his income for the year 1508;[111] the revenue of

[105] Hocquet, 'Un musicien tournaisien', 168.

[106] BrusBR 7386–7394, fos. 26 ff. contains a description of these ceremonies and the preparation for them, written by the new court historiographer, Jean Lemaire de Belges; this is published in part in Jean Lemaire de Belges, *Œuvres*, ed. J. Stecher, 4 vols. (Leuven: Lefever, 1882–91), iv. 243–66. The date of 18 Aug. sometimes seen in the literature for this event appears to come from a handwritten entry ('Le 18 aout 1507') added later at the beginning of the description, but the account itself cites the July dates as well as the correct days of the week for them. The account does not list any individual chapel singers.

[107] Published in SG 29, item 29 (date incorrectly given as 23 Aug.).

[108] From CaulletM, 158, no. 221: 'Dominus Petrus de la Rue ... absens capax per privilegium 1507' after de Meulenaere, 'Notanda ex computibus', 'Tableau de résidence et d'absence ... 1500 ... [ad 1609]'; also given in RobijnsP, 243. The citation is likely to date from spring 1508, close to the end of the fiscal year.

[109] Charles's itinerary for the year is given in GachardCV, ii. 5–6.

[110] Published in SG 29, item 30; also in RobijnsP, 242, with slight differences.

[111] From CaulletM, 158, no. 221: 'Dominus Petrus de la Rue ... absens non capax ad cothidianas canonicorum 1508' after de Meulenaere, 'Notanda ex computibus', 'Tableau de résidence et d'absence ... 1500 ... [ad 1609]'. The citation is likely to date from spring 1509, close to the end of the fiscal year; see 27 June 1509 below. RobijnsP, 243, incorrectly has La Rue eligible for his income this year.

{diaconalis domini Petri de la Rue} goes to the other canons after deducting 'service charges'.[112] {Domino canonico Petro de la Rue} receives £60 for services discharged to the church[113]

1509 (Easter = 8 Apr.)[114]

7 Apr.: letter from Marguerite to Maximilian asking for a prebend at the collegiate church of Sainte-Pharaïlde in Ghent for '"pierchon dela Rue", formerly singer of the late King my brother . . . as much for the good services that he has done for my said late brother as for me these past 15 or 16 years, and hoping that he will do again';[115] she asks for power to give 'the said pierchon' this prebend.[116] LADN L.M. N° 35294 (letter)

30 May: {Domino Petro De LaRue . . . Dominus Petrus . . . Petrus De Larue} joins collegiate chapter of Sainte-Pharaïlde in Ghent. Ghent, Rijksuniversiteitsbibliotheek, MS 567 (*olim* 61), p. 59 (*Chronicon S. Pharaildis*)[117]

June?: record of a lump-sum payment to 'pierre de la Rue' (2nd of 25) and other chapel members for the month of May 1509 for 'the good services that they have done and do daily in the said chapel . . . singing daily in discant the hours and masses of the day before monseigneur . . .'[118] LADN B2210, fo. 360^{r-v} (Compte troisieme de Jehan micault, 1509)

27 June: chapter of Onze-Lieve-Vrouwekerk, Kortrijk, confirms that 'Magister petrus de la rue' has not sent in his 'privilege' and thus the same 'Petrum' will not receive his income for 1508. RK, Onze-Lieve-Vrouwekerk 169, fo. 67^v (Acta Capituli 1489–1532)[119]

without precise date: {Dominus Petrus de la Rue}, absent from the chapter of Onze-Lieve-Vrouw, Kortrijk, is entitled to his income for the year 1509 through his privilege[120]

1510 (Easter = 31 Mar.)[121]

24 Apr.: significamus of 'domini Petrj del rue' presented to the chapter of Onze-Lieve-Vrouw, Kortrijk, enabling him to receive his revenues for the year St John's Day 1509–1510.

---

[112] From CaulletM, 146, no. 16, under 1508: 'Applicantur cotidianis canonicorum fructus prebende diaconalis domini Petri de la Rue quia non misit privilegium qui deductis XIII lib. pro servitio valent I^c XXV lib. XIX sc. V. d.' after de Meulenaere, 'Notanda ex computibus prebendarum et mense capitularis, 1500–1580'. See also RobijnsP, 243, which is slightly less complete and says the citation is from de Meulemaere's 'Documenta capituli'.

[113] From CaulletM, 146, no. 14, under 1508: 'Domino canonico Petro de la Rue pro servitiis impensis ecclesie LX lib.', after de Meulenaere, 'Notanda ex computibus prebendarum et mense capitularis, 1500–1580'. See also RobijnsP, 243, with a slightly inaccurate reading; he says the citation is from de Meulemaere's 'Documenta capituli'.

[114] Charles's itinerary for the year is given in GachardCV, ii. 6–8.

[115] 'pierchon dela Rue Jadiz chantre de feu le Roy mon frere que dieu absoille tant pour les bon services que passe a XV ou XVI ans il a faiz audit feu mon frere que a moy et esperant que encoires fera'.

[116] 'audit pierchon'. The letter is published in Bruchet and Lancien, *L'Itinéraire*, 337 and RobijnsP, 244. 'Fiat' (done) was written on the back of the letter.

[117] This was copied from earlier documents in 1726 and 1741 by J.-B. de Castillon, then prevost of Saint-Pharaïlde, according to Baron Jules de Saint-Genois, *Catalogue méthodique et raisonné des manuscrits de la Bibliothèque de la ville et de l'université de Gand* (Ghent: C. Annoot-Broeckman, 1849–52).

[118] 'des bons services quilz leur ont faiz et faisoient lors journellement en ladicte chappelle . . . chantant journellement en discant les heures et messes du jour devant mondit seigneur . . .'. VDS vii. 268–9 gives the list of chapel members. The payment, divided equally among chapel members, is the result of a *lettre patent* of 23 Apr.

[119] Published in SG 30, item 32; also in RobijnsP, 242, with a variety of slight differences in the reading.

[120] From CaulletM, 158, no. 221: 'Dominus Petrus de la Rue . . . absens capax per privilegium 1509 ad 1515', after de Meulenaere, 'Notanda ex computibus', 'Tableau de résidence et d'absence . . . 1500 . . . [ad 1609]'. Also in RobijnsP, 243. The citation is likely to date from spring 1510, close to the end of the fiscal year; see 24 Apr. 1510 below.

[121] Charles's itinerary for the year is given in GachardCV, ii. 8–9.

RK, Onze-Lieve-Vrouwekerk 169, fo. 72^r (Acta Capituli 1489–1532)[122]

June: 'pierre de la Rue' gives up his prebend at the collegiate church of Saint-Aubain, Namur. BAGR, Chambre des Comptes, Registre 20404, fo. 9^r (Comte onziesme of Phelippe Haneton; undated but within section for June [1510])[123]

12 June: {Petrus de Vico} resigns his prebend at Saint-Aubain, Namur. NAE, Archives ecclésiastiques 104, fo. 14^r (Acta capitularia, 1507–33)[124]

19 June (13th day before the calends [first] of July): in connection with the resignation of his prebend at the collegiate church of Saint-Aubain, Namur, 'petro di la Rue' (later in document: 'petro de la Rue') of the diocese of Tournai is to be paid 12 cameral ducats per year, half on the feast of St John the Baptist and half at Christmas. This will be paid to him, or to someone he designates in Namur, by Thomas the Abbot of the Monastery of St Peter in Bevino of the Benedictine order in Namur, or by his successor. La Rue's successor to the prebend, Johannes aux Brebis, is to arrange all of this. ASV, Reg. Lat. 1240, fos. 142^r–143^v (papal bull and mandate)[125]

27 Dec., Friday, Mechelen: 'pierre dela Rue' paid 11s. (2nd of 27). LADN B3464 N° 121705 (*escroe*)[126]

without precise date: {Dominus Petrus de la Rue}, absent from the chapter of Onze-Lieve-Vrouw, Kortrijk, is entitled to his income for the year 1510 through his privilege[127]

1511 (Easter = 20 Apr.)[128]

10 Jan., Friday, 1511 mod. style, Mechelen: 'pierre de la Rue' paid 11s. (2nd of 27). LADN B3464 N° 121707 (*escroe*)

4 Feb. (Tuesday), 1511 mod. style, Mechelen: 'pierre de la Rue' paid 11s. (2nd of 28). Ibid. N° 121709 (*escroe*)

9 Feb. (Sunday), 1511 mod. style, Mechelen: 'pierre de la Rue' paid 11s. (2nd of 28). Ibid. N° 121711 (*escroe*)

without precise date: {Dominus Petrus de la Rue}, absent from the chapter of Onze-Lieve-Vrouw, Kortrijk, is entitled to his income for the year 1511 through his privilege[129]

1511–12

'petrus de vico de la Rue cantor principis' pays 30 st. to the Confraternity of Illustre Lieve

---

[122] Printed in SG 30, item 35; RobijnsP, 242, mistakenly gives the folio number as 77.

[123] Given in part in DouillezM, no. 69. Félicien de Menil, *L'École contrapuntique flamande au XVe et XVIe siècle* (Paris: E. Demets, 1905), 148, says incorrectly that he resigned his prebend at Kortrijk in 1510.

[124] Currently missing from the archives; the entry is cited in BrusBR MS II 1200 Carton 9, notes made by Alexandre Pinchart; in this case the information was provided by someone else. The material was described as 'Diplôme de Maximilien et Charles, Bruxelles, 12 juin 1510, donnant à Jehan aux Brebis, le canonicat vacant par la résignation de Petrus de Vico'. Fétis, *Biographie universelle*, 2nd edn., v. 201, incorrectly states that this is found in Pinchart, *Archives*, i, §42.

[125] Brought to my attention and kindly transcribed by Richard Sherr. La Rue's procurator in Rome for this was Wilhelm Enckewort.

[126] Printed in VDS vii. 274–5. DoorslaerC, 156, does not cite this list specifically but says, incorrectly, that La Rue is listed at a salary of 7s. per day in 1510. He does cite this list in Van Doorslaer, 'Gilles Reyngoot', 169, but incorrectly, as 22 Dec.

[127] From CaulletM, 158, no. 221: 'Dominus Petrus de la Rue . . . absens capax per privilegium 1509 ad 1515', after de Meulenaere, 'Notanda ex computibus', 'Tableau de résidence et d'absence . . . 1500 . . . [ad 1609]'; see also RobijnsP, 243. The citation is likely to date from spring 1511, close to the end of the fiscal year.

[128] Charles's itinerary for the year is given in GachardCV, ii. 9–10.

[129] From CaulletM, 158, no. 221: 'Dominus Petrus de la Rue . . . absens capax per privilegium 1509 ad 1515', after de Meulenaere, 'Notanda ex computibus', 'Tableau de résidence et d'absence . . . 1500 . . . [ad 1609]'. See also RobijnsP, 243. The citation is likely to date from spring 1512; see 14 Apr. 1512 below.

Vrouwe, 's-Hertogenbosch for his 'death duty'. 's-HAI, Rekeningen 1507–13, fo. 267^r[130]

1512 (Easter = 11 Apr.)[131]

29 Mar., Monday, 1512 mod. style, Mechelen: 'pierre de la Rue' paid 11s. (2nd of 27). LADN B3465 N° 121761 (*escroe*)

30 Mar., Tuesday, 1512 mod. style, Mechelen: 'pierre de la Rue' paid 11s. (2nd of 27). Ibid. N° 121762 (*escroe*)

3 Apr., Saturday, 1512 mod. style, Mechelen: 'pierre de la Rue' paid 11s. (2nd of 27). Ibid. N° 121764[132] (*escroe*)

4 Apr., Sunday, 1512 mod. style, Mechelen: 'pierre de la Rue' paid 11s. (2nd of 27). Ibid. N° 121766 (*escroe*)

7 Apr., Wednesday, 1512 mod. style, Mechelen: 'pierre de la Rue' paid 11s. (2nd of 28). Ibid. N° 121767 (*escroe*)

13 Apr., Tuesday, Mechelen: 'pierre de la Rue' paid 11s. (2nd of 28). Ibid. N° 121769 (*escroe*)[133]

14 Apr.: *significamus* of 'domini Petrj delarue' accepted for the 1511 income from the prebend at Onze-Lieve-Vrouwekerk, Kortrijk. RK, Onze-Lieve-Vrouwekerk 169, fo. 78^r (Acta Capituli 1489–1532)[134]

15 Apr., Thursday, Mechelen: 'pierre de la Rue' paid 11s. (2nd of 28). LADN B3465 N° 121771 (*escroe*)

16 Apr., Friday, Mechelen: 'pierre de la Rue' paid 11s. (2nd of 28). Ibid. N° 121773 (*escroe*)

17 Apr., Saturday, Mechelen: 'pierre de la Rue' paid 11s. (2nd of 28). Ibid. N° 121775 (*escroe*)

18 Apr., Sunday, Mechelen: 'pierre dela Rue' paid 11s. (2nd of 28). Ibid. N° 121777 (*escroe*)

4 May, Tuesday, Brussels: 'pierre dela Rue' paid 11s. (2nd of 25). Ibid. N° 121783 (*escroe*)

12 May, Wednesday, Brussels: 'pierre dela Rue' paid 11s. (2nd of 23). Ibid. N° 121784 (*escroe*)

15 May, Saturday, Brussels: 'pierre dela Rue' paid 11s. (2nd of 23). Ibid. N° 121785 (*escroe*)

24 July, Saturday, Brussels: 'pierre dela Rue' paid 11s. (2nd of 25). Ibid. N° 121788 (*escroe*)

2 Aug., Monday, Brussels: 'pierre dela Rue' paid 11s. (2nd of 25). Ibid. N° 121789 (*escroe*)

18 Aug., Wednesday, Brussels: 'pierre dela Rue' paid 11s. (2nd of 25). Ibid. N° 121792 (*escroe*)

7 Sept., Tuesday, Mechelen: 'pierre dela Rue' paid 11s. (2nd of 24). Ibid. N° 121794 (*escroe*)

14 Sept., Tuesday, Mechelen: 'pierre dela Rue' paid 11s. (2nd of 25). Ibid. N° 121797 (*escroe*)

5 Oct., Tuesday, Mechelen: 'pierre dela Rue' paid 11s. (2nd of 25). Ibid. N° 121798 (*escroe*)

29 Oct., Friday, Brussels: 'pierre dela Rue' paid 11s. (2nd of 25). Ibid. N° 121801 (*escroe*)

1 Dec., Wednesday, Mechelen: 'pierre dela Rue' paid 11s. (2nd of 26). Ibid. N° 121804 (*escroe*)

without precise date: {Dominus Petrus de la Rue}, absent from the chapter of Onze-Lieve-Vrouw, Kortrijk, is entitled to his income for the year 1512 through his privilege[135]

1513 (Easter = 27 Mar)[136]

31 Jan., Monday, 1513 mod. style, Mechelen: 'pierre de la Rue' paid 11s. (2nd of 26). LADN B3466 N° 121816 (*escroe*)

---

130 Published in Smijers, 'De Illustre Lieve Vrouwe Broederschap . . . 1500 tot Sint Jan 1525', *TVNM*, 14 (1932–4), 74. See also RobijnsP, 238.

131 Charles's itinerary for the year is given in GachardCV, ii. 10–11.

132 This chapel list is the most likely candidate for the one printed in LIS viii. 105, though none of the 1512 lists matches the published one exactly.

133 RobijnsP, 237, 241, mistakenly gives the date as 8 Apr.

134 Published in SG 30, item 41.

135 From CaulletM, 158, no. 221: 'Dominus Petrus de la Rue . . . absens capax per privilegium 1509 ad 1515', after de Meulenaere, 'Notanda ex computibus', 'Tableau de résidence et d'absence . . . 1500 . . . [ad 1609]'; see also RobijnsP, 243. The citation is likely to date from spring 1513; see 26 Apr. 1513 below.

136 Charles's itinerary for the year is given in GachardCV, ii. 11–12.

4 Feb., Friday, 1513 mod. style, Mechelen: 'pierre dela Rue' paid 11s. (2nd of 26). Ibid. N° 121817 (*escroe*)

10 Feb., Thursday, 1513 mod. style, Mechelen: 'pierre dela Rue' paid 11s. (2nd of 26). Ibid. N° 121818 (*escroe*)

18 Feb., Friday, 1513 mod. style, Mechelen: 'pierre de la Rue' paid 11s. (2nd of 26). Ibid. N° 121820 (*escroe*)

23 Feb., Wednesday, 1513 mod. style, Mechelen: 'pierre de la Rue' paid 11s. (2nd of 26). Ibid. N° 121824 (*escroe*)

24 Feb., Thursday, 1513 mod. style, Mechelen: 'pierre dela Rue' paid 11s. (2nd of 26). Ibid. N° 121826 (*escroe*)

25 Feb., Friday, 1513 mod. style, Mechelen: 'pierre dela Rue' paid 11s. (2nd of 26). Ibid. N° 121827 (*escroe*)

26 Apr.: the privilege of 'magistri petrj dela Rue' for his revenues for 1512 from his prebend at Onze-Lieve-Vrouwekerk, Kortrijk, is accepted. RK, Onze-Lieve-Vrouwekerk 169, fo. 85ʳ (Acta Capituli 1489–1532)[137]

30 July: date of letters patent from Charles, by which La Rue is to be paid £32 as reimbursement for the money he paid to take possession of a prebend and canonicate at Onze-Lieve-Vrouw in Dendermonde (given to him by Charles on an unknown date through his position on the benefice rolls); the prebend was then taken away from him by Charles and given instead to Gilles Vanden Bossche, generating this reimbursement[138]

without precise date: {Dominus Petrus de la Rue}, absent from the chapter of Onze-Lieve-Vrouw, Kortrijk, is entitled to his income for the year 1513 through his privilege[139]

1514 (Easter = 16 Apr.)[140]

22 May: the privilege of 'magistri petri dela Rue' for his revenues for 1513 from his prebend at Onze-Lieve-Vrouwekerk, Kortrijk, is accepted. RK, Onze-Lieve-Vrouwekerk 169, fo. 92ʳ (Acta Capituli 1489–1532)[141]

15 July: {Peter vander Straeten} becomes a member of the Confraternity of Our Lady in Antwerp. Antwerp, Kathedraalarchief, Onze-Lieve-Vrouwe-Broederschap, 1 (1513/14), fo. 158[142]

Oct., Brussels: 'Rue' paid 11s. daily (2nd of 28). LADN B3467 N° 121908 (*escroe*)[143]

unknown date: 'pierchon dela Rue' receives £32 promised to him on 30 July 1513 as reimbursement for the loss of his Dendermonde prebend. LADN B2237, fo. 328 (Registre Compte de Jean Micault, 1514)[144]

without precise date: {Dominus Petrus de la Rue}, absent from the chapter of Onze-Lieve-Vrouw, Kortrijk, is entitled to his income for the year 1514 through his privilege[145]

---

[137] Published in SG 31, item 46.

[138] Payment was not actually made until 1514; the record of the payment (LADN B2237, fo. 328) is the source of this information.

[139] From CaulletM, 158, no. 221: 'Dominus Petrus de la Rue ... absens capax per privilegium 1509 ad 1515', after de Meulenaere, 'Notanda ex computibus', 'Tableau de résidence et d'absence ... 1500 ... [ad 1609]'; also given ibid. 147, no. 34 (under 1513), after de Meulenaere, 'Notanda ex computibus prebendarum et mense capitularis, 1500–1580'. See also RobijnsP, 243, who cites de Meulenaere, 'Documenta capituli'. The citation is likely to date from spring 1514; see 22 May 1514 below.

[140] Charles's itinerary for the year is given in GachardCV, ii. 13–14.

[141] Published in SG 31, item 50.

[142] Published in Schreurs, 'Petrus Alamire', 26 n. 38.

[143] This *escroe* is much larger in format than previous ones, and every day in the month is listed, suggesting a new method of recording wages.

[144] Most of document is in VDS vii. 117, and RobijnsP, 243 (after VDS).

[145] From CaulletM, 158, no. 221: 'Dominus Petrus de la Rue ... absens capax per privilegium 1509 ad 1515',

1515 (Easter = 8 Apr.)[146]

5 Jan.: Charles attains his majority[147]

4 Aug.: declaration of debts owed to Charles's household for the months of May and June 1515, based on a list drawn up on 30 June;[148] 'Pierre de la Rue' (2nd of 26) is owed £33 11s. (= 11s. per day).[149] LADN B3346, fo. 46r (Compte ixe de pierre boisot, 1515)

25 Oct.:[150] ordinance drawn up by Charles; listing of chapel members includes {Pierre de La Rue dessus} (3rd of 34) at 11s. per day. BAGR, MS divers 796, fo. 64 (*État de la maison de Charles Quint*)[151]

without precise date: {Dominus Petrus de la Rue}, absent from the chapter of Onze-Lieve-Vrouw, Kortrijk, is entitled to his income for the year 1515 through his privilege[152]

1516 (Easter = 23 Mar.)[153]

21 Jan.: 'pierre de la Rue chantre de la chappelle domestique du Roy' receives £33 11s. for his May–June 1515 wages.[154] LADN B2251, fo. 491 (Compte dixiesme de Jehan Micault, 1516)

22–3 Jan.: King Ferdinand of Spain dies in the night[155]

14 Mar.: Charles assumes the title of King of Castile[156]

17 Apr.: *stagium* of 'venerabilis virj dominj petrj de vico huius ecclesie canonicus' presented to the chapter of Onze-Lieve-Vrouwekerk, Kortrijk by Jacobus de Thielt so that La Rue can take up residence on the following 23 June. RK, Onze-Lieve-Vrouwekerk 169, fo. 104^r (Acta Capituli 1489–1532)[157]

2 May: 'venerabilis vir dominus petrus de la Rue' personally presents his privilege to the chapter of Onze-Lieve-Vrouwekerk, Kortrijk, for his 1515 income. RK, Onze-Lieve-Vrouwekerk 169, fo. 104^v (Acta Capituli 1489–1532)[158]

16 June: 'petrus de la Rue' draws up his last will and testament in Kortrijk.[159] RK, Onze-Lieve-Vrouwekerk, Testamenten O.L.Vrouw, no. 36

18 June: Jacob de la Rue, successor to {Domini Petri De La Rue}, takes over the prebend at Sainte-Pharaïlde, Ghent. Ghent, Rijksuniversiteitsbibliothek MS 567 (*olim* 61), p. 66[160]

after de Meulenaere, 'Notanda ex computibus', 'Tableau de résidence et d'absence … 1500 … [ad 1609]'; also given ibid. 147, no. 39 (under 1514): 'Domini canonici Johannes Carondelet, Petrus de la Rue … absentes capaces per privilegium', citing de Meulenaere, 'Notanda ex computibus prebendarum et mense capitularis, 1500–1580'. RobijnsP, 243 has a shorter version said to be from de Meulenaere's 'Documenta capituli'. The citation is likely to date from spring 1515.

146 Charles's itinerary for the year is given in GachardCV, ii. 14–17.
147 GachardCV, ii. 55.
148 Not 2 June, as RobijnsP, 25, says.
149 La Rue did not receive this money until Jan. 1516.
150 The date of the ordinance is wrongly given as 15 Oct. in VDS vii. 277, and 27 Oct. in RobijnsP, 237, 240.
151 The ordinance is given on fos. 63^r–103^v; this is a later 16th-c. copy of the original, as the script, spelling, and omissions make clear. A 17th-c. copy is found in BAGR E&A 23, item 2, and was published in GachardCV, ii. 491–501 (the chapel statutes appear on 495–6), as well as VDS vii. 278–81, and Schmidt-Görg, *Nicolas Gombert*, 337–8. Neither version is complete; the 17th-c. copy omits the list of chapel members, for example. At the same time, 17th-c. copy provides the full statutes governing the chapel, whereas the 16th-c. copy makes several omissions in this section.
152 From CaulletM, 158, no. 221: 'Dominus Petrus de la Rue … absens capax per privilegium 1509 ad 1515', after de Meulenaere, 'Notanda ex computibus', 'Tableau de résidence et d'absence … 1500 … [ad 1609]'; see also RobijnsP, 243. The citation is likely to date from spring 1516; see 2 May 1516.
153 Charles's itinerary for the year is given in GachardCV, ii. 17–19.
154 See 4 Aug. 1515. Although dated Jan., the payment was recorded among the entries for Apr.
155 GachardCV, ii. 56.   156 Ibid.17.   157 Published in SG 32, item 59.
158 Published ibid., item 61; most of it also published in RobijnsP, 242.
159 The testament is published in CaulletM, 46–9; portions of its execution are ibid. 49–52.
160 This manuscript was copied from earlier documents in 1726 and 1741 by J.-B. de Castillon, then

23 June: official residence in Kortrijk begins

2 Aug.: 'dominis petrus de la Rue huius ecclesie canonicus' completes 40 days' residence for the year '1515' at Onze-Lieve-Vrouwekerk, Kortrijk. RK, Onze-Lieve-Vrouwekerk 169, fo. 107ʳ (Acta Capituli 1489–1532)[161]

without precise date: {Dominus Petrus de la Rue}, resident at chapter of Onze-Lieve-Vrouw, Kortrijk, for the year 1516[162]

1517 (Easter = 12 Apr.)

23 June: 'petrus de la Rue' present at general chapter meeting of Onze-Lieve-Vrouwekerk, Kortrijk. RK, Onze-Lieve Vrouwekerk 169, fo. 111ʳ (Acta Capituli 1489–1532)[163]

without precise date: {Dominus Petrus de la Rue}, resident at chapter of Onze-Lieve-Vrouw, Kortrijk, for the year 1517[164]

1518

without precise date: {Dominus Petrus de la Rue}, resident at chapter of Onze-Lieve-Vrouw, Kortrijk, for the year 1518[165]

20 Nov.: La Rue dies in Kortrijk; the date given in the account of the execution of the will 'domini petri de la Rue diaconi . . . defuncti XXᵃ die mensis Novembris anno domini Millesimo quingentesimo decimo octavo'[166] and on the epitaph of his tombstone '{Petrus de Vico} . . . Obiit anno Domini 1518, xx die novembris'.[167] A slightly different date is suggested by the reckoning of accounts for the year at Onze-Lieve-Vrouwekerk, Kortrijk: '{dominus canonicus Petrus de la Rue} non vixit nisi quatuor mensibus et XXV diebus'[168]

[after 20 Nov.]: £3 paid for the diaconal garment of 'magistri Petri de la Rue'[169] at Onze-Lieve-Vrouwekerk, Kortrijk. RK, O.L.V. 5 (Computus Fabricae 1500–30), 1518, p. 4

1519

4 Feb.: final calculation of La Rue's will in Kortrijk. RK, Onze-Lieve-Vrouwekerk, Testamenten O.L.Vrouw, no. 36[170]

without specific date: Johannes Hanneton is the successor to {domino Petro de la Rue} at Onze-Lieve-Vrouwekerk, Kortrijk, but Hanneton's first year's income goes to the estate of {magistri Petri de la Rue}[171]

prevost of St. Pharaïlde, according to Baron de Saint-Genois, *Catalogue méthodique*.

161 Published in SG, 32, item 63; and also (less completely) in RobijnsP, 242.

162 From CaulletM, 158, no. 221: 'Dominus Petrus de la Rue . . . residens 1516 ad 1518', after de Meulenaere, 'Notanda ex computibus', 'Tableau de résidence et d'absence . . . 1500 . . . [ad 1609]'; see also RobijnsP, 243. The citation is likely to date from spring 1517.

163 See SG 33, item 66.

164 From CaulletM, 158, no. 221: 'Dominus Petrus de la Rue . . . residens 1516 ad 1518', after de Meulenaere, 'Notanda ex computibus', 'Tableau de résidence et d'absence . . . 1500 . . . [ad 1609]'; see also RobijnsP, 243. The citation is likely to date from spring 1518.

165 From CaulletM, 158, no. 221: 'Dominus Petrus de la Rue . . . residens 1516 ad 1518', after de Meulenaere, 'Notanda ex computibus', 'Tableau de résidence et d'absence . . . 1500 . . . [ad 1609]'; see also RobijnsP, 243.

166 Published in part in CaulletM, 49, 'quondam domini Petri de la Rue diaconi dum viveret antedicte ecclesie etiam canonici in ea defuncti XXᵃ die mensis novembris anno domini millesimo quingentesimo decimo octavo'.

167 See the discussion of the epitaph and its sources in Ch. 1.

168 Cited by CaulletM, 147, no. 52, after de Meulenaere, 'Notanda ex computibus prebendarum et mense capitularis, 1500–1580'. See the discussion in Ch. 1.

169 'Item pro Indumento diaconali magistri Petri de la Rue, iii L'; see also CaulletM, 155, no. 175, 'Pro indumento diaconali domini Petri de la Rue canonici diaconi', from de Meulenaere, 'Notanda ex computibus fabrice de anno 1500 [ad 1600]'.

170 Published in part in CaulletM, 49–52.

171 From CaulletM, 158, no. 221: 'domino Petro de la Rue successit dominus Johannes hanneton absens,

1520

10 Oct.: record of donation made to Onze-Lieve-Vrouwekerk, Kortrijk, by 'quondam domini petri dela Rue' via Johannes de Vico; also recorded 27 Mar. 1521. RK, Onze-Lieve-Vrouwekerk 169, fos. 143ʳ (1520) and 148ʳ⁻ᵛ (1521) (Acta Capituli 1489–1532)[172]

1522

3 Jan., mod. style: record of donation for the daily Salve service at Onze-Lieve-Vrouwekerk, Kortrijk by {quondam venerabilis viri magistri Petri dela Rue} via Jacob van Tielt. RK, Kapittelkerk van O.-L.-Vrouw to Kortrijk, Oorkonden, without number[173]

1524

15 Oct.: Onze-Lieve-Vrouwekerk, Kortrijk, given a parchment book of discant, complete and not torn, by Vincentius de Fossatis, chaplain and former *magister cantus*; the gift was originally from {quondam Magistrj petrj dela Rue}. RK, Onze-Lieve-Vrouwekerk 169, fo. 181ʳ (Acta Capituli 1489–1532)[174]

1540

28 July: Johannes Pedis is deprived of the office of *magister cantus* at Onze-Lieve-Vrouwekerk, Kortrijk, because he was negligent in teaching and training the young men and because of his other demerits. He has to bring back each and every songbook belonging to the church from the gift of {magistri petri de la rue} and others. RK, Onze-Lieve-Vrouwekerk 170, fo. 85ʳ (*Acta Capituli* 1532–1564)[175]

29 July: when Petrus Maessins, new *magister cantus* of Onze-Lieve-Vrouwekerk, Kortrijk, gives up the office, he will have to return the 7 songbooks bound in boards; the printed one is the gift of Carolus van Halewyn; the other six are the gift of 'quondam magistri petri de la Rue'. Of these six, one was written on parchment in *maxima forma*; the others are of average shape bound in parchment. RK, Onze-Lieve-Vrouwekerk 170, fo. 85ᵛ (Acta Capituli 1489–1532)[176]

sed fructus hujus anni sunt magistri Petri de la Rue pro primo anno suo post mortem', after de Meulenaere, 'Notanda ex computibus', 'Tableau de résidence et d'absence . . . 1500 . . . [ad 1609]'; see also CaulletM, 147, no. 52, after de Meulenaere, 'Notanda ex computibus prebendarum et mense capitularis, 1500–1580', 'Dominus Johannes Haneton absens sed fructus hujus anni sunt magistri Petri de la Rue pro primo anno suo post mortem'; and RobijnsP, 243.

[172] Cited by SG 33–4, item 75.

[173] Published in J. De Cuyper, 'Een Godsdienstige Stichting van de beroemde komponist Pierre de la Rue in de Kapittelkerk te Kortrijk', *Verslagen en Mededelingen van De Leiegouw: Vereniging voor de Studie van de lokale geschiedenis, taal en folklore in het Kortrijkse*, 13 (1971), 295–7.

[174] Published in SG 35, item 94: 'dominus vincentius de fossatis huius ecclesie capellanus et dudum magister cantus deliberauit in capitulo duos libros discantiales integros non laceratos vnum pergamencum ex dono quondam Magistrj petrj dela Rue / et aliud impressum ex dono quondam Magistri karoli van halewyn huius ecclesie dum viuerent canonicorum'.

[175] Published ibid. 46–7, item 209: 'Eodem die dominj de capitulo euocato coram eis domino Johanne pedis presbytero capellano huius ecclesie priuarunt eum officio magistri cantus eo quod negligens fuit in docendis ac instituendis iuuenibus et propter alia sua demerita / prohibentes eidem exercitium dicti officij magistri cantus iniungentesque quod omnes et singulos libros cantuales spectantes ad ecclesiam ex dono magistri petri de la rue et aliorum reportaret hic in capitulo quod ipse fecit sine mora.'

[176] Published ibid. 47, item 211: 'xxixᵃ die julij anno xvᶜ xlᵒ fuerunt hic in capitulo deliberatj magistro cantus petro maessins ac sue custodie commissi et concrediti septem libri cantuales ligati in asseribus (ex quibus vnus est impressus spectans ad hanc ecclesiam ex dono quondam magistri Caroli van Halewyn et sex alij ex dono quondam magistri petri de la Rue huius ecclesie dum viuerent canonicorum / ex quibus sex libris est vnus conscriptus in pergamine in maxima forma Item adhuc duo alij libri mediocris forme ligati in membrana qui solent deferri ad capellas cum aliquot alijs codicillis conscriptis non compactis / quos vniuersos et singulos libros et codicillos cantuales habebit idem magister cantus reddere quando renunciabit siue cedet officio magistri cantus.'

Dates mistakenly cited

1476: cited by Fétis[177] as year of Philip the Fair's *Etat de l'hôtel*, which comes from 10 Mar. 1497

1477: Ambros[178] claimed, without citation, that the Burgundian court accounts of that year included La Rue as a chapel singer. No evidence supports this claim.

1482–5: Staehelin claimed that the singer variously known as piero delapiazza tenorista/Misser Pietro tenorista/Misser pietro d..... tenorista/Misser Piero tenorista cantore del duomo/Piero de platea tenorista/Misser pietro de pratio tenorista, who worked in Siena Cathedral, was La Rue; van Benthem, Meconi, and D'Accone disagree, largely on the basis of the form of his name[179]

2 Apr. 1485: date given by Pinchart for the *escroe* of 2 Apr. 1496 mod. style[180]

7 Nov. 1495: date given by Robijns[181] for the *escroe* of 27 Nov. 1495

Mar. 1496: date frequently cited for Philip's *Etat de l'hôtel* of 10 Mar. 1497[182]

16 Feb. 1498: date given by Robijns[183] for the *escroe* of 26 Feb. 1498 mod. style

28 Apr. 1498: date given by Robijns[184] for the *escroe* of 28 Aug. 1498

7 Jan. 1499: date given by Robijns[185] for the *escroe* of 12 Jan. 1499 mod. style

30 June 1499: date given by Robijns[186] for the *escroe* of 30 Jan. 1500 mod. style

1 Apr. 1501: date given by Prizer[187] for the *escroe* of 9 Apr. 1501 mod. style

19 May 1502: date given by Van Doorslaer[188] for the *escroe* of 19 Mar. 1502 mod. style

7 July 1502: date given by Robijns for the *escroe* of 6 July 1502[189]

7 Aug. 1502: date given by Robijns[190] for the *escroe* of 12 Aug. 1502

2 Oct. 1502: date given by Robijns[191] for the *escroe* of 9 Oct. 1502

7 June 1503: date of the *escroe* mistakenly considered by Van Doorslaer[192] to include the *grande chapelle*; it is instead an *escroe* for Juana's household

1 June 1504: date of a non-existent *escroe* cited by Robijns[193]

10 Apr. 1505: date of a non-existent *escroe* cited by Robijns[194]

22 July 1505: date given by Van Doorslaer[195] for the *escroe* of 23 July 1505

3 Mar. 1506 mod. style: date given by Robijns[196] for the *escroe* of 5 Mar. 1506 mod. style

21 Mar. 1506 mod. style: date given by Robijns[197] for the *escroe* of 22 Mar. 1506 mod. style

22 June 1506: date of a non-existent *escroe* cited by Robijns[198]

12 July 1506: date of a non-existent *escroe* cited by Robijns[199]

---

[177] Fétis, *Biographie universelle*, 2nd edn., v. 200.

[178] Ambros, *Geschichte der Musik*, iii. 235.

[179] Martin Staehelin, 'Pierre de la Rue in Italien', *Archiv für Musikwissenschaft*, 27 (1970), 128–37; Jaap van Benthem, 'Introduction to Workshop III: Josquin and La Rue', in Willem Elders (ed.), *Proceedings of the International Josquin Symposium, Utrecht 1986* (Utrecht: Vereniging voor Nederlandse Muziekgeschiedenis, 1991), 101–2; Meconi, 'Free from the Crime of Venus', 2676–8; Frank A. D'Accone, *The Civic Muse: Music and Musicians in Siena during the Middle Ages and the Renaissance* (Chicago and London: University of Chicago Press, 1997), 231.

[180] Pinchart, *Archives des arts*, iii. 165; cited by various other writers.   [181] RobijnsP, 235, 240.

[182] e.g. DoorslaerC, 156.   [183] RobijnsP, 235, 240.   [184] Ibid. 235, 239.

[185] Ibid. 236, 241.   [186] Ibid. 241.

[187] Prizer, 'Music and Ceremonial', 127 n. 39, which also incorrectly gives the document number for this as B2152 N° 70529 (the number for 2 Oct. 1495).

[188] DoorslaerC, 56. In his articles 'Nicolas et Jacques Champion, dits Liégeois, chantres au début du XVI° siècle', *Mechlinia*, 8 (1930–1), 4–13, and 'Gilles Reyngoot', he lists numerous dates for *escroes* supposedly containing the chapel, but any date given in those articles that is not included here in App. A is erroneous.

[189] RobijnsP, 236, 241.   [190] Ibid.   [191] Ibid. 236.

[192] DoorslaerC, 57; the document is BAGR E&A 13 N°336p; it was also cited as containing a chapel list in Gachard, 'Notice sur quelques collections', 444.

[193] RobijnsP, 236.   [194] Ibid.   [195] DoorslaerC, 57.   [196] RobijnsP, 237.

[197] Ibid. 241.   [198] Ibid. 237, 241.   [199] Ibid. 237; is this supposed to be 22 July 1506?

1506: Picker[200] mentions a report from the Venetian ambassador to the court that supposedly lists members of the chapel; the report does not do this

28 Mar. 1512: date of a non-existent *escroe* cited by Robijns[201]

1 Apr. 1513: the date is cited by Caullet[202] as having a chapel *escroe*. He has misquoted his source (Vander Straeten),[203] where the *escroe* is dated 1513 o.s., thus 1514 mod. style (but see below)

1 Apr. 1514: Van Doorslaer[204] claims that La Rue is no longer on the chapel pay lists; Vander Straeten[205] prints a list labelled 'Wednesday, 1st day of Apr., the year 1513 before Easter' that does not include La Rue. Since the list was made before Easter, the date given is old style and thus was supposedly for 1 Apr. 1514. But 1 Apr. 1514 was Saturday, not Wednesday, and Easter in 1513 was 27 Mar. in any case. Vander Straeten thus erred in his transcription: the list he was copying was LADN B3470 N° 122139, for 1 Apr. 1517 (which was indeed after La Rue left the chapel), and reads 'Mercredi, premier jour d'avril l'an mil cincq cens et seize avant Pacques'. Easter in 1517 was on 12 Apr. and the first of Apr. was a Wednesday; Vander Straeten misread the *seize* as *treize*.

---

[200] PickerCA, 26. See Eugenio Albèri (ed.), *Relazioni degli ambasciatori veneti al Senato*, 1st ser., 1 (Florence: Tipografia all' insegna di Clio, 1839), 3–30.

[201] RobijnsP, 237.   [202] CaulletM, 53.   [203] VDS vii. 276–7.   [204] DoorslaerC, 156.

[205] VDS vii. 276.

Appendix B
Chronology of Sources

The sources are indicated in approximate chronological order. For works presumed authentic, all sources are given. For those currently considered inauthentic (see App. D), only sources that attribute the piece to La Rue are included;[1] exceptions are the chansons by Robert de la Rue (attributed only to de la Rue), none of which has been included.[2] All sources from the Habsburg-Burgundian scriptorium (here indicated as 'HB scriptorium') are included whether they contain music by La Rue or not, permitting a chronological overview of his position within this complex of manuscripts. Sigla for court manuscripts are given in bold.

Sigla for printed books are principally from RISM; manuscript sigla are primarily from *CC*. 'Brown' references are to Howard Mayer Brown, *Instrumental Music Printed Before 1600: A Bibliography* (Cambridge, Mass., and London: Harvard University Press, 1965). Dates, provenances, and destinations for manuscripts are normally from *CC* unless otherwise indicated; exceptions are those for the Habsburg-Burgundian court manuscripts, where material is from *TA* or my own evaluations of the sources. Information on provenance and destination is somewhat more detailed than usual to provide a greater sense of who knew La Rue's music. All dates are modern style.

Contents listed under sources are presented in alphabetical order. Shortened uniform titles are given for pieces, though alternative names and other information are occasionally provided. Attributions are presented as they appear in the sources, except that the rebus form of La Rue's name uses *la* instead of the note itself.[3] Attributions for the sacred works are taken from LRE unless they differ from what is there, in which case they are based on my own observations. Attributions for secular works are based on my own observations.

The following abbreviations and identification marks are used:

*	unicum
**	only source to attribute the work to La Rue (not including unica)
+	inauthentic work
[ ]	no contemporary attribution to La Rue
S	Superius
A	Altus
T	Tenor
B	Bassus
anon.	anonymous
attr.	attribution

VatC 234 (*c*.1498–1503; HB scriptorium, for courtier Philippe Bouton)
Credo, 6v (De *la* Rue)
Missa Almana (P de *la* rue)

---

[1] For source information on inauthentic secular works, see Meconi, 'Style and Authenticity'. Source information on some inauthentic sacred works can be found in LRE.

[2] See Meconi, 'Style and Authenticity', 100–13, and ead., 'French Print Chansons'.

[3] For those who are curious, LRE distinguishes between void and coloured longs used in the rebus.

BolC Q17 (1498 or later;[4] northern Italy, probably Florence or vicinity)
  Pourquoy non (P. de *la* ruee)

TrentBC 1947/4 (late 15th–early 16th c.; connection with Maximilian's court?)[5]
  Een vrolic wesen+ (anon., but says 'Der alt Discant gehört da Rue'**; setting by Pipelare; S
    not written out)

MilD 3 (*c.*1500; Milan, for cathedral choir, under the direction of Gaffurius)
  Missa sine nomine I+ (index: petricon de la rue; crossed out and replaced by 'de Brumel')

BrusBR 11239 (*c.*1501? N. France? Savoy? ultimately owned by Marguerite)[6]
  Ce n'est pas jeu (de la rue; has only S and T, *prima pars*)
  Il viendra le jour désiré (anon.)
  Pourquoy non (anon.; missing end of A and B)
  Pourquoy tant (attr. page missing; residuum of A and B only)
  Tous les regretz (de *la* rue)
  Vexilla regis/Passio domini (de la rue)**

1501 Harmonice musices odhecaton A (Venice: Petrucci, after 15 May)
  Pourquoy non (Pe. de larue; up a fifth)

1502² Canti B (Venice: Petrucci, 5 February)
  Ce n'est pas jeu (Pe.de.la rue)
  Fors seulement, 4v, II+ (Pe.de.la.rue)**
  Tous les regretz (Pe. de. la rue)

SGallS 461 (no earlier than 1502, *c.*1510–15? Switzerland?)[7]
  Fors seulement, 4v (Pirson)

1503² new edition of 1501 *Harmonice musices odhecaton A* (Venice: Petrucci, 14 January)
  Pourquoy non (Pe. de larue; up a fifth)

1503³ reprint of 1502² *Canti B* (Venice: Petrucci, 4 August)
  Ce n'est pas jeu (Pe.de.la rue)
  Fors seulement, 4v, II+ (Pe.de.la.rue)
  Tous les regretz (Pe. de. la rue)

1503 Misse Petri de la Rue[8] (Venice: Petrucci, 31 October)
  Missa Almana (Pe. dela rue; as *Missa Sexti, ut, fa*)
  Missa de beata virgine (Pe. de la rue)
  Missa L'homme armé I (pe de la rue)
  Missa Nuncqua fue (Pe. de la rue)
  Missa Puer natus est (Pe de la rue)

OxfBA 831 (*c.*1503–8; HB scriptorium; fragment)
  no La Rue

---

  [4] See Meconi, 'The Manuscript Basevi 2439', 171.
  [5] See Strohm, *The Rise of European Music*, 523.
  [6] See the discussion in Ch. 4.
  [7] On the possibility of a later dating see David Fallows, introduction to *The Songbook of Fridolin Sicher around 1515: Sankt Gallen, Stiftsbibliothek Cod. Sang. 461* (Peer: Alamire, 1996), 5–8.
  [8] RISM L718. The collection was listed in the 1566 inventory of Raimund Fugger the Younger (see Kellman, 'Josquin and the Courts of the Netherlands and France', 202), as well as in Conrad Gesner's *Pandectarum sive partitionum universalium* of 1548 (see Lawrence F. Bernstein, 'The Bibliography of Music in Conrad Gesner's Pandectae [1548]', *Acta musicologica*, 45 (1973), 119–63 at 147).

1504² new edition of 1501 *Harmonice musices odhecaton A* (Venice: Petrucci, 25 May)
Pourquoy non (Pe. de larue; up a fifth)

1504³ Canti C (Venice: Petrucci, 10 February)
Mijn hert (De la rue)
Pourquoy tant (anon.)

JenaU 22 (1504–5; HB scriptorium, sent to Frederick the Wise)
Missa Almana (index: de La Rue; no title)
Missa Assumpta est Maria (index: Rue)
Missa Cum iocunditate (index: Rue)
Missa de beata virgine (index: Petrus de *la* Rue)
Missa de Sancto Antonio (index: Petrus de *la* Rue; no title)
Missa L'homme armé I (index: Petrus de *la* Rue; missing Agnus II)
Missa Nuncqua fue (index: Rue)
Missa Puer natus est (index: Rue de *la*)

VienNB 1783 (1504–5; HB scriptorium, originally for Philip the Fair but given to Manuel I of
    Portugal and Marie of Spain)
Missa Almana (Rue)
Missa Assumpta est Maria (Rue)
Missa Cum iocunditate (Rue)
Missa de beata virgine (anon.; no title; with *Salve sancta parens* text)
Missa de Sancto Antonio (Rue; no title; with *O sacer anthoni* text)
Missa L'homme armé I (Rue de *la*, at end of piece)
Missa Puer natus est (P de la Rue)

BrusBR 9126 (1504–5; HB scriptorium for Philip and Juana)
Gaude virgo* (P. de *la* Rue)
Magnificat sexti toni (P. de *la* Rue)
Magnificat octavi toni* (P delarue)
Missa Almana (P. de *la* Rue; no title)
Missa de Sancto Antonio (P. delarue; no title; with *O sacer anthoni* text)
Missa L'homme armé I (Petrus de *la* Rue)
Missa Sub tuum presidium (Rue)
Salve regina VI (P de *la* rue)**

1505² Motetti libro quarto (Venice: Petrucci, 4 June)
Salve regina II (Petrus de la rue)

FlorC 2439 (*c.*1505–8; HB scriptorium, for an unidentified member of the Agostini-Ciardi
    family of Siena)
Autant en emporte le vent (Rue)**
A vous non autre (Rue**; with altered text)
Dedans bouton* (Pierson de la Rue)
De l'oeil de la fille du roy (Rue)**
Fors seulement, 4v (Rue; Perison in index)
Il viendra le jour désiré (Rue)**
Ma bouche rit* (Rue; Perison in index)
Mijn hert (Rue)
Plorer, gemir, crier/Requiem* (Rue)
Pour ce que je suis (Rue**; as *Puisque je suis*)

Pourquoy tant (Rue; Perison in index)**
Sancta Maria virgo (Rue)**
Si dormiero (Rue)**
Tous noble cueurs (Rue)**
Trop plus secret (Rue)

VerBC 756 (*c.*1505–8; HB scriptorium)
Missa de Sancto Antonio (anon.; no title; with *Agnosce O vincenti* text)

VatS 41 (*c.*1505–7 to before Nov. 1512;[9] Rome, for Cappella Sistina)
Missa de beata virgine (P. DE LA RUE in illumination; Perisson de la rue in index)

VatS 23 (*c.*1505–7 to before Nov. 1512;[10] Rome, for Cappella Sistina)
Missa Puer natus est (anon.)

VatS 42 (after 1505–7 and before Nov. 1512;[11] Rome, for Cappella Sistina)
Regina caeli* (Petrus de la rue)

VienNB Mus. 15495 (*c.*1508–10; HB scriptorium, for Maximilian and Bianca Maria Sforza)
no La Rue

BrusBR 228 (*c.*1508–before March 1516; HB scriptorium, for Marguerite of Austria)[12]
[Aprez regretz]* (anon.)
Autant en emporte le vent (anon.)
[Ave sanctissima Maria] (anon.)
A vous non autre (anon.)
[Ce m'est tout ung]* (anon.)
Ce n'est pas jeu (anon.)
[C'est ma fortune]* (anon.)
[Changier ne veulx]* (anon.)
Considera Israel (anon.; only *Doleo super te* given)
[Cueurs desolez/Dies illa]* (anon.)
De l'oeil de la fille du roy (anon.)
[Dueil et ennuy] (anon.)
?[Dulces exuvie] (anon.)
[Helas, fault il]* (anon.)
Il est bien heureux* (anon.)[13]
[Il me fait mal]* (anon.)
[J'ay mis mon cueur]* (anon.)
[Je ne dis mot]* (anon.)
[Je ne scay plus]* (anon.)
[Las, helas, las, seray-je repris?]* (anon.)
[Maria mater gratie/Fors seulement] (anon.)
[Me fauldra il]* (anon.)
Mijn hert (anon.)

---

[9] Date from Richard Sherr, *Papal Music Manuscripts in the Late Fifteenth and Early Sixteenth Centuries* (Renaissance Manuscript Studies, 5; Neuhausen: American Institute of Musicology–Hänssler-Verlag, 1996), 73 and 150.

[10] Dated ibid. 73 and 142.

[11] Dated ibid. 73 and 167.

[12] See Meconi, 'Style and Authenticity', 7–10, for this date.

[13] The attribution to La Rue comes from Pietro Aaron, *Toscanello in musica* (Venice: Bernardino and Matheo de Vitali, 1529), *Aggiunta*, sig. N iii^v.

[Plusieurs regretz]* (anon.)
Pour ce que je suis (anon.)
Pourquoy non (anon.)
Pour ung jamais (anon.) .
[Quant il advient+]* (anon.)
[Quant il survient]* (anon.)
Secretz regretz (anon.)
[Se je souspire/Ecce iterum+]* (anon.)
[Soubz ce tumbel+]* (anon.)
Tous les regretz (anon.)
Tous noble cueurs (anon.)
Trop plus secret (anon.)
Vexilla regis/Passio domini (anon.)

AntP R43.13 (*c.*1508–20; HB scriptorium; fragment)
no La Rue

[1508] 1509[1] *Missarum diversorum autorum liber primus* (Venice: Petrucci, 15 March)
Missa de Sancto Antonio (Piero de la rue)

LonBLH 5242 (*c.*1509–14; France, for Françoise de Foix;[14] possibly commissioned by Charles de Bourbon)
A vous non autre (anon.)

MunBS 53 (*c.*1510; presumably Vienna, for Maximilian's court chapel)
Credo*, 4v (Petro de *la* rue)

FlorC 2442 (*c.*1510–15? France? gift from Bernardus Rinuccini to a member of Strozzi family? missing B book)
Dicte moy bergère+ (P. de *la* Rue)**
Pourquoy non (P. de *la* Rue; up a fifth)
Tous les regretz (P. de *la* Rue)

FrankSU 2 (*c.*1510–20? German format)
Missa Nuncqua fue (missing attribution page; missing S and B of Kyrie I; only S is present for Benedictus; missing Agnus)
Missa O gloriosa domina (missing attribution page; transposed down a fifth; portions of Credo, Sanctus and Agnus only)
Missa Puer natus est (missing attribution page; missing Agnus II and parts of Kyrie)
?[Missa sine nomine II] (missing attribution page; missing part of Kyrie and Credo and all of Sanctus and Agnus)
Missa Sub tuum presidium (missing attribution page; parts of Sanctus and Agnus only)
Missa Tous les regretz [original version with 2 duos for Benedictus] (missing attribution page; missing parts of Kyrie, Credo, Sanctus, and all of Agnus II and III)

WrocU 428 (*c.*1510–30, 1516? possibly Frankfurt an der Oder or vicinity)
Si dormiero (anon.; as *[O] mitis mater Christi*)

BrusBR IV.90 and IV.1274/TourBV 94 (1511; Bruges; S, A, and T books)
Mijn hert (anon.; S and T parts switched; A and T incomplete)

---

[14] Françoise de Foix (1495–1537), a cousin of Anne of Brittany, married Jean de Laval-Montmorency in 1509 and became the official mistress of Francis I in 1515.

VatS 45 (1511–14; Rome, for Cappella Sistina)
  Credo de villagiis (Pe. de La rue/Pe. de la Rue)
  Missa Almana (P. de *la* Rue; as *Missa Pourquoy non*)
  Missa Ave Maria (Pe. de *la* Rue)
  Missa Cum iocunditate (Pe de *la* Rue; text corrections *c.*1576–7)
  Missa Nuncqua fue (Person de la Rue; missing Agnus)

OxfBLL a.8 (1512–before March 1516; HB scriptorium; fragment)
  no La Rue

SGallS 530 (*c.*1512–21; Konstanz, by St Gall organist Fridolin Sicher;[15] keyboard tablature)
  Pourquoy non (anon.; up a fifth)
  Si dormiero (Alexander)
  Trop plus secret (anon.)

BasU F. X. 1–4 (*c.*1512–24; Basel, probably for Bonifacius Amerbach)[16]
  Ach hülff mich leid+ (Pirson)**
  Pourquoy non (Pirson; up a fifth)
  Tantque nostre argent durra+ (pirson)**
  Tous les regretz (pirson alias PE. DE.*la* rue; in T; SAB = Pirson)
  Trop plus secret (S = pe. De *la* rue; ATB = Pirson)

BasU F. IX. 22 (by 1513? Basel and/or Freiburg,[17] for Bonifacious Amerbach; keyboard
    tablature)
  Si dormiero (Isac)

LonBLR 8 G. vii (by October 1513; HB scriptorium, for Henry VIII and Catherine of
    Aragon)
  ?[Absalon fili mi] (anon.)
  Ave regina caelorum (anon.)
  Considera Israel (anon.; only *Doleo super te*)
  ?[Dulces exuvie] (anon.)
  Vexilla regis/Passio domini (anon.)

VatP 1982 (*c.*1513–23; Rome, for Giulio de' Medici[18] or other family member; S book only)
  Cent mille regretz (Pierson de la Rue)**
  Missa Ave Maria (P. De la rue; no title)
  Missa Tous les regretz (Rue; later version; no title)

MunBS F (*c.*1513–25; HB scriptorium, for Henry VIII and Catherine of Aragon but received
    by Wilhelm IV, Duke of Bavaria)
  110 La Rue

MunU 239 (1514–17;[19] Basel, probably by students of Glarean)
  Missa Puer natus est (Petri Platensis; missing Agnus II and part of Sanctus)

---

[15] *St. Galler Orgelbuch: Die Orgeltabulatur des Fridolin Sicher (St. Gallen, Codex 530)*, ed. Hans Joachim Marx and Thomas Warburton (Schweizerische Musikdenkmäler, 8; Winterthur: Amadeus, 1992).
[16] Amerbach (1495–1562) was a Basel lawyer and humanist.
[17] See John Kmetz, *Die Handschriften der Universitätsbibliothek Basel: Katalog der Musikhandschriften des 16. Jahrhunderts* (Basel: Universitätsbibliothek Basel, 1988), 76.
[18] Pope Clement VII from 1523.
[19] Judd, *Reading Renaissance Music Theory*, 158, suggests a slightly later date (the 1520s) as a plausible time of copying.

RegB C 98 (early 16th c.; probably S. Germany or Austria)
  Salve regina II (anon.)
  Salve regina VI (anon.)

AntP M 18.13/3 (early 16th c.; presumably Low Countries; fragment)
  Missa de Sancto Job (attr. page missing; contains only CT and B of Agnus)

1515[1] *Misse Antonii de Fevin* (Venice: Fossombrone, 22 November)
  Missa Sub tuum presidium (Pierzon; as *Missa quarti toni*)

JenaU 7 (between July 1515 and March 1516; HB scriptorium, for Maximilian? but sent to
    Frederick the Wise)
  Missa de Sancta Anna (attr. page missing; bits of Agnus missing)
  Missa de Sancto Job (Petrus de la Rue)
  Missa Inviolata (Petrus de la Rue)
  [O salutaris hostia] (anon.; substituted for Osanna I in *Missa de Sancta Anna*)

VienNB Mus. 15496 (between July 1515 and March 1516; HB scriptorium, for Charles V); all
    La Rue
  Missa Alleluia (Petrus de la Rue)
  Missa Ave Maria (Petrus de la Rue)
  Missa de Sancta Anna (Petrus de *la* Rue**; Tenor = *Felix Anna*)
  Missa de sancta cruce (Petrus de *la* Rue)
  Missa de Sancto Job (Petrus de *la* Rue)
  Missa Inviolata (Petrus de *la* Rue)
  Missa Sub tuum presidium (Petrus de *la* rue)
  [O salutaris hostia] (no special attr. for motet; replaces Osanna I in *Missa de Sancta Anna*)

MontsM 773 (completed by March 1516; HB scriptorium, for Marguerite?); all La Rue
  Missa Alleluia (P. de *la* rue; lacks Sanctus and bits of other movements)
  Missa Ave Maria (attr. section missing; parts of Kyrie and Agnus missing)
  Missa de feria (p. de *la* rue; missing part of each movement)
  Missa de Sancta Anna (attr. page missing; much missing; only Credo is complete)
  Missa de sancta cruce (P. de *la* rue; missing parts of Kyrie)
  Missa de Sancto Job (attr. page missing)
  Missa Inviolata (de *la* Rue; parts of all movements missing)
  Missa O gloriosa domina (Petrus de *la* rue; no title; with *O gloriosa margareta* text; only
    source for 2v Agnus II; missing two small sections of mass)
  Missa O salutaris hostia (rus de *la* rue; attribution mutilated? portions of Gloria and
    Agnus missing; only one part notated)
  [O salutaris hostia] (anon.; replaces Osanna I in *Missa de Sancta Anna*)

JenaU 9 (before March 1516; HB scriptorium, for Henry VIII and Catherine of Aragon, but
    acquired by Frederick the Wise)
  no La Rue

JenaU 2 (before March 1516; HB scriptorium, for Frederick the Wise)
  Missa Ista est speciosa (Petrus de la Rue; as *Missa de Sanctissima Virgine maria*)
  [Missa L'homme armé II] (anon.)

VienNB Mus. 15497 (before March 1516; HB scriptorium, for Ulrich Pfinzing, treasurer at
    Maximilian's court)
  Kyrie in festo pasche*, 4v (Petrus De *la* Rue)

Missa Ista est speciosa (missing attribution page; missing parts of Kyrie)
Missa Tous les regretz [original version with 2 duos for Benedictus] (Petrus de *la* Rue;
    missing Agnus II)

BrusBR 215–16 (before March 1516; HB scriptorium, for Charles Le Clerc)[20]
Missa de septem doloribus (Petrus de *la* Rue)
[Missa de septem doloribus II+]* (anon.)

VatS 160 (between July 1515 and March 1516; HB scriptorium, for Leo X)
Credo de villagiis (Petrus de *la* rue; inserted into Obrecht, *Missa Sicut spina rosam*)

VatS 34 (between July 1515 and March 1516; HB scriptorium, for Leo X); all La Rue but one
Missa Conceptio tua (attr. page missing; missing Kyrie I and part of Christe)
Missa de feria (Pe de *la* rue)
Missa Ista est speciosa (missing attr. page; missing parts of Kyrie)
[Missa L'homme armé II] (anon.; missing parts of Kyrie and Gloria)
Missa pascale (missing attr. page; missing part of Kyrie)

MechAS s.s. (between July 1515 and March 1516; HB scriptorium, for Charles V); all La Rue
    but one
Missa Alleluia (Petrus de *la* Rue)
Missa Ave Maria (anon.)
Missa Conceptio tua (anon.)
Missa de feria (anon.; missing Agnus II; no title)
Missa de sancta cruce (anon.)
Missa pascale (anon.; no title; with *Resurrexi* text)

VatV 11953 (*c.*1515–16; court of Maximilian I;[21] B book only)
Ce n'est pas jeu (anon.)
Mijn hert (anon.; down a fifth)
Missa L'homme armé I (anon.; Sanctus, Osanna, and Agnus III only)
Pourquoy non (P De la Rue; up a fifth)
?[Sailliés avant] (anon.)
Tous les regretz (Rue)
Trop plus secret (P. De la Rue)

MunBS 65 (*c.*1515–16; Munich, for Wilhelm IV, Duke of Bavaria)
Missa Cum iocunditate (Petrus de *la* rue; missing Agnus I)
Missa pro fidelibus defunctis (P de *la* rue; as *Missa pro defunctis*)

TongerenSA 183 (*c.*1515–17; HB scriptorium; presumably used in Tongeren; fragment)
Missa Almana (attribution page missing; fragment of Gloria only)

CasAC M (D) (*c.*1515–18; Casale Monferrato, possibly commissioned by Guglielmo Marchio
    Paleologo, Marquis of Monferrato)
Missa Ave Maria (Pierson de *la* Rue)

MunBS 6 (*c.*1515–26? HB scriptorium, for Wilhelm IV, duke of Bavaria)
no La Rue

UppsU 76b (*c.*1515–35; Troyes or vicinity?)
[O salutaris hostia] (anon.)

[20] Le Clerc, Seigneur de Bouvekercke, was a highly placed administrator for Maximilian, Philip, and
Charles V.
[21] Birkendorf, *Der Codex Pernner*, i. 39, 101–4.

1516[1] *Liber quindecim missarum electarum quae per excellentissimos musicos compositae fuerunt* (Rome: Antico)
  Missa Ave Maria (P. dela Rue)
  Missa O salutaris hostia (P. de la rue; only one part notated)

AntP B 948 IV (*c.*1516; HB scriptorium; presumably used in Antwerp; fragment)[22]
  Missa de beata virgine (attr. page missing; parts of S and T of Credo only)

AntP M 18.13/1 (*c.*1516; HB scriptorium; presumably used in Antwerp; fragment)
  Missa Assumpta est Maria (attr. page missing; portions of Sanctus only)
  Missa Ave Maria (attr. page missing; fragments of each movement)
  Missa Conceptio tua (attr. page missing; portions of Credo, Sanctus, Agnus I)
  Missa Puer natus est (attr. page missing; Gloria plus parts of other movements)

BrugRA Aanw. 756 (*c.*1516? HB scriptorium; presumably used in Wingene; fragment)
  Missa Ave sanctissima Maria (attr. page missing; fragments of Agnus only)

UtreC 47/1 (*c.*1516–17? HB scriptorium; fragment)
  Missa Tous les regretz (attribution page missing; fragments of superius for Christe and Kyrie II)

UtreC 47/2 (*c.*1516–17? HB scriptorium fragment)
  no La Rue (no music at all)

JenaU 4 (after 14 March 1516; HB scriptorium, sent to Frederick the Wise)
  [Kyrie pascale], 5v (anon.)
  Missa Ave sanctissima Maria (no attr.; as *Missa de beata virgine*)
  Missa Conceptio tua (anon.)
  Missa de septem doloribus (Petrus de la Rue)
  Missa Incessament (Pe. Rue)
  Missa Ista est speciosa (Petrus de la Rue; as *Missa quinque vocum*)
  Missa pascale (anon.; no title; with *Resurrexi* text)

JenaU 20 (*c.*1516–18; HB scriptorium, for Frederick the Wise)
  Magnificat primi toni* (Pe. de *la* rue)
  Magnificat secundi toni (Pe. de *la* Rue)
  Magnificat quinti toni (Petrus de *la* Rue)**
  Magnificat sexti toni (Pe. de *la* Rue)
  Magnificat septimi toni (Pe. de *la* Rue)**

VatS 36 (March 1516–*c.*1521; HB scriptorium, for Leo X); all La Rue but one
  Credo, 6v (petrus de la rue)
  Credo L'amour du moy (Petrus de *la* rue)**
  Missa Alleluia (anon.)
  Missa Ave sanctissima Maria (missing attr. page; missing Kyrie and part of Gloria; followed by Te decet laus 'loco deo gracias')
  Missa de septem doloribus (attr. page missing; missing parts of Kyrie)
  Missa de virginibus* (Petrus de *la* rue; with *O quam pulchra* text)
  Missa O gloriosa domina (PETRUS DE LARUE; no title; with *O gloriosa Margaretha* text)
  Missa pro fidelibus defunctis (anon.)
  [Te decet laus+]* (anon.)

---

[22] In *CC* under AntP M 18.13/1.

JenaU 8 (March 1516–c. 1521; HB scriptorium, for Frederick the Wise)
    Credo L'amour du moy (anon.)
    Missa Incessament (petrus de *la* Rue)

MunBS 7 (March 1516–c. 1521; HB scriptorium, owned by Wilhelm IV, Duke of Bavaria)
    no La Rue

BrusSG 9423 (c.1516–21; HB scriptorium; presumably used at Sint Goedele, Brussels;
    fragment)
    Credo, 6v (Petrus de la Rue; fragments only)

BrusSG 9424 (c.1516–21; HB scriptorium; presumably used at Sint Goedele, Brussels;
    fragment)
    [Ave sanctissima Maria] (anon.; fragments of S2 and B2)
    Credo de villagiis (anon.; fragments only)

GhentR D 3360b (c.1516–21; HB scriptorium; Ghent use? fragment)[23]
    Missa Ave sanctissima Maria (de la Rue; fragments of Kyrie only)

FlorBN II.I.232 (c.1516–21; Florence)
    Considera Israel (P.DELERVE)
    Quis dabit pacem* (P. DELARVE/P de la Rue)

JenaU 5 (c.1516–25; HB scriptorium, for Frederick the Wise); all La Rue but one
    Missa Ave sanctissima Maria (no attr.; missing portions of Agnus)
    Missa Conceptio tua (attr. page missing; missing Kyrie I and parts of Christe)
    Missa de feria (Petrus de la rue; as *Missa quinque vocum*)
    Missa O gloriosa domina (Petrus de la Rue; as *Missa quatuor vocum*)
    Missa pascale (Petrus de la Rue; as *Missa quinque vocum*)

CambraiBM 18 (probably after 1517; Cambrai, for cathedral choir)
    Missa Ave Maria (anon.)
    Missa de Sancto Antonio (anon.; as *Missa O sacer anthoni*)

RegB C120, first part (c.1518–19; court of Maximilian, Innsbruck?)[24]
    ?Il fault morir* (Pirson)
    Pour ung jamais (anon.; as *fraw margretsen lied*; has *si placet* voice)

JenaU 12 (c.1518–20; HB scriptorium, for Frederick the Wise); all La Rue?
    Missa Alleluia (Petrus de la Rue)
    Missa Ave Maria (attr. page missing)
    Missa de sancta cruce (attr. page missing; missing parts of Kyrie and Credo)
    Missa pro fidelibus defunctis (Pe de la Rue)
    Missa sine nomine I* (Petrus de la Rue; no title)
    ?[Missa sine nomine II] (anon.; no title)
    Missa Sub tuum presidium (Petrus de la Rue)
    Missa Tous les regretz [original version with 3v Benedictus] (Petrus de la Rue)

JenaU 3 (c.1518–20; HB scriptorium, for Frederick the Wise)
    no La Rue

VatG XII.2 (c.1518–21; Rome, for Cappella Giulia)
    Missa Incessament (anon.; Osanna and Agnus II only)

---

[23] The fragments were used in a rent register of the Cistercian nuns from the Ghent abbey Ter Haeghen.
[24] Birkendorf, *Der Codex Pernner*, i. 27.

VatP 1980–1 (*c*.1518–23; Rome, probably for Giulio de' Medici, future Pope Clement VII; T and B books only)
Incessament (anon.)
Missa Ave Maria (anon.; without title)
Missa Incessament (*la rue*)

WolfA A (1519–20; Munich, for Wilhelm IV, Duke of Bavaria)
Missa Incessament (Petrus De Larue; missing Agnus I)
Missa pro fidelibus defunctis (PETRUS DE LARUE; as *Missa pro defunctis*)

VienNB 9814 (*c*.1519–25; HB scriptorium, owned by Raimund Fugger the Elder?)
O domine Jhesu Christe* (Rue)

VienNB Mus. 18825 (*c*.1519–25; HB scriptorium, for Raimund Fugger the Elder)
no La Rue

[1520] reprint of 1515[1] *Misse Antonii de Fevin* (Fossombrone: Petrucci)
Missa Sub tuum presidium (Pierzon; as *Missa quarti toni*)

1520[3] *Motetti novi e chanzoni franciose a quatro sopra doi* (Venice: Antico)
En espoir vis* (La rue)

1520[4] *Liber selectarum cantionum quas vulgo Mutetas appellant sex quinque et quatuor vocum* (Augsburg: Grimm and Wyrsung)
Pater de coelis deus (Petrus de *la* Rue)

BrusBR IV 922 (*c*.1520–1; HB scriptorium, for Pompeius Occo of Amsterdam)[25]
[O salutaris hostia] (anon.)

RegB C120, second part (*c*.1520–1; S. Germany, probably Augsburg)[26]
Fors seulement, 4v (P: De *la* rue)
Leal schray tante+ (*la* rue; as *Carmen in re*)
[Plus aultre+]* (anon.)
Tous les regretz (Josquin)
Trop plus secret (p: *la* rue)

BerlS 40026 (*c*.1520–4; Pforzheim, by town organist, Leonhard Kleber;[27] keyboard tablature)
Tous les regretz (anon.)
Trop plus secret (anon.)

ModD 3 (1520–4, additions to 1530; Modena, for cathedral choir)
Magnificat quarti toni II+ (Pe. de la Rue)**

ModD 4 (1520–30; probably Modena, for cathedral choir)
Missa de beata virgine (anon.; Credo only)

AntP M 18.13/2 (*c*.1520–34; HB scriptorium fragment)
no La Rue

[c. 1521][?]: see 1524

BrusBR 6428 (1521 or later; HB scriptorium, for Marguerite?); all but one La Rue
Missa Ave sanctissima Maria (attr. portion missing? missing portions of Gloria)

---

[25] Occo (*c*.1480–1537) was a merchant and a representative of the Fugger banking firm. One fascicle in the book (not containing La Rue's work) dates from several years earlier.

[26] Birkendorf, *Der Codex Pernner*, i. 27.

[27] *Die Orgeltabulatur des Leonhard Kleber*, ed. Karin Berg-Kotterba, 2 vols. (Das Erbe deutscher Musik, 91–2; Frankfurt: Henry Litolff, 1987).

Missa Conceptio tua (attr. portion missing? no title; missing portions of Kyrie I)
Missa de sancta cruce (Petrus de la Rue; portions of Kyrie missing)
Missa de septem doloribus (attr. page missing; missing parts of Kyrie and Agnus)
Missa Ista est speciosa (attr. page missing; missing parts of Kyrie and Gloria)
Missa pascale (attr. portion missing? missing part of Kyrie)

JenaU 21 (1521–5; HB scriptorium, owned by Frederick the Wise)
Missa Sancta dei genitrix (Petrus la vie)
Missa Tandernaken (Petrus de la Rue)

VienNB Mus. 18832 (c.1521–5; HB scriptorium, for Raimund Fugger the Elder)
Magnificat quinti toni (anon.; Esurientes only)
Missa de feria (anon.; Agnus II only)
Missa de septem doloribus (anon.; Pleni only)
Missa Ista est speciosa (anon.; Pleni only)

VienNB 4809 (c.1521–5; HB scriptorium, for Raimund Fugger the Elder)
no La Rue (all Josquin)

VienNB 4810 (c.1521–5; HB scriptorium, owned by Raimund Fugger the Elder)
no La Rue

VienNB 11778 (c.1521–5; HB scriptorium, owned by Raimund Fugger the Elder)
no La Rue

MunBS 34 (c.1521–6? HB scriptorium, for Wilhelm IV, Duke of Bavaria)
Salve regina I (De la Rue)
Salve regina II (Petrus de la Rue)
Salve regina III* (Petrus de la Rue)
Salve regina IV* (Rue)
Salve regina V* (Petrus de la Rue)

VienNB Mus. 15941 (c.1521–31; HB scriptorium, for Raimund Fugger the Elder; missing S book)
Ave regina caelorum (index: Rue)
Salve mater salvatoris (index: Rue**)

SubA 248 (c.1521–34; HB scriptorium); all La Rue
Missa Assumpta est Maria (Rue; as *Missa de assumptione beate marie*, missing end of Agnus III)
Missa Ave Maria (Rue; as *Missa de annuntiatione maria*)
Missa Cum iocunditate (attr. page missing; missing part of Kyrie and Agnus)
Missa de beata virgine (Rue; as *Missa de domina*)
Missa O gloriosa domina (Rue; very last part of mass found separately from rest of mass)
Missa Puer natus est (Rue; missing part of Agnus II; as *Missa de nativitate Christi*)
Missa Tous les regretz [original version with 3v Benedictus] (Petrus de la Rue; missing A and most of B for Benedictus and all of Agnus)

1522 Missarum decem a clarissimis musicis ... (Rome: Giunta)[28]
Missa Ave Maria (Piere dela Rue)

VienNB Mus. 18746 (1523; HB scriptorium, owned by Raimund Fugger the Elder)
[Adieu comment]* (anon.)

---

[28] Based on 1516[1].

Cent mille regretz (anon.)

[Dueil et ennuy] (anon.)

D'ung aultre aymer* (Rue)

Fors seulement, 5v (Rue**; only source, but appears twice, second time incomplete)

Incessament (anon.)

[Je n'ay regretz]* (anon.)

[Maria mater gratie/Fors seulement] (anon.)

?[Sailliés avant]* (anon.)

Brown 1523₂ Ain schone . . .büechlein . . . dürch Hans Judenkünig (Vienna: Hanns Singryener; German lute tablature; these are adjacent in the print, with Mijn hert second)

Mijn hert (anon.)

Trop plus secret (anon.)

VienNB Mus. 18688 (1523 or later; Ebenfurt, Lower Austria, largely by Stephan Crauss;[29] German lute tablature)

Trop plus secret (anon.)

MontsM 766 (*c.*1523? HB scriptorium, for Charles V?)

[Kyrie pascale], 5v (anon.)

Missa de feria (missing attr. page; missing except for bits of A and B of Agnus III)

Missa de sancta cruce (Petrus de la Rue)

MunBS 5 (*c.*1523–31; Munich, for Wilhelm IV, Duke of Bavaria)

Missa Cum iocunditate (Pe: de larue; missing Agnus II)

1524 = [*Motetti et carmina gallica*] (place and publisher unknown; [*c.* 1521⁷])[30]

Incessament (anon.)

BrusBR 15075 (*c.*1524–34; HB scriptorium, for John III and Catherine of Portugal); all La Rue

Missa Ave sanctissima Maria (Petrus de la Rue; as *Missa sex vocum*)

Missa Conceptio tua (Petrus de la Rue)**

Missa de feria (Petrus de la rue)

Missa de sancta cruce (Rue)

Missa de septem doloribus (Rue; as *Missa quinque vocum de doloribus*)

Missa Ista est speciosa (de la Rue; as *Missa Quinque vocum*)

Missa pascale (de la Rue)

BasU F. IX. 25 (first quarter 16th c.; probably Basel or vicinity)

Missa Tous les regretz (anon.; later version; A and T books only)

BolSP 38 (*c.*1525; Bologna, for Church of San Petronio)

Missa de beata virgine (anon.; Credo only; as *Patrem Cardinal*)

CambraiBM 4 (*c.*1526–30; Cambrai Cathedral)

Missa Incessament (anon.)

Missa Puer natus est (anon.)

---

[29] Arthur J. Ness, 'Sources of Lute Music', *New Grove II*, 45.

[30] Altus book only, from an original set of four. This was not published by Antico; see Martin Picker, 'The Motet Anthologies of Andrea Antico', in Edward H. Clinkscale and Claire Brook (eds.), *A Musical Offering: Essays in Honor of Martin Bernstein* (New York: Pendragon, 1977), 211–37; and Catherine Weeks Chapman, 'Printed Collections of Polyphonic Music Owned by Ferdinand Columbus', *JAMS* 21 (1968), 34–84 at 71, item 74. The sole exemplar is in Bologna, Civico Museo Bibliografico Musicale, where it forms the second part of R141, a collection of four unrelated altus partbooks.

MunU 328–331 (by 1527; probably Augsburg, for Ieronimus Welserr)[31]
Secretz regretz (anon.; as *Carmen in la*)

VatP 1976–79 (*c.*1528–31; HB scriptorium, for Queen Anne and King Ferdinand of Bohemia and Hungary)
Ave regina caelorum (anon.)
Considera Israel (P. Rue)
Delicta iuventutis (anon.)
Salve mater salvatoris (anon.)

DresSL 1/D/505 (*c.*1530; probably Wittenberg or vicinity)
Passio domini nostri+ (Petrus de la rue)**

's-HerAB 72A (1530–1; HB scriptorium, for Confraternity of Our Lady in 's-Hertogenbosch)
no La Rue

's-HerAB 72B (1530–1; HB scriptorium, for Confraternity of Our Lady in 's-Hertogenbosch)
Missa Cum iocunditate (Rue; missing parts of Kyrie)
Missa Incessament (P. Rue)

's-HerAB 72C (1530–1; HB scriptorium, for Confraternity of Our Lady in 's-Hertogenbosch)
no La Rue

VienNB 11883 (first 3rd 16th c.; HB scriptorium [in part], owned by Raimund Fugger the Elder?)
no La Rue

CoimU 2 (after 1530; Flanders)[32]
Missa Ave Maria (P. De la Rue; missing Agnus III)
Missa Cum iocunditate (Petrus de la rue)
Missa Iste confessor domini+ (Petrus de la Rue/P. de *la* rue**; missing Agnus II; really by Févin [*Missa O quam glorifica*])

UlmS 237 (*c.*1530–40; central Germany)
Mijn hert (anon.; down a fifth)

Brown 1532₂ Musica Teusch . . . durch Hans Gerle (Nurenberg: Formschneider; German lute tablature)
Ce n'est pas jeu (anon.)

c.1532 [c. 1535][14] [*Lieder zu 3 & 4 Stimmen*] ([Frankfurt: Egenolff]; S book only)
Ce n'est pas jeu (anon.)
Mijn hert (anon.)
Si dormiero (anon.)

Brown 1533₁ Tabulatur auff die Laudten . . . Hans Gerle (Nuremberg: Formschneider; German lute tablature)
Si dormiero (index: Isaac)

VienNB Mus. 18810 (by 1533; probably Augsburg or Munich)
Adieu florens+ (petri de la rue**; as *Carmen*)

---

[31] Welserr was first noted as the owner in Meconi, 'Style and Authenticity', 33. Biographical information about his life that I have uncovered since then will appear in a forthcoming essay on this collection.

[32] Jacobijn Kiel has recently determined that the main scribe of CoimU 2 also worked on MontsM 765 and ToleF 23; see ead., 'Terminus post Alamire? On Some Later Scribes', *Yearbook of the Alamire Foundation*, 5 (forthcoming). I am grateful to Dr Kiel for sharing her recent thoughts on the manuscript with me (private comm., 6 June 2000).

Een vrolic wesen+ (petri de la rue**; down a fifth; really by Pipelare)
Jouyssance vous donneray+ (Petri de la Rue;**[33] as *Iam sauche*; really by Claudin)
Leal schray tante+ (petri de la rue; as *Carmen*)
Si dormiero (Henricus Isaac; as *Guretzsch*)
Secretz regretz (petri de la rue**; as *Carmen*)
Tous les regretz (petri.de.la.Rue)

1534[5] *Liber tertius . . . mótetos* (Paris: Attaingnant)
[Ave sanctissima Maria] (S & B = Verdelot; A = Claudin)

CivMA 59 (*c.*1534–7; Cividale, for Collegiate Church of Santa Maria Assunta)[34]
Missa de Sancto Antonio (anon.; no title)

KasL 53/2 (dates 1534 to 1546 in MS; Kassel, for Count Philip of Hesse; S book only)
Si dormiero (anon.)

KasL 24 (dates 1534 to 1550 in MS; Kassel, for Count Philip of Hesse)
Laudate dominum* (Pirson/P de *la* rue)

[c. 1535][14:] see *c.* 1532

LonBL 19583 (*c.*1535; Ferrara, for Ercole II d'Este, Duke of Ferrara; A partbook only)
En l'amour d'une dame+* (P de la rue)

ZwiR 78/3 (*c.*1535–45; probably Zwickau, owned by city scribe Stephan Roth)
Si dormiero (anon.)

KasL 38 (dates 1535–66 in MS; Kassel, for Count Philip of Hesse)
Credo, 6v (Pirson)
Credo Angeli archangeli* (Pirson)

1536[13] *Der ander Theil des Lautenbuchs* (Nuremberg: Petreius; German lute tablature)
Si dormiero (Hainricus Finck)
Mijn hert (anon.)

1537 Sebald Heyden: *Musicae, id est, Artis canendi*[35] (Nuremberg: J. Petreius)
Missa L'homme armé I (Petri de la Rue; Agnus II only)
Missa O salutaris hostia (Petri de la Rue; Pleni only)

*Brown 1537*₁ reprint of Brown 1532₂[36] *Musica Teusch . . . durch Hans Gerle* (Nurenberg: Formschneider; German lute tablature)
Ce n'est pas jeu (anon.)

BerlGS 7/KönSU 1740 (*c.*1537–44; perhaps Königsberg, for Matthias Krüger; B [BerlGS 7] physically extant, S and A missing, T and Vagans exist on microfilm)
Domini est terra+* (P de Larue)
Missa Cum iocunditate (Petri de la Rue; missing Agnus II?)
Missa L'homme armé I (de *la* rue; missing Agnus III; part of Pleni reworked as a trio; all but Agnus II transposed up a fourth)

1538[3] *Secundus tomus novi operis musici . . .* (Nuremberg: H. Grapheus)
Delicta iuventutis (index: Petrus de larue)**

---

[33] The work also appears anonymously elsewhere in this manuscript.
[34] See Lewis Lockwood, 'Sources of Renaissance Polyphony from Cividale del Friuli: The Manuscripts 53 and 59 of the Museo Archeologico Nazionale', *Saggiatore musicale*, 1 (1994), 249–314.
[35] Theoretical treatise.
[36] La Rue's song was dropped from the later revised and augmented edition (Brown 1546₉).

1538[8] *Symphoniae iucundae atque adeo breves* . . . (Wittenberg: G. Rhaw)
Ave regina caelorum (Petrus de la Rue; as *Ave apertor caelorum*)
Salva nos domine+ (attributed to PETRVS DE LA RUE**, but = Agnus III of *Missa Salva nos* by Isaac)

1538[9] *Trium vocum carmina* (Nuremberg: Formschneider)
Sancta Maria virgo (anon.; prima pars only)
Si dormiero (anon.)
Tous nobles cueurs (anon.; down a fifth)

RegB B220–222 (c.1538; Salzburg?)[37]
Missa L'homme armé I (Petrus de la Rue; Pleni only)
Virga tua+ (Petrus de la rue/P de la rue)**

StuttL 45 (c.1538; Stuttgart, for Ulrich, Duke of Württemberg)
Missa Nuncqua fue (anon.; no title; missing Agnus)

1539[1] *Liber quindecim missarum à praestantissimis* . . . (Nuremberg: J. Petreius)
Missa Tous les regretz (Petrus de la Rue; original version with Benedictus for 2 duos)

1539[2] *Missae tredecim quatuor vocum* . . . (Nuremberg: H. Grapheus)
Missa Cum iocunditate (Petrus de La Rue; Credo is missing A part (5th voice); collection is otherwise 4v masses)
Missa de Sancto Antonio (Petrus de La Rue; prepared from 1509[1])
Missa O gloriosa domina (Petrus de La Rue/Petrus de LaRue; down a fifth; missing parts of Sanctus and Agnus)
Missa Sub tuum presidium (attr. PETRVS DE LA RUE; missing Agnus I and part of Sanctus; S, T, B, and T index: Iosquin)

NurGN 83795 (c.1539–48, plus additions 2nd half 16th c.; Torgau, under direction of Johann Walther, for use in Pfarrkirche or Schlosskirche; T and B books only)
Incessament (anon.; as *Sic deus dilexit/ Incessament*)
Magnificat secundi toni (Pe. de la rue; has new Esurientes)
Magnificat quarti toni (anon.)
Magnificat sexti toni (Pe. de *la* rue; has alternative Sicut locutus)
Missa Incessament (anon.)

MunBS 260 (1539–50; probably Low Countries, possibly owned by Johann Heinrich Herwart of Augsburg)
Missa de feria (anon.; Agnus II only)
Missa Ista est speciosa (anon.; Pleni only)

GriefU 640–641 (1539–88; presumably Barth, for [and by] local minister Joannes Soldeke; S and B books only)
Si dormiero (anon.)

VienNB Mus. 15499 (1540; probably German origin)
Missa Nuncqua fue (anon.; lacks Agnus; no title)

1540 Sebald Heyden: *De arte canendi* (Nuremberg: J. Petreius)[38]
Missa L'homme armé I (Petri de la Rue; Agnus II only)

---

[37] Date given in Winfried Kirsch, 'Josquin's Motets in the German Tradition', in *JosCon*, 261–78 at 274.
[38] Theoretical treatise; the Pleni from the *Missa O salutaris hostia* found in 1537 Heyden has been dropped from this treatise, which is essentially a revised edition of the earlier work.

1540[7] *Selectissimae necnon familiarissimae cantiones* (Augsburg: M. Kriesstein)
  ?[Absalon fili mi] (IOSQVIN)
  Da pacem domine (PETRVS de la Rue)

MontsM 769 (*c.*1540; Brussels, at court of Mary of Hungary)
  Magnificat septimi toni (anon.)

MunBS 1516 (*c.*1540; probably Augsburg)
  Mijn hert (anon.)
  Pour ung jamais (anon.; as *Pour vous james*)

BerlPS 40013 (*c.*1540; Torgau, for Pfarrkirche)
  Incessament (anon.; as *Sic deus dilexit/Incessament*; [later hand: Josquin D.p. oder Pierre de
    la Rue])
  Magnificat secundi toni (Pe. de *la* rue; has new Esurientes)
  Magnificat quarti toni (anon.; has alternative Sicut locutus)
  Magnificat sexti toni (Pe: de *la* rue; has alternative Sicut locutus)

SGallS 463 (*c.*1540 or slightly later; Glarus or vicinity, by (and for) Aegidius Tschudi, student
    of Glarean; S and A only)
  Incessament (Petrus de la Rue)
  Mijn hert (Iacobus Obrecht)
  Pourquoy non (index: Petrus de La Rue; piece listed only there; is not in MS proper)

ErlU 473/4 (1540–1; Heilbronn, for the Cistercian monastery)
  Missa Tandernaken (anon.; missing Benedictus, Agnus II and III)

WeimB B (1540–4; Torgau, perhaps for Wittenberg Schlosskirche)
  Incessament (anon.; as *Incessament/Sic deus dilexit*)
  Missa Coronata+ (Petri de Larue**; Kyrie, Gloria, and Credo only;[39] = *Missa de beata
    virgine* by Josquin)

CambraiBM 125–8 (1542; probably Bruges, for Bruges merchant Zeghere van Male)
  Mijn hert (anon.)

1542[8] *Tricinia* (Wittenberg: G. Rhaw)
  Missa Cum iocunditate (Petrus a Rue; Benedictus only, as *Si esurierit inimicus*)
  Missa Inviolata (Petrus de la Rue; Benedictus only, as *Omnes peccaverunt*)
  Pour ung jamais (Petrus de la Rue/Petrus a Rue; as *Nos debemus gratias*)**

MunBS 1508 (1542 or later; Germany or the Low Countries, owned by Johann Heinrich
    Herwart of Augsburg)[40]
  Incessament (anon.)

after 1542 Kamper Liedboek (Kampen? Johannes Petrcius? table of contents cites anonymous
    Mijn hert; probably La Rue's; music not extant)[41]

MunU 327 (*c.*1543; probably Augsburg)
  Missa Nuncqua fue (anon.; no title; tenor book only; missing Agnus)

[39] Sanctus and Agnus copied elsewhere in the manuscript and attributed to Josquin ('Iosquini').
[40] For the date, see Meconi, 'Style and Authenticity', 37.
[41] All that remains of the print are a table of contents and fragments of A and B books. The contents of
the books and their order are almost identical to [*c.* 1535][14], vol. 2, which contains La Rue's *Mijn hert*, making
it likely that the *Mijn hert* listed here was also La Rue's. See Nanie Bridgman, 'Christian Egenolff,
imprimeur de musique: A propos du recueil Res. Vm/7 504 de la Bibliothèque nationale de Paris', *Annales
musicologues*, 3 (1955), 77–177; and C. W. H. Lindenburg, 'Het "Kamper" liedboek', *TVNM* 16 (1940), 48–62.

MunBS C (1543–4; Munich, probably commissioned in memory of Wilhelm of Bavaria's sister)

Missa Incessament (Petrus de *la* rue [but uses bass clef for note])

Missa pro fidelibus defunctis (Petrus de *la* rue; as *Missa pro defunctis*; with elaborate miniatures depicting funeral service)

MunBS 47 (*c.* 1543–50; Munich, for Wilhelm IV, Duke of Bavaria)

Missa pro fidelibus defunctis (Petrus de Larue; as *Missa pro defunctis*)

VatS 154 (1543–60; Rome, for Cappella Sistina)

Missa Incessament (anon.)

1544⁴ Postremum Vespertini Officii opus, cuius priores partes . . . (Wittenberg: G. Rhaw)

Magnificat quarti toni (Petri de La rue)**

HeidU 318 (1544) Inventory of library of Palatine Count Ottheinrich at Neuburg

Missa Ave Maria (petrus de larue/Pe: De Larue; 2 copies)

Missa Conceptio tua (pe: De Larue/P de Larue)

Missa de feria (P de Larue)

Missa de sancta cruce (P de Larue)

Missa de septem doloribus (De Larue/P de Larue; as *Missa de doloribus M. virginis*)

Missa de virginibus (de Larue; as *Missa Pulchra es*)

Missa Incessament (petrus de *la* rue)

Missa Ista est speciosa (pe: De larue/P de Larue)

Missa Mediatrix nostra (pe: De. Larue/p. de la rue)

Missa Nuncqua fue pena maior (pe: De larue/P de larue; as *Missa Nunquam fierit*)

Missa O salutaris hostia (pe de larue)

Missa pascale (pe: De Larue/P de Larue)

Missa pro fidelibus defunctis (Pet: de *la* rue; as *Missa pro defunctis*)

Missa sine nomine (petri de Larue/Petri de Larue; no title)

Missa Sub tuum presidium (pe: de Larue/petri de larue/Pierzon; as *Missa in mi*/*Missa Quarti thoni*; 3 copies)

Pater de coelis deus (P. De Larue)

Petre amas me (pe: De Larue/pe: De larue; 2 copies)

Tous les regretz (petrus Delarue)

GothaF A98 (1545; Torgau, for Schlosskirche)

Incessament (anon.; as *Incessament/ Sic deus dilexit*)

1545⁶ Bicinia gallica, latina . . . (Wittenberg: G. Rhaw)

Missa Ave sanctissima Maria (anon.; Pleni only; as *Deus meus eripe me*)

Missa de feria (PE. DE LA RUE; Agnus II only, as *Ne temere quid loquaris*)

Missa Incessament (PETRUS DE LA RUE/PE. DE LA RUE; Pleni only, as *Non salvatur rex*)

Missa Sancta Dei genitrix (PETRVS DE LA RUE; Pleni only, as *Miserere mei deus*)

1545⁷ Secundus tomus biciniorum . . . (Wittenberg: G. Rhaw)

Missa L'homme armé I (anon.; Pleni only, as *Quaerite Dominum*)

Missa Tandernaken (PE. DE LA RVE; Benedictus and Agnus II only, as *Amicus fidelis* and *Frange esurienti* respectively)

HerdF 9820 (*c.*1545–50? probably German)⁴²

---

⁴² A collection of scores, apparently for study purposes; see David Fallows, 'The Herdringen Scores', in

Missa O salutaris hostia (P de la rue; Kyrie, Osanna, and Benedictus only; score format)

HerdF 9821 (*c.*1545–50? probably German)[43]

Missa Ave Maria (Pierde La rue; portions of Kyrie and Sanctus only; score format)

Missa Sub tuum presidium (Pier de la rue; Kyrie and first section of Gloria only; score format)

1547¹ Glareani Dodecachordon[44] (Basel: H. Petri)

Missa de Sancto Antonio (Petrus Platensis; Christe only)

Missa L'homme armé I (Petri Platensis; Agnus II only)

Missa O salutaris hostia (Petri Platensis; Kyrie I only)

Missa O salutaris hostia (ex Petro Platensis; Pleni only)

BolC B57 (after 1547; Naples?) Cimello: Della perfettione delle quattro note maggiori[45]

Missa L'homme armé I (anon.; Agnus II only)

Missa O salutaris hostia (anon.; Kyrie I only)

WarN 564 (1548; Krakow? keyboard tablature destroyed in Second World War, but microfilm remains)[46]

Si dormiero (Josquin)

StuttL 38 (1549; Stuttgart, for Ulrich, Duke of Württemberg)

Missa Cum iocunditate (petrus de la Rue)

1549¹ Lamentationes Hieremiae Prophetae . . . (Nuremberg: Montanus & Neuber)[47]

Lamentations+ (Nvmeri excellentissimi Musici, Petri de la Rue Flandri**; Tenor partbook title page, among list of composers included: Petro de la Rue, Flandro; portions of the work are attributed to Févin elsewhere in the print)

1549¹⁶ Diphona amoena et florida . . . (Nuremberg: J. Montanus & U. Neuber)

Le renvoye+ (PYRSON DE LARUE/PIRSON DE LARUE**; as *Num stultum est mortem*)

Missa de Sancto Antonio (Pirson; Benedictus only)

Missa Incessament (Pirson; Pleni, Benedictus, and In nomine only)

Missa Nuncqua fue (PIRSON; Benedictus only, as *Libertatem quem maiores*)

UtreH s.s. (*c.*1549–50; probably Wittenberg)

Lauda anima mea dominum (anon.)

VienNB Mus. 16746 (first half 16th c.; possibly SW German origin)

Missa Puer natus est (anon.; no title; Kyrie, Pleni, and Agnus only)

BarcBC 681 (first half 16th c.; Vich)

Credo, 6v (anon.)

BerlPS 40634 (first half 16th c.; Stuttgart or vicinity? A and B books only)

Missa Tous les regretz (anon.; later version)

Missa de Sancto Antonio (anon.; as *Missa Ecce advenit*)

Conference Packet for *Josquin: International Conference, New Directions in Josquin Scholarship*, Princeton University, *29–31 October 1999*, 410–25.

[43] Ibid.   [44] Theoretical treatise.   [45] Theoretical treatise.   [46] LRE ix, pp. xc–xci.
[47] This print is the only one of several sources to attribute any part of the Lamentations to La Rue. Dresden 1/D/7 (not in *CC*; destroyed in the Second World War) had two excepts from the Lamentations, but their attribution is not known. 1538¹, Rhau's *Selectae harmoniae . . . De Passione Domini*, included parts of the Lamentations but labelled them as being by 'incerto Symphonista'. See LRE viii, pp. xxxiv–xxxv.

MilA 46 (mid-16th c.? probably Italy)
  Missa Cum iocunditate (Josquin; no title; with *Dirige* text)
  Missa Sub tuum presidium (P. de la Rua.; as *Missa quarti.*)

EisS s.s. (mid-16th c. with later additions; Eisenach)
  Missa de beata virgine (Petrus de Larue; Kyrie only; as *Kyrie Coronatum*)

LeidGA 1443 (mid-16th c., with additions *c.*1564–7; probably Amsterdam, used by St Peter's
    Church in Leiden, where additions were made)
  Missa Puer natus est (De la Rue; parts of Kyrie, Gloria, and Credo only)

ParisPNC 1591 (mid-16th c.; probably Augsburg)[48]
  Salve regina I (petrus de l.... [illegible])

RegT 3/I (mid-16th c.; probably S. German; B book only)
  Trop plus secret (anon.)

1550 Trente sixiesme livre contenant XXX chansons . . . (Paris: Attaingnant, 1549 o.s.)
  Cent mille regretz (Josquin)
  Incessament (Josquin)

HeilbS X/2 (early 1550s; Frankfurt am Main?[49] B book only)
  Si dormiero (anon.)

1552²⁹ Hortus musarum . . . (Leuven: P. Phalèse; lute tablature)
  Incessament (anon.)

1553⁶ Tomus tertius Psalmorum selectorum . . . (Nuremberg: J. Montanus & U. Neuber)
  Lauda anima mea dominum (Petrus de la Rue)**

1553³³ Horti musarum, secunda pars (Leuven: Phalèse; for superius [mensural notation] and
    lute [tablature])
  Incessament (anon.)

1554 Johann Zanger: *Practicae musicae praecepta* (Leipzig: Georgij Hantzsch)[50]
  Missa Cum iocunditate (Petri de larue; Et incarnatus only; four voices only)
  Missa L'homme armé I (Petri de Larue; Agnus II only)

DresSL Pirna IV (1554; Pirna, for Stadtkirche St Marien)
  Missa de beata virgine (petri de Larue; as *Missa Coronatum*; end of Gloria newly com-
      posed by unknown composer)

1555¹¹ Tertius tomus Evangeliorum . . . (Nuremberg: J. Montanus and U. Neuber)
  Pater de coelis deus (Petrus de la Rue)

LeipU 51 (*c.*1555, with slightly later additions; Leipzig, maybe under direction of Thomas-
    kirche cantor Melchior Heger; T and B partbooks only)
  Ave regina caelorum (anon.; as *Ave apertor caelorum*)
  Missa L'homme armé I (Petri de la Rue; missing Agnus II)

1556 Hermann Finck: *Practica musica* (Wittenberg: Georg Rhau)[51]
  Missa Cum iocunditate (anon.; initial section from Sanctus only)
  Missa de beata virgine (anon.; Kyrie I only)

1556 enlarged edition of above published same year[52]

---

[48] Place of compilation for the La Rue piece, which is first in the manuscript.
[49] Probably copied from [*c.* 1535]¹⁴.   [50] Theoretical treatise.   [51] Theoretical treatise.
[52] Theoretical treatise.

Missa Cum iocunditate (anon.; initial section from Sanctus only)

Missa de beata virgine (anon.; Kyrie I only)

Brown 1556₅ Lautten Buch…Wolffen Heckel (Strasburg: Urban Wyss Rechenmeister; German lute tablature)

Incessament (anon.)

1558²⁰ Tabulaturbuch auff die Lauten … durch Sebastian Ochsenkhun (Heidelberg: J. Kohlen; lute tablature)

?[Absalon fili mi] (Iosquin de Pres)

LeipU 49 (*c.*1558, with slightly later additions; Leipzig, maybe under direction of Thomaskirche cantor Melchior Heger)

Missa Tous les regretz (anon.; later version; Kyrie and Gloria only = Lutheran mass; no title)

1559 Inventory of Mary of Hungary's library[53]

7 masses and 'çiertas obras' in a paper manuscript (Pedro de la Rue)[54]

7 masses in a parchment manuscript (Pedro De la Rue)[55]

8 masses (La Rue)[56]

9 masses (De la Rue)[57] = MontsM 773?

Magnificats and 'otras obras' (Pedro de la Rue)[58]

1559² Tertia pars magni operis musici (Nuremberg: Montanus & U. Neuber)

?[Absalon fili mi] (IOSQVIN DE PRES; JOSQVIN)

1560 Livre de mélanges (Paris: Le Roy & Ballard; S book only)

Incessament (De la Rue)

StuttL HB 26 (*c.*1560; Bavaria)[59]

Missa Cum iocunditate (anon.; no title or text; Et incarnatus only; missing altus)

1562²⁴ later edition of *Brown 1556₅ Lautten Buch…Wolfen Heckel* (Strasburg: Christian Müller; German lute tablature)

Incessament (anon.)

1567¹ Suavissimae et iucundissimae harmoniae… (Nuremberg: T. Gerlach)

Da pacem domine (Petrus de La Rue)

1572² Mellange de chansons… (Paris: Le Roy & Ballard)

Incessament (DE LA RUE)

VatS 45 (*c.*1576–77; Rome; text corrections made)

Missa Cum iocunditate (Pe de *la* Rue)

LonBL 4911 (*c.*1580; probably Edinburgh or Aberdeen for use in song school for boys)[60]

Missa Cum iocunditate (anon.; tenor of Sanctus, bars 1–25 only)

Missa L'homme armé I (anon.; Agnus II only)

---

[53] The collection of nine masses reappears in the 1597 library inventory of Philip II; other entries seem very similar.

[54] VDS vii. 481; the manuscript appears to be listed again on p. 489.

[55] Ibid. 488.   [56] Ibid.   [57] Ibid. 489.

[58] Ibid. 482; the manuscript appears to be listed again on p. 490. The description reads 'ques de los ocho tonos de Pedro de la Rue, en que ay Manificas y otras obras', implying the existence of a *Magnificat tertii toni*. See a similar but clearer entry in the 1597 inventory of Philip II's library, which may refer to this manuscript.

[59] Theoretical treatise.   [60] Theoretical treatise.

1587 lost first edition of 1590[30] and 1594[3]

1590[30] Iacobo Paix: *Selectae, artificiosae et elegantes fugae* . . .[61] (Lauingen: L. Reinmichel)
    Missa L'homme armé I (Petri Platensis; Petri Plat.; Agnus II only)
    Missa O salutaris hostia (Petri Platensis; Pleni only)

1592 Lodovico Zacconi: *Prattica di musica*[62] (Venice: Girolamo Polo)
    Missa Cum iocunditate (Petrus della Rue; altered beginning of Confiteor only; tenor
    only)
    Missa Cum iocunditate (Pietro della Rue; portion of Agnus I only; tenor only)
    Missa de Sancto Antonio (Pietro della rue; conclusion of Credo only; altus only)

1594[3] Iacobo Paix: *Selectae, artificiosae et elegantes fugae* . . .[63] (Lauingen: L. Reinmichel)
    Missa L'homme armé I (Petri Platensis; Petri Plat.; Agnus II only)

1596 another edition of Zacconi: *Prattica di musica*[64] (Venice: Bartolomeo Carampello)
    Missa Cum iocunditate (Petrus della Rue; altered beginning of Confiteor only; tenor
    only)
    Missa Cum iocunditate (Pietro della Rue; portion of Agnus I only; tenor only)
    Missa de Sancto Antonio (Pietro della rue; conclusion of Credo only; altus only)

1597 Thomas Morley: *A Plaine and Easie introduction to practicall musicke*[65] (London: Peter
    Short)
    Missa O salutaris hostia (Petrus Platensis; Kyrie I only)

1597 inventory of Philip II's library – no music
    Credo Angeli archangeli (Patrem, a ocho vozes), in manuscript of works by Pedro de la
    Rue[66]
    8 Magnificats, including otherwise unknown Magnificat tertii toni (existence implied by
    entry 'de ocho tonos de Magníficat de música, de Pedro de la Rua'); 'algunos ynnos' as
    well?[67]
    7 masses in parchment manuscript (Pedro de la Rue)[68]
    7 masses in paper manuscript (Pedro de la Rue)[69]
    9 masses in parchment manuscript (Pedro de la Rua)[70] = MontsM 773?
    10 masses in parchment manuscript (Pedro de la Rua)[71]
    Missa Cum iocunditate, in a manuscript of his works (Pedro de la Rue)[72]
    Missa Tous les regretz (Pedro la Rue)[73]
    Salve Jesu, 6v, otherwise unknown (Pedro la Rue)[74]
    first work (la Rue) in manuscript of 'Regina, Salve y motetes'[75]

---

[61] Collection of canons.   [62] Theoretical treatise.
[63] Collection of canons; it drops the Pleni from the *Missa O salutaris hostia* that had appeared in 1590[30].
[64] Theoretical treatise.   [65] Theoretical treatise.
[66] Andrés, 'Libros de canto', 123, no. 71; VDS viii. 373.
[67] Andrés, 'Libros de canto', 109, no. 31; VDS viii. 367.
[68] Andrés, 'Libros de canto', 94, no. 3; VDS viii. 365.
[69] Andrés, 'Libros de canto', 94, no. 4; VDS viii. 365.
[70] Andrés, 'Libros de canto', 126, no. 22; VDS viii. 375.
[71] Andrés, 'Libros de canto', 95, no. 27; VDS viii. 367.
[72] Andrés, 'Libros de canto', 156, no. 170; VDS viii. 379.
[73] Andrés, 'Libros de canto', 123, no. 76; VDS viii. 369.
[74] Andrés, 'Libros de canto', 124, no. 87; VDS viii. 370.
[75] Andrés, 'Libros de canto', 111, no. 65; VDS viii. 372.

MontsM 766?[76]
MontsM 769?[77]

1618 Giovanni Battista Rossi: *Organo de Cantori*[78] (Venice: Gardano)
Missa L'homme armé I (Pier de la Rue; Kyrie I only, T and B)

[76] If the manuscript cited in Andrés, 'Libros de canto', 124, no. 87, and VDS viii. 370, is the same as MontsM 766, then La Rue's *Kyrie pascale*, *Missa de sancta cruce*, and a fragment of his *Missa de feria* were included in Philip's collection.

[77] According to *CC* ii. 180, this manuscript, which contains La Rue's *Magnificat septimi toni* without ascription, was also included in the inventory.

[78] Theoretical treatise.

Appendix C
Literary and Theoretical Citations

In the following excerpts, arranged chronologically, abbreviations have been expanded silently and spelling has usually been modernized. La Rue's name has been kept as it appears in the original; the names of other composers are sometimes modernized in the translations.

*c.*1498
Jean Molinet (1435–1507), *Nymphes des bois* (BNF fr. 24315, fo. 96ʳ)

Nymphes des boys deesses des fontaines
Chantres expers de toutes nations
Changez voz voix fort cleres et haultaines
En cris trenchantz et lamentations
Car atropos tres terrible satrape
A vostre Okgam atrape en sa trape
Vray tresorier de musique et chef doeuvre[1]
Grand dommage est que la terre le coeuvre
Acoultrez vous dhabitz de doeul
Josquin **perchon** brumel compere
Et pleurez grosses larmes doeil
Perdu avez vostre bon pere
Requiescat in pace
Amen[2]

Nymphes of the woods, goddesses of the fountains,
Expert singers of all nations,
Change your strong, clear, lofty voices
Into trenchant cries and lamentations,
Because Atropos, terrible satrap,
Has caught your Ockeghem in his trap.
True treasurer of music and masterpiece,
Great loss it is that the earth covers him!
Clothe yourselves in mourning,
Josquin, perchon, Brumel, Compère,
And cry great tears from your eyes;
You have lost your good father.
May he rest in peace.
Amen.

---

[1] An extra line of text, 'Doct, élégant de corps et non point trappé', is found in Josquin's setting, possibly added by Josquin himself. See Lowinsky, *The Medici Codex*, text vol., 214. The fact that Molinet never wrote a poem of thirteen lines adds credence to this suggestion.

[2] The poem also appears in FlorL 666 and 1545¹⁵, in Josquin's setting of the poem, with different spellings.

1516

Heinrich Glarean (1488–1563), *Isagoge in musicen* (Basel: J. Froben, 1516)

Citation 1: Chapter 4, Concerning the Intervals and Consonances, sig. C[1]ᵛ
Sed, & haec, & quod magis miror, tonus cum diapente, & disdiapason a **Petro Platensi** symphonista doctissimo nonnuncumque usurpatae sunt, magis forsitan ut voces excelsissimae luderent, cumque belle consonarent. (But both of these [the diapente plus the double octave; ditone plus the double octave], as well as the major sixth plus double octave—which surprises me still more—are all sometimes used by the learned polyphonist Petrus Platensis, more perhaps in order that the highest voices should be brought into play than that they should make beautiful consonances.³)

Citation 2: Chapter 10, Concerning the Final, Expansion, Recognition and Mixture of the
  Modes, sig. E[1]ʳ⁻ᵛ
Ad hanc etiam formam **Petrus Platensis**, Symphonistes nostra aetate clarissimus, septimum tonum cum octavo in unam cantilenam pulchre coniunxit. Et Iacobus Hobrechth ingeniosissimus primum & secundum. Quoties autem hoc fit, dicuntur permiscent toni, quod facile videbit qui diapason species memoria tenet. Quod si sunt cantus a regula liberi, ij bono Musico non minus noti esse possunt cumque optimi, eiusdem enim est bene & male canere. (According to this plan, Petrus Platensis, a most distinguished contemporary polyphonist, has combined in beautiful fashion the seventh and eighth modes in a single melody. Also the highly skilled Jacobus Obrecht has done the same thing with the first and second. Whenever this happens the modes are said to be mixed, as anybody will easily see who has mastered the octave species. But though these melodies are free from the rule, they can be learned by a good musician as well as the regular ones, for it is simply a matter of singing a given melody well or badly.⁴)

1517

Andreas Ornithoparchus (*c.*1490–?), *Musice active micrologus* (Leipzig: Valentin Schumann, January 1517; another edition in November of the same year⁵)

Book II, Chapter 8, de diminutione (subsection: De diminutione)
Nunc ad rem redeo et Amusos illos atque ridiculos Phormiones (quorum plures musice provintiam: proh pudor: invasere) Harmoniarum non compositores: ymmo corruptores, non musarum, sed furiarum alumnos: virorum minimo dignor honore. Ridenda enim sunt cantica in ipsis musice fontibus non radicata. licet quantumvis consona sint. Quoniam non artifex artem, sed ars artificem decorat . . . Fides itaque nec ulla prestetur componistis, nisi inveniantur arte probati. Quorum autem probata est auctoritas, ij sunt: Joannes Okeken, Joannes Tinctoris, Loyset, Verbonet, Alexander agricola, Jacobus Obrecht, Josquin, **Petrus de larue**,⁶ Henricus Jsaack, Henricus Fynck. Antonius Brummel, Matheus Pipilare,

---

³ Translation from Frances Berry Turrell, 'The *Isagoge in musicen* of Henry Glarean', *Journal of Music Theory*, 3 (1959), 97–139 at 124.
⁴ Ibid. 136.
⁵ Reprinted in 1519, 1521, 1524, 1533, 1535, 1540, 1555; an English translation by Dowland was published in 1609. The 1521 publication may be a ghost edition, and no copy survives of the 1540 edition. A facsimile of the November edition was published as Andreas Ornithoparchus, *Musicae activae micrologus libris quatuor digestus* (Hildesheim and New York: Georg Olms, 1977); as well as id. and John Dowland, *A Compendium of Musical Practice: Musice active micrologus by Andreas Ornithoparchus/Andreas Ornithoparcus His Micrologus, or Introduction: Containing the Art of Singing by John Dowland*, facs. edn., ed. Gustave Reese and Steven Ledbetter (New York: Dover, 1973).
⁶ The citation is the same in the edition of 1519; I have not seen the other editions.

Georgius Brack, Erasmus Lapicida, Caspar Czeys, Conradus Reyn, et similes: quorum poemata ex artis radicibus emanare conspiciuntur.[7] (Now come I to the matter, and leave these unlearned ridiculous *Phormio's*, many whereof (the more is the shame) have violently invaded the art of *Musick*, as those which are not compounders of Harmonies, but rather corruptors, children of the furies, rather than of the Muses, not worthy of the least grace I may doe them. For their Songs are ridiculous, not grounded on the Principles of the Art, though perhaps true inough. For the Artist doth not grace the art, but the Art graceth the Artist. [Therefore a Componist doth not grace Musicke, but contrarily: for there be that can make true Songs not by Art, but by Custome, as having happily lived amongst singers all their life-time: yet do they not understand what they have made, knowing that such a thing is, but not what it is. To whom the word our Saviour used on the Crosse, may be well used: *Father pardon them, they know not what they doe.*] Wherfore allow of no Componists, but those, who are by Art worthy to be allowed of: now such are *Ioan. Okeken, Ioan: Tinctoris, Loyset, Verbonet, Alex: Agricola, Iacobus Obrecht, Iosquin, Petrus de Larue, Hen: Isaack, Hen: Finck, Ant: Brummel, Mat: Pipilare, Geor: Brack, Erasmus Lapicida, Caspar Czeys, Conradus Reyn*, and the like: whose Compositions one may see doe flow from the very fountaine of Art.[8])

Pierre Moulu (?1484–*c*. 1550), motet *Mater floreat florescat* (FlorL 666, fos. 51ᵛ–55ʳ (copied Rome, 1518))

Mater floreat florescat modulata musicorum melodia Crescat celebris dufay cadentia prosperetur preclaris Regis busnoys Baziron Subtiles glorientur Triumphet alexander magnificus Congaudeat Obreth compere Eloy hayne **la Rue** [altus: **la rue**] memorabiles Josquin Incomparabilis Bravium Accipiat.[9] (Mother music, measured melody, may she flourish and prosper. May the celebrated Dufay's cadence grow and may the famous Regis be made to prosper; glory to the subtle Busnois and Baziron. May the magnificent Alexander triumph and may rejoice with him the memorable Obrecht, Compère, Eloy, Hayne, and La Rue. May the incomparable Josquin receive the prize.[10])

1518

Another appearance of *Nymphes des bois* (see under *c*.1498) (FlorL 666, fos. 125ᵛ–127ʳ (Rome), motet-chanson setting by Josquin)

Josquin **piersson** brumel comper[11]

1519

Another edition of Ornithoparchus: *Musice active micrologus* (see under 1517)

1520

Giovanni del Lago (*c*.1490–1544), letter to Giovanni da Legge (29 February 1520, VatV 5318, fos. 107ʳ–108ʳ)[12]

---

[7] Ornithoparchus and Dowland, *A Compendium of Musical Practice*, 60.

[8] Ibid. 169–70 (in the original: 49–50/sig. P 1ʳ–ᵛ).

[9] Lowinsky, *The Medici Codex*, facs. vol., fos. 51ᵛ–55ʳ.   [10] Ibid., text vol., 73.

[11] Josquin's motet-chanson first appeared in 1508¹, but without its French text.

[12] All information is from *A Correspondence of Renaissance Musicians*, ed. Bonnie J. Blackburn, Edward E. Lowinsky, and Clement A. Miller (Oxford: Clarendon Press, 1991), 766–70.

Et queste tali congiunte, o ver exachordi acquisti, non sono dalli regolari differenti se non di luogo, perché anchora loro sono nella diatonica et naturale progressione di sei sillabe, cioè ascendendo . . . et così descendendo . . . Ma le predette congiunte sono state usate da compositori, così antichi come moderni, ne' loro concenti per sua comodità, come Dufai in una sua canzone 'Le serviteur' fatta del primo tuono irregolare, et 'Venus tu m'a pris' de Orto, et 'Porquoi non', {**Petrus de la Rue**}, et la messa sine nomine, Jo. Mouton, et 'O beata infancia' de Loyset Pieton, et molti altri canti, motteti, et messe . . .[13] (These *coniunctae*, or transposed hexachords, are no different from regular ones except in location, for they also have the diatonic order of the six syllables, ascending and descending. They have been used in works by old and modern composers, such as Dufay's *Le serviteur*, de Orto's *Venus tu m'a pris*, *Porquoi non* by {Petrus de la Rue}, Mouton's *Missa sine nomine*, Loyset Piéton's *O beata infantia*, and many other works.[14])

*c.*1520
S'ensuivent plusieurs belles chansons (Geneva: Jacques Viviane, n.d.)[15]

Chanson .xli. Sus nimphe des bois

Reveillez vous tous chantres naturelz
Qui endurez fantaisie de cervelle
Venés nous veoir et vous nous trouverez
Deliberez: si nous sommes enrhumez
N'en murmurez ce fait nostre chapelle
L'ung se brumelle l'autre se josquinelle
{**Pierresonelle**} et l'autre se compere
Quant nous souvient de Brumel nostre pere

Ne plourez plus dame de court
Cessez vostre doulent amere
Monsieur reviendra quelque jour
Ce que n'est fait se pourra faire[16]

Awaken, all you natural singers
Who put up with a caprice of the mind.
Come and see us and you will find us.
Resolve: if we have caught a cold,
Don't complain if this makes our chapel sound
The one foggy [brumelle], the other 'josquinelle',
One stony {Pierresonelle} and the other the same [compere]
When we remember our father Brumel.

Cry no more, courtly lady,
Cease your bitter suffering.
Monsieur will return some day.
What isn't done can be done.

---

[13] *A Correspondence of Renaissance Musicians*, 767–8.
[14] Condensed translation after ibid. 769–70.
[15] All information on this collection is taken from van Benthem, 'La magie des cris trenchantz', 124.
[16] Ibid.

1521
Teofilo Folengo [Cocaius] (1491–1544), *Opus Merlini Cocaii, poete Mantuani Macaronicorum* (Toscolano: Alexander Paganini, 1521)[17]

Chapter 20, fo. 196ʳ (later editions pp. 390–1)

> O ventura bonis felicia secla diebus,
> Florida monstrabit cum Musica sacra Leonis
> Sub spe Pontificis quantum sit grata tonanti
> Nascere Phoebei decus o Iosquine senatus,
> Nascere qui primos in hac arte merebis honores.
> O felix Bido, Carpentras, Sylvaque, Broier,
> Vosque Leoninae cantorum squadra capellae,
> Iosquini quoniam cantus frifolabitis illos,
> Quos Deus auscultans coelum monstrabit apertum.
> Missa super voces Musarum, lassaque far mi,
> Missa super sextum, Fortunam, missaque musquae,
> Missaque de Domina, sine nomine, duxque ferare.
> Partibus in senis cantabitur illa Beata,
> Huc me sidereo, se conge, Preter, et illud
> Compositum Miserere Duca rogitante Ferare.
> Nascere phoebeae laus ergo prima cohortis
> O Iosquine Deo gratissime, nascere mundo
> Composite diu, quem clamet Musica patrem.
> Magnus adorabit tua tunc vestigia Brumel,
> Iannus motonus, **Petrus de robore**, festa
> Constans Iosquinus qui saepe putabitur esse.
> Tuque pater franchine novas componere normas
> Incipe, et antiquas remove[18] squallore sepultas.

> O happy age, destined to come in the good days
> When flourishing sacred music under the hope of Pope Leo
> Will show how pleasing it is to the thunderer.
> Be born, O Josquin, the glory of the senate of Phoebus.
> Be born, you who will win first honours in this art.
> O happy Bido, Carpentras, Sylva and Broier,
> And you, band of the singers of the Leonine chapel,
> Because you will sing elegantly those songs of Josquin.
> Listening to these, God will show the heaven opened.
> Missa super voces Musarum, and lassa far mi,
> Missa super sextum, Fortunam, and Missa musquae,
> And Missa de Domina, sine nomine, and dux ferare.
> It will be sung in six parts, this Beata,
> Huc me sidereo, se conge, Preter, and

---

[17] Folengo's work had a long and complex publishing history with four main versions appearing in 1517, 1521, *c.*1539/40, and 1552 (the last printed posthumously). Only the 1521 edition contains the passage in question; this version was reprinted in 1522, 1572, 1581, 1613, 1692 and possibly at other times. A summary of its publishing history is found in [Teofilo Folengo] Merlin Cocai, *Le Maccheonee*, 2 vols., 2nd edn., ed. Alessandro Luzio (Bari: Gius. Laterza & Figli, 1927–8), ii. 367–75.

[18] In the original: removet.

That Miserere composed at the request of the Duke of Ferrara.
Be born, therefore, first glory of the cohort of Phoebus,
O Josquin, most pleasing to God, be born to the world,
You who are going to compose for a long time, whom music acclaims as father.
Great Brumel will adore your footsteps,
Iannus Motonus, Petrus de robore, festa constans
Who often will be thought to be Josquin.
And you, father Franchinus, begin to create new rules
And remove the old ones, buried in squalor.

?Another edition of **Ornithoparchus**, *Musice active micrologus*[19] (see under 1517)

1522
Reprint of **Folengo** (see 1521)

c.1523?

Jean Daniel (*c.*1480/*c.*1501–*c.*1550), noël *Ung gracieulx oyselet*; appears in Jean Daniel, *S'ensuyvent plusieurs noels nouveaulx* ... (no publication information)[20]

Sur: Le Chant de la Grue	Sung to: The Song of the Crane
Ung gracieulx oyselet	A graceful little bird
Est venu en noz village,	Has come to our village,
Chantant ung chant nouvellet	Singing a new song,
Sans tenir propos vollage.	Bringing us the truth.
Il nous dit que Dieu est né,	It tells us that God is born,
Pour nous saulver ordonné,	Ordered to save us,
Et paix en terre est venue.	And peace on earth has come.
De joye en dance ma grue.	My crane dances for joy.
Noel!	Noel!
Dieu gard de mal le varlet	God protect from harm the one
Qui fait si jolys messaige;	Who brings such a pleasing message.
Il n'estoit pas tout seullet	He wasn't alone
A chanter si doulx langaige.	In singing such a sweet speech.
Les cieulx en ont résonné,	The heavens have resounded with it;
Tous instrumens ont sonné	All instruments have sounded
Si hault qu'en fendoit la nue.	So loudly that the clouds have burst!
De joye en chantoit ma grue.	My crane sings for joy.
Noel!	Noel!
Alexandre tout de het	Alexander all gaily
Sur trois parties fist raige	Had a big success with three parts.
Prioris le doucelet	Prioris the soft one

---

[19] This might be a ghost edition, never published but rather a mistake by Fétis; see Ornithoparchus, *A Compendium of Musical Practice*, p. viii.

[20] Date from Henri Chardon, *Les Noels de Jean Daniel dit Maitre Mitou, Organiste de Saint-Maurice & Chapelain de Saint-Pierre d'Angers, 1520–1530, précédes d'une étude sur sa vie et ses poésies* (Le Mans: Edmond Monnoyer, 1874), p. xlvii. The song was published, sometimes with changes, in other editions from *c.*1525–6, *c.*1537, between 1547 and 1566, between 1555 and 1597, *c.*1573–95, and *c.*1595. For a later version of the song, see Adrienne F. Block, *The Early French Parody Noël*, 2 vols. (Studies in Musicology, 36; Ann Arbor: UMI Research Press, 1983), ii. 145–6.

Y monstra bien son ouvraige.
Josquin si est adonné,
Qui par sus tous a tonné,
Aussi a fait {**De La Rue**},
Tant qu'en a dancé ma grue.
Noel!

Showed well his skill.
Josquin is so involved
That he drowned everyone out.
{De La Rue} did the same,
So that my crane danced.
Noel!

Aussi s'es meut Loyselet
Qui besongna de couraige,
Puis Fenin le proprelet
Ne mist ses oeuvres en caiges.
Robinet n'est étonné,
Qui si bien a bourdonné.
Chascun pousse à sa charrue
Et je fais dancer ma grue.
Noel!

Loyset is also so moved
That he's giving his all.
Then Févin, the proper fellow,
Doesn't hide his talent.
Robinet isn't astonished,
Who has sung the bass so well.
Each does his part
And I make my crane dance.
Noel!

Avons trouvé l'aignelet
Tenant bien pauvre mesnaige:
Le divin enfantelet
N'avoit pas royal paraige.
Trestous l'avons adoré
Et humblement vénéré;
Marie tous nous salue
Et tousjours dançoit ma grue.
Noel!

We have found the little lamb
Enduring well the poor surroundings.
The divine little infant
Wasn't dressed royally.
We have all adored him
And humbly revered him.
Mary greets us all
And my crane was always dancing.
Noel!

En ce petit hostelet
Richard fort ne fut saulvaige,
Deschanta ung motelet,
Dieu scet s'il estoit ramaige!
Gascoigne y fut bien nommé.
Et Mouton fort renommé.
Moullu tant doulcement rue,
Et tousjours dance ma grue.
Noel!

In this little inn
Richafort wasn't wild,
Singing a little motet.
God knows he can make a lot of noise!
Gascongne was well-named there
And Mouton well renowned.
Gentle Moulu was very excited
And my crane is always dancing.
Noel!

La bénigne dame oyoit
Des musiciens l'usaige;
A Joseph point n'ennuyoit
Qui avait plaisant visaige.
Divitis y a chanté,
De La Fage deschanté.
Chascun chante et diminue,
Et je fais fancer [*sic*] ma grue.
Noel!

The blessed lady heard
The work of musicians.
We can tell from Joseph's face
That he quite enjoyed himself.
Divitis sang there;
De la Fage has discanted.
Each sang with ornamentation,
And I make my crane dance.
Noel!

Janequin vint au roollet
Bien jouant son personnaige,
Claudin monstra son collet
Autant que nul de son aage.

Janequin came to the *roollet*
Playing well his part.
Claudin put in an appearance
Showing that he wasn't old.

Chascun a si bien joué	Each played so well
Que Jesus en est loué	To honour Jesus
En mainte façon congrue,	That they were almost able to do him justice.
Je lui présente ma grue.	I present my crane to him.
Noel!	Noel!

Or faisons, comme on souloit,	Since each is filled with music,
Au benoist Jesus hommaige.	Let's pay homage to the blessed Jesus.
Heureux sommes s'il vouloit	Happy are we if he wants
Nous préserver de dommaige,	To preserve us from harm,
Nous rendre par sa pitié	To deliver us by his pity,
Nostre roy plain d'amytié	Our king full of kindness,
Et tout faux conseil corrue,	And to prevent false counsel.
Si ferons dancer la grue.	All that will make the crane dance.
Amen.[21]	Amen.

1524

Republication of **Ornithoparchus**, *Musice active micrologus*, in Cologne, as *De arte cantandi micrologus*[22] (see under 1517)

1525

Pietro Aaron (*c.*1480–after 1545), *Trattato della natura et cognitione di tutti gli tuoni di canto figurato* (Venice: Bernardino Vitali, August 1525)[23]

Citation 1: Chapter 4, Dichiaratione del primo et secondo tuono, sig. bii^r

Alcuni altri sono terminati nel medesimo luogo & detti del secondo tuono, questi facilmente si comprendono per el cont[i]nuo processo discendente come ... Cenest pas di **Pierazzon de larue** (Certain other compositions, ending on this same step [G sol re ut], are said to be of the second tone; these are readily recognized by their extended downward range, such as ... *Ce n'est pas* by Pierazzon de larue[24])

Citation 2: Chapter 4, sig. b ii^r

Alcuni altri finiranno in D la sol re ... quando ascenderanno infino alla quinta o sesta voce, saranno del primo ... o sia el B molle o no Fours seu lament di **Pierazzon de Larue** (Certain other compositions end on D la sol re ... When they ascend as far as the fifth or sixth step, and especially when they ascend still further, they will be of the first tone, whether with a flat signature ... or without, as in *Fours seu lament* by Pierazzon de Larue[25])

Citation 3: Chapter 6, Dichiaratione del quinto et sesto tuono, sig. c i^v

Cioe ... el Santus et Agnus dei della messa de virgine maria di **Pierazzon de larue**, gliquali non altrimenti saranno chiamati rispetto allo ascenso et processo suo. ([In a discussion of composers adding flats to works in mode 5] Namely ... the Sanctus and Agnus Dei of the

---

[21] Text from Chardon, *Les Noels de Jean Daniel*, 7–9.

[22] Copies in the Houghton Library, Harvard University.

[23] All citations are taken from Pietro Aaron, *Trattato della natura et cognitione di tutti gli tuoni di canto figurato non da altrui piu scritti: A Facsimile of the Venice, 1525 Edition* (New York: Broude, 1979).

[24] Translation after Oliver Strunk (ed.), *Source Readings in Music History: The Renaissance* (New York: W. W. Norton, 1965), 23.

[25] Ibid. 24. This piece is actually a setting by Pipelare, but it is attributed to La Rue in 1502², which was the source for many of Aaron's examples.

mass of the Virgin Mary by Pierazzon de larue, which cannot be otherwise assigned in view of their upward range and procedure[26])

Citation 4: Chapter 7, Dichiaratione del settimo et ottavo tuono, sig. c ii[v]
Alcuni altri finiranno nella positione di G sol re ut . . . la Gloria della vergine maria di **Pierazzon de larue** per spetie fine & continuo ascenso saran chiamati del settimo tuoni. (Certain other compositions end in the position G sol re ut . . . the Gloria of the Virgin Mary by Pierazzon de larue should be assigned to the seventh tone by species, final, and extended upper range.[27])

c.1525-6

Another edition of **Jean Daniel**, noël *Ung gracieulx oyselet*, appears in Jean Daniel, *Noels nouveaulx*[28] (no publication information; see *c.*1523?)

1529

Pietro Aaron, *Toscanello in musica* (Venice: Bernardino and Mattheo de Vitali, 1529)[29]

Citation 1: Aggiunta, sig. Niii[v]
Piero de larue, in una canzona chiamata. Il est bien, quasi nel principio a la parte del controbasso sopra una breve, ha segnato el b molle in ♮ mi acuto per il diapénte imperfetto, ne la parte del suo controalto. (Piero de larue in a chanson called *Il est bien*, near the beginning of the bass part on a breve, has shown the *b molle* in ♮ mi acute because of the imperfect diapente with the contralto.[30])

Citation 2: Aggiunta, sig. Niii[v]
De gli quali per esser moderni, forse non presterrai a loro indubitata fede: ma io che questo in fra di me ho considerato, voglio per piu chiarezza, & satisfattione tua, adducere alcuni altri al proposito nostro antichi, come Orto, Alessandro agricola, **Pierazzon de larue**, Iapart, Compere, Isach, & Obreth. (Since all these are moderns, you may not have unshakeable faith in them, but I have considered these things carefully, and I wish to show you for your greater clearness and satisfaction some other pertinent examples from our ancients, such as Orto, Alexander Agricola, Pierazzon de larue, Japart, Compère, Isaac, and Obrecht.[31])

Citation 3: Aggiunta, sig. Niii[v]
Da poi **Pierrazon de larue**, sopra del canto. Por quoy, ha segnato in A re el ♭, per una quinta col tenore imperfetta a mezzo la prima riga del controbasso. (Pierrazon de larue in the song *Pour quoy*, has shown the ♭ on A re because of an imperfect fifth with the tenor in the middle of the first line of the contrabass.[32])

1531

Jacobus Meyerus, *Flandricarum rerum tomi X* (Antwerp: Guilielmus Vorstermann, 1531)[33]

---

[26] Strunk, *Source Readings in Music History: The Renaissance*, 26.   [27] Ibid. 27.
[28] See Block, *The Early French Parody Noël*, i. 135, no. 38; the date is from ibid. 37.
[29] This is a revision of Aaron's *Thoscanello de la musica* (Venice: Bernardino et Matheo de Vitali, 1523), to which an Aggiunta has been added. A third edition was published in 1539 and a fourth in 1562; each is apparently the same as the 1529 edition. All citations are from Pietro Aaron, *Toscanello in musica* (facs. edn., Bibliotheca musica bononiensis, Sez. II, 10; Bologna: Forni, 1969).
[30] Pietro Aaron, *Toscanello in Music: Book II, Chapters XXXVII–XXXX/Supplement*, trans. Peter Bergquist (Colorado Springs, Colorado: Colorado College Music Press, 1970), 19.
[31] Ibid.   [32] Ibid.
[33] The book was also published in July of the same year by Hubert Crokus in Bruges; in this edition the

Book 9, fo. 52^v

Foecunda insuper genitrix est Flandria laudatissimorum cantorum. Siquidem vocum nobilitate quacumuis Christiani orbis gente certare potest. Testes sunt Alexander nuper Philippi principis cantor **Petrus Vicanus** cantor maximi Pirncipis [*sic*] Caroli, Adrianus Vuillardus Rosilaria oriundus, cantor regis Ungariae, Thomas Martinus cum fratribus Petro ac Ioanne, patria Armentarius, monachus nunc (ut audio) Cartusiensis in Ambianis. (Moreover, Flanders is a rich mother of most excellent singers. In fact, it can contend in excellence of voices with whatever people of the Christian world that you like. Examples are Alexander [Agricola], recently singer of King Philip [the Fair], Petrus Vicanus, singer of the very great emperor Charles [V], Adrianus Vuillardus [Willaert], born in Roulears, singer of the King of Hungary, Thomas Martinus with his brothers Petrus and Johannes, native of Armentières, now (as I hear), a Carthusian monk in Amiens.)

1533

Giovanni Maria Lanfranco (*c*.1490–1545), *Scintille di musica* (Brescia: Lodovico Britannico, 1533)

Dedication, fo. ii^v

Et quantumque Iosquino oltre il segno di tanti altri nelli harmonici componimenti si trapassi, non possiede pero se non la sua stanza, lasciando la loro a **Pierson della Rue**, ad Agricola, a Giovan Moton, a Riccaforte, et a gli altri antichi, se antichi e lecito chiamarli.[34] (And however much Josquin surpassed the mark of so many others in the composing of harmonies, he possesses, for all that, only his own place, leaving theirs to Pierson della Rue, Agricola, Jean Mouton, Richafort, and to the other ancients, if it is permitted to call them ancients.[35])

Republication of **Ornithoparchus**, *Musice active micrologus*, in Cologne, as *De arte cantandi micrologus* (see under 1517)

1535

Republication of **Ornithoparchus**, *Musice active micrologus*, in Cologne, as *De arte cantandi micrologus* (see under 1517)

1537

Martin Luther (1483–1546), *Tischreden*, no. 3516, Ser. 15, Mathesius L. 724a

Prima Ianuarii anni 1537. Egregias cantilenas post coenam cecinerunt. Quas cum admiraretur Doctor Martinus, dixit cum singultu: Ach, wie feine musici sindt in 10 jahren gestorben! Iosquin, {**Petrus Loroe**}, Finck et multi alii excellentes. Die welt ist gelerter leuthe nimmer werth, sed vult habere rudissimos asinos, quales sunt Lypsenses, qui has positiones theologicas defendere conantur. (Tenens in manu positiones illorum.) Deinde conclusit: Wer do blindt ist, der sol nicht sehen.[36] (1 January 1537. After dinner they sang exceptional

passage in question appears on fo. 53^r.

[34] Giovanni Maria Lanfranco, *Scintille di musica*, facs. edn., ed. Giuseppe Massera (Bibliotheca musica bononiensis, Sez. II, 15; Bologna: Forni, 1970).

[35] Barbara Lee, 'Giovanni Maria Lanfranco's Scintille di musica and its Relation to 16th-Century Music Theory' (Ph.D. diss., Cornell University, 1961), 58.

[36] Martin Luther, *D. Martin Luthers Werke: Kritische Gesamtausgabe, Tischreden*, 6 vols. (Weimar: Hermann Böhlaus, 1912–21), iii. 371–2.

songs. When Dr Martinus admired them, he said with a gasp: 'Oh, what fine musicians have died in the last ten years! Josquin, {Petrus Loroe}, Finck, and many other excellent ones. The world is unworthy of its learned people, but prefers to have the most ignorant asses, such as the Leipzigers who try to defend these theological positions' (referring to those positions held in his hand). Therefore he concluded: 'None is so blind as he who will not see.')

Sebald Heyden (1499–1561), *Musica, id est Artis canendi, libri duo* (Nuremberg: J. Petreius, 1537)

Citation 1: Introduction, sig. Aii^v–Aiii^r
Quas vero Fugas non abs quibuslibet, sed ab illis optimis ac laudatissimis Musicis Iosquino, Oberto, **Petro de la rue**, Henricho Isaac, & similibus huc nobis commodato acceptas pueri sciant, ut & hoc nomine hos nostros libellos tanto pluris habeant, dum sciant, ita huc adscripta exempla, non tantum optima, sed & velut miracula quaedam, Musicae artis aestimanda esse. (But the boys should realize that I have received these *fugae* on loan not from any old source, but from the best and most approved musicians: Josquin, Obrecht, Petrus de la rue, Heinrich Isaac, and the like. So that they may hold these books of ours in the greater esteem for this reason as well, provided they know that the examples thus written down here are to be regarded not just as the best, but even so to speak as miracles of the musical art.[37])

Citation 2: Book II, Chapter 7, pp. 90–1
Alterum Argumentum **Petri de la Rue** est, ex Lomme arme ipsius. Fuga quatuor vocum ex unica. In qua Diminutus Discantus, Tenor proportionatus, Altus & Bassus integri hic imperfectus, ille perfectus canendi sunt. (The other argument is by Petrus de la Rue, from his *Lomme arme*, a *fuga* of four voices from one in which the discantus is sung *diminutus*, the tenor *proportionatus*, the altus *integer perfectus*, and the bassus *integer imperfectus*.) (Music example = Agnus II from *Missa L'homme armé I*)

Citation 3: Book II, Chapter 8, p. 108
Quis Cantus est Secundi Toni. Secundi Toni est, quicunque cantus cum re finali fa Semiditonum frequentius repetit . . . Exemplum. Duo, **Petri de la Rue**. O salutaris hostia (Which song is the second tone. The second tone is whatever song with a 're' final repeats the 'fa' *semiditonus* frequently . . . Example. Duo, Petrus de la Rue. *O salutaris hostia*.) (Music example = Pleni from *Missa O salutaris hostia*)

c.1537
Another edition of **Jean Daniel**, noël *Ung gracieulx oyselet*; appears in *Les Grans noelz nouveaulx* . . . (Paris: Pierre Sergent)[38] (see *c.1523*?)

1539
Pietro Aaron, *Toscanello in musica*, 3rd edition (see under 1529)

1540
Sebald Heyden, *De arte canendi, ac vero signorum in cantibus usu, libri duo* (Nuremberg: J. Petreius, 1540)

---

37 Translation after Judd, *Reading Renaissance Music Theory*, 98.
38 Date from Block, *The Early French Parody Noël*, i. 39.

Caput septimum: De unica Tactuum aequabilitate, in quantumlibet diversis cantuum speciebus seruanda: Deque mutua variorum Signorum resolutione . . . Attamen priusquam hoc praestem, certa argumenta Cantionum ex optimis Musicis adducam, quae, cum a nemine cantari possint, qui diversas Tactuum species usurpare velit. Per hoc utique convincent, omnia signa quantumlibet diversa, ad eiusdem Tactus Proportionem accommodari posse, & ex arte debere. . . .Tertium argumentum **Petri de la Rue** est, quod eandem necessitatem confirmat. Fuga quatuor vocum ex unica. In qua Diminutus Discantus, Tenor proportionatus, Altus & Bassus integri. hic imperfectus, ille perfectus canendi sunt.[39] (Chapter 7: Concerning a single, uniform tactus used in every different kind of song, and concerning the mutual resolution of various signs. . . . But first let me say that I will give definite proof in songs of the best composers, songs which, since they cannot be sung by anyone who tries to use different kinds of *tactus*, will fully demonstrate through this that all signs, however diverse, in conformity with the art can and must be fitted to the measurement of the same tactus. . . . Third proof confirming the same rule, by Petrus de la Rue. *Fuga* of four voices proceeding from one, in which the *discantus* is sung *diminutus*, the *tenor proportionatus*, the *altus integer perfectus*, and the *bassus integer imperfectus*.[40]) (Music example = Agnus II from *Missa L'homme armé I*)

Republication of **Ornithoparchus**, *Musice active micrologus,* in Cologne, as *De arte cantandi micrologus* (see under 1517)[41]

1545[15]

another appearance of *Nymphes des bois* (see under *c.*1498): *Le septiesme livre contenant vingt & quatre chansons . . . de . . . Iosquin des pres* (Antwerp: Tylman Susato), fos. 13ʳ, 13ʳ, 13ʳ, 14ᵛ, motet-chanson setting by Josquin:

Iosquin brumel pirchon (A and T: pierchon) compere

1547
Heinrich Glarean, *Dodecachordon* (Basel: H. Petri, September 1547)

Citation 1: Book II, Chapter VI, p. 75: What is necessary to establish 12 modes, if indeed our eighth mode has been correctly separated from the others.
Quam inde falsam facile ostendemus. Si enim septimus Modus in sua diapente de tertio loco semitonium in secundum deiecerit, ut ex ut sol fiat re la, prorsus incidet in primum Modum. Quo pacto **Petrus Platensis** Missam: Puer natus, licenter immutavit.[42] (We shall easily show in what manner this is false. For if the seventh mode drops the semitone in its fifth from the third position to the second position, so that *re la* is formed out of *ut sol*, it will fall completely into the first mode. Petrus Platensis has freely changed the *Missa Puer natus* in this way.[43])

Citation 2: Book II, Chapter XI, p. 91: Concerning the mutual interchange of modes
Quamquam quis Modus est, qui non ad diversa applicari queat modo sit in genium ad eam

---

[39] Sebald Heyden, *De arte canendi: A Facsimile of the 1540 Nuremberg Edition* (Monuments of Music and Music Literature in Facsimile, Second Series: Music Literature, 139; New York: Broude, 1969), 110, 112.

[40] Sebald Heyden, *De arte canendi*, trans. Clement A. Miller (Musicological Studies and Documents, 26; n.p.: American Institute of Musicology, 1972), 97, 99.

[41] No copy extant; see Ornithoparchus, *A Compendium of Musical Practice*, p. ix.

[42] Henricus Glareanus, *Dodecachordon: A Facsimile of the 1547 Basel Edition* (New York: Broude, 1967), 75.

[43] Heinrich Glarean, *Dodecachordon*, 2 vols., trans. Clement A. Miller (Musicological Studies and Documents, 6; n.p.: American Institute of Musicology, 1965), i. 113.

rem felix, quale aut Iodoci Pratensis, aut **Petri à Platea,** aut similium.[44] (Yet what mode is there that cannot be applied to different songs, provided that the happy genius of such as Iodoci Pratensis, Petrus à Platea, or similar men, is present?[45])

Citation 3: Book II, Chapter XVIII, p. 113: Concerning the second octave species and the one mode belonging to it.

In Poëtica pulchrum est eximios sequi uates, ita Virgilius Theocritum Hesiodum ac Homerum sequi non dubitavit. In musicis vero, Dij boni quàm hoc quibusdam turpe videtur, si quis vel Iodocum Pratensem, in hoc negocio propé Virgilium, vel Ioannem Ockenheim eruditissimum virum, vel **Petrum Platensem** suavissimum modulatorem sequi conetur. Cum illi tamen cantus naturam ingenio ac arte imitati, egregiam laudem iure meruerint.[46] (In poetry it is a fine thing to follow distinguished masters, as Virgil did not hesitate to follow Theocritus, Hesiod, and Homer. Yet in music, good gods, how shameful this seems to some, if anyone should attempt to follow either Iodocum Pratensem, nearly comparable to Virgil in this matter, or Ioannem Ockenheim, a very erudite man, or Petrus Platensis, a most pleasing musician, although these men have expressed the nature of song with ingenuity and artistry, and have justly merited surpassing praise.[47])

Citation 4: Book II, Chapter XXVI, p. 134: Concerning the seventh octave-species and its two modes.

Porrò ad hunc Modum multae sunt iucundissimae cantiones, ut in mille Responsorijs Introitibusque patet. Viri Galilaei huius est Modi, Intr[o]itus. Item: Puer natus est nobis, quem **Petrus Platensis** Gallus elegantissime quatuor instituit vocibus, ex Mixolydio tamen Dorium instituens non absque licentia, sicut postea Ioannes Mouton in Ionicum eundem mutavit: Responsoria, ut Cives Apostolorum: &, Summae Trinitati, Utrunque oppido eleganter hunc Modum referens. Quae exempla, ubique obvia studiosis, examinanda veniunt.[48] (Moreover, many extremely pleasing songs are in this mode, as is evident in a thousand Responsories and Introits. The Introit Viri Galilaei is in this mode, also Puer natus est nobis, which the Gallic Petrus Platensis has set most elegantly in four voices, yet forming the Dorian from the Mixolydian with freedom, just as Ioannes Mouton later changed it into the Ionian, and such Responsories as Cives Apostolorum and Summae Trinitati, each of which reflects this mode very beautifully. The examples should be examined wherever they are met with by the studious.[49])

Citation 5: Book II, Chapter XXXVI, p. 164: That modes are recognized principally by the octave division, which is made through the fourth and fifth consonances.

Aeolius inter G ac g, ad quam formam est Tenor **Petri Platensis** in missa de S. Antonio, & in vulgata Cantione Basias me, quam Iodocus à Prato instituit potest & esse inter c ac D, si fa fuerit in b clavi, ut in Sacris solemnibus.[50] (The Aeolian moves between G and g, and the tenor in the *Missa de S. Antonio* of Petrus Platensis follows this form, and also the tenor in the commonly known song *Basias me*, which Iodocus à Prato has set; it can also occur between *c* and *C*, if *fa* is on the *b* key, as in sacred songs.[51])

Citation 6: Book III, Chapter XIII, p. 241: Examples of the twelve modes, and first of the Hypodorian and Aeolian.

---

44 Glareanus, *Dodecachordon: A Facsimile*, 91.

46 Glareanus, *Dodecachordon: A Facsimile*, 113.

48 Glareanus, *Dodecachordon: A Facsimile*, 134.

50 Glareanus, *Dodecachordon: A Facsimile*, 164.

45 Glarean, *Dodecachordon*, i. 130.

47 Glarean, *Dodecachordon*, i. 151.

49 Glarean, *Dodecachordon*, i. 170.

51 Glarean, *Dodecachordon*, i. 197.

Quo sit ut numeris respondeant etiam cantiones, et quod ad Monadem attinet, Hoc est duarum vocum concentum ex una voce, duo exempla ponemus. Alterum ex Iusquini Hercule in sua sede positum ac finitum in D. Alterum per diatessaron levatum in G, sed non absque fa in b clavi, ut in Dorio Hypodorioque frequenter fieri solet ex **Petri Platensis** Missa. O Salutaris Hostia. In priore exemplo Inferior vox diapente infra incipiens semibrevi praecedit. In posteriore contrarium fit, Nam Tenor incipit, & sequitur Basis in diapente post integrum tempus. Eiusdem alterum exemplum ex **Petro Platensi**.[52] (Because it happens that songs also correspond to numbers and because it pertains to the monad, namely, a harmony of two voices arising from one voice, we shall present two examples, the first from Josquin's *Missa Hercules*, placed on its proper tonic and ending on D, the second from *Missa O Salutaris Hostia* of Petrus Platensis, raised to G through the fourth, but not without *fa* on the *b* key, as frequently happens in the Dorian and Hypodorian. In the first example the lower voice, beginning below the fifth, precedes it by a semibreve. The opposite occurs in the following example, for the tenor begins and the bass follows at the fifth below after a complete *tempus*. . . Second example of the same mode [Hypodorian] from Petrus Platensis.[53]) (Music example = Pleni from *Missa O salutaris hostia*)

Citation 7: Book III, Chapter XIII, p. 243

Scio multam nos illis alijs quoque debere gratiam, qui apud me in magna sunt existimatione, cum ob ingenij acrimoniam, tum ob non proletariam Musicae rei eruditionem, quod de Okenhemio, Hobrechtho, Isaaco, **Petro Platensi**, Brumelio, atque alijs, quos enumerare longum esset, hoc in libro saepe testati sumus.[54] (I know that we owe much gratitude to the others [besides Josquin] who are held in great veneration by me, not only because of a high degree of talent, but also because of an uncommon erudition in musical matters, which we have often declared in this book concerning Okenhemio, Hobrechtho, Isaaco, Petrus Platensis, Brumelio and others whom it would take long to enumerate.[55])

Citation 8: Book III, Chapter XIV, p. 276: Examples of the Hypophrygian

Huius quidem integrum nullum, quod sciam, invenitur, sed ut fingi queat, superiore volumine docuimus. Apud **Petrum Platensem** defectum supernè ditono inveni, adiecto infernè tono, cum tamen ea missa esset ad Aeolium intonata Modum, supernè deficiens Tono, quem infernè habet, ut ad finem Capitis 36. superioris libri ostendimus . . . Haec Cantio praeter expectatum authori excidisse videtur, Cuius Tenor, ut diximus, huius Modi finalem habet clavem, supernè ditono ab eius diapason deficiens, infernè tonum adijcit. Reliquae voces à Phrygij natura haud multum absunt. Cum tota missa ad Æolium sit instituta Modum ab authore, ut iam diximus . . . Hyperaeolij alterum exemplum, Author **Petrus Platensis**[56] (So far as I know no complete example of this mode has been found, but we taught in the previous book that it can be composed. In Petrus Platensis I have found an example lacking a major third above and adding a whole tone below; however, since this Mass is sung according to the Aeolian mode, lacking a whole tone above which it has below, as we have shown at the end of Chapter 36 of the preceding book . . . . The following song seems to have escaped the composer involuntarily. Its tenor, as we said, has the final key of this mode, lacking by a major third its octave above, and adding a whole tone below. The remaining voices are not far removed from the nature of Phrygian, although the entire Mass has been arranged according to the Aeolian mode by the composer, as we have already

---

52 Glareanus, *Dodecachordon: A Facsimile*, 241; example on 242.
53 Glarean, *Dodecachordon*, ii., 249; example on 308.
54 Glareanus, *Dodecachordon: A Facsimile*, 243.   55 Glarean, *Dodecachordon*, ii., 249.
56 Glareanus, *Dodecachordon: A Facsimile*, 276; example on 278.

said . . . Another example of the hyperaeolian—Petrus Platensis, author.)⁵⁷ (Music example = Christe from *Missa de Sancto Antonio*)

Citation 9: Book III, Chapter XXIV, p. 363: Examples of the connection of two modes and also in passing, a eulogy of Josquin des Prez.

Unde & quidam non inepte, alterum Virgilio, alterum Ovidio comparari merito posse contendunt. Quod si admittimus, **Petrum Platensem**, mirum in modum iucundum modulatorem cui potius quàm comparabimus? ita Isaacum fortassis Lucano. Feum Claudiano, Brumelium Statio, sed ineptus haud immerito videar, de ijs tam ieiune pronuntiare, ac iure forsitan audiam illud vulgatum.⁵⁸ (From this some aptly maintain that the one [Josquin] could justly be compared to Virgil, the other [Obrecht] to Ovid. But if we allow this, to whom shall we compare Petrus Platensis, a wonderfully pleasing composer, other than to Horace? So perhaps Isaacus to Lucan, Feum [Févin] to Claudian, Brumelius to Statius; but I may seem truly inept to speak about them so sketchily, and perhaps I may justly hear the well-known saying: 'Let the cobbler stick to his last.'⁵⁹)

Citation 10: Book III, Chapter XXVI, pp. 444–5: Concerning the skill of *symphonetae*
Sed admirabilius longè est **Petri Platensis** Exemplum, quod aemulatione haud dubie Iusquini eadem proportione, caeterum quatuor diversis signis praescripsit. In eo Basis ac Altus absque diminutione incedunt, hic perfecti, illa imperfecti temporis, Cantus vero cum diminutione imperfecti item temporis. Tenor sesquipla ratione constat, non omnino difficile cantatu, si quis Hemioliam recte intromiscuerit. Hypodorij est Modi, quanquam fine claudicans. Id alij resoluerunt, nobis satius visum est, nudum proponere. Neque ob id lector iure succensere nobis poterit, quando tàm multa alia bona fide indicaverimus, si ipsi etiam quaedam discutienda relinquimus . . . **Petri Platensis** IIII vocum fuga ex unica ad Hypodorium . . . Idem **Petrus Platensis** Missam totam quatuor item vocum ex unica instituit. O salutaris hostia, literis innuens cuiusque vocis & principium & finem. Cuius unum dúntaxat Kyrie adponere placuit cum initii resolutione, ut ex his Lector, quae nimis multa sunt, reliqua facilius ad eandem formam discutiat. Sanè vocum initia hisce IIII produntur literis, S.C.T.B. & S quidem supremae vocis, nos Cantum vocamus, C.Contratenoris, nunc Altum nominant. T. Tenoris. B. Baseos. Finis etiam eisdem, sed semicirculo tectis literis indicatur . . . Eiusdem **Petri Platensis** IIII vocum fuga ex unica sed aliter, ad eundem Hypodorium.⁶⁰ (But far more astonishing is the example of Petrus Platensis, which undoubtably in emulation of Josquin, he prefixed with the same proportion and moreover with four different signs. In it the bass and alto move without diminution, the latter in *tempus perfectum*, the former in *tempus imperfectum*, but the cantus moves in a diminution of *tempus imperfectum*. The tenor has a one and one half ratio, not very difficult to sing if one has correctly intermingled the *hemiola*. The song is in the Hypodorian mode, although it is incomplete at the end. Others⁶¹ have resolved it, and we thought it sufficient to present it. Therefore, the reader cannot be justly irritated with us if we have left some examples for him to solve, since we have conscientiously disclosed so many others . . . In the hypodorian, a fuga of four voices arising from one voice, by Petrus Platensis [Music example = Agnus II from the *Missa L'homme armé I*] . . . Petrus Platensis also has composed an entire Mass, *O salutaris hostia*, of four voices arising from one; he indicates the beginning and the end of each voice by letters. We decided to present only one Kyrie, with the resolution of its beginning, so that

---

⁵⁷ Glarean, *Dodecachordon*, ii. 254–5; example on 350–1.
⁵⁸ Glareanus, *Dodecachordon: A Facsimile*, 363. ⁵⁹ Glarean, *Dodecachordon*, ii. 265.
⁶⁰ Glareanus, *Dodecachordon: A Facsimile*, 444–5. ⁶¹ Glarean is referring here to Heyden.

from these examples, which are far too numerous, the reader may investigate the others in the same way. The beginnings of the voices are indicated by the four letters S.C.T.B; namely, S for the highest voice, which we call *cantus*; C for the contratenor, now called alto; T for the tenor, and B for the bass. Their ending is indicated by the same letters covered by a semicircle ... Also in the hypodorian and by Petrus Platensis. A fuga of four voices arising from one, but in another way[62]) (Music example = Kyrie I from the *Missa O salutaris hostia*)

after 1547[63]
[**Giovanthomaso Cimello**] (*c.*1510–after 1579): *Della perfettione delle quattro note maggiori* (BolC B57)

Citation 1: fo. [11]^r, top
Musical example = Agnus II from the *Missa L'homme armé I*, headed 'Unusquisque manebit in sua vocatione'[64] (Each one shall remain in his calling), and followed by 'nulla dies sine linea maximum in punctis' (No day without the maximum limit in *punctis*)

Citation 2: fo. [11]^r, bottom
Musical example = Kyrie I of *Missa O salutaris hostia*, headed 'semper pacem habebunt' (They will always have peace), and followed by 'O vos felices qui tot et tanta perfruimini in pace' (O you happy ones who are delighted by so many and in so much peace)

between 1547 and 1566
Another edition of **Jean Daniel**, noël *Ung gracieulx oyselet*, appears in *Les Grans noelz . . .* (Paris: Jehan Bonfons)[65] (see *c.*1523?)

1552
François Rabelais (1494–1553/4), *Le Quart livre des faicts et dicts heroïques du bon Pantagruel* (Paris: Michel Fezandat, 1552)

Prologue to the 1552 edition[66]
Et me soubvient (car j'ay mentule, voyre diz je memoire, bien belle, et grande assez pour emplir un pot beurrier) avoir un jour de Tubilustre, es feries de ce bon Vulcan en may, ouy jadis en un beau parterre Josquin des prez, Olkegan, Hobrethz, Agricola, Brumel, Camelin, Vigoris, de la fage, Bruyer, Prioris, Seguin, {De la rue}, Midy, Moulu, Mouton, Guascoigne, Loyset compere, Penet, Fevin, Rouzée, Richardford, Rousseau, Consilion, Constantio festi, Jacquet bercan chantans melodieusement Grand Tibault, se voulent coucher . . . Neuf Olympiades et un an intercalare aprés (ô belle mentule, voire diz je, memoire. Je soloecise souvent en la symbolization et colliguance de ces deux motz), je ouy Adrian villart, Gombert, Janequin, Arcadelt, Claudin, Certon, Manchicourt, Auxerre, Villiers, Sandrin, Sohier, Hesdin, Morales, Passereau, Maille, Maillart, Jacotin, Heurteur, Verdelot, Carpentras, Lheritier, Cadeac, Doublet, Vermont, Bouteiller, Lupi, Pagnier, Millet, Du mollin, Alaire,

---

[62] Glarean, *Dodecachordon*, ii. 274–6; examples on 524–6.

[63] James Haar, *The Science and Art of Renaissance Music*, ed. Paul Corneilson (Princeton: Princeton University Press, 1998), 152, places the treatise in the 1540s; its dependence on Glarean puts it after the appearance of *Dodecachordon* (see ibid. 158).

[64] Haar, ibid. 157, notes the reliance on 1 Cor. 7: 20, 'Unusquisque in qua vocatione vocatus est in ea permaneat'.

[65] Date from Block, *The Early French Parody Noël*, i. 141. Ibid., ii. 147, implies that it appears twice in this volume (her S3 and S4).

[66] Earlier versions of *Le Quart livre* have a different prologue.

Marault, Morpain, Gendre et autres joyeulx musiciens en un jardin secret soubz belle feuillade au tour d'un rampart de flaccons, jambons, pastez et diverses Cailles coyphées mignonnement chantans. S'il est ainsi que coingnée sans manche. . . .[67] (And I remember (because I have a member, I mean memory, quite beautiful, and big enough to fill a pot of butter) having heard once, on a day of Tubilustrium, the holiday of the good Vulcan in May, Josquin des Prez, Ockeghem, Obrecht, Agricola, Brumel, Camelin, Vigoris, de la Fage, Bruhier, Prioris, Seguin, {De la rue}, Midy, Moulu, Mouton, Gascongne, Loyset Compère, Penet, Févin, Rousée, Richafort, Rousseau, Conseil, Constanzo Festa, and Jacquet de Berchem singing melodiously in a flowerbed *Grand Tibault se voulent coucher*. Nine Olympiads and an intercalary year later (oh beautiful member, I mean memory, I often confuse the symbolism and relation of these two words), I heard Adrian Willaert, Gombert, Janequin, Arcadelt, Claudin, Certon, Manchicourt, Auxerre, Villiers, Sandrin, Sohier, Hesdin, Morales, Passereau, Maille, Maillard, Jacotin, Le Heurteur, Verdelot, Carpentras, Lhéritier, Cadeac, Doublet, Vermont, Le Bouteiller, Lupi, Pagnier, Millet, Du Mollin, Alaire, Marault, Morpain, Le Gendre, and other joyous musicians in a secret garden under beautiful foliage around a rampart of bottles, hams, pies, and various quails, beautifully arranged, singing *S'il est ainsi que coingnée sans manche*.)

Adrianus Petit Coclico (1499/1500–62 or later), *Compendium musices* (Nuremberg: Johannes Montanus & Ulrich Neuber, 1552)[68]

Citation 1: Preface to Noric Youth, sig. A2ʳ

Nam qui hactenus eam artem iuventuti proposuerunt, maxima ex parte (ut absit invidia verbo) tantum Theorici, non practici fuerunt, nec eo docendi modo, quo Principes Musicorum Iosquinus de Pres, **Petrus de La Rue,** & alij, quos mundus suspicit, & admiratur, usi sunt. (Those who have previously exposed this art to youth have been, for the most part, only theorists (and I mean no disparagement in this term), not practical musicians, nor, in their teaching, have they used that method that the princes of music, Josquin des Près, Petrus de La Rue and others whom the world esteems and admires used.[69])

Citation 2: Concerning the types of musicians, sig. [Biv]ʳ⁻ᵛ

In tertio genere, sunt Musici praestantissimi, & ceterorum quasi reges, qui non in arte docenda haerent, sed theoriam optime & docte cum practica coniungunt, qui cantuum virtutes, & omnes compositionum nervos intelligunt, & vere sciunt cantilenas ornare, in ipsis omnes omnium affectus exprimere, & quod in Musico summum est, & elegantissimum vident, & in omnium admiratione sunt, quorum cantilenae, vel solae sunt admiratione dignae. Inter hos facile princeps fuit Iosquinus de Pres, cui ego tantum tribuo, ut eum omnibus ceteris praeferam. In hoc etiam genere sunt peritissimi Musici, & artificiosissimi Symphonistae: **Petrus de La rue,** Brumel, Henricus Isaac, Ludovicus Senfel, Adrian Willarth, Le brun, Concilium, Morales, La fage, Lerithier, Nicolaus Gombert, Criquilon, Champion, & Iaquet, Pipelare, Nicolaus Paien, Courtois, Meyster Ian, Lupi, Lupus, Clemens non Papa, Petrus Massenus, Iacopus de Buis, & innumeri alij, quos omitto brevitatis gratia. (In the third type, there are the most outstanding musicians and almost as kings of the others, men who do not specialize in teaching the art, but join together theory

---

[67] François Rabelais, *Œuvres complètes* (n.p.: Gallimard, 1994), 530–1.

[68] All citations are from Adrian Petit Coclico, *Compendium musices* (facs. edn., ed. Manfred F. Bukofzer (Kassel and Basel: Bärenreiter, 1954)).

[69] Translation after Adrian Petit Coclico, *Musical Compendium (Compendium Musices)*, trans. Albert Seay (Colorado Springs, Colorado: Colorado College Music Press, 1973), 1.

and practice in the best and [most] learned way, men who understand the virtues of songs and the full details of compositions, and truly know how to embellish melodies, to express in them all the emotions of all kinds. They see what is highest and most elegant in music and are in the admiration of all, men whose melodies alone are worthy of admiration. Among these the chief is easily Josquin des Prez, to whom I owe so much and whom I prefer to all the others. In this type are such most skilled musicians and artful symphonists as: Petrus de La Rue, Brumel, Heinrich Isaac, Ludwig Senfl, Adrian Willaert, Le Brun, Consilium, Morales, Lafage, Lheritier, Nicolas Gombert, Crecquillon, Champion and Jacquet, Pipelare, Nicolas Payen, Courtois, Maistre Jan, Lupi, Lupus, Clemens non Papa, Petrus Massenus, Jacob Buus and innumerable others, whom I omit for brevity's sake.[70])

Citation 3: Concerning elegance and ornamentation or method of performance in singing, sig. Hiii[v]

Qualem enim quisque Praeceptorem nactus est in iuventute, talis efficitur cantor, quod videre licet in Belgicis, Hannoniensibus & Gallis, qui singulare quoddam donum in canendo prae alijs nationibus habent. Vixerunt apud hos Musicorum principes plurimi, Iosquinus de Pres, **Petrus de La rue**, Iacobus Scampion, et alij, qui admirandis, & suavissimis clausularum elegantijs usi sunt, horum virorum relictus odor in scholis illarum regionum adhuc reservatur, ac a Musices studiosis hauritur, dum discipuli Praeceptores fideliter imitantur. . . . Quandoquidem vero in his regionibus perpauci sunt, qui praecipuorum veterum Musicorum in canendo suavitatem calleant, consultum duxi aliquot exempla ad scribere, quae ad omnes clausulas possint applicari, dum silent syllabae, aut verba quae notis supponuntur. (Whoever has found such a teacher in his youth makes the kind of singer that ones sees in the Belgians, men from Hainaut, and the French, who have a special gift in singing above those of other nations. Among these men have lived most of the princes of musicians, Josquin des Près, Petrus de La rue, Jacob Scampion and others, who have performed the smoothest and [most] elegant passages that must be admired. The influence of these men, left in the schools of these regions, is still preserved and is continued by scholars of music, since their pupils faithfully imitate their teachers . . . since there are, in our own regions, only a few who in their singing understand the smoothness of these extraordinary old musicians, I have decided to write out a few examples . . . [71])

Citation 4: Concerning the rules of counterpoint, according to the doctrine of Josquin des Pres, [sig. Iiiii[r]]

Si enim hominum aures offenderet, cur non magis Iosquini, **Petri de la Rue**, & eorum successorum, quibus hae fuerunt delicatissime. Cur non Imperatorum, Regum, Principum, Pontificum, qui huius artis ignaros in Cantorum suorum cumulum recipere dedignantur. (If it [counterpoint] has offended the ears of men, why not more those of Josquin, Petrus de la Rue, and their successors, whose ears were most delicate? Why not those of emperors, kings, princes, and popes who scorned to receive men ignorant of this art into the group of their singers?[72])

1554
Johann Zanger (?1517–87): *Practicae musicae praecepta* (Leipzig: Georgij Hantzsch, 1554)[73]

Citation 1 (in a discussion of modus minor imperfectus), sig. I 4[v]
Et licet rarissima exempla, uitio fortassis exscribentium, reperiantur per modum minorem

---

[70] Coclico, *Musical Compendium*, 8.   [71] Ibid. 20.   [72] Ibid. 21.
[73] My thanks to Bonnie Blackburn for kindly supplying the citations from this treatise.

imperfectum signata, eo quod quantitates cum tempore imperfecto, conueniant. tamen memini me in uetusto codice uidisse exemplum, **Petri de larue**, in Missa, cum iocunditate, ubi ni fallor author innuit ex more Ecclesiae, summa maiestate & reuerentia hoc genus cantionis esse occinendum. (And although very rare examples are found marked with modus minor imperfectus, perhaps because of the fault of the scribes, because the quantities agree with imperfect tempus. Still, I remember having seen an example in an old codex, in the *Missa Cum iocunditate* of Petrus de larue, where, unless I am mistaken, the author agreed, in accordance with the church, that this type of song ought to be sung with the greatest majesty and reverence.) (Music example = Et incarnatus of the *Missa Cum iocunditate*, four voices only, without altus)

Citation 2 (in a discussion of canons), sig. S 4^v
Fuga **Petri de Larue** .4. uocum ex unica, ubi tripla ad signa temporis refertur. (Fugue of Petrus de Larue, 4 voices from one, where the tripla refers to the signs of tempus.) (Music example = Agnus II of the *Missa L'homme armé I*)

1555
Reprint of **Ornithoparchus**, *Micrologus active micrologus* (see under 1517)[74]

between 1555 and 1597
Another edition of **Jean Daniel**, noël *Ung gracieulx oyselet*, appears in *La Grand Bible des noelz* . . . (Lyons: Benoist Rigaud)[75] (see *c.*1523?)

1556
Hermann Finck (1527–58), *Practica musica* (Wittenberg: Georg Rhaw, 1556; original edition)[76]

Citation 1: Book I, De Musicae Inventoribus, sig. Aij^r
Circa annum millesimum quadringentesimum & octuagesimum & aliquanto post alij extiterunt precedentibus longe praestantiores. Illi enim in docenda arte non ita immorati sunt, sed erudite Theoricam cum Practica coniunxerunt. Inter hos sunt Henricus Finck, qui non solum ingenio, sed praestanti etiam eruditione excelluit, durus vero in stylo. Floruit tunc etiam Iosquinus de Pratis, qui vere pater Musicorum dici potest, cui multum est attribuendum: antecellit enim multis in subtilitate & suauitate, sed in compositione nudior, hoc est, quamvis in inueniendis fugis est acutissimus, utitur tamen multis pausis. In hoc genere sunt et alij peritissimi Musici, scilicet, Okekem, Obrecht, **Petrus de larue**, Brumelius, Henricus Isaac, qui partim ante Iosquinum, partim cum illo fuerunt, et deinceps Thomas Stoltzer, Steffanus Mahu, Benedictus Ducis, & alij multi quos brevitatis gratia omitto. (Around the year 1480 and a little after there lived others who were far ahead of their predecessors. They were not involved to so great an extent with the art of teaching, but skilfully combined theory with practice. Among them was Heinrich Finck, who excelled not only by virtue of his talent, but by his superior intellect, but was hard, however, in style. Then there flourished Josquin des Prez, who can truly be called the father of musicians, to whom a great deal is to be attributed; he surpassed a great many in subtlety and charm, but in composition was somewhat bare, in that, although he was skilled in the invention of *fugae*, he made use of a great many

---

[74] See Ornithoparchus, *A Compendium of Musical Practice*, p. ix.
[75] Date from Block, *The Early French Parody Noël*, i. 131.
[76] An expanded edition was published in the same year. Citations for the original edition are from Hermann Finck, *Practica musica* (facs. edn., Hildesheim and New York: Georg Olms, 1971).

rests. There are other skilled musicians belonging to this group, such as Ockeghem, Obrecht, Petrus de larue, Brumel, and Heinrich Isaac, who in part lived before Josquin and in part at the same time, and then Thomas Stoltzer, Stefan Mahu, Benedictus Ducis, and many others whom I omit for the sake of brevity.[77])

Citation 2: Book II, De Tactu, sig. F iii[r]–[iv][r]
Sequuntur exempla ad tactum Maiorem, Minorem & Proporcionatum. (Examples follow showing major tactus, minor tactus, and proportionate tactus.) (Music example, anonymous and labelled 'Hoc est exemplum ad tactum maiorem' [This is the example of major tactus] = Kyrie I of the *Missa de beata virgine*)[78]

Citation 3: Book III, De Canonibus, sig. Cc[v]
Descende gradatim. Quando aliqua clausula, in cantilena quae plurium vocum est, in una tantum voce saepius ponitur, tunc ea singulis vicibus per secundam deprimenda est . . . (Descend step by step. When any clausula, in a song for many voices, is frequently placed in only one voice, then it is put down by a second that way each successive time.) (Music example on sig. Hh ij[v]–Hh iij[r] = initial Sanctus of the *Missa Cum iocunditate*)

Hermann Finck, *Practica musica* (Wittenberg: Georg Rhaw, 1556; expanded edition)[79]

1558
Gioseffo Zarlino (1517–90), *Le istitutioni harmoniche* (Venice: [Pietro Da Fino], 1558)[80]

Citation 1: Part III, Chapter 28: A Composition Must Begin with a Perfect Consonance
Ma non è però da lodare, che due parti siano distanti ne i loro principij dalla parte del Soggetto, o nel grave, o nello acuto, l'una per una Quarta, & l'altra per una Quinta: perciohe allora queste parti verrebbeno ad esser distanti l'una dall'altra per una seconda, & nel pigliar le voci farebbeno dissonanza, & potrebbe essere, che l'una di esse parti facesse il suo principio sopra una chorda, che no sarebbe del Modo, sopra'l quale è fondata la compositione, o cantilena. Et quantunque tale avertimento sia buono, tuttavia non è necessario, quando il Soggetto principale della compositione, fusse composto con tale arteficio, che l'una parte cantasse sopra l'altra in Fuga, o Consequenza, di modo che due di loro cantassero sopra la parte principale del Soggetto, nell'acuto, over nel grave, l'una distante dall'altra per una Quinta, overo per una Quarta: overamente che l'una fusse distante dal Soggetto per una Quarta, et l'altra per una Quinta, o per altro intervallo; Si come si puo vedere nel motetto,[81] Pater de celis deus, che fece **P. della Rue** a sei voci, & nel motetto Virgo prudentissima, che gia composi à sei voci, nel quale tre parti cantano in fuga, o consequenza, due verso l'acuto, & una verso il grave per gli istessi intervalli; & nel pigliar le voci si ode un tal incommodo.[82] (However it is not praiseworthy when two parts enter at a distance from the subject, above or below, of a fourth *and* a fifth, for then they would form a second between themselves. The entrance would then sound dissonant, and one of the voices might begin out of the mode of

[77] Translation after Frank Eugene Kirby, 'Hermann Finck's Practica Musica: A Comparative Study in 16th Century German Musical Theory' (Ph.D. diss., Yale University, 1957), 77.

[78] My thanks to Bonnie Blackburn for kindly bringing this example to my attention.

[79] Hermann Finck, *Practica musica* (facs. edn., Bibliotheca musica bononiensis, Sez. II, 21; Bologna: Forni, 1969); citations and locations are the same as in the original edition.

[80] Reprinted in 1561 and 1562; the third revised edition appeared in 1573 (this drops the reference to *Missa Ave Maria*) and again in 1588, the latter time as vol. 1 of Zarlino's complete works.

[81] The indication *a sei voci* is included in the 1573 edition.

[82] Gioseffo Zarlino, *Le istitutioni harmoniche: A Facsimile of the 1558 Venice Edition* (Monuments of Music and Music Literature in Facsimile, Second Series, Music Literature, 1; New York: Broude, 1965), 175.

the composition. Although generally inadvisable, such an entrance is acceptable when the principal subject of a composition is so written that one part sounds above the other in fugue or consequence and two of them enter a fourth or fifth apart singing the subject in the upper or lower register. The same holds also when one part starts a fourth away from the subject and the other a fifth or other interval. These exceptions may be observed in the six-voice motet 'Pater de coelis deus' of P. della Rue, and in my six-voice motet 'Virgo prudentissima', in which three voices are in fugue or consequence at the same intervals, two above and one below. There is some disturbance to the ear when the voices enter.[83])

Citation 2: Part III, Chapter 66: Some Advice about Compositions for More than Three Voices

Sarà anco lodevole il comporre Quattro parti sopra una, ponendone alcune in Fuga, & alcune nella Imitatione; come fece **P. della Rue** nella messa O Salutaris hostia; & Adriano anche, con molta leggiadria, nella messa Mente tota; delle quali l'una, & l'altra si trova a Quattro voci.[84] (It is also admirable to write four voices on one, some in fugue, others in imitation, as P. della Rue did in the mass 'O salutaris hostia' and Adrian very gracefully in the mass 'Mente tota', both for four voices.[85])

Citation 3: Part IV, Chapter 26: Ninth Mode

In questo Modo si ritrova composta l'Antifona Ave Maria gratia plena, laquale ne i libri antichi si trova terminata tra le sue chorde naturali in cotal modo; che nelli moderni si trova scritta più grave per una Diapente. Et che ciò sia vero, da questo potemo comprendere, che **P. della Rue** compose la Messa a quattro voci sopra questa Antifona nelle chorde vere, & essentiali di tal Modo.[86] (The antiphon *Ave Maria gratia plena* is composed in the ninth mode. In the ancient books this antiphon is found within its natural notes, as is seen in Example 23, whereas in the modern books it is written lower by a diapente. We may understand that this is true from the fact that P. della Rue composed a Mass for four voices on this antiphon in the true and essential notes of the ninth mode.[87])

*c.*1560

StuttL HB 26; anonymous treatise on music, copied in Bavaria, fos. 51^r–52^r

Music example = *Et incarnatus* section of the Credo of the *Missa Cum iocunditate*, presented without ascription or other identification.[88] Voices presented successively (S, T2, T1, B; missing A)

1561

Reprint of **Zarlino**, *Le istitutioni harmoniche* (Venice: Francesco Franceschi Senese)

1562

Pietro Aaron, *Toscanello in musica*, 4th edition (see under 1529)

---

[83] Gioseffo Zarlino, *The Art of Counterpoint: Part Three of* Le Istitutioni Harmoniche, *1558*, trans. Guy A. Marco and Claude V. Palisca (New Haven and London: Yale University Press, 1968), 57–8.

[84] Zarlino, *Le istitutioni harmoniche*, 265–6.

[85] Zarlino, *The Art of Counterpoint*, 240.

[86] Zarlino, *Le istitutioni harmoniche*, 330.

[87] Gioseffo Zarlino, *On the Modes: Part Four of* Le Istitutioni Harmoniche, *1558*, trans. Vered Cohen (New Haven and London: Yale University Press, 1983), 78.

[88] Information from LRE ii, p. xxiii. The citation would appear to come from Zanger's *Practicae musicae praecepta*.

Reprint of **Zarlino**, *Le istitutioni harmoniche* (Venice: Francesco Franceschi Senese)

1563
Claudius Sebastiani (fl. 1557–65), *Bellum musicale inter plani et mensuralis cantus reges* (Strasburg: Pauli Machaeropoei, 1563)

From Chapter 27
Tertio, *Practici theorici*, caeterorum Principes, qui canere et componere, et composita intelligere noverant. Josquinius Des pres, {**Petrus de la rue**}, Brumel, Henricus Isaac, Ludovicus Senfel, Adrian Vuillart, Lebrun, concilium, morales, La fage, lheritier, Nicolaus Gombert, Thomas Crequillon, Champion, Petrus Massenus, Iacquet, Pipelari, Nicolaus Paien, Courtois, Luxi [*sic*], Lupus, Clemens non Papa, Homerus Herpoll, Claudin, etc. Divus Bernhardus, Beatus Gregorius, Berno Abbas.[89] (Third, practical theorists, the leaders of all the rest, who knew how to sing and compose and understand compositions: Josquinus Despres, {Petrus de la Rue}, Brumel, Henricus Isaac, Ludovicus Senfel, Adrian Vuillart, Lebrun, Concilium, Morales, Lafage, Lheritier, Nicolaus Gombert, Thomas Crequillon, Champion, Petrus Massenus, Jacquet, Pipelari, Nicolaus Paien, Courtois, Luxi [Lupi], Lupus, Clemens non Papa, Homerus Herpoll, Claudin, etc. St Bernard, Blessed Gregorius, Abbot Berno.)

1565/70
MunBS A II. Medallion by Hans Müelich, under a picture of Lasso's Munich choir (fo. 187ʳ)

AUTORES PMUSICES [*sic*] PRAECIPUI ET EXCELLENTISSIMI[90]
(Distinguished and Most Excellent Authors of Music)

Iacobus hobrecht	Christo: Morales	Claudin
Jusquinus	Nicolas Gombert	Antonius Brumel
Joannes Moutton	Petrus Mancicourt	Ludovicus Senfl
Hadrianus Williart	Joan: Richafort	Thomas Stolzer
Clemens Janequin	Thomas Crequillon	Joan Courtois
Ciprian Rore	Lupus Lupi	Sandrin
Leo pa: card dec M.DI	Clemens non papa	Schlaconius epis: Viennensis
Petrus pirson de la rue	Joha: Ockenhain	ERASMUS Rodero
Certon verdelot	Henricus YSAC	
	Orlando di Lasus	

between 1565 and 1574
Pietro Gaetano, *Oratio de origine et dignitate musices*, Venice, Museo Correr, MS Cicogna 906, fos. 19ʳ–20ᵛ

Included in the *tertiam aetas*: Ocheghen, Josquin de pres, Brumel, Fevim, Monton, {**Petrus de larue**}, Andreas de sylva[91]

---

[89] Burbure, 'Étude sur un manuscrit du xviᵉ siècle', 38, corrected. My thanks to Bonnie Blackburn for pointing out the similarity between this list of musicians and that of Coclico.

[90] Information after Martin Staehelin, *Die Messen Heinrich Isaacs*, 3 vols. (Berne and Stuttgart: Paul Haupt, 1977), ii. 127–8. A colour reproduction is found in Ignace Bossuyt, *Flemish Polyphony* (Leuven: Davidsfonds, 1994), 59.

[91] The date, citation, and folio numbers are taken from Owens, 'Music Historiography', 321; the manuscript's location and shelf number were kindly supplied by Bonnie Blackburn.

1572
Reprint of **Folengo** (see 1521)

1573
Zarlino, revised edition of *Le istitutioni harmoniche* (Venice: Francesco Franceschi Senese)[92]

Drops Citation 3 but retains the two earlier ones, on pp. 203–4 and 327.

c.1573–95
Another edition of **Jean Daniel**, noël *Ung gracieulx oyselet*, appears in *La Grand Bible des noelz* . . . (Paris: Nicolas Bonfons)[93] (see *c.*1523?)

c.1580
LonBL 4911. Anonymous, *The Art of Music collecit out of All Ancient Doctouris of Music* (probably Edinburgh or Aberdeen)[94]

Citation 1: Chapter 15 (the chapter on canons), fo. 33^v
The Twelft Canon. In this exempile the tenor followand fro the propre seit is removit, quhilk is in C, B, A, and G eftir the precept of th auctor is degradit. Per C, ♯, simul A, ruit in G. (Music example = initial Sanctus from the *Missa Cum iocunditate*, tenor only)

Citation 2: same chapter, fo. 41^r
Heir followis diveris exemplis conform to the rewlis within writtin quhilkis ar veray necessar to be had for information of studentis of music desyrand to exersize their ingyne in speculation of that art. Quhairfor, be thir exemplis followand they may persaif the progression of diverss conceptis of harmony. (Music example on fo. 43 = Agnus II from the *Missa L'homme armé I*)

1581
Reprint of **Folengo** (see 1521)

1588
Zarlino, reprint of *Le istitutioni harmoniche* as vol. 1 in *De tutti l'opere*, based on the 1573 edition (Venice: Francesco Franceschi Senese)[95]

1592
Lodovico Zacconi (1555–1627), *Prattica di musica* (Venice: Girolamo Polo, 1592)[96]

Citation 1: Book III, Chapter 46, In che cosa circa le regole Musicali i Prattici non convengano con i Theorici (Where the practitioners do not agree with the theorists on the rules of music), fo. 162^{r-v}

---

[92] Gioseffo Zarlino, *Istitutioni harmoniche* (facs. edn., Ridgewood, NJ: Gregg Press, 1966).
[93] Date from Block, *The Early French Parody Noël*, i. 24.
[94] All information on this treatise is taken from Judson Dana Maynard, 'An Anonymous Scottish Treatise on Music from the Sixteenth Century: British Museum, Additional Manuscript 4911' (Ph.D. diss., Indiana University, 1961), 94, 118, 127–8.
[95] Facsimile in Gioseffo Zarlino, *Music Treatises*, ed. Frans Wiering (Thesaurus musicarum Italicarum, 1; Utrecht: Universiteit Utrecht, 1997).
[96] All citations are found in Lodovico Zacconi, *Prattica di musica*, 2 vols., facs. edn. (Bologna: Forni, 1967). My thanks to Bonnie Blackburn for bringing the citations in this treatise to my attention.

Alla qual cosa non si trova Prattico che ancora gli habbia assentito; perche se gli havesse assentito, in tante compositioni si troverieno alcuni essempii che ce lo demonstraria. Solo si trova **Petrus della Rue** nel Tenore della sua Messa cum iocunditate che usa queste figure. Le quali in prima vista paiano che sieno conforme à queste regole: ma poi considerandole bene le sono tutte contrarie: perche nel primo essempio, se è vero la regola delle pause come è verissima che tanto sia una pausa quanto che una figura tacciuta: quelle due maggiori seconde haverieno sei figure, e nondimeno la prima non è perfetta; ne anco le sei sono per doi Tempi ternari, che l'ultima viene à esser alterata. Di piu ancora a se le cinque che li seguitano dopò per regola havesse l'ultima alterata non haveria havuto bisogno di punto di alteratione, ne meno gli l'haveria posto se havesse creduto che tal cosa non fosse stata ragionevole. (As regards this matter, there is no practitioner who agrees with it, because if there were agreement with it, proof of it would be found in passages in many compositions. It is only found in the tenor of Petrus della Rue's *Missa Cum iocunditate*, which uses these notes. Which at first sight might appear to agree with these rules, but then considering them carefully, they are totally opposite to them, because in the first example, if the rule concerning rests is true (as it truly is, for a pause is like a note but it is not sung), those two long notes would equal six notes, and yet the first is not perfect; nor are the six grouped into two ternary tempora, since the last has come to be altered. And furthermore, if the last of the five that follow afterwards were altered according to the rule, there would be no need for a point of alteration, nor would it have been put there had the composer thought that this was not reasonable.) (Music example = two sections from the beginning of the Confiteor from the *Missa Cum iocunditate*; tenor only)

Citation 2: Book III, Tavola universale, fo. 189ʳ
Pietro della Rue nel Credo della Messa di S. Ant. fa quel punto di divisione per osservar le regole Th[e]oricale azzennate di sopra delle cinque figure inferiori. (Pietro della Rue, in the Credo of the *Missa de Sancto Antonio*, uses this point of division to observe the theoretical rules indicated above in the five smaller notes.) (Music example = conclusion of the Credo from the *Missa de Sancto Antonio*; altus only)

Citation 3: Book III, Tavola universale, fo. 190ʳ
Pietro della Rue nel Agnus Dei della Messa Cum iucunditate, se il punto stà per divisione è male ma se stà per perfettione della Massima è bene. (In the Agnus Dei of Pietro della Rue's *Missa Cum iocunditate*, if the dot stands for division it is bad, but if it stands for perfection of the maxima, it is good.) (Music example = portion of the Agnus I from the *Missa Cum iocunditate*; tenor only)

*c.*1595
Another copy of **Jean Daniel**, noël *Ung gracieulx oyselet*; appears in BNF MS fonds fr. 14983[97] (see *c.*1523?)

1596
Republication of **Zacconi** (Venice: Bartolomeo Carampello, 1596) (see 1592)[98]

---

[97] Date from Block, *The Early French Parody Noël*, i. 120. Ibid., i. 146, implies that this noel is also in Paris, Bibliothèque de l'Arsenal, MS 3653, but that manuscript is not listed as a concordance ibid. ii. 147.
[98] Two facsimile editions are available: Lodovico Zacconi, *Prattica di musica*, 2 vols. (Bibliotheca musica bononienses, Sez. II, 1; Bologna: Arnaldo Forni, 1983); and Lodovico Zacconi, *Prattica di Musica utile e necessaria si al compositore, si anco al cantore (1596)/Prattica di Musica Seconda parte (1622)* (Hildesheim and New York: Georg Olms, 1982).

1597
Thomas Morley (1557/8–1602), *A Plaine and Easie Introduction to Practicall Musicke* (London: Peter Short, 1597)[99]

But to come to those *Canons* which in one part have some others concluded, here is one without any *Canon* in words, composed by an olde author, **Petrus Platensis**, wherein the beginning of everie part is signified with a letter S. signifying the highest or *Saprema* [sic] *vox*, C. the Counter, T, Tenor, and B. the base, but the ende of everie part hee signified by the same letters inclosed in a semicircle, thus: [music example = Kyrie I from the *Missa O salutaris hostia*, but without text or identification] But least this which I have spoken may seeme obscure, here is the resolution of the beginning of everie part [gives the first three notes, in proper clef, of Cantus, Altus, Tenor, and Bassus]. Of this kinde and such like, you shall find many both of 2, 3, 4, 5. and sixe parts, every where in the works of *Iusquin*, **Petrus Patensis** [sic], *Brumel*, and in our time, in the Introductions of *Baselius & Calvisius* with their resolutions and rules how to make them, therfore I wil cease to speake any more of them . . .[100]

1607[21]
Giulio Cesare Monteverdi (1573–?1630–1), 'Dichiaratione della lettera stampata nel Quinto libro de suoi madregali', in Claudio Monteverdi, *Scherzi musicali a tre voci* (Venice: Amadino, 1607)[101]

Prima prattica intende che sia quella che versa intorno alla perfetione del armonia; cioè che considera l'armonia non comandata, ma comandante, & non serva ma signora del oratione; & questa fu principiata, da que' primi che ne nostri caratteri composero le loro cantilene a più di una voce, seguitata poi, & ampliata, da Occhegem, Iosquin de pres, **Pietro della Rue**, Iouan Motton, Crequillon, Clemens non papa, Gombert, & altri de que' tempi perfetionata ultimamente da messer Adriano, con l'atto prattico, & dal Eccellentissimo Zerlino con regole giudiciosissime.[102] (By First Practice he understands the one that turns on the perfection of the harmony, that is, the one that considers the harmony not commanded, but commanding, not the servant, but the mistress of the words, and this was founded by those first men who composed in our notation music for more than one voice, was then followed and amplified by Ockeghem, Josquin Desprez, Pietro della Rue, Jean Mouton, Crequillon, Clemens non Papa, Gombert, and others of those times, and was finally perfected by Messer Adriano with actual composition and by the most excellent Zerlino with most judicious rules.[103])

1609
Dowland translation of **Ornithoparchus**, *Micrologus* (see under 1517)

---

[99] Thomas Morley, *A Plaine and Easie Introduction to Practicall Musicke* (facs. edn., The English Experience, 207; Amsterdam and New York: Theatrum Orbis Terrarum and Da Capo Press, 1969); mod. edn., *A Plain and Easy Introduction to Practical Music*, ed. R. Alec Harman (New York: W. W. Norton, 1953).

[100] Morley, *A Plain and Easy Introduction*, 283–5; Morley, *A Plaine and Easie Introduction*, 173. My thanks to Bonnie Blackburn for bringing the similarity to Glarean's description to my attention.

[101] Reprint edn. = 1609[25].

[102] Facsimile in Claudio Monteverdi, *Tutte le opere*, 17 vols., ed. G. Francesco Malipiero (Asola: n.p., 1926–66), x. [69–72]; modern edition in Claudio Monteverdi, *Lettere, dediche e prefazioni: edizione critica*, ed. Domenico de' Paoli (Rome: di Sanctis, 1973), 398–9.

[103] Oliver Strunk (ed.), *Source Readings in Music History: The Baroque Era* (New York: W. W. Norton, 1965), 48.

1609²⁵
Reprint of **Monteverdi** 1607²¹

1613
Reprint of **Folengo** (see 1521)

1618
Giovanni Battista Rossi (fl. 1585–1628), *Organo di cantori* . . . (Venice: Bartholomeo Magni, 1618)¹⁰⁴

Citation 1: Chapter 14, Della fuga detta volgarmente Canon, & de' motti che vi si pongono, p. 13

Pier della Rue fà una Messa senza motti, & guide, & mette una parte sola con queste quattro letter C.B.T.S. sopra le figure, cioè contr'alto, Basso, Tenore, è [sic] Soprano, & è facile da cantarsi: doue pone il B. hà da comminciar à cantare il Basso, è cosi si dice dell'altre lettere . (Pier della Rue makes a mass without words or guides and gives only one part, with these four letters, C.B.T.S., above the notes, namely contralto, bass, tenor, and soprano, and it is easy to sing it: where the B. is placed, one has to begin to sing the bass; it is thus for the other letters as well.) (This reference is to the *Missa O salutaris hostia*).

Citation 2: Chapter 14, p. 14

Pier de la Rue il primo Kyrie del la Messa l'omme armè, fa cosi [example = first nine breves of T and B]. Si vede che il primo Basso và cantato per il segno del tempo imperfetto: & la seconda parte per il tempo perfetto, doue la longa vale sei: & nel tempo imperfetto quattro. Nel terzo Kyrie ne vanno due di questo Basso di sotto contra tre del primo Basso, difficilissimo da cantarsi. (Pier de la Rue, the first Kyrie of the *Missa L'homme armé*, goes as follows. You see that the first bass must be sung according to the sign of *tempo imperfetto*, and the second part (i.e. tenor, derived from the bass) according to *tempo perfetto*, where the long is worth six, and in *tempo imperfetto* [it is worth] four. In the third [i.e. second] Kyrie two of this latter bass are set under three of the first bass, which is extremely difficult to sing.) (Music example = T and B of Kyrie I, *Missa L'homme armé I*)

Citation 3: Chapter 27, Delli essempi di Prolatione, p. 37

Questo punto di dicchiaratione non lo mette altrimenti **Pier della Rue**, nella Messa l'omme armé, nel basso, doue dice, Passus & sepultus est, ne meno nel tenore, in quelle parole sepultus: però bisogna che il cantore sia molto oculato d'istesso fa nel soprano. (Pier della Rue does not place the point of division otherwise in the *Missa L'homme armé* in the bass where it says 'Passus et sepultus est', nor in the tenor on that word 'sepultus'; therefore it is neccessary for the singer to be very aware of the same fa in the soprano part.)

Citation 4: Chapter 30, Con una tavola si puo haver cognitione d'ogni cantilena, p. 57

Di simili passi vedete **Pier della Rue** nella Messa della Madonna: & nella Messa puer natus: & nella Messa, Numqua fue pena mayor. (For similar passages [examples of perfect breves] see Pier della Rue in the Messa della Madonna [*Missa de beata virgine*], and in the *Missa Puer natus* and in the *Missa Numqua fue pena mayor*.)

Pedro Thalesio (*c.*1563–*c.*1629), *Arte de canto chão com huma breve instrucção* (Coimbra: Diogo Gomez de Loureyro, 1618), p. 64¹⁰⁵

---

¹⁰⁴ All citations are taken from Rossi, *Organo de cantori*. . . . My thanks to Bonnie Blackburn for bringing Citations 1 and 3 to my attention.

¹⁰⁵ All information on this treatise is taken from Stevenson, 'Josquin in the Music of Spain and Portu-

Sobre esta Antiphona [Ave Maria] compos {Pierres de Larue}, hua Missa do nono tono. (On this antiphon [Ave Maria] {Pierres de Larue} composed his mass of the ninth tone.)

1628
Revised edition of Thalesio, *Arte de canto chão com huma breve instrucção*

mid-17th century
Instrumentälischer Bettlermantl (Edinburgh University Library, ref. Dc. 6. 100), pp. 295–6

Caput duodecimum et ultimum: De ratione in hac arte progredienti. Decimo. Quatuor sunt genera symphonistarum. Primum genus Josquio, {Petro de Darne}, et aliis ipsorum coetaneiis auferibitur, hi ex fugis suas constituunt cantilenas, et multa artis inferunt exempla, sed in cantionibus quatuor vocum sunt nudi, Secundum genus Heinrico, Isaac, Ludovico, Senflio, Joanni Baltero, et aliis similibus attribuitur, qui in chorali cantu, vel in contrapuncto fracto, seu florido excelluerunt. Tertium genus imputatur Nicolao Gumberto, Jacob Clementi, Crequiloni, et aliis hi ex fugis constituunt cantiones, sed plenas cudunt harmonias sine multis pausis. Quartum genus Orlando, Adriano, Wilhar, Jachet, de Alexandro Utendal, et Regnardo tribuitur, quorum cantiones non nunquam fugis mixta sunt, et miram praeferunt suavitatem propter Semitoniorum positam, et applicationem singulorum vocabulorum.[106] (Twelfth and Last Chapter: To a person progressing in this art. Item 10. Four are the Types of *Symphonistae*. The first type will be taken from Josquio, {Petro de Darne}, and others of that throng, who construct their songs from *fugae* and produce many examples of art, but in songs of four voices they are bare. The second type is allotted to Heinrico Isaac, Ludovico Senflio, Joanni Baltero [Walther], and others who are similar, who excelled in choral songs, even in *contrapuncto fracto* or *florido*. The third type is ascribed to Nicolao Gumberto, Jacob Clementi, Crequiloni, and others who make songs out of *fugae* but strike full harmonies without many pauses. The fourth type is assigned to Orlando, Adriano, Wilhar, Jachet, Alexandro Utendal, and Regnardo, whose songs are sometimes mixed with *fugae* and display amazing sweetness because of the location of semitones and placement of individual vocables.)

1662
João Álvares Frouvo (1608–82), *Discursos sobre a perfeiçam do diathesaron*... (Lisbon: Antonio Craesbeeck de Mello, 1662)[107]

Cites a consonant fourth in La Rue's *Missa de beata virgine*

1692
Reprint of **Folengo** (see 1521)[108]

---

gal', 238–9; and id., 'Thalesio [Talesio], Pedro', *New Grove II*. According to the former, 239, 'Pierre de la Rue deserves praise, according to Thalesio, for having correctly chosen Mode IX for his "Missa Ave Maria" published in the 1516 collection dedicated to Leo X, *Liber quindecim missarum*. La Rue's movements begin with c G A and end on the A chord approved by Thalesio.' Stevenson's citation comes from the revised edition of 1628.

[106] Citation kindly provided by Noel O'Regan.

[107] All information on this treatise is taken from Stevenson, 'Josquin in the Music of Spain and Portugal', 243; and id., 'Frouvo [Frovo], João Álvares', *New Grove II*. According to the latter, the treatise was 'substantially complete by 1649'.

[108] This edition is cited in Josquin des Prez, *Werken*, Missen 2, afl. 17, no. 7, p. v.

Appendix D
Catalogue of Works

For full source information for the sacred music consult LRE; for secular music see Meconi, 'Style and Authenticity'. Only sources additional to those cited therein are listed below. Under sources and in footnotes I have attempted to point out the more fragmentary sources, though complete information is found only in LRE. An asterisk indicates a work with a single source; brackets mark works lacking a contemporary attribution. A question mark indicates works whose authenticity remains uncertain. Theoretical citations are without music unless otherwise indicated. Titles in italics are alternative names for a work; these are also given in parentheses under the composition's main entry.

Abbreviations

Ag	Agnus	LRE	La Rue, *Collected Works*
ant	antiphon	M	Meconi, 'Style and Authenticity'
BVM	Blessed Virgin Mary	P	PickerCA
C	Credo	Sa	Sanctus
c.f.	cantus firmus	*Tp*	*Musique profane* portion of *Trésor musical*, ed. Van Maldeghem
G	Gloria	*Tr*	*Musique religieuse* portion of the preceding
K	Kyrie		

MASSES

Title	Edition	Sources	Remarks
Missa Agnosce o Vincenti			Alternative name for the *Missa de Sancto Antonio* from VerBC 756.
Missa Alleluia, 5v	LRE I	5 (4 attr.)	Unidentified c.f.
Missa Almana, 4v (*Missa Pourquoy non*) (*Missa Sexti ut fa*)	LRE I	7 (6 attr.) TongerenSA r83 (fragment of G)	Unidentified model (not La Rue's chanson).
Missa Assumpta est Maria, 4v (*Missa de assumptione beate marie*)	LRE I	4 (3 attr.)[1]	Uses 1st ant for Lauds for the Assumption of the BVM.
Missa Ave Maria, 4–5v (*Missa de annuntiatione Maria*)	LRE I	15 (9 attr.)[2]	Uses ant for the Annunciation. C expands to 5v.

Missa Ave sanctissima Maria, 6v (Deus meus eripe me) (Missa sex vocum) (Missa de beata virgine)	LRE I	8 (2 attr.)³ BrugRA Aanw. 756 (fragment of Ag) GhentR D 3360b (fragment of K)	Entirely canonic; normally 6 ex 3. Parody mass on La Rue's motet. Unknown *O dulcis amica Dei* in final Ag. Motet *Te decet laus* appended in VatS 36. Possible inspiration for Appenzeller's (lost) 6v *Missa Ave sanctissima Maria*.
Missa Conceptio tua, 5v	LRE II	7 (1 attr.)⁴	C.f. is the Magnificat ant for the Conception of the BVM. Tr & T2 in canon in Ag I.
Missa Coronatum			Alternative title for the *Missa de beata virgine* in DresSL Pirna IV.
Missa Cum iocunditate, 4–5v (Missa Dirige) (Si esurierit inimicus)	LRE II	19 (13 attr. to La Rue)⁵ Sa opening in 1556 Finck enlarged edn. 1554 Zanger (Et incarnatus only) 1592 Zacconi (C and Ag I fragments only)	Uses 5th ant for 2nd Vespers for the Nativity of the BVM. C expands to 5v. Incorrectly ascribed to Josquin in MilA 46. Theoretical citations (with music): 1554 Zanger, 1556 Finck, 1556 Finck enlarged edn., StuttL HB 26, LonBL 4911, 1592 Zacconi.
Missa de annuntiatione Maria			Alternative title for the *Missa Ave Maria* in SubA 248.
Missa de assumptione beate marie			Alternative title for the *Missa Assumpta est Maria* in Sub A 248.
Missa de beata virgine, 4v (Kyrie Coronatum) (Missa Coronatum) (Missa de domina) (Missa Salve sancta parens) (Patrem Cardinal)	LRE II	12 (6 attr.)⁶ 1556 Finck and 1556 Finck enlarged edn. (K I only)	Uses K IX, G IX (with 'Spiritus et alme' trope), C IV, Sa IX, and Ag XVII. Theoretical citations: (with music) 1556 Finck, 1556 Finck enlarged edn.; (without music) 1525 Aaron *Trattato*; 1618 Rossi.
Missa de beata virgine			Alternative title for the *Missa Ave sanctissima Maria* in JenaU4.

¹ AntPM 18.13/1 has fragments of Sa only.   ² HerdF 9821 is a score of parts of K and Sa only.   ³ 1545⁶ has Pleni only.   ⁴ AntPM 18.13/1 has portions of C, Sa, and Ag I only.
⁵ 1542⁸ has Benedictus only; 1544 Zanger and StuttL HB 26 have Et incarnatus only; 1556 Finck (and 1556 Finck, enlarged edn.) has Sa only, bars 1–25; LonBL 4911 has the T of Sa only, bars 1–25; 1592 Zacconi has fragments of C and Ag I only.
⁶ AntPB 948 IV has fragments of C only; BolSP 38 and ModD 4 have C only; EisS s.s. has K only; 1556 Finck (and 1556 Finck, enlarged edn.) has K I only.

Title	Edition	Sources	Remarks
Missa de doloribus M. virginis			Alternative title for the *Missa de septem doloribus* in HeidU 318.
Missa de domina			Alternative title for the *Missa de beata virgine* in SubA 248.
Missa de feria, 5v (Missa quinque vocum) (Ne temere quid loquaris)	LRE II	9 (5 attr.)[7] VienNB Mus. 18832 (Ag II) MunBS 260 (Ag II) 1545[6] (Ag II)	Uses G XV and C I. Inspired Févin's *Missa de feria*. All movements built on canon between T1 & T2.
Missa de nativitate Christi			Alternative title for the *Missa Puer natus est* in SubA 248.
Missa de Sancta Anna, 4v (Missa Felix Anna)	LRE II	5 (1 attr.)[8]	?Uses ant to the Magnificat for St Anne in the use of Paris.[9] Uses motet *O salutaris hostia* in place of 1st Osanna.
Missa de sancta cruce, 5v (Missa Nos autem gloriari)	LRE III	7 (5 attr.)	C.f. Nos autem gloriari from the introit for both the Finding of the Holy Cross and the Exaltation of the Holy Cross. Pleni related to Ag II of Josquin's *Missa L'ami baudichon*.
Missa de sanctissima virgine Maria			Alternative title for the *Missa Ista est speciosa* in JenaU 2.
Missa de Sancto Antonio, 4v (Missa Agnosce o Vincenti) (Missa Ecce advenit) (Missa O sacer Anthoni)	LRE III	11 (7 attr.)[10] BerlPS 40634 1592 Zacconi (fragment of C)	Uses 1st ant for Vespers for St Anthony Abbot. Theoretical citations (with music): 1547 Glarean, 1592 Zacconi; (without music) 1547 Glarean.
Missa de Sancto Job, 4v (Missa Floruit egregius)	LRE III	5 (3 attr.)[11]	Based on chants from the rhymed office for St Livinus as used in Pipelare's *Missa Floruit egregius*. Ag I built on 2v canon in lowest voices.
Missa de septem doloribus, 5v (Missa de doloribus M. virginis) (Missa quinque vocum de doloribus)	LRE III	6 (3 attr.) VienNB Mus 18832 (Pleni)	Uses texts for the invitatory to Matins and the sequence[12] for the 7 Sorrows of Mary as well as an unidentified 'Trenosa compassio'; chant models unknown. Osanna II uses the superius of the concluding phrase of Josquin's *Ave Maria . . . virgo serena*. A and T2 in canon in Ag I.

	LRE	No. (attr.)	Notes
*Missa de virginibus, 4v (Missa O quam pulchra) (Missa Pulchra es)	LRE III	1, with attr.	Unidentified model(s).
Missa Dirige			Alternative name for the Missa Cum iocunditate from MilA 46.
Missa Ecce advenit			Alternative name for the Missa de Sancto Antonio from BerlPS 40634.
Missa Felix Anna			Title from the tenor rubric of the Missa de Sancta Anna in VienNB Mus. 15496.
Missa Floruit egregius			Alternative name for the Missa de Sancto Job from MontsM 773.
Missa Incessament, 5v (Missa Sic deus) (Non salvatur rex)	LRE IV	12 (8 attr.)[13] 1545[6] (Pleni)	Parody mass on La Rue's chanson. All movements built on 2v canon in lowest voices.
Missa in mi			Alternative title for Missa Sub tuum presidium in HeidU318.
Missa Inviolata, 4v (Omnes peccaverunt)	LRE IV	4 (4 attr.)[14]	Uses Marian sequence Inviolata, integra et casta es Maria.
Missa Ista est speciosa, 5v (Missa de sanctissima virgine Maria) (Missa quinque vocum)	LRE IV	8 (3 attr.)[15]	Uses ant 'de commemoratione beata virgine'.
Missa L'homme armé I, 4v (Quaerite dominum)	LRE IV	18 (14 attr.)[16] BolC B57 (Cimello; Ag II only) 1554 Zanger (Ag II only)	Uses the L'homme armé melody. Also uses Tant que nostre argent in bassus of Ag III. K I (T/B), Christe (A/T), K II (T/B) built on 2v mensuration canons.

[7] MontsM 766 has part of Ag III only. [8] BrusBR IV 922 and Upps76b have O salutaris hostia only.

[9] M. Jennifer Bloxam, Review of Pierre de la Rue, Opera omnia, vols. r-3, in Notes, 51 (1994-5), 407-10 at 409, suggests this as a possible source for the pre-existent material.

[10] 1547[1] (Glarean) has the Christe only; 1592 Zaccon: has a fragment of C only. [11] AntP M 18.13/3 has Ag fragment only; 1549[16] has Benedictus only.

[12] Jennifer Bloxam has suggested that the sequence text may be a contrafact for chant from another feast, generating a situation parallel to that of La Rue's use of the chants for St Livinus in his Missa de Sancto Job (pers. comm., 13 Feb. 1996); my thanks to Professor Bloxam for generously sharing this insight.

[13] 1549[16] has Pleni, Benedictus, and In nomine only. [14] 1542[8] has Benedictus only. [15] VienNB Mus. 1883? and MunBS 260 have Pleni only.

[16] 1537 Heyden, 1540 Heyden, 1547[1] (Glarean), BolC B57 (Cimello), 1554 Zanger, LonBL 4911, 1590[30], and 1594[3] have Ag II only; RegB B220-222 and 1545[7] have Pleni only, VatV 11953 has the Sanctus, Osanna, and Ag III only; and 1618 Rossi has part of K only.

Title	Edition	Sources	Remarks
[Missa L'homme armé II], 4–5v	LRE VII	2 (no attr.)[17]	Ag II = 4 ex 1 mensuration canon. Theoretical citations (with music): 1537 Heyden, 1540 Heyden, 1547 Glarean, BolC B57 (Cimello), 1554 Zanger, LonBL 4911, 1618 Rossi; (without music) 1618 Rossi. Uses the *L'homme armé* melody. Ag expands to 5v. All movements built on 2v canon; voices vary.
Missa Mediatrix nostra			Lost; known from HeidU 318 inventory (see Lambrecht, *Das 'Heidelberger Kapellinventar'*, 215, 243).
Missa Nos autem gloriari			Alternative name for the *Missa de sancta cruce* from c.f. text in all sources but JenaU 12.
Missa Nunqua fue pena maior, 4v (Libertatem quam maiores) (Missa Nunquam fierit)	LRE IV	8 (4 attr.)[18]	Based on Urrede's villancico. Theoretical citation: 1618 Rossi.
Missa Nunquam fierit			Alternative title for *Missa Nunqua fue pena maior* in HeidU 318.
Missa O gloriosa domina, 4v (Missa O gloriosa Margaretha) (Missa quatuor vocum)	LRE V	6 (5 attr.)[19]	Based on the hymn *O gloriosa domina*.
Missa O gloriosa Margaretha			Alternative name for the *Missa O gloriosa domina* from VatS 36 and MontsM 773.
Missa O quam pulchra			Alternative name for the *Missa de virginibus* from VatS 36.
Missa O sacer Anthoni			Alternative name for the *Missa de Sancto Antonio* from VienNB 1783, BrusBR 9126, and CambraiBM 18.
Missa O salutaris hostia, 4v	LRE V	8 (7 attr.)[20] BolC B57 (Cimello; K I only)	Totally canonic; normally 4 ex 1. No known model. Theoretical citations (with music): 1537 Heyden, 1547 Glarean, BolC B57 (Cimello), 1597 Morley; (without music) 1558 Zarlino, 1618 Rossi.

Missa pascale, 5v (Missa quinque vocum) (Missa Resurrexi)	LRE V	6 (2 attr.)	Uses 7 chants from the Easter liturgy.
Missa Pourquoy non			Alternative title for the *Missa Almana* in VatS 45.
Missa pro defunctis			Alternative title for *Missa pro fidelibus defunctis* in HeidU 318, MunBS C, MunBS47, MunBS 65, and WolfA A.
Missa pro fidelibus defunctis, 4–5v (Missa pro defunctis) (Requiem)	LRE V	6 (5 attr.)	Uses appropriate chants from the Requiem mass.
Missa Puer natus est, 4v (Missa de nativitate Christi)	LRE V	11 (6 attr.)[21]	Uses introit for the 3rd mass on Christmas Day. Theoretical citations: 1547 Glarean, 1618 Rossi.
Missa Pulcbra es			Alternative title for *Missa de virginibus* in HeidU 318.
Missa quarti toni			Alternative name for the *Missa Sub tuum presidium* from 1515[1] and MilA 46.
Missa quatuor vocum			Alternative title for the *Missa O goloriosa domina* in JenaU 5.
Missa quinque vocum			Alternative title for the *Missa de feria* in JenaU 5; for the *Missa Ista est speciosa* in BrusBR 15075 and JenaU 4; and for the *Missa pascale* in JenaU 5.
Missa quinque vocum de doloribus			Alternative title for the *Missa de septem doloribus* in BrusBR 15075.
Missa Resurrexi			Alternative name for the *Missa pascale* from a c.f. text in all sources.
Missa Salve sancta parens			Alternative name for the *Missa de beata virgine* from VienNB 1783.

17 Both sources are Habsburg-Burgundian manuscripts; first suggested as La Rue's in Franz Xavier Haberl, *Bibliographischer und thematischer Musikkatalog des päpstlichen Kapellarchives im Vatikan zu Rom* (Leipzig: Breitkopf & Härtel, 1888) [supplement to *Monatshefte für Musikgeschichte*, 19–20 (1887–8)], 13–14, 87. The attribution was accepted by RobijnsP, 161, and RubsamenMGG, 232, but questioned by StaehelinNG, 476.

18 1549[16] has Benedictus only.   19 FrankSU 2 has portions of C, Sa, and Ag only.

20 1537 Heyden and 1590[30], Pleni only; 1597 Morley, K I only; 1547[1] (Glarean), Pleni and K I only; HerdF 9820, K, Osanna, and Benedictus only, in score format.

21 VienNB Mus. 16746 has K, Pleni, and Ag only; LeidGA 1443 has parts of K, G, and C only.

Title	Edition	Sources	Remarks
Missa Sancta dei genitrix, 4v (Miserere mei deus)	LRE VI	2 (2 attr.)[22]	Uses an unidentified 7-note ostinato. Uses the *L'homme armé* melody briefly in the bassus of C. Pleni = 3 ex 1 canon (SAB); Ag II supposed to be 2v canon (S1 & S2?); music missing.
Missa Sexti ut fa			Alternative title for the *Missa Almana* in 1503 Petrucci.
Missa sex vocum			Alternative title for the *Missa Ave santissima Maria* in BrusBR 15075.
Missa Sic deus			Alternative title for the *Missa Incessament* given in RubsamenMGG.
Missa sine nomine, 4v			Mass without title in HeidU 318 inventory; possibly an already known La Rue mass.
*Missa sine nomine I, 4v	LRE VI	1, attr.	
?[Missa sine nomine II], 4v	LRE VII	2 (no attr.)[23]	
Missa Sub tuum presidium, 4v (Missa in mi) (Missa quarti toni)	LRE VI	8 (7 attr.)[24]	Uses the Marian antiphon. 1539[2] attributes it to both La Rue and (incorrectly) Josquin.
Missa Tandernaken, 4v (Amicus fidelis) (Frange esurienti)	LRE VI	3 (3 attr.)[25]	On a Flemish popular song.
Missa Tous les regretz, 4v	LRE VI	10 (5 attr.)[26] UtreC 47/1 (fragments of K only)	Parody mass on La Rue's chanson. Survives in two separate versions.
Requiem			Alternative modern title for the *Missa pro defunctis*.

MASS MOVEMENTS

Title or Incipit	Edition	Sources	Remarks
Kyrie Coronatum			Alternative title for the Kyrie of the *Missa de beata virgine* in EisS s.s.

Title	Edition	Sources	Remarks
*Kyrie in festo pasche, 4v	LRE VII	1, with attr.	Uses K I (Easter Kyrie).
[Kyrie pascale], 5v	LRE VII	2, no attr.[27]	Uses K I (Easter Kyrie). K I, Christe, K II built on 2v canon; voices vary.
*Credo, 4v	LRE VII	1, with attr.	
Credo, 6v	LRE VII	5 (4 attr.)	
*Credo Angeli archangeli, 8v	LRE VII	1, with attr.[28]	Based on Isaac's 6v motet for All Saints, which uses the tenor of Binchois's *Comme femme*.
Credo de villagiis, 4v	LRE VII	3 (2 attr.)	Based on C I. Used as C in Obrecht's *Missa Sicut spina rosam* in VatS 160.
Credo L'amour du moy, 4v	LRE VII	2 (1 attr.)	Based on the monophonic chanson *L'amour de moy si est enclose*.
Patrem Cardinal			Alternative title for the Credo of the *Missa de beata virgine* in BolSP 38.

MAGNIFICATS

(all Magnificats are *alternatim*, even-verse settings)

Title	Edition	Sources	Remarks
*Magnificat primi toni, 3–6v	LRE VIII	1, with attr.	Sicut locutus est = 6 ex 3 mensuration canon. Sicut erat = 6 ex 3 canon.
Magnificat secundi toni, 2–4v	LRE VIII	3 (3 attr.)	

22 1546[6], which has the Pleni only (as a contrafact), attributes it to PETRVS DE LA RVE. JenaU 21, a court manuscript, has a garbled ascription to Petrus la vie, but it did not originally read 'Petrus alamyre', as some claim (Flynn Warmington, private comm., 28 Nov. 1999).

23 FrankSU 2 has G and parts of K and C only; JenaU 12 is a court source. The mass was first suggested as La Rue's in Karl Erich Roediger, *Die geistlichen Musikhandschriften der Universitäts-Bibliothek Jena: Notenverzeichnis* (Claves Jenenses: Veröffentlichungen der Universitätsbibliothek Jena, 3; Jena: Walter Biedermann, 1935), 25x. RobijnsP did not include this work, but RubsamenMGG, 232 did; it was questioned by StaehelinNG, 476. The work is quite possibly not La Rue's at all.

24 FrankSU 2 has Sa and Ag only; HerdF 9821 has K and part of G only, in score.   25 1545[7] has Benedictus and Ag II only, each as a contrafact.   26 LeipU 49 has K and G only.

27 Both sources are Habsburg-Burgundian manuscripts; it was first suggested as La Rue's in Roediger, *Die geistlichen Musikhandschriften*, 7x, and has been readily accepted since then.

28 The attribution in the source is confirmed in the 1597 inventory of manuscripts owned by Philip II (see Andrés, 'Libros de canto', 123, no. 71, and VDS viii. 373).

Title	Edition	Sources	Remarks
Magnificat tertii toni			Lost; existence implied by statements in inventories of the libraries of Mary of Hungary (1559) and Philip II (1597).[29]
Magnificat quarti toni, 3–4v	LRE VIII	3 (1 attr.)	
Magnificat quinti toni, 2–4v	LRE VIII	2 (1 attr.)	
Magnificat sexti toni, 3–5v	LRE VIII	4 (4 attr.)	
Magnificat septimi toni, 3–4v	LRE VIII	2 (1 attr.)	
*Magnificat octavi toni, 2–4v	LRE VIII	1, with attr.	

MOTETS

Title or Incipit	Edition	Sources	Remarks
?[Absalon fili mi, 4v]	LRE IX	4 (no attr. to La Rue)[30]	Probably written for Maximilian on the death of Philip the Fair.
			Influenced the motet of same name in 1538.[31] inspired a parody mass in BolSP 31.
Amicus fidelis			Contrafact of the Benedictus from the *Missa Tandernaken* in 1545.[7]
Ave apertor caelorum			Alternative text for *Ave regina celorum* in 1538[8] and LeipU 51.
Ave regina celorum, 4v (Ave apertor caelorum)	LRE IX	5 (2 attr.)	Marian antiphon, possibly modelled on a chant.
[Ave sanctissima Maria], 6v	LRE IX	3 (no attr. to La Rue)[32]	6 ex 3 canon, on Marian text. Used as model for La Rue's mass of the same name.
Considera Israel, 4v	LRE IX	4 (2 attr.)[33]	David's lament for Jonathan from II Samuel; probably written for Marguerite on the death of Philip the Fair. Influenced by Josquin's *Planxit autem*. Quarta pars *Doleo super te* also circulates independently.
Cum coelum mutatur			Contrafact of *Si dormiero* in *Tr* 19 (1883), 12.

Delicta iuventutis, 4v	LRE IX	2 (1 attr.)	Uses antiphon for peace. Two versions of the text, each drawing briefly on the office for the dead. Possibly written to commemorate the death of Philip the Fair.
Deus meus eripe me			Contrafact of the Pleni of the *Missa Ave sanctissima Maria* in 1545[6].
Doleo super te			Quarta pars of *Considera Israel*.
Frange esurienti			Contrafact of the Agnus II from the *Missa Tandernaken* in 1545[7].
*Gaude virgo, 4v	LRE IX	1, with attr.	Possibly based on psalm tone 7. Text attributed to St Thomas Becket.
Lauda anima mea dominum, 4v	LRE IX	2 (1 attr.)	Sets Ps. 146. Uses the tonus peregrinus.
*Laudate dominum, 4v	LRE IX	1, with attr.	Sets Ps. 117. 3 ex 1 canon (SAT) plus a free voice.
Libertatem quam maiores			Contrafact of the Benedictus from the *Missa Nunqua fue pena maior* in 1549[16].
[Maria mater gratie/Fors seulement], 5v	P 257	2 (BrusBr 228 and VienNB Mus. 18746), no attr.[34]	2nd bassus uses the tenor of Ockeghem's rondeau.

[29] VDS vii. 482, 'Yten, un libro . . . ques de los ocho tonos de Pedro de la Rue, en que ay Manificas y otras obras'; 491, 'Y mas otro libro . . . ques de los ocho tonos, de Pedro De La Rue, en que ay Magnificas y otras obras'; Andrés, 'Libro de canto', 109, 'de ocho tonos de Magnificat de música de Pedro de la Rua con algunos ynnos'. LRE viii, p. xiv, inexplicably says that Philip's library was destroyed by fire in 1557. This cannot be the case, as we know from the inventory of 1597.

[30] Attributed to Josquin in 1540[7], 1558[20], and 1559[2]; anonymous in court manuscript LonBLR 8 G. vii. Suggested as La Rue's by van Benthem, 'Lazarus versus Absalon'; Joshua Rifkin, 'Problems of Authorship in Josquin: Some Impolitic Observations with a Postscript on *Absalon fili mi*', in Willem Elders (ed.), *Proceedings of the International Josquin Symposium, Utrecht 1986* (Utrecht: Vereniging voor Nederlandse Muziekgeschiedenis, 1991), 45–52; and Meconi, 'Another Look at *Absalon*'. Although the identification is not air-tight, La Rue is still the most plausible candidate for authorship for now, despite questioning of the reattribution by Milsom, Review of Pierre de la Rue, 479–82; and Nigel St. John Davison, '*Absalom fili mi* Reconsidered', *TVNM* 46 (1996), 42–56.

[31] Richard Sherr, 'Resonances of *Absalon fili mi* in the Sixteenth Century', in *Abstracts of Papers Read at the Meeting of the American Musicological Society: Sixty-Seventh Annual Meeting, November 15–18, 2001*, ed. Mark Evan Bonds (n.p.: American Musicological Society, 2001), 49.

[32] Attributed incorrectly to Verdelot/Claudin in 1532[5] and anonymous in court manuscript BrusBR 228; first published as La Rue's in *Tr* 18 (1882), 13 and widely accepted as his thereafter (though StaehelinNG thought it might be by Verdelot).

[33] BrusBR 228 and LonBLR 8 G. vii have *Doleo super te* only.

[34] Sources are both from the court; first published as La Rue's in *Tr* 19 (1883), 7; see PickerCA, 90, for supporting arguments.

Title or Incipit	Edition	Sources	Remarks
Miserere mei deus			Contrafact of the Pleni from the *Missa Sancta dei genitrix* in 1545[6].
Ne temere quid loquaris			Contrafact of the Agnus II of the *Missa de feria* in 1545[6].
Non salvatur rex			Contrafact of the Pleni of the *Missa Incessament* in 1545[6].
Nos debemus gratias			Contrafact of *Pour ung jamais* in 1542[8].
*O domine Jhesu Christe, 4v	LRE IX	1, with attr.	
O Maria virgo mittis			Tenor incipit for *Sancta Maria virgo.*
[O] mitis mater Christi			Alternative name for *Si dormiero* from WrocU 428.
Omnes peccaverunt			Contrafact of the Benedictus of the *Missa Inviolata* in 1542[8].
[O salutaris hostia], 4v	LRE II, IX	5 (no independent attr.)[35]	Text in honour of the Blessed Sacrament. Substitutes for the Osanna I in the *Missa de Sancta Anna*; also circulates separately.
Pater de coelis deus, 6v	LRE IX	2 (2 attr.)	3 ex 1 canon (S, A2, T2), plus three free voices. Sets a collection of responses associated with the Trinity. Theoretical citation: 1558 Zarlino.
Petre amas me			Lost; known only from the HeidU 318 inventory, where it is cited as having two sections.
Quaerite dominum			Contrafact of the Pleni from *Missa L'homme armé I* in 1545[7].
*Quis dabit pacem, 4v	LRE IX	1, with attr.	Textless; title found in the MS index only. A text beginning with these words (from Seneca and possibly Poliziano) was set by Isaac for the death of Lorenzo de' Medici.
*Regina celi, 4v	LRE IX	1, with attr.	Marian antiphon; uses the appropriate chant.
Salve Jesu, 6vv			Lost; cited in the 1597 inventory of the manuscripts of Philip II.[36]
Salve mater salvatoris, 4v	LRE IX	2 (1 attr.)	Text is a prayer for the Assumption of the BVW, adapted with references to Marguerite of Austria as governor of the

Some similarities to the chant sequence of the same name.

Work			Notes
Salve regina I, 4v	LRE IX	2 (2 attr.)	4 ex 1 canon. Marian antiphon. Canon melody influenced by chant.
Salve regina II, 4v	LRE IX	3 (2 attr.)	Marian antiphon; uses the appropriate chant.
*Salve regina III, 4v	LRE IX	1, with attr.	Marian antiphon; uses the appropriate chant.
*Salve regina IV, 4v	LRE IX	1, with attr.	Marian antiphon; uses the appropriate chant, superius of Dufay's *Par le regard*, and superius of Binchois's *Je ne vis oncques la pareille*. *Alternatim* setting.
*Salve regina V, 4v	LRE IX	1, with attr.	Marian antiphon; uses the appropriate chant. *Alternatim* setting.
Salve regina VI, 4v	LRE IX	2 (1 attr.)	Marian antiphon; uses the appropriate chant.
Sancta Maria virgo, 3v	LRE IX	2 (1 attr.)	Sacred tricinium.[37] Incipits only.
Sic deus dilexit			Bassus shares material with *Il viendra* and *Pourquoy tant*. 2.p. is the model for Craen's *Ecce video*. Written before 9 May 1502.[38]
Si dormiero, 3v (Güretzsch) ([O] mitis mater Christi)	LRE IX	14 (1 attr. to La Rue)	Contrafact for *Incessament mon pauvre cueur lamente* in BerlPS 40013, GothaF A98, NurGN 83795, and WeimB B. Sacred tricinium belonging to family of 'si' works;[39] also attributed (incorrectly) to Isaac, Agricola, and Finck.
Si esurierit inimicus			Contrafact of the Benedictus of the *Missa Cum iocunditate* in 1542.[8]

---

[35] BrusBR IV 922 and Upps76b are the only sources to transmit the motet independently; in the remaining three it substitutes for the first Osanna. Since Ambros, the work has been generally accepted as La Rue's despite no attribution other than the general mass ascription.

[36] See Andrés, 'Libros de canto', 124, no. 87, and VLES viii. 370.   [37] On this genre, see Meconi, 'Sacred Tricinia'.

[38] Date of publication of Craen's *Ecce video*, which borrows from *Sancta Maria virgo*.   [39] See Meconi, 'Sacred Tricinia'.

Title or Incipit	Edition	Sources	Remarks
Vexilla regis/Passio domini, 4v	LRE IX	3 (1 attr.)	Uses the text and tune of the hymn for the Holy Cross (*Vexilla regis*, sung at Vespers on Passion Sunday); also uses texts from two Gospel passages (St Matthew) as well as the formulae of Chronista and Christus from the Passion lessons.

SECULAR WORKS

Title or Incipit	Edition	Sources	Remarks
Abandon			Title for *C'est ma fortune* in *Tp* 22 (886), 12; and title for *Pour ung jamais* in *Tp* 23 (887), 7.
*[Adieu comment], 5v		1 (VienNB Mus. 18746) without attr.[40]	Incipits only. Lowest 2 voices in canon.
Amour			Title for *Aprez regretz* in *Tp* 22 (886), 23.
Amour méconnu			Title for *Pourquoy non* in *Tp* 21 (885), 13.
*[Aprez regretz], 4v	P 347	1 (BrusBR 228), without attr.[41]	Rondeau cinquain.
Attachement			Title for *A vous non autre* in *Tp* 23 (887), 13.
Autant en emporte le vent, 4v	P 204	2 (1 attr.)	Rondeau cinquain.
A vous non autre, 3v	P 373	3 (1 attr.)	Text altered (probably for Marguerite) in 2 sources.
Carmen			Alternative title for *Secretz regretz* in VienNB Mus. 18810.
Carmen in la			Alternative title for *Secretz regretz* in MunU 328–331.
*[Ce m'est tout ung], 4v	P 215	1 (BrusBR 228), without attr.[42]	Rondeau quatrain.
Ce n'est pas jeu, 4v	P 188	6 (2 attr.)	Theoretical citation: 1525 Aaron *Trattato*.
Cent mille regretz, 5v	M 288	3 (1 attr. to La Rue)	Lowest 2 voices in canon. Incorrectly attributed to Josquin in 1550 Attaingnant.

Title	No.	Sources	Notes
*[Changier ne veulx], 4v	P 343	1 (BrusBR 228), without attr.[44]	rondeau quatrain.
Cruels tourments			Title for *Plusieurs regretz* in *Tp* 22 (1886), 19.
*[Cueurs desolez/Dies illa], 5v	P 330	1 (BrusBR 228), without attr.[45]	Motet-chanson and rondeau cinquain. Uses the 3rd verse of the responsory *Libera me* from the Requiem mass. Written on the death of Jean de Luxembourg, Seigneur de Ville, in 1508 (a portion of text has the acrostic VILLE). Text by Jean Lemaire?
Déception			Title for *Helas, fault il* in *Tp* 22 (1886), 13.
*Dedans bouton, 4v	M 294	1, with attr.	Written for a member of the Bouton family of courtiers?
De l'oeil de la fille du roy, 4v	P 184	2 (1 attr.)	Rondeau cinquain. For Marguerite.
Discrétion			Title for *Trop plus secret* in *Tp* 21 (1885), 5.
[Dueil et ennuy], 5v	P 195	2 (BrusBR 228, VienNB Mus. 18746), without attr.[46]	Lowest 2 voices in canon.
?[Dulces exuvie], 4v	F 265	2 (BrusBR 228, LonBLR 8 G. vii), without attr.[47]	Latin secular work on text from *Aeneid*.
*D'ung aultre aymer, 5v	M 301	1, with attr.	Incipits only. 2nd tenor uses the tenor of Ockeghem's rondeau.
*En espoir vis, 4v	M 314	1, with attr.	Double canon.
Fatalité			Title for *Il est bien heureux* in *Tp* 21 (1885), 15.
Ferme constance			Title for *Changier ne veulx* in *Tp* 22 (1886), 21.
Fors seulement, 4v	M 325	3 (3 attr.)	Incipits only. Altus uses the superius of Ockeghem's rondeau.

[40] See Lawrence F. Bernstein, 'Chansons Attributed to Both Josquin des Prez and Pierre de la Rue: A Problem in Establishing Authenticity', in Willem Elders (ed.), *Proceedings of the International Josquin Symposium, Utrecht 1986* (Utrecht: Vereniging voor Nederlandse Muziekgeschiedenis, 1991), 125–52.

[41] See *Tp* 22 (1886), 23; PickerCA, 66–7; Milsom, Review of Pierre de la Rue, 482.

[42] See *Tp* 21 (1885), 7; PickerCA, 66–7; Milsom, Review of Pierre de la Rue, 482.

[43] See *Tp* 22 (1886), 12; PickerCA, 66–7; Milsom, Review of Pierre de la Rue, 482.

[44] See PickerCA, 66–7; Milsom, Review of Pierre de la Rue, 482.

[45] See *Tp* 22 (1886), 88; PickerCA, 88; Milsom, Review of Pierre de la Rue, 482.

[46] See *Tp* 21 (1885), 3; PickerCA, 76; Bernstein, 'Chansons Attributed to Both Josquin des Prez and Pierre de la Rue'; Milsom, Review of Pierre de la Rue, 482.

[47] See *Tr* 18 (1882), 18; Milsom, Review of Pierre de la Rue, 482.

Title or Incipit	Edition	Sources	Remarks
Fors seulement, 5v	M 329	2 appearances in 1 source[48] (1 attr.)	Incipits only. Superius uses the superius of Ockeghem's rondeau. Lowest 2 voices in canon.
Fortune contraire			Title for *Je ne scay plus* in *Tp* 23 (1887), 29.
Fraw margretsen lied			Alternative title for *Pour ung jamais* in RegB C120.
Güretzsch			Alternative name for *Si dormiero* in VienNB Mus. 1881o.
*[Helas, fault il], 4v	P 323	1 (BrusBR 228), without attr.[49]	Theoretical citation: 1529 Aaron *Toscanello*.
*Il est bien heureux, 4v	P 207	1, without attr.[50]	
?*Il fault morir, 6v	M 337	1, with attr.	Incipits only. Uses the tenor of Compère's *Tant ay d'ennuy/O vos omnes*.
*[Il me fait mal], 3v	P 355	1 (BrusBR 228), without attr.[51]	Perhaps intended as a response to *Me fauldra il*; text possibly by La Rue.
Il viendra le jour désiré, 4v	P, 443	2 (1 attr.)	Possibly intended as a response to *Pourquoy tant*. The bassus shares material with *Pourquoy tant* and *Sancta Maria virgo*.
Incessament mon pauvre cueur lamente, 5v (Sic deus dilexit)	M, 344	15 (3 attr. to La Rue)	A rondeau cinquain text exists but La Rue apparently sets the refrain only. Lowest 2 voices in canon. Attributed incorrectly to Josquin in 1550 Attaingnant.
Indifférence			Title for *Ce m'est tout ung* in *Tp* 21 (1885), 7.
*[J'ay mis mon cueur], 3v	P 410	1 (BrusBR 228), without attr.[52]	Uses the refrain of a monophonic virelai.
*[Je n'ay regretz], 5v	P 404	1 (VienNB Mus. 18746), without attr.[53]	Incipits only. Built on 2v canon (T1/B).
*[Je ne dis mot], 6v	P 406	1 (BrusBR 228), without attr.[54]	6 ex 3 canon.
*[Je ne scay plus], 3v	P 404	1 (BrusBR 228), without attr.[55]	
La grande destinée			Title for *Ce n'est pas jeu* in *Tp* 20 (1884), 21.

*[Las, helas, las, seray-je repris?], 4v	P 320	1 (BrusBR 228), without attr.[56]	Rondeau cinquain. Text by the courtier Aubigny le seigneur?
Lief, begheeft my niet			Title for *Mijn hert* in *Tp* 21 (1885), 21.
*Ma bouche rit, 4v	M 359	1, with attr.	Incipits only. Tenor uses the tenor of Ockeghem's bergerette and material from his *Je n'ay deuil*.
*[Me fauldra il], 4v	P 351	1 (BrusBR 228), without attr.[57]	Text probably by Marguerite of Austria. Probably paired with *Il me fait mal*.
Mijn hert, 4v	P 229	?r3 (2 attr.)[58] New partbook: BrusBR IV.1274 (goes with BrusBR IV.90 and TourBV 94)	Flemish song. Serves as model for (a) parody mass by Gascongne, (b) anonymous 3v setting (in 1538⁹ and elsewhere), (c) 3v setting by Cornelius Rigo de Bergis, and (d) anonymous 4v *Salve regina* (in MunBS 34). Assigned incorrectly to Obrecht in SGallS 463.
Patience			Title for *Quant il survient* in *Tp* 21 (1885), 9.
Pitié			Title for *Tous nobles cueurs* in *Tp* 23 (1887), 11.
Plainte			Title for *Me fauldra il* in *Tp* 22 (1886), 25; and for *J'ay mis mon cueur* in *Tp* 24 (1888), 5.
*Plorer, gemir, crier/Requiem, 4v	M 371	1, with attr.	Motet-chanson using the plainchant introit from the Requiem mass. Probably intended as a lament for Ockeghem.
*[Plusieurs regretz], 4v	P 339	1 (BrusBR 228), without attr.[59]	
Pour ce que je suis, 4v (Puisque je suis)	F 219	2 (1 attr.)	Originally a rondeau cinquain?
Pourquoy non, 4v	P 211	9 (6 attr.)[60]	Model for Gascongne's parody mass.

48 The scribe of 18746 erroneously began copying the piece a second time, but stopped after entering three of the voices; see Meconi, 'Style and Authenticity', 134–6.
49 See *Tp* 22 (1886), 13; PickerCA, 75–6. 50 Attributed to La Rue in the *Aggiunta* to Pietro Aaron's *Toscanello in musica* (1529). 51 See *Tp* 22 (1886), 27; PickerCA, 75–6.
52 See PickerCA, 79. 53 See Bernstein, 'Chansons Attributed to Both Josquin des Prez and Pierre de la Rue'. 54 See PickerCA, 76; Milsom, Review of Pierre de la Rue, 482.
55 See PickerCA, 75; Milsom, Review of Pierre de la Rue, 482. 56 See PickerCA, 66–7; Milsom, Review of Pierre de la Rue, 482. 57 See *Tp* 22 (1886), 25; PickerCA, 75–6.
58 BrusBR IV.90, BrusBR IV.1274, and TourBV 94 are counted as a single source, as all were originally from the same set of partbooks. The Kamper Liedboek may have originally contained this piece; see App. B under 'after 1542'. 59 See PickerCA, 66–7; Milsom, 'Review of Pierre de la Rue', 482.
60 SGallS 463 (included in this count) lists the work, attributed to La Rue in its index, but the piece is not in the manuscript.

Title or Incipit	Edition	Sources	Remarks
Pourquoy tant, 4v	P 440	3 (1 attr.)	Theoretical citations: 1520 Del Lago letter; 1529 Aaron Toscanello.
Pour ung jamais, 3v (Fraw margretsen lied) (Nos debemus gratias) (Pour vous james)	P 368	4 (1 attr.)	Probably intended to be paired with Il viendra. The bassus shares material with Il viendra and Sancta Maria virgo. Sets a strophic text by Marguerite of Austria. A si placet altus appears in RegB C120.
Pour vous james			Alternative name for Pour ung jamais in MunBS 1516.
Puisque je suis			Alternative name for Pour ce que je suis from FlorC2439.
*[Quant il survient], 4v	P 223	1 (BrusBR 228), without attr.[61]	Rondeau quatrain.
Regrets			Title for Tous les regretz in Tp 20 (1884), 16; and title for Secretz regretz, ibid. 23.
Sacrifice			Title for Il me fait mal in Tp 22 (1886), 27.
?[Saillés avant], 5v		2 (VienNB Mus. 18746; bassus in VatV 11953), without attr.[62]	Incipits only.
Secretz regretz, 4v (Carmen) (Carmen in la)	P 192	3 (1 attr.)	
Tous les regretz, 4v	P 180	9 (6 attr. to La Rue)	A rondeau cinquain text by Octavien de Saint-Gelais is available, but only the refrain appears in musical sources. Attributed (incorrectly) to Josquin in RegB C120.
Tous nobles cueurs, 3v	P 371	3 (1 attr.)	A full rondeau cinquain text by Octavien de Saint-Gelais exists, but La Rue sets the refrain only, and rondeau performance will not work.
Tristesse et ennuy			Title for Dueil et ennuy in Tp 21 (1885), 3.
Trop plus secret, 4v	P 200	10 (4 attr.)	

DOUBTFUL AND SPURIOUS WORKS[63]—SACRED

Title or Incipit	Edition	Sources	Remarks
[Anima mea liquefacta est], 4v	P_358		Published as La Rue's in Tr 18 (1882), 20. By Weerbeke, to whom it is attributed in FlorBN Magl. 178 and elsewhere.
Coelum, terra Mariaque			Title for Proch dolor in Tr 19 (1883), 20.
*Domini est terra, 4v	LRE IX	1, with attr.[64]	2 voices currently missing. Unlikely on stylistic grounds.
Lamentationes Hieremiae, 2–6v	LRE VIII	16 (1 attr. to La Rue)	Attributed to La Rue in 1549[1]; portions also attributed to Févin and Forster; Févin is doubtless the author of the first part, but the remainder is probably by Stephan Mahu, to whom it is attributed in 1568[2]
Magnificat quarti toni II, 4v	Josquin edition[65]		Attributed to La Rue in ModD 3, but to Josquin, Agricola, and Brumel elsewhere; probably by Josquin, to whom it is attributed in VatS 44.
Missa Coronata, 4–5v	Josquin edition[66]		Attributed to La Rue in WeimB B, but by Josquin (his *Missa de beata virgine*).
*[Missa de septem doloribus II], 4v	LFE VII	1 (no attr.)[67]	Unlikely on stylistic grounds.
Missa Fors seulement			Claimed by Ambros as La Rue's, but apparently the one by Pipelare.[68]
*Missa Fortuna desperata, 4v		1 (attributed to 'Periquin')[69]	Uses T of the Italian song *Fortuna desperata*.

[61] See Tp 21 (1886), 9; PickerCA, 67; Milsom, 'Review of Pierre de la Rue', 482.

[62] See Bernstein, 'Chansons Attributed to Both Josquin des Prez and Pierre de la Rue'. Jaap van Benthem, 'Einige wiedererkannte Josquin-Chansons im Codex 18746 der Österreichische Nationalbibliothek', TVNM 22 (1971–7), 18–42 at 21–9, argues for Josquin as the composer.

[63] Source information in this section is selective.

[64] Only a microfilm copy survives of the now lost tenor book (KönSU 1740) that contained the attribution.

[65] Josquin des Prez, Werken, Motetten 5, af. 47, Bundel 21, p. 62.   [66] Ibid., Missen 3, afl. 30–1, no. 16, p. 125.

[67] The sole source is court MS BrusBR 215–16; the rr ass is first mentioned in an ambiguous manner in Fétis, Biographie universelle (1st edn.), vi. 49: 'On y trouve la messe à cinq voix de Larue, de septem doloribus ... une autre messe, aussi de septem doloribus, à quatre voix, et un Stabat mater dolorosa à cinq voix, sur le thème de la chanson française: Comme femme de reconfort, par le même maître.' Fétis's phrase, 'by the same master', presumably applies to Comme femme, does it apply as well to the four-voice Missa de septem doloribus? Fétis's son, Édouard, obviously thought both were by La Rue; see Les Musiciens belges, 118, where his reference to a Brussels Royal Library manuscript containing two masses by La Rue and a Stabat mater on Comme femme can only refer to BrusBR 215–16, where the Septem doloribus masses are the only polyphonic masses included.

[68] Ambros, Geschichte der Musik, iii. 236.

[69] Curiously, Weckerlin, La Chanson populaire, 115, refers to an otherwise unknown Fortuna disperata mass supposedly by La Rue contained in a library of either Munich or Vienna.

Title or Incipit	Edition	Sources	Remarks
Missa Iste confessor domini, 4v	LRE VII		By Pierrequin de Therache. Attributed to La Rue in CoimU 2; but by Févin (his *Missa O quam glorifica luce*), to whom it is attributed in court MS VienNB Mus. 1497 and elsewhere.
Missa Jesum liate, 4v			Misreading in VDS viii. 379 of *Missa Cum iocunditate.*
Missa [super] Pater noster			Ambros claims one is in a Brussels codex, but no such mass is known.[70]
Num stultum est mortem			Contrafact for *Le renvoye* in 1549.[16]
Passio domini nostri, 4v	Rhau edition[71]		Attributed to La Rue in DresSL 1/D/505; but by Longueval, to whom it is attributed in FlorBN II.I.232. Also attributed to Obrecht and Jo. a la Venture (= Longueval?).
*[Proch dolor/Pie Jhesu], 7v	P 304	1, without attr.	Published as La Rue's in *Tr* 19 (1883), 20. Written for the death of Emperor Maximilian (1519); hence not by La Rue. PickerCA, 90, suggests Josquin as the composer.
Salva nos domine, 4v	Rhau edition[72]		Attributed to La Rue in 1538[8].
[Salva nos domine], 6v	Medici Codex[73]		By Isaac (Agnus III from the *Missa Salva nos*).
[Sancta Maria succurre miseris/ O werde mont], 4v	P 270		By Mouton; the *New Grove* 1st edn. Mouton entry[74] says a conflicting attr. exists for La Rue, but that is a confusion with the 4v work of the same name (also not by La Rue).
[Stabat mater/Comme femme], 5v	Josquin edition[75]		Published as La Rue's in *Tr* 19 (1883), 5. By Franciscus Strus, to whom it is attributed in BasU F.X.1-4.
*[Te decet laus], 5v	LRE I, IX	1, without attr.[77]	By Josquin; first cited as La Rue's by Fétis.[76] Follows the *Missa Ave sanctissima Maria* in VatS 36 with heading 'loco deo gracias'. Unlikely on stylistic grounds.
Virga tua, 2v	LRE IX		Setting of the Gradual text from the Requiem mass

Title or Incipit	Edition	Sources	Remarks
Virgo prudentissima, 6v			Attributed to La Rue in RegB B220–2, but more likely by Pipelare, to whom it is attributed in 1545.[76]
			By Zarlino, whose statement about the motet was thought by Vander Straeten to refer to La Rue as author.[78]

SECULAR

Title or Incipit	Edition	Sources	Remarks
Ach hülff mich leid, 4v	M 278		Attributed to La Rue in BasU F.X. r-4. Also attributed to Josquin, Noel Bauldeweyn, and Hans Buchner; probably by Buchner, to whom it is attributed in SGallS 530.
Adieu florens, 4v (Carmen) (Carmen in sol)	M 283		Attributed to La Rue in VienNB Mus. 1880. By Pietrequin Bonnel, to whom it is attributed in FlorBN Magl. 178.
Amours fait moult/Il est de bonne beure né			Alternative names for *Tant que nostre argent durra* in numerous sources.
Au feu d'amour, 4v	M 286		Attr. to 'La Rue' in 1541[6] and elsewhere refers to Robert de la Rue.
Buccucia dolce chiu che canamielle, 4v	Canzone edition[79]		Attr. to Piersson in 1548[11] thought by Ambros[80] to be La Rue actually refers to Perissone Cambio.
[Car dieu voulut], 4v	P 251		Published as La Rue's in Tp 21 (1885), 29. Actually by Agricola (= 2. p. of *Je n'ay deuil que de vous*), to whom it is attributed in FlorBN Magl. 178 and elsewhere.
Carmen			Alternative title for *Adieu florens* and for *Leal sebray tante* in

[70] Ambros, *Geschichte der Musik*, iii. 236.   [71] Georg Rhau, *Musikdrucke aus den Jahren 1538 bis 1545 in praktischer Neuausgabe*, ed. by Hans Albrecht et al. (Kassel: Bärenreiter, 1955–), x. 34.
[72] Ibid. iii. 149.   [73] Lowinsky, *The Medici Codex of 1518* (1st edn.), vi. 49.   [74] Howard Mayer Brown, 'Mouton, Jean', *New Grove*, 659.
[75] Fétis, *Biographie universelle* (1st edn.), vi. 49.   [76] Josquin, *Werken*, Motetten 2, afl. 21, Bundel 8, p. 51.   [77] The motet was published as part of La Rue's *Missa Ave sanctissima Maria* (and thus implicitly considered his) by Laurence Feininger; see La Rue, *Missa Ave sanctissima*, ed. Feininger.
[78] VDS iii. 213.
[79] *Adriaan Willaert and his Circle: Canzone villanesche alla napolitana and Villotte*, ed. Donna G. Cardamone (Recent Researches in the Music of the Renaissance, 30; Madison: A-R Editions, 1978), 3.
[80] Ambros, *Geschichte der Musik*, iii. 238. The unnamed madrigals by Perisone published by Gardane in Venice in 1544 cited by Fétis, *Biographie universelle* (2nd edn.), v. 203, and Goovaerts, 'Delarue (Pierre)', *Biographie nationale*, v, cols. 325–8 at 327, are coubtless works of Cambio.

Title or Incipit	Edition	Sources	Remarks
Carmen in re			*VienNB* Mus. 1880.
Carmen in sol			Alternative title for *Leal schray tante* in RegB C120.
Dicte moy bergère, 4v (Schanson)	M 297		Alternative title for *Adieu florens* in MunU 328–31. Double canon.
Donzella no men culpeys			Attributed to La Rue in FlorC 2442; perhaps by Josquin, to whom it is attributed in HerdF 9820.[81] Alternative name for *Mais que ce fust secretement* from VatG XIII.27.
D'ung desplaisir, 4v	M 306		Attribution to 'De la Rue' in 1538[10] and elsewhere refers to Robert de la Rue.
[Du tout plongiet/Fors seulement], 4v	P 237		Published as La Rue's in *Tp* 21 (1885), 27. By Brumel, to whom it is attributed in FlorC 2439 and elsewhere.
Een vrolic wesen, 3v	Barbireau edition[82]		TrentBC 1947/4 states that the superius of this setting (and presumably the rest as well) is by La Rue; Barbireau, to whom it is attributed in SegC s.s. and elsewhere, is the more likely composer.
Een vrolic wesen, 4v	M 308		Attributed to La Rue in *VienNB* Mus. 1880. By Pipelare, to whom it is attributed in FlorC 2439 and elsewhere.
Elle a bien ce ris, 4v	M 311		Attribution to 'D. la rue' in MunBS 1508 refers to Robert de la Rue; the work is possibly by Claudin de Sermisy, to whom it is attributed in 1543[14] and elsewhere.
*En desirant ce que ne puis avoir, 3v	2794 edition[83]		Attribution to 'Pietrequin' in FlorR 2794 refers to Pietrequin Bonnel.
*En l'amour d'une dame, 5v	M 316	1, with attr.	Only altus voice extant. Unlikely on stylistic grounds.
Epitaphe			Title for *Soubz ce tumbel* in *Tp* 22 (1886). 2

Exortum est in tenebris

[Fama malum], 4v	P 296	Contrafact for *Fors seulement II* in SegC s.s. Text from the *Aeneid*. Published as La Rue's in *Tr* 19 (1883), 3. PickerCA, 96, discusses the possibility of de Orto as the composer.

Fidélité

Fors seulement II, 4v (Exortum est in tenebris)	P 233	Title for *Je n'ay deuil* [Agricola] in *Tp* 21 (1885), 23.

Iam sauche

[In pace/Que vous madame], 3v	P 451	Attributed to La Rue in 1502[2], but by Pipelare, to whom it is attributed in SegC s.s. and elsewhere. Alternative name for *Jouyssance vous donneray* from VienNB Mus. 1881o.
[Je n'ay deuil que je ne suis morte], 4v	P 226	Published as La Rue's in *Tr* 19 (1883), 15. By Josquin.
[Je n'ay deuil que de vous], 4v	P 247	Published as La Rue's in *Tp* 21 (1885), 19. By Ockeghem, to whom it is attributed in FlorC 2439 and elsewhere.
*Je suys a moy, 4v	M 349	Published as La Rue's in *Tp* 21 (1885), 23. By Agricola, to whom it is attributed in FlorBN Magl. 178 and elsewhere.
Jouyssance vous donneray, 4v (Iam sauche)	M 351	'La Rue' in 1536[5] refers to Robert de la Rue. The work may be by Mittantier, to whom it is given in the index of the same print.
Las que plains tu, 4v	M 353	Attributed to La Rue in VienNB Mus. 1881o, but by Claudin de Sermisy, to whom it is attributed in 1536[2] and elsewhere.
Leal schray tante, 4v (Carmen)	M 355	'La Rue' in 1541[6] and elsewhere refers to Robert de la Rue. Attributed to La Rue in RegB C120 and VienNB Mus. 1881o.

[81] Discovered by David Fallows, who kindly brought it to my attention.

[82] Jacques Barbireau, *Opera omnia*, ed. Bernhard Meier, 2 vols. (Corpus mensurabilis musicae, 7; Amsterdam: American Institute of Musicology, 1954–7), ii. 11.

[83] George Morton Jones, The "First" Chansonnier of the Biblioteca Riccardiana, Codex 2794: A Study in the Method of Editing 15th-Century Music, 2 vols. (Ph.D. diss., New York University, 1972), ii. 158.

Title or Incipit	Edition	Sources	Remarks
(Carmen in re)			Possibly by Josquin, to whom it is attributed in ZürZ Z. XI. 301.
Le renvoye, 2v (Num stultum est mortem)	M 357	3 (1 attr.)	S uses the S of Compère's chanson. Unlikely on stylistic grounds.
Mais que ce fust secretement, 3v (Donzella no men culpeys) (Mesque se fut secretement)	Compère edition[84]		Attribution to 'Pierquin' and variants thereof in BolC Q17 and other sources refer to Pietrequin Bonnel; also attributed (incorrectly) to Compère.
*Ma mère hellas, 4v	M 368		Attribution to 'La Rue' in 1536[5] refers to Robert de la Rue.
*Mes douleurs sont incomparables, 3v	2794 edition[85]		Attribution to 'Pietrequin' in FlorR 2794 refers to Pietrequin Bonnel.
Mesque se fut secretement			Alternative name for *Mais que ce fust secretement* in numerous sources.
*[Quant il advient], 5v	P 300	1 (BrusBR 228), without attr.[86]	Unlikely on stylistic grounds.
*Qu'en dictez vous suis je en danger, 3v	2794 edition[87]		Attribution to 'Pietrequin' in FlorR 2794 refers to Pietrequin Bonnel.
Philosophie			Title for *Quant il advient* in Tp 22 (1886), 10.
*[Plus aultre], 4v		1 (RegB C120), without attr.[88]	Incipit only of the motto of Charles V. Unlikely on stylistic grounds.
Résignation			Title for *Je n'ay deuil* [Ockeghem] in Tp 21 (1885), 19.
*Sans y penser a l'aventure, 3v	2794 edition[89]		Attribution to 'Pietrequin' in FlorR 2794 refers to Pietrequin Bonnel.
Sebanson			Alternative title for *Dicte moy bergère* in HerdF 980o.
Secrète douleur			Title for *Se je souspire* in Tp 23 (1887), 19.
*[Se je souspire/Ecce iterum], 3v	P 384	1 (BrusBR 228), without attr.[90]	Motet-chanson on the death of Philip the Fair. French text and first Latin text probably by Marguerite of Austria; perhaps music too.[91] 2.p. uses text from Lamentations and the reciting tone for

[Si dedero], 3v	P 464		Published as La Rue's in Tr 19 (1883), 15. By Agricola.
*Si le changer, 4v	M 374		Attribution to 'De la Rue' in 1554[21] refers to Robert de la Rue.
[Si sumpsero], 3v	P 467		Published as La Rue's in Tr, 19 (1883), 15. By Obrecht.
*[Soubz ce tumbel], 4v	F 275	1 (BrusBR 228), without attr.[92]	Setting of Jean Lemaire's 'L'epitaphe de l'amant vert'. PickerCA, 76, and others suggest Josquin as composer.
Souverain bien			Title for *Car dieu voulut* in Tp 21 (1885), 29.
Tant que nostre argent durra, 4v (Amours fait moult/Il est de bonne heure né/Tant que nostre argent durra)	M 376		Attributed to La Rue in BasU F.X. 1–4; also attributed to Japart and Busnoys; probably by Japart, to whom it is attributed in FlorBN BR 229 and elsewhere.

[84] Loyset Compère, *Opera omnia*, ed. Ludwig Finscher, 5 vols. (Corpus mensurabilis musicae, 15; [Rome]: American Institute of Musicology, 1958–72), v. 67.

[85] Jones, 'The "First" Chansonnier', ii. 165.   [86] See *Tp* 22 (1886), 10; Milsom, Review of Pierre de la Rue, 482.   [87] Jones, 'The "First" Chansonnier', ii. 294.

[88] La Rue's authorship was suggested by Birkendorf, *Der Codex Pernner*, i.74, 152, 162, 177, 232–3, 244; iii. 89.   [89] Jones, 'The "First" Chansonnier', ii. 160.

[90] See Milsom, Review of Pierre de la Rue, 482.   [91] For the possibility that Marguerite is the composer, see Picker, 'Musical Laments', 139–43.

[92] See *Tp* 22 (1886), 3; Milsom, Review of Pierre de la Rue, 482. Charles Van den Borren, 'Le Moyen Age et la Renaissance', in Ernest Closson and Charles Van den Borren (eds.), *La Musique en Belgique du Moyen Age à nos jours* (Brussels: La Renaissance du Livre, 1950), 15–144 at 100, also mentions La Rue's name in connection with the work.

Bibliography

AARON, PIETRO, *Thoscanello de la musica* (Venice: Bernardino et Matheo de Vitali, 1523).

—— *Toscanello in Music: Book II, Chapters XXXVII–XXXX/Supplement*, trans. Peter Bergquist (Colorado Springs, Colorado: Colorado College Music Press, 1970).

—— *Toscanello in musica* (Venice: Bernardino and Mattheo de Vitali, 1529; facs. edn., Bibliotheca musica bononiensis, Sez. II, 10; Bologna: Forni, 1969; 3rd edn., Venice: Marchio Sessa, 1539; 4th edn., Venice: Domenico Nicolino, 1562).

—— *Trattato della natura et cognitione di tutti gli tuoni di canto figurato non da altrui piu scritti* (Venice: Bernardino and Mattheo de Vitali; facs. edn., New York: Broude, 1979).

Adrian Willaert and his Circle: Canzone villanesche alla napolitana and Villotte, ed. Donna G. Cardamone (Recent Researches in the Music of the Renaissance, 30; Madison: A-R Editions, 1978).

ALBÈRI, EUGENIO (ed.), *Relazioni degli ambasciatori veneti al Senato*, 1st ser., 1 (Florence: Tipografia all'insegna di Clio, 1839).

AMBROS, AUGUST WILHELM, *Geschichte der Musik*, 5 vols. (Breslau: F. E. C. Leuckart, 1862–82).

ANDRÉS, ALFONSO, 'Libros de canto de la Capilla de Felipe II', *Musica sacro-hispana*, 10 (1917), June, 92–5; July, 109–11; Aug.–Sept., 123–6; Oct.–Nov., 154–6; Dec., 189–90.

Anthologie des maîtres religieux primitifs des XVᵉ, XVIᵉ et XVIIᵉ siècles, ed. Charles Bordes, 6 vols. (Paris: Bureau d'édition de la Schola Cantorum, 1893; repr. New York: Da Capo, 1981).

APEL, WILLI, *The Notation of Polyphonic Music 900–1600*, 5th edn. (Cambridge, Mass.: Mediaeval Academy of America, 1953).

AUDA, ANTOINE, 'La Transcription en notation moderne du "Liber Missarum" de Pierre de la Rue', *Scriptorium*, 1 (1946–7), 119–28.

BAINI, GIUSEPPE, *Memorie storico-critiche della vita e delle opere di Giovanni Pierluigi da Palestrina*, 2 vols. (Rome: Società tipografica, 1828; repr. Hildesheim: Georg Olms, 1966).

BARBIREAU, JACQUES, *Opera omnia*, ed. Bernhard Meier, 2 vols. (Corpus mensurabilis musicae, 7; Amsterdam: American Institute of Musicology, 1954–7).

BELLERMANN, HEINRICH, *Die Mensuralnoten und Taktzeichen des XV. und XVI. Jahrhunderts* (Berlin: Georg Reimer, 1858).

BENT, MARGARET, 'Accidentals, Counterpoint and Notation in Aaron's *Aggiunta* to the *Toscanello in Musica*', *Journal of Musicology*, 12 (1994), 306–44.

BENTE, MARTIN, *Neue Wege der Quellenkritik und die Biographie Ludwig Senfls: Ein Beitrag zur Musikgeschichte des Reformationszeitalters* (Wiesbaden: Breitkopf & Härtel, 1968).

BENTHEM, JAAP VAN, 'Einige wiedererkannte Josquin-Chansons im Codex 18746 der Österreichische Nationalbibliothek', *TVNM* 22 (1971–2), 18–42.

—— 'Introduction to Workshop III: Josquin and La Rue', in Willem Elders (ed.), *Proceedings of the International Josquin Symposium, Utrecht 1986* (Utrecht: Vereniging voor Nederlandse Muziekgeschiedenis, 1991), 101–2.

—— 'Lazarus versus Absalon: About Fiction and Fact in the Netherlands Motet', *TVNM* 39 (1989), 54–82.

—— 'La Magie des cris trenchantz: comment le vray trésorier de musique échappe à la trappe du très terrible satrappe', in *Théorie et analyse musicales/Music Theory and Analysis*

1450–1650: Actes du colloque international Louvain-la-Neuve, 23–25 septembre 1999/Proceedings of the International Conference Louvain-la-Neuve, 23–25 September 1999, ed. Anne-Emmanuelle Ceulemans and Bonnie J. Blackburn (Publications d'histoire de l'art et d'archéologie de l'Université catholique de Louvain, C; Musicologica Neolovaniensia, Studia 9; Louvain-la-Neuve: Département d'histoire de l'art et d'archéologie, Collège Érasme, 2001), 119–47.

BERGMANS, PAUL, *Les Musiciens de Courtrai et du Courtraisis: notes d'une conférence faite au Cercle historique et archéologique de Courtrai le 30 mars 1911* (Ghent: C. Vyt; Courtrai: L. Beyaert-Sioen, 1912).

'Bericht über die Reise des Erzherzogs Philipp von den Niederlanden nach Spanien 1501', in Joseph Chmel (ed.), *Die Handschriften der k.k. Hofbibliothek in Wien, im Interesse der Geschichte, besonders der österreichischen*, 2 vols. (Vienna: Carl Gerold, 1840–1), ii. 554–656.

BERNSTEIN, LAWRENCE F., 'The Bibliography of Music in Conrad Gesner's Pandectae [1548]', *Acta musicologica*, 45 (1973), 119–63.

—— 'Chansons Attributed to both Josquin des Prez and Pierre de la Rue: A Problem in Establishing Authenticity', in Willem Elders (ed.), *Proceedings of the International Josquin Symposium, Utrecht 1986* (Utrecht: Vereniging voor Nederlandse Muziekgeschiedenis, 1991), 125–52.

—— 'French Duos in the First Half of the Sixteenth Century', in John Walter Hill (ed.), *Studies in Musicology in Honor of Otto E. Albrecht* (Kassel: Bärenreiter, 1980), 43–87.

—— 'Josquin's Chansons as Generic Paradigms', in Jessie Ann Owens and Anthony Cummings (eds.), *Music in Renaissance Cities and Courts: Studies in Honor of Lewis Lockwood* (Warren, Mich.: Harmonie Park Press, 1997), 35–55.

BETHUNE, LE BARON, *Epitaphes et monuments des églises de la Flandre au XVIme siècle d'après les manuscrits de Corneille Gailliard et d'autres auteurs* (Bruges: L. De Plancke, for the Société d'émulation pour l'étude de l'histoire et des antiquités de la Flandre, 1900).

BIRKENDORF, RAINER, *Der Codex Pernner: Quellenkundliche Studien zu einer Musikhandschrift des frühen 16. Jahrhunderts (Regensburg, Bischöfliche Zentralbibliothek, Sammlung Proske, Ms. C 120)*, 3 vols. (Collectanea musicologica, 6/1; Augsburg: Bernd Wißner, 1994).

BLACKBURN, BONNIE J., 'For Whom Do the Singers Sing?', *Early Music*, 25 (1997), 593–609.

—— 'Lorenzo de' Medici, a Lost Isaac Manuscript, and the Venetian Ambassador', in Irene Alm, Alyson McLamore, and Colleen Reardon (eds.), *Musica Franca: Essays in Honor of Frank A. D'Accone* (Stuyvesant, NY: Pendragon, 1996), 19–44.

—— 'Masses Based on Popular Songs and Solmization Syllables', in Richard Sherr (ed.), *The Josquin Companion* (Oxford: Oxford University Press, 2000), 51–87.

BLOCK, ADRIENNE F., *The Early French Parody Noël*, 2 vols. (Studies in Musicology, 36; Ann Arbor: UMI Research Press, 1983).

BLOCKMANS, WIM, and PREVENIER, WALTER, *The Promised Lands: The Low Countries under Burgundian Rule, 1369–1530*, trans. Elizabeth Fackelman, rev. Edward Peters (Philadelphia: University of Pennsylvania Press, 1999).

BLOXAM, M. JENNIFER, 'Communication', *JAMS* 45 (1992), 166–7.

—— 'In Praise of Spurious Saints: The *Missae Floruit egregiis* by Pipelare and La Rue', *JAMS* 44 (1991), 163–220.

—— 'Masses Based on Polyphonic Songs and Canonic Masses', in Richard Sherr (ed.), *The Josquin Companion* (Oxford: Oxford University Press, 2000), 151–209.

—— Review of Pierre de la Rue, *Opera omnia*, vols. 1–3, in *Notes*, 51 (1994–5), 407–10.

—— 'A Survey of Late Medieval Service Books from the Low Countries: Implications for Sacred Polyphony 1460–1520' (Ph.D. diss., Yale University, 1987).

BLUME, FRIEDRICH, *Renaissance and Baroque Music: A Comprehensive Survey*, trans. M. D. Herter Norton (New York: W. W. Norton, 1967).

BOORMAN, STANLEY, and JAS, ERIC, 'Clibano, Jheronimus de', *New Grove II*.

BOSSUYT, IGNACE, *Flemish Polyphony* (Leuven: Davidsfonds, 1994).

BOTTÉE DE TOULMON, AUGUSTE, *Agnus dei de la messe super l'homme armé de Pierre de Larue: lettre adressée à M. le Conseiller G.-R. Kiesewetter* ([Paris: Imprimerie royale, 1838]).

BRENET, MICHEL, *Palestrina* (Paris: Félix Alcan, 1906).

BRIDGMAN, NANIE, 'Christian Egenolff, imprimeur de musique: à propos du recueil Res. Vm⁷ 504 de la Bibliothèque nationale de Paris', *Annales musicoloques*, 3 (1955), 77–177.

BROWN, HOWARD MAYER, 'In Alamire's Workshop: Notes on Scribal Practice in the Early Sixteenth Century', in Ludwig Finscher (ed.), *Datierung und Filiation von Musikhandschriften der Josquin-Zeit* (Wolfenbütteler Forschungen, 26; Quellenstudien zur Musik der Renaissance, 2; Wiesbaden: O. Harrassowitz, 1983), 15–63.

—— *Instrumental Music Printed before 1600: A Bibliography* (Cambridge, Mass., and London: Harvard University Press, 1965).

—— Introduction to *Uppsala Universitetsbiblioteket Vokalmusik i handskrift 76a* (Renaissance Music in Facsimile, 19; New York and London: Garland, 1987).

—— 'Mouton, Jean', *New Grove*.

—— 'Music and Ritual at Charles the Bold's Court: The Function of Liturgical Music by Busnoys and his Contemporaries', in Paula Higgins (ed.), *Antoine Busnoys: Method, Meaning, and Context in Late Medieval Music* (Oxford: Clarendon Press, 1999), 53–70.

BRUCHET, MAX, and LANCIEN, E[UGÉNIE], *L'Itinéraire de Marguerite d'Autriche, gouvernante des Pays-Bas* (Lille: L. Danel, 1934).

BURBURE, LÉON DE, 'Étude sur un manuscrit du XVIᵉ siècle, contenant des chants à quatre et à trois voix; suivie d'un *Post-scriptum* sur le *Bellum musicale*, de Cl. Sebastiani', *Mémoires couronnés et autres mémoires publiés par l'Academie Royale des Sciences, des Lettres et des Beaux-Arts de Belgique*, 33/6 (1882), 1–44.

BURNEY, CHARLES, *A General History of Music from the Earliest Ages to the Present Period (1789)*, 2 vols. (New York: Harcourt, Brace, 1935).

BUSNOYS, ANTOINE, *Collected Works, Part 3: The Latin-Texted Works*, ed. Richard Taruskin (Masters and Monuments of the Renaissance, 5; New York: Broude Trust, 1990).

BUTKENS, CHRISTOPHE, *Supplement aux Trophées tant sacrés que profanes du Duché de Brabant* (The Hague: Chrétien Van Lom, 1726).

CARTER, TIM, 'Rossi, Giovanni Battista', *New Grove II*.

CASON, T. ELIZABETH, 'The Dating of Munich 3154 Revisited', paper presented at the Josquin Symposium, Duke University, 19–20 February 1999.

CATTIN, GIULIO, 'Canti, canzoni a ballo e danze nelle Maccheronee di Teofilo Folengo', *Rivista italiana di musicologia*, 10 (1975), 180–215.

CAUCHIES, JEAN-MARIE, 'La Signification politique des entrées princières dans les Pays-Bas: Maximilian d'Autriche et Philippe le Beau', *Publication du Centre européen d'études bourguignonnes (XIVᵉ–XVIᵉ s.)*, 34 (1994), 19–35.

CAULLET, GUSTAVE, *Musiciens de la collégiale Notre-Dame à Courtrai d'après leurs testaments* (Kortrijk: Flandria, 1911).

Census-Catalogue of Manuscript Sources of Polyphonic Music, 1400–1550, 5 vols., vol. 1 ed. Charles Hamm and Herbert Kellman; vols. 2–5 ed. Herbert Kellman (Renaissance Manuscript Studies, 1; Neuhausen-Stuttgart: American Institute of Musicology–Hänssler-Verlag, 1979–88).

CHAPMAN, CATHERINE WEEKS, 'Printed Collections of Polyphonic Music Owned by Ferdinand Columbus', *JAMS* 21 (1968), 34–84.

CHARDON, HENRI, *Les Noels de Jean Daniel dit Maitre Mitou, Organiste de Saint-Maurice et Chapelain de Saint-Pierre d'Angers, 1520–1530, précédes d'une étude sur sa vie et ses poésies* (Le Mans: Edmond Monnoyer, 1874).

CHASTELLAIN, GEORGES, *Chronique des ducs de Bourgogne*, 6 vols. (Collection des chroniques nationales françaises, 42–7; Paris: Verdiere, 1827–8).

CHORON, ALEXANDRE ÉTIENNE, and FAYOLLE, FRANÇOIS, *Dictionnaire historique des musiciens artistes et amateurs, morts et vivans . . . précédé d'un sommaire de l'histoire de la musique*, 2 vols. (Paris: Valade, Lenormant, 1810–11).

COCLICO, ADRIANUS PETIT, *Compendium musices* (Nuremberg: Johannes Montanus & Ulrich Neuber, 1552; facs. edn., ed. Manfred F. Bukofzer, Kassel and Basel: Bärenreiter, 1954).

—— *Musical Compendium (Compendium Musices)*, trans. Albert Seay (Colorado Springs, Colorado: Colorado College Music Press, 1973).

COMPÈRE, LOYSET, *Opera omnia*, ed. Ludwig Finscher, 5 vols. (Corpus mensurabilis musicae, 15; [Rome]: American Institute of Musicology, 1958–72).

Correspondance de l'empereur Maximilien Ier et de Marguerite d'Autriche, sa fille, gouvernante des Pays-Bas, de 1507 à 1519, ed. M. Le Glay, 2 vols. (Paris: Jules Renouard, 1839; repr. New York: Johnson Reprint, 1966).

A Correspondence of Renaissance Musicians, ed. Bonnie J. Blackburn, Edward E. Lowinsky, and Clement A. Miller (Oxford: Clarendon Press, 1991).

COUSSEMAKER, CHARLES-EDMOND-HENRI DE, *Notice sur les collections musicales de la bibliothèque de Cambrai* (Paris, 1843; repr. Hildesheim and New York: G. Olms, 1975).

CRÉTIN, GUILLAUME, *Œuvres poétiques*, ed. Kathleen Chesney (Paris: Firmin-Didot, 1932).

CROLL, GERHARD, and LINDMAYR-BRANDL, ANDREA, 'Weerbeke, Gaspar van', *New Grove II.*

CROSS, RONALD, 'Matthaeus Pipelare: A Historical and Stylistic Study of his Works' (Ph.D. diss., New York University, 1961).

CRUICKSHANK, C. G., *The English Occupation of Tournai 1513–1519* (Oxford: Clarendon Press, 1971).

CUYLER, LOUISE, *The Emperor Maximilian I and Music* (London, New York, and Toronto: Oxford University Press, 1973).

D'ACCONE, FRANK A., *The Civic Muse: Music and Musicians in Siena during the Middle Ages and the Renaissance* (Chicago and London: University of Chicago Press, 1997).

DANIEL, JEAN, *S'ensuyvent plusieurs noels nouveaulx . . .* (N.p.: n.p., n.d.).

—— *Noels nouveaulx* (N.p.: n.p., n.d.).

DAVISON, NIGEL ST. JOHN, '*Absalom fili mi* Reconsidered', *TVNM* 46 (1996), 42–56.

—— 'Continental Cousins of the *In Nomine* Family?', *Music Review*, 52 (1991), 1–11.

—— 'The Motets of Pierre de la Rue' (D.Mus. diss., University of Edinburgh, 1961).

—— 'The Motets of Pierre de la Rue', *Musical Quarterly*, 48 (1962), 19–35.

DEAN, JEFFREY J., 'The Repertory of the Cappella Giulia in the 1560s', *JAMS* 41 (1988), 465–90.

DE CUYPER, J., 'Een Godsdienstige Stichting van de beroemde komponist Pierre de la Rue in de Kapittelkerk te Kortrijk', *Verslagen en Mededelingen van De Leiegouw: Vereniging voor de Studie van de lokale geschiedenis, taal en folklore in het Kortrijkse*, 13 (1971), 295–7.

DELPORTE, JULES, 'A travers chants', *Revue liturgique et musicale*, 14 (1930–31), no. 5, 124–7; no. 6, 154–5, supplement.

DEVAUX, JEAN, *Jean Molinet: Indiciaire bourguignon* (Bibliothèque du XVᵉ siècle, 55; (Paris: Honoré Champion, 1996).

DIJCK, CHRISTIAAN MARIA VAN, *De Bossche optimaten: Geschiedenis van de Illustre Lieve Vrouwebroederschap te 's-Hertogenbosch, 1318–1973* (Bijdragen tot de geschiedenis van het Zuiden van Nederland, 27; Tilburg: Stichting Zuidelijk Historisch Contact, 1973).

DOMMER, ARREY VON, *Handbuch der Musikgeschichte* (Leipzig: Fr. Wilh. Grunow, 1868).

DOUILLEZ, JEANNINE, 'De Muziek aan het Bourgondische-Habsburgse Hof in de Tweede Helft der XVde Eeuw' (diss., University of Ghent, [1967]).

DUGGAN, MARY KAY, 'Queen Joanna and her Musicians', *Musica disciplina*, 30 (1976), 73–95.

DUPIRE, NOEL, *Jean Molinet: La Vie—Les Œuvres* (Paris: E. Droz, 1932).

EDMUNDS, SHEILA, 'The Medieval Library of Savoy', *Scriptorium*, 24 (1970), 318–27; 25 (1971), 253–84; 26 (1972), 269–93.

EDWARDS, WARWICK, 'Text Underlay in Marguerite of Austria's Chanson Album Brussel 228', *Jaarboek van het Vlaamse Centrum voor Oude Muziek*, 3 (1987), 33–47.

Een vrolic wesen, ed. Richard Taruskin (Miami: Ogni Sorte, 1979).

EITNER, ROBERT, *Biographisch-bibliographisches Quellen-Lexikon der Musiker und Musikgelehrten der christlichen Zeitrechnung bis zur Mitte des neunzehnten Jahrhunderts*, 10 vols. (Leipzig: Breitkopf & Härtel, 1900–4).

—— *Verzeichnis neuer Ausgaben alter Musikwerke aus der frühesten Zeit bis zum Jahre 1800* (Berlin: T. Trautwein [M. Bahn], 1871).

—— et al., *Bibliographie der Musik-Sammelwerke des XVI. und XVII. Jahrhunderts* (Berlin: L. Liepmannssohn, 1877).

ELDERS, WILLEM, 'Number Symbolism in Some Cantus-Firmus Masses of Pierre de la Rue', *Jaarboek van het Vlaamse Centrum voor Oude Muziek*, 3 (1987), 59–68.

—— 'Who Was Josquin', in id. (ed.), *Proceedings of the International Josquin Symposium, Utrecht 1986* (Utrecht: Vereniging voor Nederlandse Muziekgeschiedenis, 1991), 1–14.

Encyclopädie der gesammten musikalischen Wissenschaften oder Universal-Lexikon der Tonkunst, ed. Gustav Schilling, 6 vols. (Stuttgart: Franz Heinrich Köhler, 1835–8; repr. Hildesheim and New York: Georg Olms, 1974).

FALLOWS, DAVID, 'Alamire as a Composer', *Yearbook of the Alamire Foundation*, 5 (forthcoming).

—— *A Catalogue of Polyphonic Songs 1415–1480* (Oxford: Oxford University Press, 1999).

—— *Dufay* (London and Melbourne: J. M. Dent, 1982).

—— 'The Herdringen Scores', in conference packet for *Josquin: International Conference, New Directions in Josquin Scholarship, Princeton University, 29–31 October 1999*, 410–25.

—— Introduction to *The Songbook of Fridolin Sicher around 1515: Sankt Gallen, Stiftsbibliothek Cod. Sang. 461* (Peer: Alamire, 1996).

—— 'Jean Molinet and the Lost Burgundian Court Chansonniers of the 1470s', in Martin Staehelin (ed.), *Gestalt und Entstehung musikalischer Quellen im 15. und 16. Jahrhundert* (Quellenstudien zur Musik der Renaissance, 3; Wiesbaden: Harrassowitz, 1998). 35–42.

—— 'Other Editions', *Early Music*, 18 (1990), 657–8.

—— 'Robert Morton's Songs: A Study of Styles in the Mid-Fifteenth Century' (Ph.D. diss., University of California, Berkeley, 1978).

—— *Songs and Musicians in the Fifteenth Century* (Aldershot: Ashgate, 1996).

—— 'Specific Information on the Ensembles for Composed Polyphony, 1400–1474', in Stanley Boorman (ed.), *Studies in the Performance of Late Mediaeval Music* (Cambridge: Cambridge University Press, 1983), 109–59.

FALLOWS, DAVID, "'Trained and Immersed in All Musical Delights": Towards a New Picture of Busnoys', in Paula Higgins (ed.), *Antoine Busnoys: Method, Meaning, and Context in Late Medieval Music* (Oxford: Clarendon Press, 1999), 21–50.

—— and Jander, Owen, 'Tenor (2)', *New Grove II*.

FEININGER, LAURENCE K. J., *Die Frühgeschichte des Kanons (um 1500)* (Emsdetten: Heinr. & J. Lechte, 1937).

FÉTIS, ÉDOUARD, *Les Musiciens belges* (Brussels: Jamar, [1849]).

FÉTIS, FRANÇOIS-JOSEPH, *Biographie universelle des musiciens et bibliographie générale de la musique*, 8 vols. (1st edn., Brussels: Leroux, 1835–44).

—— *Biographie universelle des musiciens et bibliographie générale de la musique*, 8 vols. (2nd edn., Brussels: Firmin-Didot, 1860–5).

—— 'Mémoire sur cette question: "Quels ont été les mérites des Neerlandais dans la musique, principalement aux 14ᵉ, 15ᵉ et 16ᵉ siècles; et quelle influence les artistes de ce pays qui ont séjourné en Italie, ont-ils exercée sur les écoles de musique, qui se sont formées peu après cette époque en Italie?"', in *Verhandelingen over de vraag: Welke verdiensten hebben zich de Nederlanders vooral in de 14ᵉ, 15ᵉ en 16ᵉ eeuw in het vak der toonkunst verworven; en in hoe verre kunnen de nederlandsche kunstenaars van dien tijd, die zich naar Italien begeven hevven, invloed gehad hebben op de muzijkscholen, die zich kort daarna in Italien hebben gevormd?* (Amsterdam: J. Muller, 1829).

FINCK, HERMANN, *Practica musica* (Wittenberg: Georg Rhaw, 1556; facs. edn., Hildesheim and New York: Georg Olms, 1971).

—— *Practica musica*, expanded edn. (Wittenberg: Georg Rhaw, 1556; facs. edn., Bibliotheca musica bononiensis, Sezione II, 21; Bologna: Forni, 1969).

FINSCHER, LUDWIG, *Loyset Compère (c. 1450–1518): Life and Works* (Musicological Studies and Documents, 12; n.p.: American Institute of Musicology, 1964).

FOLENGO, TEOFILO, *Histoire maccaronique de Merlin Coccaie*, ed. Gustave Brunet (Paris: Adolphe Delahays, 1859).

—— (as Cocai, Merlin), *Le maccheonee*, 2 vols., 2nd edn., ed. Alessandro Luzio (Bari: Gius. Laterza & Figli, 1927–8).

—— (as Cocai, Merlin), *Le opere maccheroniche*, 2 vols., ed. Attilio Portioli (Mantua: C. Mondovi, 1882–3).

—— *Opus Merlini Cocaii, poete Mantuani Macaronicorum* (Toscolano: Alexander Paganini, 1521; later editions, 1522; 1572; Venice: Horatium de Gobbis, 1581; Venice: Beuilacquam, 1613; Amsterdam: Abrahamum a Someren, 1692).

FORKEL, JOHANN NICOLAUS, *Allgemeine Geschichte der Musik*, 2 vols. (Leipzig: Schwickertschen, 1788–1801).

—— and Sonnleithner, Joseph (eds.), *Geschichte der Musik in Denkmälern von der ältesten bis auf die neueste Zeit* (n.p.: n.p., n.d.)

Fors seulement: Thirty Compositions for Three to Five Voices or Instruments from the Fifteenth and Sixteenth Centuries, ed. Martin Picker (Recent Researches in the Music of the Middle Ages and Early Renaissance, 14; Madison: A-R Editions, 1981).

Fortuna desperata: Thirty-Six Settings of an Italian Song, ed. Honey Meconi (Recent Researches in the Music of the Middle Ages and Early Renaissance, 37; Middleton, Wis.: A-R Editions, 2001).

FOX, CHARLES WARREN, Review of *Josquin des Prés: Motetten, Bundel XXI–XXII*, ed. M. Antonowycz, and Pierre de la Rue, *Drie missen*, ed. René Bernard Lenaerts and Jozef Robijns, in *Notes*, 19 (1961–2), 687–8.

FREEDMAN, RICHARD, 'Mureau, Gilles', *New Grove II*.

—— 'Music, Musicians, and the House of Lorraine during the First Half of the Sixteenth Century' (Ph.D. diss., University of Pennsylvania, 1987).

FRIS, VICTOR, 'Tableau de la Flandre au début du XVIe siècle d'après Antonio De Beatis et Jacques de Meyere', *Bulletin de la Société d'histoire et d'archéologie de Gand*, 18 (1910), 42–91.

FRUOVO, JOÃO ÁLVARES, *Discursos sobre a perfeiçam do diathesaron* . . . (Lisbon: Antonio Craesbeeck de Mello, 1662).

FULLER, DAVID, LEDBETTER, DAVID, and JOSEPHSON, NORS S., 'Champion', *New Grove II*.

GACHARD, LOUIS PROSPER, *Collection des voyages des Souverains des Pays-Bas*, i: *Itinéraires de Philippe le Hardi, Jean sans Peur, Philippe le Bon, Maximilien et Philippe le Beau; Relation du premier voyage de Philippe le Beau en Espagne, en 1501, par Antoine de Lalaing, Sr de Montigny; Relation du deuxième voyage de Philippe le Beau, en 1506, par un anonyme* (Mémoires de l'Academie royale de Belgique, 1; Brussels: F. Hayez, 1876).

—— *Collection des voyages des Souverains des Pays-Bas*, ii: *Itinéraire de Charles-Quint de 1506 à 1531; Journal des voyages de Charles-Quint, de 1514 à 1551, par Jean de Vandenesse* (Mémoires de l'Academie royale de Belgique, 1; Brussels: F. Hayez, 1874).

—— 'Notice sur quelques collections d'états de la maison des princes, et spécialement sur celle qui est conservée aux Archives du Royaume', *Compte rendu des séances de la Commission Royale d'Histoire ou Recueil de ses Bulletins*, 2nd ser., 6 (1854), 435–48.

—— *Rapport à Monsieur le ministre de l'intérieur sur différentes series de documents concernant l'histoire de la Belgique qui sont conservées dans les archives de l'ancienne chambre des comptes de Flandre à Lille* (Brussels: M. Hayez, 1841).

GAFFURIUS, FRANCHINUS, *Practica musicae*, trans. Clement A. Miller (Musicological Studies and Documents, 20; n.p.: American Institute of Musicology, 1968).

GERBER, ERNST LUDWIG, *Historisch-biographisches Lexicon der Tonkünstler*, 2 vols. (Leipzig: J. G. I. Breitkopf, 1790–2).

—— *Neues historisch-biographisches Lexikon der Tonkünstler*, 4 vols. (Leipzig: A. Kuhnel, 1812–14).

GLAREAN, HEINRICH, *Dodecachordon* (Basel: H. Petri, 1547; facs. edn., New York: Broude, 1967).

—— *Dodecachordon*, 2 vols., trans. Clement A. Miller (Musicological Studies and Documents, 6; n.p.: American Institute of Musicology, 1965).

—— *Dodecachordon: Basileae MDXLVII*, trans. and ed. Peter Bohn (Publikationen älterer praktischer und theoretischer Musikwerke, 16; Leipzig: Breitkopf & Härtel, 1888).

—— *Isagoge in musicen* (Basel: J. Froben, 1516).

GOOVAERTS, ALPHONSE, 'Delarue (Pierre)', *Biographie nationale* [Belgium], v. 325–8.

La Grand bible des noelz . . . (Lyons: Benoist Rigaud, n.d.).

La Grand bible des noelz . . . (Paris: Nicolas Bonfons, n.d.).

Les Grans noelz . . . (Paris: Jehan Bonfons, n.d.).

Les Grans noelz nouveaulx . . . (Paris: Pierre Sergent, n.d.).

GUICCIARDINI, LUDOVICO, *Descrittione di tutti i paësi bassi* (Antwerp, 1556).

HAAR, JAMES, *The Science and Art of Renaissance Music*, ed. Paul Corneilson (Princeton: Princeton University Press, 1998).

HABERL, FRANZ XAVIER, *Bibliographischer und thematischer Musikkatalog des päpstlichen Kapellarchives im Vatikan zu Rom* (Leipzig: Breitkopf & Härtel, 1888) [supplement to *Monatshefte für Musikgeschichte*, 19–20 (1887–8)].

HÄBLER, KONRAD, *Der Streit Ferdinand's des Katholischen und Philipp's I. um die Regierung von Castilien 1504–1506* (Dresden: Albanns'sche Buchdruckerei [Christian Teich], 1882).

HAEN, FRITZ DE, 'A Magnificat Quarti Toni with a Fourfold Ascription', in Willem Elders (ed.), *Proceedings of the International Josquin Symposium, Utrecht 1986* (Utrecht: Vereniging voor Nederlandse Muziekgeschiedenis, 1991), 117–23.

HAGGH, BARBARA, 'Binchois and Sacred Music at the Burgundian Court', in Andrew Kirkman and Dennis Slavin (eds.), *Binchois Studies* (Oxford: Oxford University Press, 2000), 1–25.

—— 'Itinerancy to Residency: Professional Careers and Performance Practices in 15th-Century Sacred Music', *Early Music*, 17 (1989), 359–66.

—— 'Music, Liturgy, and Ceremony in Brussels, 1350–1500', 2 vols. (Ph.D. diss., University of Illinois at Urbana-Champaign, 1988).

—— 'Recovering Meaning in a Manuscript: Brussels, Bibliothèque Royale, MS 215–216, and its Repertory for the Seven Sorrows of the Virgin', *Yearbook of the Alamire Foundation*, 5 (forthcoming).

—— 'The Status of the Musician at the Burgundian Habsburg Courts, 1467–1506' (Master's thesis, University of Illinois, 1980).

HAWKINS, JOHN, *A General History of the Science and Practice of Music*, 2 vols. (2nd edn., London: J. Alfred Novello, 1853; repr. New York: Dover, 1963).

HEESTERS, W., and RADEMAKER, C. S. M., *Geschiedenis van Sint-Oedenrode* (Bijdragen tot de Geschiedenis van het Zuiden van Nederland, 24; Tilburg: Stichting Zuidelijk Historisch Contact, 1972).

HERMELINK, SIEGFRIED, 'Ein Musikalienverzeichnis der Heidelberger Hofkapelle aus dem Jahre 1544', in Georg Poensgen (ed.), *Ottheinrich: Gedenkschrift zur vierhundertjährigen Wiederkehr seiner Kurfürstenzeit in der Pfalz (1556–1559)* (Heidelberg: n.p., 1956), 247–60.

HEYDEN, SEBALD, *De arte canendi, ac vero signorum in cantibus usu, libri duo* (Nuremberg: J. Petreius, 1540; facs. edn., Monuments of Music and Music Literature in facs., 2nd ser.: Music Literature, 139; New York: Broude, 1969).

—— *De arte canendi*, trans. Clement A. Miller (Musicological Studies and Documents, 26; n.p.: American Institute of Musicology, 1972).

—— *Musica, id est Artis canendi, libri duo* (Nuremberg: J. Petreius, 1537).

HIGGINS, PAULA, 'Busnoys, Antoine', *New Grove II*.

—— '*In hydraulis* Revisited: New Light on the Career on Antoine Busnois', *JAMS* 39 (1986), 36–86.

HOCQUET, ADOLPHE, 'Archives de Tournai: tables alphabétiques des testaments et des comptes de tutelle et d'exécution testamentaire (xvᵉ siècle)', *Annales de la Société historique de Tournai*, 10 (1906).

—— 'Un Musicien tournaisien dit courtraisien', *Revue tournaisienne* (Sept. 1911), 167–8.

HOFFMANN-ERBRECHT, LOTHAR, 'Ein Frankfurter Messenkodex', *Archiv für Musikwissenschaft*, 16 (1959), 328–34.

HÖFLER, CONSTANTIN R., 'Depeschen des venetianischen Botschafters bei Erzherzog Philipp, Herzog von Burgund, König von Leon, Castilien, Granada, Dr. Vincenzo Quirino 1505–1506', *Archiv für Österreichische Geschichte*, 66 (1885), 45–256.

IMRIE, MARTYN, 'La Rue Masses', *Early Music*, 24 (1996), 699–701.

INGRAM, SONJA STAFFORD, 'The Polyphonic Salve Regina, 1425–1550' (Ph.D. diss., University of North Carolina, 1973).

Inventaire sommaire des archives départementales du Nord, Archives civiles, Série B, ed. Abbé Dehaisnes, Jules Finot, and A. Desplanque, 8 vols. (Lille: L. Danel, 1872–1906).

JAS, ERIC, 'Choirbook Fragments', in *TA* 166–7.

—— '*Sicut lilium inter spinas*: Het muziekleven te 's-Hertogenbosch rond de Illustre Lieve Vrouwe Broederschap', in *Kloosters, kronieken en koormuziek: Cultuur in bourgondisch 's-Hertogenbosch 1450–1629* (Brabantse lezingen, 6; 's-Hertogenbosch: Het Noordbrabants Genootschap, 1991), 41–60.

—— 'Vienna, Österreichische Nationalbibliothek, Handschriftensammlung, MS 11778', in *TA* 147.

JOACHIM, NICOLAS, *Aperçu historique sur la maîtrise de la cathédrale de Tournai (Xme–XXme siècle)* (Tournai and Paris: Casterman, 1942).

JONES, GEORGE MORTON, 'The "First" Chansonnier of the Biblioteca Riccardiana, Codex 2794: A Study in the Method of Editing 15th-Century Music', 2 vols. (Ph.D. diss., New York University, 1972).

JOSEPHSON, NORS SIGURD, 'The Missa De Beata Virgine of the Sixteenth Century' (Ph.D. diss., University of California, Berkeley, 1970).

Josquin des Prés und andere Meister: Weltliche Lieder, ed. Friedrich Blume (Das Chorwerk, 3; Berlin: Kallmeyer, 1929).

JOSQUIN DES PREZ, *Werken*, ed. Albert Smijers, Myroslaw Antonowycz, and Willem Elders (Amsterdam and Leipzig: Vereniging voor Nederlandse Muziekgeschiedenis, 1921–69).

JUDD, CRISTLE COLLINS, 'Reading Aron Reading Petrucci: The Music Examples of the *Trattato della natura et cognitione di tutti gli tuoni* (1525)', *EMH* 14 (1995), 121–52.

—— *Reading Renaissance Music Theory: Hearing with the Eyes* (Cambridge: Cambridge University Press, 2000).

JUST, MARTIN, *Der Mensuralkodex Mus. ms. 40021 der Staatsbibliothek Preußischer Kulturbesitz Berlin: Untersuchungen zum Repertoire einer deutschen Quelle des 15. Jahrhunderts*, 2 vols. (Würzburger musikhistorische Beiträge, 1; Tutzing: Hans Schneider, 1975).

KAHMANN, B., 'Antoine de Févin: A Bio-Bibliographical Contribution', *Musica disciplina*, 4 (1950), 153–62; 5 (1951), 143–55.

KARP, THEODORE, 'Rhythmic Irregularities in La Rue's *Missa de Sancto Antonio*', *Israel Studies in Musicology*, 5 (1990), 81–95.

KELLMAN, HERBERT, 'Brussels, Bibliothèque royale de Belgique MS 6428', in *TA* 71.

—— 'Brussels, Bibliothèque royale de Belgique MS 9126', in *TA* 73.

—— 'Josquin and the Courts of the Netherlands and France: The Evidence of the Sources', in *JosCon*, 181–216.

—— (ed.), *The Treasury of Petrus Alamire: Music and Art in Flemish Court Manuscripts 1500–1535* (Ghent and Amsterdam: Ludion, 1999).

KERVYN DE VOLKAERSBEKE, PHILIPPE, *Les Églises de Gand*, 2 vols. (Ghent: Hebbelynck, 1858).

KESSELS, LEON, 'The Brussels/Tournai Partbooks: Structure, Illumination, and Flemish Repertory', *TVNM* 37 (1987), 82–110.

KIEL, JACOBIJN, 'Terminus post Alamire? On Some Later Scribes', *Yearbook of the Alamire Foundation*, 5 (forthcoming).

KIESEWETTER, RAFAEL GEORG, *Geschichte der europäisch-abendländischen oder unsrer heutigen Musik: Darstellung ihres Ursprunges, ihres Wachsthumes und ihrer stufenweisen Entwickelung; Von dem ersten Jahrhundert des Christenthumes bis auf unsre Zeit. Für jeden Freund der Tonkunst* (Leipzig: Breitkopf & Härtel, 1834).

—— 'Die Verdienste der Niederlaender um die Tonkunst', in *Verhandelingen over de vraag: Welke verdiensten hebben zich de Nederlanders vooral in de 14', 15' en 16' eeuw in het vak der toonkunst verworven; en in hoe verre kunnen de nederlandsche kunstenaars van dien tijd, die zich naar Italien begeven hevven, invloed gehad hebben op de muzijkscholen, die zich kort daarna in Italien hebben gevormd?* (Amsterdam: J. Muller, 1829).

KIRBY, FRANK EUGENE, 'Hermann Finck's *Practica Musica*: A Comparative Study in 16th-Century German Musical Theory' (Ph.D. diss., Yale University, 1957).

KIRSCH, WINFRIED, 'Josquin's Motets in the German Tradition', in *JosCon*, 261–78.

KMETZ, JOHN, *Die Handschriften der Universitätsbibliothek Basel: Katalog der Musikhandschriften des 16. Jahrhunderts* (Basel: Universitätsbibliothek Basel, 1988).

KNIGHTON, TESSA WENDY, 'Music and Musicians at the Court of Fernando of Aragon, 1474–1516' (Ph.D. diss., University of Cambridge, 1983).

KREIDER, JOHN EVAN, 'The Masses for Five and Six Voices by Pierre de la Rue', 2 vols. (Ph.D. diss., Indiana University, 1974).

—— 'Pierre de la Rue's *Incessament* and its Musical Descendents', in Albert Clement and Eric Jas (eds.), *From Ciconia to Sweelinck: Donum natalicium Willem Elders* (Amsterdam: Rodopi, 1994), 167–78.

—— 'Works Attributed in the Sixteenth Century to both Josquin des Prez and Pierre de la Rue', in Willem Elders (ed.), *Proceedings of the International Josquin Symposium, Utrecht 1986* (Utrecht: Vereniging voor Nederlandse Muziekgeschiedenis, 1991), 103–16.

KREITNER, KENNETH, 'Very Low Ranges in the Sacred Music of Ockeghem and Tinctoris', *Early Music*, 14 (1986), 467–79.

LA FAGE, ADRIEN DE, *Essais de diphthérographie musicale*, 2 vols. (Paris: O. Legouix, 1864).

LA MARCHE, OLIVIER DE, *Mémoires d'Olivier de la Marche, Maître d'hotel et capitaine des gardes de Charles le téméraire*, 4 vols., ed. Henri Beaune and J. d'Arbaumont (Paris: Renouard, 1883–8).

LAMBRECHT, JUTTA, *Das "Heidelberger Kapellinventar" von 1544 (Codex Pal. Germ. 318): Edition und Kommentar*, 2 vols. (Heidelberger Bibliotheksschriften, 26; Heidelberg: n.p., 1987).

LANFRANCO, GIOVANNI MARIA, *Scintille de musica* (Brescia: Lodovico Britannico, 1533; facs. edn., ed. Giuseppe Massera, Bibliotheca musica bononiensis, Sez. II, 15; Bologna: Forni, 1970).

LA RUE, PIERRE DE, *Collected Works*, 9 vols. to date, ed. Nigel St. John Davison, J. Evan Kreider, and T. Herman Keahey (Corpus mensurabilis musicae, 97; Neuhausen–Stuttgart: American Institute of Musicology/Hänssler-Verlag, 1989–).

—— *Drie Missen*, ed. René Bernard Lenaerts and Jozef Robijns (Monumenta musicae Belgicae, 8; Antwerp: Vereniging voor Muziekgeschiedenis, 1960).

—— *Liber Missarum*, ed. [Antonio] Tirabassi (Mechelen: Maison Dessain, [1941]).

—— *Missa Assumpta est*, ed. Ludwig Finscher (Musica divina, 18; Regensburg: Friedrich Pustet, 1966).

—— *Missa Ave sanctissima Maria*, ed. Laurence Feininger (Documenta polyphoniae liturgicae Sanctae Ecclesiae Romanae, ser. I. B. 1; Rome: Societas universalis S. Ceciliae, 1950).

—— *Missa Cum iucunditate for 4 and 5 voices*, ed. Nigel Davison (Mapa Mundi Series B: Franco-Flemish Church Music, 3; London: Bruno Turner, 1978).

—— *Missa L'Homme armé I zu 4 Stimmen*, ed. Nigel Davison (Das Chorwerk, 114; Wolfenbüttel and Zürich: Möseler, 1972).

—— *Requiem und eine Motette zu 4–5 Stimmen*, ed. Friedrich Blume (Das Chorwerk, 11; Wolfenbüttel: Möseler, 1931).

—— *Vier Motetten zu 4 Stimmen*, ed. Nigel Davison (Das Chorwerk, 91; Wolfenbüttel: Möseler, 1962).

LECOUVET, F. F. J., 'Les Enfants de chœur et les maîtres de musique de la cathédrale de Tournay—Fête des Innocents', *Messager des sciences historiques des arts et de la bibliographie de Belgique* (1856), 147–76.

LEE, BARBARA, 'Giovanni Maria Lanfranco's Scintille di musica and its Relation to 16th-Century Music Theory' (Ph.D. diss., Cornell University, 1961).

LEMAIRE DE BELGES, JEAN, *Œuvres*, 4 vols., ed. J. Stecher (Leuven: Lefever, 1882–91).

LENAERTS, RENÉ BERNARD, 'The 16th-Century Parody Mass in the Netherlands', *Musical Quarterly*, 36 (1950), 410–21.

Liber quindecim missarum: Brumel Missa 'De beata virgine', P. de la Rue Missa 'Ave Maria', ed. Henry Expert (Les Maîtres musiciens de la Renaissance française, 8; Paris: Alphonse Leduc, 1898).

LINDENBURG, C. W. H., 'Het "Kamper" liedboek', *TVNM* 16 (1940), 48–62.

LOCKWOOD, LEWIS, 'Josquin at Ferrara: New Documents and Letters', in *JosCon*, 103–37.

—— 'Sources of Renaissance Polyphony from Cividale del Friuli: The Manuscripts 53 and 59 of the Museo Archeologico Nazionale', *Saggiatore musicale*, 1 (1994), 249–314.

—— and Brobeck, John T., 'Braconnier, Jean', *New Grove II*.

Louis XII et Philippe le Beau, ed. Berthold Zeller (L'Histoire de France racontée par les contemporains, 37; Paris: Librairie Hachette, 1889).

LOWINSKY, EDWARD E., *The Medici Codex of 1518: A Choirbook of Motets Dedicated to Lorenzo de' Medici, Duke of Urbino*, 3 vols. (Monuments of Renaissance Music, 3–5; Chicago and London: University of Chicago Press, 1968).

—— and Blackburn, Bonnie J. (eds.), *Josquin des Prez: Proceedings of the International Josquin Festival-Conference held at The Juilliard School at Lincoln Center in New York City, 21–25 June 1971* (London, New York, and Toronto: Oxford University Press, 1976).

LUTHER, MARTIN, *D. Martin Luthers Werke: Kritische Gesamtausgabe, Tischreden*, 6 vols. (Weimar: Hermann Böhlaus, 1912–21).

MAAS, CHRIS, 'Josquin—Agricola—Brumel—de la Rue: een authenticiteitsprobleem', *TVNM* 20 (1964–7), 120–39.

MACEY, PATRICK, 'Conflicting Attributions for *De profundis*: Josquin and Champion', in conference packet for *Josquin: International Conference, New Directions in Josquin Scholarship, Princeton University, 29–31 October 1999*, 99–121.

—— et al., 'Josquin (Lebloitte dit) des Prez', *New Grove II*.

MARVIN, MARY BETH W[INN]: *see under* WINN (MARVIN).

MAYNARD, JUDSON DANA, 'An Anonymous Scottish Treatise on Music from the Sixteenth Century: British Museum, Additional Manuscript 4911' (Ph.D. diss., Indiana University, 1961).

McMURTRY, WILLIAM, Introduction to *Chansonnier of Hieronymus Lauweryn van Watervliet: London, British Library Ms. Add. 35087* (Peer: Alamire, 1989).

MECONI, HONEY, 'Another Look at *Absalon*', *TVNM* 48 (1998), 3–29.

—— 'Art-Song Reworkings: An Overview', *Journal of the Royal Musical Association*, 119 (1994), 1–42.

—— 'Foundation for an Empire: The Musical Inheritance of Charles V', in Francis Maes (ed.), *The Empire Resounds: Music in the Days of Charles V* (Leuven: Leuven University Press), 18–34.

—— 'Free from the Crime of Venus: The Biography of Pierre de la Rue', *Revista de musicología*, 16 (1993), 2673–83 (*Actas del XV congreso de la Sociedad Internacional de Musicología: Culturas musicales del Mediterráneo y sus ramificaciones, Madrid, 3–10 abril 1992*, v. 121–31).

—— 'French Print Chansons and Pierre de la Rue: A Case Study in Authenticity', in Jessie Ann Owens and Anthony Cummings (eds.), *Music in Renaissance Cities and Courts: Studies in Honor of Lewis Lockwood* (Warren, Mich.: Harmonie Park Press, 1997), 187–214.

MECONI, HONEY, 'The Function of the Habsburg-Burgundian Court Manuscripts', *Year-book of the Alamire Foundation*, 5 (forthcoming).

—— Introduction to *Basevi Codex: Florence, Biblioteca del Conservatorio, MS 2439* (Peer: Alamire, 1990).

—— 'Josquin and Musical Reputation', in Barbara Haggh (ed.), *Essays on Music and Culture in Honor of Herbert Kellman* (Paris and Tours: Minerve, 2001), 280–97.

—— 'La Rue, Pierre de', *New Grove II*.

—— 'The Manuscript Basevi 2439 and Chanson Transmission in Italy', in *Atti del XIV congresso della Società Internazionale di Musicologia (Bologna 1987)*, ed. Angelo Pompilio et al. (Turin: EDT, 1990), iii. 163–74.

—— 'Ockeghem and the Motet-Chanson in Fifteenth-Century France', in Philippe Vendrix (ed.), *Johannes Ockeghem: Actes du XLe Colloque international d'études humanistes, Tours, 3–8 février 1997* (Paris: Klincksieck, 1998), 381–402.

—— 'Pierre de la Rue and Secular Music at the Court of Marguerite of Austria', *Jaarboek van het Vlaamse Centrum voor Oude Muziek*, 3 (1987), 49–58.

—— Review of Pierre de la Rue, *Opera omnia*, vols. 1–3, ed. Nigel St. John Davison, J. Evan Kreider, and T. Herman Keahey, in *JAMS* 48 (1995), 283–93.

—— 'Sacred Tricinia and Basevi 2439', *I Tatti Studies: Essays in the Renaissance*, 4 (1991), 151–99.

—— 'Style and Authenticity in the Secular Music of Pierre de la Rue' (Ph.D. diss., Harvard University, 1986).

—— 'What is La Rue Doing in *Nymphes des bois*?', paper presented at Conference on Medieval and Renaissance Music, London, August 1986.

MENDEL, HERMANN, and REISSMANN, AUGUST, *Musikalisches Conversations-Lexikon* (Berlin: Robert Oppenheim, 1870–9).

MENIL, FÉLICIEN DE, *L'École contrapuntique flamande au XVe et XVIe siècle* (Paris: E. Demets, 1905).

MEYERUS, JACOBUS, *Flandricarum rerum Tomi X* (Antwerp: Guilielmus Vorstermann, 1531).

MILLER, CLEMENT A., 'Gaffurius's *Practica Musicae*: Origins and Contents', *Musica disciplina*, 22 (1968), 105–28.

MILSOM, JOHN, Review of Pierre de la Rue, *Opera omnia*, vols. 2–3, in *Early Music*, 21 (1993), 479–82.

MOLINET, JEAN, *Chroniques de Jean Molinet (1474–1506)*, ed. Georges Doutrepont and Omer Jodogne, 3 vols. (Brussels: Palais des académies, 1935–7).

—— *Les Faictz et dictz de Jean Molinet*, 3 vols., ed. Noël Dupire (Paris: Société des anciens textes français, 1936–9).

MONTEVERDI, CLAUDIO, *Lettere, dediche e prefazioni: edizione critica*, ed. Domenico de' Paoli (Rome: di Sanctis, 1973).

—— *Tutte le opere*, 17 vols., ed. G. Francesco Malipiero (Asola: n.p., 1926–66).

MONTEVERDI, GIULIO CESARE, 'Dichiaratione della lettera stampata nel Quinto libro de suoi madregali', in Claudio Monteverdi, *Scherzi musicali a tre voci* (Venice: Amadino, 1607; repr. 1609).

MOREAU, CLAIRE, 'L'Obituaire de la Collégiale Sainte-Ode d'Amay: édition et commentaires' (thesis, Université de Liège, 1983).

MOREAU, ÉDOUARD DE, *Histoire de l'église en Belgique*, 5 vols. and supplement (Brussels: L'Édition universelle, 1945–52).

MORLEY, THOMAS, *A Plain and Easy Introduction to Practical Music*, ed. R. Alec Harman (New York: W. W. Norton, 1953).

—— *A Plaine and Easie Introduction to Practicall Musicke* (London: Peter Short, 1597; facs. edn., The English Experience, 207; Amsterdam and New York: Theatrum Orbis Terrarum and Da Capo Press, 1969).

NAEGELE, PHILIPP, 'Ambros, August Wilhelm', *New Grove II*.

NEDDEN, OTTO ZU, 'Zur Geschichte der Musik am Hofe Kaiser Maximilians I', *Zeitschrift für Musikwissenschaft*, 15 (1932–3), 24–32.

NELSON, BERNADETTE, 'Ritual and Ceremony in the Spanish Royal Chapel *c*.1559–*c*.1561', *EMH* 19 (2000), 105–200.

NESS, ARTHUR J., 'Sources of Lute Music', *New Grove II*.

NIERMEYER, J. F., *Mediae Latinitatis lexicon minus: A Medieval Latin-French/English Dictionary* (Leiden: E. J. Brill, 1976).

NUGENT, GEORGE, and JAS, ERIC, 'Gombert, Nicolas', *New Grove II*.

O'REGAN, NOEL, 'The *Instrumentälischer Bettlermantl* and Gallus Dressler's *Precepta Musicae Poeticae* of 1563/4', in J. P. Campbell (ed.), *Proceedings of the International Interdisciplinary Conference on Instrumentälischer Bettlermantl, August 1997* (forthcoming).

Die Orgeltabulatur des Leonhard Kleber, ed. Karin Berg-Kotterba, 2 vols. (Das Erbe deutscher Musik, 91–2; Frankfurt: Henry Litolff, 1987).

ORNITHOPARCHUS, ANDREAS, *De arte cantandi micrologus* (Cologne: H. Alopecius, 1524; reprint edns., I. Gymnicus, 1533, 1535, 1540).

—— *Micrologus, or Introduction: Containing the Art of Singing*, trans. John Dowland (London: Thomas Adams, 1609; facs. edn., as *A Compendium of Musical Practice*, ed. Gustave Reese and Steven Ledbetter, New York: Dover, 1973).

—— *Musice active micrologus* (Leipzig: Valentin Schumann, Jan. 1517; reprint edns., November 1517, 1519, 1521, 1555; Hildesheim and New York: Georg Olms, 1977).

OSTHOFF, HELMUTH, *Josquin Desprez*, 2 vols. (Tutzing: H. Schneider, 1962–5).

OWENS, JESSIE ANN, 'Music Historiography and the Definition of "Renaissance"', *Notes*, 47 (1990–1), 305–30.

PERKINS, LEEMAN L., 'Ockeghem, Jean de', *New Grove II*.

PICKER, MARTIN, 'The Chanson Albums of Marguerite of Austria: Manuscripts 228 and 11239 of the Bibliothèque Royale de Belgique, Bruxelles' (Ph.D. diss., University of California, Berkeley, 1960).

—— 'The Chanson Albums of Marguerite of Austria: MSS 228 and 11239 of the Bibliothèque Royale de Belgique, Brussels', *Annales musicologiques*, 6 (1958–63), 145–287.

—— *The Chanson Albums of Marguerite of Austria: MSS 228 and 11239 of the Bibliothèque Royale de Belgique, Brussels* (Berkeley and Los Angeles: University of California Press, 1965).

—— 'Divitis, Antonius', *New Grove II*.

—— 'The Habsburg Courts in the Netherlands and Austria, 1477–1530', in Iain Fenlon (ed.), *The Renaissance From the 1470s to the End of the 16th Century* (Englewood Cliffs, NJ: Prentice Hall, 1989), 216–42.

—— 'More *Regret* Chansons for Marguerite d'Autriche', *Le Moyen Français*, 5 (1979), 81–101.

—— 'The Motet Anthologies of Andrea Antico', in Edward H. Clinkscale and Claire Brook (eds.), *A Musical Offering: Essays in Honor of Martin Bernstein* (New York: Pendragon, 1977), 211–37.

—— 'Musical Laments for King Philip of Castile and his Musician Alexander Agricola', *Revista de musicología*, 16 (1993), 2684–95 (*Actas del XV congreso de la Sociedad Internacional de Musicología: Culturas musicales del Mediterráneo y sus ramificaciones, Madrid, 3–10 abril 1992*, v. 132–43).

PICKER, MARTIN, 'A New Look at the "Little" Chansonnier of Margaret of Austria', *Jaarboek van het Vlaamse Centrum voor Oude Muziek*, 3 (1987), 27–31.

—— 'Orto, Marbrianus de', *New Grove II*.

—— Review of Pierre de la Rue, *Drie Missen*, ed. René Bernard Lenaerts and Jozef Robijns, in *JAMS* 16 (1963), 262–6.

—— 'Three Unidentified Chansons by Pierre de la Rue in the *Album de Marguerite d'Autriche*', *Musical Quarterly*, 46 (1960), 329–43.

PIETZSCH, GERHARD, *Quellen und Forschungen zur Geschichte der Musik am kurpfälzischen Hof zu Heidelberg bis 1622* (Wiesbaden: F. Steiner, 1963).

PINCHART, ALEXANDRE, *Archives des arts, sciences et lettres*, 3 vols. (Ghent: L. Hebbelynck, 1860–81).

PIRRO, ANDRÉ, 'Jean Cornuel vicaire à Cambrai', *Revue de musicologie*, 10 (1926), 190–203.

—— *Histoire de la musique de la fin du XIVᵉ siècle à la fin du XVIᵉ* (Paris: Librairie Renouard, 1940).

PREVENIER, WALTER, and BLOCKMANS, WIM, *The Burgundian Netherlands* (Cambridge: Cambridge University Press, 1986).

PRINTZ, WOLFGANG CASPAR, *Ausgewählte Werke*, 3 vols., ed. Helmut K. Krausse (Berlin and New York: Walter De Gruyter, 1974–93).

—— *Historische Beschreibung der edelen Sing- und Kling-Kunst* (Dresden: Johann Georgen, 1690).

PRIZER, WILLIAM F., 'Music and Ceremonial in the Low Countries: Philip the Fair and the Order of the Golden Fleece', *EMH* 5 (1985), 113–53.

RABELAIS, FRANÇOIS, *Œuvres complètes* (Paris: Gallimard, 1994).

—— *Le Quart livre des faicts et dicts heroïques du bon Pantagruel* (Paris: Michel Fezandat, 1552).

REESE, GUSTAVE, 'Maldeghem and his Buried Treasure: A Bibliographical Study', Notes, 6 (1948–9), 75–117.

—— 'The Polyphonic "Missa de Beata Virgine" as a Genre: The Background of Josquin's Lady Mass', in *JosCon*, 589–98.

REIFFENBERG, FRÉDÉRIC AUGUSTE LE BARON DE, 'État de l'hôtel de Philippe-le-Bel, duc de Bourgogne, en l'an 1496, à Bruxelles', *Compte-rendu des séances de la Commission royale d'histoire ou Recueil des ses bulletins*, 11 (1846), 677–718.

—— 'Lettre à M. Fétis, directeur du conservatoire de Bruxelles, sur quelques particularités de l'histoire musicale de la Belgique', in *Le Dimanche, récits de Marsilius Brunck*, 2 vols. (Brussels: Louis Hauman, 1834), ii. 259–329.

Rentboek van het begijnhof van Dendermonde (1499), ed. Jan Broeckaert (Dendermonde: Snelpersdruk Aug. de Schepper Philips, 1901).

RHAU, GEORG, *Musikdrucke aus den Jahren 1538 bis 1545 in praktischer Neuausgabe*, ed. Hans Albrecht et al. (Kassel: Bärenreiter, 1955–).

RIEMANN, HUGO, *Musik-Lexikon* (Leipzig: Bibliographisches Institut, 1882).

RIFKIN, JOSHUA, 'Busnoys and Italy: The Evidence of Two Songs', in Paula Higgins (ed.), *Antoine Busnoys: Method, Meaning, and Context in Late Medieval Music* (Oxford: Clarendon Press, 1999), 505–71.

—— 'Problems of Authorship in Josquin: Some Impolitic Observations with a Postscript on *Absalon fili mi*', in Willem Elders (ed.), *Proceedings of the International Josquin Symposium, Utrecht 1986* (Utrecht: Vereniging voor Nederlandse Muziekgeschiedenis, 1991), 45–52.

ROBIJNS, JOZEF, 'Eine Musikhandschrift des frühen 16. Jahrhunderts der Verehrung unserer Lieben Frau der Sieben Schmerzen', *Kirchenmusikalisches Jahrbuch*, 44 (1960), 28–43.

—— 'Pierre de la Rue als overgansfiguur tussen Middeleeuwen en Renaissance', *Revue belge de musicologie*, 9 (1955), 122–30.

—— *Pierre De la Rue, circa 1560–1518: Een bio-bibliographische studie* (Universiteit te Leuven, Publicaties op het gebied der geschiedenis en der philologie, ser. 4/6; Gembloux: J. Duculot, 1954).

—— 'Rue, Pierre de la', *Nationaal Biografisch Woordenboek*.

RODRÍGUEZ-SALGADO, M. J., 'Charles V and the Dynasty', in Hugo Soly (ed.), *Charles V 1500–1558 and his Time* (Antwerp: Mercatorfonds, 1999), 26–111.

ROEDIGER, KARL ERICH, *Die geistlichen Musikhandschriften der Universitäts-Bibliothek Jena: Notenverzeichnis* (Claves Jenenses: Veröffentlichungen der Universitätsbibliothek Jena, 3; Jena: Walter Biedermann, 1935).

ROSENBERG, MARIANNE, 'Symbolic and Descriptive Text Settings in the Sacred Works of Pierre de la Rue (c. 1460–1518)', *Miscellanea musicologica*, 1 (1966), 225–48.

ROSSI, GIOVANNI BATTISTA, *Organo di cantori* (Venice: Bartholomeo Magni, 1618; facs. ed., Bibliotheca musica Bononiensis, Sez. II, 57; Bologna: Arnaldo Forni, 1984).

RUBSAMEN, WALTER, 'La Rue, Pierre de', *Die Musik in Geschichte und Gegenwart*, viii, ed. Friedrich Blume (Kassel: Bärenreiter, 1960).

—— 'Pierre de la Rue als Messen-Komponist' (Ph.D. diss., University of Munich, 1937).

—— 'Some First Elaborations of Masses from Motets', *Bulletin of the American Musicological Society*, 4 (1940), 6–9.

—— 'Unifying Techniques in Selected Masses of Josquin and La Rue: A Stylistic Comparison', in *JosCon*, 369–400.

SACHS, KLAUS-JÜRGEN, 'Pierre de La Rues "Missa de Beata Virgine" in ihrer *copia* aus *varietas* und *similitudo*', in Werner Breig, Reinhold Brinkmann, and Elmar Budde (eds.), *Beiträge zu einer Problemgeschichte des Komponierens: Festschrift für Hans Heinrich Eggebrecht zum 65. Geburtstag* (Wiesbaden: Franz Steiner, 1984), 76–90.

SAINSBURY, JOHN S., *Dictionary of Musicians, from the Earliest Ages to the Present Time*, 2 vols. (London: Sainsbury, 1825; repr. New York: Da Capo, 1966).

SAINT-GENOIS, BARON JULES DE, *Catalogue méthodique et raisonné des manuscrits de la Bibliothèque de la ville et de l'université de Gand* (Ghent: C. Annoot-Broeckman, 1849–52).

—— *Notice sur le dépôt des archives de la Flandre orientale* (Ghent: L. Hebbelynck, 1841).

SANDERUS, ANTONIUS, *Chorographia sacra Brabantiae* . . . (Brussels: Philippum Vleugartium, 1659).

St. Galler Orgelbuch: Die Orgeltabulatur des Fridolin Sicher (St. Gallen, Codex 530), ed. Hans Joachim Marx and Thomas Warburton (Schweizerische Musikdenkmäler, 8; Winterthur: Amadeus, 1992).

SCHAAL, RICHARD, 'Zur Methodik quellenmäßiger Datierung der Werke Pierre de la Rues', in Hans Albrecht, Helmuth Osthoff, and Walter Wiora (eds.), *Kongress-Bericht, Gesellschaft für Musikforschung Lüneburg 1950* (Kassel and Basel: Bärenreiter, [1950]), 80–2.

SCHACHT, MATTHIAS HENRIKSEN, *Musicus danicus eller Danske sangmester*, ed. Godtfred Skjerne (Copenhagen: H. Hagerup, 1928).

SCHMIDL, CARLO, *Dizionario universale dei musicisti* (Milan: G. Ricordi, 1887).

SCHMIDT-GÖRG, JOSEPH, 'Die Acta Capitularia der Notre-Dame-Kirche zu Kortrijk als musikgeschichtliche Quelle', *Vlaamsch jaarboek voor muziekgeschiedenis*, 1 (1939), 21–80.

—— *Nicolas Gombert: Kapellmeister Kaiser Karls V.: Leben und Werk* (Bonn: L. Rohrscheid, 1938; repr. Tutzing: Hans Schneider, 1971).

SCHREURS, EUGEEN, 'Petrus Alamire: Music Calligrapher, Musician, Composer, Spy', in *TA* 15–27.

SEBASTIANI, CLAUDIUS, *Bellum musicale inter plani et mensuralis cantus reges* (Strasburg: Pauli Machaeropoei, 1563).

Sechzig Chansons zu vier Stimmen aus der ersten Hälfte des 16. Jahrhunderts von französischen und niederländerischen Meistern, ed. Robert Eitner (Publikationen älterer praktischer und theoretischer Musikwerke, 23; Leipzig: Breitkopf & Härtel, 1899).

SENN, WALTER, *Musik und Theater am Hof zu Innsbruck: Geschichte der Hofkapelle vom 15. Jahrhundert bis zu deren Auflöslung im Jahre 1748* (Innsbruck: Österreichische Verlagsanstalt, 1954).

S'ensuivent plusieurs belles chansons (Geneva: Jacques Viviane, n.d.).

SHERR, RICHARD, 'Chronology of Josquin's Life and Career', in id. (ed.), *The Josquin Companion* (Oxford: Oxford University Press, 2000), 11–20.

—— *Papal Music Manuscripts in the Late Fifteenth and Early Sixteenth Centuries* (Renaissance Manuscript Studies, 5; Neuhausen: American Institute of Musicology–Hänssler-Verlag, 1996).

—— 'Resonances of *Absalon fili mi* in the Sixteenth Century', in *Abstracts of Papers Read at the Meeting of the American Musicological Society: Sixty-Seventh Annual Meeting, November 15–18, 2001*, 49 (n.p.: American Musicological Society, 2001).

SMIJERS, ALBERT, 'De Illustre Lieve Vrouwe Broederschap te 's-Hertogenbosch', *TVNM* 11 (1923–5), 187–210; 12 (1926–8), 40–62, 115–67; 13 (1929–32), 46–100, 181–237; 14 (1932–5), 48–105; 16 (1940–6), 63–106, 216; 17 (1948–55), 195–230.

SPALATIN, GEORG, *Friedrichs des Weisen Leben und Zeitgeschichte*, ed. Chr. Gotth. Neudecker and Ludw. Preller (Jena: Friedrich Mauke, 1851).

SPARKS, EDGAR H., *Cantus Firmus in Mass and Motet 1420–1520* (Berkeley and Los Angeles: University of California Press, 1963; repr. New York: Da Capo, 1975).

SPUFFORD, PETER, *Monetary Problems and Policies in the Burgundian Netherlands 1433–1496* (Leiden: E. J. Brill, 1970).

STAEHELIN, MARTIN, 'La Rue, Pierre de', *New Grove*.

—— *Die Messen Heinrich Isaacs*, 3 vols. (Berne and Stuttgart: Paul Haupt, 1977).

—— 'Pierre de la Rue in Italien', *Archiv für Musikwissenschaft*, 27 (1970), 128–37.

STAFFORD, WILLIAM COOKE, *A History of Music* (Edinburgh: Constable, 1830).

STERNDALE BENNETT, WILLIAM, 'La Rue, Pierre de', in *Grove's Dictionary of Music and Musicians*, 2nd edn. (London: Macmillan, 1904–10); 5th edn. (London: Macmillan, 1954).

—— 'Rue, Pierre de la', in *A Dictionary of Music and Musicians (A.D. 1450–1889)*, 4 vols. (London: Macmillan, 1879–89), iv. 778.

—— 'Rue, Pierre de la', in *Grove's Dictionary of Music and Musicians*, 3rd edn. (1927–8); 4th edn. (1940).

STEVENSON, ROBERT, 'Anchieta, Juan de', *New Grove II*.

—— 'Frouvo, João Álvares', *New Grove II*.

—— 'Josquin in the Music of Spain and Portugal' in *JosCon*, 217–46.

—— 'Thalesio, Pedro', *New Grove II*.

—— 'The Toledo Manuscript Polyphonic Choirbooks and Some Other Lost or Little Known Flemish Sources', *Fontes artis musicae*, 20 (1973), 87–107.

STROHM, REINHARD, *Music in Late Medieval Bruges* (Oxford: Clarendon Press, 1985).

—— *The Rise of European Music 1380–1500* (Cambridge: Cambridge University Press, 1993).

—— and Kempson, Emma, 'Isaac, Henricus', *New Grove II*.

STRUNK, OLIVER (ed.), *Source Readings in Music History: The Baroque Era* (New York: W. W. Norton, 1965).

—— *Source Readings in Music History: The Renaissance* (New York: W. W. Norton, 1965).

SUREMONT, PIERRE JEAN, *Opuscule apologétique sur les mérites des célèbres musiciens belges, inventeurs ou régénérateurs de la musique aux 14e, 15e, et 16e siècles* (Antwerp: Veuve J. S. Schoesetters, 1828).

SWING, PETER GRAM, 'Parody and Form in Five Polyphonic Masses by Mathieu Gascongne' (Ph.D. diss., University of Chicago, 1969).

TERLINDEN, VICOMTE, 'Limburg Stirum (Thierry-Marie-Joseph, comte de), *Biographie nationale* [Belgium], xxxiii. 443–6.

THALESIO, PEDRO, *Arte de canto chão com huma breve instrucção* (Coimbra: Diogo Gomez de Loureyro, 1618; rev. edn., 1628).

TIRABASSI, ANTONIO, *Grammaire et transcription de la notation proportionnelle et sa transcription moderne: Manuel des ligatures* (Brussels: Van Damme & Duquesne, 1930).

—— 'L'Interpretation traditionelle des œuvres de Pierre de la Rue', *Musica sacra*, 42 (1935), 250–7; 43 (1936), 37–41, 116–30.

—— *La Mesure dans la notation proportionnelle et sa transcription moderne* (Brussels: Maison Delvigne, 1927).

Trésor musical: Collection authentique de musique sacrée et profane des anciens maîtres belges recueillie et transcrite en notation moderne, 29 vols. each of *Musique profane* and *Musique religieuse*, ed. Robert-Julien Van Maldeghem (Brussels: C. Muquardt, 1865–93).

Trienter Codices I: Geistliche und weltliche Kompositionen des XV. Jahrhunderts, ed. Guido Adler and Oswald Koller (Denkmäler der Tonkunst in Österreich, 14–15; Vienna: Artaria, 1900).

TURRELL, FRANCES BERRY, 'The *Isagoge in musicen* of Henry Glarean', *Journal of Music Theory*, 3 (1959), 97–139.

VAN DEN BORREN, CHARLES, 'Le Moyen Age et la Renaissance', in Ernest Closson and Charles Van den Borren (eds.), *La Musique en Belgique du Moyen Age à nos jours*, 15–144 (Brussels: La Renaissance du Livre, 1950).

—— Review of Jozef Robijns, *Pierre de la Rue (circa 1460–1518), een bio-bibliographische Studie*, in *Revue belge de musicologie*, 9 (1955), 165–7.

VAN DE PUTTE, F., 'Epitaphes copiées, en 1629, par Christophe van Huerne, seigneur de Schiervelde', *Annales de la Société d'Émulation pour l'Étude de l'Histoire et des Antiquités de la Flandre*, ser. 3, 16/4 (1871), 280.

VANDER STRAETEN, EDMOND, *La Musique aux Pays-Bas avant le XIXe siècle*, 8 vols. (C. Muquardt, G.-A. van Trigt, Schott, 1867–88; repr. New York: Da Capo, 1969).

VAN DOORSLAER, GEORGES, 'Aperçu sur la pratique du chant à Malines au XVe siècle', *Annales de l'Académie royale d'Archéologie de Belgique*, ser. 7, vol. 7 (1930), 465–84.

—— 'La Chapelle musicale de Charles-Quint en 1522', *Musica sacra*, 40 (1933), 215–30.

—— 'La Chapelle musicale de Philippe le Beau', *Revue belge d'archéologie et d'histoire de l'art*, 4 (1934), 21–57, 139–65.

—— 'Gilles Reyngoot: chantre-compositeur—xve–xvie siècles', *Mechlinia*, 7 (1928–9), 167–71.

—— 'Herry Bredemers organiste et maître de musique 1472–1522', *Annales de l'Académie royale d'archéologie de Belgique*, 66 (1914), 209–56.

—— 'Nicolas et Jacques Champion, dits Liégeois, chantres au début du xvie siècle', *Mechlinia*, 8 (1930–1), 4–13.

'La Vierge aux sept glaives', *Analecta Bollandiana*, 12 (1893), 333–52.

WAGNER, PETER, *Geschichte der Messe* (Kleine Handbücher der Musikgeschichte nach Gattungen, II/1; Leipzig: Breitkopf & Härtel, 1913).

WALTHER, ANDREAS, *Die burgundischen Zentralbehörden unter Maximilian I. und Karl V.* (Leipzig: Duncker & Humblot, 1909).

WALTHER, JOHANN GOTTFRIED, *Musikalisches Lexicon, oder Musicalische Bibliothec* (Leipzig: W. Deer, 1732).

WARMINGTON, FLYNN, 'Jena 4, Charles V, and the Conquest of the Infidels', in *Abstracts of Papers Read at the Meeting of the American Musicological Society: Sixty-Seventh Annual Meeting, November 15–18, 2001*, ed. Mark Evan Bonds (n.p.: American Musicological Society, 2001), 48–9.

WEAVER, ANDREW H., 'Aspects of Musical Borrowing in the Polyphonic *Missa de feria* of the Fifteenth and Sixteenth Centuries', in Honey Meconi (ed.), *Early Musical Borrowing* (New York: Garland, forthcoming).

WECKERLIN, J. B., *La Chanson populaire* (Paris: Firmin-Didot, 1886).

WEGMAN, ROB C., 'Agricola, Bordon and Obrecht at Ghent: Discoveries and Revisions', *Revue belge de musicologie*, 51 (1997), 23–62.

—— *Born for the Muses: The Life and Masses of Jacob Obrecht* (Oxford: Clarendon Press, 1994).

—— 'Communication', *JAMS* 45 (1992), 161–5.

—— 'Ghent', *New Grove II*.

—— Introduction to *Choirbook of the Burgundian Court Chapel: Brussel, Koninklijke Bibliotheek Ms. 5557* (Peer: Alamire, 1989).

—— 'Obrecht, Jacob', *New Grove II*.

—— 'Who Was Josquin', in Richard Sherr (ed.), *The Josquin Companion* (Oxford: Oxford University Press, 2000), 21–50.

—— Fitch, Fabrice, and Lerner, Edward R., 'Agricola, Alexander', *New Grove II*.

WESNER, AMANDA ZUCKERMAN, 'The Chansons of Loyset Compère: Authenticity and Stylistic Development' (Ph.D. diss., Harvard University, 1992).

—— 'The Chansons of Loyset Compère: A Model for a Changing Aesthetic', in Jessie Ann Owens and Anthony Cummings (eds.), *Music in Renaissance Cities and Courts: Studies in Honor of Lewis Lockwood* (Warren, Mich.: Harmonie Park Press, 1997), 483–501.

WIESFLECKER, HERMANN, *Kaiser Maximilian I.: Das Reich, Österreich und Europa an der Wende zur Neuzeit*, 5 vols. (Munich: R. Oldenbourg, 1971–86).

—— *Maximilian I.: Die Fundamente des habsburgischen Weltreiches* (Vienna: Verlag für Geschichte und Politik; Munich: R. Oldenbourg, 1991).

WINN (MARVIN), MARY BETH, 'Octavien de Saint-Gelais: Complainte sur le départ de Marguerite', *Le Moyen Français*, 5 (1979), 65–80.

—— '"Regret" Chansons for Marguerite d'Autriche by Octavien de Saint-Gelais', *Bibliothèque d'humanisme et Renaissance: Travaux et documents*, 39 (1977), 23–32.

—— '"Regrets" in French Chanson Texts of the Late XVth Century', *Fifteenth-Century Studies*, 1 (1989), 193–217.

WOLFF, HELLMUTH CHRISTIAN, *Die Musik der alten Niederländer* (Leipzig: Breitkopf & Härtel, 1956).

WOOLDRIDGE, H. E., *The Oxford History of Music*, ii: *The Polyphonic Period, Part II, Method of Musical Art, 1300–1600* (Oxford: Clarendon Press, 1905).

WRIGHT, CRAIG, *Music at the Court of Burgundy 1364–1419: A Documentary History* (Musicological Studies, 28; Henryville, Ottawa, and Binningen: Institute of Mediaeval Music, 1979).

—— and Fallows, David, 'Burgundy', *New Grove II*.

WYMANS, G., 'Un dépôt ressuscité: Les Archives de l'État à Tournai', *Archives et bibliothèques de Belgique*, 37 (1966), 186–96.

ZACCONI, LODOVICO, *Prattica di musica* (Venice: Girolamo Polo, 1592; facs. edn., 2 vols., Bologna: Forni, 1967; reprint edn., Venice: Bartolomeo Carampello, 1596; facs. edns., 2 vols., Bibliotheca musica bononienses, Sezione II, N. 1 (Bologna: Arnaldo Forni, 1983); *Prattica di Musica utile e necessaria si al compositore, si anco al cantore (1596)/Prattica di Musica Seconda parte (1622)* (Hildesheim and New York: Georg Olms, 1982)).

ZANGER, JOHANN, *Practicae musicae praecepta* (Leipzig: Georgij Hantzsch, 1554).

ZARLINO, GIOSEFFO, *The Art of Counterpoint: Part Three of* Le Istitutioni Harmoniche, *1558*, trans. Guy A. Marco and Claude V. Palisca (New Haven and London: Yale University Press, 1968).

—— *De tutti l'opere* (Venice: Francesco Franceschi Senese, 1588).

—— *Le istitutioni harmoniche* (Venice: [Pietro Da Fino], 1558; reprint edns. Venice: Francesco Franceschi Senese, 1561, 1562; facs. of 1558 edn., Monuments of Music and Music Literature in facs., Second Series, Music Literature, 1; New York: Broude, 1965).

—— *Le istitutioni harmoniche*, rev. edn. (Venice: Francesco Franceschi Senese, 1573; facs. edn., Ridgewood, NJ: Gregg Press, 1966).

—— *Music Treatises*, ed. Frans Wiering (Thesaurus musicarum Italicarum, 1; Utrecht: Universiteit Utrecht, 1997).

—— *On the Modes: Part Four of* Le Istitutioni Harmoniche, *1558*, trans. Vered Cohen (New Haven and London: Yale University Press, 1983).

Index of Manuscripts and Printed Sources

Index of Compositions by or Attributed to La Rue

General Index